<u>"The Ego Identity Crisis"</u>
Handbook for Enlightenment

A step-by-step guide to realizing the Self

by Brian Nager

RTN Publishing
Orlando, Fl 32810
United States of America

Web Site: www.RevealingTruthNow.com
Email: RTNpublishing@revealingtruthnow.com

ISBN: 0-9764672-0-8
LCCN: 2004195401

Printed in the United States of America

Legal Disclaimer Note: Any meditative practices or techniques presented within this book should be first consulted with a doctor and implied by one's own consent. When reading this book, you dismiss the publisher, RTN Publishing, and the author, Brian A. Nager, from any and all outcomes or results due to practicing the techniques presented within or from reading any of the material in this book.

A Word of Caution

This book, "The Ego Identity Crisis," is written to help all beings who read it dismantle their current belief system, which then reveals Truth as Self. The Truth is not found in any beliefs, for they are dualistic and disillusioned to a degree. This book is not intended to reprogram the ego mind, but to deprogram it. Any beings who are entrenched in religious or spiritual belief systems may become offended or irritated if they are not ready to let go of their current ideals. There are certain sections and chapters in the book that are specifically made to resurface beliefs and religious ideals as to deprogram them; however, it can make one feel very uncomfortable and upset. So any religiously dedicated being may not want to read this book, for it may cause them distress if they are not ready to heal.

The teachings in this book are a step-by-step guide that aids one in clarifying the path of enlightenment so as to experience the Higher Self, the divine aspect of God, in which is free from all pain, suffering, and worry. This book is not a belief, nor is its purpose to reinforce any belief system. This path is the journey of eventually recognizing one's self as the Higher Self, which is love, peace, and happiness, thereby bringing forth the higher qualities of Light (Truth) to the lower dimensions that have currently chosen to deny it. And by this, the relief of suffering is under way.

*As with all information, one should read at their own risk.

Note: Due to the fact that nearly 2 billion beings on earth are Christians, those were the views that were mostly corrected within the religious section of this book. It, by no means, is intended to be a personal attack against the religion or the practitioners. It should be noted that all religions have errors within them, along with some Truths.

Acknowledgments

I first and foremost thank the universe for being perfection, and for allowing my beingness to transfer Truth onto paper with as little distortion as possible.

I would also like to give a special thanks to my editor, Linda Lord, who graciously offered to edit the book free of charge as a service to the universe, and for her countless hours of preparation that went into getting the work ready for publication.

I also thank my family and wife for having the patience to continue standing by me while I devoted nearly every hour of the week for almost two years, without income, to complete this book. And for their understanding and love that allowed me to accomplish part of my Self-appointed mission to help all beings be at peace.

To all of you………Thank you.

Expression of Self

The cover states that Brian Nager is the author of this book. However, he humbly denies having any immediate authorship. Instead, he states, "That which is of the universe, belongs to the universe and cannot be claimed by a manifestation of it." He is simply a channel of the divine, which pours through him as Truth. The book simply is a product of the universe, an expression of the higher levels of consciousness and the qualities that are of the Unmanifest. It simply is Truth.

"If this book is helpful and inspiring to you, then give the credit and praise to the Universal Whole. May Truth be recognized by all who read it; Love Be Thy Name… one's innermost Source of purity, stillness, and peace."

How To Use This Book

The Setup

The first part of this book is designed to supply general information and to create intrigue, which then develops the inner drive to search for Truth. The second part creates an understanding that not all that is perceived is all that there is, which educates the ego on various metaphysical topics. The third part explains the differentiating dimensions of form and nonform, while the fourth part helps one understand the basis of illusion (ego), which creates suffering and has been accepted as the only level of reality; it also provides the step-by-step knowledge that is needed to transcend the ego. The fifth part provides information that allows one to understand how to raise one's level of consciousness. The sixth and final part of the book answers, explains, and clarifies the many questions that have been asked throughout the author's many teachings.

The Information

This book is specifically designed to help one transcend their ego by answering the hidden questions within one's mind. These questions, if left unanswered, create the illusion that suffering is a reality that has to be endured—thus blocking the love of God that is provided to help the being experience existence as Love and Peace, which is Truth (God), at all times. The answers provided within this book are sufficient in and of themselves to help anyone, no matter what crimes or sins have been committed, to transcend their ego, the source of suffering and limitation.

As the explanations are read, the ego's many questions will resolve and then dissolve into oblivion. As the ego answers its own questions, which blocks Truth or one's happiness from being experienced on a daily basis, that being raises in its inherent level of consciousness. As one's level of consciousness raises, a new awareness will be revealed, thus allowing one to experience Truth on a higher level.

As one's awareness increases, a new level of reality emerges, with heightened levels of joy, happiness, and peace. This occurs because a being surrenders aspects of their ego to God, willfully allowing the Power of God into their lives, thus increasing their ability and capacity to love all things unconditionally and nonjudgmentally. This then brings about a worry-free existence that allows one to focus all energy on existing in the Now, while not contemplating what should have been done in the past and what to do in the future.

As complete transcendence of the ego becomes one's reality, this book may be further utilized to increase one's level of awareness to an even more heightened level, thus allowing the Divinity of God to pour through and as one's Self as a continual blessing upon the universe.

The information within this book is written by an enlightened sage (2nd Gold), whose purpose is to help all beings realize their 'True Universal Identity' that will willfully help others as well.

To What Frequency Should This Be Read?

This book should be read until one is enlightened; it is capable of doing so. The level of Truth presented within this book will be hard for the ego to comprehend, due to a differing nature and context or understanding. The ego, a linear mechanism, is not capable of realizing the Nonlinear Truths that are presented within. However, the Nonlinear Truths are presented within a seeming linear format to increase the chance for comprehension. Let it be known that no ego can truly understand what enlightenment or Truth is. It has to be experienced by Self-Realization, or by transcending the ego.

When this book is read the first time, approximately 30% of the book will be realized. On the second reading, the book will be about 60 to 70% realized; almost capable of enlightenment. And as the Truth of the book, in which is identical to the Truth of the Self, is realized completely, one is enlightened. If the book is read a third, fourth, or fifth time, enlightenment is more or less certain; but only if the being is completely 'willing' to give up

6

their ego identity and all of its attachments. It can however, be read a fewer number of times while still providing the same outcome.

The book will be understood the second time with more clarity due to one's increase in level of consciousness that was acquired during the first reading. As the second read is under way, the greater Truths that are read again will be seen with ease and understood with clarity. It is important to understand that one's level of consciousness allows for that same level of understanding Truth. So with an increased level of consciousness, one will have an increased awareness for the higher Truth. The book, when reread, may actually feel as if it were a different book with a dissimilar context, although displaying a greater reality.

If one has 100% 'Will' to transcend the ego and surrender their identity to God as false and illusory, enlightenment is then instantaneous. However, the ego, which is trying to convince itself to transcend itself, is really only tricking itself into believing that it can be done. The ego is the trickster; it cannot trick itself; the source of illusion. This is why so many beings do not themselves become enlightened—because they are trying to convince themselves (the ego) that they want to be enlightened. The ego never wants to be enlightened; that would terminate its existence. All that can be done is to answer the questions that the ego has pondered. God provides for and is enlightenment; it is not of the ego's doing.

So this book is formatted in a way that will show the ego why it is necessary to give up the boundaries and attachments that it has unknowingly set for itself. It does not know that there is a greater Truth or happiness; it can only experience that which it has been led to believe. So by reasoning with the ego, the greater Truths slip into the being's energetic field disguised as linear information, and by this process, enlightenment is made possible.

Carrying the Higher Frequency

This book not only holds the appropriate information that is needed in order to resolve the illusory thought forms of the ego, but carries with it the Higher Self's frequency of Truth that cannot

7

be read, measured, understood, or perceived. Instead, the high level of consciousness (frequency) is transferred from the book to the being's energetic field, thus prompting the revelations to flow.

The frequency of Truth is imbued upon each page. So with every page that is read, one's level of awareness/consciousness is increased just a little more: some days, with quantum leaps, and other days, with a small hop. No matter what the progress, though, the end result is the same—enlightenment.

So just by carrying this book with one's self, the inherent energy imprinted within it reinforces the energetic field and level of consciousness of the individual. But as the book is read, the frequency of Truth transpierces one's energetic field, heralding the emergence of the Self. However, *studying* this book *relentlessly* is perhaps one of the most effective ways for one to become enlightened. This is a 100% pure obsession with the Truth of one's existence.

Slight increases of awareness will usually be known and felt by the ego as just a more open-minded viewpoint on life, although, as enlightenment becomes one's condition, it will be henceforth be known as Truth and not just as an interesting concept. The level of Truth that this book provides can genuinely help one exceed the lower levels of enlightenment, which is sufficient and complete in and of itself, as well as raise one to the level of the Avatar (3rd Gold) or *Universal Identity* (the highest expression of Self in this realm).

The frequency that has been imprinted upon this book is specifically intended to create enlightened beings who dwell within God's love and are a direct expression of Truth. The author's true hope in writing this book, though, is for all beings to become Self-Realized to the degree of a 'Saint,' a being who is and goes beyond ordinary perceived means to help all individuals become Self-Realized. This is God's direct channel as the 'universal helper.'

This book has been written with not just 'inner peace' and 'world peace' in Mind, but *Universal Peace*, which is the liberation of all of the souls within the hells, restricted heavens, and physical dimension proper. God has allowed for it, so it is really all just a matter of Will.

The Daily Practice

This is the method which expedites the spiritual devotee's journey. If followed correctly, with purity of heart, enlightenment can become one's existence in less than a year. The author used this system (which he pondered for many years at first) and became enlightened in less than 6 months with no meetings with a guru or help from any other. ***the book part, #3, 5, and 7, is obviously different from the authors readings.**

To Be Done Every Day

1. *Wake up and Pray for others and self. (15 minutes)*
2. *Directly after Prayer, introspectively meditate. (30 minutes)*
3. *Read as much of this book of Truth as possible.*
4. *Do what needs to be done within the day while keeping in mind the greater context of life, God (Oneness).*
5. *Read the book in one's spare time. If no spare time, then make some. Always practice learned principles.*
6. *At night, pray and meditate introspectively (30-40 minutes), and then meditate to still the mind (one-minded focus). 15 minutes*
7. *Read some of this book before bedtime.*
8. *Pray for the Universe, family, friends, enemies, and self to become Self-Realized. Go to bed, then wake up and start over again.*

A Note to the Reader

As you read this book, the ego will bring up many questions. Some of these will inspire and spur on the ego to acquire knowledge; but in opposition, there may be many days when the ego will believe that all that is written within this book is false. When the ego feels positive change, it becomes motivated and enthralled with the enlightenment process. However, when the ego experiences a massive release of negative karma, or a progressive quantum leap in consciousness, the ego can become slightly depressed and may temporarily feel abandoned by God. One should not let this brief moment of illusory negativity affect them.

In addition to this feeling of abandonment, the ego will then question all spiritual practices that are currently under way, many of which will be denied as false practices or a 'waste of time.' There may be a tendency to go back to the conventional practice of religion, which reinforces the ego identity's feeling of separateness, uniqueness, and belongingness. This only furthers the being's evolution back to the illusory and away from the Reality of the Unmanifest.

It needs to be realized that any **'low feelings'** or **depressed sensations** that one feels when going through the enlightenment process **are normal** and **only temporary**. It is some of the residual negative karma being transcended which instills fear within the ego. As the 'low points' pass, a momentary feeling of love and peace will prevail throughout certain points in time. When enlightened, this state of increasing happiness and ecstatic bliss will become one's beingness as the Self. It will, at that time, then become a permanent condition that one will simply 'be' for all of eternity, and one will realize that all worries that the ego once had were just an attempt to save its identity and to keep one from knowing Truth.

It is also normal for the ego to begin judging other egos, spiritual beings, spiritual texts, and religions, in order to identify and understand its level of importance among the others. The 'judgmentalism' will pass as one transcends the ego. One should make sure that they do not allow the ego to get wrapped up in 'judging things.' It is a way for the ego to create a new identity as 'spiritually advanced' or 'smarter than others.' That judgment in and of itself is an illusion that should be bypassed and ignored. It is important to keep in mind that all beings are simply misguided due to the lack of Truthful knowledge, and that all beings really believe that they know what reality is. Unfortunately, they are just confused souls; however, this is only until Truth is revealed.

To become enlightened, it is necessary to ignore any and all temptations to stop or slow one's spiritual evolution. It is absolutely mandatory to drive through all of the worries that the ego will use to stop one from progressing through the path of enlightenment. This book is Truth, with no lies or biased beliefs. Trust in this book, study this book, absorb the frequency of this book, become obsessed with Truth, surrender the ego to God, and be enlightened. All is well with God as the Unmanifest, which is beyond the Higher Self.

How the Ego Will Feel on the Path of Enlightenment

- *It will question the path and the Truth presented.*
- *It may label the Truth as false or unbelievable.*
- *It may deny God as presented within texts of Truth, because these do not conform to a conventional religion's theory.*
- *At times the being will believe Truth and then instantly deny Truth, as if overnight the being suddenly changes view.*
- *It may denounce all religions as false.*
- *It may denounce all spiritual teachers as false.*
- *It may feel that the book of Truth was just made up.*
- *It may feel hopeless and directionless.*
- *It may feel as if it needs to seek a spiritual guru; this is not necessary, but very helpful. One's Higher Self is the only guru needed, which one already has and is.*
- *It may feel that it is smarter than others (pride).*
- *It may feel that all beings are dumb for believing in the manifest, various religions, overall beliefs, etc.*

11

- *It may want to teach other egos to reinforce its identity of 'spiritual pride.'*
- *It may become depressed or sad, thinking God has abandoned them because they are going the 'wrong way.'*
- *It may want to choose to go back to a more conventional and accepted religious practice.*
- *It may try to force others to learn what they are learning; however, it needs to be realized that it is their choice to make, and so it should not be forced upon them.*
- *It may begin to doubt the authenticity of the teachings of Truth and enlightenment itself.*
- *It may feel tingling in the nerves, headaches, and wooziness.*
- *It may experience an increase in dreams, thus making the ego want to dream. **Wanting** to dream is 'ego will.'*
- *It may feel special, due to its knowledge and inherent level of consciousness that affects all others positively.*
- *It may feel as though it should stay away from all others who do not follow the same path. **Aversion** is also a product of the ego that is based on judgment.*
- *It may believe that it shouldn't care if someone dies, thus showing less compassion towards the bereaved family members. Sometimes too much understanding of reality is portrayed to the ego as uncompassionate and careless.*

These temporary feelings that the ego will go through should not be feared, but instead accepted and learned from. When one feels as if they are having a 'bad day,' it should be realized that it is either themselves transcending negative karma, experiencing ego resistance, or experiencing the ego coming back into one's life as the focal point of existence. In any attempt, one should stay calm, relax, and realize that it will pass. To feel better, one may pray, read a book of Truth, meditate, say a high-powered mantra, seek help from a being who is higher in consciousness, or write down one's experiences in a journal.

<u>The Blessing</u>

This book has not only been charged with some of the highest levels of Truth ever presented within this dimension, but it has the energetic imprint of the Higher Self (mid 3rd stage Gold— refer to Appendix 1A).This book has been charged with some of the highest frequencies ever experienced by any currently living or deceased being.

Beyond the ordinary means of writing, each book has been blessed, which inherently heightens the level of consciousness even further. The frequency contained within this book is close to the Avatar's (highest level of enlightenment [3rd Stage Gold] for this dimension) awareness of Reality.

The information within this book is sufficient to dissolve the structure of the ego that keeps the individual within the illusory dimension of the manifest, as well as perpetuates it. As the ego dissolves by exposure to the power presented within this book, the Self shines forth with brilliance, thereby reminding one of their True nature as love and peace.

As one intentionally picks up this book, the frequency transfers to that being little by little. By intense concentration, such as while reading, the frequency is allowed to transpierce one's energetic field even more, thus bringing in 'the blessing' of Truth on a daily basis. One needs to simply surrender all to God and allow the frequency presented within this book to enter one's being. By this energetic exchange, the condition known as 'enlightenment' will become one's reality.

Clarifying Terminologies

(All terms referring to God are capitalized to express Divinity.)

Terms Used for God as Unmanifest:

> The Source, Supreme Reality, Absolute Reality,
> Absolute Truth, Unmanifest, Nonlinear,
> Nondualistic, True Self, the Formless, Real Reality

Terms for God as Higher Self:

> Higher Self, Self, Divinity, Awareness, Pure Consciousness,
> Love, Peace, Higher Truth or Truth

Terms for God as Totality:

> All, All That Is, One Mind, Universal Whole, Universal Self

Terms Used for Enlightenment:

> Self-Realization, Self-Revealed,
> God-Consciousness, Aware of Self, Awareness

Terms Used for the ego:

> lower self, illusory self, source of suffering, self, sin

Terms Used for the manifest dimension:

> manifest, illusory, world of form, linear reality,
> dualistic reality, false reality, perceived reality,
> ego reality, the 'unreal'

Terms Used Interchangeably (yet they differ in quality):

> Consciousness and Awareness

Terms Used for the Upper Astral Dimensions:

> Heavens, Higher Levels of Consciousness

Terms Used for the lower astral dimensions:

hells, lower level of consciousness, sin

The Use of the Term 'God'

Within this book, the term 'God' is used to express the 'creative source' from which all of the manifest or material came. It refers to the infinite potentiality that is the Unmanifest substrate, in which is the matrix that provides for the universal consciousness.

This term was chosen because it has a universal meaning that the majority of this realm has become accustomed to. Although the term is recognized as meaning the 'Creator,' it is not to be thought of as the traditional conceptualizations and/or dualistic and linear beliefs, which impose the various limitations that contradict the very meaning of infiniteness.

The term 'God' is used within this book to convey the creative potentiality of the highest, nonform energy that is capable of actualizing into the various manifest forms. It is a pure reference to that which can only be known as unlimited and infinite, the Unmanifest (unlimited, potential, nonform energy).

The term, when used in this book, does not denote any religionistic viewpoints and/or beliefs that have been expressed by the many churches, leaders, followers, or religions. The use of the term 'God' does not denote a personified being with unlimited and/or supernatural powers, but rather a type of energy that is unlimited and infinite by the sheer nature of its existence, which is the reason for, the sustenance of, and the spawning of all manifest existence.

When the term 'God' is used in written expression, its meaning and nature of energy as existence is the Nonlinear, Nondualistic, and Unmanifest. This is the only Reality and/or dimension that may infer infiniteness, boundlessness, and limitlessness. Whereas the physical dimension, as well as the spiritual manifest dimensions of the 'heavens and hells,' are restricted and limited, the essence of God is beyond all manifestations that imply limitations and/or restrictions. Thus God as the unlimited 'Source' is the Unmanifest quality of nonform energy that is drawn in and/or summoned by the 'will' of all beings as creation, in which the major leaps in temporal time are recognized or witnessed as evolution.

The above-stated terminology for 'God' is used when describing the ultimate and infinite source of potentiality of the Unmanifest. But it should be recognized that **God as Totality** is 'All That Is,' the creator, the created, and consciousness. All form and nonform, as well as all karma, heavens, and hells, are a product of a distortion of Truth, which was provided by the Unmanifest and thus activated as a limitation instilled by the flailing and ignorant qualities of the 'egoistic will.' These various limitations of consciousness, ranging from heavily to slightly occluded, are known as the 'astral dimensions' or 'universal consciousness.' The totality of karma is the expression of existence that is termed 'universal consciousness.' So **God as Totality** is 'All That Is.'

The Use of 'Single Quotes'

All words that have loose meanings, such as 'bad,' will have single quotation marks around them to indicate that one should not take them as literal fact, but rather, just as a label that egos use—for example, In Reality, nothing is 'good' or 'bad.' Also, terms such as 'All That Is,' 'Oneness,' and others may be put in single quotes to indicate that they are just labels. Labels that most teachers of spirituality use, such as 'Oneness,' are expressed in this book to help readers become familiar with various spiritual topics. These labels have been chosen because they do express the closest essence of what the author is trying to convey. So the single quotation marks surround some terms to be remembered, while others just emphasize a 'figure of speech' that egos usually use.

All words in **bold** or *italics* are intended for one to pay extra attention to, or to introspect on relentlessly.

Repetition of Words, Phrases, and Essences

In many instances throughout the book, a phrase, comment, quote, thought, practice, or essence is repeated. This is done on purpose. The reason behind this is that the ego breaks down or deprograms when it is constantly bombarded with topics of Truth that a being has a 'better' grasp of. And while a new reader may go through the book and not understand the topics presented within, as that reader raises in consciousness, and a word or phrase is brought up repeatedly, that being will have a new understanding of what the essence of that Truth is. The more that one reads this book, the higher in consciousness one transcends, which makes the book understandable on a whole new level.

One cannot understand the entirety of this book unless they are at the same level of consciousness as the book. So specifics, or 'main points,' are brought up at certain times throughout the chapters so that the reader can see the term with a whole new level of consciousness, which yields a whole new understanding. Likewise, as the book is read a second and third time, the book will feel as if it is brand new or never been read. The writings within will have a whole new 'ring' to them, due to one's raised level of consciousness, thus one's transcension is continually perpetuated.

Meaning of Cover Design

The black cover represents the darkness of illusion, while the gold words express that Truth is present in All things; no matter how negative it may seem. The blurry or out-of-focus tree is to represent that the realm of form is an illusion that lacks clarity and purity. But through attuning one's mind to the Truth (gold words) when in the illusory dimension of form, such as the current one we are in and term earth, we can transcend the illusion of form that is suffering and experience the Higher Self, which is love, peace, and happiness that is always present and accessible.

The tree does not represent a 'tree of life.'

Table of Contents

Chapter	Title	Page

Part 6   "Revealing Truth Now"

Appendix

Section One
Clarifying Concepts

"To Know Truth, One Must Abandon Belief"
—BN

Note: First chapter goes over the life path of author in order to express a certain path that he chose to travel to search for Truth. This section was only included in the book so that it could inform others of an ego's spiritual journey. It is felt that this particular path can connect with many spiritualists that are currently searching for Truth, but misguided, as was he. He is no longer this ego identity, therefore, it is not an attempt to boast or prove.

Also, do not mind the references to the psychic experiences or phenomena; for they are a brief explanation of the ego's previous path and *is not what this book is about*. In addition, the explanations of how the psychic phenomena occur or what it is are written from the basic psychic explanation (with some light of Truth) and not from an enlightened view (complete Truth). It would be too difficult for the ego to comprehend the enlightened understandings of these phenomena, so they will be explained in the enlightened context in the subsequent book, Being That Which Is.

Chapter 1
<u>Preplanned by Karma</u>
(Past ego lifestyle)

My Choice, My Path — But Predestined

As a result of past karma, I was destined to be born into an American family in the state of Florida, on January 10, 1979, at St. Joseph's hospital in Tampa. I was born at about 7:11 a.m. My birth weight was 9 pounds, 15 ounces, which was probably a pretty tough pregnancy for my mother to go through. After I was born, my mother took me home and proudly showed me to her friends, saying, "I have a little baby boy." These friends became very close to me; they were virtually relatives.

Fortunately, I was born without any medical problems or birth defects, except that my immune system was awfully weak. I got sick about every month, and took a lot of medication for as long as I can remember, at least until the age of 20. Other than being sick, I had no other 'real' problems.

The neighborhood that I was born into was developmental or new, which means that no one was really aware of who their fellow neighbors were going to be. All one can really do is hope for the best.

When old enough, I was put into a private religious pre-school, Lake Magdalene Methodist, which was also a church. After preschool, I moved up to kindergarten within the same school. While in preschool and kindergarten, making friends was a problem. I had a few, which I actually preferred anyway, but making many friends was a challenge.

When I had birthday parties, my mom would invite the entire class, but they weren't all my friends. Even so, I tried to make friends when possible. It seemed to be the only way to fit into society. My mother told me to try to be more outgoing, but I just felt like I was on another wavelength than other people.

I can actually remember all of my friends' names throughout my school career. Getting picked on was also common while I

23

was in school. When I graduated from Lake Magdalene Method-ist, with certain views about religion ingrained in my mind, I trans-ferred to Seminole Presbyterian Elementary, which differed in teachings, for 1st grade.

As I went to this new school, I noticed that things were different. I couldn't quite place it, but I knew that the two schools were dissimilar. My mother never told me that these were two different religions; I was not really sure that my parents knew that they were. I think that they just figured that a Christian religion is a Christian religion. While younger, though, I was convinced enough to believe that they were the same. I also started to notice that this religion was very strict.

They used to show us a video called "Hell's Bell's." This video was basically intended to 'scare us straight' by making us feel that we were going to 'hell' if we watched Madonna, Michael Jackson, Aerosmith, and Guns n Roses videos, and so forth. If we watched anything that had to do with sexual innuendos, drugs, or rock 'n' roll, we were told that we were going to hell. I remember our teachers would tell us if we did 'good things' we would go to heaven and 'bad things' would take us to hell. But they typically used force (control), which is a product of the ego; only 'Divine Will' or the 'Power of God' can create change. One cannot be forced to change, they must decide for themselves.

Later in life, I actually caught up with many individuals who went to school with me at Seminole Presbyterian. Nearly all had chosen to try all of the things that the teachers had taught us were 'bad.' This is due to the fact that the 'ego force' only creates fear, curiosity, animosity, and rebellion. All of the teachers thought that they were doing the right thing and teaching us the way to heaven, but instead they just scared most of the children and made them want to figure it out for themselves.

In addition, the children whom I had gone to school with at Seminole had misbehaved a lot; usually when the teacher wasn't looking. They were not shown why to be loving, but rather, by the teacher's force, were scared into behaving properly only when the 'public eye' was upon them. At any other instant, they seemed to be just as unruly as the other children in the public schools.

I was also led to believe that only Jesus was God, and that we were nothing. We were only something when we accepted Jesus as our savior. And obviously, if we chose another religion or path, we were "going to hell." The children were told that they were all predestined for hell, and that their way was the only way to go to heaven; all other beings were on their way to hell.

Everything told to me within, that the religion just didn't seem right. I had a deep inner feeling that was telling me not to believe what the teachers were saying. Every time a teacher spoke to the class about something, it seemed as if the students outwardly agreed but internally questioned it. If one actually questioned their faith to the teacher, one would be punished for having a lack of faith or questioning God. But all I wanted was information that made sense to me or made me feel that my faith was there.

Throughout the latter stages of school, I remained quiet. I did not have many friends; in fact, I only had one real friend (Chris). With Chris, I seemed like a normal, talkative kid. But on my own I didn't talk much, because I was always pondering existence.

I was constantly thinking and wondering about why I was here and what life was about. I would rather sit under a tree and think about life than make more friends. When thinking, I realized that I had felt, since about the age of 2 or 3, that I had an important mission—that somehow, I was supposed to impact the world. Due to that feeling, I was determined to find out who I was and what purpose I was to serve.

While I was progressing through private school, my parents decided to put me into a public school when in the 8th grade. This obviously brought about many changes. I started to see people from many different religions and races (there was only one black child in my previous school—Michael). There were also many different personalities among the children, which showed what the Christian-free, or unprogrammed and nonreligious, viewpoints looked like. I really began to question faith then—not faith in God, but faith in religion. I felt like there was no need for religion, and that there was something more important than anything I had ever been taught before, but no one knew it.

During my years at the public junior high school, I made

about 4 friends (more than before). I still got picked on almost every day, though. Apparently my physical appearance and odd persona just made me an easy target. I used to feel really depressed and that my life was horrible. I felt like I got picked on because I didn't look 'cool.' I used to look at my face in the mirror and cry, saying, "Why did God make me so ugly?" I would blame my parents and God for all of my mishaps or unfortunate turns of events. My parents tried to comfort and console me, but their efforts didn't heal me. My parents gave me a great life, even though I didn't see it that way at the time. However, school is another story, one with many ups and downs.

When in public school, I was surrounded by people who seemed as if they were never taught the 'Ten Commandments,' or any good morals for that matter. The students could be so cruel. They would pick out a small defect and make it the topic of gossip. They would sometimes make me feel too embarrassed even to go to school. These were just things that I had to deal with while in school, like most other children.

Throughout public junior high and high school, I did not practice any religion. Instead, I just tried to fit in with any group that I could. There was no way that I could ever be cool, and so I ended up hanging around a group that I felt most comfortable in. This group was thought to be better than the 'cool group'; they were the 'indifferent group,' the group that didn't try to impress anyone or make any friends. They were just being who they were, not caring about others' comments. They were interested in poetry, music, writing, art, and being independent, although many times they were viewed as rebellious. Some were viewed to be a misfortune by my parents because they were known to be involved with drugs as well. I hung around with them to try to develop some of my interests, such as writing poetry and playing the guitar. However, I was also influenced by drugs from time to time. It didn't feel wrong to examine *all* possibilities of life while still looking for answers, although most choices were the 'wrong paths.'

My new friends were basically hippies in the new generation. Similarly, their parents were the hippies of the old generation. So poetry, music, and drugs were commonplace with them as well. This obviously made me feel accepted and comfortable with my friends and their parents. I could look into my areas of interest, which were also my friends' interests. But I noticed something while doing drugs with my friends: that I didn't really do it for fun. Instead, I did drugs to see reality through a 'different perspective.'

I actually studied drugs in my spare time, not just because it was my area of interest, but because it was different and not like what I had been led to believe was 'evil' or 'satanic' by my previous schooling; it felt innocent and harmless. I thought at the time that maybe there was something else to life that I was also not aware of, and I was determined to find out what that might be.

By this time, I had stopped doing drugs as I kept on seeking the answer to life. I started to look in alternative places. Thus began my interest and main focus in the health field. I was interested in vitamins, minerals, herbs, working out, eating right, and alternative healing methods. This triggered a massive, compelling drive to study constantly. I would study all day long, at work, at school (my interests only), and when I had any free time. I wanted not only to study health, but to know it better than anyone else in the world.

I had a strong desire to know everything better than others; it was my ego exhibiting 'pride.' I studied so much that I would get headaches from forcing myself to learn in an excessive quantity. Using my newly acquired knowledge, I got a job at an alternative health food store and studied nutrition and herbs continuously, until I could repeat from memory most of the lines from the books. While at that store, I also met a person who changed the way I look at the 'unknown'; her name was Allison.

Allison and I went on some dates and I learned a lot about her and from her; although I did not know it at the time. She was a recovering alcoholic and had some prior problems with attempted suicide. I was a little uncomfortable because I had never met someone who had tried to kill themselves. I have to admit, it was a bit 'dark' or 'spooky' for that immature time in my life. All of this aside, the realization set in that all people have made mistakes and that one should not be judged for what has occurred in the past. So

I brushed it aside and tried to understand, even though the thought was always lurking in the back of my mind. I went to some of her AA meetings as well, to provide some support for her. That was also very weird for me at the time, because I was no older than 19 and had not experienced much in my life, let alone gone to an AA meeting.

When discussing interests, I discovered that she was into 'astral projection,' 'telekinesis,' and 'telepathy.' I thought that she was crazy after that, and that possibly this way of abstract thinking resulted from being an addict and doing drugs. I told her that it wasn't possible and that she was 'nuts' for even trying it. She felt sad that I had said that and told me it was an interest of hers and I should respect it. I said sorry, but still thought she was a little strange. I responded with, "Don't you think that if it were real, that everyone would be doing it or that it would be a common occurrence in everyday reality?" She replied, "Well, I don't know," and I said, "Exactly," with the implication that it was all a myth or fallacy. This was my programming from all of those years at a Christian school that made me so 'narrow minded' at the time.

I was very logical and thought that all 'things' had an answer or a rational explanation; only later in my life would I find out differently. She believed that there were many unknown 'things' out there that were not yet discovered. I thought that the way she thought was a side-effect of alcoholism. As our relationship ended, all that was left were the thoughts that she had put into my head to the effect of, "The unknown is known to the ones who know."

Some months later, I was walking through a bookstore (somewhere I never went) and just looking around. I had nothing else to do, and so I figured I would 'kill some time.' So I walked by a book section that I always thought was 'satanic' because my previous school had conditioned me to believe so. As I walked up to the section called 'metaphysics,' a book that I didn't touch actually fell on the ground. I didn't think anything of it, until I saw that it was the same book that Allison had showed me earlier. After that, it was a little 'spooky.' So for fun and curiosity, I picked up the book and read the back to see what it was about. It was interesting, but I never once thought that it could be real. I ended up reading some of the pages, and before I knew it, I bought the book. However, I still thought that it was a fictional story or imaginary. I figured that I'd read the book all the way through and apply some of the meditations to the ones that I already did for relaxation. "After all, it can't hurt," I thought. I started to tell my roommates about what I was trying to do, and as 'karmic proof,' they thought I was 'crazy.' Just as I had believed Allison to be, my peers and family treated me the same way.

I meditated for 2 to 5 hours per day and practiced the techniques presented in the book for astral projection; which is when the soul leaves the physical body at will. I thought that it was imaginary and was trying to prove it to be so, all so I could say, "Ah ha, I knew it was all made up." As I continued, I applied these meditation techniques and noticed that I just felt better all around and had more energy. I still didn't think anything of it; I just thought that it was because I was resting more than usual.

After about 10 to 15 days, though, I started to feel all of the symptoms that were to be expected when astrally projecting, except for the 'out of body' experience. I tried and tried with a passion to see if it was right now, instead of proving it wrong. So my intentions had actually switched. On the 21st day, I went through the meditations again to see what happened. After I applied the meditations presented within the book that I had been reading, nothing happened. This infuriated me and I made an ultimatum with God. I swore and cursed, and threw my book across my room while saying, "If there is a God, show me!" I was disappointed, feeling let down, and went to sleep crying because I thought that there was no hope and that there was no God. Then I finally drifted off to sleep.

Then suddenly, I awoke from my sleep but could not move my physical body. I was overwhelmed by these 'coursing vibrations' and the feeling of an 'electrical shock' in the back of my head. The vibrations were so powerful that I thought that something must be wrong. However, I kept my intention strong and followed what I had read in books. They had said to feel a slipping movement and so I did. I actually felt as if I were slipping off of my bed and then rolled over onto my stomach and face down onto the floor.

When I was on the floor, I actually thought that I had 'physically' slipped off my bed, and so I tried to stand up but couldn't. I was trying to use my physical arms, but with a glance, I realized that I had no physical arms. So I remembered what the books had instructed; they had said to feel your way up because it is a mental realm. So I did. And like clockwork, I slowly started to rise as if in my physical body, but slightly different. I had never felt so alive and full of love. I looked at my hands like the books had said and they were supposed to look disfigured or like ice melting, but they didn't. Instead, they looked like beams of subtly colored light shooting out in all directions, especially at my face. Then I turned toward my physical body and shocked myself. I was directly looking at my physical body while 'it' was sleeping. This was obviously the turning point in my life, when I realized that the physical body was not my existence, but instead, the soul was. I realized that the soul was the source of the experience and not the physical body, as I was previously led to believe by my past religion and social conditioning. So as I went to my physical body, I dove in, like tap water pouring into a cup, and I awoke saying out loud, "This is the dream; that was real!" And from that point on, I knew a higher level of reality that makes the physical realm feel like the dream.

After this extraordinary event in my life occurred, I tried to do it again, right after the first one. This time I actually went into a lucid dream, which is where you know you are dreaming, but it feels as real as if you were operating in the physical dimension. As I moved around in this mental dreamland, I noticed that I could create or manifest things by simply thinking about them. I could change scenery if I got bored with the one I was in; I could do anything. It was like being 'God,' but a smaller version. Then I woke up again and quickly noticed the difference between the out-of-body (OBE) experience and the lucid dream. They were nothing the same; they felt different and were experienced differently. After my first lucid dream, a repeat performance felt necessary, and at the very least, exciting and intriguing. So I meditated, while trying to keep the excitement subdued, to experience either an

OBE or a lucid dream. But this time it was different.

On the third attempt, I experienced a very high-powered 'vivid dream,' which absolutely blew my mind again. Everything was so real, but I didn't know I was dreaming until I was awake and reflected back on my experiences. The differences between the three were unmistakable. I experienced a dramatic difference between the OBE, lucid dream, and vivid dream, the three experiences that are commonly confused with each other, because it is difficult to distinguish amongst them (by the novice practitioner). I now know that I was destined to see that there are other things that are not consciously known to man, but that do exist in other dimensions. I had a strong feeling, when awake, that I should help all people know this revelation and the difference between the conscious, subconscious, unconscious, and many other spiritually experienced realities.

As I returned to everyday life with a profound difference in perception, everything seemed to be transformed, different, connected, and full of life. I also saw many individuals who had no idea what reality they were even living in. It was as though they just accepted what reality they were given (physical) but denied the Real Reality. At this time I was not enlightened but thought that this was the real reality (mistaken).

After experiencing OBEs, lucid dreams, and vivid dreams, as well as seeing spirits and astral phenomena, I was determined to study more about this realm of the Spiritual Manifest to figure out what is real and what is not. I was convinced that I was here to find the difference between these realms and to teach others why. I started to look into psychic phenomena, but still with an extremely skeptical approach. Even though I saw another reality, I still didn't believe that one could be a psychic. This was the result of being programmed by a Christian school that made its students believe that these practices were 'satanic,' or that it was impossible to directly communicate with spirits. So I inherently felt the same. But I worked relentlessly to find out the truth about psychics.

I started to gather books on the subject of psychic phenomena. I applied their meditations and ended up proving the psychics right. Once again, I was convinced through my own experiences that psychics were real. Some are 'false,' though, and one should be skeptical when speaking to them until they are proven otherwise.

As of July 5, 2003, I can tell you from my own personal experiences that **all the psychic phenomena listed below and discussed in subsequent pages are true:**

Psychic or Spiritual Phenomena*

Psychokinesis ([seemingly] moving 'things' with the mind)
Psychometry (feeling and interpreting energy with the hands)
Clairaudience (hearing spiritual/astral realms/spirits)
Clairvoyance (seeing energy, spirits, auras)
Clairsentience (feeling energy with the aura)
Claircognizants (Knowing beyond your capability)
Channeling (energy being sent through oneself)
Mediumistic (allowing spirits to share your body)
Astral Projection (leaving your body at will)
Lucid Dreaming (knowing you're dreaming while dreaming)
Healing with Hands (channeling energy to others)
Divination (I-Ching, runes, pendulum, kinesiology)
Connect with Higher Self (meditation and enlightenment)
Communicating with Deceased (talking with passed spirits)
Communicating with Angels and Spirit Masters
Telepathy (picking up others' mental frequencies)
Communicating with Spirit Guides
Tarot Cards (half psychic and half divination)
Astrology (all matter [moon, stars, suns, etc.] affects beings)
Archetypes (sounds, symbols, words, imagining)
Crystals, Gems, and Stones (have healing energies)
Karma Predestines Life's Path
Spontaneous Recovery by Accepting God (faith healing)
Kundalini Energy and Chakras
Enlightenment (becoming One with the Source)
Healing with Prayer and Positive Thinking

*Note: It is important to note that not all so-called psychics are psychics. These 'imposters' tend to ruin the credible psychics' reputations, thus creating disbelief by the public. The only phenomenon that I have not experienced yet is that of levitation (where the physical body floats off the ground at will). Because I have proven so many phenomena to be true, I am not even pursuing the skill of levitation. I believe it can be possible. I

*believe that all things are possible; it is really all just a matter
of personal experience and faith. What one experiences is what
one believes. And if one doesn't experience something but believes, one has what is termed faith. Faith is all that is needed,
but most people want proof.*

Throughout the many paths I chose, all seemed to inspire and intrigue me; however, a constant and unwavering 'void' remained. This void was an emptiness that no psychic skill or spiritual experience could fulfill. I felt as if I was at the 'end of the road,' as well as disappointed and confused about what to do next.

As life seemed to go in an endless spiral downwards, nothing within this physical dimension could make me happy or at peace with myself. After all, thousands of unanswered questions remained within my being. Much to my dismay, I had acquired so much knowledge throughout my previous explorations into the astral realms that it seemed as if no other being whom I heard speak, who wrote books, or who was in the same region of the world knew any more about spirituality than I did. My ego was plagued by 'pride.'

With this depressing knowingness, I stopped meditating and gave up all hope for close to a year. Then inspiration spurred me on to search for more answers. This time, I wasn't going to cease until all was known. At the time, I felt as if God had prompted me to learn so that I could be a facilitator or educator of spiritual truth; really just *divinely inspired.*

Beginning on that day, I began to introspect into the deepest parts of my being. My mind was running rampant with thoughts, as if it was never going to turn off unless God showed himself to me or did something drastic. I began to read more spiritual books, research philosophy, practice yoga (again), and meditate 2 to 3 times a day. This time there would be no giving up until I knew the Truth about existence.

Throughout my many meditations, I saw and felt the presence of many spiritual beings, such as spiritual guides, angels, and other astral dwellers. I experienced so much that I was convinced I must be close to some sort of 'spiritual doorway.' I just didn't know what it was or where I was headed. I still was not satisfied because 'I,' in my mind, had not experienced God.

The search continued, but with a new awareness that my life's experience (journey) was changing as well. I felt a deeper connection with nature and with all animals, and could understand all beings a little better than before. Other than that, I felt no extraordinary change in my life. It just felt as though I was more understanding and compassionate to others, and that my point of view had changed as never before.

So I continued meditating and researching sacred texts relentlessly. I saturated my mind with spiritual texts that provided Truth; at the time I was not aware of how powerful this was. Previously, I thought that enlightenment was a goal for the 'weak minded' because of its generally 'easy-*sounding* concepts' and teachings. However, with the application of some teachings, it then became known that these concepts were Truths that I could not completely comprehend; I just 'thought' I could.

My meditations, in which I spent most of my day, became increasingly more beneficial and powerful. I did not exactly know why, but I felt as if I was bound to find out. So I just let God take me and I surrendered myself to the Infinite Presence of the Unmanifest. Much to my surprise, nothing happened. I felt as though my sincerity was at its maximum potential and that there was nothing else for me to give. So as I got up from my meditation, I told myself that I didn't need proof, that I believed with all of my heart and would just let things happen of their own accord.

The next day, I went to my mother-in-law's store and worked on the computer as I always did. I was searching the Internet for sites on enlightenment, and was just probing for anything that I might have missed. I kept on researching Truth, but at the same time wasn't really sure what that even was. So with blind faith, I just followed my heart and vowed to continue following the path of enlightenment. Although this vow was not spoken, or consciously even registered as being said, it was as if a sincere part of my being had surfaced and summoned the love of God.

As I turned off the computer, I had got up out of my seat and looked around. It was as if everything had melded together, or as if thousands of thoughts were within One Mind. It was not completely understood, but it was obviously very different from my previous everyday beingness. As I continued out the door, while hardly containing myself, I noticed that all life seemed to take on an animated feeling, so that the flowers, trees, sky, and concrete road had a special feeling to them. One feeling did not feel different than the other, but rather, it was all the same and felt as One, but alive.

This power that was flowing throughout my body seemed to operate it without thought or preparation. It was as if all was already preplanned and happening of its own. This power not only coursed ever so gently throughout my body, but at the same time, it felt as if it was the universe's energy—like I was in a connective energetic web of energy that was within and throughout All. I knew of its infiniteness, but could not accurately describe it. I could feel the connection of All, but could not comprehend it. It just was what it was as a feeling of 'Allness' and completeness that was the basic substrate of all that had ever manifested and currently is.

The wisdom came not only with an innate knowingness, but was reinforced by something so powerful that it was hard to place. It was that this inner connective energy was love, and that love was not a separate energy, or an emotion. It became understood that love was wisdom, which was awareness, which was God as formlessness. So then it became apparent that God as pure formlessness was Truth; the very thing that I was looking for could not even be seen, but instead was the underlying, Unmanifest energy of All That Is.

I now didn't have to read any books of enlightenment; I was the Self that the books spoke of. That became the day that I could write an accurate book on the subject of Self-Realization. And hopefully, that I would be able to aid other beings in their quest for remembering their True Self and not the illusory self that so many beings still focus on.

From an enlightened standpoint, I now reflected on my previous ego's lifestyle and occurrences. It became apparent that the very 'thing' that kept me from realizing my True Self was that of the illusory self (ego). So I studied the ego's every move and analyzed my life even further. It was seen that the ego was an illusory identity that maintained a feeling of independence or separateness from God, as well as from all other beings.

The main faculty of the ego that allowed for and reinforced this notion of division was 'judgment.' It was also seen that judgment is the very illusion that limits the amount of love that one wishes to experience, whether knowingly or unknowingly. If one chooses to be an ego, they simply elect to limit the amount of love, peace, and happiness that can be felt. But if they choose to abandon it, they experience peace, love, and happiness for all of eternity with no possibility of pain and suffering.

So from that day forward, I vowed to be a source of inspiration and wisdom to all of the beings in the world, while simultaneously being a source of love and compassion to all that exists. I saw all life with the potential to have their Divinity activated by Truth; like a candle turning into a halogen bulb in an instant when one wants change. All that is needed is direction and will, and that direction is Truth, and Truth is existence that provides for the Light of consciousness which spawns and is all life.

So with the Truth being known in the accompaniment of such splendor and fulfillment, who could turn their back on God once more? As Truth is revealed, one's locus of existence becomes that which is revealed—the Self. So to realize the Self is to be an expression of God as Truth, which is love, light, peace, and happiness. When this is known, one would not want to know another type of reality that provides 'subtruths.' Pure love and happiness is Reality as the Unmanifest essence.

Summing Up Life

This brief summary of the path that I chose was written to help you understand that destiny is what revealed itself to me in my life, as it does to all beings. From my past life, I acquired a certain amount of karma, which allowed me to be placed into a specific life within the physical dimension. Because of my past karma, this planet in this galaxy, the country of the United States, the state of Florida, the city of Tampa, the neighborhood, the family with siblings and other relatives, the house, the school, the friends, the sports, the thoughts, and the emotions were preselected and inherently created and were my destiny that unfolded as existence within the manifest.

As one is born into the world, they are placed by past-life karma into a 'life' that will help them learn their specific lessons and fix their accumulating karma. When one is put into a body and takes on the lifestyle of that destiny, they are given infinite possibilities to change destiny at 'will.' As one changes karma, one changes their destiny, which outwardly changes their lifestyle and outcomes. So if one is not happy with their lifestyle, they must change their karma by positively changing their lifestyle, habits, intentions, and actions. As this 'will' changes, so does destiny, which means that every positive thought, intention, or action one has changes their destiny or outcome for the better. The outcome will increase their future level of happiness, their capacity to love, and their understanding of the Real Reality. They will always feel fulfilled, experience God, experience a better future, and reincarnate no more (unless desired).

In sum, changing choice changes destiny. So always have a positive 'will,' because this creates a positive outlook and positive choices. Positive 'will' creates positive change, because positive 'will' summons the action of the Divine Destiny. Each choice creates a new destiny, but Divine Will guarantees positive destiny. So devote one's life to God and Divine Will will flow through one's Self while continuously manifesting a more positive destiny for one's own existence as well as others.

Don't Concentrate on the Astral Dimensions

If enlightenment is one's goal, then do not concentrate on becoming a psychic or studying psychic phenomena. This will actually slow one's spiritual evolution greatly. As one focuses on form, one stays away from or denies God (formlessness). The physical dimension and the astral dimensions are those of 'form.' Wherever energy concentrates into a pattern, such as an idea, thought, language, dream, word, or astral phenomenon, it is considered form. To 'stay in' or 'concentrate on' form is to stay away from God, because God is nonform.

Just because one does not perceive something doesn't mean that it doesn't exist. God is Unmanifest (invisible and nonform) and always present and available; just trust in this. So if one exercises their 'will' to do astral things such as OBEs, psychic skills, dreaming, and so forth, one would be exercising their 'ego will.' 'Ego will' is not 'Divine Will.' 'Ego will' comes from one's own wants and desires, which are at lower levels of consciousness. These wants and desires are needed and sought after to fill an emptiness or void that was created from the constant rejection of one's True Nature (Self/God). Unlike what is preached in the various religions, it is not 'satanic' or 'evil' unless one's 'will' is as well.

If a good heart and good intentions are dominant, then a certain level of 'Divine Will' is present, and the negative qualities of the being will usually not prevail. However, if negative intentions are in one's mind, then negative intentions are achieved and negative karma is assumed. So do an OBE once or twice if it needs to be proven to one's self, but then move on and never look back. Do not keep doing it, because it will bring one's karma down, since 'ego will' is being practiced instead of Divine Will (God's Will).

'Proof,' to the ego, can be used to replace 'faith' for the experiences that the being **will not** accept as 'Real.' It should not, however, be dwelt upon. If one chooses to have 'proof' replace 'faith,' then walk the safe path—the path of Enlightenment. All will be revealed in the end (proof) when the Self is revealed. If one has faith and does not need proof, then follow the path of Enlightenment as well, and be complete and fulfilled.

Watch Out for Deceivers

The majority of the world is filled with deceivers. The unfortunate thing is that they do not even know they are the deceiver that they speak of themselves. What is even more confusing is that they go around telling everyone to watch out for deceivers. These deceivers are beings who either knowingly or unknowingly try to make one fall victim to the darkness (dualistically speaking) or the illusory dimension of the manifest.

They are very hard to pick out because they appeal to the 'ego will' or one's desires and wants. They also speak in and of the linear dimension of reality, which is the reality that the ego mind was meant to function in, not the Self/Spirit/God. 'Linear reality' is the existence that can be perceived by the ego senses, which detect form within time, space, and distance, or have a rational explanation. These 'deceivers' will camouflage or hide the 'ego will' in spiritual-sounding texts or identities such as priests, pastors, ministers, gurus, saints, sages, or spiritual masters. So when one listens to the pastor, they think they are getting pure truth because:

1. *The pastor works for the church and no one could work for the church or a religious institution unless they really knew what they were talking about, right?*

2. *They make sense and they are rational ('ego will' is rational and linear; God is nonlinear and beyond rational).*

3. *This person is nice (the 'ego will' of people can appear nice to the outside world, but has hidden intentions [gaining power, having control and a following, feeling important, feeling like they are helping, which satisfies the ego]).*

4. *They read from the Bible or some other sacred text (linear/rational/logical egos cannot truly interpret the Nonlinear Truths presented within the Bible).*

5. *They have a large following (the 'ego' appeals to the 'ego will,' which makes one ego follow another—Truth does not have to be present, only rationality).*

6. *They have a PhD and teach theology (one can't study God; studying is linear, rational, and logical; one can only experience God, which very few have ever done)*

7. *I've studied with them or gone to their church for ten years and they have always had good sermons.*

> *(The church's definition of 'good' is basically following their morals or the 'Ten Commandments' and not trying to experience God—their way is faith, not direct experience. It should also be added that the human mind cannot distinguish 'Truth' from 'fallacy.')*

8. *My family practices this religion, and so it can't be that bad (chances are that one's family doesn't know the 'Truth' of existence, and if not, their ego's judgment cannot be trusted).*

9. *They wrote a book, or made a video and CDs, so they must know what they are talking about. (There are many books which are false or just 'half-truths'; it is almost impossible to find a 'Book of Truth' unless one has already experienced God or Truth.)*

10. *The person speaking is so passionate on the subject that they are speaking about that it must be true ('ego will' unknowingly distorts truth and makes one think it is true by rationality, which unknowingly fools the followers into believing).*

It is also important to note that not all of these identities that are taken on are false. There are some beings who speak the 'whole truth.' There are also some who 'think' they are speaking the 'whole truth,' yet it is a distorted truth that their ego has generated. Until the ego is transcended or purified, through the understanding of one's true existence or taking the path of enlightenment (which so many religious leaders say is 'satanic'), that being cannot be completely trusted due to their own unknown 'ego will's' distortions of reality. They usually mean well, but often lead others astray, which can create loss of religion and loss of hope after many years. Only 'enlightened beings' can lead one to an experience with God. All others speak 'fallacies' or 'half-truths,' which cannot be completely trusted.

If one cannot find a book by an enlightened being, an enlightened being to study with, or a person who is at least a purified ego (whose predominant emotion is unconditional love—no judgment should be present), then one should keep on looking. Never leave your soul in the hands of an unenlightened being. By following the proper meditations and studying the books on enlightenment, Self-realization can happen in less than a year. It does not take a guru or a religion to reach enlightenment. All it takes is your 'Will' to do so, or devotion to God and the continual questioning and dismantlement of one's ego. It does not take 'lifetimes' to reach enlightenment, as was previously thought. It just takes one's undying devotion to do God's Will and the complete abandonment of the ego.

This book will not only help one become an 'enlightened being,' it will also help one understand the different realms of existence. The teachings within this book have been presented in such a way that one's level of consciousness will rise with every page that is read, thus allowing one to transcend their ego. This book is designed to attract the ego's attention by creating interest, intrigue, desire, wants, and a feeling of specialness. Then after the ego has been attracted to the book, it reads a couple of pages and begins to feel as if life is more than what has been shown, which makes it feel as though there is something else that very few people know. This makes the ego feel special when it is presented with the fact that it may experience the 'Real Reality.' As this special and exclusive feeling keeps the ego's attention by sounding rational and logical, it slowly starts to raise one's level of consciousness by allowing the Truth to enter into their energetic field. As it changes one's level of consciousness via Truth, one's ego will start to recede while the Divine Will starts to come forth as Self.

As Divine Will takes over and leads one's life for them, one's perception of the world will change to a perfect and positive view. It will then be impossible to see any imperfections in the world. So all beings will not just look perfect, but the divinity within them will be known at all times. One will not be able to judge anyone anymore. In fact, one can't even try to judge, because the perfection that all beings radiate is known and felt at all times. One will also have a complete understanding of how all things work in the spiritual realms and how form manifested in the spiritual and physical levels of existence from the Unmanifest. One will see that all 'things' that were allowed to take form did so because the conditions within the spiritual dimensions allowed the manifestation to take place in the physical world because it was 'willed' so. One will see that all things are connected as One. One will feel compassion, which is a nonjudgmental understanding for all beings.

As enlightenment becomes one's self as Self, one will feel compelled to help all beings raise their level of consciousness. One will also karmically heal all beings when near them. One's prayers will become very effective due to the constant positive irradiation that one's Self emits. One's enlightened existence can offset most of the negativity on the entire planet. One will be able to know when spiritual teachings are 'false' or 'true,' because spiritual vision is acquired and usually used at all times. And one will realize that the world is full of perfect souls who have been severely disillusioned or misdirected by the 'ego's will,' thus perfectly expressing their level of consciousness as it should be.

My Soul's Path of Inquiry

During my soul's evolution, I have met many people who are certain that they know what they are talking about. I have also been misled a couple of times, and believed what they told me was true because it made so much sense. They appeal to the 'ego will,' but unless one knows how the ego works, it will not be recognized and one will fall victim to their ignorance. I have met very convincing beings who have had me believe everything that they've said; because my previous ego was always a rational thinker, it only believed people who spoke in rational or logical speech patterns.

So it believed in the scientific approach, or "show me proof" method. When one doesn't know what path to take, or is confused about exactly what 'spirituality' is, the scientific/logical/rational/provable ego mind will keep one from it. It will delay progress and can even make one go backwards in spiritual evolution. Fortunately, I did not get trapped by the seduction of psychic skills and OBEs. But believe me, I almost did because I was obsessed with having OBEs and improving my psychic skills. And I did not realize that there was more to spirituality than the astral dimensions. I also did not realize that I was supposed to evolve to a higher state of enlightenment. This was obviously information that the everyday person has no clue about, and neither did I. I thought that the more psychic I got, the more evolved I got. However, this is not the case. Luckily, I stopped digressing back into the astral dimensions and continued on my path of enlightenment. I know that the majority of the beings who inhabit this world need or want to see proof in order to believe. That is why this method of Enlightenment, which appeals to the ego and then dissolves it, was developed; however, one must have faith until 'proof' is experienced at the end as Self.

This method was developed to help all beings bypass psychic phenomena, but to have some information as well as some proof (through knowledge and experience) that it exists. It will allow one to have 'direct proof' through various meditative practices, instead of being forced to adapt to having faith without proof. If one can have 100% faith without proof, it would be a faster path to enlightenment; but almost no beings currently have this impermeable faith or they would already be enlightened.

Just remember not to get involved in trying to be psychic; this is only satisfying the 'ego will' because of the feeling of specialness or uniqueness that it creates. No one being is more special than another; we are all the same, because we are all One. This book's methods will allow one to realize the fallacy in the world, how to avoid it *at first*, but then how to resolve it by adding light and love as Truth. This book is the direct route to enlightenment through the process of understanding the nature of the ego and its inherent levels of consciousness, as well as the universal karmic laws and various levels of divinity.

The ego has to be shown proof or it will not believe it is true. Instead, it might hope it is true, but it will not believe. If one truly believes in God, then death is actually anticipated, because all is known and there is no fear. There is no fear because all is fulfilled by the presence of the 'Divine Source' (permanent inner fulfillment). Understand that 'spiritual proof' is not a belief, it is a 'realization,' just as enlightenment is proof, or a 'realization' and not a belief. Unfortunately, those who are not enlightened or psychic do not necessarily believe very strongly. But those who are do believe because they experience reality very differently. This is how the 'perception of reality' changes throughout one's path; as consciousness changes, so does reality.

Chapter 2
<u>Enlightenment Confusion</u>

Inaccuracies in the 'Age of Enlightenment'

Throughout time, man has pondered existence. The fact that something greater could exist seemed possible, plausible, and, at the very least, intriguing and inspiring. This prompted man to begin a spiritual journey that will last throughout the end of *time* (within the perceived linear reality). As part of the philosophical viewpoints manifested by man's ego since the beginning, new techniques and theories were developed to aid in the journey. There is only one problem with this movement, which is termed the 'Age of Enlightenment': although people's intentions were honest, they were going about it using many misguided theories.

The history books usually identify the 'Age of Enlightenment' as being in the 18th century, but it really originated many centuries before Christ. Since the first thinking being, the questions, 'What is this,' 'Where am I,' or 'Who am I,' have always plagued the mind. These questions provided a springboard for people to jump into a new dimension; however, a lack of understanding and realization blocked their spiritual progress.

There is only one Truth, and it is subjective. However, the ego prompted man to think that 'thought and reason' were the keys to realization. Many beliefs were created and broken through, but the fact remains that people were not completely helping each other become Self-Realized.

People's living conditions definitely improved, and an increased emphasis on scholastic achievements shaped our political and economic environment. Science was made into the driving factor that was thought to bring the understanding of God closer by way of 'proof,' or evidence and reason. At best, however, this so-called 'Age of Enlightenment' is and should be renamed the 'Age of Linear Reasoning.' During this period, only a handful of philosophers, such as Socrates (enlightened), his student Plato, and several others can be considered teachers of enlightenment.

The 'Wrong' Direction

During the 'Age of Enlightenment,' which should never be confused with actual Enlightenment, ego methodologies such as linear thinking and reasoning were thought to be of great importance. Science and theology flourished, along with the belief that the truth of existence was going to be found. In fact, this age was considered an 'intellectual movement,' where scholars and philosophers abounded. Although thinking solves many problems within the linear dimension, the actual enlightenment process meant abandoning all thought and all of its processes—not something that anyone was willing to do at this time.

This age compelled people, first and foremost, to improve the structure of society. The understanding of God would have been looked at as spectacular and wanted, but in essence, people were living to improve the current conditions of their countries and dictatorships, and not their spirituality. The reforms included changes in government, schooling, arts, politics, family, social structure, morality, and 'thinkingness'; these are all beneficial but lacking in Absolute Truth.

This age included the 'Renaissance Humanist' movement during the 14th and 15th centuries. Its main focus was to celebrate the many creations of God, mainly humans. The development of 'Hedonism' as a religion was the evident result. Prior to this movement, the churches were against the lower emotions and positionalities of the ego, even though it wasn't stated that way. The churches that were not Hedonistic were against expressing overly affectionate relationships, having promiscuous sex, and falling for the traps of Satan—which were desire, cravings, pride, exhibitionism, deception, and enjoying the pleasures of the flesh. Even so, the Humanists did what they wanted to do, as long as they were not caught or executed for it. During this time, witches were also said to exist, and people were killed for even questioning the current religion. The mainstream religions at that time were Catholicism and Protestantism.

These religions constantly battled one another through

thoughts, will, and force. They would both declare that the other religion was a follower of Satan, and in so doing, they tried to deter others from joining the other religion and gaining patronage. At the same time, the churches controlled one's choice of faith. So if one was told to become a Protestant, and the Catholic Church found out, the person would be executed if they refused to convert back to the governing religion. This constant turmoil created more conflicts between the churches and governments, which would go to war to attempt to remedy this by forcing each other to surrender their beliefs.

Enlightenment is about inner peace, which leads to outer peace, which leads to worldly peace, which creates universal peace. So the churches obviously were not yet enlightened themselves. In fact, the churches were ignorant, deceitful, malicious, argumenttative, controlling, judging, punishing, and basically enslaved the entire population. All of these qualities are emotions and positionalities of the ego, and are not a property of God. Therefore the churches were actually unholy places at the time, and their leaders were unholy as well.

The churches controlled whom one knew, where one went, what one knew, and all of the literature that one was able to read. All texts, books, or any other type of literature were reviewed by the state and the church, which would have the final editing rights and say-so, if they even allowed something to be published. Any organization or person saying anything argumentative, or proving anything other than what the church spoke or taught of, was imprisoned, banned, or executed.

Not too differently from today, in various parts of the world at this time, every church proclaimed their own special way of practicing religion as the only way to salvation. So the only reason that Christianity flourished was because the state and the church didn't allow otherwise. So our nations were not really formed by God; rather, in a sense they were formed by the controlling aspect of the egos within the churches that distorted the pure Truth of God.

Another aspect of the controlling nature of the church during this period, as well as a demonstration of its ignorance, was that any interpretations taken from the Bible were not only considered, but revered, as the highest of truths. Much of the Bible was based on metaphorical and analogous stories that were meant to help one overcome and dissolve the ego. However, these were taken to be literal, and even to this day are often thought to be the truth. The stories, when translated, understood, and realized correctly, as they were meant to be, definitely and undeniably convey a high level of Truth. Much of the Bible was indeed based on observations made by man. Unfortunately, the observations made by man were made by the ego of man, and therefore are not very accurate, since the ego's job is to distort Higher Truth into subtruth or fallacy.

As a result, most churches tried to contradict the facts of the linear dimension that were proved by science. For example, when Galileo proved that the earth revolved around the Sun, and not the Planets around the Earth (as the church had previously believed because the Bible said so), the Catholic Church threatened him. They told him to denounce his claim as a mistruth. Galileo was forced to denounce his claim that was held under a Catholic providence; however, later the publications were moved to a Protestant district where his claim could be announced with confidence without punishment from the greater controlling and restricting church.

Keep in mind that the Bible has some very high levels of consciousness imprinted within it, which is a very high level of Truth. The only misinterpretations and misunderstandings in the Bible are due to the constructs of the ego, which will not allow the whole Truth to flow unrestricted or unhindered to and as the essence of the being. As soon as Truth is thought to be perceived, it is misunderstood due to the nature of the ego, because the linear/dualistic ego mind is trying to understand Nonlinear teachings. This is like trying to understand the essence of air when studying the structure of a solid. No understandings or realizations will come from this, due to the misplacement of focus.

Beyond the control of the churches were independent 'thinkers' who avoided the restrictions of society. These thinkers, called 'philosophers,' pondered the meaning of life, but again, some were very misguided. They, as well as psychoanalysts and theologians, studied the manifest for answers about the Unmanifest; which entails attempts to understand the Unmanifest or Nonlinear Truths by the study and utilization of manifest or linear/dualistic concepts, theories, and structures. These 'thinkers' studied problems within society, such as social structure and morality, along with political and economic problems. They challenged the churches on many ideas, even if it meant risking death or imprisonment, because they were on a crusade to fix the world's problems. They wanted to make it a 'better place.'

These 'thinkers' questioned everything that they could 'think of,' but within that statement lies a paradox, because the Truth about Enlightenment is in 'nonthinking.' This means to clear one's mind and just be. In the beginning, introspection, a way of internal questioning that helps to resolve the viewpoints of the ego, was utilized with much benefit, because it brought the questions that blocked Truth from being known into conscious awareness. This helped to loosen the grip of the ego, allowing Truth to prevail with clarity. So the Truth is not in what one 'thinks' they know, but in what one doesn't 'think' they know. This goes against what many believe today, that "Knowledge is power."

There is a difference between *knowingness* and *knowing about*. *Knowingness* is knowing what one is as the highest aspect of consciousness because they are it. In contrast, *knowing about* entails utilizing the ego to dualistically 'study about' something that the ego believes is separate. Therein lies the illusion.

This is simply because the ego blocks Truth, which blocks realization. Therefore the ego must be abandoned in order to experience Truth. One's emotional attachment to the world, the viewpoint that is held of the world, the knowledge that one has, the relationships that one thinks they have, the thoughts that they think they have, the life that they have been led to believe that they have, and the identity that one has with the body must be unlearned or abandoned. However, one must not really forget their identity, but rather become unattached to 'who they think they are' in order to remember 'who they really are.' Truth is egoless, and so the ego must be abandoned for realization to occur. A *samadhi* is a mini-enlightened state that is an egoless experience, and enlightenment is a permanent realization of Truth.

This leads one to the realization that the Vedic religion, Krishna, Buddha, the Bodhisattvas, and Jesus had tried to explain without explaining, which is the only way the Truth could be properly conveyed. However, people wanted proof. So these spiritual masters spoke of Nonlinear Reality in linear terms, the first and foremost error in teaching enlightenment. However, there is no other way to teach 'ego stubborn' people the Truth. So the level of Truth had to be decreased a little so that it made more sense to others. As these levels of 'truth' were understood and realized more and more, these teachers increased the levels of 'Truth' to help beings spiritually evolve to a higher level of consciousness. But these Truths were not realized by many, leading to mass confusion. People still seek the Truth as if it had never been found or presented before.

There is only one Truth; however, people's egos seem to believe that only their religion is the Truth and that all other religions and/or methods of knowing God are inferior. These thoughts, as well as the belief that Truth has not been already presented, must be abandoned. Truth is just what one is, albeit in the higher aspect. So in essence, one is just being what the ego has learned to be and has temporarily just forgotten to be what one really is— God (in and as the highest aspect of beingness—Unmanifest).

The Incorrect Reason To Become Enlightened

One chooses to start upon the pathway of enlightenment for many reasons, but some of them are self-serving (such as pride, identity acquirement, control, power, and money). As the pathway of enlightenment is under way, some of the ego is dissolved as Truth begins to enter consciousness. This helps one refocus their purpose for enlightenment, away from the selfish and onto the selfless. Even so, some of the remnants of the broken-down ego may resurface even if the individual is enlightened. As one enlightens and the ego is transcended, the spirit rejoices as it is free, but the ego remains on 'standby' with the various temptations of 'will.' This is why the term 'transcended' is a more accurate term than 'dissolved.' The term 'dissolved' leads one to believe that the ego has no more existence, and that it would be an impossibility to regain it. This is false. A 'being' is 'free will'; therefore, one may simply 'will' to become absorbed within the ego's traps and desires again—if prompted and lessons were not learned, of course. 'Transcended' means 'to go beyond the limited bounds of'—in this case, an ego. So it is possible and has been done before by other enlightened beings.

Just because one is enlightened doesn't mean that they will never again be tempted by the ego or other nontruthful beings to be self-serving once more. In fact, sometimes temptations grow. Buddha and Jesus spoke of many instances when they were tempted by 'sinful beings' while they were enlightened. Even if one is tempted, there are no emotional or mental ties to what these beings try to tempt one with, whether sex, money, power, or control. This is how they try to pull one back into the false reality of illusion and suffering. In actuality, they just want to share their pain.

The path of enlightenment should be for one reason only: to become that light of Truth and spread it to others. To enlighten in order to help others is very hard to imagine at lower levels of consciousness, but as one's level of consciousness raises, their motives are changed by way of inspiration. Thus they are concerned with helping all others spiritually evolve. Whether it is done in word or in silence, it is done.

If one hopes to become a widely known mystic or healer, then enlightenment is not for them. If one wants to be a psychic or have special powers, then enlightenment is not for them. If one wants to develop certain skills so others view them as powerful, or so they feel looked up to or admired and respected, then enlightenment is not for them. If one wants to become an enlightened sage just so they can charge for advice that others do not know, then the path should be reconsidered. Enlightenment is a path of Truth, the highest of high Truth. It should be undergone to save one's self and all of humanity. The benefit should not be looked at selfishly, for as one enlightens, they help save many souls. Enlightenment should be a selfless act. Enlightenment should be taken as a path only when one wants to change for the better, thus helping others. Even if the ego's motives overshadow the Truth in the beginning, inspiration as Divinity will eventually overcome one as Self and refocus one's endeavors.

When enlightened, one is the 'singular Self' of all beings; therefore, one is aware of being One. When one has come to this realization, they are Self-identical with all beings. Not connected, just One, because connection implies that there is something to be connected to—a dualism. This leads to the conclusion that every thought an enlightened being has affects all mankind, due to their beingness, which directly affects other egos' beingness. This is due to the enlightened being 'being' everywhere and everyone at all times. So their positive thoughts and 'beingness' actually lift and reinforce the universal energetic field, as well as the beings that they pray for, thus spreading positivity. In the same way, the negative thoughts of the ego will negatively affect mankind as well.

What Not To Expect When Enlightened

Many people believe that some sort of astral party, ceremony, initiation, signs, flags, lights, spirit beings, or other 'form' will be set off or come to greet them when enlightenment is attained. This is not so. Some beings experience sounds or lights, yet most others experience nothing. Some beings are tempted from the 'dark side' (so to speak), yet others have no confrontations at all. Some people become enlightened when in sleep and others in wakefulness, some during meditation and others when on the computer or playing with their children. Enlightenment can and will come at any time, whenever one is ready. Only God knows.

Enlightenment, when attained, is an infinite, all-encompassing, profound love, which surrounds one as a gentle embrace from and as the Unmanifest. It is and provides for one to be positive while simultaneously making one not see the negative. It allows for one to see (so to speak) the Source of Divinity within all 'things' or beings. When the ego's positionalities cease, beingness is experienced in the Now. Enlightenment seems to transform all 'beings,' 'things,' or 'perceived reality,' into an 'astral-like' dimension, such as making the physical dimension not feel as concrete or solid as it once did. It begins to feel like that which it is, a mental zone; a universe charged by 'will,' one with endless possibilities and known to be perfect 'as is.' So with nothing that needs to be changed or controlled, life 'as is' can be experienced as perfect and beautiful.

Only God's Help Transcends

The *very* important fact to *always* keep in mind is that one can push through the borders of the ego to the door of enlightenment, but <u>*cannot*</u> force their way over to an enlightened state. One must just allow 'Thy Will' or God's Will to enlighten them when they are ready. Force is a product of the ego; therefore, it cannot be used to transcend itself into infinite Power. It is like using water to get rid of water; it makes no sense. If the enlightened state is without the ego, then clearly the ego is not allowed to exist there.

This is why so many beings are 'trying' to get enlightened, but cannot because they are 'trying' too hard. To 'try' is a positionality of the ego. Just 'try' to get to the door of enlightenment, and then let go and relax. The door is easily signified by an increase in the number of 'mini-enlightened' states of awareness, known as 'samadhis.' The more frequent the samadhis, the closer one is to the door; having two or three a week, during meditation and spontaneously in a fully awake state, denotes being very close.

No matter how much one wants to be enlightened, one must simply surrender all positionalities, desires, cravings, and wants, and let the Self or God's Will take over. Complete humility and surrender of the ego to God/Source will allow for its transcension to take place. When one surrenders the ego, analogously speaking, one gives it up and says, "I don't need it anymore; I get it now." That's the sign or the permission that God needs (so to speak—because God needs and wants nothing), allowing the Self to become realized, thus transcending the limitations of the ego.

Why Churches Believe Enlightenment Is 'Evil'

This is because the egos of the religious leaders who speak

for the churches are naïve. It is because Jesus and Buddha did not speak the same language; therefore, their terminology differs. Jesus and Buddha taught the same lessons, but due to the lack of interpretation and translation of the religious texts, error is obviously immanent. Most Buddhists (not all) realize that Jesus and Buddha taught the same lessons, but many church leaders would rather die than admit that. The Christian churches have severely distorted Truth to what they still call truth. There is only one Truth; it is seen in all the great religions and is the same Truth, although distorted in varying amounts.

Only the ego of man *judges* what is truth or what is not, because only the ego can *judge*. Truth was spoken by both, yet interpreted differently by different egos. Buddha said, "I am one with everything," and Jesus said, "The Father and I are One," which is the same thing, yet the churches obviously disagree. Jesus even said, in the New Testament (John 10:34-35), "Is it not in your Law, I have said, you are gods? (NIV)." This clearly states that Jesus wanted us to know that we are gods; however, we are not realized yet. This is why the difference in capital lettering between 'gods' and 'God.' He brought the word of God, because he was 'God-Realized' and his words were the 'Word of God.' 'Gods' is used to show us that we are of the same God, but not yet realized to be so. Jesus wanted us to realize that we are God and that we are all One. This was an attempt by Jesus to help us remember that we are, in our highest aspect…God.

The churches, however, only believe that God is the trinity—that is, the Father (God), the Son (Jesus only), and the Holy Spirit (God's Grace, but selectively given to people who are Christians). Even though they call themselves the 'children of God,' they still think that only Jesus is the Son of God (the only child) and nothing else.

They think that God is infinite, yet God is only 'three things or entities' (the trinity). This leaves out almost everything in existence and also contradicts the belief that God is infinite. "How can God be infinitely everywhere, except here (man), here (hell), and there (physical)?" This indicates that the belief that someone who could even conjure up such an idea as 'One with everything' would be 'satanic.' The churches' distorted beliefs are due to ignorance, or not knowing.

I have heard many preachers say that "Buddha is in hell," or that "he was possessed by demons." This is pure ignorance on the part of the church and the individual. It is also a way for the church to instill fear in the hearts of mankind, making them depend on that specific religion for salvation. The 'speaking out' of the preacher's ego is representative of the fear of the church. First, this exhibits mainly ignorance; second; pride and righteousness (to prove to others that they are right and everyone else who is not following them is wrong); third; selfish control (an attempt to control the people); fourth, fear of abandonment by 'followers' and having their beliefs challenged; and fifth, 'wanting' to have followers to fulfill their selfish greed and desires (which therefore makes them believe that happiness is something that has to be acquired). The emptiness that they are trying to fill is actually due to the lack of Truth, which is the lack of God. It is important to note that all religions have some distortions of Truth, some modest and others greater.

The beings who display these traits are self-serving because they more or less serve their ego. They think that they are the holiest of people and know the way to salvation. Unfortunately, the ego usually has such a strong grip upon many Christians that salvation can be nearly impossible for many of them—even when they are convinced that they are saved. This contradiction in thought is purely because they still follow and give in to the special needs and desires of their ego. It is also due to the fact that they have never been taught the actual origination of sin, the ego—which they still have.

Almost all Christians still believe that the origination of sin is 'Lucifer,' one 'bad guy' who is trying to harm everyone. This depiction is actually an example of egos displacing their anger and blame onto the unseen forces of some other being. It is a way to not take 100% responsibility for their sins. Therefore, they feel that they should be wary of 'Satan' and watchful of demons, and they really *hate* 'Satan.' The 'hatred' that they feel toward Satan is a sin in and of itself, because hate originates from the ego—that which provides and is the lower level of consciousness. The story of Lucifer in the Bible was used to illustrate how **all** souls descended from the Source; thus, all egos who are entrapped in the lower levels of consciousness can really be said to be 'Lucifer.' Christians take this very literally, though. Because of all of the misinterpretations and mistranslations that are conveyed in the Christian religion, its followers usually believe in Jesus, are confused about the Bible (even though they usually think that they know everything about it), and still give into sin (the ego). Meanwhile, they go around *hating* sin, sinners, demons, and Satan, which inherently makes them fall into the trap of the ego and fall victim to sin because of their own ignorance of Truth. To 'hate hatred' is ridiculous and a trap that condemns one's self.

The examples provided by many churches, portrayed by their preachers, are the vanities of the self-serving ego, which are inherently picked up and learned by the audience, who in turn become followers because of the fear of eternal damnation instilled into them. They follow the traits of the preacher's ego because they assume that the preacher is 'holy' (which means 'Divine Serving and Enlightened'), but they are usually not. In fact, nearly all preachers have many ego problems or sins that they have not yet resolved and that currently rule their life. To be an ego and to teach egos is to teach these beings how to be another quality of ego, thus creating a mirror image of the preacher and his/her inherent traits; therefore, it is a classic case of a 'sinner teaching a sinner,' or more accurately, an 'illusionist teaching an illusionist.'

The negative traits of some preachers' egos are pride (feeling as if they are better than non-Christians), righteousness (feeling as if they are right and everyone else is wrong), judgment, classification (wrong or right religions), contempt for sinners, control, aversion (not wanting to be around nonbelievers), disgust (for anything that does not fall within their ideals), and the feeling that they are special. These traits carry over and infect their followers negatively. These Christians therefore act out and portray the same ego positionalities as the preacher.

It is not their fault if they act or behave like these types of preachers. They were just programmed with a different type of ego program. 'Truth' is not found by or in programmings of the ego; it is found by simply unprogramming the ego. Therefore, one must abandon the traits of the ego to reveal the 'Supreme Reality' or essence of Truth; the very thing that Christians hold beloved (besides Christ), just like many others in the world, is their ego, not Absolute Truth. This creates difficulties when one tries to release or unprogram another 'church being.' These beings will verbally attack one by making fun of another's ideals or what one thinks is Truth. What the 'church beings' don't know is that they covet their own thoughts and ego, which is a sin: "Thou shalt not covet." So anything that opposes what they covet in their ego (thoughts, beliefs, beingness) as important will be defended by all means necessary. This inherently brings about the fighting spirit or, in other words, the 'evil ego' or 'the sinner' of that being.

If one is truly enlightened, any conflicting beliefs will not anger or irritate them. Instead, they will respect what is said and offer a sign of compassion (a handshake, hug, apology, prayer, or comforting comment) to stabilize the negative effects of the sinning ego. Right after the event with the argumentative ego has taken place, the enlightened being will pray and try to help the other being as much as they can. On the other hand, the average Christian will usually mutter 'sinful things' under their breath or think judgmental thoughts in an attempt to show themselves that they are better than the other because they are a Christian and the other is not (judgment, pride, condemnation, anger, contempt, disgust, and aversion, or trying not to ever run into that person again, unless it is an attempt to prove themselves right, a sign of righteousness and pride). This is obviously a drastic difference in character; one helps others and the other hinders (*not all Christians are this way*).

All seeming problems are within the ego; if all were enlightened, no problems would exist. So if all religions and/or spiritual sects concentrated on the Truth in their spiritual teachings, all would be saintly. Unfortunately, the egos in various religions are competing to show each other which religion is more correct, thereby judging, classifying, and degrading all others who are not approved by their religion. This creates not only war, but an internal and external unpeaceful existence. This is why religion divides people and countries.

If all churches, temples, and synagogues were to drop their pride and get together to examine what Truths are in each others texts and teachings, then a compromise could be reached. If compromises were made and the common Truth was known by all beings, then people would be more open to the experience of God, rather than just 'thinking' that they 'know about' God; an ego quality and expression of dualism (the thinker and the thought-about).

One reason that many people are not currently religious is because they don't know why there are so many religions. They think to themselves, "Out of all of these religions, how do I know which one is correct?" If the simple Truth is adhered to by all religions, then one will feel free to join any religion, as long as the Truth is told. This will bring the possibility of peace within this lifetime. If this attempt is *never* made, then war, sexism, hatred, racism, and any other type of 'ism' or crime will be a common occurrence and part of reality.

The Religion Business

Thousands of years ago, churches were developed to deliver a certain amount of Truth to the masses. Currently, however, religions and churches have been transformed into businesses. They ask for more money at every sermon that one goes to; sometimes charging thousands of dollars just to get married 'under God' for 15 to 30 minutes. Money is fine when needed, but it sometimes comes into the churches in excess of millions every year.

This much money is not needed to tell the Truth. Enlightened beings tell it for free every single day, but the ego will always charge or want something in return, whether it is admiration, respect, control, to feel powerful or godlike, to feel knowledgeable, to feel as if it is doing something 'good,' or to be in a position with leverage. The bottom line is that the Truth, which is ignored and condemned by religions, should be spoken of liberally. It should be free. It should be seen as the only Truth. After all, all religions are based purely on Truth (God/Source/Unmanifest).

Why Doesn't Everyone Follow Truth?

Truth is the furthest thing from the standards of what and where we currently think (with the ego) we are. Therefore, it is a long stretch to believe that it is even a possibility. This fact remains due to the ego mind, which each being covets.

This ego mind is rational, logical, chronological, dualistic, and can only perceive things in the linear dimension. The absolute 'seemingly opposite' (which is perceived this way by the ego, but has no actual reality) is that of Truth. It is Nonlinear, Nondualistic, cannot be perceived, cannot be proven, cannot be conveyed perfectly in words, and cannot be experimented with; therefore, it seems to be a myth or fallacy.

Another reason is 'defense.' The release of attachments brings fear to the ego, which feels threatened and will defend itself and the perceived identity that it has created for itself. As a result, it convinces itself that Truth can't be real, providing a strong foundation for why one should not undergo such a quest. The ego is a defense mechanism in and of itself. It will defend that which it has claimed or possesses as 'rightfully' belonging to it at all costs. Its feeling of losing its existence (or part of it) is obviously not very appealing to the ego. So it can be seen that it serves itself because it likes itself; that is the ego's main function (maintaining separateness).

Many people feel as if the 'spiritual journey' of enlightenment is a waste of time. This is part of the ego's defense system as well. It will make one feel unmotivated, uncomfortable, lazy, tired, and prideful, and convince one that the mission is wasteful and unnecessary. These feelings obviously do not prompt one to go out and do something that may reveal Truth. So in the beginning of the process of enlightenment, one may actually have to *__force__* themselves to study, meditate, and be nice to others. This is the quality of 'resistance' that the ego displays. With time, it no longer needs to be forced because the positive qualities become one's self as Self and display their attributes in perfect concordance with Self.

Not many people have become enlightened, and few people know anyone who currently is or ever was, as far back as Biblical times or even earlier. Only about 80 people in the world are currently enlightened out of nearly 6 billion earthly inhabitants. Because enlightenment has typically been considered as impossible for most, most beings do not even attempt to seek it. So it is a very rare phenomenon indeed. At the same time, people always seem to go in the direction of the masses. So whatever religion is common, or most popular, will more than likely be picked as the source to find God. It is easier to 'follow the norm' than to be different.

Some people have been so programmed by society, their family, the church, and their friends that they would never go against any of them. Instead, they would rather just 'fall back in line' with the rest of the egos who do not want to change from self-serving to other-serving.

Furthermore, many people feel as if they have messed up their life so much that there is just no hope for them. On the contrary, many people who ask for God's help at a crucial time in their life usually get it, if they are sincere. When one has committed many sins and is asking for forgiveness and to start a new life, God's love and Power will flow forth and surely change their life. This only happens when one gives all of who they are 'wholeheartedly' to God. This process is called 'surrender,' or 'humility.' In the past, many people have asked God for help and have been changed overnight from a sinner to a saint. This is known as 'instant or spontaneous transcension.'

There are always those elite few who deny God at any cost. They do not like 'nice things' or 'nice people.' They view them as 'sissies' or 'pansies.' They think that it is 'cooler' to be 'tough guys' or 'macho.' So treating people like dirt, not respecting animals, doing drugs, and of course, making fun of other people at their expense is what they enjoy doing. And some of these people just like the feeling (power, control) that they get when they steal or kill something. Remember that 'like attracts like,' and so a person who denies the Power of God is trying to show the *force* of their ego in many forms, such as *pulling* in friends with the same lifestyle and attributes (for example, drug users hang around with other drug users).

Many people believe that enlightenment is something that

only the blessed may receive, such as historical figures like Buddha, Quan Yin, Jesus, St. Francis of Assisi, Mother Mary, and Krishna. This goes back to the fact that they just don't feel worthy (a positionality of the ego) to become enlightened. This helps them fall further from grace (so to speak). Just ask yourself, "Who were they before enlightenment?" It is simple; they were just average individuals with thoughts, emotions, and an ego who believed in many theories, but they strived to uncover Truth. As they became Self-Realized, they emerged as the Higher Self, which is Divinity.

Simply, though, the most common reason for not following the way of Truth is that the being still wants to be self-serving. They do not want to give up the ego. They like their desires and cravings. Some like suffering and pain, while others like the rollercoaster rides of pleasure and pain that synchronistically follow each other. There are also others who will not give up the material possessions that they feel are 'real' because they are felt to be their only tangible proof of happiness. They like their identity, thoughts, beliefs, friendships, and lifestyles. These beings, unless converted, may remain hopeless until they decide themselves to become a channel of God.

A very common factor that prevents one from following Truth is that one didn't know that there was Truth to follow. At least 90% of people are not even aware that there is Truth that can be followed which eradicates all of the ego's suffering. This is due to ignorance and plain naïveté. The world is not educated in Truth. That is why so few people are enlightened today, and ever have been. Even if Truth were made available to everyone today, few would still be enlightened. Why is this the case, since teachings of Truth are available now and have been for centuries? It is because the ego likes where and what it is. It lacks interest and enthusiasm, and is neither fully motivated nor willing to completely change its ways. In addition, there is a lack of enlightened teachers to affirm the path that one has chosen.

The teachings are also very hard for egos to follow and comprehend. In fact, even if an ego studies Truth, it would more than likely stop trying to learn because of the belief that 'they think they know it.' Thinking can indeed be detrimental in progressing through the stages of evolution and enlightenment. One must keep in mind that 'thinking' is dualistic—the 'thinker and the thought of'—and a trait of the ego, meaning that it is a linear event, an illusion. That which is linear is manifest and not capable of knowing the Unmanifest. Herein lies the illusory claim: to 'think' that one knows what enlightenment is. If one is not enlightened, then they have no clue what enlightenment is. They just fallaciously think that they do. To think that they know is a notion that a 'prideful ego' makes, or one who would rather believe in their thoughts than experience it as Truth and know it by direct experience, contact, and beingness.

Note: Chapter 3 contains very **blunt and straightforward information** thats purpose is to deprogram the religious mind. If irritation arises, then it is due to the ego surfacing and taking control with its beliefs; thus it gets irritated when its beliefs or way of existence get challenged. This feeling of mental insecurity leads to the ego being fearful of its transcension, which is obviously displeasing and uncomfortable. It is no different than being forced to put a gun to your head and pull the trigger when you don't want to; it is against its will. **(All egos go through this; they are all <u>resistant</u> to a degree.)** This is why the Truths presented herein are troubling to the ego. This should be noted and introspected on until the reasons for irritation are known, deprogrammed, and surrendered to the Source. Only after this is done will one's beingness feel peaceful and blissful. Those who get irritated and put the book down are only protecting their ego and denying union with All That Is. **One who has no positionalities (which is a product of the ego) can never get irritated at another's views.**

Chapter 3
Religious Misinterpretations

Lack of Understanding

Religious leaders 'study about' their religion of interest at a school. In other words, they study how man has 'perceived' God, which inherently creates their religion's view of God. This leads man to think of God as a personified being with an ego, who thinks just like us. For instance, "Our God is a Righteous God" means that God is very prideful and that "he" (in reference to being a person or being male—incorrect) likes to be right. Righteousness is a human emotion that we inherit from our ego, because we feel as though we must prove ourselves to other people.

God does not have an ego (this is an ego quality) because God is All That Is. When you are everything that ever was, is, and ever could be, what is there to prove? Whom do you prove it to when you are All that exists? There is no other to prove anything to, because all existence is God. Because virtually all religious leaders have had no direct experience of God, they speak blindly. They may have had no experience of God or just a small experience that shows only a part of Truth. It is a classic case of the blind leading the blind.

Religious leaders think they have the answer to existence, or truth (as they call it), but they don't. In fact, they market it like that by saying, "Buy this CD and get a profound message of truth," but it is really only their version of perceived truth that they think is real. Therefore, they are misleading the masses due to the public's interest in the unknown, the ego's readiness to learn, and the inherent ignorance of most religious followers. Unfortunately, these leaders' limited perception of the True Reality is actually helping people learn about the exact opposite (ignore the dualism) of God in some cases, or at best, a distorted truth about God.

It is not societies' fault for being naïve; all they want is the truth about their existence. Unfortunately, True Reality is blocked by the ego's perception. So it is also not the leaders' fault for misleading the masses, because they think that they are helping. These leaders were trained by 'misled' or 'misinformed' individuals who seemed very convincing. These original 'misled' individuals, who taught the teacher, thought they were telling the Truth, but this is only because they were in turn taught by other 'misled' individuals who thought that they were telling the Truth. So most of the information that they have received is actually incorrect, but they have been 'misled' to believe that it is 100% correct. So technically no one is to blame, only ignorance, a predominant quality of the ego.

Throughout time, man has thought that they have heard God, talked to God, seen God, or even touched God, and because man doesn't understand the very essence of God, they believe it. Even today, one can go to church or turn on the television and hear the pastor, bishop, priest, or minister claim that God talks to them a couple of times a week (that they "heard God's message"). People also view God as a person, as evidenced by constant references to God as 'He' or 'Him.' This falsely perceived person, or 'super-being,' is seen as someone who listens only if one prays to him, someone who is everywhere at once (in human form), someone 'out there' (heaven), someone who judges us for our sins, someone who is righteous or prideful, and someone who will let us into heaven if we choose the right religion and go every Sunday, practice at home, and so forth.

Understand that God is not a person, God is the infinite creative energy, the Unmanifest potentiality that allows the manifest to form. God has no gender (such as male or female energy); this is just a concept in our physical, limited reality that helps us judge and see separations between 'things.' God is not somewhere, such as heaven. God is everywhere infinitely (omnipresent) as a formless energy of love and peace. God does not judge us; instead, God simply lays out infinite destinies and allows us to choose our own fate by 'free will.' Whether it is heaven or hell is purely a product of a being's choice. God is only pure unconditional love and peace, nothing more.

In some religions and regions of the world, the populace even believes that it is all right to kill in the name of Allah or God (whatever label you choose). What's really comical is that religious leaders have trained their misled followers to think that anyone who tries to show them the real Reality or Truth is actually the 'Anti-Christ' or a 'Satan worshipper.' It is amazing how much people and religious leaders don't know about God, their Creator, their own essence. No religious leaders want to have their faith or their "point of view" questioned.

Most religious leaders have big egos, are very prideful, want admiration, adore themselves for having a large following, and lead people astray because they don't really know what they're talking about. Their egos would rather believe that they are right, and they do not search for the Truth simply because they can't handle the fact that they may be wrong.

How Some Religious Leaders Train

It is not a complicated process to become a religious leader. In fact, to become an ordained minister, one can simply go online and fill out an application. Also, many egos don't realize that about 95% of religious leaders are trained in theology—which is basically teaching people to believe misleading transcriptions and translations (because these are linear, rational, and dualistic) of an already altered religious or sacred document. Just because something is written in a book doesn't mean that it is 100% correct. Just because a document is 1,000 to 2,000 years old and considered sacred doesn't mean that it is 'holy' ('Whole' or 'One with God'). In fact, the older the document, the more chance of mistranslations.

Keep the preceding in mind as you journey through this spiritual quest called life. Always keep an open mind but do not believe anything except the Truth. Remember that theology doesn't teach 100% truth. It is usually about 30 to 40% truth and the rest is metaphors and analogies for living life spiritually (not to be taken literally, as though these things actually happened) or the process of transcending the ego. However, most religious leaders often teach these stories (metaphors) as fact. If they were meant as an example of the journey of the ego, these leaders might instead translate it into a 'real life' physical story. They wouldn't know that it referred to the ego, since these religious leaders don't even know what an ego is.

Some of the camps that one can go to become a Christian minister are in desolate places, which could actually be of some benefit. This is because trainees escape from everyday reality, which can really help one spiritually evolve. Unfortunately, the trainees are bombarded with theology and beliefs that replace Truth as truth. Then they are put through what seems to be just psychological conditioning. They do physically strenuous activities until they give out mentally and physically, to make them understand their physical and mental capabilities, as well as their limits. Most of the trainees who are under duress throw up, and some even pass out. This is an example of 'minister training camp.'

This training may be beneficial for an athlete, but it is not going to make one a better minister. Jesus didn't say "know thyself" in the sense of knowing one's physical, mental, and emotional limitations. Instead, Jesus said, "know thyself" as in "Know Thy Self." This means to understand the limitations, positionalities, and control factors that keep the ego in control, and to question one's motives and remove the ego in order to know the Higher Self. Once the ego's motives are questioned and unraveled, the ego will soon lose its grip upon the soul. Once the Higher Self is realized, only God can be experienced and known as unconditional love, peace, and serenity from that point on. This is just another misunderstanding that many Christians seem to have. But keep in mind that they are not to blame for following that path, because the ego mind cannot discern Absolute Truth from fallacy. This is because Absolute Truth is the Unmanifest energy that cannot be recognized and interpreted by the manifest and linear structure of the ego. These two 'programs' (so to speak) are incompatible.

Most people are more likely to follow a religion than their own spirituality (Self), because they are too lazy (no offense) to spend countless hours and/or years searching for the Truth. Not many are that committed. They would rather just go to church for their weekly or monthly dose of religion, so that they feel as if they are making some effort. Sometimes an individual will read a book of Truth and feel that they should look into it, but they often don't. Usually it is because they think that it is not that important, or they are willing to settle for less, or they don't currently believe in it, or it is too difficult to understand. The ego does not want the Truth to be discovered, because this means that there will be no need for the ego once the Real (egoless) Reality of the Self is known. Since the ego does not want to die, it obviously will enjoy going to a 'place of worship' that is teaching misleading information. This only strengthens the ego's grip, because fallacy reinforces and strengthens the ego as well as its traits. Fallacy is the fuel that the ego runs on.

If most religions taught the Absolute Truth, then many more people would be enlightened and a much more profound Truth would prevail today, which is not the case. The only way to find the Truth is to go against what one's ego says or makes one feel, and to examine the possibilities. Faith is following one's heart; True Faith is following the Truth of the Unmanifest ('against the grain'), and enlightenment comes when 'knowingness' becomes one's Self. However, one should be sure to follow the Absolute Truth (nonform) and not the illusion (form) of comfort and familiarity.

Religious Theology (Good or Bad)

Theology stretches a little beyond using the measurability of physical existence within the Newtonian Linear Paradigm of Reality (time, space, and distance). This paradigm basically says, "If we can't measure or perceive something, then it doesn't exist" (the scientific arena). Theology helps one to believe in the unseen, to an extent. It would help one to become enlightened if it didn't impose false beliefs upon people. Theology is primarily belief oriented, an approach that does not typically use 'Absolute Truth' as its premise.

Anyone who is enlightened can pick up a sacred text or document and see the many fallacies or misinterpretations of God, just in the way that God is described. The mistranslations are known because an enlightened being experiences and knows God on a daily basis, which provides a foundation for comparing their ex-

periences with written text. An enlightened being has a more profound sense of spiritual awareness than the average person. Less
than .000001% of the world is enlightened, or knows the True
Reality of being 'One with God.' This does not by any means
denote specialness; rather, it simply infers that Truth is being denied on a daily basis in order to fulfill the whimsical wants of the
ego's desires. So the majority of society is not enlightened because they don't want to be, not because it is a difficult task. It
only takes one physical, emotional, or mental attachment to block
one from the realization of Truth. So if one is not enlightened, it is
no one's fault but their own, because they deem it more important
to hold onto their attachments than to experience God as Truth.
This is why the complete surrender of the ego is important. It alone
provides the grounds for enlightenment.

The manifest world, and most churches, view almost anyone who says that you can be "One with God" as a heretic. This
obviously stops most people from taking the alternate path. People
who fear the truth usually just follow the mainstream view and
adapt to whatever religion they feel 'comfortable' in. For instance,
Buddha was (and the word means) enlightened and the church
views him as being possessed by Satan or demons, yet he was one
of the most peaceful, humble, unconditionally loving, and accepting beings who ever walked the face of the earth. The church coun-
teracts this by saying, "Well, Satan is a master of disguise and a
deceiver who tells many lies that cannot be detected by humans";
in effect, this keeps their followers from asking questions about
enlightenment that the church leaders can't answer.

Anything that religious leaders don't know the answers to
is called demonic if it sounds mystical, miraculous, or spiritual.
This is all because theologians really only understand the *linear
thought forms of dualism*; they do not **know** the Unmanifest Presence of God. Remember that God is Nonlinear and Nondualistic.
So what theologians know are some linear concepts about a spiritual being, his life, and his view of God, which leads to the creation of a religion. The theologians, however, do not themselves
understand the Absolute Truth of Nonlinear reality. Plainly put,
they don't 'know' God, but they think that they **know about** God.

Only the ego claims to **know about** something; the enlightened being 'knows' because that Reality is what they are.

"If an ego looks for God, he/she will never find him," is a statement that represents the dualistic thought processes (the seeker and the sought) that do not exist in Absolute Reality. All who dwell in duality do not dwell within God (Nonduality) as Absolute Truth. Why? Because God is Nondualistic and Nonlinear, since there are no separations in the Oneness (infiniteness) of God. If one thinks dualistically, then they have elected to stay separated from God (because of the opposites that rule their perceived reality). So it can be seen that theology does in fact teach in linear, rationalized, dualistic terms, and it teaches that people are separated from God. Thus most church leaders could actually be the deceivers that they talk about so frequently. The one who is the deceiver does not realize it, because they were led to believe that what they **know about** is real or true.

Because these religious leaders sound so rational (since they think in a linear/dualistic way, like the masses), make some sense, are nice looking, wear decent clothes, and are decent individuals, people trust them and are misled as well. All of these linear, dualistic, and rational leaders mislead the masses because their information sounds so acceptable and easy to understand. If it makes sense to the people, the religious leaders aren't questioned; therefore, their followers' egos just accept and believe everything that is said. In addition, the ego doesn't want to know the Truth because it fears death, or the resolution of its 'self.' So the ego constantly questions the Nonlinear (God) and wants to label it as false so that one won't have an interest in the subject, thus preserving the ego's existence within this lifetime.

If one appeals to the ego by keeping it interested in the subject (Truth), it will begin to fade. As it fades away, the divine inspiration of God's Radiance will illuminate as Truth, which is Reality, while giving one a strong sense of purpose to devote one's life to a higher purpose and realizing the Self, or becoming enlightened. As one feels this inspiring Presence of God, they will then devote their entire lifetime to studying every instant of existence. This continual unraveling of the ego, done by introspection, will ensure that being's transcendence and keep one on the path of Truth.

False Teachings Create Loss of Faith

When an ego is born, its parents shape it to their specifications of what they perceive as being 'good' or 'bad,' because it was what they were taught by their parents, or they think it is beneficial. Most egos are born into a family and brought up in a religion that imprints upon them certain beliefs and traditions. It is almost as though religion is inherited, because one doesn't really have a *say in it* until they are older (18 or more years). By that time, one usually just adapts to the conditions, beliefs, and traditions of the family (either against one's will or because one now believes what they were unknowingly trained by the rest of society to believe). One feels that if they don't believe, family, relatives, and religious society will think that they are just trying to be different. A society or family may even believe that the individual is trying to rebel or withdraw from the 'norm.' But this is not so.

Instead, one feels an inner pulling (intuition or divine guidance) to try to discover whether the reality that one dwells within is the 'real reality,' or whether there is something greater. This inner spark of God is calling one back to the Source; its message is Love. God is always there for each soul and loves them unconditionally, no matter what they have done in the past. God forgives all beings for all sins and will accept them back home as if they had never left. If one just allows the Divine Will to operate through them while devoting their life to Truth, love will be experienced on an unparalleled level.

Unfortunately, most ancient or sacred texts that initially contained high levels of Truth have been mistranslated, whether religious leaders want to admit it or not. This is because the ego mind works in and as the linear reality and therefore needs sufficient information and rationalization to interpret something as a fact and as something of value to teach others. The Supreme Reality (God) cannot be rationalized or understood by the linear mind, due to its irrational, illogical, Nonlinear, and Nondualistic nature. So when spiritual masters such as Jesus, Buddha, and Krishna

70

tried to explain what cannot be understood by the linear ego mind, people rationalized what was said and put into their own terms what they 'thought' (linear and dualistic term) these masters were saying. And when people witnessed a great miracle of Jesus, they 'saw' (linear/dualistic term), or perceived it from their position (referring to location) in space, time, and distance (dualistic/linear terms), and interpreted what happened. So people's egos could only perceive their (linear/dualistic) reality, which was different from Jesus' (Nonlinear/Nondualistic) Reality as One with God.

Beings existing in two different realities (manifest and Unmanifest) cannot and will not perceive (so to speak) 'things' in the same way. For instance, if Jesus said, "The Father and I are One," this was inconceivable to people, and they assumed that he said something else. Then, as stories were told around the village for decades, they changed in their level of truth and understanding. So 75 years later, when the stories had changed, had drama added, and were misinterpreted considerably, the Bible was written by man, marking the day when civilization began to be misled. The problem is not the Bible; instead, it is that man misinterpreted Jesus' original teachings as an enlightened being, thus creating many false teachings because of the intermingling of Nonlinear (Truth) and linear (illusion) realities. At the time, mankind did not understand one reality and was not capable of comprehending it through normal thought (Nonlinear/Nondualistic), and the other reality was false due to its linear, dualistic nature.

There are many translations of the Bible, yet almost all are not how Jesus would have intended them to be written. These Bibles are dreadfully misinterpreted and are leading many followers astray, even if they are not aware. Many Christian religious leaders in fact start to question their own faith in God and the existence of an afterlife. They sometimes seek advice from metaphysical or spiritual counselors, the very beings whom they used to call heretics. Some become involved with astral projection to prove to themselves that there is an energy body residing throughout the physical body that may leave 'at will' to go into infinite worlds of pure energy they call the afterlife. However, while some religious leaders doubt their own faith and seek other spiritualists for help, they are often too proud to admit it. But they do manage somehow to keep on preaching to everyone else that "they should stay on track and live their life through God." Why should one trust a teacher who doesn't even trust in themselves or their teachings? (Note: <u>Some</u> religious leaders do teach higher truths.)

Why Does God Let Bad Things Happen to Me?

This is a statement that is heard all the time. People are constantly blaming God for *all* the mishaps in their life, yet they thank God for only a *few* of their many achievements, or perhaps none. The ego is quick to blame God or others so that it doesn't have to take responsibility when it is wrong, yet it will take all responsibility when something is done right. It can then feel like it has never made a mistake, or that the ego didn't bring something on itself (a karmic lesson). Sometimes, the ego will feel responsible for thanking God if it is pressured into saying so.

For instance, a football player (a star quarterback) has a great season, and wins a trophy and the Superbowl. When the interviewer asks whom he thanks for the great season, the player's ego responds, "I thank the coach, the players, and God," even though his ego feels (deep down) that he himself is really the one to thank for everything. Even though the coach and players helped, naturally the player thinks that "I have the trophy and was selected for the interview, so therefore I am the most valuable player and did all of the work, or at least most of it." The player doesn't have to be religious, spiritual, or even believe in God, but he thanks God because that's what's expected and what everyone else does in front of the spotlight.

The ego would feel wrong if the player didn't thank God and everyone else who has been interviewed had. The ego would rather die than feel wrong. So it caves in under the pressure and says some simple words that have no meaning to the player's ego, but have great meaning to the onlookers. The ego appears respectful, humble, and of high moral value, because he is putting on a show that he is a 'believer,' when really the ego is thinking, "I'm awesome, I'm the greatest, I'm going to make so much money, everybody loves me, people want to be me, I'm going to be in commercials, I can get any girl I want, etc…" Remember that the ego's only service is to itself. It serves only its own pleasures, desires, vanity, and sense of "I" (separateness).

God is pure unconditional love, peace, and joy. God is not and does not know of anything else. Hate, distrust, murder, mishaps, disease, sudden death, or anything else of so-called 'evil' intent is a product of our own ego mind. God is the Unmanifest that is the basic underlying, formless, infinite, creative energy that allows for the manifest to form, as well as being All of creation, referred to as *God as Totality*.

So the ego is what separates all beings from knowing their True nature as God. As we stepped out of God's Love and shaded ourselves from the light ('the fall from grace'), 'negative' emotions developed that brought the ego's level of consciousness down to the level where so-called 'negative qualities' were perceived to manifest, such as disease, illness, and emotional and mental problems.

God created (and is) All. All is One. There are no separations, which means there is no need for control (when there is nothing to control), desire (when one is already fulfilled), deceit (when there is no one to deceive). Illness doesn't exist, because Spirit was never meant to have physical bodies. So there would be no 'body' to get sick or ill. We elected to separate from God, create a physical body, and live in the physical realm. This means that we bring upon ourselves any misery that may come. So one shouldn't blame God for what the ego has willed upon itself. God is always around and throughout us, showing nothing but unconditional love and support. If God had 'wants,' they would be for us to 'wake up' and notice that maybe this perceived physical reality isn't the right one, or the 'Real Reality' of happiness, love, and peace.

The power of God manifests as signals and miracles all the time, but we just don't perceive them because of our limited perception. Every time we experience love, we experience God a little. Every time we experience peace, happiness, contentment, or joy, we experience God. So the question is really, "Why would we choose this life that can have downfalls and negativity, when we could be experiencing nothing but pure love, joy, and peace?"

Remember that God is the creative energy that provided for the manifest reality, in which all egos have the ability to 'will' whatever they want. So the 'ego will' is what concentrated energy into crystallized patterns that created this domain known as the 'physical world,' along with all of the astral dimensions. God is continuous creation that allows the egos to 'will' for the creation of things, events, and destinies. So the Unmanifest, manifest, ego will, and universal karma are all of the contributing factors that allow for the various 'life experiences' on one's particular pathway. If it is felt to be undesirable, then choose Divine Will and be transported to that level of consciousness that yields a more positive reality and destiny. All that 'happens' is a direct result of one's totality of karma and the universal influences that were 'willed' to be a part of one's existence. All happens exactly as it should; there are no mistakes or accidents possible.

Confusion about God

Everywhere in the world, religion seems to rule part of every country. Whether the religion is any of the several branches of Christianity, Taoism, Hinduism, Judaism, Islam Faith (Muslim), Spiritualism, Brahma Kumari, Catholicism, or one of the many Buddhist religions, the main Truth of the Unmanifest is present, although somewhat misinterpreted or distorted by the ego. All religions have a sense of a 'higher power,' which they usually call God. However, in different parts of the world it may be called by different names, such as Atman, Brahma, Divine Source, Universal Energy, Infinite One, Almighty One, Vishnu, Omnipotent One, Transcendental Krishna, and many others. Unfortunately, the ones who tried to show the masses the True Reality, or the nature of existence of being One with God, were idolized and worshipped instead.

For instance, Jesus, Krishna, Buddha, Muhammad, Kuan Yin, and many others taught about the Source from which all beings come, or the Truth behind one's physical existence. However, instead of people devoting their life to Truth and worshipping God, they have worshipped the messenger instead. Does it make any sense to worship and praise the mailman if he delivers a highly desirable message? Jesus never said to make graven images of him, or to worship him and his life, but it happened. Jesus simply taught people to understand the real reason why they are here in this physical lifetime and how to follow the path of Truth. Because people had a relationship with Jesus and not with God, they saw Jesus do miracles, which made them feel closer to Jesus, and therefore they worshipped him instead. But people were naïve and did not realize that everything that Jesus did was not Jesus doing it, but rather, God doing it through him.

When Jesus said, "The Father and I are One," he did not mean that he himself was actually the highest power of God. What he meant was that he realized that 'All is One,' which means that all beings are One as the 'Totality of Creation,' as well as One as the Unmanifest. There are no separations in Unmanifest Reality; these idealizations of separation only exist within our ego mind, which by its nature is only capable of perceiving its own selective viewpoints and not the 'whole picture.' When one is enlightened, all is known as One. Jesus very much saw himself and all others as One with God. This is also why Jesus said, "Do unto others as you would have them do unto you," to show people that all of one's actions affect not only other people, but one's self as well. This is because all seemingly independent beings are really just the many manifestations of the 'Universal Self.' So all beings are connected, not by physical bodies, but by and as the 'Universal Whole.' People in Jesus' time took his statement literally, because they did not understand Jesus, and the same is true in our time. Believers carried on the legend of Jesus, which led to a book called the Bible. So when Christians worship God, they are actually worshipping Jesus, not God as Unmanifest.

As the Bible was being preached, the Religion of Christianity was taught. This is a great accomplishment and one to be proud of, except for one major detail: it was taught differently than Jesus intended. Jesus never said to name the religion after him (Jesus the Christ = Christianity). Jesus never said to worship him or statues of him. Jesus never said that he was God, although God's Will did manifest Truth in the form of words and essence through him. People were supposed to be worshipping the only God (Unmanifest), or realizing the True Reality of existence as being One with the Unmanifest. All of this confusion really arose because Jesus spoke of the Nonlinear dimension and people tried to rationalize it within linear reality. This created many misinterpretations, which were so rational that Christianity currently attracts around 1.8 billion followers worldwide.

Buddhism faces the same predicament. Buddhism was formed to carry on Siddhartha Gautama's teaching. Known as the Buddha after he became enlightened, he too walked around the country, healed with his hands, and told people that he was "One with everything." He too could manifest something out of thin air, and he also taught about a Higher Truth or God. However, Buddha did one thing correctly: he did not speak of a God. Instead he spoke of the Supreme Reality, which was the same as experiencing the Unmanifest (God). He did not talk about the concept of God, because this would lead egos in a dualistic search for God and lead to many idealizations about what they thought God was. This creates false thoughts and belief patterns, strengthening the illusion that blocks one from realizing Truth.

If one thinks that God is someone to be found, then they will never become enlightened, because they are thinking dualistically (the finder and that which is found), or using the ego's linear formatting, which is incapable of understanding the Nonlinear/Unmanifest/Nondualistic. Buddha knew that he should teach people to transcend the realm of duality by analyzing and then abandoning the ego. Therefore, he showed his followers small steps to take that would eventually lead them to experiencing the Supreme Reality of the Unmanifest (God). This branch of Buddhism still exists, but other, smaller branches also teach similar pathways of living. Some resemble the main branch of Buddhism, but others vary greatly from the Truth.

Buddhism has around 500 million followers, about 1.3 billion fewer followers than Christianity does. Why? Buddhism is much more difficult for most people to understand, because it doesn't talk about the traditional concept of God. This makes some people think that it is a good way of living a moral life, but not a way of knowing God. Because the Buddhist religion teaches the Nonlinear, it doesn't make sense to people trying to rationalize it with the linear mind. It also requires dedication and discipline, which unfortunately is more than most of society is willing to give. Most people like the fact that they can go to church once in a while and just remember to accept Jesus as their savior before they die in order to go to heaven. (Note: There are some Christians who do practice every day.)

Not all, but many Christians believe that one can lead almost any lifestyle they want, and as long as one accepts Jesus in their heart they will be saved. This is their 'secret' to get into heaven. People within other religions also tend to believe the same of the spiritual teacher they follow. This belief is very much misinformed, however, and is not how the subtle energetic realms of existence or karmic laws work. To experience God, one must transcend the ego, be selfless, and love others unconditionally. Just to get into 'heaven' or the higher astral dimensions, one must simply be an honest and respectful person. Even though almost all religious followers are taught that one must devote their entire life to God, very rarely do they do that. Every second of one's life should be devoted to or be an expression of God's Will, not when one gets around to it when they are not busy. This does not mean that once in a while one can just say in prayer that they devote themselves to God. One needs to have God (Truth) in every thought that they have and every action that they do.

If the information is not true, then why are there so many religious followers? The more that something makes sense and is rational or logical, the more that egos believe it. If something doesn't make a lot of sense, it is then rationalized until it does and can be understood and followed. This means that as soon as any enlightened being speaks, the words are most likely misinterpreted by the listener because they are rationalizing the words that can't be rationalized instead of just accepting the light (Truth) that comes forth with it. They can't help it; it is the only way that people know how to think.

The ego's only capability is to 'think' within the linear reality or dimension. This means that it has to be measured in time, space, or distance, to be thought to be within existence. If something cannot be perceived or rationalized, then the linear-minded ego dismisses Nonlinear truths as false. For example, spirits who have been seen by egos are labeled true by those who have seen them, but false by those who haven't. Just because some egos have not seen spirits doesn't mean that they don't exist; it simply denotes that their limited perception has not yet seen or detected them. Most people are nonbelievers until they have an experience that proves otherwise.

Unfortunately, the souls who show themselves to spiritual seekers are often mislabeled as God, angels, or something else. The ego labels any manifesting spirit that is of a trustworthy nature as God, or if Christian, as Jesus, if Buddhist as Buddha, and so forth. This spirit, however, could be an untrustworthy being who is trying to deceive the ego into believing that it is God, because the naïve ego makes many assumptions with no real proof or understanding. The ego just sees, rationalizes, and then labels the object (spirit) as whatever it feels is appropriate at the time.

What Does "Sell Your Soul to the Devil" Mean?

This age-old saying has frightened and confused many individuals, because of the context in which it is used. Churches say it to scare their followers into doing the right thing, or at least they think so. The churches also don't fully understand what this means, but they preach it anyway, because it was written in a book that they swore they would follow to the best of their ability and realization. Religious leaders are not yet able to understand, because their level of consciousness or ability to realize 'truth' is too low. Just go to many different religious leaders and ask one question that has only one answer. To one's surprise, one will get several different answers that conflict with each other. But there is only one Truth, which means there is only one answer.

It all comes down to this. The Truth is God's Light as existence. To deny Truth is to step away from the Light of God; which means to deny or reject God, although it won't seem that way at the time. The ego will make one think that they are right, or it will justify 'wrongdoing' in order to think that it is still a 'good soul' (dualistically speaking). As people look at others and judge them, they think the person is 'good or bad.' There is only one Truth; however, there are two decisions one can make: to accept or deny Truth. The ego does such a good job at making one feel separate from others and God that one really thinks that they are their own self and different from others. One point that should be taken into consideration is that one's ego put them here (by denying God) in the first place. Is one sure that they still want to let it take control of their life, while keeping them from the light of God?

Think of the ego as dark clouds that block one from the sunlight of truth. It is shielding the sense of "I" or one's feeling of being separate and not 'One with All.' The ego likes this feeling of being in control and (thinking that it is) choosing its own destiny, neither of which will it give up easily. It knows that when one finally decides to abandon the ego, or 'heal it,' that its perceived reality and feeling of being separate are gone. So it feels as though it is dying. It is obviously not looking forward to its complete dissolution or perceived death, which is not pleasant to the ego. This is because the ego's only real job is to satisfy needs and wants, and to feel fulfilled any way it can. So technically, it is just doing its job to keep one 'lost in the dark.' It is also important to note that the ego does not think that anything is wrong or that they are without God. It can make one believe that they are independent from God as well as having God at the same time, which is not possible.

Most religious leaders think that they are (dualistically) with God, but it is really their ego that (dualistically) *thinks* they are with God. For example, they frequently say, "I have been appointed by God to deliver you from your sins." This type of statement is egotistical and prideful. In other words, they are exhibiting very low levels of consciousness merely by making this statement. Someone who has transcended the ego would never make such a claim. Until one's ego has been transcended, it will think that everything logical and linear is exactly how it is supposed to be. Remember that it only knows the reality that has been shown to it as long as the ego has existed in this incarnation. So the information in this book will look 'crazy' to the ego, unless there is a hole in the 'darkness' through which the 'light of God' can penetrate and bring in Truth.

Truth can be presented specifically to appeal to the ego. It will then open up and break down the ego's barrier that keeps it from the Truth of its existence. Thus, a being begins the ascension or purification process, which will eventually lead to enlightenment, or being an expression of God as Truth.

For the sake of clarity, the universal levels of consciousness are listed below to reference the main emotions and ego viewpoints on a scale of desirability, from the least to the most desirable. The least desirable attributes have a lower level of consciousness or frequency, while the most desirable emotions and viewpoints have higher levels of consciousness or frequency.

The Universal Levels of Consciousness

Energies having lower levels of consciousness:
——**Listed Lowest to Highest**——
Humiliation (you humiliate others and yourself), Apathy, Blame, Guilt, Despair, Regret, Anxiety, Craving, Desire, Grief, Fear, Desire, Anger, Hate, Scorn, Pride (Righteousness), Affirmation (wanting constant admiration and affirmation that you are a good person)

Energies having a 'neutral' stand with regard to negative/positive:
——**All are about the Same**——
Integrity, Faith, Honesty, and Respect

Energies having higher levels of consciousness:
——**Listed Lowest to Highest**——
Faith, Courage, Trust, Optimism, Willingness, Acceptance, Reason, Understanding, Reverence, Love, Joy (filled with a lot of love), Serenity (always feeling fulfilled), Ego Peace (knowing all is perfect), Ego Bliss (over-flowing with love and joy), Enlightenment (One with All—the end of the ego and its emotions and viewpoints), Enlightenment Bliss and Peace, Universal Identity

All emotions or viewpoints that are below enlightenment (except unconditional love) are a block that shades one from the 'Light of God,' or the True Reality. The True Reality is one of unconditional love and infinite knowingness. Until love becomes completely unconditional, it still is hindered by the ego's perception that judges what not to love. And until a being has transcended the ego's perception completely, it will not know the Higher Truths of Reality.

So in essence, the phrase "Selling your soul to the devil" means that one is choosing the path of the ego. One does this by allowing the ego to keep a firm grip or control on one's perceived reality. The ego will try to retain control by keeping itself fueled with negativity and illusion. So every lower emotion or viewpoint, which is basically any emotion or positionality that is below unconditional love, is an ignorant choice to accept, because of the inherent limitations and suffering that it brings. Every time one chooses an emotion or viewpoint below unconditional love, one is choosing to deny God (to a certain extent). The soul is only saved for certain if the predominant energy in the human energy field is that of unconditional love. This can be considered the point of 'salvation,' what Jesus taught as, "Love thy neighbor."

One's level of consciousness determines the level of 'heaven' or 'hell' that can and will be accessed. The lower heavens of form (remember that God Unmanifest is formless) can be reached or predestined as long as the human level of consciousness is fixed predominantly at the level of truth and integrity. This level simply means to devote one's life to be honest with others and honest with one's self. So as long as one is honest and respects others, one will probably enter the lower heavens, where it is pleasant, comfortable, secure, and resembles being in a happy memory. The lower heavens of form do not portray the Real Reality, but give one a beautiful and trusting atmosphere in which to spend eternity.

Once one enters, a decision can be made (if allowed) to determine whether one would like to reside there, reincarnate (re-embody), or finally know the Truth of Existence by raising one's level of consciousness to transcend the ego completely. For those who want to guarantee their 'heavenly placement' and see the 'Real Reality' of Formlessness, Beauty, Perfection, and Unconditional Love—then transcend the ego completely and don't look back.

All truth will be revealed in the end. Finally, the Reality of One-ness of the Supreme Reality can be known (the reality of the higher Self) and not 'perceived' (an ego function). Since the ego is tran-scended, there is no more personal karma and no more reincarna-tion. All is complete and One.

So the saying, "Selling your soul to the devil," simply means devoting one's life to staying away from the light of God. One way to devote one's life to 'dwelling in the dark' is by being an expression of the lower emotions (such as hate, resentment, deceit, anger, revenge, desire, and control), worshipping or call-ing upon the lower astral entities (aleister crowley in spirit, de-mons, etc...), or astral subgods (god of fire, wind, volcanoes, kitchen god, etc...). The other way to "sell your soul to the devil" is simply to follow the way of ignorance. This means that by adapt-ing and believing the ways of the ego, one is kept from the light of God.

By taking the latter path, one doesn't realize that they are doing anything 'wrong.' Unfortunately, mankind is so blinded by the ego that it makes them believe what they are doing is right with God, even though its actions contradict God. The easiest way to stay on the path of God is to choose to be an expression of unconditional love, which is a higher level of consciousness that bypasses the judgmental ego. One cannot go wrong with love, compassion, and peace.

Chapter 4
Understanding Spirituality

The Simple Task

As the ego takes on the many trivial vicissitudes of life, it often gets distracted from its actual goal. Because the ego has had many previous incarnations, it starts anew in each conscious existence with a 'blank slate,' meaning that each soul begins its brand-new existence with a type of 'spiritual amnesia.' For if it knew the Truth of one's existence, it would have become Self-Realized due to the compelling nature of fearing the lesser astral dimensions (hells), rather than learning its lessons. This is the wrong reason for becoming enlightened. By those grounds that 'force' one to strive for God, one will not Truly learn their lessons.

Instead, one should evaluate one's life and try to focus on the constant, never-changing context of Reality (God). Enlightenment is a goal for those beings who choose God (Truth) due to their undying and pure devotional love for God (Truth), not because they fear hell or 'bad things' happening to them. So throughout the many changes in one's life, one fact is certain: Truth never changes and is the ever-constant fact of existence that one can always trust in.

Throughout history, though, egos have made Truth seem a lot more difficult than it really is. It means simply devoting one's life to the higher purpose (God) with 100% certainty, belief, and trust that All is well. One must also choose love and peace above all other temptations or aspects of the ego's life. Because God is love, to express love is to express or channel a quality of God. The more that one expresses love, the more enlightened they become.

So one's only True goal in life is to love God (Truth) above all other aspects of life. One must not only love God, but any chance one has, one must choose to be a pure expression of love and peace to all beings in the universe; this includes the lower astral dimensions as well as the upper, the seeming enemy and the saint, and the bugs and plants as much as the human beings and angels. In other words, one must stop passing judgment and just accept 'all' as a perfect expression of 'beingness' at the level of consciousness that it has either knowingly or unknowingly chosen to be a vehicle of.

In addition, the being who seeks enlightenment should endlessly seek the Truth both day and night. To focus on the manifest world is to become attuned to the impermanent illusion that fades away with time. But to focus on God is to become attuned with the Absolute Truth that is permanent and never changes or fades, thus revealing one's True nature of infinite love, peace, and happiness, which always provides compassion to all.

Starting with a Common Belief

While reading this book, many Truths will be thought by the ego to be false, out of the ordinary, unbelievable, or just plain wrong. Many of these Truths will be denied due to the ego's conflicting perception of what it feels is God, or a quality of God. So with this said, it would be wise to start with a common belief that can help all beings interpret this book and Reality a little better.

Just ask yourself the following: "Do you believe that God (Reality or existence) is infinite?" If you reply yes, then you would also have to agree that God cannot be measured. If you believe that God cannot be measured, then you would have to believe that God is formless. This is because a table, tree, person, planet, and so forth, or only that which is form, can be measured. Since the essence of God is formless, then God is Unmanifest (infinite formless creative energy), Nonlinear, and Nondualistic. This is due to the fact that the linear dimension (physical and spiritual manifest) and dualistic reality is based on the dimension of form that is within the measurability of time, space, and distance (linear), which would inherently limit God and therefore deny God's infiniteness. So it can now be stated that God is Unmanifest or formless, infinite, Nonlinear, and Nondualistic, as its essence, as well as unperceivable and undetectable. Just the same, all that stems from the Source (God) is of the Source and can not be excluded from being an aspect of God as All that Is (form and nonform).

True Faith Is Believing in the Unmanifest

Many people, or ego beings, have discredited and denied the Presence of God as existence, because they misunderstand what God is. The ego is only capable of knowing other egos (structurally energetic programs) and the current manifest dimension in which it operates (earth). It does not know archangels (very high levels of Self) firsthand, nor does it see into the astral dimensions (heavens and hells) at will. Just the same, it does not know God directly, although it may think it can. This is due to the differing nature or qualities of energy. It is analogous to cold air thinking it knows or has experienced hot air. This is an impossibility, because once cold air mixes with hot air, the temperature of the cold air is raised and therefore it is not cold air any more; it is now warm air. So there cannot be a relationship between the two, because when they truly meet, they both change in temperature, therefore changing their very nature while merging as one. So cold air cannot know hot air, but it can become hot air itself if enough heat is added.

The same goes for the ego; once it mixes with the Presence of God, the ego no longer exists. This shows that the ego (illusion) doesn't meet God (Real) or have a relationship with God (Reality), but it can be transcended and the True Self realized as already One with God. This is due to the Presence of God as Light, which changes the very nature (raises the level of consciousness) of the currently experienced ego 'beingness.' So for an ego to believe that they have a personal relationship with God is false, or an illusion.

An ego is linear and can only function and interpret form. God is Nonlinear and cannot be perceived by that which is form, functions in the linear, believes in or is a quality of dualism, and can only perceive form (ego). However, when a being gives up its 'ego will,' one can then adopt the higher (love, peace) qualities of energy of God known as *Divine Will*. This allows a being to surrender its ego (belief in illusion) to God and realize its infinite Presence as the Unmanifest. It allows one to experience the infiniteness of God, not through a relationship (a linear term and ideology), as the ego mistakenly thinks, but instead, through shedding the illusory belief of separateness that allows one to experience Truth.

That Which Cannot Be Perceived Is Real

All egos believe that they can tell the difference between truth and falsehood; however, this is not so. Absolute Truth is completely formless due to its Unmanifest (formless) nature. Since the ego is only capable of comprehending form, or the manifest, the Unmanifest nature of God will and can never be understood by the ego's energetic structure. But just because the ego is incapable of perceiving and comprehending the nature of God does not mean that God does not exist.

Throughout one's life, there has constantly been energy around the ego that it has not perceived. For instance, if one blows a dog whistle without knowing that it produces a sound which human ears cannot perceive, the ego will think that the whistle is broken, or that it doesn't produce a sound; therefore it says that the sound doesn't exist. But a dog knows differently, due to its more sensitive perception. The same goes for gamma and infrared rays, which cannot be perceived by the ego; however, scientific equipment can pick them up.

Similarly, there are many subatomic particles that science is just currently discovering within our ego world of form. This field is called 'quantum physics' and 'mechanics.' Some branches known as 'Nonlinear Theoretics' try to make comprehensible the True nature of Unmanifest energy. Scientists do not believe this to be God, nor do they discredit it. Quantum physics can be solved to a certain degree due to the energies of form, although on a much smaller scale than most scientists are used to; however, Nonlinear Theoretics will never and can never be solved by the ego. This is where the dimension of form (the scientific arena) and the dimension of the formless (the spiritual arena) merge. At this point, scientists who require proof either stop conducting experiments or become spiritual devotees themselves. They discover that all perceived events or things have only one answer, which is the nature of God (Unmanifest/Truth).

The ego, which currently lives and operates within the

manifest, can only perceive and interpret the manifest. This is because egos have been programmed to function within a certain range of frequencies, these being water, air, solid, and plasma, as well as the frequencies in between. Just as a computer is programmed to interpret and use only the frequencies that its 'maker' designed it to respond to, the ego can only interpret the frequencies that the 'creator' made it to respond to. So if a Macintosh computer can't recognize or operate with an IBM computer program, the Macintosh computer will not perceive that the IBM program exists. With this said, one can now know that the ego cannot perceive God due to its differing qualities of energy; it would be like asking the 'Frogger' program to run a computer mainframe or motherboard. Programs aren't the mainframe, but they are a part of it. In the same way, egos cannot control or interpret God, and neither are they God, but they are a part of *God as Totality*.

There is a 'Divine Spark' within each of us that is not limited to gender, race, thoughts, ideologies, or form. And it is completely Unmanifest energy, not only because it is an expression of the properties of God, but because it is God. It is the *Unmanifest Self*. It is the part of *God as Totality* that is always with us and can be contacted at any time. However, the ego does not know that it is there due to its nature in the world of form, which cannot interpret or perceive the formless quality of God that is always present. Some religions teach about this aspect of God, but not many truly understand it.

Just as the ego cannot perceive or understand God, it cannot tell the difference between Truth and falsehood. This is because God is Truth, and the manifest is falsehood or illusion. So the ego mind can operate fairly well within this illusory world of the manifest, but it cannot detect the Presence of God (Unmanifest), although it usually thinks it can. Many 'preacher egos' (church leaders) can be heard telling how they have spoken to God, seen God, or felt God, usually to gain control over their congregation by feeling important and being respected as a 'holy individual.' These individuals, if not enlightened (99+% are not), are operating under the control of the ego, which does not allow them to experience God, although these individuals will argue that point until their last days.

Do Not Put Limitations on God

Due to the ego's inability to understand or perceive God, the ego tends to idealize a God that it can comprehend more easily. It takes traits that it already knows and projects them upon that which is 'traitless.' For instance, the lower ego emotions, such as hate, anger, vengeance, wrath, humiliation, shame, pride, and judgmentalism, are placed on the idealized figure of God. This allows the ego to understand a 'creator figure' that it actually has created itself. The ego feels as if God is a more powerful being than itself, but with the same traits or limiting qualities of the ego, simply because these are familiar. Unfortunately, when this is done, the ego really starts to believe in the traits that it assumes God to have, and therefore envisions an angry and vengeful God.

Egoistic qualities such as these, which are an expression of the limited and manifest, impede upon the realization of the infinite. So to say that God is male (God is usually referred to in the Bible as 'He') limits God from being the female quality as well. To say that God is gold limits God from being any other color. To think that God is everywhere and infinite, but not on earth, in the physical universe, or in ourselves, limits God and contradicts the infinite quality of God. So this shows how the ego cannot conceive of infiniteness, because it always tries to limit the limitless with its beliefs. To believe that God prefers a certain individual over another limits God's unconditional love and makes God judgmental (an ego trait that limits infinite love), for example, 'damning the sinners' and 'helping the worshippers' get to heaven. All of these egoistic concepts are ridiculous and illusory. The more that an ego tries to conceive of the infiniteness of God, the more that the ego ignorantly limits God. Only the ego is limited, not God.

The True Reality — Becoming One with God

Not by looking into the depths or the vastness of the ocean, nor by looking into the seemingly enormous sky can we even have the slightest hint of the infinite, ever-creating, expansion of the energy of the Divine or the Absolute of All That Is. By taking the time to actually think or to try to rationalize the infiniteness of the Absolute energy source just shows how naïve man can actually be. God is beyond all measurable means. The human mind is incapable of thinking or rationalizing the essence of God. The ego is only equipped to operate in the Newtonian Paradigm of Linear Reality, meaning that the mind cannot understand something unless it can be measured, rationalized, or perceived in the "so-called reality" of time, space, distance. This is the scientific view of life, in which people need or want to see proof; few just have faith anymore. If it is impossible to perceive God through one's senses, and if God cannot be measured by mathematical equations or rationalized by the mind, then faith is all one can have—or is it?

The 'Real Reality' of the Unmanifest exists only in or as the Nonlinear dimension, which is beyond the Newtonian Paradigm (linear) that measures our 'so-called reality' of the physical. There are methods, or a way of life, that can help one achieve enlightenment (to be an expression of the light of God as Self), or at least achieve a huge jump in spiritual awareness. These spiritual pathways will, in time, allow one to experience the infinite, interconnected, forever-expansive web of energy that is intrinsic to All. It can also be referred to as the infinite sea of energy, if this helps one comprehend it more easily. The boundaries that humans create, by using their ego minds, separate us from each other and God. But through reading this book, as realizations come forth through stunning revelations, the illusory world of the manifest will be dissolved, and from this, only total oneness can and will be experienced for all of eternity.

When enlightened, there is no 'you' or 'me' or 'I'—there is only One. By taking this path, one's *Higher Self*, or the Spark of God inside, will dissolve one's ego (one's perceived sense of 'I' or separateness), transcend all personal karma, and realize that they are 'One with Everything.' One will transcend all opposites (the world of duality) and see that there is no 'bad or good,' no 'positive or negative,' no 'seer and seen,' and no 'knower and the known.' There will be no difference between anything that is living or dead, including plants, animals, or humans. All things will be seen as they are—with each as a perfect expression of its existence. One will see the Divinity of God in all, and see that all things are perfect in their own essence. Neither dirt, money, nor gems will seem to have any differences, and they will all appear to be perfect and 'unjudgeable.' One will see all beings as equal and perfect. A murderer and a philanthropist will appear the same, except that their egos are on different paths.

It is important to keep in mind that only the Unmanifest Self truly exists, not the physical body or the personality, which are a direct expression of the 'ego.' The Spark of God and the Supreme Reality (God) of all beings exist, and all else is an illusion. The Truth refers to the 'Real Reality,' or Source of existence of All that is created. This infers that only Truth exists as Reality, and all other forms of reality are a type of distorted truth or illusory existence. If one is concerned with enlightenment, only Truth is the formless Reality (Unmanifest), and all else is a distraction from Truth. So if one seeks God, then simply seek and follow the Truth, and the essence of All That Is will be revealed.

The pathway of enlightenment does not take lifetimes to achieve, as previously thought. The revelation of Oneness, typically referred to as 'God-Consciousness,' can be instantaneous or gradual, depending on whether one chooses the proper path (pure Truth) or one with many distortions.

The following chapters are organized so as to appeal to the ego, which creates acceptance and then raises one in consciousness. After the gradual breakdown of the barriers of the ego, Truth is then revealed as the Source. The book is designed to allow one to experience God's Unmanifest energy in small increments by having a series of small revelations (egoless experiences), which will serve to gain the ego's trust in the path that is chosen. The ego will then unknowingly begin to fade away as the Presence of Truth illuminates the once-dark soul, as if lit candles were gradually being added to a dark room.

When this book is read, one's frequency will increase more and more until the ego's grip is loosened; thus the *Higher Self* is closer to being revealed. The book is designed to educate the ego and keep its interest while one learns about the realm of metaphysics, the Spiritual Manifest, spiritual healing, meditation, and the Unmanifest qualities of God. It will also be the ego's source of proof that paranormal or spiritual 'things' can be possible. Even though metaphysics (chakras, auras, and other Spiritual Manifest phenomena) are clarified for general knowledge and understanding, they are not the main focus of this book. Instead, the main focus is to help one understand spiritual energy, to follow the path of enlightenment, and to help all beings rapidly evolve spiritually.

Are Religion and Spirituality the Same?

Religion and spirituality are not the same. There are many religions, each with its own beliefs, concepts, rituals, and sacred texts. Churches have kept their traditions going strong because of the immense number of followers and the fact that they do teach some truth about the nature of existence. Unfortunately, they unknowingly teach a lot of fallacy as well. In fact, most religious leaders bash the idea of being 'One with God' and tell their followers that it is 'satanic,' or that they worship 'devil spirits.' If that is true, then Jesus is satanic, because he stated, "I am one with the Father."

These misunderstandings come about simply because the churches do not understand Truth, or the 'Real Reality' of being One with God. Because most churches have a lot of pride, they will never admit that they don't know the whole truth; and the enlightened being is so humble that he doesn't go around blabbing everything he knows or has experienced. However, if one asks the enlightened being what they know, it can be felt that they are a direct expression of Truth that has a profound sense of Reality.

Spirituality is the study of the Truth of existence, or understanding the spiritual energy that is intrinsic to All That Is. Spiritual energy is an intrinsic factor (meaning the creative and crucial substrate) of life. Just think about it. Which came first, religion or spirituality? Spirituality has always been present and has always existed. Spirituality is not a religious set of beliefs; it is a fact. Spirituality is the basic understanding that the 'Source of Divinity' (or God) is the reason why all beings and ostensible 'things' exist, and that the 'Infinite Self' can never be destroyed.

It is knowing that one's Spirit is not only a part of God (not separate, but One), and that one doesn't need a religion or a church to reveal Truth because, as Jesus said, "Your body is a temple," the home for the soul, where it can worship at any time. However, most religions misinterpret this as, 'Your body is sacred because God created it, so don't mess it up with piercings, tattoos, and toxins.' If they told everyone that they could just stay at home and devote themselves to God with prayer and meditation, then no one would go to church and they would lose their following and their religion would diminish.

Beliefs are formulated by the illusory ego; Truth is already one's Self in the highest and least deluded aspect of one's being-ness. Remember that religions differ due to the varying opinions of what other egos think Truth to be. The ego is distortion, so the Truth that the ego believes it knows is already incorrect, because it 'thinks' while using the ego. One doesn't need beliefs, only Truth. Truth just is Reality, and beliefs are a distortion (opinion) of reality.

How This So-Called Reality Came About

In the beginning, we were all 'One' and chose to separate from God (the beginning of the ego and dualistic/linear/manifest reality) because we wanted something different. We wanted a new reality over which we could have more control. We wanted a place where we could control our reality and be its boss. So, in essence, we all wanted to try our hand at playing God within our seemingly self-created, made-up reality. Unfortunately, other beings started to intrude, and we all fought for control and power over the various energy dimensions. The more beings who passed by the energy plane, the more they enjoyed the reality that was created by the ego's mental faculties and creative abilities. "What could be better?" they thought. Everything that the ego thought of was manifested and became a part of its perceived reality.

These worlds, or different realities, were created in what are termed the 'Astral Dimensions' (these will be explained later in the book, but redefined as the 'Spiritual Manifest'). The energy world is blank, like one's mind when relaxed in a deep trance. Then, as one thinks of something that is of some interest, it manifests and appears in one's mind, which in the astral dimensions manifests as the new, perceived reality, which is willed into expression by the ego. As more beings inhabit the newly created worlds, they perceive the already created energy patterns again and again; these soon crystallize into a permanent energy pattern (more dense energy). The more that a being perceives and experiences an energy pattern, the more that energy pattern 'hardens' or 'crystallizes.' This is all because concentration, or the 'intense focused energy' of the perceived energy pattern, reaffirms, strengthens, and forms a newly subcreated (created below the Truth of God) energy domain that is thought to be real. These manifested and concentrated energy patterns have created this so-called 'reality of form,' which all beings have now accepted as the *only* reality within existence.

As the energy becomes more and more concentrated, it crystallizes into permanent energy patterns that we perceive as solid, but still permeable form. As this form is concentrated on, the energy world vibrates and changes, from one energy domain (or level of consciousness) that is vibrating at a higher frequency closer to that of formlessness, to an energy domain that is vibrating at a lower vibration of concrete thoughts and solid form. So as the energy realm slips into the lower energy domains, it grows closer to the lowest level of reality, one of solids. As more energy is concentrated upon, the more dense or solid it becomes. This in turn created what scientists call the 'Big Bang Theory.' When the energy world crossed from the Unmanifest to the spiritual manifest to the physical manifest, in an explosive, immediate, and crystallizing transformation, it was then termed 'physical reality,' a reality of form and limitations, one that could be measured and perceived.

Scientists, evolutionists, and spiritualists were all right to a certain degree. By the Power of the Unmanifest, the physical reality of the manifest was allowed to be created. After the seeming start of creation, by God as Unmanifest and 'willed' by all our egos, the small one-celled organisms that we developed to carry spirit all came here, starting to evolve and adapt to the climate and conditions of the physical, limited reality. So all beings who chose to separate from God and create their own reality are now stuck in the manifest dimension with no prior memory of the *Absolute Reality*, which is One with God.

This new experience became known as 'all there ever could be' by all who lived in the limited reality. The reality that egos partly created was discovered to be seemingly imperfect because of all of its limitations. Egos now felt separated from God and noticed that love was not as present as it used to be. Because this lack of love created an empty feeling, a lack of fulfillment, egos searched for an external means to create happiness. They also started to show off to others, which led to a sense of pride and happiness. It also provided for security, because they protected their territory and attracted mates. They felt very insecure, however, as they noticed that life didn't last long; death was the newest experience that no beings were prepared for or knew of. So on the physical plane, loss was now experienced, followed by despair, regret, grief, sadness, confusion, insecurity, and perhaps hatred on the part of those who were left so suddenly.

This world now isn't perceived exactly how egos want it to be, and so depression has set in as well. Because they have no prior memory of the perfect reality with God (spiritual amnesia), beings think that this limited reality is the only one, and that no other can be experienced. Thus, we are stuck here until we figure out the Truth of our existence and devote our lives to doing God's Will. After realization (enlightenment) occurs, one can then leave the manifest dimension and return to the true existence of being the Higher Self and then eventually as the Unmanifest.

Some egos will disagree, saying, "What is in your mind stays in your mind and you know that it is not real." In response, first, the ego is programmed to deny God or Truth. Remember that the ego's job is to create its own sense of 'self,' or independence. It does not wish to lose its apparent sense of separate identity because of the joy that comes from being admired, respected, adored, and loved. It knows that if one abandons the ego, the *True Self* is realized and the ego dies. Obviously the ego does not want to die; therefore it seeks many identities, which brings a sense of temporary fulfillment that hides Truth.

Second, keep in mind that when the energy body leaves the physical body, one is now experiencing the astral dimensions. This new world, at least to the ego, can be experienced through astral projection and near-death experiences. These experiences—in which energy is changed, manipulated, created, and passed through as if it were air—will give anyone a new perspective on life. All thoughts that one thinks are sacred are in fact shared with all that exists. These thoughts are now known not to be independent or owned by the 'thinker.' They have always existed, and forever will exist, in the energy dimensions of the Spiritual Manifest. This universe is created by energy and thoughts. It is a mental zone and all thoughts and ideas already exist there; we just 'will' them into expression.

Third, what is reality? Reality is whatever one perceives the world to be. Note that a blind person and a person with sight have two different realities, because they experience their worlds differently. To a sea animal, water is its reality and it cannot conceive of the concept of air or space (perhaps they think that a fisherman is a god). That sea animal tells other sea animals (hypothetically) that he saw god, but no one believes him. It is rare that a sea animal has seen god (a fisherman) and gone back into reality (water) to proclaim it. Due to the fact that the other sea animals have not experienced this reality that the 'one' sea animal has talked about, they think he is crazy.

Lastly, while one dreams, don't the tables, characters, or scenery look and feel real? So what exactly is real? If it is whatever the mind perceives to be real at the time, then dreams are as real as the physical. Because when one is dreaming, they don't think they're dreaming; the mind thinks the dream is really happening. So if one dreams that they are about to die, they wake up! Why? Because the ego thought that it was real! So it is apparent that whatever one perceives or subjectively experiences at any moment is in fact real to them. It is the only reality that they can know and the only one that they can understand. So one cannot expect other egos to understand how they perceive reality, or how it is possible to experience all of creation as One. It just won't make sense to other egos. All one can do is walk the 'path of Truth,' or the path of enlightenment, which allows one's self to show others what was done to experience God. The understandings will fall into place, and they will come back and thank the teacher for freeing them of this 'limited reality' that they had so blindly accepted before.

Every soul's mission is to once again realize that it is a part of something greater, that we are all whole, that 'All is <u>One</u>.' It is a purely spiritual journey that helps one bypass the mundane qualities of this manifest existence and realize their True nature, that of being completely Unmanifest and an inherent quality of God.

Are There Two Different Realities?

There is an 'Absolute Reality' and there is also a 'perceived reality,' but this is just a separation of the whole. The perceived reality is the manifest reality provided by the dualistic and linear 'thinkingness' of the ego. The (True) Absolute Reality is Nonlinear and Nondualistic, meaning that it is Unmanifest (formless) and cannot be perceived. When 'things' are not perceived by the ego, they are not experienced as real phenomena. The physical dimension or perceived reality must be perceived, measured, or mathematically solved for its inhabitants to 'think' that it is real. If it is not, then it is either considered wishful thinking, a myth, or just a fictional story.

In the dualistic aspect of the linearly perceived reality, there are seeming oppositions, which imply that everything is separate and has its own identity. So there are thought to be opposites to everything—for example, this/that, left/right, happy/sad, up/down, high/low, bad/good, life/death, light/dark, or hot/cold. This shows a relationship between the 'experiencer and the experienced,' the 'knower and the known,' the 'thinker and the thought of,' and the 'judger and the judged.' It allows one to witness many different 'things' that all seem to follow independently their own paths or destiny. This false 'dualistic reality' shows that 'things' happen by chance and not as a consequence of Divine Will, ego, or karma.

The ego does not want to feel out of control. So, to feel in control, it makes itself believe that everything happens in life because it decided that a consequence should happen. The thought that nothing 'bigger' can control or dictate its life actually establishes the ego's sense of security, independence, and control over life.

Having a dualistically perceived reality continuously engrains or imprints the idealistic view that all 'things' have a 'spatial' relationship with one another. Because the ego makes itself think that all is separate, distance and location can be mapped out. This further reinforces and strengthens the ego's feeling of separateness from 'things' that it perceives. Now the locations of 'many' different things can be seen, heard, tasted, felt, smelled, and known as separate entities that are stored in the ego mind as an expression of its identity. The more that one sees 'things' as separate, the more one begins to identify with everything having its own location and identity. This also brings in the arbitrary ego quality of judgment.

With judgment, egos see and compare many different things, which then are stereotyped and categorized within their mental filing systems as 'likes and dislikes.' This begins to reinforce the idea of positives (I like) and negatives (I don't like) or, in other words, what we desire or do not desire. Because of this, we now start to judge all things in our perception, ranking them according to their degree of importance.

If we judge something as good and feel we need it, we now have a desire to own or possess it. This positive judging results in compliments toward people or things. For instance, one would say, "I think you are beautiful." This feeling creates a mild desire, which can escalate into an obsessive ego want/desire that controls one's life and feelings. One can become completely overcome by desire, thus creating an alter ego or an animalistic personality that emerges when one is overcome by an intense emotion or drive, and causes one to do things that are wild and out of control in the heat of the moment. A feeling of loss occurs if the desired person rejects the 'desirer' by being smug or rude, or by ignoring them. When egos 'like' something, the longer they think about it or remain around it, the stronger the desire becomes. This is the point when an emotional attachment to an object/person can get out of control. The ego loathes the idea of being out of control and will take drastic measures to regain a 'secure feeling' of being 'in control.' These drastic measures, such as 'covering up a crime,' are usually viewed as being 'unlawful' in the perceived physical reality.

On the opposite end of the spectrum, if the ego dislikes something or finds it repulsive, rude or judgmental comments abound. The ego places importance on itself by showing others and itself that it is not like the thing that it perceives to be repulsive. The ego therefore unconsciously and subconsciously reinforces the feeling of separation, which then strengthens the ego's hold on its version of reality. The ego not only feels better for not being whatever it thinks is repulsive, but it feels stronger and more important, because in a way the ego is complimenting itself.

The ego only listens to itself. This is a common, everyday occurrence. If one tells someone else the right way to do something, that person's ego rejects the idea, simply because the ego answers only to itself. So the ego has to want help in order to listen or get help. If the ego doesn't want help, then it will reject help because of its own pride. Pride is basically when the ego thinks that it is right and it cannot be proven wrong, or when the ego won't admit that it is wrong.

The only reason for wanting something is because one doesn't have it, or at least enough of it. If one lacks something, a want is created that needs to be fulfilled. This is where all of the ego's desires come from. It sees 'many separate things' out in the world and does not feel connected to anything. So the ego tries to find something that will replace this feeling of incompleteness, or having a 'lack of.' In linear/dualistic society, everything feels separate, which creates a feeling of desire (a need to fill the void). But within this perceived reality, with so many things to get and to have, one's desires are constantly strengthened and reinforced because one always will have a feeling of emptiness if not fulfilled. With one's ego mode of thinking in the dualistic realm, emptiness is only there to be filled. Unfortunately, it thinks it should be filled with the things or objects that are seen, which leads to acquiring materialistic things. But with the ***True Reality***, if one seeks to give love and to be an expression of the Unmanifest, while not focusing on the material realms, infinite fulfillment will be one's Reality.

The ***True Reality*** is One; it is one of immeasurable status, which means that it is Nonlinear (beyond the measurement of time, space, and distance). This means that nothing is separate and All is One. In this Reality, All is not perceived, but rather known and experienced as One. There is nothing to learn, see, or think about, because all simply is what it is: formless and perfect. Only unconditional love and peace can be experienced. There is no cause and effect, 'because' (contradictive humor) nothing causes anything to happen. When all is One, there is not two, since there is no other thing or entity to cause anything to happen to another. Remember ('it takes two to tango'), there is no two—only One. There are no opposites, because there is nothing to be opposite to (this would imply two). There is no higher or lower (this states that something is above or below). There is no location, distance, or spatial relationship, because there are no separations between anything.

The Supreme Reality (God as Unmanifest) allowed for the manifest to take shape <u>as the conditions *(karmic lessons that were willed to be learned by the egos)* were necessary for creation</u>. The Unmanifest is within the manifest and is an intrinsic factor for the manifest to be an aspect of creation. Although the manifest is treated as reality (by the unenlightened), the Unmanifest is the Supreme Reality or Ultimate Truth. This Reality is formless but allows the manifest to form. So since it allows for creation and provides for creation, it is deemed the ***Source*** that all 'comes' from.

The ego considers form as reality because it is tangible. Just the same, scientists study physical form because it can be perceived, measured, controlled, and it provides proof. Although the manifest is considered form, it is technically not really 'solid' form. Instead, it can be better known as a more concentrated plane of energy that the ego perceives as 'form.' For instance, when one is out of their body (astral projection/near-death experience), they can be tricked into thinking that there are limitations that hold them back, such as an impassable wall that no one can go beyond. However, this is all just a product of the mind. If one thinks that they cannot do something, then they can't. The ego is a 'limit-making machine.' It is what keeps one from realizing the Truth. There is energy everywhere that cannot be perceived, but it can be experienced by any soul if thought to be a possibility. Remember that the ego creates only limitations, not Reality.

A Little Reminder of God

It is important to keep in mind that God has never left anyone, but rather, some beings have elected to leave God. Even so, as one rejects the existence of God, God remains throughout body, mind, and existence, although clouded by one's ego. When one asks for help, however, instantaneous Love can be experienced. This Love that is experienced is the reason one exists. Without God, there is no Truth. Without Truth, there is no Love. Without Love, there is no existence. Many people do not actually understand the difference between love, lust, and like, which are often confused with each other.

When you 'like' something, you desire to be around it or to have possession (a controlling emotion) of it. When you 'lust' for something, you are infatuated by the physical aspects of the object. With the infatuation, a deep desire and craving for the object is constant. When you 'Love,' however, it doesn't matter what something looks like or how someone acts; it cannot change the purity and overwhelmingly positive feeling of perfection that radiates from the experience. Love (not sex, which is lust) can be experienced between animals, humans, plants, and bugs. But do not forget where Love comes from. Love does not come from animals, humans, plants, bugs, or nature; instead, it comes directly from God. God allows us to experience Love through other beings as a 'connective experience' whose purpose is to remind us of our *True Nature*, which is One with God as Love.

For one to claim that they own love is for them to claim to own the very essence of God—which is Love. This obviously is not a possibility; the creation (ego) can not own the creator (God). That is like an atom claiming to own the universe, or a table claiming to own the carpenter. The absurdities are obvious.

So What of Destiny?

The so-called 'cause and effect' theory works for the ego's perceived dimension of form, but unfortunately, it doesn't actually exist in the real underlying substrate of the Unmanifest. In the *Absolute Reality* of All there Is, nothing can cause anything. This is due to the fact that all is 'Whole' and not separate. One 'thing' has to influence another 'thing' in order to cause 'something' to happen. Since the underlying matrix of energy or consciousness (Unmanifest) is already total and complete, only 'Oneness' exists, but the ego tricks itself into believing that everything is separate and has its own identity. Fortunately, the *Higher Self*, the part that is aware of being connected with the whole, knows that All is One and that there is no specific thing that causes anything else to happen. So this reveals the ego's notion of itself—as a separate entity roaming around the world of form, while creating its own destiny and not needing God for help or existence—as a fallacy. Without God, no decisions could be made or 'will' could be exercised, nor would there be any existence for egos or beings to exist within. Without God, nothing is possible, so not only is God existence, but the possibility for choice and 'beingness' as well.

All possible pathways that can be accessed or followed have a planned outcome or destiny, which means that any path that one wishes to take is already planned. As the ego's choice (will) changes, so do the path and the outcome. However, these are still within the all-knowing universe, which has all destinies infinitely preplanned. Just because one changes paths slightly doesn't mean that they escape their inherent destiny (the main path); they simply choose another avenue along that same pathway of destiny, thus yielding an outcome that is close to what would have previously taken place. If an ego decides to 'will' another destiny to occur, however, the outcome may completely change to a different preplanned destiny. This is because God is the infinite potentiality of stored and preplanned destinies; one just has to choose (by will) the one that they desire at the time.

The ego denies preplanned destiny because it doesn't like

the idea of not controlling its reality. It would feel as if it were not needed to make decisions, think, speak, and physically move. Due to the ego's fear that it is not needed and that existence is autonomous, the ego makes itself believe that it is indeed in control of anything and everything that happens within its realm of existence—although certain things that it doesn't understand, such as the process of birth and death, are thought to come from and go to an unknown source. Since science doesn't really know what activates the brain and body at birth, it is termed a 'miracle,' because it is beyond linear perception and complete understanding.

The Universe knows where everything is located. Nothing can escape the knowingness of the Supreme Reality. As a grain of sand shifts, so does destiny. Destiny is not confined just to individuals. Everything in the *Universe of Totality* influences every outcome. Some shifts in energy can be measured by physical means, and other shifts cannot be measured because they occur in a more subtle state of existence. Because we don't constantly have access into the knowledge of destiny or the future, this is something that the ego constantly worries about. If one chooses the path of Truth (God), then only positive outcomes are available.

God Is Always Available for Help—Just Ask!

Remember that there is always a 'worse' down side to whatever down side one perceives at the time. Rest assured that even if the physical body and mind are pleading with a killer to live and let one's self go, one's soul and consciousness are karmically pulled out so that only the appropriate amount of pain that one needs to go through will be experienced: no more, no less. One's consciousness can be divided or split, so even if one's body is moving around and displaying the personal aspects of self, one may not be in the part of consciousness that feels pain. A split part of one's consciousness is then karmically pulled out so that nothing horrific will be experienced, except whatever one's current level of consciousness allows them to feel. Instead, if karmically allowed, one will only experience unconditional love and peace. So as one sits in love and peace, one may observe one's thought-to-be 'former self' (body) being beaten by the killer while learning a certain lesson for that time.

God will always help one if asked. Even when one continuously rejects the idea of God, God is there with one's self as Self waiting for them to see the light of love and acceptance. No matter if one is a so-called 'satanist,' God is there for them to call out to for help so that they can see the Truth. If eternity goes by and one is in 'hell,' God is there waiting to be realized. When realization occurs, the soul will be home (as Self) wishing they had never left.

The problem here is the ego. It is so corrupted and feels so separated from God that it is not able to realize that God is there for and as help. So what seems simple—just to ask God for help—is really something that might never happen. If it does, it may take hundreds, thousands, millions, billions, or even trillions of years, just to realize that one can just say with sincerity, "God help me." When one expresses this, they can try all over again, hopefully choosing a more positive destiny.

Destiny and Good Deeds

Once one realizes that destiny is preset, then pick a path within the 'Heart and Mind of God' to assure the best possible outcome. The more unconditional love (not sex), compassion, or understanding that one gives away, the more love one will receive from God. In psychic work, there is a contradiction, or least so it seems. Psychics teach one how to pull energy from the Universal Energy System into one's aura. They will continue to tell one to protect one's self from psychic attack, or unforeseen negative energies that will drain one from love and other positive energies. This in turn will leave one unbalanced and in need of healing (part of this is true, and is explained later).

The real reason that people feel drained from love (positive) energies is that they are negatively ego charged; therefore, they are not choosing to be a channel of Divine Love. The people who think that they are getting drained of positive energy are, but it is because they don't give enough love to others. In other words, they are stingy with love in fear that they will run out of that positive energy. On the contrary, if one gives loving energy to others, one's flow will increase because now God's Will is being done, and one will start feeling more fulfilled than ever. In order to do God's Will, one must love all beings unconditionally. For instance, if one holds the door open for someone, gets a turtle off a busy highway, or helps a stranded driver, they feel good because they have allowed or 'Willed' themselves to be a channel of Love and compassion.

This happens all because one was 'selfless' (God's Will) and gave loving energies to others. When one is 'selfish' (ego's will), one feels drained because they are blocking God's Will, which is forever helping, loving, and selfless. If one emulates God's Will, it will allow God's energies to flow through one to help others in need, infinitely. Since one is no longer blocking God's Will, the ego can now take a back seat in life. Consequently, the ego's grip will loosen more and more as one does 'good' or 'positive' things for everyone else except one's self.

Wherever one goes, no matter what the circumstance, it is possible to do good things for all beings. Even if the being does not acknowledge the good deed, one shouldn't get upset, because the universe knows and loves one for it. At first, one will have to think about doing 'good things' for people; it will not come easily. As the ego is trained to stay out of life, it weakens and inevitably fades away. In time, as one operates within God's Will, one will find that it comes effortlessly, and one feels better.

Just because one does a 'good deed,' don't ask or expect a thank you in response. The response, which one's self wants, is only going to satisfy the ego. Remember that the ego wants respect, admiration, and thanks. Do not use the ego to do 'good deeds'; instead, use God's Will and work humbly. Another example is that if one works at a tipping establishment and doesn't get tipped, don't get mad or rude with the person; just put a smile on one's face and say, "Thank you, come again" (and actually mean it). One just gave a selfless act toward humanity, which means that one just positively affected the entire world. One doesn't need a 'thanks' or acknowledgement for the act; just know that God appreciates one doing Divine Will 'down on earth as it is in heaven' (so to speak—ignore the personification).

Eventually, as one allows God to work continuously through one's self as Self, one's destiny gets reselected from the infinite, preset positive paths that were not chosen before, thus yielding a more positive outcome. Even if it does not look or feel positive, believe that it is. Rewards may be reaped in the physical or the spiritual, but if they are expected, then it is the ego 'desiring' it.

What Is An Enlightened Being?

Enlightenment means 'awakened to Self' or 'dwelling in the light of God.' An enlightened being is someone who has transcended the ego, which in turn has freed their soul through the direct realization of being One with God. And since they have transcended their ego, which is negative karma, they also never have to reincarnate again. Just the same, they no longer perceive the linear/dualistic as reality; rather, they see it as illusion. As they function within the linear realm of form, the infinite expression of Divine Love and Truth is brought to all beings. They see no separation in the reality that we live in, only Oneness, or a constant unification of all things. They see no 'evil' in the world. They see no one who is 'bad,' but they may see a being who is misdirected and in need of some help. The Presence of the Self, or the Divine Radiance of God, is detected as coming from within and as All. They see all beings as perfect in their own essence, with no need for judgment. All just is.

These beings live completely for and as Truth, while allowing God to channel through them as love, peace, and compassion to all beings with whom they come in contact. Their only function is to help all beings spiritually evolve by dissolving the lower levels of consciousness (ego) that have blinded and entrapped many beings in the realm of suffering. Wherever these enlightened beings go, they emit Divine Radiance to all life, thus helping all beings experience love, peace, and happiness.

They do not see any imperfections in the world, nor anything to solve or change. Because the physical world and bodies only exist within the 'illusory realm,' known as the manifest (earth), they see no importance in fixing an 'illusion.' They focus on what exists and is most Real, the ***Supreme Reality***—known as the 'Spirit of God' to most people, and the 'Divine Presence' or the 'Unmanifest Source of All That Is' to the spiritually adept, or simply 'Truth' to the Enlightened One.

The Benefits of Enlightenment

One who is enlightened <u>may</u> (enlightened does not mean psychic) be able to see into various dimensions of existence or astral realms, but always experiences God continuously. This being <u>may</u> be able to communicate with beings from that realm, but usually sees no reason for it. For the enlightened one knows that their presence alone is sufficient to help all that exists to evolve spiritually. Because the enlightened being subjectively (by their experience) knows the ***Real Reality***, these spiritual occurrences can now be perceived without shock or 'being spooked,' as it would the ordinary. It simply seems completely normal; to them it is just another aspect of reality. Keep in mind that the most important connection is with God, or the Unmanifest Self, not deceased relatives or other worldly beings (that is just a diversion from Truth).

Many times the Enlightened being sees (internally knows, which translates into a 'seeingness') light illuminating from all that exists as Divinity. The aura and the chakras <u>may</u> be perceived during the rest of their physical existence, but this is not of any interest to the enlightened being. Chakras and auras can help the psychic diagnose certain energetic problems, but the enlightened being knows that any and all beings who are not enlightened need help, regardless of their chakra size or the color of their aura. If a being is an ego, they are currently operating within a lower level of consciousness and need help. The enlightened being can significantly raise a being's level of consciousness, which may spontaneously heal mental, emotional, spiritual, and some physical problems, if karmically allowed. The 'Radiance of God' is always flowing throughout and emanating from the enlightened being. This Radiance will affect in a positive way all beings who 'willfully' allow it to do so.

The enlightened being's Radiance can significantly offset the negativity that millions of ego inhabitants have brought into the world. This means that they are transmuting (changing the negative into positive) the negativity of the world, or saving mankind from their own sins (negativity). They realize that they don't have to touch (healing with hands) someone to heal them; they can simply think of them and they are healed—although perhaps not in the way that the ego wanted or expected itself to be healed. True healing has no limits or boundaries, because it is manifesting from the Unmanifest, which is the Nonlinear (immeasurable) Reality. The ego just thinks that boundaries exist, which may actually prevent healing through prayer, thought, or 'Will' within the limited linear physical reality. Boundaries are all the ego knows, so that is its reality. However, without the ego, the enlightened being's ability to heal others is not limited or restricted by any means except the other ego being's will, which may resist the healing.

The enlightened being does not have to think about being nice, loving, or compassionate; they just are. It is an expression of Divinity, because this is their reality. In other words, it is all they know, and now are. When the ego has been transcended, all aspects of the personality that they once were no longer exist, meaning that a criminal could become enlightened or transcend the ego and never think about a 'bad deed' ever again. They will only positively benefit humanity for the rest of eternity. This is because the ego was the criminal, not the Spirit. The Spirit, or the Higher Self, is complete and pure, with nothing to gain. All it knows is love. All it wants to do is selflessly help others. The enlightened being loves anyone and will offer to help them even if they have tried to inflict harm on them previously.

The enlightened being <u>may</u> also have paranormal abilities (to the ego), such as manifesting from the Unmanifest or creating something out of thin air. For instance, Sai Baba has been noted to create what westerners call 'holy ash,' and what he terms 'Vesbhuti.' He just waves his hand in the air and creates ash that seems to come from nowhere. This ash is said to have healing properties, as he does. People have spontaneously healed just being near him, because the radiance flows through him to others at all times. Just as Jesus spontaneously healed others or created bread out of thin air, these seemingly miraculous events are normal to the enlightened being but stun the average person.

The enlightened being always feels fulfilled or full of love and joy. They are sometimes overwhelmed by the joy and can go into catatonic (unmoving) states. They know the so-called 'secrets' of the universe and how all is created. This joy and peace of Mind will flow from them and into other beings, which creates an obvious uplifting effect. Because they now know the method of manifestation, many times they too can manifest. Whether manifesting physical things, attitudes, love, or positive energy, their demeanor is still humble and not done out of gain or admiration.

Because the enlightened being no longer operates under the control of the ego, they are a pure reflection of God being with us. They only allow God's Will to operate and flow through them to continuously benefit all beings, while being completely selfless. Their only true wish is for 'world peace,' not so that they can be happy (because they already are), but for all others to be happy. They know how this can be accomplished and are 'usually' working on it in the spiritual dimensions through prayer and increasing positive energy with thought formations and Will.

Most of the physical realm is not yet ready to accept the information provided by the enlightened being. As much as people say they want 'peace on earth,' they really don't. They are too attached to the vicissitudes of the troubled ego lifestyle and the emotional, mental, and physical attachments that come from existing under the control of the ego. As long as the ego exists on even the most seemingly innocent level, it is only there for self-gain. The ego only serves itself, not others. If one serves others by choice or will, one is allowing God's Will to operate through one's self. This 'Will' slowly dissolves the grip of the ego and leads to the transcendence of the lower self (ego). To serve others by the use of Divine Will, which is expressed through compassion and action, is known as the path of the heart, one of the paths of enlightenment. But to serve others with the wisdom of God is the pathway of the Mind, an enlightened path more rarely taken.

The enlightened being knows all as One and sees no separations in reality. They feel as if everything is another aspect of themselves and sometimes try to explain this to others. They know reality as the Nonlinear/Nondualistic realm of existence at all times, as 'pure existence.' They do not think it; they just know it because they are it. They teach others from their own subjective experience. What they know is not learned from books; it is their reality and what they are, a higher and more pure level of consciousness known as Divinity. Because they no longer see the ostensible truths of linear reality, they do not see opposites such as good and bad, dark and light, high and low, near and far, male and female, smart and dumb—they see only the Absolute Reality, or the Divinity that shines forth from All. No matter their seeming outward appearance, their purity is seen and known. They accept all who come for help and even those who deny and criticize them.

Creation from the Unmanifest to the Manifest (Manifestation of the Universal Mind)

Everything that could ever be created in the manifest already exists in the Unmanifest as unlimited potentiality. 'Things,' which can only be manifest (created in form), are created because they arise from the Unmanifest (formless potential) energy when willed by the universal consciousness to be an energetic expression. The energetic patterns are then 'energized' and concentrated into a more dense energetic pattern; they then exist as a certain vibratory rate or frequency. The ego/mind complex, or the totality of personal karma, is vibrating at a certain rate or resonance, which sets the level of consciousness that displays inherent character traits or qualities. This allows all energetic patterns that vibrate at the same rate as the consciousness of a specific individual to be accessed by that individual with the congruent level of consciousness that is their current state of existence, which is portrayed as the essence of their 'personhood.' This means that all energetic patterns that match the energetic frequencies of a specific individual's consciousness can be accessed and expressed as a trait of that person. The person believes they have 'ownership' of these traits, whether thoughts, ideas, actions, words, and so on, when in reality any and all thoughts, actions, or words are and have already been created prior to the visible expression.

This means that there was no creation date for any thoughts, actions, or words; these simply existed because they were a product of the infinite potentiality of God as Unmanifest (the Source) and the Universal Consciousness. Without that trait having already been created, it could never have been expressed by the ego. An ego can only *express* the qualities of its current level of consciousness; since All comes from the Source, only God can really be said to create. It is the provider and the creation system as the Totality of Existence. This is because God is Unmanifest, and all that is created is allowed to by way of the manifestation process (universal consciousness 'willing it' into expression), or energy potential coming from the Unmanifest and crystallizing into the energetic pattern of form, which thus becomes and is referred to as manifest. So the ego calls for something to be created, or 'wills it so,' but God allows it to manifest. Unfortunately, the ego doesn't always know what's best (for example, hell).

One constantly accesses information from the universal consciousness without knowing it. This is because the ego always claims to own every thought or action as it enters consciousness, but it is given freely by the universe as the ego unconsciously (wills) asks for it. After the vibrational rates of both the 'energy pattern' and the 'individual' match, manifestation on a mental, emotional, or even physical level can take place. The 'energy pattern' that enters the individual's unconscious mind gets charged with the individual's inherent energy. When the 'energy pattern' gets charged with this energy, it lowers to a lesser level of consciousness (that is, more dense, getting closer to the physical dimension due to the focused concentration, which solidifies form), which then shifts dimensions. Keep in mind that these finer energy vibrations (less tangible or concrete) are not in the physical manifest, but instead are within the astral dimensions or universal consciousness, which are the same and are called the 'Spiritual Manifest.'

These lower energy patterns thus become more dense and closer to the existence of the physical planes of 'matter.' They then enter the individual's subconscious, where they become charged with even more energy. As the additional charging takes place, the 'energy pattern' becomes more crystallized and enters the realm of consciousness, where it can then be referred to as a 'thought pattern' by the individual, or felt to be a quality of form.

All thoughts are just energetic patterns, or organized and structured energy, within the manifest dimension. The organized energy doesn't have to make sense to the ego's consciousness, but it does belong there if it entered its consciousness by way of the ego, mind, karma, or will, which are one and the same. The ego/mind/karma complex's 'will' sets one's current vibrational state, or level of consciousness, which basically predetermines one's thoughts, actions, outcome, and destiny. This means that one's thoughts are preprogrammed to (as well as a product of) a specific level of consciousness. One does not create any thoughts; instead, a being just connects to or taps into their level of consciousness, which is set within the various levels of consciousness that have been provided by, and that are, the universe. So all beings at the same level of consciousness simply share the aspect or quality of energy that is a product of that level of consciousness, referred to as 'ego mind' for the lesser levels of consciousness (lower self), as 'Aware Mind' for the upper (enlightened) levels of pure consciousness (Higher Self), and as 'Pure Mind' for the Unmanifest Reality of Absolute Truth (the Unmanifest [infinite, nonform] Self).

No one is an independent individual; they are just borrowing energy (so to speak) from the collective universal consciousness, which is a composition of many different frequencies 'willed' into existence and expressed by all types of beings. So all beings really just steal their identity; they do not create it. No matter how different one tries to be, they are just following the crowd like everyone else. Everyone steals an identity; few abandon it. The only aspect of one's self that is even 'real' is the Unmanifest Self (God); all else is just an illusion.

Throughout time, the level of consciousness of mankind, as a whole, has raised significantly. This allows new ideas or thoughts of the physical dimension to be experienced as creation. Ideally, we want to think of mankind as progressing or getting smarter. However, as our vibrations raise we connect to different levels of consciousness, experiencing a new reality. This exposes all beings to a new, perceived reality as 'timeless inventors' or the 'extremely imaginative.' So all that we think we create is actually stolen from the Unmanifest as potentiality and the universal collective consciousness, which fuels one's egoistic traits and identities. Each and every soul's 'beingness' is shaped by their 'will' to be an expression of the many various types of frequencies that come from the universal consciousness in a local appearance of mixtures known as the energetic field (aura) and displayed as 'character traits' or personality.

Not only does this energy pattern, now a thought pattern, come into our consciousness, but it reveals what we believe and perceive can be created as reality—no more, no less. All actions of the physical body, such as walking, jumping, driving a car, talking, thinking, and eating, are predetermined by the individual's current level of consciousness and usable frequency range. All energy that the individual can portray or act out is predetermined by the ego and its karmic resonance. So every motion made by the physical body is already known and has been created before it is performed by the ego as a trait. By choice and current level of consciousness, then, the ego's outcome is inevitable and predestined. All is and already has been created in and as the infiniteness of the universe; the ego simply chooses to express one of its many inherent character traits that it believes originated within its own self.

Since the ego always wants to feel as if it is in control, it rejects this concept, thus denying Truth, which is God. So if one were to think (hypothetically), "Well, I could just shoot myself and go against my prior level of consciousness and prove it wrong because I'm not a demented person," one would then prove this to be right. Remember that choice and level of consciousness are a part of the reality in which existence ensues. As one chooses to shoot one's self, one chooses the lower emotion of pride (trying to prove one is right), which therefore momentarily lowers one's level of consciousness and changes one's destiny or outcome in that instant of exercising 'lower ego will.' As the individual lowers thought patterns to those of a lower vibrational state, this affects not only the consciousness of that specific individual but the entire consciousness of the universe, affecting all **unenlightened** beings negatively. Remember that all enlightened beings have transcended the ego and therefore have transcended all personal karma. So these enlightened beings remain unaffected by any use of an ego's 'lower will.' Unfortunately, however, the use of a lower being's 'egoistic will' brings negative energy into play in the universe, adversely affecting all beings as a whole through the connective tie of universal karma. Universal karma (the collection of all universal energies and the personal karma of all beings) is subject to the influences within lower consciousness, which stem from the ego being's use of 'will' and lower the level of consciousness of the universal whole.

Even though that 'lower' level of consciousness has already existed, the ego still thinks that the negatively perpetuated thought forms were created by the use of their own 'will,' which invoked the energy of that specific level of consciousness. So in essence, that negative energy was not created, it was simply chosen to be felt or expressed by that individual, and for others to feel it as well. As it was chosen, it was expressed as an emotion, mental state, or physical action. So, for example, when others perceive a being who is a product of a lower level of consciousness expressing the personality of a so-called 'evil-doer,' that being is thought by others and its self to be the originator or creator of the personality trait. Therefore, other egos see and label the originator of that action as 'evil' or 'mean.'

Throughout the evolution of the soul (ego), the individual with a higher level of consciousness can choose to regress in or decrease its inherent vibratory state. This allows them to access the lower dimensions, or the energy planes that supply the lower vibrational emotions, thoughts, 'evil deeds,' etc…. Thus, if one's vibrational state is high, one can go low, by choice or 'will.' However, if one is low, one can only go lower. One may not go higher due to the lack of karmic privilege. To be able to go higher in level of consciousness, one must transcend some of the ego and adopt the higher qualities of consciousness (love, peace, joy, and understanding). This process, however, is usually not as rapid as the option to decrease one's vibrational state. To go higher may take lifetimes if one is not properly informed or directed, but to go lower may take an instant.

Section Two
<u>Metaphysical Study</u>

"The mind attempts to control reality by perception and programming, but the Mind is Reality."
— BN

Chapter 5
<u>Understanding Meditation</u>
(<u>Decreasing Brainwaves</u>)

The Main Focus

This chapter focuses on the basics of meditation. It teaches various seemingly simple techniques used throughout the ages in many different cultures. Many people try to claim that they invented these techniques; however, that is their ego talking, and it shows a lack of research into the past. This chapter discusses the different ways to decrease brainwaves, as well as the keys to deep relaxation, breathing techniques, mental focus, and syncing the hemispheres of the brain. The most important key of all, though, is intention. One must really want to meditate to achieve phenomenal results.

As meditation is practiced 'religiously' (so to speak), healing may result on many levels. It is not uncommon for mental and emotional disorders to disappear spontaneously, but it is always wise to consult a physician for advice. Physical ailments may also disappear or go into remission. Throughout history, meditation has been cited for all kinds of healing effects. Religious and scientific texts also confirm the importance of introspection, breathing, energy balancing, and meditation. Currently, many people do not know much about meditation; thus most techniques can only be learned from books, seminars, and workshops. Perhaps the future will yield more meditative knowledge within the social environment.

As stated before, intention, or 'will,' is the most important factor in any spiritual quest. This energizes and inspires one to try their best and to stop at nothing. Deeper states of relaxation and meditation can be attained when one's 'will' is the energizer.

Meditation requires 'fixity of focus,' also known as 'one-minded' deep concentration, which is an asset that benefits any meditator. If one is sleepy, then it is not the best time to meditate.

One needs to be alert and able to concentrate on the task to reap the benefits.

Sleep is not the same as meditation. When one sleeps, their astral body either leaves the physical confines of the body, unknown to the sleeper, or it may yield an internal projection into the deep subconscious of one's mind, known as 'dreaming.' The ego becomes energized and activates the dream state. This actually reduces one's level of consciousness by a small amount. While one is trying to dream or induce an out-of-body experience, the level of consciousness also decreases. However, meditation and intention during the next day can raise one's consciousness, counterbalancing any residual negativity.

Setting Up an Altar

Before one begins the process of meditation or prayer, a comfortable and inspiring sacred place should be selected or created. This means that one should find a comfortable spot in the house or outside in the garden that is peaceful, quiet, and inspiring, and can be accessed at any time when at home. The best place for meditation is a section of the house that is a bit removed from ordinary life. This can be a vacant room, a section of the bedroom, or a big, unused closet that can be transformed into a meditation and prayer room. The room should have its own thermostat that regulates the temperature to a comfortable degree—not too cold or hot.

This room should be clean and 'clutter free,' which aids in keeping the mind clear. As the mind is clear, the body feels relaxed, and vice versa. For instance, walk into a very dirty room in the house and note how you feel, then clean it and see and feel the difference. A clean, uncluttered room just feels more comfortable and relaxing. The reason for this is that all 'things' create energetic waves. So a mixture of many different 'things' in a room creates an occluded atmosphere with disruptive patterns of energy that all impede on each other. Having 150 pieces of 'junk' in a room is like turning on 150 radio stations all at once. It is complete chaos, not to mention very hard to relax to, or within.

Items that have a very soothing and calming effect, such

as a waterfall, plants, 'feng shui' crystals, or statues, may be placed throughout the room. But don't add too many; this would just create chaos as well. The room should have one focal point; it is usually wise for it to be a low desk with a flower and a couple of rocks, sand, or crystals. This act incorporates the natural phenomena of nature, which are able to balance energies within the auric field. Put balancing energies on the sides of the desk, such as a flower and sand on one side and a couple of crystals, rocks, and stones on the other side. A main archetypal figure, such as Buddha, Jesus, or an Angel, may be placed in the middle as the focal point. Archetypes will be explained in the latter part of this chapter. As meditations change, so may focal points. Or one may choose to not use archetypes; it is an individual preference.

This clutter-free desk will allow one to remove easily, or to move, any of the items. Colors may also be draped over the desk to bring that vibrational quality to the meditation. Just as focal points or archetypes may change throughout one's practice, so will colors. It is important to note that all healing images can simply be thought of and the healing qualities will and can be used, so there is really no need for any focal points if the ability to visualize comes easily.

The desk, and the objects on it, create the 'sacred space' that inspires one to search their soul. This 'sacred space' also entrains one's brainwaves and consciousness levels. As one meditates in the same place for a couple of weeks, the feeling of safety and relaxation that is acquired in meditation is associated with the 'sacred space.' Thus, every time one enters the room and prepares to meditate, it becomes easier to relax and enter into deeper levels of trance. The 'sacred space' also becomes charged with one's psychic (immediate life force) energy from the energetic field; this imprints one's energy on everything in that room, making it easier for one to get back into a state of heightened consciousness or awareness. So it is important that each person has their own 'sacred space' with their own energy imprinted on it. When one is enlightened, the whole universe becomes one 'sacred space.'

This 'sacred space' should be kept clear of all drugs, medicine, alcohol, money, or any other objects that create a sense of worry, appeal to the cravings or desires of the ego, or have been handled by numerous people. The room should be cleansed with incense (sage, lavender, moldavite, or other high vibrational scents and oils), sounds (songs, notes, singing bells, musical instruments, or words of high vibrational energy), crystals (amethyst, smoky quartz, lapis lazuli, moldavite, tektite, or other stones that emit high-frequency energies), and most important, (positive) prayers or intent.

This room should be treated with the utmost respect. One should not enter it unless in a 'good mood' or having 'good intentions.' If one enters it with the lower emotions or viewpoints of the ego, such as worry, fear, regret, hate, anger, revenge, pride, or righteousness, it will imprint the room with negative energy. This obviously would put disruptive energies into this so-called 'sacred space,' which should be kept a 'Holy' room. These disruptive energies make it more difficult to reach the desired states of consciousness. Room clearing will be discussed later, in the chapter called *Raising Consciousness Level.*

In front of the low-level desk, a mat, prayer rug, chair, zafu, zabuton, or meditation chair may be used. Make sure it is comfortable but not too comfortable. One doesn't want to fall asleep while meditating, because it is not beneficial for elevating consciousness (one decreases in consciousness when sleeping). Just make sure that the seat is comfortable enough so that the body feels no pain. Be certain that one can remain seated for at least 30 minutes without pain.

Reasons for Meditating

The term meditation ('medi' refers to medicine) basically refers to 'internal medicine,' but not to western standards of medicine. Instead, it is a noninvasive, nonpill–popping way of reflecting on and introspecting inside the mind (ego), which is what creates the seeming disturbances in a being. It is a way to explore the mind and the universal consciousness, thus understanding the various levels of consciousness and gaining compassion and insight into the various expressions of existence—self, others, and creation.

Meditation is also done to calm the mind and body while breaking down the ego a little at a time, hopefully to realize the Self. Meditation is done for many different reasons, all depending on what the meditator is trying to accomplish—whether it is to silence the mind and have no thought; work with the chakras and energize the aura; increase psychic receptivity; raise one's level of consciousness; do astral projection, past-life regression, or dream recall; stabilize mental and emotional problems; contemplate the meaning of existence; gain intuitive insight; become enlightened; or just relieve stress and relax. Whatever one's goal, meditation can definitely help.

There are also many ways to meditate. Depending on the desired effect, one can use different meditations. Some meditations require working with mantras, archetypes, mandalas, tratak (open-eye meditation), Dharana Yantra, nature, colors, chakras, auras, crystals, incense, oils, breathwork, and many other techniques. This chapter discusses various methods of meditation to heal the soul and still the mind.

What Is Hypnosis?

Hypnosis is the process of reducing the brainwaves, thus stilling the mind. As the mind becomes still and thoughts slow down, clarity is produced. The first prerequisite is to be willing to be hypnotized, the second is to trust the hypnotist, the third is to be deeply relaxed, the fourth is to follow the hypnotist's directions, and finally, one must be willing to let go of inhibitions and accept **all** suggestions. Most people, however, are not that willing or trusting.

Hypnosis is a great way to delve into the lower self or the ego. In so doing, problems may be looked at and examined with more clarity than when one is in a mentally rampant waking state. All topics, intentions, and motives may be seen for what they really are, whether desirable or undesirable. Hypnosis may be used to help rectify current problems, which are, of course, a product of the ego. During a waking state, one's superficial thoughts can be seen or acted on. Unfortunately, the ego's unconscious and subconscious motives and intentions are usually unknown to the in-

121

dividual, and are thus acted on without wisdom, or Divine Understanding.

Hypnosis is only one of many meditation techniques. It really just consists of the first steps of meditation: willingness, relaxation, and decreased brainwaves. 'Self-hypnosis' basically means using the same methods on one's self; it is a way of examining the ego, but the true essence of meditation is really to transcend the ego and to become Self-Realized. Unfortunately, many hypnotists are not themselves enlightened and usually base their practice on psychology, which is 'linear reasoning.'

This psychological method of hypnotism works well for analyzing a problem and seeing that one has a problem, but not really for understanding, from a more in-depth or spiritual standpoint, why one's ego has the problem. Sometimes, as the problem rises to the surface through hypnosis, the person relives past trauma. Hypnotists and psychologists view this as a 'breakthrough'; however, it usually just forces someone to relive a traumatic experience, without the Truth that is needed to heal properly.

One can raise their level of consciousness through the route of enlightenment, thus transcending all their problems and not reliving painful experiences. In comparison, the person who relives an experience using a hypnotist's or psychologist's methods often does not raise their level of consciousness. Instead, they may even go down, because the emotions and viewpoints of the ego that are relived through hypnotism have their own specific charge that relates to a corresponding consciousness level. These emotions are usually regret, greed, lust, pain, anguish, and fear, or others that are on a very low level of consciousness. So reliving or merely thinking of any of these low-level emotional and mental states, or viewpoints, will decrease the level of consciousness for the being experiencing them, if Truth is not presented for Nonlinear healing (Self).

Many beings feel refreshed after being hypnotized; this could be for a variety of reasons. Perhaps one's level of consciousness has been raised and the problem has been understood and released. One may feel elated after a session because the brainwaves are reduced, so that one feels stressfree and relaxed. Furthermore, one may feel comforted to know of a problem that was apparently afflicting them. Lastly, one could have experienced a very trying and tiring emotional outburst during a hypnotic session. Compared with not crying, versus crying and feeling the trauma, the former seems very different and stressfree. One may feel happy because they feel such a vast difference between their previous state of misery, compared with their normal, everyday state. This normalcy now feels striking, compared with the lower emotional state experienced during hypnotism.

Hypnotism is a valid form of therapy and can help to cure many ego problems. However, it may take several sessions, which can be costly, and it will not readily equip one with the necessary skills to transcend the lower self. It could, though, lead one's self to the path of 'self-inquiry,' which will help one transcend all of one's seeming problems and opposites; this may release the ego.

Meditation may seem like the best path for silencing the mind, but for enlightenment, 'self-inquiry' is all that is really needed. To clarify confusion, however, the combination of many meditation techniques can help one transcend the ego more quickly. In the end, all that is needed is 100% Will and surrender to God.

Reducing Brainwaves (Beta, Alpha, Theta, Delta)

The brain uses energy in pulses or beats per second (bps). This energetic term is called hertz. Hertz means 'beats per second,' but it is more commonly known as 'cycles per second' (cps). The more energy the brain uses, the higher the hertz level or cps.

In its most awake state, the brain operates at 14 or more cps; this level is called the beta state. The next level is about 8 to 13 cps; this level is known as the alpha state. The slower levels of functioning, around 4 to 7 cps, are termed the theta state. The lowest level that the brain can operate at is 1 to 3 cps, which is called the delta state. These states not only show the energy being consumed by the brain, but they also show the current state of the individual (see the chart below).

Reducing brainwaves is not the same as reducing levels of consciousness. Brainwaves have to do with the brain, and are activated by the use of the 'thinking mind,' and levels of consciousness have to do with a being's energetic frequency, although the two are integrated. Reducing brainwaves is a prerequisite to acclimating the 'self' to the trance state. The lower the cps of the brain, the deeper the level of trance that can be attained. The higher the brainwaves, the more active the ego. The lower the brainwaves, the less active the ego. As a person lowers the brain's cps by using breathing, visualizing, and muscle relaxation techniques, the ego can be witnessed and introspected upon. As its many questions are answered, the ego lessens its grip, thus raising consciousness.

Brainwave Level	Meditative State	Cycles Per Second
• Beta	Wide Awake State	14+
• Alpha	Light Meditative State	8-13
• Theta	Dream and Deep Meditative State	4-7
• Delta	Deepest Meditative State	1-3

Different Stages of Trance

As one's brainwaves decrease, the level of trance increases. When one operates in the physical realm, there are many demands placed on the ego. These demands create a constant drive to act that obviously increases brainwaves to the beta (awake) state and hinders relaxation. This in turn affects one's ability to bring about a deeper level of trance and a higher quality meditation. First-level trance is when the consciousness that is felt to be located in the ego's brain is felt to be reflected onto the etheric energy body (the first-layer energy body closest to the physical body).

Light Trance

The first level of trance, 'light trance,' is attained when one's brainwaves reduce from the beta state to the alpha state. Mental clarity accompanies this state of decreased brainwaves. Thoughts seem to slow down and can be analyzed to a fuller extent. This is when one can study how the ego claims thoughts as its own. Thoughts always are seen as uncontrolled and rampant as meditation is started, but with control, these slow and can be seen as concepts, statements, sentences, questions, fragments, and confusion. The ego only takes credit for a thought that arises out of universal consciousness when it is relevant to the situation at hand; thus it seems to 'make sense.'

A sensation of warmth and tingling that travels throughout the body is felt almost as a buzzing sensation. This condition makes one feel as though they are 'glowing with light.' The energy carries with it a deep sense of relaxation and peacefulness. In fact, one also tends to feel a bit removed from reality, but in essence, they have just moved one step closer to *True Reality*. If one moves 6 more energy bodies out, Truth becomes realized to a larger degree. When one always functions from the 7th level of the auric field, they are said to be enlightened.

In this light trance state, sounds feel muffled when in the background, but sharp or isolated sounds feel very pronounced. These sounds can be felt to travel through the body in waves of energy, like a ripple in a pond. Continual sounds can feel like a massage of the energy body. Many people like to do sound meditations with singing bells or tuning forks. It can be very healing and a truly unique experience.

This state can be attained by 5 to 25 minutes of deep, controlled peaceful breathing called 'pranayama.' The length of time it takes to reach the desired condition depends on willingness, alertness, energy reserve, and skill level. After one receives a massage or relaxes to the peaceful sound of a waterfall, they are more than likely in a light trance state. One can operate in it but will sacrifice some of the 'warm, fuzzy, glowing' feeling. When one has attained this state, they usually do not want to move. As one slowly resumes what is felt as the 'real state' for humans, they tend to feel revitalized, balanced, and peaceful for the rest of the day.

Full Trance

As the brainwaves are reduced from the alpha to the theta state, full trance is attained. This state of awareness is accompanied by an increase in warmth and tingling that may overpower one, so that the physical body is no longer felt. All sounds seem to be muffled by about 80%. The combination of the physical body's numbness, the muffled sounds, and the deep relaxation make one feel as though they have forgotten where they are.

This allows one to travel into their thought processes with all of their awareness. This is the best state for self-inquiry and uncovering the Truth about one's existence. Thoughts are so sluggish that they can be examined from all angles. Astral projection or out-of-body experiences (OBEs) are also easier from this state.

This is the best state to raise one's level of consciousness. Using high vibrational items such as crystals, archetypes, or colors can bring it on very rapidly. Working with the higher chakras will also do the same. From this state of awareness, it is easy to slip into sleep if one is not mentally energized or alert enough. The deep unconscious and subconscious can be accessed with ease after one has acquired proficiency in reaching the 'full trance' state.

Deep Trance

As one passes through the different levels of trance, and the brainwaves have been reduced to the lowest level of functioning, the 'delta waves' that bring forth 'deep trance' can be felt. Within this state of awareness, the body feels as if it doesn't exist. Energy can be so strong that one becomes exhausted by the overuse of their energetic capacity. With much experience, this level can be attained and held for a substantial time. In this level, consciousness is barely hanging on and the body is completely asleep. It takes a lot of mental control to remain conscious. Usually, this state is referred to as Yoga Nidra, psychic sleep, or yogi blackout. During this state, the body is sleeping and revitalizing every cell in the body, while consciousness is awake but hardly functioning. The mind does not think, and 'astral sight,' a common 'byproduct,' provides for unique spiritual experiences.

'Real Time Sight,' also known as astral sight, is when one sees by way of awareness and not by the physical faculty of the eyes. 'Seeing' is the best way to describe the condition, but in actuality, the awareness of the energy bodies just senses everything as energetic patterns. These patterns are picked up as 'forms' by the astral senses or awareness, but are translated to the mind as sights. The awareness 'sees' into the 'real-time' dimension (which is a level of the astral dimension) by being aware of the form within it.

The 'real-time' dimension is one level of consciousness higher than the physical dimension. This means that it looks exactly like the physical dimension, except for physical laws such as gravity and solid matter. Spirits, thoughts, dreams, and energy can be easily seen in this dimension. Astral sight can be used during the lesser types of trance, such as the full trance, but this usually requires great skill. When astral sight is attained in a deep delta trance, things are just seen; they are not really questioned at all. In fact, to question anything or even to think would require a great effort. So the 'things' that are seen are just accepted, because consciousness is barely functioning and the brain hardly differs from a deep, unconscious state of sleep. Because thinking is so hard in this trance state, only fragments of the experience may be remembered. With practice come ease and greater remembering.

Why One Can't Seem To Relax

This is because the brain is activated and is still needed to perform many tasks. The brain interprets movement, speech, computing, hearing, thinking, touching, seeing, and other voluntary and involuntary actions. So these functions must be shut off, or at least slowed down considerably. The chakras of the energy body may be overly active as well, thus pulling extra energy into the body; this energy is usually not needed. For instance, indigestion, anxiety, nervousness, obsessive-compulsive disorders, shallow breathing, overactive mind, attention deficit disorder, nerve pain, headaches, shakiness, and fast talking are common if the chakras are overactive; just a simple energy body tune-up is needed.

This is why many religions teach yoga and meditation, or prayer. They are an easy way to shut off or slow down the mind. The yogis learned that if you increase the energy flowing through the body's circuitry, the nerves become overstimulated and worn out. As the neurons constantly fire, the body becomes overworked. As this overstimulation slows down and eventually stops, the body's muscles, nerves, and mind feel a huge difference between the active state and when the activity is stopped altogether. This results in a deeply relaxed feeling. This activity also allows the body to burn up extra energy that would fuel the body and the mind's mental functions.

Someone who undertakes the practice of yoga also adds many health benefits, such as flexibility, strength, balanced physical body and functions, balanced energy body and functions, elimination of wastes, increased oxygenation, better mental control, increased immune system, antiaging benefits, better concentration, and calmer mental states. Yoga and progressive muscle relaxation are the two principles that should be applied in order to get into a deep state of relaxation, which then yields deeper meditations.

Medications such as caffeine, ephedra, or any other stimulants overwork the neurons and the mental functions, making it hard to attain a proper state of deep relaxation. Even if really deep states of relaxation and meditation cannot be attained, high levels of consciousness can still be achieved, although they are a little harder to feel. It is beneficial to do yoga or stretch for 10 to 15 minutes while deep breathing before meditation is attempted.

The Importance of Breathing

Breathing not only is a way for the physical body to respirate and oxygenate its cells, but it is the foremost way to circulate energy. This energy, which is known as prana, Ch'I, Ki, Universal Energy, Orgone Energy, or any of a number of other labels, is the nurturing energy that allows manifest life to sustain itself (besides the Unmanifest). It supports the structure of all cells, atomic forms, and physical and spiritual laws.

Without the Unmanifest Presence of God, which is the supportive substrate of energy, every cell, atom, or molecule of energy would simultaneously implode and become nonexistent. And with every breath drawn, the physical body pulls in the atmosphere, which includes the necessary elements for existence, such as oxygen and subtle energy. Simultaneously, the energy body expands with each breath and absorbs energy from the Universal Energy Field, which nourishes and supports the soul. Without oxygen the physical body could not exist, and without subtle energy (consciousness) the soul could not exist, but without God (Unmanifest; beyond consciousness) nothing would exist.

Different Types of Breathing Methods

There are many types of meditations, each of which requires different breathing methods to achieve the desired result or condition. Different breathing methods change the quality of meditation and the level of trance, as well as the level of consciousness. If a deep level of relaxation is attained while one is at least in a state of full trance, the chances for increasing one's level of consciousness are far greater. When these precepts are taken into account, and meditative aids such as archetypes, colors, crystals, mantras, mudras, prayers, or other high vibrational energies are used, extremely high levels of consciousness can be attained. Not only will one definitely feel this extraordinary quantum leap in level of consciousness, but they will assume that other people can feel their energy as well. Sometimes others may, but usually they will be positively affected on an unconscious or subconscious level.

The chart below lists many beneficial methods of breathing that have been practiced for centuries. They will produce positive and quantifiable results. These breathing techniques should be practiced for at least 10 to 20 minutes at a time, sometimes longer. Full concentration should be placed on these exercises, until one achieves the desired effect.

Type of Breathing	How To Breathe
Pranayama (Rhythmic Breathing)	Inhale is equal to exhale, and hold on inhale and hold on exhale. *Sample Meditation:* **Inhale for 5 seconds, then hold for 4 seconds. Exhale for 5 seconds, then hold for 4 seconds.**
Breath Retention (Clear the Mind)	Follow pranayama, but have a long hold on the inhale and on the exhale. *Sample Meditation:* **Inhale 5 seconds, then hold for 15 seconds. Exhale 5 seconds, then hold for 15 seconds.**
Circular Breath (Circular Image and Motion with Breath)	**On inhale, feel the breath and visualize the energy starting from your feet and bring it out in front of body to the top of your head in a circular motion. Then follow through with an exhale that goes in a circular motion behind the body from the head to the feet.**
Breath Awareness (Being Aware of Breathing)	**Simply allow your body to breathe in its natural, slow rhythm. Do not alter the way your body breathes; just follow it with your mind. Be aware of your breath.**
3-Stage Breath (Lower Abdomen, Middle, Chest)	**Breathe in and blow out your lower abdomen first, then blow out your stomach, and then your chest. Follow by exhaling and releasing air from the chest, then the stomach, and then the lower abdomen.**
3-Stage Wave Breath (Lower Abdomen, Middle, Chest, then Same Sequence on Exhale)	**Breathe in and blow out your lower abdomen first, then blow out your stomach, and then your chest. Follow by exhaling and releasing air from the lower abdomen, then the stomach, then the chest.**

Type of Breathing	How To Breathe
Breath Bounce (Awareness Travels with Breath)	On the inhale, bring awareness from the feet and feel the energy come up through the body one appendage at a time (toes, feet, lower legs, knees, upper legs, hips, lower abdomen, stomach, spine, upper chest and back, neck, face, eyes, and head). Then exhale awareness back down.
Forced Exhale (Get Rid of Stagnant Energy)	Inhale for about 6 seconds, and hold for 8 seconds. Then exhale fully as hard as you can, expelling all air from the lungs, thus dispelling all of the stagnant (unmoving) energy.
Double Inhale Breath (Supersaturate with Energy)	Inhale for 4 seconds at 75% of lung capacity, then hold for 4 seconds. Inhale on top of inhale all the way to 100% maximal lung capacity. Hold for 8 seconds, and then release very slowly (about a 10-second exhale).
Deep Breathing (Relax, Center, Ground, Saturate)	Inhale for 8 seconds while blowing out the stomach like a balloon. Then hold for 8 to 10 seconds and release very slowly (about a 10-second exhale).
Alternate Nostril Breathing (Polarize Hemispheres, Balance)	Plug the right nostril with the right thumb, and inhale through the left nostril; be aware and follow the path of the air. Then exhale through the right nostril. Inhale through the right nostril, then exhale through the left. Always breathe slowly; continue for 5 to 10 minutes.
Color Breath (Raise Level of Consciousness) (Stabilize Energy, Charge Aura/Chakras)	Inhale color, then exhale color through the mouth. Visualize the exchange taking place. Then inhale color, and then exhale color down to the feet. Repeat with low colors to high vibrational colors—red, orange,

Type of Breathing	How To Breathe
	yellow, green, blue, indigo, violet, and gold.
Negativity Release Breath (Cleanse Aura and Chakras)	Inhale sparkling white and gold color, hold for 8 to 10 seconds, and then exhale very slowly (about a 10-second exhale).

Progressive Muscle Relaxation

For thousands of years, many different religions or spiritual sects have taught deep relaxation through progressive muscle relaxation. It has been called many things under different labels, but the fact remains: it is *very* beneficial.

Deep relaxation is the process of releasing stagnant or unmoving energy throughout one's being. This method of energy removal not only helps physical energy recirculate, but the subtle energy that is parallel to the physical also begins to move. The 'nadis,' or subtle energetic pathways, are parallel to the physical nerves. Thus, as the physical nerves are stimulated, the subtle (immediate) energy within the 'nadis' is stimulated as well.

Progressive muscle relaxation is a common technique in which one <u>progressively</u> contracts and relaxes the muscles, usually starting from the toes, all the way up to the top of the head (crown). For instance, one contracts their toes for 5 seconds, and then relaxes for 10 to 15 seconds. During the relaxation period, one then concentrates on the relaxed feeling, noting the difference between the contracted state and the relaxed state. After 3 repetitions of the toes, one then moves on to the calves, following the same procedure. Similarly, one follows upwards, through the hamstrings and quads, the butt and hips, the lower abs and lower back, the upper abs and upper back, the shoulders, the arms, the neck, and then the face and head. Throughout the duration of the muscle relaxation practice, one should focus on *pranayama*. But right afterwards, one should focus on either *breath awareness*, *color breath*, *circular breath*, or *breath bounce*.

If one does not have time to meditate, then one should try *whole body tensing*, or contracting all one's muscles at one time, rather than going by muscle groups. For everyday practice, the whole body tensing technique should be used. However, when one is very alert and wants to enter into a very deep meditation, the progressive method should be used. *Whole body tensing* is similar to the progressive method, in that one contracts their whole body for about 5 to 10 seconds, then releases and concentrates on the relaxed feeling. Three repetitions should also be done, or until the practitioner feels deeply relaxed and stressfree.

Other than breathing itself, this practice is probably the most common type of relaxation method found throughout various sacred texts and ancient teachings to help one to increase their subtle energetic reserve, and to quiet the mind to an extent so that healing becomes easier. If the progressive practice cannot be done every day, it may be practiced just a couple of times a week. *Whole body tensing* can be done before every meditation, and only takes about 5 minutes or less to complete.

Increasing Energy Body Awareness

The process for increasing awareness in the body, or 'soma,' is quite simple. Energy is increased within the physical body, but also in the energy bodies. It can be learned in a matter of days; although it may take a couple of months to become very skilled.

The methodology behind increasing awareness seems to come from the fact that the human mind has stored sensory information that can be accessed by the mind of the ego and the human brain. The ego mind has felt and remembered every cell in one's body. So one must only learn how to remember and access the already-stored information. In a way, this is a type of kinesthetic approach to the matter. But instead of remembering and accessing the feeling or worldly motions that the entire body goes through, one must simply learn how to remember and access the feelings and locations of each cell in the body.

It sounds difficult, because it is not often that a person tries to remember the location of a cell. However, a person does not access one cell at a time. Instead, one learns to locate and feel hundreds of cells with ease. This technique has been around for ages, even though many people claim to have just developed it. They may call it different things, but the methodology is inherently the same.

The technique is best applied after progressive muscle relaxation, followed by kinesthetic methods and trigger words, then Energy Body Awareness. These different techniques show one how to focus their awareness and increase energy in the physical body and energy bodies. The techniques involve visualization, remembered sensations, kinesthesia, and the use of certain breathing methods.

The most basic practice that elicits a response from the subtle energetic body is simply to use one's mind to think about a part of the body; a toe, legs, and fingers are the easiest. One just closes their eyes and thinks about their toe with every part of their being. Imagine how it would feel if one's 'astral hand' were touching their physical toes. A slight tingling sensation will be felt, maybe some warmth and 'buzzing.' While holding concentration on one's toes, move awareness to the upper part of the foot, as well as the sole and heel. Do the same until the warm tingly feeling has consumed them all. While maintaining concentration on the feet and toes, move the awareness up a little at a time; if one moves too fast, all awareness may be lost and one will need to start over, either at or near the beginning. Move up the entire body in this fashion, little by little. End with the top of the head. When finished, and the entire body is tingling, concentrate on the entire body glowing.

Throughout this practice, one should focus on the breathing method of 'pranayama.' When the exercise is finished, one should focus on 'color breath,' 'breath awareness,' 'bounce breath,' or 'circular breath.' This will enhance one's meditative state greatly. It is also very beneficial to work with the many chakras and various levels of the energy bodies.

If it is easier, one may try to feel as if water, in the form of a river or waves, is flowing up one's toes throughout one's body. One may try to feel what it would feel like if their astral arms were wrapping up their physical body with a giant Ace bandage or thick string. Or one may try to visualize a paint brush that goes all over their body, and stimulates each and every skin cell. It can be very helpful to visualize the paintbrush painting one's self from within the actual body, as well as outside. This seems to activate more subtle energy pathways. Whatever seems to be the easiest method for activating the chakras and energy bodies should be used.

Using Kinesthetic Meditation (Falling, Rising)

This is a method of remembering and instilling the feeling of falling. This feeling has been memorized by the ego mind and every neuron in the human body, so all one has to do is remember it and subjectively feel the falling sensation. As the sensation is created in the mind, it should be continuous and gentle. The various techniques that one should try to visualize and subjectively remember are the following: elevator, jumping off a cliff, parachuting, paragliding, walking down stairs, walking or running down a hill, sliding down a slide, sliding down a decline, and doing a series of minihops off a series of boxes or stairs. Not only should these methods be remembered with feeling (the most important part), they should be visualized as if they were actually happening in that instant. They should be imagined and felt to be as real as possible.

The falling technique actually tricks one's ego mind into relaxing and letting go. When the ego is 'off guard,' so to speak, it slips into the next level of the energy body, which is known as the etheric. This 'slipping' feeling transfers the focus of consciousness from the localized area of functioning, thought to be the human brain, and into the etheric (energy) body, which brings forth an 'expansion of awareness.' It is simply a way to refocus one's mind from the most 'concrete and illusory' to the more 'abstract and meaningful.' As consciousness <u>seems</u> to expand, one shifts their focus from the 'thinking mind' of the ego to the 'Aware Mind' of the Self, thus increasing one's awareness of reality.

This falling effect is very beneficial for entering into the desired level of trance; however, the opposite may aid in raising one's level of awareness—that is, the falling technique may be used for expanding awareness, but the rising technique may be used to experience the outermost levels of awareness to the extent possible (depending on a being's current state). So one meditates and uses the falling technique to enter a trance (the 1st to 3rd layer of the energy body), and then uses the rising technique to shift

135

their awareness into the outer layers (higher frequencies) of the energy body. While this increases one's level of awareness, one can only increase their awareness to the extent placed upon themselves by the limiting factors (beliefs) of their ego.

Example

Think, visualize, and feel… do not speak the following:

"…Walk into an elevator and allow the mechanism to shut itself slowly…As you face forward and see the doors close slowly, you look to the left and see a control panel that will allow you to access any floor that you would like…You decide to go down one floor at a time, so you press the button with the number 10 on it…This moves the elevator slowly down, and as the potential or stored energy picks up speed, you feel a shift in the elevator's weight. Some of its energy is transferred through you as if it were a part of you. As you rock back and forth and feel a sinking feeling, you are lowered with ease by this machine…As you reach the next floor, number 9, you decide to proceed to the next floor…As you press the number 9, you feel the sinking (Trigger Words) feeling, but with safety in the well-built machine… as you progress down, deeper and deeper (TWords) towards your inevitable goal… (Continue down to the last floor, level 0) As the last floor is reached, a feeling of courage and trust fills your being, giving you the confidence to undertake the biggest challenge of all… It remains within the safety of 'God's Grace,' so as the elevator doors open, you leap out of the elevator and fall through the unending infinite depth of pleasurable and harmonizing velvet black energy*…"

*Note: This black energy balances one's energetic system as the ego mind lowers its brainwaves. While 'velvet black' harmonizes and stabilizes negative energy, it also lowers one's level of consciousness for a brief time (hours or a day).

Using Trigger Words To Help with Relaxation

This is a common way to reach the appropriate state of relaxation. The technique, which hypnotherapists and psychologists have used for years, can be used by one's self, but it usually works better when coming from the intellect of another. If one becomes sleepy or overly relaxed, it brings on a sense of incoherency and abstraction. Words such as deep, down, further, lower, relaxed, heavy, let go, sleepy, and trance bring, by way of association, a feeling of letting go, which leads to relaxation.

If 'trigger words' are used in the beginning of one's meditation, it can greatly increase the depth of relaxation. This obviously improves clarity of mind, which benefits meditation because of the lowered brainwaves and the decreased mental processes. These words go well with the kinesthetic methods listed above.

Example

"...Feel yourself floating down, down, down...deeper and deeper into a warm, cozy, relaxing trance...As you feel yourself getting heavier and heavier, a slight and continuous sinking feeling pulls you down into a deeper state of trance..., one with no worries, no stress, and completely surrounded by the 'Grace of God.'"

Using Archetypes for Relaxation

All 'things' are allowed to manifest from the unlimited Unmanifest potential and the universal consciousness. These 'things,' which are known as 'form,' are created by a series of energetic frequencies that seemingly merge together, thus creating a specific pattern at a certain level of consciousness that can be recognized by the objective faculty of the ego mind. Whether something is a thought, picture (in mind or out of mind), solid object, word, or texture, it is still an energetic pattern of 'form.' This 'form' holds a specific level of consciousness or level of truth, whether heavily distorted or mildly occluded.

This archetype, or energetic pattern, can be seen objectively in the physical dimension or within the mind of the ego. When the archetype is visualized, the level of 'power' (consciousness) transfers to the being who maintains the image. This raises or lowers the individual's level of consciousness, depending on the level of consciousness of the archetype. The longer the image is held within the mind's eye, the more of that energy transfers to the being. Archetypes for increasing the level of consciousness are discussed in the chapter, *'Raising Consciousness Level.'*

The archetypes that will instill a deep sense of relaxation are as follows: water, gentle breeze, beach, river, mountains, stream, clouds, garden, trees, flowers, green pastures, pool, waterfall. Any other archetypes or associations that one finds relaxing can also be used. When archetypes are used, they should be visualized and felt with kinesthesia, as if one were actually there experiencing the deeply relaxing event. The longer that the archetype is held and felt in mind, the greater the energy transfer that occurs. If one has a 'bad' correlation or association, such as 'a fear of water,' it should obviously not be used. If one of the archetypes works, stick with it, unless change is felt to be necessary.

Using Colors for Relaxation

Just as archetypes can be used to create a feeling of relaxation or increase the level of consciousness, so may colors. Colors, in a sense, are archetypes; instead of being patterns, or merged frequencies, they are the frequencies themselves.

These colors, when visualized, actually start to manifest around one's physical body, through the physical body, and throughout one's energetic bodies. The colors used to balance and harmonize the energy bodies are as follows: deep blue, soft (sky) blue, velvet black, white, and soft green. Colors should be used as archetypes and held in the mind through visualization and subjective experience; the energy transfer is inevitable.

Example

After one has reached an appropriate level of trance, the meditation can be amplified by the use of soothing colors.

"...As you feel deeply relaxed, with no worries in mind, a door manifests in front of you (in the mind's eye). This door has a doorknob (symbolizing readiness, agreement, and acceptance). As it is turned, the door easily and slowly swings open, revealing a room of color. As you walk in a velvety-black energy (smooth black with sparkling and swirling white energy), you become entrenched and immersed within it. It consumes your body with peace and stillness. As you walk through this energy, you breathe it in (physically and visually), then you exhale it down into your physical body, feeling it travel down your body and outwards throughout the energy bodies. As you continue to walk, the velvety-black, soothing energy passes right through you, undisturbed, as if it did not know of your presence. The energy feels as though it accepts you, heals you, and yet does not 'feel' you physically. As the energy passes through your body, it absorbs any imbalances and harmonizes the body."

All of the previous exercises should be done for about 5 to 20 minutes. When the comfortable and pleasurable feeling dies down, or nullifies itself (so to speak), it is time either to move on with another color; to use a mantra, mudra, archetype, prayer; or to finish the meditation.

Syncing the Hemispheres

If the two hemispheres of the brain—the left and the right—are synced, a very deep level of trance can be attained. Syncing means to lower the cps of the right and the left hemispheres at exactly the same speed. This is more difficult than it sounds, because the two hemispheres naturally run at different cps. The problem can be overcome when one is correctly taught how.

By analyzing the two hemispheres of the brain, methods can be discovered to lower the cps. For instance, the right hemisphere is very creative and abstract. This side of the brain is not good at following directions in a logical or rational manner. However, the subconscious and unconscious mind can be accessed through it, which is very healing and beneficial. At the same time, visualization is easier for this side, so creativity is very common. Artists, writers, poets, psychics, philosophers, and visionaries usually access this part of their brain throughout the day.

The left hemisphere is the 'opposite' (so to speak) of the right. This left hemisphere is the logical and rational side of the being that deals with the planning, sorting, and categorizing of events or 'things.' Lawyers, planners, mathematicians, accountants, scientists, psychologists, and usually teachers are predominantly left-brained. It is also very common for a person to be a little of both. Many scientists who are only concerned with the linear dimension sometimes break the mold and look beyond. This stimulates the other side of the brain and accesses the subconscious and unconscious mind. Accessing the deeper levels of mind brings about more creativity, as well as new and revolutionary ideas, concepts, and theories.

The easiest way to sync the hemispheres is by using visualization and logic at the same time. Counting is logical (left) and visualizing (right) is creative. So there actually is truth to the 'counting sheep' method, or visualizing stairs while 'feeling one's self fall' and counting backwards. One may also use mantras. One should find the method that works for them and stick to it. The 'visualizing logic' method is very popular and is also a very efficient technique.

Mantra Sync

The mantras used to sync the hemispheres should be long—for example: *"I will not harm life; instead, I will love life. No matter how big or small, no matter how significant or insignificant, I will respect All things, because All things have a purpose."* The length of the mantra forces the left side of the brain to focus logically on the *progression or sequence of words*, while the right hemisphere needs to *focus visually* on the words and the *understanding* of the message. Try to conceive of the entire concept ('big picture,' and meaning) of the mantra each word at a time, or focus on the form and structure of the words as well as the essence.

This mantra may need to be said 10 times on some days and 100 times on others. Sometimes it is just easier to enter a trance state, while on other days it may seem impossible. Also, sometimes a mantra needs to be changed, to keep one's focus. After all, some mantras become tiring or boring, or a lesson may be learned and a new lesson needs to be recited. However, some methods or mantras may be effective every time they are used.

The Counting Method

As with the ***counting method***, while the right hemisphere *visualizes* the numbers, the left hemisphere should focus on counting the numbers *slowly*. The numbers should be counted backwards in descending order because this makes one feel relaxed. Almost like trigger words, the reverse motion or direction of the order of logic creates a relaxed feeling as it syncs the hemispheres. With this in mind, start at 10, 20, 30, 50, 100, or wherever you feel comfortable. The act of finishing is not important, just the motion and direction of the order of logic and the 'fixity of focus' itself.

Often a trance will come on suddenly and one will even forget they were counting. One should not try to remember what they were doing, unless the trance state has not yet been attained. If one wants to resume counting or meditative practice, then slowly return to one's focus and breathe. If the trance state is prevalent and one tries to remember what they were just doing, the trance state may be broken accidentally. One may focus on imaginary numbers in the mind while counting very slowly, or focus on imaginary objects such as sheep, pencils, dogs, cats, angels, or stars while counting. It is usually very helpful if one counts imaginary objects; such as sheep.

One may instill the use of ***trigger words***, count backwards, while kinesthetically feeling the dropping motion as one imagines one's self walking down stairs, while counting the stairs as one comes across them; one may also visually see the numbers on the stairs for added effect. This incorporates many different methods and would definitely increase the benefits of the meditation. If only counting and visualization are done, synchronizing the hemispheres (hemi-sync) is possible. If all of the above are done, however, one will have greatly improved results.

Unknowingly Lowering Levels of Consciousness

No being, unless a 'satanist,' or someone who is involved in some sort of lower secular cult, wants to lower their level of consciousness. As one lowers their level of consciousness, more negative karma is acquired, dampening one's spiritual evolution and slowing the progress of enlightenment.

The levels of consciousness do fluctuate greatly through-out one's life, especially from day to day if one is an emotional being. If one has lower qualities of the ego such as pride, guilt, shame, remorse, hatred, deceit, revenge, and so on, the level of consciousness is lowered continuously, or it remains at a stand-still at whatever level contains the specific type of energy that predominates in one's energetic field.

Most spiritual adepts, however, do not know that some meditations, or seemingly harmless intentions, in fact lower one's level of consciousness. Astral projection, or out-of-body travel, decreases one's level of consciousness significantly. The act of 'willing to dream' also lowers one's level. If the intention to do the above is strong and unwavering, the levels of consciousness will drop very low, which may result in one feeling 'spacey' and overall not at their best. They may feel depressed that day, or for the week. They may even feel nothing, which is more disturbing. Since they may not know their consciousness level has dropped, they may see no reason to raise it again or to stop being an expres-sion of that lower energy.

If one shifts attention and 'will' to the physical dimension, the level of consciousness will drop as if it were focused on the dream world or astral dimensions, simply because all of these are the worlds or dimensions of form; and form is illusion. They are illusion, just as the ego is illusion. That which is illusion (the ego) is capable of interpreting only illusion (the world of form). Just as the physical dimension and the ego are to be transcended, the in-tent to dream or travel the astral dimensions must be made to sub-side, ignored, and transcended. All form is illusion; only the form-less Unmanifest is the True Reality. So one should bypass all form and align one's self with the formless and real. This is why the book does not discuss learning how to dream, vivid dreaming, lucid dreaming, remembering dreams, psychic development, and astral projection.

Understand that the above spiritual illusions are still <u>many times</u> at a higher level of truth than the physical dimension, but not always. If one has not yet tried to transcend the ego, or has not followed any spiritual precepts, then chances are that one's level

142

of consciousness will not go down if these activities are attempted because they are already so low. If one is trying to transcend the ego, however, then these intentions will only hold them back by further decreasing their overall level of consciousness.

Astral projection, dreaming, and psychic development are not evil; in fact, they can at times be very illuminating and quite revealing about spirituality. Only at higher levels of consciousness, or when the decision to become enlightened has been 'willed,' does one usually bypass the illusory realms of the 'Spiritual Manifest.' When one is at higher levels of consciousness, the effects of lowered consciousness can be quite staggering, even depressing. Thus, the evoked emotional states and energetic imbalances caused by a lesser illusory practice often deter one from any further action or interest.

It is important to note that just because psychics focus on the finer frequencies of form, they are not 'satanic' or 'evil,' as most churches believe. The churches fear this ability to interpret higher energies that are not normally (to the ego in this dimension) perceived, because the ability is something unfamiliar. Thus fear stems from ignorance. However, most psychics are at a higher level of consciousness than most religious leaders. But this should not make one believe that a psychic is at a higher level of consciousness than all religious leaders. Psychics can be at very low levels of consciousness, in the middle, and close to an enlightened state. So clearly, one's level of consciousness does not denote the amount of psychic ability.

Chapter 6
Chakras and Energy Flow

What Are Chakras?

Chakra, a Sanskrit term, is translated as 'wheel' and also means 'circular motion.' The term refers to the many *Energy Centers* in the energy body that are integrated with the physical and the Supreme Reality of All That Is. The word 'chakra' is found in Hindu and metaphysical documents. Chakras are the interconnected keys that directly tap into the universal consciousness.

These energy centers are found all over the body, usually in specific locations, such as around major organs, joints, glands, and the meridian network. The tertiary chakras, the smallest in size, exchange energy through the skin. Minor chakras are usually found around the joints and some organs. The most commonly talked about energy centers are the major chakras, which, as their name indicates, are the largest of them all.

The two functions of the chakras are to metabolize energy and to direct energy flow. Energy is exchanged from the universal energy field, the 'aura' of the self, the aura of others, and energies around plants, animals, and other objects. A chakra 'metabolizes,' or breaks down, energy into different frequencies or vibrational rates, so that it can be used by the energy body or the physical body. After the energy is metabolized, it is pushed out or pulled into the energy body. The chakras can push energy out of the body to dispel negativity, get rid of excess energy, or send positive energy to those in need. The chakras also pull in energy to charge vital organs in the physical body, dissolve negativity, and harmonize the energy bodies.

Unconsciously, the energy exchange takes place continuously, whether one is aware of it or not. This is why sometimes one notices that after they walk into a room and talk to a person for a couple of minutes, they leave feeling completely drained and exhausted. Unknowingly, the other person is 'leaching' energy from them because their energy body needs a little boost. Naturally, higher pressures of energy flow to lower pressures (gradation) to balance them out (harmonization), when willed. The two energy fields are trying to harmonize by balancing energy levels, such as in a symbiotic relationship. If one is the being who is now drained of energy, then think of it as a good deed towards humanity. If one doesn't want to feel drained all the time, there are methods of spiritual protection that one can use to prevent energy from being drained, while keeping one shielded from negativity. However, one can learn how to concentrate and direct energy flow with the mind and breath, if one would like to learn how to heal one's self and others.

Unfortunately, not everyone's chakras are working properly. In fact, many beings' chakras are clogged, deformed, shut down, or just not working correctly. This is because most people concentrate on improving the physical body and not on spending time on the spiritual. So problems arise from sheer neglect and an intrinsic ignorance of the spiritual bodies.

The condition of the chakras reflects the health of the individual—not just their physical health, but their emotional and mental health as well. The evolution of the spiritual soul and its level of awareness are also represented. The cleaner the chakras, the cleaner the soul. In addition, when they are operating properly, the chakras act as a filter that protects the energy body from negative debris. By diagnosing the shape, color, direction, and size of the chakras, one can determine a being's current state of health. Experienced healers use clairvoyant sight and psychometry, but other forms of divination, such as the pendulum or kinesiology, may also be used. Diagnosis is not really needed, however, since all beings who are not 'ego transcended' have obvious problems—the ego.

Anatomy of the Spirit (Part 1: Chakras)

All colors are a reflection of certain levels of consciousness (frequencies). Each color has its own unique energy attributes or qualities. There are thousands of colors in the world, with different shades, tints, and hues; however, only the primary colors are discussed here. These subtle colors are red, orange, yellow, green, blue, indigo, and violet, better known as ***ROYGBIV***. These are the main colors that the chakras use for healthy and balanced everyday function.

Other subtle energetic colors can also be metabolized to help one increase their soul's spiritual evolution and make enlightenment more probable; these colors are white and gold. They have the strongest effects in heightening one's consciousness level compared with the others. The other colors (ROYGBIV) help one to regulate energy while cleansing and purifying the 'ego self.'

Warning: ROYGBIV can cleanse the ego self, but the ego will not be transcended from most charka work. Because charkas and auras are form, the formless qualities of energy of the Higher Self can not be experienced. For beginners, though, this is a great way to have tactile or visual proof that can captivate the ego into continuing the pursuit of spiritual work. Once proof, if needed, has been acquired and the ego is satisfied, the practice should be dropped and the path of enlightenment should be followed directly. Chakra work helps one develop psychic abilities and harmonize the energy bodies, although, when enlightened, these skills are not needed or wanted.

All chakras look like wind tunnels, or funnels. These funnels comprise smaller funnels, which are referred to as 'petals' in the Hindu and Buddhist religions. The tertiary and minor chakras are only made up of one funnel, but the major chakras are made up of a varying quantity, depending on the chakra.

The lowest chakra (Root) has the lowest frequency, as well as the fewest petals. The highest chakra (crown) has the highest frequency and the most petals. Each chakra has a different number of petals, and each different frequency has its own color. Colors are made up of certain frequencies, which in turn reflect their inherent qualities of light. Each quality of light as color represents one's innate level of consciousness, which comprises many emotional, mental, physical, and spiritual views.

- *The **Root Chakra** is the lowest energy center on/in the body. Due to its location, its corresponding color is red. Red has the lowest vibrational frequency, and therefore this chakra has the fewest petals (4). It is located between the anus and the genitals. The large (open) part of the chakra faces the ground, connecting one to 'ground energies.' The smaller part of the chakra is between the legs and attaches at the bottom of the spine (tailbone).*

  The root chakra is the first energy center to become completely developed. After one is born, the root chakra slowly develops. This chakra controls one's feelings of stability and security—that is, one's 'basic needs.' It is also involved in 'potty training.' The negative attributes that manifest if the chakra does not properly develop are destruction, despair, humiliation, blame, regret, abdication, and despondence. Once this chakra becomes developed, the next chakra begins to take form, balance, and harmonize.

- *The **Navel Chakra** is located right above the root chakra, but on the front of (as well as behind) the body, instead of underneath. This chakra, the next lowest from the bottom chakra, is located about 2 inches below the bellybutton. The navel chakra is orange. The frequency of orange is higher than red but lower than yellow. This chakra has 7 petals. Due to its frequency, the navel chakra has more petals than the root chakra, but fewer than the solar plexus chakra.*

  The navel chakra starts to develop a little while the root is still developing. When the root is completely developed, however, the body can now exclusively concentrate on working with the navel chakra. When the navel chakra begins to form, it helps one manifest a sense of ambition and vitality, as well as an understanding of sexuality. If it is not properly developed, negative attributes result, such as anger, withdrawal,

148

craving (deep desire), feeling trapped, fear, denial, aggression, and hate. This chakra may take 5 to 7 years to develop. The next chakra, the solar plexus chakra, develops a little while the navel chakra is still developing.

- *The **Solar Plexus Chakra** is the third highest energy center from the root up to the crown. It is located above the navel chakra but below the heart chakra. The solar plexus chakra is located just underneath the xyphoid process, which is right below the sternum (remember that the ribs connect in the middle of the chest at the sternum). This chakra is yellow and has 10 petals, or small vortices, within it.*

  This chakra is the powerhouse for the ego. Not only can it be used to energize psychic activities (known as the psychic battery), it is also considered the 'ego will' center. As it develops, the individual usually starts to exhibit a more separate personality, meaning that a being starts to do things on its own and does not cling to parents as much. The individual starts to think of itself as its own person and starts to go through the identity crisis stage of life. This is when it starts to dress how it feels, or identifies who it is by its likes and dislikes, all of which reinforces the ego.

  Although the solar plexus chakra can be a hindrance when one is trying to reach enlightenment, it can help one have a stronger 'will' when trying to direct one's life and goals within the physical. When this chakra is working correctly, the individual can appear to be confident. However, when it is not working properly, the person may appear 'egocentric' (overcharged) or extremely introverted/shy (underactive). This chakra usually finishes developing before a person reaches the age of 24. However, it is possible to finish development before or after this age. During the final stages of development of the solar plexus chakra, the energy body usually starts to divert all energy to the heart chakra, so the next stage of life may unfold.

- *The **Heart Chakra**, the fourth highest chakra from the root to the crown, is located in the center of the sternum and has 12 petals. The specific frequency of this chakra emits an emerald-green color. If it is too dark or too light, it is not working properly. The chakra is positioned above the solar plexus and below the throat chakra.*

    The heart chakra controls 'matters of the heart' (not the physical heart; although it affects that as well). It allows the individual to love 'things' or 'beings.' Unfortunately, this can allow one to create false relationships with these 'things' in place of God's love—for example, 'love of money' or 'love of house.' When this chakra is working properly, the individual feels connected to nature and finds it very easy to love and form relationships. When the chakra is closed, the individual is distant and not affectionate. When the chakra is open and charged, the individual is loving, understanding, and peaceful.

    This chakra starts to develop a little when relationships are formed (with family, friends, girl/boyfriends, animals, etc...). When unconditional love is experienced, which is different from love, the heart chakra develops faster. Most people finish developing the heart chakra when they have had an unconditional love relationship with another, just like they have with their family.

- *The **Throat Chakra** is located a little bit below the center of the throat, above the heart chakra and below the brow chakra. It is 'sky blue' in color and has 16 petals. This chakra has to do with voicing opinions, emotions, thoughts, and ideas. It is also a being's emotional center—the sympathetic and empathetic* *center of the body.*

When this chakra is working properly, one's emotional state is balanced and wisdom and calmness are vocalized. If the chakra is overcharged, an individual may have sudden emotional outbursts, feel another's feelings, or just talk too much. If the chakra is undercharged, then the individual does not voice their opinions, emotions, ideas, or thoughts; this person usually appears untalkative or unsociable. If the chakra is blocked, the individual most likely has, or had, an emotional problem that has blocked the healing process.

The throat chakra usually starts to develop when the individual learns to voice their own opinions or feelings. It develops faster in females than in males because of society's programming (for instance, "guys don't cry"). Males can indeed be programmed to be more emotional or empathetic, and women can be programmed to be tough. This programming depends on the factors influencing an individual, such as family, friends, society, morals, ethics, city, state, country, neighborhood, and schooling. The chakra usually develops when one is in the mid-20s, but can take longer.

- *The **Brow Chakra** is located between the eyebrows and up about one-fourth of an inch. It is above the throat chakra and below the crown chakra. This chakra is also called the 'third eye.' Its vibratory rate emits an indigo color, which is a mixture of blue (throat chakra) and violet (crown chakra). It has 98 petals. The brow chakra has to do with perceived reality and spiritual vision. What is seen depends on how well the chakra functions.*

  When the 'third eye' is working properly, clarity of vision into emotional and mental matters can be expected. When it is purified, clarity of spiritual vision can be expected. When it is blocked or closed, an individual has seen something that they did not want to see and has not let go of that image. When the chakra is overcharged, the individual may feel mentally over-taxed (stressed out mentally) or may too often see spirits. When the chakra is undercharged, a lack of visualization can be expected, as well as unclear thoughts.

The brow chakra usually develops in an individual throughout the mid-20s, and one may reach the upper 30s before it completely develops, matures, and cleanses. The ego's perception is usually very clouded and impure, so the evolution of the brow chakra may take longer than the other chakras. When one purifies the ego, one perceives the real Reality clearly.

- *The **Crown Chakra** is located directly on top of the crown of the head. It opens (big end) up to the sky and the narrow end towards the head, as if to funnel or direct information into the head. It has about 988 petals and emits violet with gold sparkles from its powerful frequency. This chakra has to do with thought and 'knowingness.' Gold appears if the being is 'pure.'*

  When the crown chakra is overcharged, the individual feels as if he/she knows everything, which also may lead to pride (solar plexus energy). If it is undercharged, one may have difficulty in thinking, or may feel that their mind is unclear. A crown chakra that is blocked could mean the denial of God or a negative thought pattern about the higher reality. A crown chakra that is well balanced leads to clarity of thought and a sense of 'knowing' the Universal Reality of the Unmanifest.

All of these chakras attach deep within the physical body, but not directly to the physical body. They attach to the etheric energy body, which in turn is the link to the physical body. The etheric body takes the energy from the chakras and distributes it evenly throughout the physical and energetic bodies.

The etheric energy body is the 'blueprint' of the physical body. Any problems or energy imbalances in the physical body can be detected in the etheric body. In fact, 'healers' and 'psychics' can feel these imbalances with psychometry (feeling energy with one's etheric hand). A pendulum can also be used for finding these energetic imbalances; this is called dowsing.

The chakras are subtle energetic organs that exist in one's immediate energetic field, which is one's local consciousness that is intrinsic to and integrated with the physical body. Without the energy centers, one would not have incarnated into a physical body (one's *Unmanifest Self* does not have any chakras). Animals and plants also have chakras, but not as many as humans. As long as something is operating as a conscious being, it has a chakra system. If it has a chakra system, it has an emanating and constantly changing aura. The color changes that occur in one's immediate energetic field are prompted to change as one wills to connect to another level of consciousness. These energies simply reflect one's choices or intentions and various thought forms that denote the charge of one's beingness, which comprises various levels of truth or fallacy.

Physical Organs and Functions that Chakras Supply Energy To

Crown
Upper Brain, Pineal Gland, Muscles around the Upper Part of the Head

Brow
Lower Brain, Eyes, Ears, and Pituitary Gland, Muscles around the Face

Throat
Bronchial Tubes, Pharynx, Larynx, Thyroid Gland, Muscles around the Throat and Upper Shoulders

Heart

Lungs, Heart, Circulatory System, Thymus Gland,
Muscles around Arms, Hands, Chest, Back

Solar Plexus
Stomach, Adrenal Gland, Liver, Gallbladder,
Small Intestines, Nervous System, Pancreas,
Metabolism, Abdominal Muscles and Lower Back

Navel
Kidneys, Lower Intestines, Reproductive System,
Water-Balancing Systems/Hormones (Aldosterone),
Bladder, Muscles around Lower Abdomen

Root
Colon, Rectum, Genitals, Muscles around Legs/Feet

Psychic Skills that Chakras Supply Energy To

Crown
Claircognizance (Clear-Knowing)
 Attribute of an enlightened being, knowing
 Truth and the Divinity within All.
 Pulls in energy directly from the Source (God).

Brow
Clairvoyance (Clear-Seeing)
 Seeing Spirits, energies, and Truth.
 Some chakras around the brow chakra
 help with hearing (astral and physical).

Throat
Clairaudience (Clear-Hearing)
 Hearing voices of spirit guides, spirits, astral
 noises, and Truth in another's words.
 Clear-tasting and Clear-smelling also take place here.

Heart
Intuition
 A combination between feeling and knowing
 that is a message from the Higher Self; can be
 distorted by the ego and used for the ego's

154

own protection and fueling energy.

Solar Plexus
Clairsentience (Clear-Feeling)
Feel energy with aura or external
sensory perception.
Charges energetic bodies
(also known as Psychic Battery).

Navel
Astral Projection Energizer
Helps one leave the body when charged;
also ambition center.
Also a great Psychic Battery.

Root
Psychometry
Feeling energy with etheric energy field around
hands (this is different than Clairsentience).
Pulls in energy from the large Battery (Earth).
This is the easiest psychic skill to do.

These chakras range from the highest (Crown) to the lowest (Root) vibrational state within this manifest dimension. These psychic skills also range from the hardest (highest vibration or crown) to the easiest (lowest vibration or root). Start with the easiest and work up if psychic skills are desired; however, when one becomes enlightened, these seemingly 'special skills' are seen as normal and undesired (a distraction from Truth).

Psychic skills are also to be seen for what they are, an illusion that keeps one from realizing the True Reality of the Unmanifest. These psychic skills are only noted here so that while working with chakras to cleanse one's being, one is prepared for any spiritual phenomena that may occur.

It is important to understand that chakras, auras, and any spiritual occurrences are within the dimension of form, due to its structured energetic patterns that differ in frequency. This is the domain of the astral dimensions; for a clearer understanding that it is a dimension of form, it is termed the 'Spiritual Manifest.'

Many spiritual experiences may occur while one is cleansing the chakras; however, one needs to drive past these illusory phenomena towards the only True Reality that **cannot** be seen, heard, or perceived by any means. Remember that only the ego wants to judge form. The True Reality is what one <u>is</u> as the Unmanifest quality of the Self.

During chakra work and meditations, many spiritual phenomena can be witnessed. These can range from chaotic and frequent, to mild and rare, and depend on one's innate psychic receptivity and level of willingness and skill. The spiritual devotee should be informed about the seeming 'oddities' that may occur throughout their practice. Using the chakra's colors attunes one to the various levels of energy (psychic); white and gold colors are to enlighten.

Remember to learn how to use colors wisely. If improperly used, they could result in imbalances in the energy bodies, which could result in physical, mental, or emotional disorders, or may slow one's spiritual development. By using the chart below on chakra traits, it can be seen that one can just add white or gold to cleanse a chakra that is having problems, or white and gold can also be added to purify cloudy 'thought forms.'

Emotional States and Realities Viewed by Chakras

Crown
Balanced: Helps one think and problem solve.

Negative: Distorts thought patterns and blocks knowing the True Reality. Hinders cognitive abilities. Thoughts are cluttered.

Brow
Balanced: Helps one visualize perceived reality and other realities. Helps one visualize ideas and thoughts.

Negative: Distorts visual perception. Blocks visual perception of the True Reality.

Throat

Balanced: Helps one empathize and sympathize with others. Helps one vocalize emotions and ideas.

Negative: Distorted speech patterns. One will not vocalize feelings or emotions. Is very irritated and depressed. Speaks lies or distortions, not Truth.

Heart

Balanced: Helps one love self, others, and nature. Makes one Selfless. Helps beings understand others via a compassionate view.

Negative: One overly loves or hates 'self' and does not like the feeling of love. Doesn't like nature and most pets. Is uncomfortable in loving situations.

Solar Plexus

Balanced: Helps one feel the joy of life, energetic, self-empowered, makes one very talkative and self-expressive.

Negative: Is egotistical and egocentric. Has addictive personality; can be loud or extreme (overly shy). Is materialistic; only thinks of self-gain or how to pleasure oneself. Feels anxiety, stress, and pride.

Navel

Balanced: Helps one feel ambitious and creative.

Negative: Doesn't see any reasons to create or to develop any artistic abilities. Feels lazy or lethargic. Feels destructive and despairing. Views life as tragic.

Root

Balanced: Helps one feel a sense of security and that needs are fulfilled. Life or existence feels stable.

Negative: Feels a lack of security; has excessive needs and wants. Personally views sex only as lust, not love. Only experiences lust, not love. Is angry at others and at self. Is easily enraged. Would rather destroy than love something. Thinks it's cool to be bad, instead of good. Seeks revenge.

Experienced Reality Through Chakras as Enlightened

Crown
Knowingness; Awareness replaces thinkingness; One simply expresses pure Truth as Wisdom.

Brow
There is nothing negative to see because purity is seen in all beings. One has 'spiritual vision' and sees love, compassion, and Truth in All.

Throat
One expresses only Truth through speech and recontextualizes other beings' statements, thus adding Truth and light to their being as well as the universe.

Heart
One feels unconditional love for All and channels Love to All beings. To be a channel of God is to be a channel of Unconditional Love.

Solar Plexus
The Divine Will operates one's life for them. The ego is finally dissolved and does not control 'Self.' Since Divine Will wants nothing, neither does one's Self. There is nothing to be acquired because there is no want. Motivation comes from the inspiration of Self.

Navel
There is no need to be creative because All that could be created already is. 'Creations' come from the pure Unmanifest essence, which then is the manifest. One only 'wills' to be an expression of creation if it will benefit mankind and deliver Truth and Love.

Root
There are no needs or wants. All is fulfilled from the Divine. There is no reason to fear death because what lies on the other side is closer to the True Reality than that which is currently being experienced in the physical. When All is known, one realizes that fear is a product of the mind, the mind is a product of the ego, and the ego is illusory because only the Unmanifest Self Truly exists as one's beingness. One no longer fears for their survival; they Trust in God that all is well. They allow the Higher Power to lead their life.

Religious Texts Describe Chakras and Auras
As seen in many religious paintings, a radiant golden glowing light emanates from the heads of certain religious figures. In

movies, Angels are represented with 'Halos' above their heads to imply their Divinity. Jesus, Buddha, Krishna, St. Francis of Assisi, Mother Mary, and many others are also shown with this mysterious golden light around their heads. This so-called 'Halo' is actually the crown chakra and their mental body. It is usually violet in color for the impure, but 'pure' souls have one that is golden in color. The color 'gold' represents a pure being with a life devoted to God/Truth. Even though chakras or halos are found in many religious paintings, they are also found around all other beings' heads, although usually in a different color.

The crown chakra is the energy center that connects one to the higher frequencies, known as 'God-Consciousness.' The Christians call it a 'Halo' and the Hindus, spiritualists, metaphysicians, and some other groups call it a chakra; some even attribute the golden glow to the outermost level of the aura. Whatever one wants to call it, it is the same thing. Some religions hold the closed-minded view that chakras are 'evil' or 'demonic,' while the 'Halo' is a mark of Divinity. Without True spiritual vision, one cannot tell the difference between what is Truth or just misleading. Many religions do not want to admit that they are wrong (because of ego pride), so they just keep on preaching the unchanged teachings, even if new realizations occur.

Even ancient cave drawings have depicted the halo and the aura around different beings. Astral projection, also known as out-of-body experiences (OBEs), are also shown in cave drawings and described in ancient sacred texts. This just shows that whether one is religious, spiritual, or none of the above, 'bits of truth' or spiritual phenomena can happen to anyone regardless of their status, religion, creed, dogma, or beliefs; it is all a matter of faith.

A few thousand years ago, religious leaders and kings thought that since they were in power, God would select them for any spiritual revelations, or that they would be shown and taken to heaven. In fact, they were upset if a commoner or a peasant had any spiritual experiences that they did not. This was punishable by death and taken as blasphemy or heresy. The egos of these kings and religious leaders thought that by displaying power and by being leaders in the physical world, that God would choose them above all others. So anyone who said differently was tortured and killed.

On the physical plane of existence, power, prestige, admiration, and leadership are what people hold to be virtuous and of value. However, God <u>unconditionally</u> loves All and is not concerned with the idealisms of the ego or what it views to be important. Instead, God remains accessible for any beings who choose to leave the world of desire, vanity, and form by realizing the Supreme Reality where form is nonexistent and formlessness is Truth. If the choice is made, and one transcends the ego or the independent sense of 'I', then the Higher Self is revealed and one will finally be realized to of always have been home (Truth). Naïvely, it just didn't know it could choose happiness and leave suffering by following Divine Will, or its 'True Essence' calling one back.

The Bible contains many references to metaphysics that most Christian leaders simply overlook, don't understand, or deny, in effect to save their pride. A 'big stand' that Christian leaders think they have is that Jesus never spoke of reincarnation... or did He? In several verses in the book of Matthew, Jesus stated that Elias had reincarnated and come back as John the Baptist.

The Bible also speaks of incense and oils, such as when the wise men brought frankincense (very high frequency) and myrrh to the baby Jesus. They also brought gold; not only can this be used as currency, but it also has a very high vibrational color (subtle parallel) that can help to boost the frequency of the people around it (if charged with 'good intent'). Maybe the gift of gold was an attempt to keep the baby Jesus a 'pure child.' If the story of the wise men is true, then why would the wise men travel so far to bring just three 'simple gifts'? Why not bring more for the 'King of Jews' or the 'Son of God,' unless the power of the gifts was more important than anything else that could be given.

The Bible also refers to crystals, rubies, and other gemstones that have a unique and mystical quality. Crystals and gemstones are used even today by experienced healers and novice practitioners. They emit a unique energy or vibration that can be very healing. They can be used to add light to areas (of darkness) that need a boost.

In the Bible, astral projection is very briefly referred to in the statement, "Whilst the silver cord ever be loosed." The silver cord refers to the energy connection between the astral energy body and the physical body. It is used to send information or energy back to the physical body, like a telepathic linkage. It also supplies the energy body with energy that comes from the physical, and vice versa. The silver cord tends to pull one's 'astral body' back in and can be a hindrance when one is too close to their physical body. Many people ask how to separate from the silver cord, which is the energy connection, because it can be problematic. There are many other connections between the Bible and metaphysics, but they will not be covered extensively in this book.

The caduceus, which we know as the symbol for health and also as a medical symbol, really portrays the path of the Kundalini. The caduceus shows a serpent wrapping around a staff. The staff is a representative symbol of the spine and main meridian (Sushumna), and the serpent is the Kundalini. The Kundalini is the potential energy that lies dormant at the base (in a *coiled shape*) of the spine and travels upward during the process of realization. Various realizations help one become enlightened and occur when one is truly healed: There is nothing to heal, but our perception of reality.

Modern-Day Connections to Chakras

Many expressions that have entered into language throughout the years correspond to the body's energy centers and the presence of auras. Modern-day mankind uses the terms and phrases frequently, and yet few know their origin or fully understand them. Instead, they insist that there are no such 'things' as chakras and auras. Some people go to extraordinary measures to try to prove them to be folklore, imaginary, or even 'satanic.' If the chakras are 'satanic,' then so are **all** people and animals. The chakras and auras are a part of us that cannot be denied. The following sections show the connection between the metaphysical (spiritual) and the physical world.

Clarifications of Subconscious Meanings

One of the most common sayings heard around the world is, "I'm feeling blue." This is said to reflect the emotional expression of being depressed, or not 'energetically uplifted.' Subconsciously, the color blue is the prevailing energy pattern that fuels one's current emotional state. The color blue is related to the throat chakra, etheric energy level, and emotional stress. It is the color that regulates empathetic and sympathetic feelings in the energy bodies. Due to the fact that the blue energy patterns store most of the emotional distress in one's life, the color blue is felt or seen in mind to help the soul by directing focus or concentration to the energy level that is in need of the healing.

When beings fall in or out of love, they express it in many ways, most commonly by referring to the 'heart.' A saying that is used very frequently is, "You broke my heart." Western civilization thinks this is just a figure of speech, or that it relates to the actual physical heart. This is not so. The center for love is not the physical heart; the physical heart just pumps blood. However, the heart chakra (energy center) is near the physical heart and is in virtually the same location as the physical heart, but the heart chakra deals with emotional issues within relationships and deals with love on many different levels.

The expression, "You're playing on my heart strings," refers to the energetic connection between two people's heart chakras. As two beings develop a relationship and love forms between them, the heart chakras extend towards each other in the form of energetic 'cords' or 'linkages.' In a relationship, two people actually start to share and balance energy from the links. If the two people really love each other and are open to helping one another at any cost, then the chakras naturally send energy down the 'cords,' which almost resemble telephone lines, to balance energy fields. In severe cases of dependency, these invisible cords can actually remain connected to the chakras and jeopardize the health of the one whom energy is being leached from. Even after the couple separates, the cords could still remain attached undesirably at certain chakras. This is where a professional healer (metaphysician) could be helpful in removing the links. I have seen and heard of cases where a couple separates and the energy link is still there 10 to 15 years later, causing the one who is being leached from much distress. Genuine healers or meditations can be used to separate the linkages.

When one is scared or nervous, one might say, "I have butterflies in my stomach," or "I feel it in the pit of my stomach." The solar plexus chakra is the energy center that supplies energy for bioenergetic (physical) needs, as well as spiritual needs. When an organ, a gland, or an energy level needs some energy, the solar plexus chakra supplies it. The solar plexus is located right below the stomach. So when that particular chakra speeds up, it super-charges the organs and glands as well. As the stomach tightens, spasms, and increases acid production, one feels the so-called 'butterflies in the stomach' because of the excess energy that the solar plexus chakra has created.

Most people also think that the color 'red' is sexy. For instance, a red dress, red rose, red nail polish, and red lipstick are thought of as sexy or symbolizing romance and passion. The root chakra is one of the chakras that supplies energy to the genitalia of both men and women. Subconsciously, the color red is mentated and then thought of as the corresponding emotion of desire, passion, and lust. Remember that as the chakra activates, it subconsciously charges the whole being to the specific vibration of the color of that energy center. As someone gets aroused or sexually stimulated, the color red is ingrained into the subconscious mind, which is displayed in the energy bodies. This color slips in unnoticed from the Spiritual Manifest and works its way to the conscious state of awareness, where it is then thought of and used in many imaginative ways. Thoughts are not a product of just _our_ mind, they are a product of the Unmanifest creative energy that provides for the manifestation of form, which is influenced by the karma of the ego, as well as the universal consciousness, which in turn represents itself as _our_ thought or idea as soon as it enters one's beingness and the ego claims it as its property and a part of its identity.

The color yellow is used in uplifting the spirit. People paint the rooms in their houses a bright color (usually yellow) to feel energized and uplifted. There is a lot of truth to this idea. In fact, the solar plexus chakra is yellow and regulates energy needs in the energy body and the physical body. When the color yellow is in the surrounding atmosphere, it stimulates the consciousness, which stimulates the subconscious to realize the subtle parallel (*yellow level* of consciousness), which stimulates the unconscious, which in turn stimulates the overall energy package of the ego's karmic patterns. This could initiate a change of 'self' and heal by uplifting the current vibrational state to a higher one.

The color yellow not only energizes, but can make one feel more assertive, as it actually charges the ego. Since the solar plexus chakra is connected to the stomach, too much of the color yellow could cause stomach problems, digestive problems, overacidity, and nervousness. If the person has an overactive solar plexus chakra and other chakras are underactive, the solar plexus chakra usually diverts some of its energy to the other chakras to balance them. The downside of an overcharged solar plexus chakra, besides digestive problems, is that it charges the ego, which could make it harder to transcend. It could even lead to an 'egocentric' or 'grandiose' personality disorder.

The phrase used at baseball, football, soccer, or any other wound-up atmosphere is, "You can feel the energy in the air." Consciously this refers to the physical energy being expressed through screaming and other upbeat behaviors. The energy is forming or 'concentrating' because of 'like' attitudes, meaning that "like attracts like" (spiritual magnet). In the Spiritual Manifest, that is reality, although opposites attract in the physical dimension (magnet). So energies in one's energetic field (karma) attract others when they are the same. For instance, positive energy attracts positive energy and negative energy attracts negative energy. In another example, an 'alcoholic' likes to hang out with 'alcoholics' and 'churchgoers' like to hang out with 'churchgoers.' What is seen in the physical dimension is the physical attributes, but the subtle energy is what is felt. Because what is seen is what is believed to be reality, it is accepted as is by the ego, with no questions asked. However, what has allowed this atmosphere to release its potential are the 'like-minded' people who have gathered. But without the intrinsic factor of the Unmanifest, nothing would exist, not even air.

Chapter 7
The Human Energy Field

The Human Energy Field (Part 2: Aura)

An **Aura** or a '*human* energy field' (*which we will discuss*) is created as subtle energy emanates from a living organism. It is a manifestation of consciousness, a byproduct. When the chakras pull energy into the organism, it starts to circulate through the entire energetic system or the network of 'nadis' (etheric nerves). As the energy goes through the organism, it radiates from the being and infinitely outwards. Auras *also* radiate from animals and plants. Minerals, gems, stones, and crystals have auras as well, due to the programmed frequency inherent to the crystallization process.

These auras can be seen with psychic sight, which is known as clairvoyance or 'clear-seeing.' This means seeing beyond the physical dimension and into the spiritual realms of existence where energies are visible everywhere; although form still exists, it is less dense. Psychic sight is really just using one's brow chakra to pull in and interpret energy of various frequencies. These energies in the aura can also be felt with psychometry and diagnosed with a pendulum.

Subtle energy radiates as an energetic field (aura) (1) because of an organism's energy system, (2) because subtle energy pathways within nonliving matter such as crystal, stones, or gems, (3) because colors emit their own frequencies, and (4) because the energy is just a thought of the universal consciousness. Energetic or vibratory patterns are either within the spiritual manifest (less dense) planes or the physical manifest (most dense) plane, but the object's state of existence can be detected (seen, felt, heard, smelled, etc…) by the energy that is constantly radiating from these patterns (aura). All matter is composed of energy and emanates it as well. This energy is their key, which one may tap into.

All things have an energy field; some can easily be perceived, while others cannot. Even psychics cannot detect all energy. Some energy may be at too high or low a frequency for them to perceive. Although the entire world emits many vibrations, some are considered beneficial (helpful) and some are not beneficial (harmful). In Reality, however, these energies are neither 'bad' nor 'good,' but simply a reflection of one's inherent level of consciousness, which is a reflection of karma. Or, for inorganic (nonliving) objects, the energies reflect the karma that is within them by way of the manifestation process and energetic imprints from various beings.

How the Energies of Auras Affect Others

Everyone has had the experience of being downright uncomfortable when around another person. It may have seemed as if the person was draining all their energy. When one knows that they don't feel good, they usually leave, but they also don't really understand why. One just knows that somehow the experience has affected them negatively. This is because it affected them on a subtle energetic level, and the effect may also be displayed on a conscious level.

These subtle energy emanations affect all life, either in a *seemingly* positive or negative way. As one encounters beings of physical or nonphysical existence, many energy exchanges are made unconsciously and subconsciously, as well as consciously. As one encounters positive beings, positive energy exchanges take place, and when one encounters negative beings, negative exchanges occur. Fortunately, these negative energy exchanges seem to slow down as one raises their consciousness level, or evolves spiritually. Negative energy exchanges cease completely when one finally becomes enlightened.

When one is fully enlightened, negative energy is seen for what it is—an illusion. This negative energy is transmuted (changed into positive) in the presence of an enlightened being. All the enlightened being does is add the presence of light, or the 'Divine Source,' to areas where there are lower levels of light (darkness, dualistically speaking). The ego is receptive and projective, but the enlightened being is only projective as love, peace, and light.

This is how one's unconscious/subconscious/conscious and the thoughts/ideas/motives/emotions of the ego can affect other beings without anyone knowing. For example, as a disgruntled man walks through a mall feeling contempt for mankind, that negative energy freely floats and crystallizes (as the man thinks about it) into a more concentrated energy pattern within the person's energetic field. This energy, however, is not confined to that person alone. On the contrary, it affects all beings in the universe. As one thinks, whether these are negative or positive thoughts, they are brought forth into the person's aura and radiate infinitely outwards (for a lack of a more effective word; excuse the dualism), affecting all beings everywhere. Unfortunately, the closer one is to the more concentrated or crystallized negative patterns, or closer to the source (a person) of the specific energy that is charged by intent, the more it affects one negatively.

The lower levels of consciousness—energetically represented by anger, resentment, hatred, and contempt—in the person's energy field slip into another's energetic field and unconsciously, subconsciously, and consciously affect both them and others. This will manifest a similar feeling within one when passing by the person. Even if one doesn't talk to them, this energy may cling to one's field. Thus, contracting negative energy changes the way one feels and/or changes one's state of mind and/or health.

So the saying, "Healer, heal thyself," makes sense. In effect, it states that a person who is trying to help others and has a lot of problems themselves will not really help mankind, but instead will hinder it. For example, if a psychologist has emotional and mental problems, not to mention spiritual/ego problems, he will indeed affect the one seeking help. Unfortunately, the 'posing healer' will affect one negatively.

However, if the psychologist is energetically balanced, spiritually resolved, and pure, he can help one with their problems, karma, and therefore, current spiritual situation or level of consciousness. Thus, as he affects one positively, that being then affects all beings positively, which of course makes him the ultimate healer. This helps one further transcend their karma, and ultimately the ego.

The same repercussions apply when an object (any object) is touched in a negative fashion. This means that if a person simply touches something with 'ill will' or negative intentions, these thoughts and intentions can imprint negative energy patterns onto the object. As another being picks up the negative object, the imprinted energy is transferred to them. This negative energy then circulates through their energetic system and causes much distress. This distress consists of the same negative intentions or thoughts that the negative person imprinted on the object. If the person had contempt for mankind, then one might feel a little irritated or impatient on that day or the next, or perhaps for a week. When the negative imprinted object is (literally) carried with the new owner, who used to have a positive outlook on life, so-called 'bad luck' may arise. This 'bad luck' is usually just an uncomfortable or depressed feeling. It doesn't mean that one actually has 'bad luck'; however, when one doesn't feel great, their outlook on life tends not to be optimistic, and therefore this is only assumed to be 'bad luck.'

Fortunately, objects can also be charged with positive energy. For example, when a mom says, "I baked these cookies with love," she probably did. If the overall energy that prevailed while cooking was love, then that positive energy is imprinted onto the cookies. As one is near, holding, or eating the cookies, the positive or 'good vibrations' are absorbed. This is obviously uplifting, so one may actually feel more at peace or at ease that day. The world would be a happier and more caring place if all mankind had positive intentions and allowed the higher frequencies to operate through them. Then the world would be positively charged no matter where one went, thus providing a world of love, peace, compassion, and happiness. These energetic exchanges happen continuously throughout one's lifetime, even in places where one least expects it.

For example, a pregnant woman can have mood swings and feel irritated even when physical discomfort is absent. Doctors attribute this to hormonal changes, which is true. However, something else also causes the hormones to rise and the neurons to become overworked, which makes the woman feel emotionally unbalanced and irritated. The new inhabitant (baby) energetically links itself to the woman's being. As the soul of the baby enters its new vehicle (the baby body in the mother's body), the energy of the baby and that of the mother are shared. However, just because the mother is having an 'innocent little baby' doesn't mean that the soul was innocent in its prior lifetimes. In fact, it is fairly safe to say that the soul was probably misguided and made some mistakes; why else would it be reincarnating? If not enlightened, a being reincarnates. However, some beings with a higher level of consciousness do elect to come back to bring Light to the world.

If the soul is reincarnating, it is doing so to pay off past karmic debts. Karma carries over from all past lifetimes to the present one. So if the soul of the baby denied the existence of God, or the being was a murderer, rapist, or just a dishonest person in a past life, it will have a very low level of consciousness that needs to be raised. Unfortunately, this low level of consciousness comes into the mother's energy field and adversely affects it. The two energy fields balance out at almost a middle point (it is a little more complex than that, but this explanation will do for the time being); the mother's energetic frequency is lowered, which in turn raises the baby's frequency. When this happens, the mother helps the child raise its consciousness level, speeding up its spiritual evolution. This can better its chances of taking the right path and not reincarnating again. In some cases, the mother's energetic frequency is lower than the baby's, so this actually helps the mother. There are cases where the mother and child could both be low or high as well. If the mother and the baby have the same frequency, then less frequent mood changes take place because of the new inhabitant's energy. However, the mother's mood swings may also be multiplied by the physical discomfort of the pregnancy.

Exchanging positive energy can be viewed as a 'good deed' and a 'selfless act.' If one has a high level of consciousness, then their very presence can be uplifting to all of mankind. Their high energetic patterns and frequencies transmute negative energetic patterns into positive, which leads to all beings feeling better and being more peaceful. These changes in energetic fields can be small but very profound. The changes in one's energy happen throughout one's life, but rarely are they noticed, since the ego clouds one's perception and ability to experience or realize them. As one's ego constantly thinks/perceives/visualizes/idealizes/talks/acts and also governs one's morals, one's level of consciousness goes up and down. For every negative thought that one has, or self-expression of the 'ego will,' one's current level of consciousness drops. Likewise, for every positive thought or action, doing God's Will, abandoning the ego, or carrying out a 'selfless act' for just one moment, one's level of consciousness raises. So by just having the intention of being 'good' to all beings, serving God, and abandoning the ego, the consciousness level of one's self and all others will rise. One affects <u>all of humanity</u> by doing these things, because all are integrated as One. Every thought, intention, or action one has affects everything in existence.

One reason that 'care facilities' such as hospitals allow people to visit their loved ones is that visitors have a positive impact on the ill. The visitor helps to uplift the sick person, not only emotionally, but also physically and spiritually. The visitor's healthy auric energy goes to the person in need of healing. This positive energy helps the sick person release negative thought patterns and energy, encouraging their recovery and also helping them sort out other emotional, mental, and spiritual issues at the subconscious and unconscious levels. Not only does the positive energy help to speed their recovery, it also helps them to raise their consciousness level. So every positive word, thought, or intention has an effect. This is important to realize when visiting a sick person.

The most important factor is intention. If one visits their family or friends, usually intentions and thoughts are positive. However, if one is having differences with the person and cannot forgive them for it (or just doesn't like them), this creates 'ill will' or negative intentions, affecting the sick person negatively and possibly worsening their condition. Only unconditional love should be in one's heart when visiting. This invokes the power of Divine Will, which betters everyone's condition; even the healthy benefit.

Like Attracts Like and Opposites Repel

It is important to realize that physical reality and subtle energetic reality are not the same (in this instance). The laws of physics also differ on some levels. The fact that opposites attract is a property of the physical dimension, as science can document negatively and positively charged ions attracting each other, or being pulled together. However, the 'opposite' applies to the spiritual realms of existence. To clarify this point, keep in mind that physical matter does not exist in the spiritual realms. No atoms exist there. A finer energy of a higher vibratory state exists and is the context for, or envelops and is, the spiritual realm. The only subtle energy that can be measured (subjectively) in linear reality is that of the mental (mentations, thoughts, ideas, beliefs, perceptions) and emotional states (such as despair, disgust, hatred, jealousy, lust, and control). It is important to note that 'Love' is not listed, because it is not an emotion. Love is a state of awareness or a condition that one is as their highest aspect (Self). Just as the physical dimension has negative/positive attraction, the subtle energy or spiritual realms operate on the basis of 'like attracts like.'

In the subtle energy realms of existence, the energy that exists is mental and emotional energy, which is a byproduct of one's spiritual level. This means that how one thinks or emotes changes the overall charge of one's auric field. This charge is basically considered an attractor pattern. Not only does this energy emit infinitely outwards, but the energy also attracts others with the same charge in their auric field. So whatever thoughts or emotions one has continually throughout their day as a constant pattern of self-expression, others with the same thoughts or emotions are attracted to one's energetic field. However, there is one exception to the rule; if the being's ego is already willing to be broken down in an effort to elicit change, then the Higher Self will actually direct the being to seek help (hopefully from higher levels of consciousness). This is known as being 'open-minded,' or willing to change. When the ego is shown a rational/logical (the ego mind operates in a linear or rational way) option or alternative, and the

173

ego is willing to try the new path, then the ego is looking for direction or something different. The ego only looks for something different when it is not currently satisfied. When one is complete, one is satisfied. There is nothing else to be acquired or desired when one is completely fulfilled with Divine Love.

Many everyday examples illustrate how beings are pulled together by 'like-mindedness.' For example, a person who likes to hang around in bars or clubs will hang around people who like to do the same. If one is interested in metaphysics, then they will read books, go to workshops, or find friends with the same interest. It is obvious that a positive person would not want to hang out with a negative person, because the negative person would always bring the other person down to their level and maybe even make them depressed. When one has a certain emotion or thinks a specific way, they want to be surrounded by the like-minded. They want their emotions to be affirmed, agreed with, sympathized with, and empathized with. They don't want someone trying to tell them what to do to fix it (not until the ego wants to fix it); they just want affirmations that what they did was all right and that they (the ego) were not to blame.

Everyone has noticed people who tell you what 'bad thing' happened to them, as though you were a psychologist. You were just trying to say hello, and they told you about their string of 'bad luck.' These people just want you to listen and not to criticize them. They unknowingly use others as a therapeutic release to get stagnant emotions or thoughts moving through their body (circulating through the energy system). But perhaps, after telling 5 or 10 people their story, they will get tired of hearing themselves and hopefully understand what should have been done in the situation. This allows the energy or thought pattern to escape or dissipate, while releasing them from their inner torment. These people like to be around their 'own kind' in order to share the same emotions or ideas that they have been experiencing. Why? Because they get support and acceptance from them and they'll give the same back.

Churchgoers do the same thing; they would rather hang around with people from their own church. They do this because these people learn from the same book (the Bible), go to the same place every Sunday (church), have the same belief system, practice the same values, and think that the other probably got raised in a similar family as well. What do you think would happen if an 'opposite-minded' person was thrown into the mix? Let's say that an atheist was put together with an avid Christian. Do you think that this relationship would last, or, better yet, do you think that it would even begin? The answer is no... because they are not 'like minded.' In terms of subtle energetic existence, they are opposites, meaning that they repel each other. These two can talk decently together if their thoughts are on the same wavelength, for example, the current situation (or job if they are co-workers). When they meet, if both people are charged energetically equally and do the same task, then they can tolerate each other. However, when one speaks of or exhibits an opposite trait of the other (such as religious view), then they feel uneasy being next to each other. If one constantly thinks about how one doesn't believe in God, then one charges one's field to that frequency (denial of truth). As one's self is around others with different views, one's energy field is not congruent with theirs, which brings on an uneasy (repelled) feeling or a feeling that one doesn't want to open up to them.

Another example, which is good for worried parents to know, is that drug users hang around with drug users. If someone uses heroin, then they will want to hang around with a heroin user as well. Thus a parent can track their child's social patterns.

Why a heroin user would rather be with another heroin user:

1. *A 'user' can get 'high' with the like-minded friend.*
2. *They can borrow drugs from the friend.*
3. *They will sometimes get high for free (because the other friend wants someone to do it so badly that they'll even pay for it).*
4. *They can talk about doing it (which gives them satisfaction [temporary high] to talk about it).*
5. *They can see a movie together about doing drugs*

175

(temporary high/satisfaction).
6. *They meet others who do drugs (possibly turn them on to a better/different drug).*
7. *They can also talk about the low times (the ego also derives satisfaction from sharing 'bad times' that they have gone through).*

Why heroin users do not want to go to rehab:

1. *They have to admit they are wrong (the ego doesn't want to).*
2. *They have to give up a craving/desire (the ego doesn't want to).*
3. *They have to stop hanging around their friends when they go to rehab (the ego doesn't want to lose connections to drugs).*
4. *They also have to give up the temporary satisfaction of sharing good and bad times with the 'like-minded' (the ego doesn't want to).*
5. *They have to experience the disappointment of some of their friends/family/classmates (the ego never wants to be proved wrong or feel disapproval from others).*
6. *They have to hang around with and learn from nondrug users (opposite minded).*
7. *They are forced to change (force cannot truly change people; they have to want to change first).*

All of these are repelling factors, which means that the energy in the thought forms of healing is not attractive to the user. To make the user heal, the family usually forces them to get help. Remember the saying, though, "You can lead a horse to water, but you can't make them drink." **Force** (control) is a product of the ego. The force is coming from one ego to suppress (hold back) or help fix another ego. You cannot force anything to happen, because that is a 'battle of the egos.' You can simply show them the road by trying to appeal to the ego first, and then showing them Power.

Power, by contrast, is the existence of God as Unmanifest, unlimited, and infinite. Power is the only way to heal. Force can make matters even worse. By appealing to the ego, one can get on a person's same energetic frequency, which can help them understand some issues of importance. After helping them understand, one can show them the way to Power by sacrificing all of the ego's desires and cravings to God. If one truly wants to heal, then the Power will heal them instantly. The trick is really helping them understand that they want to be healed. This is the only way to change the overall charge in the energy field, by letting the ego decide that it wants to heal and then leading it to Power.

Chakra	Aura Connected To	Type of Energy Level
Crown	Ketheric Energy Body	Spiritual (7th)
Brow	Celestial Energy body	Spiritual (6th)
Throat	Etheric Template Body	Spiritual (5th)
Heart	Astral Energy Body	Bridge between
Solar Plexus	Mental Energy Body	Physical (3rd)*
Navel	Emotional Energy Body	Physical (2nd)*
Root	Etheric Energy Body	Physical (1st)*

Physical refers to dimension where spiritual energy goes to fuel activity.

The chart above shows the connection where the chakras deliver most of their energy. The different 'auric levels' are also listed in frequency from the highest (crown and ketheric) and the lowest (root and etheric). Remember that the lower vibratory chakras and auras are not worse than the higher, they are just running at a different frequency.

Ketheric Energy Body (7th level)

The Ketheric (Causal, Atmic, or Buddhic) energy body extends from the physical body and goes outward infinitely, yet one's psychic sight can only see out to about 3 to 3½ feet, where the Ketheric Template energy body seemingly ends. This is the 7th level of the aura and has the highest frequency that a human can endure in the physical body. This aura emits a powerful violet and golden frequency (when pure) that allows one to realize that All is One. When enlightenment occurs, one exists in the 7th auric level and continuously experiences God-consciousness as love and peace.

Celestial Energy Body (6th level)

The celestial energy body lies right underneath the 7th level, the Ketheric Template. It starts from the body and also radiates infinitely outwards, but can only be seen with psychic sight to end about 2 to 2½ feet from the body. Its frequency emits a gold and silver mixture, which translates into a indigo color, that creates a blissful state for the being experiencing it; this occurs when one exists within awareness of the 6th level of the aura.

Etheric Template Level (5th level)

The etheric template level is unique in that it is a reflection of the lower auric level, known as the 'etheric.' The etheric level is considered the blueprint for the physical body, while the 'etheric template' is the spiritual level for the etheric level. All healing for the physical body is possible from the 'etheric template.' If one spiritually heals the 'etheric template' level, one may heal the etheric level, which inherently heals the physical level. This 5th auric level ends about 1¾ to 2 feet from the physical body.

Astral Level (4th level)

This auric level is a multicolored (lots of green) energy field with a pinkish hue to it, sometimes called 'rose.' This energy level is usually the vehicle in which astral projection takes place. It is considered the 'bridge' between the physical and the spiritual dimensions. This frequency has the feel of unconditional love and acceptance. It extends out 1 foot to 1¾ feet from the body.

Mental Energy Body (3rd level)

The mental energy body contains the thought processes that can be tapped into and read telepathically ('tele' implies across a distance), or at least the ego thinks that it is across time and distance. Some forms can actually be seen within this aura, because the vibrations are a little more manifest or concrete compared with those of the higher levels. This level extends about 8 inches to 1 foot from the body.

Emotional Energy Body (2nd level)

The emotional energy body is a multicolored energy level associated with feelings. This auric level constantly changes colors as a person's emotional states fluctuate or change. It usually has a lot of yellows and blues. It contains the lower emotions of the ego (some higher) and extends about 3 to 8 inches from the body.

Etheric Energy Level (1st level)

This energy body extends 1 to 3 inches from the body. It is an exact blueprint (it even appears to be blue) of the physical body in energetic form. Intuitives can see or feel illness on this level. This is the easiest energy level to perceive.

What Colors Reflect in the Aura (manifest level)

Throughout the human energy field, many colors are constantly manifesting and radiating outward. Every thought that enters one's mind changes the color of one's auric field. If thoughts just flow by and one doesn't notice them, there are still remnants of those colors in the aura. These colors represent a certain frequency of which the thought pattern was a product of. It is important to remember that different frequencies create or manifest different colors. An interlocking weave of frequencies creates a pattern. This pattern is a product of the manifest, which was allowed to form by way of the Unmanifest. All energetic patterns are forms. They are form that is less dense than the physical form, but nonetheless, they are form as energetic patterns. Energy as Unmanifest is formless and is undetectable, unperceivable, and incomprehensible by any means.

These manifested patterns are the mixing of energies that

are a product of one's karma and current selection of 'will,' which energizes thought forms by taking one's karmic average of the negatives and positives. The negatives look like little gray patterns, streaks, blotches, or specks that are within the thought form. This gray color is the condition of 'ego distortion.' It is created when the 'ego will' activates a thought pattern that has a low frequency or level of consciousness, such as lying. Low levels of consciousness are low levels of light. Thus the colors that primarily denote ego distortion (known as negativity) go from dark black to gray, indicating the amount of denying light (truth) in varying levels. And showing the acceptance of light in varying amounts, starting at the lower frequencies (but still positive) and going to the higher frequencies, the colors are velvet black (black with white sparkles), red, orange, yellow, green, light (sky) blue, indigo, violet, and gold.

The lower levels of consciousness (but still within the positive range) are represented by the lower colors of velvet black, red, orange, and yellow. Compared with the higher levels of consciousness, which are green, blue, indigo, violet and gold, they are not far away from God; instead, they are vibrations that are created when truth and a lot of fallacy are mixed together. The negative (fallacy) vibrations bring down the consciousness level from the highest one (gold) for this human lifetime, creating a lower level of consciousness. The lower the color or frequency, the less truth is in it. If one adds a lot of cloudy black (negative color) to violet, it creates a darker color and lower frequency. If one adds less cloudy black (negative) to violet (positive), it brings down the vibrations much less, maybe to red or orange. If one adds just a splash of cloudy black (negative) to gold (positive), it lowers the frequency a little, maybe to blue or indigo. So basically, all colors represent a certain amount of fallacy mixed in with the ever-present Truth. This continual mixing constantly changes a being's frequency, as fallacy (ego will) is added to Truth (Higher Self). As one starts to abandon the ego, the Divine Will allows more Truth to be added to the overall frequency, or karmic resonance. Thus, negative karma is dissolved as the presence of Truth is added to what the ego created, which is the lower frequencies. This is how enlightenment is possible, by adding the presence of Light (Truth).

It is important to understand that the color red is not a negative color, nor is it 'bad.' It is simply what it is, a vibration at a certain level, which is at least around the level of truth. The color violet is also not to be looked at as better than red; it is just another frequency, or at another level. What is important is the level of purity in each color when in the chakra or auric field; a pure and vibrant red with little white sparkles indicates purity. A dark and fuzzy red with gray blotches indicates a contamination of truth with fallacy (darkness). All colors represent different frequencies that indicate the specific level of truth within an individual.

Don't think of one color as better than another color; just think of it as on another level. The Higher Self of the individual is not to blame, nor is it the fault of the ego for existing on that level, color, or frequency. The ego is not technically doing anything 'bad'; it is simply living its reality the only way it knows how, through the reality or frequency that was programmed into it. As one learns how to use colors properly, their level of reality can be changed by simply changing the frequency at which one's ego is running.

A word of advice, though: one should find out the color or frequency at which they are running. This allows one to see how they perceive reality, which gives them insight into their ego. As one understands the level they are on and of, one can then understand how certain colors affect them. Obviously, if the predominant color in one's energy field is blue, then one doesn't want to rely on red, orange, or yellow for spiritual healing, because the lower frequency that one uses mixes with the higher frequency that one is, and brings one to a lower level. This is why most psychics are at a relatively low level of consciousness (usually still positive), although higher than most of society. Psychics rely primarily on color meditations when clearing, charging, and opening their chakras. These are the metaphysical receptors that pull in spiritual (subtle energy) frequencies that transmit messages or information.

Psychics use the ***BROYGBIVW*** color meditation, which

starts with 'velvet black' to stabilize and harmonize vibrations, then proceeds to red, orange, yellow, green, (sometimes pink as well) blue, indigo, violet, white, and sometimes gold. If one totals all of their vibratory patterns, they usually average out at yellow to green—dark blue if gold is also used. By using this color meditation when one is at blue, one would stop their spiritual evolution and make enlightenment (violet) a very hard state to reach. However, fewer of the lower vibrational colors and more of the high vibrational colors could help one stay at a higher frequency, thus increasing their probability for enlightenment. It should be mentioned that using this altered psychic meditation will hinder one's psychic receptivity due to the incomplete preparation of the lower chakras, which are often used to pull in and interpret most energies.

The best way to increase one's likelihood for enlightenment when working with color meditations is to use the colors that are higher in frequency than one's self. This gives one a boost in vibration, instead of bringing one down to the lower levels or staying at the same frequency. It will definitely help one get closer to becoming Self-Realized. When one is truly enlightened, one is only at the frequency or color of violet or gold, and maybe with fractions of the other colors as well. The gold color represents pure mind and pure heart, as the Universal Identity. Violet is an enlightened frequency, but is not yet the Universal Identity. Around the heads of spiritual masters such as Jesus and Buddha, a 'gold glow' is always shown in paintings or described in text. This color represents that they are 'pure beings' who have transcended the ego.

If one has not transcended the ego and has never worked with chakras or color meditations, it is probably safe to say that they can use the color meditations to heighten their level of consciousness. This cleanses one's chakras and the various energetic fields, while adding higher frequencies to one's overall energetic package. This benefits anyone below the vibrational level of blue. As one changes in vibrational frequency (color), one then trains the energy body to adapt and change when needed. This can definitely help in healing one's emotional, mental, physical, and spiritual issues. Color meditations clean, charge, and open anyone's chakras. But bear in mind that they are primarily used to create a 'balanced ego being'; since the lower colors represent a distorted level of Truth, to a certain degree, **only violet, white, and gold should be used for one who is seeking enlightenment**.

Colors are the vibrational states that represent the individual's current state, condition, or reality. The following chart clarifies the frequencies or perceived realities that a being can experience. The chart is a very brief overview of conditions, states of awareness, or perceived realities in which beings can operate. However, many more emotional, mental, physical, and spiritual states can be exhibited (colors are to be used in meditations with white and gold sparkles—this keeps intentions pure).

Colors of Subtle Energies and What They Mean

Violet (Highest Frequency, besides Gold)

Positive (Clear):
Has spiritual insight, sees Universal picture; knows truth, imaginative.

Negative (fuzzy or with blackness):
Has negative spiritual information, doesn't know truth, denies Truth, denies positive information.

Overcharged (not pure):
Thinks they are better than others, thinks they are special, thinks too much, thinks they are God-like.

Indigo (Higher than ROYGB)

Positive (Clear):
A visionary, visual learner, has great intuition, knows higher truth, has spiritual vision.

Negative (fuzzy or with blackness):
Distorted vision, can't see higher truth or reality, receives negative psychic information.

Overcharged (not pure):
Constantly sees images, receives psychic information, seems irrational.

Sky Blue (Higher than ROYG)

Positive (Clear):
Is empathetic, sympathetic, vocalizes oneself, speaks wisely.

Negative (fuzzy or with blackness):
Doesn't see a reason to express one's self, doesn't vocalize oneself or emotions.

Overcharged (not pure):
Vocalizes too much, is overemotional, 'blows up' over little things.

Pink (Around the Same Frequency as Green)

Positive (Clear):
Loves oneself, is capable of transmuting negativity

Negative (fuzzy or with blackness):
Doesn't love Self, doesn't understand oneself

Overcharged (not pure):
Loves oneself (ego) too much

Green (Higher than ROY, Lower than BIV)

Positive (Clear):
Is capable of loving other beings/life, is compassionate, understanding, loves nature.

Negative (fuzzy or with blackness):
Doesn't love or like the feeling, doesn't understand people's actions, dislikes nature.

Overcharged (not pure):
Feels drained, pushes people to learn too much, loves material objects (money).

Yellow (Higher than RO, Lower than GBIV)

Positive (Clear):
Empowers lower self or ego, thinking, is motivated and outgoing, likes life/is optimistic.

Negative (fuzzy or with blackness):

Has low self-esteem, has no drive, is introverted, doesn't care about others, is pessimistic, doesn't like life.

Overcharged (not pure):
Is egotistical, has too much pride, has addictive personality, is selfish.

Orange (Higher than Red, Lower than YGBIV)
Positive (Clear):
Has ambition, has increased *creativity.*

Negative (fuzzy or with blackness):
Doesn't feel creative, feels low on energy, is constantly tired.

Overcharged (not pure):
Takes on too many projects that can't be completed at once, pushes self too hard to succeed

Red (Lowest color, besides the various degrees of black)
Positive (Clear):
Feels secure, needs are satisfied, feels passionate about life.

Negative (fuzzy or with blackness):
Doesn't feel Secure, doesn't feel satisfied; feels angry, lustful.

Overcharged (not pure):
Feels irritated with life, has cravings and desires, doesn't care about anyone else.

Analyzing the Most Common Frequencies

If you like to *think* or *act*, then you are expressing the 'ego will' to do something. This 'ego will' resonates at the yellow frequency. Yellow (cloudy) is the most common color in the human auric field. It represents a zest for life and a person who really likes the physical dimension when power is up (clear and charged). When power is down (cloudy and undercharged), it creates a person who is shy and has low self-esteem. When it is severely overcharged, it creates an egotistical, irritating loudmouth who only looks after themselves and who inherently displays continual selfishness that adversely affects all mankind. Not only does the 'yellow being' look out only for themselves, they are also entrapped by the many materialistic things that dominate our lives. These beings live for themselves, money, feeling good, desires, compliments, and anything else that can fulfill their deep inner feeling of emptiness.

The feeling of emptiness is created by the low level of truth in which they reside. They are in one of the lowest vibrational existences, which chooses material things and self-gain to replace the higher level of truth, which is love. When the level of love is accepted and becomes the predominant energy in a being's energy field, the healing begins. The acceptance of the condition of love is what heralds the emergence of God. God is the love that a being feels and experiences when the lower level of conditional love is first accepted. After the being acclimates to the level of conditional love, this will, in time, become unconditional when more Truth is revealed and known. The forfeit of self-gain and self-image, coupled with compassion for others, reveals the quality of unconditional love.

Blue is the other common color in society, although it is usually very 'cloudy.' This color is within this physical reality because of all of the emotional consequences of the conflicts that are perceived by egos to be reality. The emotional consequences are related to material or personal gain that brings with it the possibility of loss. Since the majority of the world is 'cloudy yellow,' this implies selfishness or self-gain. As a being acquires this self-gain in the form of material products or 'things,' a bond is formed. This bond is an emotional attachment of happiness, satisfaction, and contentment. When this physical 'thing' is taken away or lost, the being becomes sad or depressed because of the lack of happiness that ensues. As the being gets more attached to physical 'things,' more emotional states follow. This creates a multicolored pattern in which 'cloudy blue' is usually the second most predominant energy.

Thus, it can be seen why the primary auric field is a combination of 'cloudy blue' and 'cloudy yellow.' It simply represents the reality that most of the world is currently in: an emotional attachment to a false source (material thing) of external temporary happiness or satisfaction, which replaces the ever-present, unconditional love of God that is already within, but hidden by the ego. This is not to be looked at as bad, but simply the current state of awareness of the world. Society would show a significant improvement if the 'cloudy yellow and blue' turned into 'pure yellow and blue.'

Increased Awareness Brings New Level Change

With understanding, by way of unconditional love, all can be healed because that is what invokes the grace of God to facilitate positive change in level. This obviously brings about a new sense of reality, one with less pain and suffering. The level of humanity will continuously change as new viewpoints (people's/ego's points of view) are born into this physical reality. If the current state of mankind is raised to a higher vibrational level, then all of mankind will be affected positively. This will bring about a new level of reality that is experienced and known, as well as perceived.

Through the new level change, the new inhabitants born into society will be programmed to the current reality that contains a higher truth, rather than the fallacy that we have become accustomed to living within, thus creating a perfect reality by way of increased consciousness and expanded awareness. This operates only within the boundaries of unconditional love or the Divine Will, which is limitless in its utmost sense.

The Rainbow Effect

Various scriptures, teachings, paintings, and other means always show a rainbow-colored field around people, animals, and plants. For humans and animals, however, the colors are not usually clear, brilliant, and multicolored. Instead, the auric shell may look very dingy, pale, and unenergetic, with very few colors.

Furthermore, no specific colors in one's energetic field are the same as another's. An individual has the right to select the colors within which they operate. So if one chooses to be a 'cloudy dark red' by feeling angry or worrying about their security and basic needs, then they will be 'cloudy dark red.' Likewise, if an individual chooses to be very spiritual, then they may radiate a deep purple or gold color. If an individual chooses to be very prideful, then their color is usually 'cloudy yellow.' And if an individual chooses to be a 'well-rounded' character on an inner level, then a multicolored effect may be seen. So there is no certain range of colors that everyone has in their field. The 'rainbow effect' is seen on only those who have purified the lower aspects of their being—a purified ego.

This 'rainbow effect' is not actually a division of the many colors of the universal consciousness; instead, it is actually an effect that is witnessed by the limited perceptive faculties of the ego, which makes it believe that it is separate from the whole. It can be likened to water from a hose spraying in a wide pattern on a sunny day, allowing the many colors in the spectrum to be seen. The colors did not just miraculously appear through an unknown cause. Instead, they were shown, by the water's presence, to have always been there. Just as the water brought the colors into a visible pattern that has always existed and been there, one's faculty of 'will' or 'intent'(of the ego) is what allows the colors to appear as if separate from the source.

This karmic package, which is usually referred to as the 'sentient being' or 'immanent self,' is simply the local reflection of frequencies that the individual summons forth to be their beingness, whether knowingly or unknowingly. By the very belief that it is separate, the being's individuality calls forth all that it 'thinks it is' into a nearby local pattern that simply reflects who it is, how it feels, and the extent of its knowledge of Truth. The illusion of a separate consciousness is then shown by the being's seemingly independent and 'immediate reflection of consciousness,' which is termed the 'auric field,' 'bio-field,' or 'human energetic field.' The universal consciousness is the only consciousness; however, because beings have led themselves to believe that they are separate from the Source and of the universal consciousness, it is seen in auric colors, frequencies, astral dimensions, and so forth. But this perceived vision, which allows others to see the separate being's level of consciousness, is an illusory effect that holds no Truth (Higher Self—Truth and the Unmanifest—Absolute Truth).

By the varying levels of frequencies in one's energetic field, a certain range of colors and hues becomes visible. This quality of beingness, which allows for the colors to seem separate from the universal wholeness and the individual, is only energized because of the individual's belief in separateness (ego) and the aspect of will that comes forth with it. The 'vehicle of will' that reflects the being's various tendencies is simply the illusion of an immediate consciousness that resides in the sentient being. Since the belief of separateness is dualistic, then clearly it is an illusion that attempts to keep one from knowing their True Nature as One with the Whole. This is why some Buddhists believe that the 'rainbow' that appears in the sky is a reminder of our True Nature.

Chapter 8
Ego and Karma Connection

Securing Ego Identity

In the physical world, we naturally think that everything that we created was from our (showing possession or ownership, an illusion) consciousness alone. And this 'thought' helps us identify, as do other thoughts, with our ego self. The more thoughts, ideas, beliefs, and knowledge that one acquires, the more one feels as though they have a secure feeling of identity—of who they are. This identity, known as the 'ego,' helps one feel separated from society and God. The ego allows one to make various judgments of others, which places importance upon one's self and, furthermore, makes us feel separated or not connected as an integrated whole.

If someone makes a statement such as, "She is ugly; look at her hair," it is said to place importance on oneself and gather attention from others, to show them that the 'judger' is not like her, but better and more attractive. The judger's emotion stems from a lack of self-importance—basically, they do not feel 'good-looking' or 'attractive,' no matter what they look like to others. All emotions stem from a lack of being fulfilled. If one feels completely fulfilled, then there is no need to make a comment that seeks attention, because everything is perfect and needs no remark. If one was never told that they were attractive, then one will try to do almost anything to receive attention that helps them feel beautiful. People who want attention may make rude comments toward others, get involved in modeling or acting, talk loudly, swear, throw parties, boast about how good they are, write an autobiography, and brag about how many people like them or even how smart they are. No matter what the person's façade, how cocky they act, or how selfish they appear to be, it all stems from a deep, underlying feeling of a lack of something; whether it is a lack of power, wealth, status, admiration, or love, the person will try to

191

fill that void with something else, as a substitute for Truth. The ego always lacks Truth, which then prompts the constant search for fulfillment.

If one realizes that All Is One, then the understanding that there is one and not two shows that there is no other to prove something to or to try to act better than. Competition can only happen between two, not one. Once the realization, All Is One, occurs, then there is no need to comment on anything, and one always feels fulfilled with God's Unconditional Love and only sees everything as perfect and whole.

How the Ego Creates Karma

The ego is basically negative karma. Karma is an energetic accumulation of all positive and negative charges that one 'wills' themselves to be an expression of in the Now. So karma is only set by a being's current 'will' to be a certain charge. As this karma is collected, the individual's viewpoint or positionality is changed by the reality shift that occurs simultaneously. This shift in level is the change of consciousness that happens with every thought one has or act that one does, but it is only the *intention* that charges the event.

When the ego thinks or acts, it thinks and acts within its consciousness level that manifested as a result of its karma and chosen intent, thus creating its perceived reality. This perceived reality affects the ego by giving it various stimuli that can be experienced. These various stimuli are the emotional and mental states, perceptive phenomena, and all actions that the ego may access. When the ego accesses its chosen level of consciousness from the universal consciousness, it then exhibits the traits of that consciousness level. This level of consciousness is expressed because it is the product of all karma in the individual's energetic field. This energetic field is the aura, which is the local reflection of consciousness of that being. The ego operates at its currently chosen frequency (color) because of its karma; the karma sets its perceived reality and the range of choices from which it may pick (free will).

Keep in mind that the ego is composed of lower thought forms that block the realization of Truth, which the Higher Self is and continuously emits. The ego is every feeling of suffering and separateness (also loneliness) that one feels. The 'separateness' is reinforced by the individual's point of view, emotional state, mental state, thoughts, beliefs, personality, and perception of reality. This makes one feel as though every person has their own life and that we only exist because we want to. We then feel that there is no destiny and that all outcomes are created by our own terms. This gives us the belief that we are all 'in control' of our lives and, furthermore, makes us feel 'separate' and 'different' than everyone else.

This feeling of difference, brought forth by comparison, is also a product of the ego, which is called 'judgment.' Judgment allows one to feel different than others. This continuously makes one feel more or less important than what is around them, which in turn reinforces the view that places importance or nonimportance on the physical body and the personality of the ego.

The two most commonly desired things that people want in another person are a 'good body' (physical) and a 'good personality' (ego). The term 'good' is used to show how judgment occurs. When people say something is 'good,' they mean that they want it because it is desirable. If someone thinks it is desirable, they naturally 'want' it. 'Want' is another product of the ego. The ego thinks it needs something external to make it happy, satisfied, or fulfilled in some way, because of an unknown emptiness that it has. This emptiness is the lack of the Divine (God/Truth). This occurs when the ego chooses lower energies to operate on and as, rather than God. These lower energies (emotional and mental states) are an expression of the lower levels of consciousness; this is believed to be reality, but in essence, the Higher Self that the ego covers up is the True Reality. All of the negative karma that has ever been accumulated is a product of the ego. So to transcend the ego is to transcend all pain, suffering, limitation, hatred, negativity, emptiness, loneliness, and judgmentalism, all of which the ego is as an illusory entity.

Past-Life Karma

As one is born into this lifetime, past-life karma has already preprogrammed what reality the ego will perceive. This karma has already set up one's entire life destiny and all of the lessons that one needs to learn in order to transcend the ego. So the way one is born, their looks, attitude, family, neighborhood, IQ, disorders, per-sonality, friends, solar system, planet, galaxy, energy plane, and spiritual helpers decide one's lessons that will be learned, as well as the outcome of one's life. As one remains on their level of consciousness, one's destiny remains the same. But as one's consciousness level changes, so does one's destiny. So obviously, if one's level of consciousness goes down, they have more lessons to learn, which means that they have acquired more negative karma. This takes one's personal outcome or destiny to another perceived reality (energy plane or experienced existence) where the lessons can be learned, usually perceived as an undesirable level.

On the other hand, one can also acquire positive karma. This elevates the consciousness level, which means one is transcending negative karma and therefore dissolving the ego. This secures a positive outcome in life or karmic destiny. Past-life karma can be overcome in this lifetime. However, one needs to work on their karma for it to be transcended; one cannot simply hope it goes away. If past-life karma is primarily negative, then it will attract negative energy. Thus, it will be even harder to transcend, because one will eventually pick up the attributes of the negative energy that has been attracted to them, therefore creating more negative karma. It is like a really 'bad' magnet that does nothing but create doom (physically, emotionally, and mentally speaking).

It is important to realize that all karma is actually a product of the Now and not the past. It is not actually one's negative 'past deed' that made them acquire negative karma; instead, it was the level of consciousness that was elected by one's 'will' to be their beingness during the act. When the energies of that level of consciousness—which was a direct expression of the previous action, thought, or word—are chosen to be a part of one's lifestyle, they remain with one's self until one has realized the lower nature of their sin. If one naïvely chooses to be an expression of a lower energy and ignores the negative karmic repercussions, one will unknowingly remain at that lower energy and from then on will experience a more negative destiny that is concurrent with their karmic charge.

While the negative karma may have been first acquired a number of years ago by a negative act (such as robbery), in which the lower energy selected by intention was greed and selfishness, the negative energy still resides within and as them because they have not chosen to transcend that level since the act was committed. So the negative karmic repercussion was actually an event of the Now and will continually be that way until the ego chooses to transcend above that lower frequency, which brings forth a seemingly unfair amount of suffering and pain.

Linking Karma

Throughout this physical incarnation, all souls link or share karma with other beings, whether knowingly or unknowingly. This is why one should be careful not to join any 'special groups,' sects, clubs, or join with someone in marriage, unless the prior state, condition, or level of consciousness is known and accepted beforehand. In fact, just by the fact of one swearing to something, one's karma will be linked to that person, event, or object. This is all the more reason not to 'swear in' to something, unless one is ready for an energy exchange.

Fraternities and Sororities

If one really wants to belong to a specific group, one needs to analyze why. Usually it is to satisfy a want of the ego that will benefit the 'lower self' as a source of self-gain. This is not a beneficial reason to join or 'swear in' to a group.

Sororities and fraternities like to trick themselves into believing that they are a 'philanthropic group,' meaning one that helps others. This is rarely the case. These college groups are usually only positioned for self-gain. The students who join the group are more than likely trying to meet people of the opposite sex in order to have sex. Many also plan on staying up all nights of the week doing drugs, usually GHB, barbiturates, alcohol, marijuana, and sometimes LSD and Ecstasy. These are the most common drugs used in fraternities and sororities. The people in the 'college groups' also enjoy hazing. They feel a sense of power, control, and importance by making the 'pledges' do awkward things in order to be accepted. Rituals are done to <u>conform</u> everyone to a mold.

Sorority and fraternity members are obviously in the group for 'self-gain,' even though they might do one or two philanthropic deeds a year. The people who join the group are also doing it for some reasons of 'self-gain,' such as meeting others, getting connections (jobs, drugs, parties, etc.), or listing their membership on a resume. If a group does things to feel important, powerful, and controlling, and is only existing for its own self-gain, one can be certain that these groups are serving the 'ego will.' Hence, serving the ego is to deny God's Will. So mixing one's karma with a group of people who are serving their own ego is not going to benefit one in their divine mission, or help one attain enlightenment. This will in fact lower one's consciousness level to that of the whole group. If they reside at the consciousness level of desire, then one will be slowly or drastically lowered to the level of desire as well. Not only will one pick up their negative traits by hanging out with them, but when one 'swears in' to the group, one is asking one's self to link all of their karma to the karma of the people in the group. Even if one meets a lot of nice people, it doesn't mean that they have a 'pure ego.' One cannot know this until they question the motives of the people and the group. If their motives are not love, then one should not swear into or join the group if enlightenment is the goal.

Marriage

Marriage is usually one of the most anticipated events in a person's life, other than having a child. This is the most common way of linking one's personal karma with that of another being. As two people meet and fall in love, they feel that the last step that makes each person completely devoted to the other is to marry. This can be a 'good' or a 'bad' thing in terms of 'karmic linkage.' If they are both at a very high level of consciousness, then they can benefit and uplift each other while helping to overcome the current karmic conditions of their soul, thus leading to positive spiritual growth.

Unfortunately, if both beings are at a very low level of consciousness, they will inadvertently affect each another while lessening consciousness levels and multiplying negative karma. It can be said that these two beings bring out the 'worst in each other.' These two negative beings will bring each other further down the karmic scale of life because they exist on the same reality, the 'will of the ego,' which contains the lower emotions and positionalities. Neither of the two will want to change for the better, because each feeds off the negative energy in the other's lower consciousness level. This marriage will create a symbiotic and synergistic relationship in which negative energy fuels the negative fire. These beings will undoubtedly have relationship troubles and will probably seek marital counseling. Divorce is also likely, which leads to single parents and upset children, as well as hatred between the two separated parents. However, the divorce of two negative beings will most likely be the beneficial part of the marriage and can even propel them into a karmic payoff or resolution. This is accomplished when the negative person who usually feeds the other's negative fire separates from the other being, thus not fueling negative karmic conditions and propelling positive spiritual growth for both individuals, and their children.

It needs to be understood that marriage is not what is necessary to make a relationship work. Instead, it is love, understanding, and a desire to grow. And when these factors are present in any type of relationship, it will flourish beyond comprehension. Marriage is an illusion, as is having a relationship. To have a relationship infers a dualistic reality, which is an illusion because All is One and not two. In the Absolute Reality of the Unmanifest, there is no being to join to another, because All is One and there are no separate 'things' that could be connected together.

The ego makes one believe that 'things' are separate, which prompts the development of a system of guidelines for living together, called 'laws.' These laws are logical, rational, and linear; however, God is Nonlinear, cannot be rationalized, and cannot be understood with logic. So in essence, the idea of getting married or joining two together is an illusion and not True Reality. Unconditional love and commitment to one another are all that is needed for a successful relationship. Marriage is not needed, but should be understood and respected for its purpose.

Marriage is a beautiful thing, but it should be understood for what it really is, an illusion. In the physical reality it is real because the ego perceives it to be. One should realize that if they do not see it this way (real), they should be compassionate and understanding of where others are, or of what level of consciousness brings this perception and limitation of knowing.

Teaching Others

One of the most important professions in physical reality is that of the teacher. The most important of the duties of the universe, though, is that of the 'spiritual teacher.' While the teacher of the physical world educates one on the material realms of existence, the spiritual teacher educates one on understanding and experiencing their True Nature (formlessness).

The spiritual teacher is committed to helping others at all costs, while trying to reveal a higher level of truth that brings new realizations to the spiritual aspirant, which then brings forth positive change. Unfortunately, many self-proclaimed spiritual gurus or spiritual leaders/masters are spreading fallacy as though it were Truth. This is not beneficial for the spiritual aspirant and the so-called guru, for it creates negative energy that is connected by a karmic linkage.

As one agrees to teach another and the other being accepts being taught, a karmic link is created between the two. This is why it is very important to convey only the Truth and not just parts of it. If one spreads the lower truths, then the lower levels of consciousness will be accessed, bringing in more negative energy into one's field. Not only will the teacher lower the student's level of consciousness, but they will lower their own as well. So one should be careful what they teach.

Whether one teaches atheism, politics, science, theology, or enlightenment, they all contain varying levels of truth from the lower to higher levels, respectively. It is not incorrect to teach one or the other; it is merely another option that was chosen to exercise a quality of 'will,' which has a different level of truth that was either conceptualized and covered, or free from ego thought and True. So before accepting to be taught by a spiritual teacher, try to see and understand their ego motives, or, better yet, to see if they even have an ego any more (hopefully not). Always choose a teacher with a higher level of truth than one's self. This does not necessarily mean that the teacher has more knowledge, but rather, a higher realization of the Truth that can be expressed.

The educated theologian has no understanding of Absolute Truth; enlightenment is not a learned beingness, it is just what one is as the highest aspect. Remember that the realization of the Absolute Truth is experienced and not learned through years of living or from books. It is hard to discern which teachers are beneficial, so the following attributes of a true spiritual teacher are listed below.

Attributes of True Spiritual Teachers

- *Does not do anything for Self-Gain.*
- *Respects and helps all life; never does, speaks, or wills harm.*
- *Does not care or brag about having a large following.*
- *Very humble; does not claim to be more important or higher than others.*
- *Sees all beings (bugs, animals, humans, plants) as equals.*
- *Does not exhibit flashy (expensive) material items such as gold watches, money, expensive cars, houses, or clothes.*
- *Does not see any reason for using makeup or dressing nicely.*
- *Does not care about the physique of the physical body.*
- *Will go out of their way to help one **positively**, even someone who is a terrorist.*

- *Does not usually have a normal, everyday job.*
- *Spends all day devoted to God in prayer, intention, or meditation.*
- *Only cares about helping other beings become Self-Realized.*

Writing Books

Just like teaching, books are important for conveying the Truth. As a book is written, it holds the author's level of consciousness. It primarily remains a safe karmic package until it is sold in stores or given to people. As one buys the book, a 'karmic contract' is established between the author and the buyer. As the buyer reads the book, the consciousness level of the author that was conveyed in the book, via words and intention, is loaded as a vibratory package into the reader. This could be beneficial or harmful, depending on the book's overall frequency. If the author's consciousness level and the words that are written contain a low frequency, the reader will be adversely affected. The karma that was established as an unknown contract between the author and the reader will affect both parties. As the reader's consciousness level decreases, so does the author's. This is why it is important only to teach the Absolute Truth and nothing else.

Currently, about 1% of the spiritual books in bookstores teach the process of realizing the Absolute Truth. About 80% teach a very low-level truth, but at least it is still truth. The remaining 19% are absolute fallacy and misleading. In actuality, about 99% of books are misleading because their content is difficult to follow, or hard to comprehend. This makes reading seem like a 'waste of time,' because one doesn't know if the Absolute Truth is being taught or transcribed properly. And just because the book says it is teaching the Absolute Truth doesn't mean that it is. Many people like to say that they teach Truth, but really it is their ego that likes the feeling of thinking that it knows something that others don't (control issue). These books are to be avoided.

It is understood that the average person does not know what books to purchase, so a few good books are listed on the web site www.revealingtruthnow.com. But one should be careful what they read, because one doesn't karmically know what they're getting themselves into.

Books To Avoid if Enlightenment Is Sought

- *Books that say the inherent information is dangerous to the human mind, or that it is cutting edge, or special.*
- *Books that try to sell as if they were a movie, by trying to grab one with interesting words or scenarios.*
- *Books that hype themselves up to be great, or 'one of a kind.'*
- *Books that teach one that the spiritual manifest or astral dimensions are the True Reality of Oneness.*
- *Books that teach psychic skills, dream recall, OBEs, meeting with spirit guides, seeing angels (beneficial for psychic development, but not for Self-Realization).*
- *Books that tell one their book is better than others.*
- *Books that are biased (such as religious, or written from a religious ego view [closed-minded]).*
- *Books that express the Truth from the viewpoint of their ego, or positionalities.*
- *Books that teach 'bodily' sacrifice as an option or a necessity, whether human or animal.*
- *Books that teach religion, paganism, or atheism as the **only way.***
- *Books that teach witchcraft and spiritual phenomena as Truth or Reality.*
- *Books that tell one that mathematics can solve the link between humans, mind, emotions, and spiritual Truth.*
- *Books that emphasize that one can perceive Truth, or that teaches one how to perceive Truth (only the ego perceives - the Self doesn't perceive Truth, it 'is' Truth).*
- *Books that emphasize physical living **over** spiritual living.*
- *Books written by an unenlightened being.*
- *Books that explain that opposites (Polarities) are reality, such as True/False, Negative/Positive, Yin/Yang, Right/Wrong.*

- *Books that focus on astrology as the reason or cause of all.*
- *Books that teach that 'cause and effect' is part of reality.*
- *Books that say one **cannot** be God-realized.*
- *Books that criticize those who say one can be God-realized.*
- *Books that **rely** on religious research or texts for Truth.*

Unspoken Will/Intention and Thoughts

This is the 'will' or intention of an ego as its emotional states and positionalities shape the contemplative thought patterns of another individual or a society as a whole. As one thinks, one accesses the thoughts that are stored in the infinite, ever-recording, energetic computer that is the 'universal consciousness.' These thoughts can affect an individual in a 'negative' or 'positive' way. As each thought pattern is formed by the ego's will, an unspoken and unknown karmic connection is formed; this is really the connection of the 'essences' (karma) of each being. This connection transfers the positive or negative energy to the individual from the other being where it originated.

At first, the ego needs to control its thoughts in order to try to keep a 'clean mind,' which may seem impossible at times. Trying to 'control' the ego is not really possible, because the very essence of the ego is 'control'—and since the ego is the 'thinking mind,' when the ego energizes by way of using 'control,' the mind becomes more cluttered. Merely 'trying' to control an issue or part of life reinforces the ego. So to clear the mind of negative thought patterns, one needs to understand the very essence of the thought pattern itself, as well as the creative motives of the ego. When a deep understanding of the negative thought pattern is known, the energy of that thought pattern dissipates because of the unraveling of a part of the ego's nature. As one questions their own ego's motives, as well as those of others, then the ego begins to loosen its grip on the soul. As the ego weakens, the thought forms become less frequent until they are totally dissolved. After that, one no longer needs to worry about any negative karmic linkage from negative thought patterns. Only positive energy will be available, due to their constant channeling of the Divine Will, which benefits mankind.

When an individual's ego mentates or creates a negative thought pattern about another person, it affects the 'thinker and the thought of.' The ego that created the negative thought pattern is affected in a negative way, and the person whom the ego 'thought of' negatively is also affected. This is why it is important to only think 'good' about other people, even if "they have done you wrong." Most individuals believe that if someone treats them badly, then they should treat the other person badly as well. This should never happen, but it does because the ego 'wills' it to. When the ego's pride, viewpoints, or beliefs have been challenged, it feels as if it needs to prove itself in some way. This usually includes yelling, swearing, and a huge display of "I am better than you because..."

After the confrontation, a sense of animosity develops and negative thought forms about each other begin to build up and crystallize into more concentrated patterns. And as one thinks of an individual, they automatically attune and link their energy to that person. So any thought that one has affects that person's beingness or karma. If one thinks negative thoughts about the person, it will affect them negatively, as well as oneself. But the ego, even when it knows this, will ignore it and go on producing the various negative thought forms anyway. This is simply because the ego is still controlling the person, and it only really cares about itself (self-gain).

The ego cares not for the soul, for it is an impersonal aspect of the soul, like a kidnapper holding it for ransom by stupidity. It does everything it can to make one think that a soul doesn't and can't exist, or that it is a 'far-fetched idea' in which to believe. It does this while knowing that it is hiding the soul from one's current perception or awareness. This is like stealing money from a church and convincing everyone who questions you about it that you 'didn't do it,' 'someone else did,' or 'maybe you did it and you are just trying to blame it on me.' The ego will put the blame on anything else; it _may_ admit to it as long as it gets the option to escape from the wrongdoing.

It is utterly amazing and simply fascinating that the ego would rather think negative than positive thoughts about somebody. If someone 'does one wrong,' one can simply think of the person with positive intention or will, and pray for them. This positive intention adds to one's karmic field and that of the other individual, creating a positive karmic energy pattern. In this way, one can remove some of their own negative karma and at the same time remove some from the other person as well, making both individuals 'better' people. Instead, about 90% of the population would rather talk badly about others who have 'done them wrong.' By doing this, the ego is fulfilled because it makes itself feel as if the other being was entirely wrong, even if it knows that it was most of the problem. This process is called *justification*.

Everyone has met someone who has justified a previous 'wrongdoing.' *All egos* have done this to escape their own problem, letting them feel that they were mostly or entirely 'in the right.' This is obviously done to protect the ego's sense of pride, which therefore protects its identity and vanity. It is a totally selfish act, which is the ego's true nature. As one dissolves pride and the ego's identity, there is no need to defend any viewpoint or argument. One simply wishes others the best in their endeavors and prays for them to realize the Truth, just as one has. This facilitates the healing process throughout the world, rather than hindering it, as the ego has been doing since the dawn of time.

Remember that the 'ego will' is self-serving, sickening, negative, destroying, hating, wanting, obstructing, and constantly distorting the Truth while holding onto the soul, keeping one captive. On the other hand, the Divine Will is positive, healing, illuminating, unconditionally loving, perfect, helping, selfless, accepting, giving, and one's True Nature. The ego is not one's friend, but rather a sick patient who needs to heal.

Karmic Contracts

Throughout one's endless past lifetimes, one has acquired karmic contracts in the spiritual and the physical manifest. These karmic contracts are spoken, known, or unknown bonds that each soul has agreed to fulfill in an attempt to alleviate each other's past negative karma. It is a way to work silently on uplifting or raising each other's level of consciousness. However, 99% of the time, the individual with the contract does not know that they are trying to fulfill one. They just carry on with their lives as usual. Even as the individual lives their life as if nothing were planned, it still has been preprogrammed into their life, and appears as their reality.

Many circumstances can develop or require a karmic contract, such as the following:

1. *If one kills someone in a past life or this one, one may be linked to that individual in order to help 'right the wrong,' so to speak. One might serve the individual to whom one 'did wrong' as a spirit guide or as a helpful family member in a new incarnation (for example, mother and son).*

2. *One may swear to someone that they will watch over them and protect them when they die. That wish is usually granted, so one may find themselves 'in spirit' watching over others and trying to guide them.*

3. *Before incarnation into this lifetime, one may program their destiny to help others, by being a doctor, healer, minister, philanthropist, or loyal friend. This is usually because one has wronged many people in their previous lives, and this is an effort to correct it.*

4. *If one swears to God (Universe) that they will teach other people about the Truth, then they just created their karmic contract with God. People swear on their 'deathbed' that they will change and help others if they are healed, and often healing happens spontaneously.*

It is not necessarily a 'bad thing' if one breaks a karmic contract, because one just has to wait until they fulfill it, or write another one. Every split second of one's existence is creating another karmic contract by 'will,' but the major events in one's current or past life seem to create the most profound karmic linkages. Also, by waiting for the next contract to be written, one has to keep on helping until they have fulfilled their previous contract. If one makes the person that they were supposed to help, or was in a karmic contract with, go in the 'wrong direction,' one would just create more 'correcting' karmic contracts that one would have to fulfill.

No matter whether one fulfills or does not fulfill a contract, all will work out as planned, because all possibilities or outcomes have already been preprogrammed, set, and known, although not by the ego. One's destiny may change but will still work out perfectly according to Divine Will. Just because one has broken or not fulfilled a karmic contract does not mean that they will "go to hell and burn for all eternity"; it just means that one will keep on adding more negative karma to one's self, which brings about a more undesirable reality that will be perceived. This will obviously not be enjoyable, but at least one will receive more opportunities to pay off their karmic debt.

Another important realization is that God loves everyone, no matter how many karmic contracts have been broken—this happens all the time. If one swears to something and does the opposite, one is not condemned to 'hell.' However, one will be opting to accumulate more negative karma; but on the other hand, one also has infinite lifetimes to work it off and become enlightened. Just remember that God/Truth is always there for all beings and will always love them unconditionally (this means no matter what they do). To help one's self erase negative karma and add positive karma, one should just be honest with themselves and realize why they have rejected God and 'done wrong' (so to speak). This will resolve the conflict of the ego and bring Truth to the matter at hand, while resolving the negative karma.

Group Karma

Group karma is a type of karmic contract where people have lived together in the same past or current time frame and done the same things in a group; they are all connected by a karmic resonance. So as a whole they have bound themselves to work through their negative karma together. Whether they were all bank robbers, terrorists, or in a gang, they have all done their deeds together and bound themselves together by their actions and beingness.

This group may live many lifetimes together, although resembling another group with different purposes that more than likely wears different clothes and has different identities. The group may stand for political ideals, religious differences, social dilemmas, or personal strife, but all in all they are the same group that must 'right their wrongs' until the bond can be broken. It can only be broken if the group decides that it is time for self-discovery and healing. This can be done by recontextualizing their thoughts and emotional states, questioning and surrendering the ideals and motives of their ego, serving the higher purpose, or devoting themselves to helping others. This is another reason why it is important to be independent and understand that one should not join a group unless its karmic resonance is that of a higher level of consciousness or Truth. Following this simple advice can keep one from becoming linked with the karmic bonds of the ego.

In most groups in the world, there is usually a swearing-in ceremony that concludes one's initiation. As one swears in to the group, one is then linked karmically to the others. This more than likely binds one's self to their karmic fate. If one chooses to have their own destiny and not leave it in the hands of others in the group, then do not ever swear into any organization, at least not one that is lacking moral value or is self-serving, for this will surely impede one's spiritual evolution. It will only bind one's fate to the individuals who are a part of the group, thus limiting one's spiritual accomplishments and holding them back from enlightenment.

Section Three
<u>Crystallization Process</u>

"Everything is already in a state of being, but dependent upon the witnessing mind, certain realities present themselves."

—BN

Chapter 9
Essence of Creation

Linear/Dualistic Depiction of God

There are many misconceptions about creation, which is understandable because there are also many misconceptions about God. These two seemingly different concepts are one and the same: God is infinite creation, both the creator and the product.

The problem is one of ignorance, which lies within our ego/mind. This is due to the fact that the ego/mind was only set up or programmed in the linear/dualistic mode. However, God is Non-linear/Nondualistic, which poses an obvious problem. This is roughly analogous to an Englishman speaking to a Japanese man and claiming to understand what the conversation was about. A better analogy is if a human were trying to talk to the sky and claimed that a conversation took place. The experience of God is by way of subjective experience or complete submersion into the Self, not objectivity or perceptivity of the ego.

The ego/mind only operates on the dualistic scale, so God is expected to be a being who lives far away in another galaxy, universe, or spiritual dimension, who creates once in a while and watches the outcome. By watching what happens with his creation, in this 'world of chance,' he is believed to constantly judge and critique how all beings act or are. The linear concepts of space, time, distance, and perception are always added into seemingly spiritual-sounding text or stories to add comprehensibility. This shows that these stories are fictitious, misunderstood, misconceived, or projections of the ego's traits that make God seem more dramatic, vengeful, and dangerous to the nonbeliever. The ego cannot know Truth because it is not programmed to comprehend the Unmanifest, so it tends to distort Truth into something that it can comprehend. The only reality that the ego can comprehend is that of the ego's traits and delusions.

Other people's theories, stories, and depictions of God are

often taken from many different sources, such as 'hearsay' elements or myths. A large percentage (99%) of the world operates from the control of the ego's emotional and mental states, so stories have to sound interesting to other people. So man will take an unconditionally loving source of existence and transform it into a 'him' (masculine intimidation factor), and make him nonunderstanding, very judgmental, vengeful, angry, intimidating, scornful, righteous, and prideful, not to mention 'punishing.' All of these factors, when placed upon the Reality of God, make 'him' seem more exciting and powerful, therefore fueling the drama that is loved by the ego, but at the same time, blocks the Truth.

That reality and depiction of God was created because the only existence that man really knows of is the ego's reality, which was provided at birth. Since the ego's traits are believed by many to be the only possibility, these emotional and mental states are thought to be the only reality that could ever exist. This leads to people placing the ego's belief systems upon the already 'illusory thought' of a 'God being.' Since the ego has to set the reality that can be experienced, the human being cannot fathom (due to lack or programming) the existence of God 'as is,' which is the Supreme Reality, the only infinite and unconditionally loving Source.

The Essence of God

To truly know God is to be 'egoless,' or the aspect of the soul known as the Higher Self. The *Transcendent-Self* is the consciousness of God, which one's *Immanent-Self* (localized consciousness) transcends up throughout the innumerable levels of, via the process known as transcension. The Transcendent-Self is thought by many to be separate from the Immanent-Self, but really they are One and the same. God is continuously and infinitely radiating potentiality as unconditional love through the process known as manifestation that is the ever-experiencing wonder of Creation.

God is the underlying substrate Source of potentiality, known as the Unmanifest, which allows for creation, while simultaneously being the product as the manifest. God is beyond the dualistic reality that is perceived by the ego, just as God is beyond any restraint, boundary, or limitation that could ever be thought of or applied. God is beyond any means of measurement, and thus cannot be comprehended within the linear dimension of the ego or by the ego. God is beyond the astral dimensions or spiritual phenomena. God cannot be documented within the theory or construct of time or space that was created by the minds of men for the limited dimensions of linear reality.

It is an impossibility to exist outside of God, simply because God is existence; God is infinite and All. God is the Source of unconditional love, peace, and stillness, by just the virtue of being it. God is always accepting of everything. God is not subject to the lower emotional and mental states of the ego. God is not subject to feeling pain or being injured, and cannot be destroyed by any demonic beings or 'Satan.' There is no need for a war between God and Satan, because that which is unlimited and infinite cannot be destroyed by the limited, finite, and fallacious. God is the Ultimate Source of comfort and understanding, not an angry, judgmental, and punishing figure, as God is usually viewed.

God is All That Is, the creator and the created. However, the aspect that most beings refer to is that of the Unmanifest or infinite Source that is the 'Creator.' God is not separated into an infinite number of 'God Cells.' However, this theory is sometimes taught because of its ease of understanding. God is the One and only Source of purity, as perfection, beauty, peacefulness, happiness, and unconditional love (All one and the same).

God Clarified

God Unmanifest

God, which is the utmost Source of infinite potentiality, is termed the Unmanifest. This energy is nonform and excludes all that is form, for form is a distortion of Truth and the Unmanifest is nonform, Truth, and purity. **God as Unmanifest** is Nondualistic and Nonlinear, and cannot be solved by any means whatsoever. It is beyond the realm of the provable. It is the Source from which all came and All is currently a part of. It is pure love and peace.

This energy is unmoving and not subject to any external

force; thus it cannot be manipulated or changed by any means. The Unmanifest quality of God cannot be destroyed or limited in any way. It is infinite and unlimited. It is existence in and of itself, relying on no other source for sustenance.

Its very essence is beyond all form, including sound waves or light waves, whether physical or subtle in energetic nature. Just as it is nonform, no form can hinder or bind it. The Unmanifest Source of God is not even aware of form, nor is it aware of consciousness. It is purely nonform and knows nothing of any laws of the limited, linear, or dualistic, yet it provides for all of them.

God as Totality

While **God as Unmanifest** excludes all form, **God as Totality** is that very essence of the Unmanifest, as well as all that has stemmed from it. It is All That Is, the Source and the creation.

God as Totality is everything and all things, including the heavens and the hells, the ego and the Self, the Unmanifest and the manifest, the linear and the nonlinear, the 'demons' and the 'saints,' and the very substrate of form that is capable of being aware of and recognizing form, which is consciousness itself. Just the same, it is also the 'universal consciousness,' which fuels the seemingly independent consciousness. It is logic and nonlogic, the rational and the irrational. It is All That Is.

That very source of God that society reveres and worships is the Unmanifest quality, where infiniteness is expressed without limitation or restriction. But it should be understood that **God as Totality** shows the utmost, infinitely increasing levels of Power and that which hinders the expression of Absolute Truth.

These distortions of Truth are **consciousness, the ego, and form** itself. All beings on the enlightened path should recognize that **God as Unmanifest** is what they are as the highest aspect of Self (Unmanifest Self). Thus, it is the very Truth that they adhere to, which reveals the Unmanifest quality in All, known as Divinity. These two aspects of God are One and the same as Totality.

Gradation of Power and the Order of Creation

The ***Absolute Reality***, also known as the ***Supreme Reality***, ***Ultimate Reality***, ***Unmanifest Self***, or ***Supreme Spirit***, is the unlimited, boundless, and infinite potential; it is the substrate energy that remains completely still and undisturbed, just as birds do not affect or disturb the sky, but rather, simply pass through it. The Supreme Spirit is the ever-present, radiating energy that is the creative Source. This Source allows for the 'Triune Godhead' to arise as an aspect of the Universal Whole, where the essence of the Creator, Creation, and Consciousness combine as another building block of potentiality and totality.

Gradation of Power, Order of Creation, and Levels of Consciousness

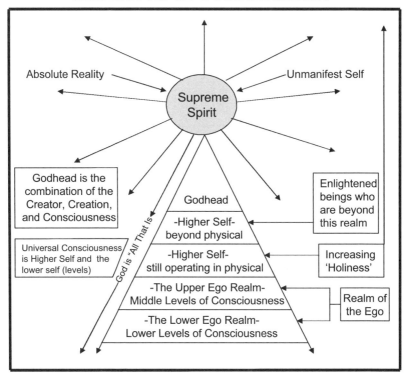

The chart above denotes the process and order of creation by varying levels of Power. It shows the corresponding levels of Consciousness, which has total equality of Power by the nature of transcendental properties. This chart does not actually represent 'cause and effect.' It represents creation as a constant creative act of Now, in which All manifests simultaneously (all arrows denote infinity, which is All).

From the only true Source of Divinity, the Unmanifest Self, the universal consciousness arises. And from this, form is born. As the higher levels of consciousness, known as the Higher Self, are transcended throughout, one goes through many pleasurable experiences, which feel as though they are a celebration of existence. And even though these levels of consciousness are not Absolute Truth, or completely Unmanifest (consciousness is still an aspect of form), they remain with and as the knowingness of being universally connected, or as One.

Just the same, there are levels of consciousness that are lower in frequency, or in nature. These realities represent and are the more restricted and limited qualities of the ego, as well as the more animalistic aspects of the 'lower self.' The lower levels of consciousness, which are still a part of the universal whole, are linear, dualistic, and completely manifest without the understanding of Oneness. From this, the ego dwells and remains entrapped within them until the error of its ways, that being ignorance, is realized and transcended by the practice of Will and the surrender of fallacy and illusion.

So out of the formless potential of the Unmanifest arises the Spiritual Dimension of Form (universal consciousness), starting with abstract forms and seemingly meaningless patterns, while progressively crystallizing and manifesting toward the more dense layers of the astral dimensions (ego realms of universal consciousness), which will be referred to as the 'Spiritual Manifest' (spiritual dimension of form). The lower that one is in universal consciousness, the more logical and rational the reality will be. Just the same, within this dimension, a being will obviously rely on its mode of perception, which uses the linear and dualistic mind (ego).

The Spiritual Manifest is a byproduct and a quality of consciousness, meaning that it was created by the mental functions, emotional states, belief systems, positionalities, and spiritual presets of the linear mind. While existing on an astral dimension where the soul seems to have lost its way, then 'purgatory,' a realm of learning, is allowed to be accessed. In a sense, **all** realms of existence are considered purgatories, because all realms are where lessons are learned; lessons **never** cease. If karma allows, then the ego can take on new lessons that may enable it to raise in consciousness and transcend its currently perceived reality. Such purgatories are available for and are every level of consciousness, heavens or hells.

The physical zone, one of many purgatories, should be considered a privilege to incarnate into. It is rare to incarnate or embody into the physical dimension. It is also the only dimension in which beings are born into, have a family, and die to exit. Numerous lessons may be learned in the physical zone, especially on earth. The lessons learned within the physical incarnation are rare and extraordinary. Many lessons learned on earth—such as those learned from birth, death, family, marriage, and children—cannot be learned elsewhere. Likewise, the relationships in this dimension are like no other; this is due to the bonding acquired through the ego's various 'ups and downs,' the trivialities within the illusory manifest. These sympathetic bonds are emotional attachments called 'friendships.' These bonds of comfort are capable of creating a strong love.

As seen from the preceding discussion, God is not just the Unmanifest nor the manifest; instead, God is All That Is, or everything that exists as Totality. The overall essence of God, the Unmanifest Self, is the Supreme Spirit that is always infinitely throughout all of creation, which energizes, provides for, and sustains consciousness. As creation, which originates in the Unmanifest as potentiality and is then 'willed' into expression by egos, manifests and crystallizes, a diverse density (if you will) of realities incessantly creates, thus forming the countless levels of consciousness that we are now trying to transcend. In essence, the very hell that we created (by way of the ego) is what we are now trying to ask God for help out of. So only with total devotion and dedication to the Truth of existence (God) can one transcend the ego and become Self-Realized. Thus one goes back to the Source with the understanding that one should not have, on any account, substituted erroneous belief for Truth in and as one's initial existential reality. By understanding the error of its ways, a being then realizes that nothing can be gained by ignoring Truth, which is existence itself as the Unmanifest Self.

It is important to note that the universal consciousness was not created eons ago. Instead, consciousness has always existed and always will. It is the 'thinking aspect' of the universal whole, or God as Totality. It is the 'universal mind,' which is one and the same as the seemingly independent minds that have their own locus in existence and are felt to be 'mobile.' The fact that these independent beings feel as though they are able to move, think, and live by themselves is an illusion and not reality. Each and every being who feels independent is merely a manifestation or a product of the 'Universal Mind.' So all beings are not separate beings; they are really just a 'thought' that the 'universal mind' is having. That is all. Just the same, all thoughts that these seemingly 'independent beings' are having are really just thoughts within their self, which is a thought also. It makes one wonder if the 'thoughts' that seemingly remain within their own mind are having their own version of reality as well. All thoughts that enter one's mind are not of their mind, but rather, of the universal consciousness. The ego just claims them.

A Warning about Illusion

The 'Spiritual Manifest,' better known as the astral dimensions, is a trap that is set to snare the unsuspecting ego in all of its endeavors. These dimensions are accessed through psychic work and astral projections. These realms can be very deceiving in that they are inhabited by confused egos; these are not souls who should be trusted for guidance. If one inhabits the astral dimensions of form, or some of the lower formless hells that are filled with pure hatred, loss, regret, fear, etc..., then they are not themselves enlightened. They are simply egos in another dimension who have lost their way. They may or may not know a higher Truth than one's self, but if they present something as Truth, it will not be Absolute. For Absolute Truth is the essence of God, which cannot be displayed, exhibited, or put into language by any means of conveyance whatsoever.

Within the Spiritual Manifest are other souls who may claim to be God, or a god, a lord, or even an angel, but these are usually false projections of that being's ego. They may claim to be 'better' than God, angels, or any spiritual master with whom one may be familiar. These disenchanted souls will use a name that either sounds impressive or familiar to one's self, such as Jesus, Buddha, Quan Yin, Master, Gandhi, etc... The names of deceased relatives may also be used, for this builds one's confidence in them. They will try to get one to trust in them, because they derive power, which is really 'force' (as in 'life force' of the ego), from controlling other beings. Their purpose is to exhibit the traits of their ego and to be self-serving while fulfilling their desires on the other's account.

The souls who reside in the lower astral dimensions (hells) are the most controlling and dangerous. Some of the more powerful (forceful) of the souls are referred to as demons, such as Satan, Mara, etc... They can actually force themselves into one's body and suppress one's consciousness, resulting in a possession. This means that a loved one whom you know who dabbles blindly (naively and without God's protection) into psychic practices can become plagued or badgered by a demonic possession. By trying to contact these otherworldly souls, one invites them into their household and sometimes into their body. Even though the psychic may not perceive the astral soul, it is there, and you can be subject to its will.

If one should practice their psychic skills, then prayer protection, good intent, good will, and gold and white light should be used to purify the mind, the ego, the house (area), etc... If 'ill will' (pride, control, etc...) are the purpose of the psychic practice, then lower astral souls will be attracted the most. Most souls yearn to be psychic, just so they can exhibit a sense of power or control over the nonpsychic. If their 'will' remains within Divine purpose

(Will), higher beings who hold more Truth are invited. This, however, does not suggest that the higher being *will* be connected with. The use of a 'control' is recommended (a book on developing psychic skills should also be examined meticulously).

The use of psychic skills can assist one in understanding Truths that ought to be learned. However, all Truth in absolute certainty is already provided sufficiently as the Unmanifest, and will facilitate one's transcension of the ego. Psychic skills are not necessary to become enlightened. In fact, they are a hindrance that may slow one's progress or spiritual evolution. Even if one is a psychic, suffering is still an element of their lifestyle. This is due to the residual remnants of the ego that still influence thought, action, will, speech, and personality. The ego is still used to judge, discern, and perceive astral souls, thereby amplifying the ego and helping it stick like glue. Whenever a psychic wants to develop into an enlightened being, the formal meditations, lifestyle (ego will), and psychic practices must be abandoned until full dissolution and abandonment of the ego (enlightenment) occur.

Many psychics and astral projectors have countless issues with this abandonment, for it is their perceived source of happiness. When psychic faculties are put on hold, there can actually be a feeling of loss. After a short while, the happiness eventually returns in extravagance, with overflowing joy and a profound sense of peace. Psychic skills actually then feel like an interference, and one does not really feel as if they even want to 'will' the phenomena to occur. Instead, the psychic (now enlightened) feels driven to help the world transcend the ego and abandon its source of sin.

Chapter 10
Difference of Dimension

What Is Considered Form?

Energetically speaking, form is considered to be energy that is arranged in a specific pattern or has been organized in some way, or, plainly put, exhibits structure. So in the physical dimension, all that egos perceive and don't perceive is form. This means that what egos feel, hear, see, taste, and smell is all form within the manifest. Most people think of form as something that is 'solid,' or with a tangible quality. This is not necessarily true in the physical energetic dimension, however, because all energy is arranged in some way, and some arrangements are not 'solids.'

These various energetic structures are what the physical dimension is composed of, besides the very substrate of the Unmanifest, which provides for all existence and consciousness, which in turn is the substrate for all creation. The 'physical manifest' is composed of the Unmanifest (first and foremost), then subtle sound vibrations, subtle light and color, and the vibrations that emanate from matter itself, known as subatomic particles. But the 'physical manifest' also contains energetic patterns of thought, emotions, ideas, and beliefs, which of course help to shape the ego's perceived reality. All contribute to how the ego perceives reality, from the solid and tangible to the subjective and imaginative.

There are two types of spiritual energy, the 'manifest' (illusion) and 'Unmanifest' (Truth). The Unmanifest is God, which is completely formless. The Spiritual Manifest, which many people mistakenly consider to be the Unmanifest, is the astral dimensions of differing levels of Truth and truth (universal consciousness).

The Spiritual Manifest is a dimension that is energetically shaped by the faculties of the ego mind, from thoughts, emotions, beliefs, or viewpoints. So it is still form, because it is energy that is arranged in patterns. These patterns can be seen, heard, felt, tasted, smelled, and intuited by psychics while on earth, or by the average person while in the astral dimensions. They are then interpreted by the ego as either fallacy or truth. The ego can only detect the dimensions of form, thus giving it access, or the ability to experience, the physical and spiritual manifest. However, the Unmanifest is Truth and has no form, meaning that an ego cannot experience the Unmanifest, but an 'egoless' being experiences an aspect of consciousness, known as the Higher Self, that is aware of the Unmanifest.

The Physical Dimension

The physical dimension is nothing but form. It was allowed to manifest by the Unmanifest because the conditions became necessary for all karmic lessons to be learned in a new type of dimension with new experiences. Even the 'things' that the ego doesn't see to be form, such as sound, air, water, fire, words, emotions, ideas, and beliefs, really are. Everything in the physical dimension is structured in a certain way, which is how one 'thing' can be known from another. This is what allows the ego to judge and decipher what is what, or the differences between two things.

Most people don't think of air as form, but the very essence of it (in the physical sense) is. Every atom in the universe has an atomic structure. This structure cannot be seen by the naked eye, but it is known by scientists. Every arrangement of an atomic structure creates different substances, such as oxygen, nitrogen, and helium, to name only a few. When atoms join, they form molecules that create even more substances, which are completely different than the atoms in their natural state before they were combined. For example, hydrogen and oxygen, which are two gases, create water, which is a completely different substance than was originally present.

Mankind has known for years that we can mix atoms to create different substances. These substances are known as 'products' in the business world. 'Products' consist of medicines, weed killers, rat poisons, acrylic, lycra, and thousands of other substances. Molecules are also mixed to form even more substances that can be marketed and sold. This is of course wonderful knowledge in the physical dimension, but does one little good for spiritual awareness and understanding.

On a finer scale of form, sound is an arrangement of different vibratory rates that, when combined with varying tones, create different pitches of sound and nuance. When mixing the tones together in a matching sequence, one calls it music. Although the arrangement of frequencies or vibratory rates and tones creates the form known as music, the tones, vibratory rates, or frequencies by themselves are arrangements that are considered form. When the notes "A" and "D" are sounded, for example, they appear to be different in tone, because the arrangement of vibrations differs in structure. When these different structures are combined, they create a specific pattern. Different patterns create different musical sounds. So all songs, 'riffs,' patterns, tunes, notes, and voices are energetic manifestations of form.

Music is not that different from the way we think. Music creates patterns, and so does thinking. As one thinks, the vibrations received from each independent object that is perceived or thought of are nothing other than form. Every thought that one has contains a series of certain frequencies that one interprets. These varying frequencies or vibratory rates create different objects that can be perceived, or ideas and beliefs that can be thought. So every thought, belief, idea, or sound that one perceives is form, because all that can be perceived is form. This is why God as Unmanifest (formless) cannot be perceived, only experienced as existence.

The physical, mental, and emotional form is important to understand, but to really know the spiritual dimension, one needs to realize the Truth of the manifestation of form in all dimensions. This allows Truth to be experienced as the levels of consciousness raise from the understanding of creation and manifestation, which are allowed by the Unmanifest, to the realization of being One.

The elements of the universe are vibrations in and of themselves. This means that Earth, Air, Fire, and Water have their own specific frequencies that can be interpreted by beings in this universe. Throughout human history, they have been revered and thought of as powerful. Although these elements were misunderstood by many different cultures, they all knew that they contained healing power.

These elements are considered the basic foundation of life in the physical sense (besides atoms and subatomic particles). Each element is very different from the others, not only in form, but also in healing abilities. Just imagining any of these elements can have a profound effect on the individual. They help to heal on a variety of levels, such as the emotional, mental, physical, and spiritual.

These elements are perceived to be different because they are not the same in their structural integrity. This is what makes one perceive and believe that they are different and not one and the same. Until the realization that All is One, everything will be judged and seen as being different. In the physical manifest, however, it does exist as such and is different in its manifested appearance in the physical world by the nature of its structure. This is because the ego perceives it this way. When the ego is transcended, the Truth will shine forth, and all will be experienced as One. Then there will be no need for healing when the soul is already pure.

The Perceived Reality of the Ego

Manifest (physical form)	Manifest (spiritual form)
Air, Fire, Water, Earth	Astral Realms
Human Body	Chakras, Energy Body
Ego (structured personality)	Ego and psychic phenomena
Dreams about the physical	Dreams (in, of, and about spiritual)
Thoughts and Beliefs	Thoughts and Beliefs
Expressed Emotions	Expressed Emotions
Neurons	Nadis
Atoms and Subatomic Particles	Subtle Energy
Physical Sound Vibrations	Subtle Sound Vibrations
Physical Lines, Circles, and Shapes	Subtle Lines, Circles, and Shapes
Solar System and Galaxies	Manifestations of Universal Mind
Physical Energetic Connections	Subtle Energetic Connections
Historical Facts	Akashic Records System
*Relationships	*Relationships

*Relationships are dualistic and only between egos.

The Unmanifest (Divine Source)

Formlessness	Existence as Peace
Supreme Reality	Truth
Unconditional Love	Oneness

No Emotions Exist here… only love, peace, and happiness.
The Unmanifest is the Ever-Present, All-Creative, Underlying, Infinite
Potential, Substrate Energy of All That Is.

Note: This comparison denotes the difference between the Physical Manifest, the Spiritual Manifest, and the Unmanifest of All That Is.

The Spiritual Manifest

The most common misconception that spiritual gurus, psychics, and other people who have experienced spiritual phenomena seem to have is that the astral dimensions are formless and the 'real truth.' They are in fact a higher energetic dimension of truth than the physical, but nonetheless, they are still a dimension of form, and not the True Reality of the Unmanifest.

The astral dimensions are a phenomenon that many beings get hung up on because they are the easiest to understand, experience, and perceive, besides the physical dimension. Because the human mind needs experience (i.e., to 'perceive is to believe') it, it tends to believe this is God's reality, rather than the Unmanifest. Some psychics will argue this point because they say that the energy they perceive is formless and fluid. They are missing one point: there would be nothing to perceive and interpret psychically if there were no patterns of interlocking frequencies that create the different thoughts, emotions, beliefs, and personalities that the energy con-veys. As long as there are patterns, there is structure. As long as there is structure, there is form. And if there is form, it is illusion.

Other psychics or mystics may argue the same point, but from the OBE (Out-of-Body Experience) positionality. They figure that since one can leave the physical body and go into the other dimensions, they are leaving the dimension of form (physical reality) and going into a world of formlessness and fluidity.

This world of formlessness is thought to be formless because one's energy body can easily pass through other objects, such as doors, walls, and people. Thus the 'world of the solids' doesn't seem to apply within this dimension, or so they think. However, if the energy still has structure (walls, ceilings, doors, astral realms) and can be perceived, whether it can be passed through or not, it is considered another dimension of form, one that is higher than the physical but lower than the Higher Self and Unmanifest.

If one is out of body in the astral dimensions and talking to spirits, then one is not experiencing God as Unmanifest. The process of going through the astral realms shows a dualistic relationship: the 'explorer and the explored' and the 'talker and the talked to.' All patterns manifest from the combination of the ego/mind complex and the Unmanifest potential. The astral realms are not necessarily 'satanic,' as some would say, but definitely could entrap one in their amazing subexistence and the brilliance of all mentations ever thought.

The astral dimensions are a mental realm of constantly creating forms, which are perceived to be real and the only reality. While the physical dimension's reality is for the ego's thoughts to remain within one's mind, the astral dimension's reality is for one's thoughts to be the external reality that manifests all around them.

All thoughts are specifically arranged patterns that manifest as various forms, which basically creates/is the astral dimensions. Every thought that has ever been 'willed' into existence by an ego has created a realm in the astral dimension. Just imagine visiting the thought forms of Ted Bundy (the murderer) or Marilyn Manson (the performer). These beings' realities are objectionable to most. Although the astral dimensions will not physically hurt one, they can frighten even the toughest person who accidentally stumbles upon these undesirable realms.

It is important to note that many astral dimensions can be pleasurable, but keep in mind that this is still a temporary satisfaction that replaces the emptiness (lack of God's love) of the ego with a lower energy/emotion. When one transcends the physical and spiritual manifest, God then can be experienced as One, as the Unmanifest, the only True existence and Source of permanent fulfillment.

Spiritual healers also tell people that there are "things that cannot be seen by ordinary sight, that it is a world of formlessness." They also state that within this existence, which they usually call the 'true reality,' that auras and chakras exist. It is great that they try to explain to people that there are different realities that can be perceived, but it is not technically the real Truth that they speak of. Chakras and auras do exist, but in the Spiritual Manifest, not in the Unmanifest. The Unmanifest is the only True Reality that can ever be experienced as Oneness. The chakras and auras that are usually manipulated by ego will are in the Spiritual Manifest. Since this is in the spiritual realms, these individuals usually just assume that because it is different than what most of our everyday reality perceives, then it must be the True Reality or the realm of God.

Another important side note is that spiritual healers mostly use their 'ego will' to heal others. They use some Divine Will, but usually 'ego will.' This 'ego will' is used because they are the ones who are 'trying' to heal the other person. The act of 'trying,' or simply having intentions to heal another, will activate the 'ego will.' Similarly, the astral dimensions are a product of the 'ego will.' So, in essence, most of the energy directed to the individual who is seeking the healing is from the astral dimensions or the healer's energetic field. This will still heal the individual temporarily, but total healing happens only when the Source of the Divine is tapped into by faith, understanding, unconditional love, devotion, and surrendering all unto God.

Some spiritual healers channel the Divine Will by radiating the pure essence of the Grace of God. These individuals can be identified by their compassion and understanding, as well as their humble demeanor. They also do not charge for most services to mankind, because it is God's Will to heal all beings, and they only serve God's Will. These beings are known as the 'enlightened ones.' They radiate the Grace of God to all beings and have no ego will. This means that they do not tap into the astral dimensions for extra power, but directly channel God's Will (the energies of the Higher Self). One does not need a spiritual healer because everyone is their own spiritual healer. All one needs to do is raise in consciousness and surrender their ego to God. When this is done and realization occurs, healing instantly takes place.

Introspection, or looking into one's self or one's ego, is the easiest way to heal. As one questions their motives, they begin to heal, thus raising one's level of consciousness past the manifest physical and spiritual, and towards the Unmanifest. Then one will experience Oneness and be completely healed.

All illness stems from the denial of God, which inherently creates an absence of the healing power of God, or the absence of the higher qualities of light. So all dark areas that are lacking in the light provided by God are due to the ego's denial of Truth. They are just false or illusory beliefs and thought patterns that invite or welcome disease and illness.

The Unmanifest

Due to its formlessness, the Unmanifest cannot be perceived, felt, or seen by the ego. It is the ever-present, all-pervading, all-knowing Source of infinite potentiality of All That Is. This infinite energy of All is what allows _**any**_ form to manifest. Therefore, nothing that one can perceive would even exist, if the Unmanifest did not allow for and support it.

So God cannot then be found, seen, heard, talked to, or idealized, because that would require the thought processes of the ego. And the ego can only think in the physical and spiritual manifest levels of existence, not in the Unmanifest. The Unmanifest requires no thinking, seeing, or hearing, or any other perceptive mediums. Basically, if one sees, hears, speaks, feels, thinks, or senses in form, one cannot understand what is formless, simply because the ego's nature is not capable of comprehending it.

The Unmanifest is complete formlessness that is the substrate for All form. This is outside the ego's reality of the linear, where things have to be perceived or measured in order to be said to exist. Since this dimension lacks form, the ego lacks belief.

The Unmanifest is the pure potential that created and allowed for the manifest to form because of the unconditional and infinite love for All. The Unmanifest can only be experienced as

Oneness, and can never be perceived. If one says that they have perceived or talked to God, then they are severely mistaken, as this would mean that God is a type of form (sound), which thus limits God and contradicts infiniteness. The claim that one has spoken to God is also perhaps the most prevalent misunderstanding that confuses others. Therefore, other beings try to pray to, talk to, or see God, rather than asking to be a vehicle of Divine Love and service.

As one's level of consciousness raises and devotion is due only to God, then the experience of the Higher Self is inevitable. When one experiences Self, nothing else will be important to them, except for the Truth that most feel compelled to convey to others. It is important to note that not much can be said about God; God cannot be summed up by all of the words in the world, because that which is form cannot completely describe formlessness. Since the ego cannot comprehend or interpret the Unmanifest, the ego must first dissolve, which then allows for the experience of God as Self; this is the only way a being can experience enlightenment/ God.

The Soul's Descent from the Unmanifest

The diagram below, the paradigm of human consciousness, shows how all of the manifest stems from the only True existence, which is the Unmanifest. The Divine Source of the Unmanifest allows for 'free will,' which created the ego. Egos developed the physical and spiritual dimensions by 'will.' Between the upper and lower ego levels of consciousness is where our egos' perceived reality currently exists.

Thus enlightenment is the process of working our way up this spiritual evolutionary ladder, back to the Divine Source. It is the process of realizing the Nonlinear dimension of the Unmanifest and transcending or escaping the inferior linear dimension of the spiritual and physical manifest that the ego has created. The diagram below shows the levels of energy from the (infinitely high) Unmanifest, all the way to the ever-expansive lower frequencies of form. The Absolute Truth is the Unmanifest, but Absolute Denial is the 'Absence of Light' or 'Rejection of God.'

"The Ego Identity Crisis"

The Absence of Light is believed by the ego to exist, but it is only illusory. The ego has chosen to reside in darkness, which is believed not to be within the Unmanifest, due to the Denial of God. It feels that which is not within Light is not within God; therefore, it feels as if it is its own source of existence and it doesn't need God. But that which has been denied as the source of existence still is the Source. It is just that the ego creates its own illusory belief, via the ego itself, its perception, and its positionalities, that it is its own being.

The Paradigm of Human Consciousness

Source of Purity and Perfection — **The Unmanifest Self** — **Absolute True Reality**

Beyond Consciousness

Nondense Energy

No Thoughts or Forms Exist

Reality of One

Levels of Self is in Varying Power

Nonlinear Reality

Higher Awareness
of True Reality

Self is 'Universal Identity'

Higher Self

(Subjective Reality)

(Can only be experienced, not perceived)
-Ego is Transcended Completely-

Level of Illumination

'Existing in the Light of Truth'

Level of Enlightenment on way up

-Heavens of Nonform-

Clarity of Reality

Beginning of the Ego on way down

Level of Transition (up or down)

Slightly Occluded Reality

Abstract Thought Forms

Level of Unconditional Love

-Weak Ego- (less ignorance)

Least Dense Spiritual Energy

-Upper Heavens of Form-

(Ego Strengthens as it forms)

Conditional Linear Reality (depends on level)

(Ego's Perceived Reality)

Upper Levels of the Lower Self

Organized Thought Forms

Unlimited Realities, but Limited Perception

-Strong Ego- (more ignorance)

Dense Spiritual Energy

-Lower Heavens of Form-

Heavily Occluded Reality

Concrete and
Comprehendable
Thought Forms

Realm where many beings of <u>differing consciousness</u> dwell together

Distorted Perception

A reality that is <u>currently</u> between the <u>upper</u> and <u>lower</u> levels of consciousness

-Ego Dominates
and Controls Reality-

(self is 'ego-identity')

Physical Manifest (World of 'Solid' Form)

Physical Form

(Newtonian Paradigm of Linear Reality) (limited perception and reality)

False Reality

-Shapeless-
low energies

'The Absence of Light' (Illusion) Beings convincing themselves that they are not within the <u>Light</u>

Nonexistence

Known as the 'Hells' (Very Heavily Occluded Reality –Confusion)

---an Illusion

-Darkness-

(Doomed by the Ego) Almost always choosing the ego over Truth

Confusion

Absolute Denial of God (completely choosing ego over God/Truth/Source/love)

This chart represents the various levels of consciousness and power, which allow for the journey of the soul, as well as its decline and ascension through the Transcendent Self. All energy as manifest comes from the potential energy of the Unmanifest. The Ultimate True Reality is known as the Unmanifest Self. This is the source of all creation. All nonform potential comes from the Unmanifest and is allowed to manifest into form when conditions are necessary for the manifestation (i.e., lessons). Since the Unmanifest Self is infinite and ever-creating, infinite souls exist, many of whom have fallen from the Grace of God, or the Divine Source as One. As the ego was developed (the beginning of dualistic reality) by our decision to examine our possibilities (curiosity), we explored the new reality by exercising 'ego will.' When the 'ego will' was used, then seemingly began the creation of the spiritual manifest, or at least it brought forth the many perceivable forms from the invisible to the visible (willed into expression). This ego was a combination of thinking, emoting, and perceiving (through chakras, not eyes).

In the beginning, as the ego thought, it willed into expression the many abstract shapes that form the basis for all humanity. These shapes, such as circles, dots, and lines, were the very beginning of form (besides consciousness). As the ego learned to mix forms, it created new designs that it found to be desirable. As the ego thought, that 'thought of' reality manifested around it; as it thought of a line, it saw a line. Over time (so to speak), the ego learned to manifest more complex patterns, which in turn created brand-new realities that were even more desirable than the last (the beginning of judgment). These perceptions of forms in the Spiritual Manifest that the ego willed into expression became its reality. This reality became all it knew and it forgot other possibilities, or the True Reality from whence it came.

Throughout the soul's descent from God (Unmanifest Self), the ego started to learn how to organize thought patterns by concentrating on them. That is the beginning of linear thought, or rational/logical thinking (seeing the separation between two objects that were created implies the linear reality of distance, time, and space). The more the ego concentrated on the thought forms, the more concrete and substantial the forms (the ego's perceived reality) became. The process of concentrating on energetic thought forms hardens them; this is called 'crystallization.' This means making form 'solid' or physical, or at least perceived to be so to the ego. The difference between the precrystallized state and the crystallized is analogous to a 'thought' (precrystallized) of a table and an 'actual' (crystallized) table in the physical world.

Due to the soul never knowing anything other than unconditional love and being One, in addition to God allowing us to have 'free will' (ego), the ego decided to try its independence and practice being a god over a realm that it thought it created itself. This brought the ego happiness, because it brought a sense of joy and love when it manifested a reality over which it was a god. The process of creating is due to love. One doesn't create something that is hated. One creates out of pure love, or there is no reason to create. So in a way, the ego got to experience True Reality by feeling love when it created something. The happiness that was experienced when creating the various astral forms was displaced onto the product that was willed into expression, rather than realizing that it is the essence of God. Unfortunately, the ego realized that form only brought temporary happiness when it was created. This is because the love of God was rapidly becoming depleted due to the use of 'ego will' instead of Divine Will. After a while, the form that it created became so unfulfilling that it made an intense internal drive to create a better product, or reality. All the ego could then do was experience a product of the 'ego will,' or lower levels of consciousness, but this was naïvely done to become fulfilled, not to keep it empty.

As the desires of the ego were fulfilled and temporary happiness was acquired, the soul drifted further away from the Source. After the soul descended further from the Truth, the Reality of Truth became incomprehensible to the soul, due to the development of the ego, which acted as a shield from the Truth. The independence made the sense of 'I' prideful, powerful, strong, and in control. But when the soul fell too far from the Source, it was lost in the ego's distortions of the Truth. So these distortions became the ego's reality and were not looked at as a perception that was only distorted and could be fixed. So now the being became trapped behind its own distortions (ego) of Truth as illusion and could not see the way back to the Source where it could be fulfilled and complete once more.

The only reason the being separated from the Unmanifest and the upper levels of consciousness, known as the Higher Self, was to try to create its own reality of form over which it could be a god or creator. That sense of power and control gave it a sense of fulfillment that could temporarily satisfy itself. The ego mistakenly mistook the pleasure of the ego for the unconditional love of God. But after falling so far from the Source, nothing but misery and emptiness could be experienced from that time on.

Because the ego was concentrated and relied upon so much, it became an entity itself, as an (illusory) impersonal aspect of the soul that does nothing but deceive. The ego lies to the soul and makes it feel that everything it can experience or that is perceived by itself is reality. This makes one feel as if life would be over when the ego is no longer around. This is why ego beings fear death, because the ego fears death. The ego thinks that when this existence that it knows is over, life is over forever. However, this is not so. When the being abandons the ego, the soul is finally free and complete, while overflowing with the unconditional love of God. The Spirit is realized to be at home within and as the Higher Self, wishing that it had never left.

In sum, the soul felt the desire to be a god and exercise control over a realm that it created (temptation and curiosity). Throughout the soul's descent, the ego was created, strengthened, and then relied upon for every thought and action. The ego made the soul feel independent, powerful, and in control of the reality that it created. The emotions gave it happiness for a while, but the ego always felt as though it had to experience more and more happiness to be fulfilled. The constant drive of trying to feel happier actually created a sense of discomfort and a feeling of emptiness by comparison and judgment. This feeling of emptiness came from the lack and denial of God's love. As the ego created constant suffering, the soul tried to re-establish the connection that it lost with the Divine Source. Since the ego became established and strengthened, it then became crystallized into a lower entity.

This lower entity is not much different than being possessed by a 'demon' or 'bad spirit,' if you will. When possessed, one doesn't know they are possessed; they simply do what feels or needs to be done to reflect the consciousness that resides within and as them. The same goes for the ego. The soul has unknowingly followed the directions and distorted perceptions of the ego. The soul does not even know that it is being misled. In fact, it thinks that the ego is itself. However, that ego believes that it is the reflecting personality and the body in which it operates. This is why the ego is afraid to die, because death marks the end of its existence. Fortunately, the soul will continue infinitely and experience only unconditional love, peace, joy, and perfection as One for all eternity when the ego is transcended.

The Absence of Light?

The condition, realm, or level of the 'absence of light' does not really exist outside of the light of consciousness. This is due to the fact that light is the *existence* that holds all form, which means that no 'thing' can exist outside of light. Keep in mind that the Unmanifest is existence itself, which provides for consciousness (light). The realm of the 'absence of light' is consequently an illusion of the ego that it has led itself to believe. The ego, knowingly or unknowingly, has actually denied God and rejected the fact that light is everywhere and All. This leads to the ego thinking that it is separate from God and in its own dimension that it has created by itself. This 'false' reality manifested by the ego is one that allows the ego to feel as if it were still in control of its own life. By denying the Light of God, it has tricked itself into believing that it exists elsewhere, such as outside God, which is an impossibility. This is not possible, because no 'thing' can exist unless it is in the Light of consciousness, which is in existence (Unmanifest). Similarly, there is no such thing as 'nonexistence.'

So all is in the Light, but the ego makes one believe that they are independent or separate from God and in control of their life's destiny; therefore excluding light. Beings existing in the

235

'absence of light' realm are <u>existing</u> because they still reside within the Light of God. No being can escape the Light of God, because All is God, and God is infinite. The ego just thinks it exists in its perceived version of where it wants to be. In essence, it exists where it <u>thinks</u> the 'absence of light' is, in the basic levels of consciousness that are below the levels that are labeled as positive, which has adapted fallacy over truth. Fallacy in the 'auric field' is simply choosing the option to believe and live one's existence according to the lowest levels of truth, or the seeming absence of it. However, the ego doesn't see it this way. Instead, it believes that all it knows is the ultimate truth and it is all that can be known. It thinks that all it perceives is all that could possibly exist. So it really thinks that it is outsmarting God, but in Reality the ego is just fooling itself into thinking that it can exist without God.

Level Availability

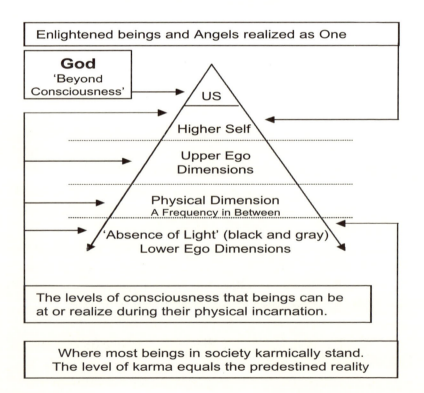

Enlightened beings and Angels realized as One

God
'Beyond Consciousness'

US

Higher Self

Upper Ego Dimensions

Physical Dimension
A Frequency in Between

'Absence of Light' (black and gray)
Lower Ego Dimensions

The levels of consciousness that beings can be at or realize during their physical incarnation.

Where most beings in society karmically stand. The level of karma equals the predestined reality

236

These lower realms of existence are the lower levels of consciousness, which are noted in sacred text as the 'hells' of existence. And just as the ego is illusion, so are the lower levels of consciousness. The beings who dwell within these realms want to suffer and enjoy being unfulfilled. These beings want company.

The ego and all of its thoughts, beliefs, conditionings, ideas, sense of self, personality, learning ability, and positionalities are all a certain degree of fallacy. Fallacy represents different levels of truth, which are not the 'whole truth.' The 'absence of light,' or the stereotyped 'pit of hell,' is absolute fallacy (denial) or the seemingly lowest level of distorted truth, while the intermediate astral dimensions, or the stereotyped 'purgatories,' are the intermediate levels of truth. In actuality, however, purgatory is available at all dimensions of existence that are not Unmanifest. The higher levels of the astral dimensions, or the lower heavens, are higher levels of truth, while the Higher Self is the 'higher heavens' of Truth, and the Unmanifest is Absolute Truth (purity) and the highest of all heavens, beyond heaven.

The beings in the 'absence of light' realm are continually fueling themselves from the light of God so that their existence is infinite and permanent. However, the ego makes itself believe that it takes care of itself, that it controls everything around it, and that it derives its own energy supply from elsewhere. So subconsciously and unknowingly, the ego is choosing nonexistence as reality, even though this is an impossibility. This is because it has tricked itself into believing that this was an option.

The reality in which the ego believes is made up, like a fairy tale springing from its own rampant imagination. The ego constantly leads itself down the wrong path, unless the higher truths are adopted and replace the lower levels of truth or fallacy. This is why one must surrender the ego (source of fallacy) and all of its prior beliefs to God in order to experience Truth/Oneness/God. When the Truths are adopted, transcension is destiny, and the absence of light within which one previously existed is realized to be an impossibility and a ridiculous mistake. This realization brings forth the understanding, or the knowing, that all is in the light and that there is no escaping it (God). By this understanding, one usually feels compelled to help others who may be suffering in the same way that they once suffered, thus making more selfless beings who live to help others be at peace.

Qualities of God/Unmanifest

The chart below denotes the qualities of the Divine Presence, in order for the ego not to be confused with the linear qualities and their innate levels of fallacy.

-Invisible
-Nonlinear
-Formless
-Stillness
-Silence
-Love
-Peace
-Happiness
-Joyful Bliss
-Beauty
-All-Creating
-Potentiality
-Complete
-Unrestricted

-Indescribable
-Stationary
-Infinite
-All-Pervading
-All-Encompassing
-Existence
-Oneness
-All-Powerful
-All-Inclusive
-Perfect and Pure
-Source
-Total
-Indivisible
-Nondualistic

These descriptive terminologies, though they cannot really describe God, can help one understand the nature of the Source. As one understands the attributes or qualities of God, an individual's quest may then take on the proper direction that would prove to be the most beneficial for that soul's evolution. Many spiritual devotees' journeys do in fact lead them astray. And many times they are prompted to become attuned to the astral dimensions or other psychic phenomena, because of their lack of knowing about the qualities or properties of God. As one is directionless, the nature of the quest may be arbitrary and confusing, thus redirecting one's path toward 'thinking' about God rather than directly 'experiencing' God subjectively.

Difference of Self

To best sum up the various realities experienced by each and every soul (some sooner than others), these should be broken into the varying degrees of Self. Where some aspects of the Self are limited, it is termed the 'lower self,' or 'ego self' (thinking mind). Then the 'Aware Mind' can be experienced as the upper levels of consciousness become one's locus of existence, known as the Higher Self. The unrestricted and unlimited Reality is termed the Unmanifest Self or 'Pure Mind.' The explanation below provides reassurance that one will not be confused.

The 'ego self' is the part of one's 'sentient (transcendental) being' or 'immediate self,' which is restricted, limited, linear, dualistic, and considered the lower states of existence. Within these lower states of existence, the lower emotional states of the ego are predominant, as are the mental states, inner and outer positionalities, and judgmental observations of the ego. This is what makes one believe that they are their own separate entity that is not a part of something as perfect as God. The ego cannot even fathom an existence in which it is One with the Source. This aspect of the sentient being's self is the source of pain and suffering.

As the lower 'ego self' is transcended, the Higher Self (which is still an aspect of consciousness, which is form) is then experienced. This is termed 'enlightenment,' or realizing that the suffering of the ego is not reality. It also allows one to know that All is One and perfectly evolving. The higher in the Self that one goes, the more pure one's consciousness becomes. Thus one progresses up through the varying levels of the Higher Self, such as *Self as Love/Light*, *Self as peace*, *Self as manifest* (pure consciousness), *Self as Logos* (subtle energetic sound), *Self as Buddha Nature* (Self as *Universal Identity*), and eventually through the Highest of Self within consciousness to the *Self as Unmanifest* (beyond consciousness itself), also known as *Mind*.

These various levels of experiential reality can only be experienced when one transcends up throughout the 'Universal

Self,' which is termed the ***transcendent mind*** or the ***universal consciousness***. One's <u>own</u> ***transcendent self***, known as the ***sentient being*** or ***immediate self***, is made up of all of the frequencies of the universal consciousness, a range of certain mixed frequencies that are changed or altered by the use of one's own 'will' or 'Will' that they choose to express. The ***immediate self*** is one and the same with the universal consciousness. The ***immediate self*** is simply the ***local reflection of consciousness and a chosen point of reference and experience*** that an aspect of the ***Universal Self*** or consciousness is currently willing to be an expression of. Each ***immediate self*** is able to choose its energetic expression at any time, and thus is a full composition of various levels of energy that range from the qualities of the ego to the Higher Self.

So each and every ***sentient being*** selects which energies they want to express. And by doing so, they become a certain expression of the various qualities of energy that they feel are necessary to use, in order to remain the expression that they currently need to be happy or to exist. This reinforces their chosen identity and/or beingness that is currently channeling the various energies of the universal consciousness. So a 'sinner' is one who chooses the lower energies of the universal consciousness, and a 'saint' is simply one who chooses the higher energies that are a direct expression of the higher levels of consciousness known as the Higher Self. This is different from the Unmanifest Self, which is beyond the realm of consciousness and frequency. So all of these different expressions of beingness, known as lower self, Higher Self, or Unmanifest Self, are all a part of the Whole and the One; it is all the oneness of ***God as Totality***.

Section Four
Understanding the Ego

"One can choose to be a servant of God and be happy, or a slave to sin (the ego) and constantly suffer."

—BN

Chapter 11
<u>The Structure of the Ego</u>

The Importance of the Ego's Structure

Understanding the structure, form, or construct of the ego is crucial. This is because one must understand what something is, how it is built or created, and how it operates, so as to help one disassemble it. If one does not understand the functions and structure of the ego, the process of transcension or enlightenment will take a very long time, perhaps lifetimes. This is analogous to an English person reading a Japanese book with no instruction from a teacher, no instruction or translation from a book, no understanding of what the words mean, and no understanding of how the sentences are structured, or of basic grammatical concepts and organizational patterns. This clearly would result in no learning or, at best, very slow progress.

The main reason that one should learn what the ego is and how it is structured is so it can be analyzed and taken apart piece by piece, by its misbeliefs, emotional attachments, and thought patterns. When the ego is analyzed and understood, Self-Realization then becomes a definite possibility within this lifetime. If done correctly, enlightenment may become one's Reality within months or a couple of years. This is much more appealing to an ego than the previous notion of taking 'many lifetimes' to become enlightened.

Analyzing the structure of the ego alone, without meditation, may bring on vast Realizations that allow the ego to become transcended completely. This is the most important aspect of enlightenment; it is called 'Self-Inquiry.' All of the great spiritual masters teach the process of looking within. Without understanding the structure of the ego, realization becomes an impossibility within this lifetime and perhaps many others. One can meditate for decades or lifetimes, every day, all day, and never become enlightened. Meditation and prayer should be used to supplement the activity of Self-Inquiry, known as ***Introspection***. This will rapidly increase one's progress.

The Ego's Main Purpose

The main function of the ego is to stay separated from the Source, or God. As all souls took the 'free-will' option that was allowed by God, we chose to descend from the Grace of God and try our luck by ourselves, so to speak. We so wanted to be just like God—all-mighty, all-powerful, ever-creating, omniscient, omnipresent, and infinitely radiating—that we chose a life that we felt we could control and manipulate to conform to our every whim. We naively thought that we could escape infiniteness and create our own kingdom of god (we being god) in some place where God was not present. This is an obvious fallacy; since God is infinite, there can be no way to exist outside of God, because God is All That Is. There is no 'existing place' that is not within God. This entirely distorted fact that we believed was possible created the illusory world; that solidified into a false reality, as separate from God, that we controlled, and created the perceived duality, or the false reality of the 'paradigm of the opposites.'

This duality is an illusion created by the newly adopted sense of ego perception, which is also an illusion. Illusion identifies, understands, categorizes, believes, trusts, follows, and perceives that which is illusion. Illusion is only capable of understanding illusion. To experience Truth, one must abandon the illusion. The illusion is simply this: "We **think** we are separate from God". That's right; it is nothing more than a **thought**. Thus begins the approach that helps one release the 'grip of sin' (which is the ego) upon a being. Resolving this thought process reveals the fact that we have never been separated from God. It is just that the ego made us believe we were, with its sense of identity, positionalities, emotions, emotional and mental attachments, mental processes, perception, and the illusion of duality created by the illusion of perception.

Nature of the Ego
(100% Correct and Definite Traits of the Ego)

1. *The ego is nothing more than an 'illusory thought' that one is separated from God.*
2. *It maintains separateness by way of the perceptive faculties, which reinforce the belief in personal identity.*
3. *It believes that it is the originator of all its actions and thoughts.*
4. *The ego blocks the Realization of Truth that in turn creates and is the source of suffering.*
5. *The only function of the ego is to exercise 'will,' which directs an infinite realm of probabilities that selects destiny at every instant of creation.*
6. *The ego is only capable of operating, understanding, and knowing about and of the linear dimension of the manifest/limited/ dualistic.*
7. *The ego's emotions and mental states rob one of True happiness (which is God, which is permanent).*
8. *The ego is incapable of understanding or experiencing God as Unmanifest.*
9. *All major religions teach one to either purify or abandon the ego, which is the cause of suffering.*
10. *The ego is only capable of being self-serving.*
11. *The ego is not 'bad'; it is just ignorant or naïve.*
12. *The ego unknowingly brings suffering when it thinks that it is helping.*
13. *The ego will deny God as the Source of happiness and Love because it fears that it will not be needed for existence and therefore abandoned.*

14. *Only the ego fears death; the spirit can never die.*
15. *The ego never created anything; it just claims ownership over the already created.*
16. *The ego 'thinks' in order to reinforce dualism.*
17. *The ego is nothing more than a 'sock puppet' reflecting and displaying its level of consciousness.*
18. *The ego reflects only the content (words, thought, actions, will) that is always within the context (meaning or level of consciousness of actions), which is within the Ultimate context of God.*
19. *The ego thinks that happiness is outside itself, which prompts the dualistic, external search.*

Process of Inquiry and Understanding the Ego

Ego's Identity

After the ego creates the illusion of separation, it assumes an identity that makes it feel as if it has control over its environment, emotions, mental states, physical body, and life's outcome. It chooses whatever identity it feels will blend in with or stick out profoundly, according to the environment that it dwells in. Most egos like to feel accepted. This feeling makes the ego want to blend in with the crowd, but have a special attribute that its peers will find extraordinary, thus creating the feeling that makes the other egos want to keep the new ego around because they admire, respect, or want to see the 'difference' of the ego. This makes the ego feel in control because it feels as if it is needed by peers, or else these peers will feel 'unamused' or 'dulled' by the absence of this new trait.

The ego judges other beings, with disgust, respect, or admiration, or as 'good or bad.' It does this in an attempt to know its place in the world, or where it stands within the levels of importance created by society. This allows it to either feel as if it needs to be more *desirable*, or to acquire more respect from others. Once its level of importance is established in the world, it judges whether to pursue another goal or trait that can also be admired by others; this inherently increases their level of importance as well.

The ego views acceptance from others as important and as a source of happiness. This 'source of happiness' is established when its dualistic mind compares the concept of having friends with having no friends. The feeling of 'no friends' or 'nonacceptance' brings about a feeling of loneliness. This feeling is obviously not very desirable or pleasing to the ego, so it seeks to acquire friendships in hopes of becoming happy.

The ego's sense of emptiness is due to the rejection of God as Oneness, or as a whole. The ego chose to have its own identity over being One with God. It traded the completion and fulfillment of God for its own false identity. It chose fallacy over Truth, in hopes that it would find another alternative source of Truth where it could rule. Unfortunately, it just created an illusion, or a false perceived reality that it made itself believe was Truth. The ego now finds an empty feeling where God's love used to be, and a sense of confusion about how to become fulfilled again. Thus the ego tries to constantly acquire 'things,' one being an identity, and the other being external, materialistic 'things' or 'items.' Both of these create a feeling of fulfillment when in the ego's possession.

One needs to keep in mind that nobody has their own identity; they just think they do. Identities are all illusions created by the illusory self, or the ego. One must realize that any identity can be programmed into the ego; therefore, no identity that one can assume is 'special.' The ego is just a manipulative machine or computer that continually gets programmed until the day it is transcended.

The Usual Identities Include:

Separateness, Specialness, Coolness, Dorkiness, Uncoolness
Stereotypes: 'Macho Man,' 'Average Joe,' 'Loner,' 'Genius,' 'Nerd,'
'Town Idiot,' 'Computer Geek,' 'Blabbermouth'

These identities create judgmentalism, which is reinforced by thought. One's identity is known by everything that one thinks they are. Identity is created by one's knowledge, beliefs, ideas, level of intelligence, what one does or doesn't know, how one dresses, whom one knows, whom one hangs out with, the school one goes to, one's family and relatives, the country and state that one lives in, the poverty level one lives in, the level of power one has, the sports one plays, one's interests and hobbies, the language one has, the accent one has, the obedience one has, the respect one receives from peers, the job one holds, etc... One must abandon these identities by realizing that they never existed in the first place. They were all just made up in one's own mind and reinforced by the perceptive faculties of the illusory ego (dualism—'perceiver and that which is perceived').

Just keep in mind that everyone assumes a role or identity in society because they have to, but in Reality there are no separations, and there are no specific identities; we are all One and the same. When one judges anything, the illusion of the many identities and duality are reinforced and believed even more to be real, therefore making it harder to realize True Reality as 'identityless.'

Abandoning the ego identity can be, and usually is, the hardest element to transcend. This and duality are usually the main blocks to realization, because one feels an overwhelming sense of loss while transcending the ego; losing one's identity is comparable to dying. It is because one comes to the conundrum, "What am I, if I am not what I had thought I was?" This creates confusion and a feeling that one has lost direction. Indeed, "What am I?" is a very important question that can only be answered by realizing the Self. The feeling of losing one's treasured and adored identity is an illusion as well. So do not worry, it will pass. As the illusion of losing one's self passes, the ultimate identity arises and is revealed: Oneness with God (Universal Identity).

Ego's Positionalities

All knowledge or learned traits bring about a positionality of the ego. A positionality has two parts: an <u>internal subjective</u> or an ego-created idea or followed belief system, or an <u>external objective</u> that relates to the 'perceiver and that which is perceived.' These two different types of positionalities create the feelings of separateness, uniqueness, specialness, and difference. Positionality reinforces duality, which brings judgmentalism, classification, and separation, and vice versa.

The ego's *internal subjectivity and imagination* are a mental process that creates a viewpoint, which it either accepts as fact or dismisses as fiction. As this experience is processed, the ego then decides it to be 'worthy' or 'unworthy' (duality) by its level of importance, which it expresses through the amount of logic or nonlogic. Items or events that are accepted as logic are usually stored within the ego mind as fact. Items or events that are nonlogical or irrational are accepted as fantasy, myth, superstition, holy, spiritual phenomena, or useless fragments of an overactive imagination. An example of this is the thought process when solving a problem within the mind: the mind thinks of many theories, but only a couple are really categorized and stored away as probable, or of any benefit for the situation at hand. However, many thoughts are discarded as nonsensical.

Examples of Internal Positionality*

- Mentally having a view about prolife or antilife
- Mentally having a view about government style.
- Mentally judging what one likes better than the other.
- A thought about a topic; problem solving.
- How one feels about different religions.
- How one feels about their level of importance.
- When one thinks about different spiritual dimensions

*Mental Position or viewpoint of a situation/being is an internal positionality.

External objectivity has to do with the perception of the ego. This type of positionality relates the viewer to what is being viewed or perceived by any means necessary. The event or person being witnessed by the ego's perceptive faculties (taste, touch, sight, hearing, smell, or psychic faculty) is relating the ego observer to the event, thing, or person being observed. This gives the observing ego a sense of 'place' within the universe due to time, distance, space, and the duality of observation, which are reinforced by the internal and external positionalities that one has. That observation makes the ego feel more concrete, or that it has its own independent reality that is specific and separate from itself.

Examples of External Objectivity*

- Looking out of the window from one's house.
- Driving a car on the road.
- Walking, running, hopping on something.
- Listening to somebody speak.
- Watching something or somebody do something.
- Analyzing duality or separateness.
- Touching a coffee cup.

*The way the perception of the ego witnesses the event, situation, or being is usually referred to as an 'external objectivity,' or an observed phenomenon.

The set of ideas, thoughts, observations, and remembered events and people that the ego has witnessed throughout its existence creates a set of different viewpoints or positionalities that make it feel more independent or separate from all others. For example, when an ego sees a tree, it knows that it is not that, or it is not a part of the tree, because the tree would have not been able to be observed or passed by. Or, when the tree is cut down, the ego does not feel pain or experience the event in the same way. This obviously amplifies the 'ego identity,' which is the very problem that keeps one from realizing their True Nature. Every view or positionality that an ego can make will reinforce the seemingly dualistic reality by placing a feeling of difference and separation between the two, thus slowing or stopping progress toward Self-Realization.

Ego's Emotional Attachments
Negativity spreads like wildfire; one level just invites the

next or lower level to activate and become inflamed. Just as 'Divine Will' attracts and is the catalyst for increasing the level of consciousness, the 'ego will' attracts and is the catalyst for decreasing the levels of consciousness. Remember the rule within the universal laws, that 'like attracts like.' Whether one has a certain belief, idea, or motive, it contains a charge that is either negative or positive. One's own negative thoughts or emotions can attract and bring forth a multitude of negative positionalities, thus taking one down in the levels of consciousness and making Self-Realization a more difficult attainment. One iota of 'insecurity' or 'pridefulness' can catapult one into a never-ending trap of the ego.

The emotions of the ego distort one's capacity for reasoning, as well as knowing Truth. Thus the emotions of the ego can make one act without reason, or irrationally. For instance, we have all heard of crimes committed in the 'heat of passion' (passionate crimes), and then the ego states after the crime is committed, "It seemed like a good idea at the time. When I saw my husband in bed with another woman, I just couldn't control myself. So I stabbed him until my mind cleared." Emotions color all activity. Those emotions are created by the ego and for the ego. Therefore, they are considered self-serving and delusional. Emotional attachments are one's block to realization and can be compared with a boat that is at full throttle but still attached by the many anchors and ties that bind it to the dock (manifest realm) and sea floor, thus not allowing it to reach its destination (Self).

Salesman's Tactics Applied to Emotional States

The 'salesman' knows these tactics well. The salesman creates a happy and comfortable environment by being friendly to the customer. So as happiness and comfort are felt by the customer, it makes it easier for the salesman to break down emotional walls. After the salesman finds out one's limitations that may restrict them from buying the 'item,' they then sympathize and identify with the customer. This makes the salesman feel like a friend and not a salesman, thus making the customer confide in the salesman like a friend.

The salesman then introduces the ego to 'the item' while creating the feeling of an emotional attachment by using visualization tactics. These create a feeling of excitement. For example, the salesman says to the potential buyer, "Just think about how all of the people will be checking you out as you drive this 'awesome car' down the street. You are bound to turn a lot of heads!" This excitement tricks the ego into believing that it needs the 'item' in order to be happy. After the 'hook' (sales pitch) is sunk into the 'fish' (customer), the salesman suddenly pulls a fast one: the feeling of 'urgency' (for example, "I'll give you this discount, but only for today"). This puts the sale into hyperdrive by creating the pressure to buy 'now.' Because the excitement is so overwhelming, the customer usually buys 'the item.' In fact, this tactic has about a 50% success rate.

These tactics are all learned in business school, or when one starts a job in sales. Salesmen are just playing with the ego to get the customer's money. All salesmen do this because they know that one cannot think rationally when emotions are involved, namely 'excitement' and 'ego-inflation.' This is because excitement, to a high enough degree, counters an inevitable feeling of loss if one were to leave 'the item' behind without purchasing it. Therefore, the customer will lean towards buying 'the item' even if they don't have the appropriate finances.

It is a widely known fact that emotions distort the ability of the ego's mind to function rationally. So it can be seen that if one understands the emotions of the ego and does not get entrapped by it, the various pitfalls in consciousness levels, created by emotional attachments, will be forfeited and the True Path to Self-Realization can be followed more accurately. The emotions and positionalities that create the inherent identity of the ego are the 'traps of sin' that are so commonly talked about. Emotions are a product of the ego that fuels its every move. So without the fuel, the ego is transcended due to its lack of power and control.

It can be seen by many religious leaders that 'salesmanship,' as well as 'showmanship,' is now a way of teaching. This is why churches are often viewed to be businesses. The pastor or religious leader starts by introducing themselves, thus creating a 'friendship' and a bond of trust. As the audience listens, the pastor makes a few statements that can be identified with, which makes the audience confident that the pastor can be trusted as knowledgeable. Due to the position that the pastor or religious leader holds, they are viewed by the audience as 'close to God' or 'holy,' even though many religious leaders are in fact very 'unholy' and self-serving. The pastor excites the audience and then sells them with subtle pressure, such as, "We do great things for society and for God; if you make a large contribution to our congregation, God will forgive your sins and bless you with more money." I have even heard a couple of pastors say, "If you don't donate money to the church, you are stealing from me, you are stealing from the church, you are stealing from God. So donate money because it pays our salary and allows us to live our life. Plus, God does not look lightly upon those who steal from him and his church" *(direct words).* Then comes the sell: passing around the donation bowls (really termed 'collection plates') while making one feel guilty if they don't contribute. At the same time, they'll tell a story from the Bible that instructs one to be giving and to give as much money as they can to the church. That's the 'pressure' and the 'sell.' On average, churches have a higher percentage rate in selling, about 70 to 80%. Therefore, they keep 70 to 80% of the audience and lose 20 to 30% permanently because of the hypocrisy of the church. Why do they have a higher selling rate? Because people feel the pressure of eternal damnation if they don't give in.

So the emotions and positionalities of the preacher's ego and those of the audience force them to make a decision on the spot; thus this is a 'pressure sale,' due to the sense of urgency. The emotions that can be felt within the church are guilt, shame, despair, regret, grief, anger, insecurity, and fear of being controlled by an 'unholy' method that the pastors supply so freely and eagerly. A 'guilt trip' should not be used by the church to force money out of its audience. Because the churches 'want and desire' money, they force (an attribute of the ego) 'unholy' energies on the audience, thus decreasing their level of consciousness at the same time as the pastors. Whether Jewish, Christian, or Muslim, religious views tend to force one to be a certain way, instead of allowing one to make their own decision or choice, which is their privilege and option of 'free will.'

Lower Ego Levels of Consciousness (darkness) — Beingness that Denies God as Reality —
(The ego emotions range from the lowest to highest of the low)

Confusion (lowest level of consciousness)

Confusion is a state in which the ego is totally confused with its identity. It doesn't know whether it is good or bad. It doesn't know why it does 'things'; it just does them because it feels compelled to do them. In some cases, a 'possession' may have taken place. In others, however, mental disorders may be the result of the confusion, or the confusion may be a result of the mental disorder. The ego doesn't know where it is in the universe (which may sound like a good thing, if one's identity is being broken to get towards enlightenment); however, it feels so insignificant that what it does doesn't even seem to matter. It feels that it is neglected and worthless. It doesn't know if it wants help or even needs help. Because of the confusion, most advice will not be heeded, nor will it feel like an option.

Humiliation

Humiliation occurs when one's identity has been challenged and degraded intensely. This overwhelming embarrassment makes one feel as if their beliefs, ideas, identity, or feelings about something are stupid, naïve, or ignorant. This then leads one to feel 'less than self,' or unfulfilled by even the ego's measures. When others make fun of or laugh at the ego's identity and beliefs, it feels disparaged, lonely, empty, fearful, and full of shame. This is the most common path that prompts many to commit self-mutilation or suicide. It may even prompt one to kill the being who made them feel the humiliation, or in return one may try to humiliate them with a vengeance.

This level of consciousness may force one to be and stay in solitude for the rest of their existence, thus staying away from that potential situation ever happening again. They obviously are antisocial, but when in social encounters, they have a very negative disposition. This is because one feels as if they have hit rock bottom, and depression is so overwhelming that they can be expected to do almost anything drastic. From this level, one may try to go lower to 'top themselves,' or they may just ask God for help because they realize that 'it can't get much worse than this.' So they hope and wish for an alternative life. If their claim and surrender to God are sincere, then the Power of God will dissolve the negativity and aid them in their transcendence.

Shame (around the same level as humiliation)

When one is deeply embarrassed or humiliated to be who they are or because of an action they have taken, this is called *shame*. When everything that they believe in, or when something that 'they are' is challenged, they feel guilty for having the emotion, belief, or identity. Thus they try to isolate themselves from others, so that the same 'identification' of the seemingly problematic 'thing' that was observed and judged by others, which created the feeling of shame, can never happen again. This level of consciousness, like humiliation, can make one feel less than adequate, or like the 'scum of society.' Shame can be compared with guilt, but in a higher capacity.

Guilt

Guilt occurs when one's identity is greatly troubling them. Abandonment of this recurrent problem is continually thought of only because unpleasant feelings come into conscious reflection constantly while one is assuming the identity or positionalities. This may also be a feeling that was triggered by not liking an action that they did, words they said, intentions they had, thoughts they had, or just being who they currently are. When one doesn't like the *guilt* that they feel, displacement is always an option. This of course leads one to blame others for what has happened, therefore sharing the guilt and pain of what they feel they are greatly troubled with.

Just because *Blame* is one level of consciousness up from

guilt doesn't mean that the individual is moving up (so to speak), or doing better than they were. On the contrary, the negative karma has now compounded, which creates a reality that is even harder to transcend above. Two wrongs don't make a right; they just make it more undesirable to be who one is.

Blame

When the ego does not want to analyze an action or intention, or the ego does not want to be caught doing an action or having an intention, it assumes the level of consciousness known as *blame*. This is an attempt not to face the reality of the outcome that their decision has created. They may blame others, or they may even accept the 'act in question,' but blame the circumstances that surrounded the event as influential or coercing. They may blame the world, the day, or the 'bad week' that they are having. They may even blame the stars, the solar system, the wind, or even God. Whatever they do, they will not fully accept the 'act in question' as their fault. This pushes the 'external conflict' into a now 'internal conflict' due to dishonesty with the Self and the self. This emotional state usually comes from intense despair that one cannot handle. The ego then pushes blame upon others so that it doesn't have to feel that it was at fault.

Despair

Despair is when the ego feels as though all is lost, and all is totally hopeless. It feels as if nothing that it can do will make it feel better, so why bother. The ego feels as if God 'has it in for them' and is trying to make their life completely miserable. They feel as though they have no friends who are willing to help and that they are all alone. This makes the ego capable of drastic measures, since it feels as though it has nothing more to live for and everybody is against it—even God. Due to a constant feeling of depression that is created with this level, suicide (or attempted) or self-mutilation can occur.

Regret

Regret is an emotional response due to having done something that does not coincide with society's current rules or morality. The ego feels 'bad' about doing the 'act in question' and is having a hard time forgiving itself. It starts to feel societal pressure because it was in error, making it hard to face society. It regrets the identity that it assumed to do the 'act in question,' and ponders forgiving oneself, blaming society or others, or staying secluded from the society that witnessed the act or identity crisis. Obviously, holding onto this regret increases one's negativity by decreasing their level of consciousness to that of despair.

Grief

Feeling a great sense of stress that affects the ego in a overwhelming way is termed *grief*. It can show up in the ego as stress, anxiety, or nervousness. If handled correctly, it can be forgiven and forgotten. The stressor needs to be analyzed so that lessons may be learned and the ego can be transcended. If grief is concentrated on and not let go, regret, blame, despair, guilt, shame, and humiliation may take place; as well as a very slow progress of the evolution of the soul. The stress can also come from others, such as a death in the family, social anxiety (extreme or constantly bothersome situations), being fired from one's job, etc…

Fear

Fear occurs when the old and known identity of the ego is falling apart; however, a new and lower level of consciousness creates another identity that creates more suffering, with much anxiety and despondence, leading to withdrawal from friends, family, social activities, and even work. This new identity, mixed with the old and known identity, creates confusion that makes the ego worry about who and what it is. It doesn't know what to expect, what to do, whom to talk to for help and comfort, or if it can handle life any more. It may feel absolutely terrified of life or the future. It may even fear the past, which brings grief and regret. If it talks over this fear with a positive being, many times this can be resolved; however, a negative being may make one's problem seem worse than it really is by perpetuating the already negative thought forms (discussed in the chapter, **'Analyzing Ego Linguistics'**).

Denial

Denial is when the ego identity refuses to admit to an act that it did, a thought that it has or had, an intention that it has, a habit that it has, people it knows, or being who it is. It is a means to run away from the reality that it has created for itself, whether an event or one's entire lifestyle and personality. This is because it is ashamed of itself for the 'act in question' and does not want to admit that it was wrong. It may not even know that the act was wrong. That would be a result of temporary confusion, misdirection, acting upon emotional impulse, and maybe even a temporary possession. One may deny themselves the truth or deny others the confession.

Nervousness

Nervousness is usually a stereotyped symptom that comes along with not being fulfilled by one's cravings, such as drugs or cigarettes. Nervousness is a common side effect of the overuse of any chakra, whether the throat, solar plexus, or root chakra. If the chakra is overactive and pulls in too much energy, nervousness is the result. It may create anger or irritation by way of the root or sacral chakra, and it may create a nervousness that comes along with pride and control, which are also associated with the solar plexus chakra. If the throat chakra is overactive, one may talk too fast, be incoherent, or just be too nervous to speak or put words into a sentence that others can understand. Deep, peaceful breathing is the most common and effective way to eliminate nervousness. Nervousness is the reason that 80% of the world's sedative intake is in the United States. The use of drugs (sedatives/barbiturates) may very well propel one into the lower states of existence and many times permanently decrease one's level of consciousness (i.e., addiction).

Craving

Craving, also referred to as 'addiction,' is basically desire in an amplified form. It occurs when desire controls one's life, thoughts, emotions, and the health of one's physical body. It can be overcome, but one must practice self-restraint and stop the ego in its tracks—not by force, but by diverting attention. One must identify the problem and then want to fix it. If not, the craving controls one's life until the end. The 'craving' level of consciousness can definitely catapult one into the lower levels of consciousness. Drugs produce this effect with ease; however, one can crave anything: food, technology, people, sex, talking, being lazy, and so on.

Desire

Any type of attachment that makes one want to do something for self-gain is *desire*. This is driven by the 'ego will,' not 'Divine Will.' To excessively want and then fulfill an act or thought is an exhibition of desire. To want to have sex, do drugs, eat food, or say something that should be held back are all expressions of the ego being self-serving. If one feels a desire, it is an emotional attachment that should be dissolved before progressing. This means, for example, having sex only with someone whom one loves, while having a monogamous relationship with them, when one *does not feel driven to by lust;* thus one can express the love during the act without the attachment of the ego's emotions that feed off lust, which is the desire. If one desires or craves ice cream, then one should not eat it until the desire passes. Love is the essence of Divine Will, so any desire or craving is a product of the ego will.

The ego can fool itself into believing that a self-serving gain or desire is actually done for other people out of love, when it is not. For instance, giving money to people seems like a noble and loving deed, but the ego may desire to be known as a 'helpful soul.' This fulfills its desire for admiration and respect among those who know what they did for others. So one must really analyze deep down their motives and intentions for doing things. Is something a self-serving deed that fulfills a desire? Or is it done out of love for God and for all of humanity, with no wants or desires for anything in return whatsoever?

Hatred

Intense dislike that can be expressed towards people or things is termed *hatred*. Hatred is usually misplaced on things: for example, 'I hate this computer.' This is just a poor way to express that one intensely dislikes something because they are irritated by it.

These individuals tend to be very aggressive physically and verbally, and also tend to be an emotional wreck. The most common statement made is, "I hate you," "I hate this," or "I hate that." This is said because they lack understanding of how to express themselves correctly. These phrases are also commonly used to make another person more angry than they already are, so in essence, they are 'stirring up the pot.'

Hatred can be programmed into one's life at any time. The usual programmings of hatred that are seen in the ego's perceived reality are 'racism' and 'sexism.' Judgment is what creates the differences that can be observed by the ego, thus creating 'likes' and 'dislikes.' Unfortunately, for this character, the 'dislike' category within the ego tends to be the most prominently expressed. This character trait, which is a part of one's ego identity, can easily be overcome if one wants to. One just needs to learn the origin of the hatred and to understand that it is all an illusion that they themselves have *willfully* programmed into their ego. If it is not seen in this way, it may never be deprogrammed.

Anger

Anger is irritation in an overdeveloped way. It can progress to hatred, if allowed to. Anger is an overwhelming sense of uncontrollable (negative) emotional responses, which stem from an already negative predisposition. When one is taught how to control it, anger dissipates. Anger is usually a product of someone offending the identity of the ego, by word, act, intention, or shared thoughts. Commonly, the ego gets angry when it tries to control a situation or a person that it can't. Beings at this level of consciousness are also very aggressive individuals. Anger, like irritation, can bring about an assortment of emotional states, such as jealousy, hatred, defilement, shame, guilt, regret, etc… It is obviously

260

not very beneficial for the soul's upward (heavenly) evolution.

Irritation

Irritation is mild anger that does not really get displayed with the full flamboyant array of emotions. Instead, it is usually seen as the ego losing patience and getting a little 'testy.' This can be seen as a being's 'breaking point.' It can easily go into anger if prompted to. One may never get irritated in their life again if they become understanding and compassionate.

Jealousy

Jealousy is a condition that is brought up into awareness many times during one's life. This is why people want a bigger house, a nicer car, more money, better-looking boy/girlfriends, etc... It is an attempt to cover up who they really are, or to accentuate the kind of lifestyle and personality that they think they have, or want. This also goes along with their false identity that they think is 'real.' It may lead to motivation to succeed in the physical life, or it may bring shame because of goals that have not been reached. Jealousy may go out of control and turn into an intense craving or desire, thus catapulting one to a lesser level of consciousness.

Control (others or situations)

Control is when the ego wants and attempts to make someone or something go their way or how they want it to be. Due to the lack of fulfillment brought on by the ego's denial of God, a new source of happiness is chosen that is assumed to bring in fulfillment; such as if the event or situation goes as planned. If the event or person doesn't go their way, an amplified feeling of loss and the fear of having lost or currently losing control manifests as reality, dropping one to the lower levels of consciousness: irritation, anger, and maybe even hatred. Control should be relinquished, so that life is just allowed to happen as it should by the Grace of God, in the Now, that is brought forth by the acceptance of God and the abandonment of the ego.

Insecurity

Insecurity is the result of an unstable (ego identity) reality being questioned. The ego then becomes defensive, controlling, angry, irritated, and sometimes hateful. All problems arise from the ego, yet all lower level of consciousness problems stem from the 'identity insecurity' of the ego. Insecurity is the main breaking point of the ego. If one is insecure, many problems may follow. If this is caught early and one is shown why not to be insecure, transcension from this level of consciousness is very possible. One needs simply to learn and realize that everything is progressing perfectly within their level of consciousness and Divine Will. If one doesn't want to deal with the insecurities that they think they have, then they must ask only God for help and transcendence.

Pride

When one's identity is challenged, an emotional roadblock is put up. This means that the ego thinks they are so right about something that they will never admit their error or admit that another being was right. They will 'stick to their guns' and won't back down. *Pride* is an attempt to block the feeling of insecurity so it never takes place. The ego will defend, sometimes irrationally, every thought, belief, idea, concept, or piece of knowledge that they have, or would rather die. Only an ego doesn't like to have its perceived reality questioned. Consciously, the ego doesn't like to have its knowledge or standpoint questioned. Unconsciously, they feel that their identity and existence are challenged; thus they apply a defense to secure their identity and perceived reality. Reinforcing identity with pride also reinforces one's feeling of separateness.

Not only does this level of consciousness indicate that an ego is overly attached to their beliefs and positionalities, but it also implies that the ego believes too much in the illusory world of the manifest. This can be seen, for example, in the bodybuilder who worships physical appearance, or even in one who believes that their personality or their physical body is who and what they are. Giving too much credit to or belief in one's body and personality as well as one's viewpoints is being prideful in one's lower self (the illusion). To think that one's mental, emotional, and physical attributes are what make up one's identity is also a main block that holds about 80% of society back from any realizations of the True Reality.

Righteousness

This is when the ego likes to initiate conversations with others, just to get into a confrontation to show that their positionality is 'better than' another being's views or beliefs. It is an attempt to prove others wrong. *Righteousness* is a technique that blocks out the potential for feeling or being insecure. It is applied to help one's sense of insecurity feel more secure. If one feels as though they are dumb, then they may try to prove others wrong, no matter what the cost, thus trying to prove all others 'dumb.'

Preachers say that God is 'righteous,' but in effect they say that God is prideful. This is an obvious misunderstanding; it can now be seen that 'righteousness' is an emotional exhibition that is based on the polarities of the ego and not of God. What they mean to say by this teaching is that God's way is the 'right way,' or the 'righteous way' (in the right), meaning that this way is the 'correct direction' if one wants to know God. This is why many religious followers *act piously*. They think that it is all right to act pridefully, or to be full of righteousness, because that is what the churches teach them and what the preacher's ego commonly displays, or to be proud of themselves (ego) and in Jesus/God/Allah/etc...

To have pride in something or someone places importance on that 'item' or 'being' that is greater than one's self and others; thus bringing forth one's judgmental values while reinforcing one's belief in duality: the linear, manifest, and their illusory identity. So in essence, pride reinforces the illusion that one is trying to escape.

Ego's Mental Processes

All mental abilities or processes are created by the current construct of the ego mind. These mental processes help one function throughout the physical incarnation and the journeys throughout the universal consciousness, but are not needed in Absolute Reality. Such things as ideas, thoughts, pictures, and memories are the main mental functions typically related to the ego mind. There are many more, however, such as organizing, classifying, recognizing, identifying, judging, prioritizing, separating, denoting importance and nonimportance, delineating events, categorizing, interpreting, and comparing all events, people, and things. This is excluding the ego's mental faction that controls the brain and bodily operations, such as movement/proprioception, neural reception and conduction, speech, the ability to function autonomously and nonautonomously, involuntary and voluntary actions, and the repair and regeneration of numerous cells.

The ego mind has no importance within the actual Unmanifest Reality. This is because the ego mind functions on structured energetic patterns, has to have structure and order, needs dualistic perception or objectivity, and is only able to function within the linear dimension—all which are inherently form. This style of operation, which is the ego mind within the linear, contradicts the Supreme Reality, which is Nonlinear, Nondualistic, and nonform.

The ego mind is a treasured commodity of and by the ego. It is, in a sense, 'in love' with its ability to reason within the logical and rational constructs of time and space (linear). It is a tool of the ego that slows the progression to spiritual unity. The ego tricks one into thinking that one can actually think on their own. It makes one feel that they would be useless without it, making one strive to be the most intelligent. It is of course supported in our society—for example, when a school gives out awards for the highest grades or the biggest scholastic improvements. In Supreme Reality, none of this is needed, nor is it important. The ego mind is form and can only interpret form; therefore, it cannot interpret or realize the nonform quality of God.

Education and schooling are of some benefit, though; they create a 'trustworthy' bond between knowledge and the ability to accept it as having value or nonvalue. They create reliability in thought processes, which allows one to choose their life's path or direction while trusting one's self fully. They can, however, be taken, and usually are, out of context. Teachers and parents always teach their children that knowledge is the <u>most</u> important part of life. That is false. The process of learning just creates more boundaries that ultimately block the ego and lock it into the false reality of form. This inherently makes transcending the ego and the limited realm of pain and suffering more difficult.

The ego mind is not given up without a struggle. As one tries to transcend thought (the ego), it continually throws thoughts into consciousness, occluding or obstructing silence any chance it gets. Silence is the 'communication' of God, or the Supreme Reality. To know silence or 'no-mind' is to know God.

The 'Silence of God' will dissolve the ego and its many functions, thus creating the fear of nonexistence. As one begins to dissect or disassemble the ego's thought processes, decrease the response to and interpretation of physical stimuli, and understand the nature of consciousness, the ego will dissolve and release its control, freeing one from **Samsara**, the karmic wheel of rebirth, as one's mind becomes silent.

Ego's Perception

The ego's perception is the ability to touch, feel, smell, taste, see, and hear; it includes the sixth sense. These all allow the ego to feel or sense itself in an area or location within the universe. All types of perception solidify the 'perceived reality' that the ego has its own identity and is separate from others and the Source. For instance, as wind caresses the body, the ego, without any other means of perception, can feel that it is somewhere (air or universe) or within something. The ego also feels heat or warmth on the skin, which identifies that it is close to a source of heat such as the sun, oven, stove burner, or someone's warm breath.

The ego, when in an elevator, can feel the shift of gravity and the weight of the body, as well as different pressures in altitude (less air pressure when higher, more air pressure when lower) as the elevator moves. This 'feeling' sense of the ego allows it to approximate where it is in the universe, thus placing itself within the dualistic and linear reality while reinforcing its 'identity of location,' such as 'in the mall,' 'on the grass,' 'in the chair,' and so forth. As dualism is reinforced by these means, Truth is hidden.

As the ego smells a scent in the air, whether food or perfume, it can detect the whereabouts or location of the item being perceived. Many times, the perceptive faculties of the ego mind work together and can pinpoint the exact location of an object accurately. As the breeze is felt from a certain direction, a smell can obviously be picked out as coming from that direction, thus pinpointing the scent over there and the ego right here, either close to or far from the smell. This perceptive process picks out two locations, self and perceived object (dualism), making the ego feel more comfortable in its whereabouts.

With all of the ego's perceptive faculties operating, a firm or concrete sense in its location within the universe is confidently established. With all senses operating at their prime, one sees where they are by all of the objects around them, feels where they are by the physical and spiritual energies in the universe, smells the scents in the atmosphere, hears sounds from all directions, and is constantly touching things that are around one's self (walking on land, swimming through water, holding the car keys, wearing clothes, opening doors, and feeling the basic movements of the physical body). This, in combination with the ego having its own thoughts, ideas, beliefs, concepts, problem-solving abilities, stored memories of past life events, knowing where it lives, knowing its likes and dislikes, and having knowledge and emotional states, plus feeling the pain or pleasures of the physical body, it is no wonder that close to 99.99999% of the world never becomes enlightened.

As the ego constantly bombards itself with its own delusions for self-gain, while covering up its fear of self-inadequacies with any fallacy that can be used, one understands that 'clearing the mind' is very important and will propagate the evolution of the soul. Daily meditation, breathing exercises, and the *'Process of Ego Release'* (Chapter 13) will allow the surface chatter of the mind to shut down. With greater clarity in mind, the ego can be analyzed and disassembled with ease through the process of introspection. When one begins to introspect and understand the nature of consciousness, the Self reveals a little more, reaffirming one's convictions of Reality and innate knowingness.

Ego's Perceived Duality

Due to a being's *free will*, the ego was created so that it could feel and think that it was separate from the Source, thus giving strength to the illusion of being an 'independent entity.' As soon as the ego made itself think that it was separate from the Source, dualism resulted by way of thought and perception, which was simultaneously inherited with the condition of becoming the ego because it is the ego. Furthermore, an eternity of illusion is certain if the path towards enlightenment is never sought. It is important to note that the very idea that 'beingness' ever existed signifies the actual beginning of dualism. This is because if one thinks that there is 'beingness,' then there must be 'nonbeingness' as well—but this is a figment of the ego's imagination, in which it may become entrapped. Likewise, the Unmanifest is existence itself, but it doesn't 'think' that it is existence or beingness; instead, it simply just is, without mentation, thought, or a reinforced feeling. When something is existence, there is no need to 'think' that it is existence; it is superfluous.

The newfound mechanism of perception allows dualism to be reinforced and falsely believed to be reality. This perception is what allows judgment, identifications, classifications, self-identity, and a false or illusory world to be examined as reality. Because the essence of the ego is illusion and can only know illusion, it is not capable of seeing or knowing Truth. The perceptive faculties of the ego mind are illusion, and they perceive illusion, create illusion, interpret illusion, judge illusion, categorize illusion, study illusion, reinforce illusion, and only believe illusion. And if the ego 'thinks' that it knows Truth, then that is an illusion also. So why follow the illusory path? Because the naïve ego simply doesn't know any other reality than the illusory. The Supreme Reality is revealed when the false positionalities of the illusory (ego) self are abandoned and surrendered to God.

So the perceptive faculties of the ego mind, combined with the ability to mentally process internal and external energetic stimuli, allow it to identify, classify, and judge 'things.' So as the ego processes the interpreted external items or 'things,' arbitrary dichotomies were developed to help the mind rationalize the illusory world so it made more sense. Such paradoxes within the ego mind created the 'belief of the opposites.' These opposites are seen and known to egos throughout the world: hot and cold, light and dark, high and low, better and worse, good and bad, small and big, pretty and ugly, smart and dumb, tall and short, fast and slow, interesting and boring, white and black, heaven and hell, heavenly and satanic, left and right, ripe and rotten, hot and cold, wet and dry, life and death, etc… The fact is that all seeming differences or opposites are just created within the mind of the ego and have no actual Reality whatsoever.

In Absolute Reality, opposites have never existed and never will. To the ego, opposites are *believed* to be within existence as Reality. False ego thinking is exhibited in such events, theories, or concepts. For example, in religious thought, there will be a battle between heaven and hell—as if the 'king of illusion' (satan) could actually defeat or even pose a threat to that which is Truth and the only infinite, immutable existence (God). The Truth of the matter is analogous to how birds fly through the sky; the sky (God) remains unaffected by the birds (satan/demons/sinners). That which is illusion cannot affect Truth. It is like swinging a bat (ego/sin) in the air (God), affecting nothing, controlling nothing, dominating nothing, and harming nothing—it just goes right through. One could say that the bat (ego/sin) may think it is affecting or controlling the air (God), but it is all just an illusion. On the other hand, Truth can dissolve illusion within a split second.

Truth is the unlimited and infinite power that 'just is' the essence of All That Is. The ego makes itself think and believe that it is separate, or not part of the whole. The force field of the ego is limited and can manipulate energy for its own purpose or self-gain. The ego can force itself to believe what it wants, but when the limitations of the force 'give in' or 'run out,' the ego will surrender to God and All will be realized as Oneness. Identity and duality can be forced to be believed by the ego for quite some time, but eventually, the infinite and unlimited power of God will dissolve the illusion that unknowingly 'causes' great suffering as long as it is perceived. So the last step of the enlightenment process is transcending the illusion of duality and the identity of a 'spiritual adept or devotee.'

The 'universal consciousness,' another aspect of the 'universal whole,' is a never-ending display or portrayal of various energies that come in a never-ending range of frequencies. These frequencies, some of which can be perceived by the ego, are then objectively interpreted by the perceptive faculties of the ego mind. In so doing, the certain range of frequencies within that it can perceive will then be said to exist; but this is only because these frequencies are within the ego's visibility. Unknown to the ego, though, are all other frequencies, which are beyond the ego's perception in the invisible realm. So the ego only decides in its mind that what it can see is 'real,' thus discarding all other energies that are in the realm of the invisible as 'false.'

This invisible realm being discussed is not the Unmanifest (even though it is invisible as well); instead, it is just the other many frequencies that are beyond the perceivable limitations of the ego, but still within the universal consciousness. This denotes the range of frequencies that is deemed as real and 'not real.' But it should be known that the ego only labels as 'real' that which it can perceive, and it only really believes in this as well.

Throughout this limited linear realm of form are seen the many objects that the ego judges. As the objects within its reality are compared, an inevitable set of similar and dissimilar values is set aside. By this there is seen 'light,' which obviously brings up the dualistic opposite of 'dark.' And as 'life' is experienced, 'death' then becomes known. Just the same, as a 'female' is encountered, a 'male' then becomes labeled and said to exist. So as the ego experiences the many perceivable forms within its realm, it then labels all 'things' as well as their seeming opposites. Thus, the scale of the visual phenomena of 'duality' is then seen to be a reoccurring theme within its reality. So the ego then naturally believes this to be 'real' and of some importance. Unknown to the ego, this very duality that the ego objectively witnesses and believes in is its very beingness itself (the structure of the ego is reinforced by opposites). Obviously, believing in this type of reality would then reinforce its feeling of being separate from everything else in the universe, such as an 'ego and every other ego,' an 'ego and God,' an 'ego and the universe itself.' And since the ego wants to be separate from everything else, it then enjoys concentrating on the dualistic nature of the linear. For every perceptive experience helps it to feel a little more stable and permanent, making the ego feel as if duality is reality and nothing else is.

❧

Chapter 12
<u>Character Differences</u>

Various Ego Identities

As the soul goes through its long evolutionary process, it assumes many identities within each lifetime. Each identity represents the soul's current level of consciousness and the overall environmental influences that have affected its development and shaped its perception of reality. As the perception of reality changes, so does the identity. Whether the changes occur on the physical level (which is easier to notice) or on the spiritual, mental, and emotional level, society *usually* perceives the identity as 'normal'; but to be without an identity seems odd to the ego. If one actually studies and observes the ego's character traits, behavior that is displayed, and the meaning of it, one can realize that there is no 'normal person,' for all beings have an identity and serve to protect it.

But if 'normal' represents the majority of beings within the context of the *__entire__* universe, where the higher power is unlimited, one can understand that to be enlightened is normal and to have an ego (lower energy) is not 'normal.' Since God is infinite and enlightened beings abound (on the higher planes of existence), then egos are really the ones who are trying to be different. It is just that all of the *visible* egos who are trying to be so 'different' are all within the manifest dimensions of the physical and the astral; therefore they cannot perceive or know of the Higher Truth and all of the beings who emanate it, meaning that egos are all on earth (or within the manifest) to understand that they are not being 'normal,' but instead are trying to be 'different.' They do this by creating an illusory identity called an ego, which expresses the many character traits that simply reflect their current level of consciousness, which they actually believe they are.

This ego creates a version of a character that it feels or thinks is a 'one-of-a-kind' identity, which to others must seem unique because of the ego's personality that puts their own stamp of 'specialness' on it. In essence, however, all beings are just pure Spirit that has created the belief (with the aspect of consciousness) that they are separated from God and are 'special' in their own way.

This false identity leads one to act pridefully in one's beliefs and knowledge, while creating competition between other egos—for example, the alcoholic who tries to *outdrink* another alcoholic, the 'pot smoker' who tries to *outsmoke* another smoker, the 'nerd' who tries to *outsmart* other nerds (and the whole school as well), the mechanic who tries to *one-up* another mechanic, the preacher who tries to *outpreach* another preacher, or the child who tries to *run faster* than the other children. All of these feeble attempts to *outdo* other egos are done to make the ego's identity— who and what it thinks it is—'special.' Disillusioned, however, the ego is trying to make a 'name for itself'…or so it thinks. Unfortunately, with that name comes the consequence of suffering. It is just trying to be recognized by other egos as 'special' or unique for an ability that is supposedly 'better' than that of others, but unconsciously it is trying to deny the presence of God with all its might.

This is where the ego who **thinks** it is very spiritual or religious says, "I'm a Christian," or, "I believe in God, so what you just said doesn't describe me." Statements such as these are an attempt by the ego to deny that it is protecting its identity by making a claim. To state one's belief, such as, "I believe in God," reinforces their identity as a 'believer identity.' A true 'identityless' being would simply say nothing, but in an effort to help others, may state Truth.

If one is not completely enlightened, then that ego is clinging to its *perceived* view of self, or 'identity.' If one ever competes with another, themselves, or an unknown idea of what one should be, then they are denying God to fulfill their identity (ego), which fuels their crisis of ignorance. After some thought, one may realize that they are competing for the title of an illusory state of existence whose purpose reinforces just a **thought** they have, such as, "I'm the best mathematics teacher in the whole school," or "I'm the best runner in the world because I won the Olympics." All physical accomplishments are illusions, just as all possibilities of an identity are illusory. So why does one compete for an illusion? Because they think that it is real. This is no different than if a con man says to a person, "I'll pay you 2 million dollars if you can jump over that 4-foot wall," then later, after the ego accomplishes that goal and waits for the prize money, it realizes that there never was any money in the first place. This shows the ego that its ostensible accomplishment was just 'wasted energy' and did not bring the happiness or fulfillment that was thought to follow.

Due to one's denial or lack of realization of Truth, which created the perceived manifest reality that one believes is the only reality, the ego searches endlessly for new accomplishments, material things, relationships, identities, or anything else that it believes will bring it happiness. But in the end, True happiness, love, and fulfillment are realized always to be a quality of God. Thus one realizes that they have spent lifetimes or eons searching for happiness, when it has existed as one's very own Self at all times, just waiting to be recognized.

Character Differences

— What are the differences between an enlightened being, an ordinary person, a preacher, and a saint?

The percentages next to a being's title represent an approximation of how many individuals like these are within the world. However, these percentages are very close to the actual percent. *(Note: for the Enlightened Being, .000001% is David Hawkins' findings for the percentage within the earthly incarnation.)*

—Enlightened Being (Sage, Mystic)—
The Levels of Consciousness of the Higher Self
Percentage of Beings within the Universe (.000001%)
These beings have completely transcended the ego and are

273

the Truth that they preach. They may speak or be silent and still; the effect on visitors is the same. They continually radiate the essence of God. They pray every instant of the day, and hold 'good intent' for all beings to become Self-Realized. They walk around the earth silently blessing all beings to be happy and at peace. Their presence uplifts the souls of mankind and lessens the grip of the ego, while simultaneously helping others transcend their karma. Their presence is a silent blessing upon all beings because of the Presence that comes forth with them.

Because these beings are Truth, they **know** Truth. All of their ego beliefs are dissolved, which then reveals the purity, perfection, and Divinity of the Unmanifest Presence within All. They unconditionally love all beings, no matter what these beings do to others or themselves. Their purpose is to help all beings spiritually evolve, or become enlightened. Because the enlightened being has no ego that controls them, their existence is a product of Divine Will, or God's Grace. They live life 100% for humanity and not for themselves (ego). The enlightened being knows and feels that All is One by way of constant subjective experience that sometimes translates into verbal transmission for the conveyance of Absolute Truth, thus benefiting all who hear them.

No one understands exactly what these enlightened beings are going through; thus they are often viewed with skepticism. Enlightenment is a very difficult Reality to explain to the ego, since it is not equipped to understand the True nature of existence of the Unmanifest, Nonlinear, and Nondualistic. Since the ego cannot truly understand or comprehend the experiences of an enlightened being, their family and friends may withdraw, either physically or verbally.

— The Saint (Example: Saint Francis of Assisi) —
The Highest Levels of Upper Ego Consciousness
Percentage of Beings within the Universe (.000006%)

Also known as 'bodhisattvas' (destined to realize the Self), these beings have felt what it is like to have no ego but currently operate within one. They have had a taste of enlightenment called a *Samadhi* but returned to their ego in order to communicate more easily with others. Just like enlightened beings, they channel the healing power of Divinity that may heal others' mental, emotional, physical, or spiritual blocks, which may manifest as disease or illness. The Presence that flows through them helps to uplift mankind as a whole (universal karma) and transcend other beings' personal karma. In extremely rare cases, some have been said to be branded with 'stigmata' (depending on their religion), *__most times not__*.

These are people who commit and live their existence about 95% for other people and 5% for themselves. Just like enlightened beings, they will go miles out of their way to help someone in need, even if the average person (ego) cannot see the need. They also see and feel that all beings are connected as a whole, even if they are not sure how. They usually do not speak of Oneness because they themselves do not feel completely 'One' due to the ego, which has set that limitation or boundary. At times, it may be hard for others to understand them, thus causing a loss of some friends and maybe the withdrawal of family.

—Preacher (an Ego Teaching Some Truth)—
Usually Low/Middle, Upper Ego Levels of Consciousness
Percentage of Beings within the Universe (1.999993%)

These beings bring some 'light' or truth to existence, but they are also occluded with many ego beliefs, superstitions, folklore, and misconceptions that block true realization; thus they are not enlightened. The block to the realization of Absolute Truth occurs because these preachers still actively use the ego, which distorts Truth into a personal belief. A preacher, unless enlightened, is theologically or belief oriented and preaches the distortions of Truth as truth. Their egos are convinced that they are right and almost no one can tell them otherwise, except a person of the church who is higher in rank (such as a cardinal, bishop, or pope).

Integrous preachers also try to help others be 'better' people. They may preach half-truths, but at least these are within the light of God. They do help people care for other beings. They help one stop and think, "Should I do this?" They reinforce life with a higher truth that has never been experienced by the lesser ego (normal society). They help people understand that the sole reason for their existence is God. They make people feel that life is more important than they had previously believed. They give people hope in life, and help others feel that life is enjoyable and not so bad after all.

Most of these churches' 'outreach programs' are phenomenal. The preachers of these churches help to coordinate philanthropies that truly touch the compassionate side of mankind, thus making one strive to be a being who dwells within the light of God and who can help to change humanity positively. These individuals make up about **1.999993%** of our society.

Preachers range from many degrees of understanding to a closed-minded view of life. This really depends on whether they are integrous or nonintegrous individuals, and the impact their environment has had on their beliefs. Their level of understanding also differs, due to the amount of their lives they want to devote to the service of God. This inherently reflects the balance of the ego and the Divinity within that has been revealed. They may be *80% serving others and 20% self-serving, 60% serving others and 40% self-serving, 40% serving others and 60% self-serving, 20% serving others and '80% self-serving*, or even *1 to 10% serving others and 90 to 99% self-serving*. Because the ego is self-serving and the Divine Will is always serving others, only a truly enlightened being who is 100% devoted to God can be 100% committed to serving others. The reason for this is that the ego does not hinder the enlightened being's unlimited capacity for the Self (unconditional love), which allows that being to serve others by interjecting the Presence of God, which spontaneously heals others. The enlightened being has no 'wants,' while the preacher is still deciding what they 'want' in order to be happy.

These individuals often preach that enlightened beings, or those who claim 'that everyone is One with God,' are demonic or 'satanic'; however, they themselves are just a realization away from the level of enlightenment. Enlightened beings do not mind these claims, for they are of the ego and fallacious. Because the enlightened being has no identity or ego, these words do not affect them adversely. Only the identity (ego) can be challenged; existence is Truth and cannot be challenged (it 'just is'). These preachers are recognized by enlightened beings, however, as making it more difficult to help others understand Absolute Truth. This is not viewed as a problem; 'it just is what it is.'

Theologians and religious beings can be very judgmental, just as they were trained to view their God to be. These religions are almost like a dictatorship, and say things such as, "Do this or go to hell," "Say this or go to hell," or, "Believe this or go to hell." They make everyone fear God in an effort to control the congregation. For instance, Catholic nuns have been known to smack or beat misbehavers with 3 rulers taped together (so it hurts more) to keep students in order at Catholic schools.

Preachers and theologians, and their congregations for that matter, are usually closed-minded and set in their unchangeable ways (programmed egos). There is usually no hope of helping them understand their True existence as One. In fact, they often become very upset or defensive when an enlightened being tries to help them understand who they are, because their ego is trying to protect its identity. For if all that they have learned is not true, they then lose their faith in their religion, and lose their trust in their perceived reality and the people who taught them. They are not prepared to let go of their beliefs and accept Truth. Most would rather die with the knowledge that they feel comfortable with, than change or unprogram their identity.

Duality rules most of the preachers, theologians, and religious beings' existence. They feel as if God is in heaven, away from humanity and the earth, while God judges us from afar, waiting for us to falter. They feel that God hates sinners and will punish them, while reserving (in some texts) a limited spot in heaven for 'Jesus believers.' They feel that if one doesn't believe exactly what they believe, than 'hell' is their destination. This means that they prejudge other beings continuously, even though the Bible says, "Thou shalt not judge" (this is also an example of Christians not following Jesus' teachings).

Along with those beliefs, most preachers feel that one must

believe that Jesus rose from the dead, or one is not a Christian. Somehow they lost the point of Jesus' sermons and teachings; they don't usually follow the teachings but still think they are 'good Christians.' In fact, there are many (**not all**) Christians that are nonintegrous people, but they feel that they will go to heaven because they believe that Jesus existed, died, and rose from the dead. A famous Christian pastor stated on her television series, "Through a recent poll, nearly 75% of Christians admit that they lie on a regular basis and nearly 91% of all people lie on a regular basis" (this denotes a nonintegrous and nontrustworthy ego for Christian followers, as well as non-Christians). She understands that Christians are not really displaying Christianity or Christ's teachings very well, so she centers many of her sermons on that fact, creating more spiritually developed Christians.

Author's Personal Note

During my first 13 years of life as a Christian in a private school, nearly all of the people whom I knew were nonintegrous and nontrustworthy, but I still thought that they were 'good Christians.' Later in my life's journey, I met people who were self-proclaimed 'die-hard' Christians, but who would steal from stores, were cheap and stingy (selfish) people, and had a negative view of life. But let it be said that ***not all*** Christians or followers of any other religion are this way; to say this would be a judgmental viewpoint, rather than an observation. The preceding section on 'preacher egos' was written to help others understand that just because one is a 'preacher' or works in a church does not mean that they are 'holy' or enlightened.

Nearly all religious followers believe that God is linear and lives in a linear environment (a limited heaven, such as heaven there and earth here, with both confined to their own designated locations), while having nonlinear (unlimited) powers, but with traits of the ego (which would show limitation and distortion). They believe that God will directly intervene and help them win the lotto, win the sports game, get an 'A' on their test, or wipe out the enemy while sending them to hell. These beliefs are really very primal and distorted. This is why I stopped going to church and a private school. I felt as though I had been programmed (brainwashed) enough, leading me to deprogram myself.

—Ordinary Trustworthy Person—
Lower Levels of Upper Ego Consciousness
Percentage of Beings within the Universe (18%)

This being operates with an ego for self-gain but also helps others once in a while. They may be seen helping others, or they may simply hold a 'good intent' within their mind most of the time. They feel pleasure from helping others, yet they would rather focus on their own life and immediate family. These beings can be trusted but are living a lifestyle that is easily coerced by the illusory pleasures of temptation. The ego still has a somewhat equal grip to that of Divinity, which is already revealed and which portrays and exhibits itself as conditional love for others and usually un-conditional love for family.

These beings usually do, or want to do, the 'right thing' (Divine Way), but the ego's temptations are a constant nuisance. By nature, these individuals are kind people. However, if the ego's temptations suck one in, they may plunge into an 'act of sin' that could trigger a downward spiral into a life of negativity. If the ego doesn't take control (ego will) of this gentle balance of 'Divine Will' and 'ego will,' loving deeds will be done on a daily basis. Once the 'ego will' takes control, however, it is almost inevitable that one plummets in level of consciousness towards the ordinary 'nontrustworthy' person. These 'trustworthy beings' only make up about **18%** of our society. To be trustworthy, one must be honest with themselves and others most of the time. So a 'trustworthy being' is not even honest all of the time.

—Ordinary Nontrustworthy Person—
Lower Levels of Lower Ego Consciousness
Percentage of Beings within the Universe (80%)
These beings choose 'ego will' over 'Divine Will' almost

all of the time. They make up about **80%** of the world. They choose to better themselves within the physical world and will step on most beings' toes, if they get in the way. They disrespect most beings through intention and will; however, they may act nicely to others to show that they are a 'nice' being, in order to preserve their identity as a 'good person.' This is done to gain the trust of individuals around them, to 'set them up,' so that when they are least aware and the opportunity arises, these beings will think, "Take what's mine, no matter what." They will lie, cheat, and steal when presented with the right opportunity, even if they seem nice, honest, and respectful. They usually look clean-cut, like 'a regular Joe,' but not always.

These beings are the very essence of self-serving. They do not wish to help others. In fact, their attitude is usually, "Why should I help them; what did they do for me?" At church, if they even go or care that they are there, they may put in a couple of dollars for a donation, but their attitude will be, "This is a waste of money." Or their intention will be to trick other people into believing that they are respectful, kind individuals. Respect and admiration are the ultimate compliments to a self-serving individual. They will do anything to get compliments from others and to have others agree with how they feel or how they think. These beings cannot be truly trusted on earth or in the astral dimensions, for they do not really care about anyone other than themselves.

Unlike 'trustworthy beings,' who are attracted to love and the more positive qualities or expressions of Divinity, 'nontrustworthy beings' are attracted to the 'nontrustworthy' qualities of the ego: pride, hatred, acting cool, acting special, being egotistical or stuck up, thinking they know it all, etc... They actually like to talk to other beings who exhibit the same qualities as themselves. These are an example of a 'good friend' to nontrustworthy beings.

—Disheartened Ego-Being—
(Part of the Ordinary Nontrustworthy)
When the ego takes too much control of one's life, it can make one feel depressed, unimportant, ugly, and a waste of exist-

ence. This severe depression, <u>created by the ego</u>, can usually make one contemplate suicide once or twice, or every single waking moment of one's existence, depending on the lifestyle that one is living. If there is some happiness, then life may be sustained only with the integration of those 'happy people or things' that are believed to bring happiness. If these are lost, then suicide or even homicide seems like a 'good deal' at the time.

These beings will usually try to convince themselves that they do not have most or any of the nontrustworthy traits of the ordinary nontrustworthy being discussed above. Instead, they say, "I don't even like myself, so I obviously am not that type of person, so I must be the ordinary trustworthy type." This is the usual response when one misunderstands the meaning of the term ego. Whether one likes themselves too much or hates themselves, it is still an expression of their ego.

These beings have created a reality where almost nothing can be done or said to cheer them up. In medicine, this is labeled depression. The person may say, "Well, I am a pretty honest person; just ask any of my friends." However, they are not honest with themselves at all. And they are so encompassed by this 'dependent reality' that they are convinced they must have something in order to be happy. They cannot even conceive of the source of happiness as being within themselves. They cannot conceive of themselves, 'this depressed wreck,' as being a part of something as wondrous as God. Therefore, their own reflection of who they are actually blocks their realization of happiness, simply because they do not feel worthy to be 'One with God.' The feeling of depression and loss is just a taste of what 'hell' really feels like, just as higher states of consciousness, *Samadhis* or mini-enlightened states, are a taste of what God feels like. It can be very hard to convince these beings that life is worth living, but it can be done only if their egos so allow.

If an enlightened being comes in contact with one of these disheartened beings who wants to change, instantaneous change may occur without warning. The enlightened being may not even say a word. All it takes is the intention or will of that disheartened ego to change and become filled with the Divine Will that the enlightened being channels. This is how spontaneous healing (change) occurs. For example, a drug user can spontaneously become a Christian missionary, or an ego on death row can spontaneously accept Jesus or Buddha as their savior. All it takes to change is *sincere* surrender to God, giving up all that one has made one's self to be (ego identity), and asking God for help. If one is not truly sincere, the ego will attempt to make one think that it wants change, but it really does not. The ego will just add 'fake sincerity' to its repertoire of what it thinks it is, furthering the ego identity crisis and choosing illusion over God once more. This basically means that if one claims to be ready to serve only God's Will, but is still clinging to the ego, then it is apparent that the ego is trying to trick God, which is impossible.

The Difference of the 'Level' of Character

All egos wonder what it would be like to be happy, peaceful, and overflowing with unconditional love. They ponder what it would be like to feel no pain, misery, loss, anger, and hatred. So essentially, everyone subconsciously wants to be enlightened. However, when presented with the option to follow the pathway of enlightenment, they usually deny it, for it seems too arduous and folly. They cannot believe that it can be possible. They feel as though it is human nature and normal to be sad and happy, smart or dumb, angry or peaceful, irritated or accepting, and so forth. They are right, from their perspective. However, they are covered in illusion from the standpoint of understanding Truth. So their ego has led them to believe the illusion that suffering is a part of reality. But with adherence to Truth, suffering disappears.

Egos are only capable of comprehending the linear dimension, or all non-God properties (in reference to Unmanifest) and expressions of fallacy (illusion). To the ego, there are no other possibilities than what exists within the limitation of what it can comprehend. So the possibility of enlightenment seems like a fantasy. It is only when the Divinity within them meets the Divinity within the enlightened being that Truth can be felt and known. As this energetic connection takes place, healing begins. This is due to the ego's relinquishment of beliefs that force God's Presence away.

The ego is damning; God is healing. As an initiation or an introduction to the Presence of God acts as a catalyst to spark Divine Will to operate through a being, without the restrictions of the 'ego will,' healing and transcension begin. Thus, the formerly controlled 'nontrustworthy ego being' now becomes a 'trustworthy ego being.' This quantum leap in spiritual evolution will save that being from many unneeded miserable experiences, which their negatively charged ego brought forth as their reality during many past lifetimes.

As the 'nontrustworthy ego' raises in consciousness, the 'trustworthy ego' emerges, like a caterpillar from its cocoon becoming a butterfly. This will be felt as a new life, a new beginning, with one ready to take a step of faith and try new things that one had not previously thought of. With Divine Will leading one's life instead of 'ego will,' life seems easier, more peaceful, and more positive, making one try new physical, emotional, and mental things, as a test to see who one (egotistically speaking) really is. As one decides to take the path of enlightenment, then one decides to see who one truly is as existence, essence, or Spirit, prompting them to learn more about theology, metaphysics, or even Truth.

This 'trustworthy ego,' if they decide to take the journey of the soul, may humbly study by themselves or scavenge every piece of spiritual material and text, in essence to 'test faith.' This 'test of faith' helps one confirm or deny what their spiritual Will was leading them to believe to be True. They may try to become psychically receptive, study the Koran, Torah, or Bible, meditate with Hindu literature, or study Truth and introspect on the meaning of existence. Whatever the method, it will provide a more knowledgeable soul. However, this is not always a 'good thing.' Too much knowledge tends to create a prideful ego, who may always say, "I know, I know; you don't have to tell me." Remember that knowledge is structured energetic patterns, patterns are form, form is within the linear, and the linear is not God or Absolute Truth. Only words that deprogram the ego by presenting Nonlinear Truths can be trusted. However, the words themselves are not even truly Nonlinear, because they are form as well.

This is why beings who feel compelled to study theology, metaphysics, or psychic phenomena sometimes develop spiritual pride, or the feeling that they 'know everything,' thus creating the feeling that no one can teach them anything because they already 'know everything.' For example, the preacher who is convinced he/she 'knows everything' because they read the Bible therefore believes everything else to be wrong or 'satanic,' and against them, the church, or their belief in God. This leads to and is judgment, where they feel as they have the power to tell people whether they are 'sinners' or not, even if they themselves are 'sinners.' Another example is the psychic whom preachers proclaim to be 'anti-Christian' or 'anti-Buddhist,' because they have been led to believe this way. There is also the vanity, or self-indulgence, of "I know": for example, "I know more than anyone because I have had such profound experiences with spirits, ghosts, nature, out-of-body experiences, or any other psychic phenomena." This becomes a 'closed-minded ego-pride' block to Truth. Spiritual pride starts bickering between psychics, spiritual "quasi-gurus," and religious leaders, who all believe they know more than the others.

One needs to understand that all of the major religions were based on the foundation of Truth that was preached by a spiritual master, whether Jesus, Buddha, or another. All spiritual masters who were Truth seekers taught the same Truth to as many beings as possible. All variations between religions lie in historical and geographical differences, as well as various cultures and ego interpretations of Truth. All of these factors create a seemingly 'newfound faith,' although it is the same Truth seeking methods that were the substrate or foundation for these religions' ability to exist in the first place.

As these differences are put aside, Truth will be seen to be the predominant factor that allows one to become enlightened by transcending the ego. When the nonbiased, nonjudgmental, Nondualistic, Nonlinear, and unconditionally loving viewpoint reigns over one's existence, enlightenment becomes Reality. This newfound 'vision' (spiritual) allows one to see Truth within all religions. When the enlightened being tries to bring Light upon religious teachings to the followers of that religion, there may be criticism due to the linear (religious) ego's inability to comprehend the Nonlinear Truth that is presented. Thus the notion of 'All being One' is thought and believed to be the proclaimed words of a heretic. But just the same, Truth will still be presented to those who want to hear.

The Multiple Ego Identity Crisis

All beings, if not enlightened, have an identity. Many egos have several identities, such as 'family man,' 'businessman,' 'churchgoer,' and 'gearhead.' Each identity is assumed at the appropriate time that would prove most beneficial for that individual. For instance, if the ego is at a car show, then the ego assumes the identity of 'gearhead'; but as that same ego goes back home to his family, he assumes the 'family man' identity. These various identities are just a mechanism that the ego uses to 'fit in' with the situation it experiences at a specific time; they reinforce the ego's belief in whom it thinks it is.

The problem with the identity of the ego is that not only does it reinforce the illusion that it is separate from God, but it judges any other beings who are not exactly the same as different in some respect. For instance, a 'gearhead' identity judges another 'gear-head' by the amount of knowledge that they have, just as a 'family man' identity judges another 'family man' as better or worse than themselves. This continual judgment happens on an unconscious and subconscious level, and is often expressed at the conscious level as a word or comment about another ego. So if a 'bodybuilder' identity sees another 'bodybuilder' identity, it will critique the other's character without cessation, whether by thought or word. It will declare some ego identities 'fat' and others 'too skinny.' It may even critique its own identity as not 'good enough,' which leads to other problems, such as bulimia or an 'Adonis complex.'

The main block to the realization of Truth that the identity provides is one's own attachment to their perceived self. As a being believes that he or she is of a specific gender, race, culture, and background, and has his or her own character traits, the ego then believes this to be a fact that it has perceived with its trusty mode of linear perception, or so it believes. Since the ego is built on the logical, rational, linear, and dualistic, and the historical and chronological timeline of life, all the seeming linear facts on which it has based all of its understandings of existence are held tightly to one's self as reality. The identity of that ego makes reality real to that individual through its own subjective experiences of life through its own perception, which its current identity has chosen to assume. So the ego genuinely feels that without its identity, "What or whom would it be?" Without all that it knows, it feels helpless, powerless, confused, and depressed. So it is easy to see why many egos like their perception of whom they are, which shows that they are not willing to give up their ego identity (identity attachment).

Identities are what an ego thinks it is in a certain aspect of its life. The listings below describe some of the countless identities that the ego assumes. The ego fears losing these identities, and thus they can be seen as an attachment to the manifest dimension. If one is attached to the illusory manifest, one cannot experience the Higher Self or the Unmanifest (Real Reality).

Analyzing Ego Identities

'Cool Guy'

The 'cool guy' identity feels as if it sets trends for the rest of society. It believes that it is responsible for the 'happening things' in the direct 'public eye' that it is within. The latest fashions and the 'coolest words' are also to be credited to this character. It feels that life is excitingly fulfilled by occasionally 'breaking the law,' such as underage drinking, doing drugs socially, driving recklessly to show off to peers and to look like a rebel, wearing clothes even if forbidden by their workplace or school, stealing a pack of cigarettes, and so forth.

Not only does this ego identity perceive itself to be 'cool,' but it desperately tries to convince others that they are 'cool' as

286

well. It also makes fun of others who are not 'cool,' by calling them names like 'dork,' 'fatty,' 'ugly,' 'four eyes,' and so on. This identity only wants to hang out with pretty women and other cool guys, but it always competes with others to be the 'coolest' (looked up to or respected) one of them all. This identity acts as though they don't want to talk to someone else if they perceive themselves to be cooler than the other person, which in effect shows that they would never hang out with the other being even if they were 'paid to.' This, to the 'cool guy' identity, feels as if it separates the 'uncool' from the 'cool,' thus establishing their 'coolness' and making themselves feel segregated from other beings who are not so 'cool.' Judgmentalism is this being's most used aspect; it denotes what is and is not 'cool.' That is their main block to Truth.

The 'Doctor'

The 'doctor' identity makes this individual feel as if they know how the entire body works. This being has been schooled, and does indeed know more than most, about the human body, but they feel as if they know more about reality than all others, except maybe religious leaders. The fact of the matter is that the 'doctor' identity knows a lot about the illusory physical body, the vehicle that carries the valuable aspect of the soul. The 'doctor' feels as if the human body is the <u>most important</u> part of life, which inherently denies the Truth of God. The pride of *knowingness* that this 'doctor' identity has about the physical aspects of life leads them to believe that they know more about existence than others, thus showing their block to Reality. To become Self-Realized, this being must stop believing that the physical body is so 'real.' They must see it as it is, a vehicle for the soul.

The 'Intelligent Scholar'

The 'intelligent scholar' believes that they know more about anything than any other ego in existence. The problem is that they have studied so much that they feel as if there is no way that anyone else could possibly have as much knowledge as they do. They also tend to judge any other egos as 'simpletons,' due to their lack of knowledge. An ancient enlightened being once said, "The more you think you know, the less you realize." So pride and judgmentalism are the major blocks to becoming Self-Realized for this character.

The 'Preacher'

The identity of the 'preacher' feels as if their religion, their way, and their sacred texts and teachers are the only way to 'get to God,' so to speak. The main problem with this is that they usually misinterpret the sacred text that they study; they then convey 'half-truths' to the congregation. And their naïve followers usually accept the information as Truth, due to their lack of wisdom and the inherent ego ignorance that they were born with.

The 'preacher' identity judges all <u>other</u> methods of getting to know God as false, or "satan's way." These beings teach their perception of truth with logical, rational, and dualistic reasoning, which further distorts truth. They believe in the linear dimension and therefore instruct their followers that the physical world is the 'real reality,' but God's heaven is a 'better' one (showing judgment).

These beings, when presented with Higher Truth from an enlightened being, actually deny it and call it 'false teachings.' This is because of many years of false or wrongful interpretation of their sacred texts that have programmed them to believe in the illusion of the linear and dualistic. It is very hard to help these beings become Self-Realized, due to their misinterpretation of sacred texts. For example, they may say, "If these teachings, which differ from mine, do not follow the path that was laid out within my sacred texts that I follow, I will not and cannot believe." These beings usually deliver 1 to 2-hour sermons of 'pure show,' lacking in Truth. In the time it would take an enlightened being to speak 200 Truths, the 'preacher' would speak about 2 or 3 'truths' (half-truths).

The main block to the realization of Truth for these beings is that they believe in the misinterpretations of their sacred texts and will not believe in the Truths presented to them by another. They also tend to judge all nonreligious beings as 'sinners' and 'damned by God,' and judge only their followers within the same religion as 'heaven bound.' So these beings do not have the ability to feel compassion, which is nonjudgmentalism and unconditional love, and which provides understanding and transmits Truth as Divinity. Their pride also blocks them from learning from a 'non-congruent (differing) religious' or spiritual being. These 'preacher' beings may go to heaven but will not be enlightened, thus prompting the next reincarnation and the karmic lessons that follow.

The 'Nerd'
The identity of 'nerd' has been given to the 'uncool'; this label has been placed on them by the seemingly 'cool guy' identity. The 'nerd' usually feels out of place and has few friends. These friends are usually very intelligent and are many times (not all) at a higher level of consciousness than most. The only dream that this individual really has is to be accepted and not made fun of. They obviously make friends with those who do not criticize them and help them feel comfortable, so they can lower their defensive guard. These beings, although seen as the most unlikely to do anything with their lives in high school, tend to be the most successful beings on the planet (in worldly terms).

While many ego beings deny God and the path of enlightenment, the 'nerd' identity seems to be attracted to it. They like the idea of 'all being equal,' since that was not how they were previously treated in their life. These seemingly 'far-fetched' concepts for other egos are actually easier for the 'nerd' to comprehend, since a large part of their life is spent contemplating the meaning of existence. All in all, the 'nerd' just wants inner-peace. The main block to realization of Truth for the 'nerd' is feeling insignificant to others, indicating that those with this identity have a hard time seeing themselves 'as good' as others.

The 'Computer Geek'
The main problem of the 'computer geek' is their thinking and mode of interpretation. They are very logical thinkers; these beings often get degrees in 'logistics,' 'statistics,' and 'computer programming.' Their egos are just like a computer: very logical.

The problem is that God is not within the dimension of logic and rationality. So as much as the ego learns to compute the idea of the Unmanifest, it becomes difficult due to their conflicting programs.

The 'computer geek' is usually categorized as a 'nerd' by peers in elementary and high school. Many of these individuals seek the computer as a means for a new friend, who does what is programmed, never judges them, and provides fun through programming and gaming. And since verbalization is not needed for expression from the ego to the computer, this individual is trained to be introverted as well.

The 'computer geek' loves to be around the 'like-minded,' as does any other ego. This can be witnessed at computer conventions, electronic boutiques, and so forth. They love to get together and speak logic. The main blocks to Truth for this being are usually the logic-minded aspect of the self and their attachment to the computer itself. By giving up the logical side of life, the Self that is beyond logistics and statistics may be revealed.

The 'Athlete'

The 'athlete' identity feels as if they must dominate in all that they do. They are very competitive. And if they lose, they may have a very harsh view of themselves. If they win, they feel 'in control' and judge others as incompetent or insufficient. They live to dominate in their chosen sport, as well as many other areas in life. They also tend to have very high standards that set the limit for their being and lifestyle. If these standards are not met, they feel as if they have failed in life.

These beings usually have a lot of pride, which undoubtedly reinforces their opinion of themselves. If anyone challenges their identity, or the way that they view themselves, a competition is born. These individuals not only compete to dominate in their sport, but really to get the reputation that comes along with it. For example, if they are the 'fastest runner in the world,' they will try to tell as many people as possible. This reinforces their opinion of themselves, which makes them feel as if they are the greatest in sport and in life.

These beings give too much truth to that which is insignificant: the physical body, physical sports, and worldly success. These 'athletes' desire to be around friends who will reinforce their ego identity with compliments and ego inflation. The main block to realizing Truth is 'pride of self' and the error of emphasis on physical goals, rather than spiritual. Some athletes are actually addicted to the various 'exercise highs' that accompany strenuous activity, such as "runner's high." In these cases, the athlete depends on this source of happiness instead of God.

The 'Drug User'

'Drug users' are probably the most misunderstood beings on the planet, because they have such a wide array of emotional and mental states. They can be very hard to pinpoint due to the fact that every 'drug user' identity seems to have its own specific traits. Some are actually searching for an alternate reality, such as the Truth, while other 'drug user' identities do it for fun, to escape the pain in their current lifestyle and world, or to be accepted by their peers.

These beings usually do not accept the amount of pleasure that has been shown to them as the limit that can be experienced, so they search for other ways to be fulfilled to a higher degree. If they believe that the drugs that provided them with the new pleasure are the best 'high' they have experienced, they often push them on others, in effect to allow other ego beings to experience the same escape from reality, like they have never felt before.

They believe that this 'high' is and must be the very best, and they think, "Why else would it be illegal?" Research shows that the 'trustworthy ego' is usually peer pressured to do drugs, but the 'nontrustworthy ego' is trying to escape reality in an attempt to hide their pain. The 'soul searcher' ego does drugs as an experiment, to see what it is like, in an attempt to see all sides of reality from different viewpoints. These beings can be 'trustworthy' or 'nontrustworthy'; it varies. With this said, it should also be noted that almost all beings who do drugs are below the level of integrity, which means, in lay terms, that they are 'hellbound.' Every time a drug is taken, whether mild ones such as cigarettes and alcohol, or serious ones such as barbiturates, heroin, cocaine, LSD, or marijuana, a being's level of consciousness decreases, bringing about a seeming 'worse' or 'less fortunate' reality, many times prompting suicide and even homicide.

A major block for these individuals is that they are often not willing to change, because they have not been shown an alternate reality that provides an adequate amount of sustained happiness and peace. Another unfortunate side effect of the 'drug user' identity is that they seem always to say, "What's the difference in what I do; what I do to myself doesn't affect anybody else." This could not be further from the Truth. Every thought, action, and will changes the universal karmic charge, which then either benefits or hinders the spiritual evolution of mankind. So as that 'drug user' identity lowers a being's level of consciousness, they are bringing the rest of the society with them, not only damning themselves, but the world and its inhabitants.

The 'Family Man'

The 'family man' has usually been programmed by his own parents to have certain standards in raising a family. If these parents were loving, then their children will most *likely* be loving as well; but if these parents were abusive, usually abuse will occur. Not only will they display the traits that were imprinted on them throughout their childhood, but they will also have some of their own ideas that they will try to integrate within their family.

The most difficult type of 'family man' identity is the one who tries to prove himself as the 'best dad' all of the time. They compete with other parents, other children's notions of what would be a 'good parent,' and their own notion of what would be a 'good parent.' They are constantly trying to be the best in every aspect of 'familyhood,' such as 'the provider,' 'the playful dad,' 'the homework tutor,' 'the funnyman,' and so forth. The problem with these characters is that they push themselves so hard that they forget to enjoy existence because they are in a constant state of competition with everybody's notion, as well as their own, of "what a good parent is."

These beings can be absolutely crushed if they are outdone by another parent. They may then feel inadequate, as if they are a failure in that aspect of life. To regain their status, however, they may try to 'outdo' the next participant, whomever that may be. They are constantly trying to preserve their identity as the 'good parent' and 'family man.'

The main block to realization is that of giving too much truth to the illusion—in other words, believing in the fallacy of relationships within the manifest. Egos are not the True Reality, just as relationships between egos are not the True Reality. Egos may feel and think that they are separate, but all beings have the same Spirit, which is the Unmanifest (God).

The 'family man' loves the relationship part of the family so much that he will not admit that his children are not really his (only separations allow for relationships, which is dualistic). Just the same, no ego likes to be told that they don't *own* their children. All egos are in fact their own entity as a part of the whole. There is no such thing as ownership in the universe; that would require a being claiming to own a part of God, which is an impossibility. Likewise, God doesn't own us, because *God as Totality* is us (All). That would be the same as the universe claiming to own an atom; it doesn't have to, because **it is** all atoms, subatomic particles, and so forth. *God as Totality* is All That Is.

The 'Loser'

The 'loser' identity feels as if it has failed at everything, no matter what the occasion. It doesn't attempt many things because it believes that it would just 'screw it up,' or fail. This being is often perceived as lazy and unmotivated, but really they are just not confident in themselves or their abilities. Throughout life, this being may be back and forth from several remedial jobs, and is usually fired due to a lack of enthusiasm, which translates into poor levels of productivity. They may live with their parents or 'bum off' their friends for several years, as if just waiting to win the lottery or die, whichever comes first.

This being doesn't date much, because they don't have the courage to ask anyone out. They view themselves as 'hopeless' and a 'waste of space.' They often wish that they had never been born. They truly feel as if they are a 'loser' and nothing in their life will really work out for them.

The main block to realization for these individuals is that they don't have enough confidence in themselves or the courage to take the next step in the physical world, so why would they trust in an unseen power that is called God? Since they feel as if nothing else makes them happy, they think that religion or spirituality will be just the same. If they can be shown how easy it is to start 'anew,' then their life can drastically change, to the extent where they are glad just to be breathing and existing. It needs to be realized that all beings have never failed at anything; instead, they may have successfully chosen the 'wrong path' for themselves. But bear in mind that *they have done that perfectly*. What they perceive to be themselves failing is really just their level of consciousness denying the road of Truth and expressing itself with perfection. God is existence; so just to exist is phenomenal, while simultaneously being all that is needed to bring permanent satisfaction and fulfillment.

The 'Tough Guy'

The 'tough guy' identity needs always to be assured that it is able to beat up another ego, can control and manipulate someone or an event, and is feared by others. These beings are perceived to be the 'bullies' in school, whom everyone has come to know at least once in their life. Many times, this identity is formed in an abusive family, which beat up on their ego, making them feel weak and powerless. It wasn't the beating that caused them to be like that, but rather, the energy of the event, or level of consciousness that was ingrained upon them, that they still carry. This prompted the ego to become strong, or at least to try to be perceived so amongst other egos. So they tried to say 'mean things,' 'make fun,' and push others around, or maybe even strike out at another. This is usually the ego's attempt to shift focus from how weak it is in certain areas of its life, while showing other egos how strong it is behind the façade that it has led others to believe is real. It is a cover that hides how they feel, nothing more.

These beings act as though 'things' don't bother them, whether emotional, mental, physical, or spiritual. However, if these so-called 'tough guys' saw a ghost, projected into a lower astral dimension (hell), or were brought to their breaking point in the other aspects of life, they would cry like a little baby. I have seen 'tough guys' go almost insane from having one bad astral projection into the lower depths of hell. Likewise, these 'tough guys' are seen in movies as not caring whether they go to heaven or hell, but it is a guarantee that these specific identities would be terrified in even the most remote hell. This is because a hell is all of one's deepest and darkest fears come alive as reality, with no escape except through God, which is love, an energy that most tough guys tend to perceive as a 'sissy emotion.'

These beings, if shown why it is important to love, may change their view of life. The ego's pride in being a 'tough guy' is what keeps them from being loving. In their eyes, if they are seen as loving, they cannot be a 'tough guy.' Thus their main block is the denial of love. Unfortunately, without love heaven is inaccessible, as well as God.

The 'Fat' Person

This being is usually very low in self-esteem, although not always. This identity, which the ego assumes, is usually a direct reflection of its overweight physical body. It is important to note that one's self-image should not be a reflection of the physical, but that of the 'shapeless' Spirit. If one is physically obese, then the way they choose to see themselves is the way that they will feel and portray themselves to be. However, this being may choose to see themselves as a 'child of God'—that is, Spirit within a vehicle that its inherent level of consciousness had previously chosen. This being, just like other beings, is not the perceived physical self (illusion), but instead, the Spirit within. So no matter what the affliction of the body, whether crippled, ill, deformed, etc…, it is not actually the True Universal Identity that one is, but rather, the illusion that they have convinced themselves to believe that they are—the ego identity.

This being needs to realize (not think they know) that it is not the vehicle and its experiences that make the being, but how the being chooses to view life, as problem-free or as a perfect expression of existence. So one shouldn't get angry if they are fat, crippled, or whatever, for they chose this vehicle before incarnation. To view it as a mistake to have 'wound up' with this body is to view God as mistaken or in error. God doesn't make any mistakes; error is only a quality (belief) of the ego. God not only is the Source of perfection, but all that manifests from the Source is perfect as well.

The 'Emotional Dumper'

Everyone has witnessed the 'emotional dumper,' the character who elicits a conversation with another being in order to express all of their problems. These beings love drama, so naturally they feel as if these problems are a suitable topic or conversation piece. Unfortunately, the beings who are bombarded with the emotional distress and various problems usually do not know how to react. So they usually just nod and appear sympathetic. Furthermore, the being who had to endure this interaction will usually judge the character as crazy, disturbed, or emotionally imbalanced.

This being actually uses other beings with whom it converses as a release and a method of healing, even though they do not see it that way. These beings will just release all of their problems onto an unsuspecting ego bystander within a couple of minutes. So a whole months worth of emotional dilemmas can be spewed forth in about a 10-minute summary that lacks almost nothing emotionally.

Their main blocks to realizing Truth are their emotional attachments that they are not ready to let go of. These beings like to reminisce about their past experiences in order to resummon their past emotions. To tell these beings that all emotions except love are illusory would actually insult them. For they feel that emotions are important and not to be abandoned. Just the same, they enjoy the emotional side of life (the ups and downs), and the ego, for that matter.

The 'Crazy' Person

As odd as this may sound, there are actually beings who

derive pleasure from telling people that they are 'crazy.' They actually enjoy the persona who tells others that they are a bit 'out of their heads.' They can be seen telling others, "Watch out, because I'm crazy." Then they will elaborate on the fact that they do 'crazy things,' whatever those may be. They may state that they have traveled the world getting drunk and doing drugs, while getting tattoos and sleeping around. They may also bring up some events that reinforce this identity, such as being put in jail or getting in a fight. Whether they have done these crazy events or not is merely *relative* to the viewer and the being expressing it.

These beings are feverishly working to establish an identity so that the rest of society will respect and admire them for their open-mindedness and uniqueness. They are fearful of others judging them as ordinary or unadventurous. They want to be as far away from being ordinary or 'boring' as possible, or so they think. They are constructing and reinforcing this identity to cover up the inherent inadequacies that they feel they have.

The 'Arguer'

The 'arguer' likes to start an argument by recognizing all of the negatives, or even make up some that are not actually present at that time, and then get into a fight, whether physical, emotional, or verbal. Throughout this ego's day, they can be seen to start up many uneasy situations. They are typically not pleasant to be around. These beings like to be offended because it gives them another opportunity to argue.

They cannot function off of positive energy. This type of vehicle, which they selected themselves, runs only on negative fuel. Therefore, to re-energize their beingness, they pick out little details within their day, or a person to make fun of or to argue with. Their best friend is someone who will play their game and argue with others as well. Because this being fears positivity, they usually shy away from most love, peacefulness, and happiness. Happiness to them is arguing.

The 'Disappointed' Person

This type of ego is never satisfied with anything. To them,

everything appears easy and doable; even if they themselves have never been successful at anything. A typical comment from this type of being, after their house was remodeled ($10,000 worth) for free, would be, "The floor is ugly; you should have gotten tile instead of wood. I don't like what you've done with this. That's ugly, too. What color of paint is this? It is certainly not pretty." And then they develop repeating (negative) thought patterns that reinforce why this type of 'free work' was not worth it. This being is not grateful for anything. They always think that they can do it better; even if they know they can't, they will trick themselves and others into thinking that they can. Just like many of the previous identities, this being would rather be negative than positive.

The 'Complainer'

This type of ego identity is similar to the 'disappointed' person and the 'arguer.' They complain about everything possible, even if they have to 'make it up' or 'stretch the truth' to find the negative. They are like metal detectors, but they are honed in to locating negativity, as well as embellishing the response when it is found. This person seeks out negative events and world situations just to complain about them.

Other Ego Identity Examples

- 'Bodybuilder'
- 'Schoolteacher'
- 'Plumber'
- 'Electrician'
- 'Boss'
- 'Hot Girl'
- 'Negativity Magnet'
- 'Convict'
- 'President of the United States'
- 'Guru'
- 'Sexual Addict'
- 'Religious Addict'
- 'Religion Hater'
- 'Pyromaniac'

- *'Spiritual Genius'*
- *'Yoga Instructor'*
- *'Beautician'*
- *'Enlightened One'*
- *'Government Agent'*

Another identity that is commonplace is the "I have no identity" identity. An ego cannot claim not to have an identity, for it is in and of itself an identity; if not, that being would be enlightened. If enlightened, one would not claim to have an identity, or claim to not have an identity; for to make a claim is a function of the ego. When one is enlightened, they are 'identityless' but rediscovered as One with All, the 'Universal Identity' (which is not really an identity).

Identity Pride

All beings who are egos have an identity, whether they know it or not. Unfortunately, this identity comes with a certain amount of pride, which blocks a being from enjoying all aspects of life by not allowing them to step down from their perceived notion of themselves to be something different (lesser). For example, the 'CEO of a company' who is congruent with the 'businessman' identity could not step past his pride to work at a 'fastfood' restaurant, the pro athlete could never go back to the minor leagues, the 'drug user' many times makes fun of the 'straightedge' identity, the doctor would find it an insult to be demoted to being a nurse, the preacher who supposedly teaches the truth of existence would hate to have their expertise questioned and corrected, the tough guy would hate to be shown up as a 'sissy,' and just the same, a king would hate to be dethroned and demoted to being a peasant. So the ability to assume another perceived 'lesser' identity reveals the block of not letting go of the old one; this is known as 'identity attachment,' which is reinforced by *identity pride*.

The ego's identity that it has assumed to be its self sets the boundary, or the barrier. This invokes the quality of pride, which helps the ego reinforce and strengthen the identity that is on the verge of being broken apart. The ego feels that in order not to degrade its 'identity' and 'beingness,' it cannot recede in energetic quality from that which it has deemed the most important. For example, if the 'beingness' of a 'CEO businessman' is the most important quality of energy in an ego's life, it cannot and must not recede (be demoted). If such a tragedy happened, that ego would feel as if life and happiness were over, with no chance of retrieving its virtue.

It should be remembered that the ego is just a program. It can be changed or reprogrammed to whatever is needed at the time. If one feels that another being's current job is degrading, then it would be spiritually beneficial to quit and get the job that is viewed to be degrading or lesser. This would stop the judgment of the degrading job type, destroy the current identity that is impinging upon Self-Realization, and allow one to see that the ego can be reprogrammed with any information that is necessary at that current time. As the program changes, so does the identity. The True Self (Unmanifest), however, never changes and is always the same.

Identity Challenge

The identity represents the image that the ego chooses to portray. In so doing, the ego believes that this identity represents the type of character that it views itself to be. Since this identity is a compilation of the ego's inherent knowledge and expressions, it tends to view anything that is not congruent with its view or identity as a challenge. If an ego identity challenges another ego identity, pride is the latter's first expression of an attempt to preserve its identity. For example, if a nurse challenges a doctor's medical opinion, the 'doctor' identity, even if wrong, will try to prove that it is right. This is done in an attempt to 'save face,' or to preserve its identity and place in the world. The 'doctor' identity thinks, "How dare that nurse try to upstage me; I'm a doctor. It is an insult to who and what I am as a doctor. She didn't go through as much school as I did. What does she know, anyway?"

So it can be seen that the major reason for conflict in the

world is actually that of the ego's various identities clashing with pride: one belief/identity against another. Very seldom does an ego just 'give in' and allow another ego to take over (dominate) a situation. This is due to the feeling that one ego gets when its identity, morals, knowledge, and beliefs are challenged. The identity feels weakened and therefore leaves that ego feeling 'identityless,' or less than self. If an ego feels as if its identity is fading away, it loses its sense of self, or separateness and independence. This means that its whole reality comes crashing down, which leaves the ego feeling stranded, with no way back to the ordinary life that it once knew. The main function of an ego is to strengthen, maintain, and reinforce its feeling of independence (dualism), which inherently comes with the specific identity, or identities, that it has created. So without that identity, it feels lost and weak, and then begins to fear the Presence of God as the replacing identity.

Identity Crisis

This being is in the process of searching for their identity, or how they can be distinguished as unique and individual by other egos. Even though this being thinks that they have no specific identity, they actually have the identity of 'identity confusion.' Their identity is simply this: to be indescribable to others. They like the fact that other individuals can't exactly 'figure out' their specific identity. These beings are many times termed 'mysterious' or 'eclectic.' In fact, they may actually pick up that descriptive term and use it to describe themselves. They may feel as if they are 'soul searching,' but really they are really just developing the ego identity further.

As they use the various traits from this identity, they also try out character traits from other identities. One year they may be into country music and square dancing, while the next year they will be into rap music and baggy clothes. These egos with their identities may be seen as lost or confused individuals, but their ego actually knows what is going on long before it is recognized as such within that being's consciousness. That being may even feel as if they are lost and confused, but it is only the ego's deceptive plan to keep the individual looking 'mysterious' and 'eclectic.' It derives pleasure from the identity label that it has gained and all of the many things that it does, even though at times it does feel confused and unhappy. Its identity is to be indescribable as such; but bear in mind: it is an identity.

Ego Knowledge vs. the Wisdom of the Self

There are two different types of knowledge. One is linear knowledge; the other is linear knowledge that describes Nonlinear Truth. The latter educates a being so that they are capable of deprogramming the linear ego mind. The latter is the most beneficial for the soul's evolutionary process.

So one type is linear ego facts, and the other deprograms the ego. All knowledge is linear due to its structure or the nature of form; that which is Nonlinear is formless and incapable of truly existing as reality within structure. This means that there is no truly accurate description of God—or, to put it bluntly, God cannot be described, only experienced, thus showing one that only a subjective experience (revelation) reveals Truth.

Linear words that describe the Nonlinear are higher in Power (level of consciousness) and capable of creating change by adding Light to one's energetic field. They prompt one to search for the knowledge that can transform their life permanently, instead of continuously focusing on the mundane qualities of the manifest. Thus one's self is prevented from digging themselves into a deeper hole of illusion...compliments of the ego.

As knowledge is acquired and used by the processes of the ego mind, the ego feels educated or smarter. This can lead to pridefulness. But as one transcends the ego and its perceived reality, experience overrides knowledge. This knowledge is then abandoned due to the experience of Truth that proves the once before ego inherent theory of existence more eloquently. So the linear knowledge that contains Nonlinear Truths now deprograms the ego, which then reveals Truth as the essence of existence. That experience of Truth that is beyond the manifest energetic patterns called knowledge is True Wisdom. Not only does Wisdom provide revelations, but revelations bring forth new Wisdom.

So it can now be understood why an enlightened being is called a *Sage*. This is because the label *Sage* means 'wisdom' or 'wise being.' The wisdom comes from their subjective experience of the Higher Self, or True Reality. With this wisdom, they no longer *think about* what Reality is; they *know* it because they are it, speaking with respect to the Higher Self.

Chapter 13
<u>Process of Ego Release</u>

Why Should I Discard the Ego?

For one to become enlightened, the ego must be transcended. It is almost as though everyone is a schizophrenic who falls victim to their own illusions of what they perceive to be reality, when it is all just made up in their mind. As one rids themselves of this mechanism of illusion (ego), the True Reality is revealed. The majority of society believes that "what they see is what they get," so they are not even interested in understanding who or what they are in Spirit. This incapability to understand is because the ego mind within which they currently operate cannot see or understand Spirit. So this Reality that they hear about seems to them to be either fallacy or wishful thinking at best. Most beings just don't have that kind of faith.

To realize why one should transcend the ego, which they perceive to be themselves or maybe in a 'best-friendish way,' they must first realize or come to terms with the fact that the ego is not a friend and not who they are. The ego is an impersonal aspect of the soul that acts almost like a computer virus. This defective program (ego) comes upon a being and takes control, while guiding it in the direction that it and only it wants to go. It makes one think as if it has its own thoughts, but in actuality, these thoughts, ideas, concepts, words, or feelings have already existed within the universal consciousness. The ego just claims that it created these thoughts, ideas, or concepts, but this is an illusion. Only God can create; the ego just claims ownership of energetic patterns that were already created by the varying levels of God. By this, the ego feels as though it has special powers that allow it to create things, just as God infinitely does. So as the ego claims a thought that it thought that it had, it dwells on its own self-indulged glory of being the creator of something. This pleasure in being the creator is noted, thus prompting it to create more things. But in actuality, every word that can be spoken has already been spoken or is made available to be spoken by the universe. Likewise, every picture that can be created or made has already existed within God, and every concept or thought would not even be able to be thought if it weren't for God allowing us to exist and to call upon the already existing energetic pattern by the faculty known as 'will.'

One needs to understand that the ego is a 'robber' of creation. It claims to be the source of happiness, but it is not—God is. It claims to be the source of its own creation, but it is not—God is. It claims to control your life path and create your future or destiny, but it does not even do that. This is because God is the infinite potentiality of creation; therefore, anything that ever could be created already has been, although in an unseen and thought-to-be 'unthought-of' energetic structure. Just because something can be created does not mean that the ego created it; it simply means that God has already created it and will allow it to take shape when the ego 'thinks that it thinks' about it. This allows us to have pleasure in thinking that we created something.

So one can clearly see God's unconditional Love for us: God created something, the ego then stole the authenticity of the idea and creation and claimed it as its own, and this was all allowed to take place because God allowed it to, because it would make a being (an aspect of itself) feel 'happy' and loved. Just ask yourself if you would do the same. For instance, if you created a CD with this absolutely wonderful music and someone stole it from you and claimed it as their own, would you be glad that it makes them happy and allow them to steal your creation without telling another soul what happened, while resting comfortably in the fact that the other being is happy? Or would you get upset, because you are angry that someone would steal what you created and claim it as their own? Now it can be seen that God knows (in a manner of speaking) that we 'steal' the creation of the Source continuously with every thought, idea, word, concept, and belief; this is also seen when the ego claims its body and its identity as its own. The body, soul, house, car, relationship, family, and identity that the ego believes and claims to be its own are not its own. Creation is a result of Absolute Power becoming manifest when the proper conditions become a necessity for creation; therefore it is of God and a quality of God as Totality.

Understanding that the Ego Is Impersonal

The term 'personal' signifies a relationship. A relationship is a product of the dualistic/manifest realm of existence, one joining to another. In Absolute Reality, dualism is not a possibility. Therefore, there is no other 'one' to have a relationship with. Relationships are between egos, not God. For example, when one finally transcends the ego, they find out that their Higher Self is really One, thus showing that one cannot have a relationship with one's own Self. Everyone's Higher Self is exactly the same; there are no differences and no separations. Because the ego believes in separations, the ego also believes in joining through relationships. The hallmark of relationship in its ultimate form is 'marriage' and family. The Truth is that everyone is One, and there is no need for joining in marriage or through friendship. The ego believes that relationships bring happiness, when in Reality, God is that happiness that two souls experience while together. The only source of happiness and Love is God; there is no other alternative source. Happiness comes from existence, and God is existence.

The following shows what the ego does for one's being:
- *It acts like a possession and makes one do things that they wouldn't normally do.*
- *It keeps one from Truth.*
- *It lies continually to oneself and others to make it feel special.*
- *It keeps one from existing within the Absolute Reality (home).*
- *It creates pain and suffering.*
- *It creates conflict between people and the world.*
- *It makes one believe in illusion and lies, while saying that these are the Truth.*
- *It forces one to go to 'hell' (to suffer).*
- *It makes one experience loss and unhappiness.*
- *It makes one feel insecure and filled with anxiety.*

307

- *It creates addictions and illness.*
- *It makes one believe that happiness needs to be acquired, when this has existed within at all times; thus it keeps one from happiness.*
- *It makes one believe that only it can experience happiness and love, when these are really provided by one's Self infinitely.*
- *It makes one feel as if other people are more special than itself.*
- *It can make one look like a fool, incompetent, or idiotic.*
- *It is capable of killing others and hurting them.*
- *It likes to degrade other beings, as well as judge and compare.*
- *It makes one fear life, death, and unknowingness.*
- *It makes one act as though they are better than others.*
- *It thinks that people are either 'bad' or 'good.'*
- *It likes to torture and control one's self.*
- *It will compromise one's life by being deceitful.*
- *It will create wars and murder.*
- *It will rape someone for its own self-gain.*
- *It will subject one to pain, rape, or murder, because it believes that punishments are necessary to control them.*
- *It creates mental disorders and emotional disturbances because it secretly enjoys being miserable at times.*
- *It steals information from God and claims it as its own.*
- *It wishes the worst for one and their friends if one doesn't worship the ego and its wants and desires.*
- *It would rather kill one than allow it to follow Divine Will.*
- *Many times it will make one feel special, which gains one's confidence, then it will do a 180-degree turnaround and destroy one's life.*
- *Its ultimate goal is to have one spend an eternity in hell, but first one must live many lifetimes in suffering and pain.*

So, do you still want to keep this disease/illness/illusion?

If someone did all of this to you, would you still want to be their friend? Most likely not, due to their dishonest and conniving nature. Don't be afraid to abandon the ego. It has never helped you before—ever. Its only goal is to keep you separated from God by maintaining the false ego identity, while it slowly takes you further down the spiritual evolutionary ladder towards an eternity within the lower astral dimensions (hell), thus making one feel completely devoid of total happiness, pleasure, friendships, peace, or love. Its job is to keep one in the dark, away from God, and in hell, with no chance of escape or salvation. Even if the ego convinces one that it treats itself right (so to speak) this very instant or within the next 20 lifetimes, one must remember its ultimate goal—to make one suffer. One does not and cannot know when the ego plans to take one in that downward spiral towards their demise.

By reading this descriptive text on the nature of the ego, the ego's hold on one's beingness has already begun to loosen. This allows one to climb their way back up to a higher level of consciousness, because one is now aware of its very nature of 'sin.' Ultimate transcendence of the ego comes when one fully understands this 'disease' to its maximum capability. Every thought, spiritually informative text or person, or high frequency helps to disassemble the ego, thus allowing the True Self to shine forth with brilliance.

Identity Resistance

It is important to note that the ego does not want to be abandoned or healed. If one feels as if they need to be healed or are currently searching for 'self-help' books, then the Divine Will has taken over to an extent to help one realize their True nature. If a being ever begins to change in a more positive direction, then the Divine Will is inspiring them to heal.

The majority of the population does not want to heal or change. These egos are satisfied, and elect to remain within their current lifestyle, or the ego is not satisfied with life but sees no way that any methodology or person can help them out of their misery. The ego chooses not to see suffering as an option that they chose out of their own free volition. Instead, the ego likes to view suffering as something that was done to them against their will. The ego hates to admit its faults, so this is how pride is born and reinforced.

The major resistances of the ego's identity are as follows:

- *Acts interested in Truth, but one can tell that they are not.*
- *Thinks that they are happy and believes that they currently live their life within God, even when one can see or knows that they are lying and still suffering.*
- *Tries to be the center of attention to draw attention away from whomever they feel they are, while shifting emphasis to the identity that they are trying to create and reinforce.*
- *Says they'll be happy, or that they love life or existence, even if they lost their house, car, job, etc..., and one can obviously see that they are very materialistic and love their identity as it currently is with 'material things' in it.*
- *Tries to smile or act happy all of the time (for example, a forced smile or conversation that makes them feel included by others).*
- *Is convinced that they are happier than most, and even tells others that they are the happiest in the world, yet they don't understand that happiness is infinite, never-ending, and ever-increasing. So what that being is really trying to say is that they are as happy as they can be and currently have experienced within the confines or limitations of what their ego will allow them to feel or know. So basically the ego can only be as happy as its current capacity for awareness. The truly happy are modest and feel no need to prove their happiness to others by acting happy or comparing lives that proclaim their happiness for them.*
- *Believes that their ego is themselves, therefore ignoring Truth that says that 'what you think you are, you are really not.'*

- *Ignores a person (due to their pride) who is trying to talk some sense (Truth) into them.*
- *Yells at or gets irritated with a Speaker of Truth. The ego may be irritated with just the presence (without verbalization) of the enlightened being alone, due to the higher frequency that the being emits, which the ego cannot handle or comprehend.*
- *Constantly makes fun of others. By pointing out other egos' faults, it shifts attention from itself, which hides its faults and allows it to be who it wants to be.*
- *Is not interested in, or even denies change. Denies reading self-help books or hearing others speak about change, and may even make fun of a being who is trying to help or heal themselves.*
- *Acts as though it already knows everything (pride).*
- *Feels as though it hates Religious, Spiritual, or God topics.*
- *Feels uncomfortable around silence, affection, and Love.*
- *Tries to be insensitive in order to deny its own feelings or emotions.*
- *Won't change a daily routine (the identity of the being revolves around this routine; therefore, to alter the routine is to alter the character or identity of the ego).*
- *Is addicted to or constantly craving something that brings happiness to themselves (an external, dualistic source of happiness).*
- *Elects to be self-serving, rather than helping others.*
- *Feels uncomfortable helping others.*
- *Will not change who they are, how they dress, what music they listen to, or how they live because that lifestyle reflects who they are as an identity that they have created for themselves. Or it may change, but only to another ego identity.*
- *Constantly lies to others to make themselves feel more important (reinforcing identity).*

So one must, by complete and total humility, surrender the

ego and all of its positionalities to God. Any of these claims or statements reflects the ego clinging to its existence, which reinforces the identity, linear dimension, and duality that create more suffering. One must simply trust in God and surrender all that one thinks they are; after all, it's just an illusion.

The ego has a very difficult time giving up what it has been previously led to believe due to the reinforcements that have made its identity feel concrete or real. Since the ego also believes all that it feels, thinks, and perceives, the illusion of the physical dimension is then reinforced as reality, thus trapping the soul in the illusory.

<u>*Levels of Identity Reinforcement*</u>

This chart represents the many levels of reality that the ego attaches itself to.

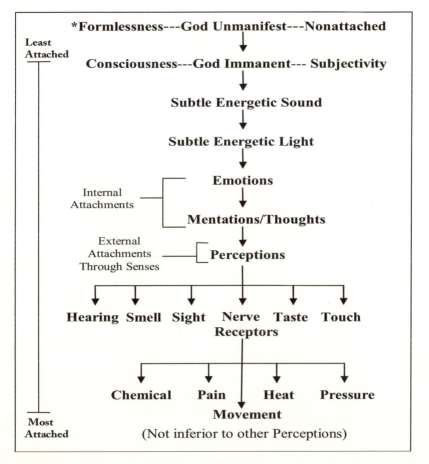

*By focusing on the Formless (upper), one may become nonattached.

Levels of Identity Reinforcement

For the many lifetimes of the ego, it has convinced itself that it knows what reality is. This is because the ego mind has control—or at least it thinks so—of the physical body. This physical body has senses such as sight, smell, hearing, taste, touch, and many neural receptors, which means that it continually receives and interprets external stimuli from the physical dimension. This reinforces the ego's feeling of 'place' within the universe, helping it know where it is within the reality that it perceives. (The chart above shows the different levels of identity reinforcement discussed in this section.)

As the ego touches a cup, it knows that it is next to or holding the cup. As it walks on the ground, neural conduction sends signals from the foot to the brain, which is interconnected with the ego mind that allows for control over its appendages and an understanding of what it is doing within the perceived reality. As another ego speaks to it, the ears allow it to hear the direction of the sound, indicating its position relative to the subject. These are just a few examples of how the ego reinforces the feeling of its independent identity. To complement the body, it also has internal senses that let the mind know what is taking place within the body.

The internal senses are known as neural receptors. These receptors detect sensory input from the skin and at the most basic level, as follows: proprioceptor (detects movement and stretch), chemoreceptor (chemicals within blood), nociceptors (pain), and others (pressure, heat, and so forth). While walking, the proprioceptors allow the mind to know that it is moving and that muscles, joints, and ligaments are stretching. As the ego's hand touches a hot toaster, the receptors allow it to train the mind not to make the same mistake again. Likewise, the chemoreceptors can detect chemicals within the blood, such as alcohol, drugs, and also its own hormone levels, to inform the ego of its internal chemistry.

So, nonstop, the ego's perceptions and internal senses are overworking the brain and simultaneously stimulating the ego, while reinforcing its belief that it is separate from others and inde-

313

pendent from God. After all, why can't this be true? The ego has all of the evidence (form) that it needs to prove (linear term) to itself that it is its own being and that the reality it has become so accustomed to is real—or is it? Although the senses reinforce the ego's identity, the 'senses' would not make much 'sense' if the ego mind did not interpret the energetic information in the first place. Without the ego mind believing in the senses by its subjective experience, no reality would exist as such. All seemingly energetic stimuli within an 'external environment' only exist within the ego mind and nowhere else.

The ego's mental processes interpret, identify, classify, delineate, judge, and place the sensory input received from the ego's bodily sensory system into the appropriate categories. The ego mind then takes the energetic patterns and tries to make sense of them (rationality). Without the ego mind to interpret the energy, the sensory input is useless and will not be noticed. It would then be as if it had never have happened, thus solving the dualistic dilemma, linear illusion, and belief that all is separate and independent. This means that without the 'senses' and the 'ego mind,' the illusion would never be perceived to exist. Thus the only True existence would be known as existence provided by awareness, and not by one's distorted and relative sensory perception.

Most Beneficial Ways To Release the Ego

The world's many religions, spiritual groups, and sects have developed numerous ways to release the ego. Each being thinks that what they do is original and that a book needs to be written about it. This is not so. There is only one prerequisite to become enlightened: this is to surrender all of the ego to God.

In some branches of Buddhism and Hinduism, complete sense withdrawal is used in order to stop the constant bombardment of external stimuli. This stops the reinforcement of the illusory self by taking away its ability to 'place itself' within the external/separate universe. If the senses are not functioning, the ego loses the grip on reality that it has. It may even become disoriented, imbalanced, or confused during the spiritual practice. This approach is very effective for meditation but will not help one become enlightened unless the greater context of the Unmanifest is kept in mind. With complete sense withdrawal, one can exist in the Now and hopefully silence the mind to experience 'No-Mind,' or True Reality, which is provided by and is the Higher Self.

Other branches of Buddhism and Hinduism focus on the Truth that is within some of the Vedic text, Buddhist scripture, or Bhagavad-Gita. This is an attempt to heighten one's level of consciousness, which increases the depth and the benefit of meditations, as well as the experience of life in general. These teachings focus on the Nondualistic and Nonlinear view of Reality, while also helping one see why all beings should be treated with the same respect and shown unconditional love.

Some branches of Hinduism focus mainly on the chakras that preserve balance within our lives. This is more of a metaphysical practice that deals with the Spiritual Manifest. Although it is of some benefit, enlightenment through these means may be impractical.

Other branches of Buddhism and Hinduism tend to focus on the Kundalini. This is the massive untapped energetic reservoir that lies at the bottom of the spine, which, when tapped, can produce an enlightening experience. The energy is released in waves, some smaller and some larger. When all of the Kundalini is raised, one becomes enlightened. The raising of Kundalini is very beneficial and can indeed help one spiritually evolve. Using this method, without the understanding of the greater context of Reality, it may take one a number of years (decades) to become enlightened. Since they are very beneficial, these techniques and teachings are provided in this book. However, unless one is taught the proper techniques by a Kundalini Yoga Master, many emotional and mental imbalances may occur, as well as physical imbalances that can lead to nausea, energetic fevers, dizziness, irritability, and low energy.

There are also other religions, such as Judaism and Christianity, that tend to focus on past events, geography, people, and past supernatural phenomena, while teaching very little Truth. In fact, due to many preachers' unenlightened nature, they actually only teach truth, not Truth. This is due to the ego of the preacher/

315

minister/bishop/etc… trying to interpret linearly the Nonlinear Truth that was already distorted and misinterpreted in their sacred texts as truth by other listening and transcribing egos in the first place. This leads to confusion and unfaithful followers who eventually drop out of the religion, lose faith, or become agnostic.

While past spiritual events can be helpful, Truth should be focused on. The fact is that many religions forget to focus on the Truth, due to their egos' ignorance of what Truth really is.

To clarify what is beneficial in releasing the ego, the following summary is provided:

- *Be **willing** to release the ego at any cost, even if it seemingly means nonexistence.*
- *Study the Truth in this book. It is a **<u>very high level</u>**.*
- *Meditate in a quiet place with as few external stimuli as possible, thus increasing the possibility of experiencing No-Mind.*
- *Question the ego and **all** its motives (introspection).*
- *Fill one's mind with only positive energy to build as many positive thought forms as possible. Not only will this help one become enlightened, it will benefit universal karma.*
- *Work with the 'Bandha Technique' that is mentioned in the latter part of the book. It helps to channel energy up to the crown chakra, which brings forth God-Consciousness.*
- *Do random acts of kindness. Help others. Be loving.*
- *Make one's life a gift to all beings by helping them get back on track.*
- *Choose Divine Will over ego will.*
- *Practice Breath Awareness; it is very beneficial.*
- *Forgive all beings from the past and present.*
- *Don't Judge others, just accept them as is—perfect.*
- *Be as humble before other people, animals, and plants as before God.*
- *Practice Mindfulness.*
- *Don't Harm Life; love, respect, and admire it—serve it for God. Be grateful for all.*
- *Compare religious texts only to find Truth within them.*

- *Read this book again and again and again. Each time will raise your level of consciousness more and more.*
- *Be consistent in one's studies—every day.*
- *Pray to God and meditate every day.*

Health and Wellness

Ego-release is just another aspect of health and wellness. While health deals with the linear/manifest/dualistic/material realm and requires healing the physical body and staying healthy, wellness refers to healing the emotional, mental, and spiritual aspects of a being. The only way to heal those three aspects is for one to transcend above them (enlightenment), or at least to purify the ego. Wellness is really just about purifying the body and the ego from toxins and staying free from toxins, whether cigarettes, pesticides, negative thought forms, or negative will. While purification can make one feel clean, mentally and emotionally stable, and uplifted, enlightenment will make one feel unconditionally loved, blissful about existence, peaceful, completely healed, and universal oneness, along with a deep understanding of universal consciousness.

Wellness to the western world seems more like psychology and health mixed together, but to the spiritual aspirant it is a way of purifying the ego of all negative energetic structures and patterns. Even though many spiritual devotees regularly cleanse their physical bodies, *this is not needed to become enlightened or even to purify the ego*. Even Jesus stated that fasting does not cleanse one of toxins: "What goes into a man's mouth does not make him 'unclean,' but what comes out of his mouth, that is what makes him 'unclean'" (Matthew 15:11 [NIV]). One must only work on purifying the ego through meditation, introspection and reflection, prayer, and aligning themselves with the Divine Will—then completely transcending it. That is all that is needed. No strict diets, no fasting, and no seclusion from the world are necessary to attain enlightenment, although at times these may be very beneficial.

'Mind'fulness

This is the process of stopping the 'ego mind' to observe the 'Mind of the Self.' To put it plainly, one must observe being aware of all actions and thoughts that one has with compassion towards themselves. The **ego mind** is the mind that is used for focusing on things with detail, such as the main or central focus of what one does. The **Aware Mind** is aware of a being's functions but does not focus on them. It is simply aware of them because they are within consciousness. While higher, pure consciousness is aware of form, the **Pure Mind of God** as the **Unmanifest Self** (Source/existence) is not.

The **Aware Mind** as 'pure consciousness' is relatively silent and recognizes all form, but does not take action in response to the illusory energies of the ego because no direct need or action is seen to be needed. It knows the motives or the will of the ego, while simultaneously knowing the 'hell' that it has created for itself. It need not see the action, or be told the thought that the ego had, because the **Aware Mind** already knows what they are spiritually—an ego-afflicted version that is a distorted reality.

The **Mind of God**, on the other hand, is existence as One. It is God as the Unmanifest. It is the Source. The **Mind of God** is existence itself, which is infinite and formless. It is the Unmanifest essence that is the building block or foundation of consciousness and form. The **Mind of God** is the **Unmanifest Self** and is not able to recognize form, sins, or any egos. It is pure formlessness as love and peace. It is not even aware of consciousness.

The **ego mind**, however, tries to distort every instance of a being's moment so that it cannot experience the True Reality. The ego's job is to keep the 'mind' busy interpreting signs, signals, concepts, and theories, while interacting within this manifest dimension, thus 'muddying the clear water,' or 'creating ripples in the still pond,' so to speak. Every ego experience and mental activity can be likened to mud thrown into a clean pond, or ripples in still water. The **ego mind** blocks the experience of the **Aware Mind**, which then blocks the realization of Unmanifest Self, or True and Absolute Reality. So it can be seen that one must discard, abandon, or heal (however one wants to put it) the ego in order to experience the **Aware Mind** aspect of **God as Totality** (enlightenment).

'Mindfulness' is really a term that is used to denote being aware of all that one does, such as being aware of taking every step while walking, or being aware of every bite while eating. This does not mean just to eat and be aware of it, it means to 'be aware' of every instant. For example, as one eats food, be aware of why the food is even in existence (God), analyze the food, give thanks for the food, be aware of the action that the arm and hand make while one is taking the food to the mouth, then analyze the way one chews and swallows it, then analyze the pathway that the food travels, and give thanks for the nourishment that the food gives one's self.

Mindfulness can be practiced everywhere at any time. In fact, it can be done all day long in every instant of existence. For example, be aware of waking up, then cleaning up and getting dressed, then eating and driving to work, and then be aware of being at work and any task that one does. If one is not doing anything significant, one may simply be aware of the motion of their breath. Also, be aware that the body breathes due to the integration of the consciousness with the brain that activates the diaphragm to contract and release numerous times without actually having to focus on it, which inherently creates the activity known as breathing.

After these awareness activities are done, it will then be discovered that there is no 'doer' of any of these actions that one has been led to believe they have 'done' in their life before. It will be understood that the interaction of consciousness levels produces an outcome at a specific level of consciousness that allows a being to have a certain and limited level of awareness due to the restrictions of the ego. Thus, with the Aware Mind, as pure consciousness, these events within the manifest realms of existence will seem to happen all on their own. There is no specific cause for anything, because everything is interlinked to Allness.

One will realize that the ego does not sustain existence, but rather, it is an impersonal aspect of the soul that can be abandoned, allowing one to reside fully within the Aware Mind/Higher Self that is aware of True existence. Remember that existence is infinite and nonexistence is an impossibility that was created to scare the soul into depending on the ego for sustenance or survival. Now that the fear of nonexistence is known to be an illusion, the **Aware Mind** allows one to exist peacefully without the fear of nonexisting. One may now understand that the ego is only the source of distraction/distortion from the Source/Self/Mind itself, thus giving one full reliance on God and the realization that one is and always has been completely safe from any illusory harm. That which is formless/Real is not subject to any harm by the manifest realms of form/illusion.

"No-Mind"

Through meditation, one may be aware of thoughts or the thinking process itself. With the **ego mind**, it believes that it creates the thoughts and ideas, but with **Aware Mind** one notices that the thoughts always existed and did not originate from the ego, as has been claimed. Thus, one can see the random thoughts that run rampant through one's mind, disturbing the 'stillness of the water' (Mind), or 'Pure Mind.'

Depending on one's level of consciousness, an infinite possibility of potentiality is already existing and waiting to be chosen as a sound, word, action, or thought. As this potentiality for the specific level of consciousness that one is currently at integrates with the manifest reality, a connection is and has been created for the manifest to flow freely into one's **ego mind**. As these thoughts, ideas, and actions continuously flow, the important and mostly relevant energetic structures (words, emotions, ideas, pictures, sensory perceptions, and understandings) are selected or picked for use in the current manifest interaction by **ego will**. As these endless energetic patterns are classified, judged, and organized, the ego now picks out what appears or seems to be the most relevant for the current situation at hand. This process of making the random selection and claiming that one owns the energetic structure or pattern takes less than one second for fast thinkers, and a little bit longer for slower thinkers. As the ego selects the random thoughts, ideas, pictures, feelings, emotions, or perceptive abilities, it then claims them as 'mine.' Sayings such as, "Hey guys, listen to what I just thought of," now seem completely absurd and ridiculous with the knowingness that no one can create anything except the Universal Whole (already infinitely created). Now this ego can be seen for what it is: confused and mistaken, or simply unaware.

To achieve the state of 'no-mind,' which refers to the abandonment of ego mind, one must transcend the ego in order to stop the seemingly endless disturbances or distractions. One may do this in a couple of ways. One way is to constantly question the ego, a process known as 'introspection.' This will deprogram and unravel the ego's structure, canceling out many of the thought forms that so readily flow throughout one's surface mind. These distractions will decrease in frequency, revealing the more profound state of awareness known as **Aware Mind** (pure consciousness—Higher Self [consciousness]), and then hopefully revealing the **Mind of God** (formless, infinite existence), which is the Unmanifest Self (beyond consciousness). At first, whole paragraphs or stories may disappear, and then sentences and fragments will soon dissipate. The state of awareness that one is trying to achieve is one of no-thoughts, known as 'no-mind.' Since the ego is the 'thinking mind,' just transcend the ego and clear the mind from all needless 'thinking.'

The other approach that is commonly used, due to the impatience of current society, is the 'fixity of focus' technique, also known as 'One Mindedness.' This requires one to find a focal point and concentrate relentlessly on it for an extended period, such as 10, 20, 30, 40, or 50 minutes, or until the supreme state of awareness is attained. In effort to concentrate on one object, the ego mind is consumed with this one object, which basically helps the ego deny any other fragment of energy that may be formed as a thought or idea. As the ego mind is overwhelmed with only **one stimulus**, all other stimuli are blocked out, due to lack of recognition. This will silence the mind by blocking out the rest of existence.

The opposite method, which is more effective, is concentration onto peripheral vision, instead of the central focus that the ego mind is more commonly used to. This actually helps the Mind activate as awareness, while the ego (focusing mind) shuts off (a little) due to the lack of 'things' to recognize and identify with. This is the best type of meditation that can be done, besides 'breath awareness,' to help one align with the **Aware Mind/Self**.

Analyzing the Ego
The questions in section are to be introspected on during meditation.

The process of introspection will alleviate the 'thinkingness' of the ego, canceling out many of the problematic thought forms while revealing a more profound level of awareness. There are no linear answers here; instead, revelations unfold as the ego mind begins to cease and the Self radiates forth as Truth.

One must sit in meditation for at least 10 minutes and relax with peaceful and rhythmic breathing known as pranayama (refer back to the meditation chapter); then the process of contemplation may begin. Each question must be thought upon for at least 15 minutes, or until one has a revelation—an 'ah-ha' or 'lightbulb' moment. When one realizes Truth, the level of consciousness will raise, which reveals more Truth. It may take all of the following questions to become enlightened, or it may take more; it may also only take one question. All depends on one's willingness and current level.

The process of introspection is as follows: pray and align one's Will with God's, relax by breathing for 10 to 15 minutes (yoga may also be used), reflect on the desired question, receive the 'ah-ha moment,' keep on prying as if there is more to it than what has been shown, try to attain another 'ah-ha moment,' write it down and reflect on it later as well, then either ask yourself another question that enters your mind or refer to one of these questions that are provided later in the chapter to stimulate the transcension process. This process uses the ego, which likes to 'think,' in order to transcend itself, and is a trick used to loosen its grip.

Author's 'Personal' Note on Introspection

About 99% of the time during my enlightenment process, introspection was used. It is much more powerful than the ego will give it credit for. Praying is very powerful and necessary for the alignment of Divine Will and showing devotion to a higher purpose. Writing down the reflective meditations is important so one may look back on the answer, which allows many more 'ah-ha moments' to follow. *One may also introspect in a normal ego waking state and reap the benefits as well*, but introspection during a meditative state often proves to be the most beneficial.

Actions

When one acts out or does something, just ask yourself why it was done: was it for self-gain, or was it to help others? Maybe it was done for pure fun, which would denote that the ego denied the happiness that God infinitely supplies and chose a temporary event that they mistakenly thought would bring them happiness. Was anyone injured during this action? If so, what was the motive for the action? Was it an accident; did one injure someone to help another, or did one injure someone for one's own sake? Ask yourself, why do I walk? Where do I walk to? Why is walking needed? Why do I breathe? Do I, the ego, breathe, or is it autonomous? Why do I think? Do I think? Where did this thought come from? What am I without my thoughts and perceptions? If I had no body or ego with perceptions and emotions, what would I be? Do I think the same as other ego beings? If not, why?

Words

Analyze what you say and why you say it. Be aware of speech and notice that it can actually carry on effortlessly without concentration from the ego. Ask yourself, what is the reason for speech? Is it needed? If words didn't exist, how would I communicate? Why doesn't everyone understand my words? Why does the content of the words that a being speaks seem to determine the content of the being itself? What is the very essence of a word? How was it created? Did I create it? Or did it already exist and I simply presented it as my own? If words didn't exist, how would

I understand myself? Would I understand myself? Do words really reflect who and what I am? If I am at a certain level of consciousness, would I still speak the same words? If I in fact spoke the same words as I did in my previous level of consciousness, would the words have a whole new meaning? What is the difference of a low level of consciousness word and a high level of consciousness word? What level of consciousness are the words that fill my mind?

Intentions and Will

As I progress throughout my day, what do I intend to do? For what? Why? Is it a way for searching for happiness outside myself? Is this 'will' or intention in accordance with the ego or the Divine? Why do I work? Is it out of love for my family or for myself? Or is it just something I have to do every day? Do I perform my duties with contempt for mankind, or do I care deeply for each and every person I meet? Do I help others spiritually evolve? Or am I a hindrance to their lifestyle and spiritual evolution? Do I want to harm people? Do I even care if anyone gets injured? Do I help beings stay safe? Is this lifestyle I lead an integrous one, or is it nonintegrous? Is my 'Will' aligned with helping all beings understand who and what they are, or do I even care? Do I carry on with life because I have to, or because I love to exist? Am I thrilled to help others, or do I even care? Do I help others so that onlookers think I am a nice, upstanding citizen? Or is it from my heart? From my being?

Thoughts, Beliefs, and Ideas

Is thinking necessary for existence? Or is it necessary for this physical incarnation? Are these thoughts mine? Or do they exist and am I just borrowing them? If I can't think, then does anyone else think either? Or do we all just steal thoughts from the infinite potentiality? Are all religious beliefs correct, or was I just programmed to believe so? Does an ego even understand Truth? What is a belief? When I think of an idea, where did the idea come from? Does God have ideas or thoughts? If I think about God, can I understand God? Is it even possible to think without God? If I don't think, will I still exist? If one is enlightened and they speak, how do they speak, if the ego has supposedly been transcended, since the ego is responsible for decisive action and decisions and aids in comprehension and communication? Is it even necessary to have a body in order to exist? Can an ego-free consciousness still communicate?

A Lesson in Forgiveness

Forgiveness is the most important aspect of enlightenment. Without it, one may never reach enlightenment. If one chooses not to forgive, the level of Love will be nearly impossible to attain. One cannot unconditionally love others if they cannot even forgive what someone has done to them in the past. Forgiveness is essential for enlightenment. This means that everybody who has done you wrong (so to speak) must be forgiven. Whether they have slapped, yelled, framed, hit, or even raped you, they must be forgiven. If anyone has killed your friend, family, child, or spouse, they must be forgiven. There are no exceptions to forgiveness.

Every event in one's life has an emotional and mental attachment associated with it. These emotional attachments are of the ego; thus they are keeping one's frequency lowered due to the low ego frequency that a being insists on holding onto. As these lower ego frequencies are forgiven, the result is 'Release.' This means that the lower ego frequencies are released and are no longer keeping one from the Truth, thus allowing one to experience their True nature.

At first, forgiveness may seem like an impossibility. But with practice and understanding, it will flow freely like water. The ego is so attached to its positionalities about certain matters that whether it was right or wrong doesn't make a difference. Whether something brings pain or happiness doesn't make the ego want to release it either. With an understanding of the wisdom attained from a text or a teacher, the ego will begin to comprehend that the process of release may make it feel better; such as 'seeking' happiness in the process of forgiveness. So the ego then forgives others for the wrongdoing and then assumes that the happiness was in the process, when really it was in the revelation attained by the Presence of God/Truth that was revealed when the clouds of the ego's nonforgiveness were released.

Forgiveness is really only possible with understanding. One must understand why to forgive. It is important to realize that everyone really doesn't understand what they are doing or why they are doing it. They feel that they are in control of their life, when in actuality, it is happening on its own due to one's current level of consciousness. If one has done something that has deeply offended you, just realize that they didn't mean it. It was an impersonal attack, or their level of consciousness was simply *naturally* expressing itself. Because of a lack of Divine guidance, the ego and its lesser 'wills' coerced or forced one to do the 'ill-action' and to speak the words. Remember that all of mankind is like a giant sock puppet reflecting its current level of consciousness. There is no 'doer' of actions; there is no 'thinker' behind thoughts; there is no personal attacker: all is a result of one's level of consciousness. So nothing was a personal attack on you; one's level of consciousness attracted the other being's level of consciousness. The outcome that presented itself was a product of the totality of consciousness of the universe, the solar system, planet, astrological signs, birthdays, country, state, city, county, area of town, building, room, air pressure, humidity level, temperature, event, people present with their consciousness levels, circumstances surrounding the event, and so forth. So everything that ever happened to one's self was a product of one's own karmic propensities, other people's levels of consciousness that interacted with them or that were around them, and the universal karmic frequency when the event occurred. All happened exactly the way it needed to be expressed.

So the real question is, "Why shouldn't one forgive another for a 'wrongdoing' that somehow affected them in an offensive manner?" There was no specific individual who brought it upon one's self; it was of the totality of the universal consciousness. Everything happens for a specific reason that is needed for one to learn a lesson. So whatever happens to one is already coming, whether one asks for it knowingly or unknowingly. People who follow their 'ego will' ask for suffering, but beings who follow their 'Spiritual Will' are blessed on a daily basis. So forgive yourself for all of your 'wrongdoings' and all others for any of their 'wrongdoings,' because neither of you knew what you were doing, or understood that an ego claimed dominance over your lives. So all pain and suffering is in the past and never needs to be experienced again. As one lets go of their emotional attachments, freedom from limitation and restriction begins with unlimited and infinite bliss and joy.

- *Forgive one's self and have compassion towards past deeds.*
- *Forgive others: family, friends, enemies, and assaulters.*
- *Forgive and Release past-life karmic connections that one may know, or not know of.*
- *Forgive any unknown thoughts that were against you.*

Emotional Attachments

E-motions are the tools that the e-go (phonetic device) uses to create motivation and drive in one's life on a material/manifest level. The emotions are created to prompt one to do something, or to stay away from it. The emotions are also used to help one remember events, people, places, and pets. The main purpose of the emotions is to reinforce the ego's identity with the 'likes' and 'dislikes' that the mechanism of the ego, known as judgment, categorizes.

These 'likes and dislikes' create an internal positionality on any event, thing, or being—for example, "I hate Billy, but I like his car." This statement or opinion, along with innumerable others, helps to create and reinforce the ego with its feeling of who and what it thinks it is (identity). More of the 'hate' opinions create a more ego-driven being, while more of the 'love,' which is usually falsely attached to an event, person, or place, manifests opinions that create a more ego-driven being as well. Only 'Love,' which is from the Divine Source, can create a spiritual being who operates as a channel of God's Will and is inspired (not motivated—ego) to serve others.

The 'love' (describes the ego's excessive likes) opinions are statements made that reflect the ego's desire to have something, because of the belief that the item, thing, person, or pet brings happiness to them; this inherently denies God's Love, which is already given and present at all times. The ego believes that the 'thing' has this feeling within it, such as, "When I get that car, I'll be so happy." This shows the ego's emotional attachment, which is associated with the false 'ego love' with the 'thing' (car), and therefore is not a Divine expression. Too much 'ego love' (excessive liking) can create a more selfish being, due to the excessive wants that are created from the desires to 'have something.' Excessive desires create cravings and addictions that can control and dominate one's life for all of eternity if not properly dealt with or realized.

If the domineering quality, or presence of, 'hate' controls one's life, then a stronger feeling of judgment and separation ensues, making one feel more independent and further from God, which creates a feeling of loneliness. This 'hate' quality prompts one to make those 'snap judgments' that create a more individualized and separated life view. Statements such as, "I hate those Jews and Spaniards," create diversity within this already seemingly divided linear realm. This 'racism' is judgment and hatred to an extreme. The negative energy acts like a magnet and attracts other negatively charged beings to participate in this 'divided act,' bringing in or attracting acquaintances of the same low level of consciousness who can bond emotionally with the already troubled ego.

As one transcends the emotional states of the ego, it can be seen that the emotions were of the ego, and all 'love' that it knew was an illusion because it was thought to come from a separate manifest form that has no capability to provide 'Love.' That being soon realizes that 'Love' can be and is only experienced because of the Divine, and that without the Divine, not only would there be no existence (which is an impossibility), there would never be the ability to experience 'Love'—or life for that matter. Therefore, since the ego provides the emotions, Love is now known to be, rather, a state of awareness, or existence itself. Remember that

God is infinite, God is Love, God is peace, God is stillness, God is happiness, God is joyful bliss, God is existence, and all of these are One and the same. So that which is not a part of the Absolute Truth (God) is a diversion (ego) and an illusion that will keep one from adopting higher values and principles, due to its feelings (emotions) of false satisfaction (acquiring love and happiness dualistically) that it thinks are true or real.

This entire manifest/dualistic/linear dimension creates the illusion of separateness, which inherently makes the ego feel as if certain material things can bring happiness. If the perceptive mode of the ego can be transcended, the awareness of God's infinite 'Love' will be felt and known to be existence itself.

Analyzing Emotional Attachments
Question where your emotions came from and why.

- *What is the feeling you get while driving your car? What is the feeling you get as another person looks at your car? Do you feel impressive, embarrassed, or happy? Do you like driving? If so, why?*
- *Do you decorate your house? Do you like it or not like it? If so, why? Do you like or dislike the neighborhood? If so, why? And as you answer why, realize that you just judged.*
- *Do you smoke cigarettes, do drugs, drink alcohol? Do you like or dislike it? Why? Do you crave anything? Why?*
- *Do you like nature? Do you feel happy when in nature? Why? Do you like to go to the mountains? Why do you like to go to the beach? Why do you feel vacations bring happiness? Is it because you hate or dislike your job?*
- *Are you in school? Do you like or dislike school? Why? How do you feel about your teachers? Why? Do you like or dislike your homework? Why? Do you stay away from other students in your school because you don't like them? If so, why? Do you judge other*

students? Why? If so, does it make you feel better than them or happy? Why do you make fun of others or critique them? Are you flawless?

- *Do you have any friends whom you can't wait to see? Why are they so special? If you feel that they are special, is it the traits of the 'ego will' or the traits of God's Will that you admire? Do your friends make you happy? If happiness cannot be acquired through another being, where does it come from?*

- *If you have a girlfriend or boyfriend, do you love them? Why can you experience 'Love'? Is it 'Love,' or is it 'ego love'? Do you desire them and their physical body, or do you respect and love them for their pure existence? Do you want to change any aspect of them? If so, why? Are you yourself perfect? Then how can you change another if you yourself do not set a 'good' example? If you see any faults of the other being, you judged them. Why? Do you feel that you are allowed to judge? Do you feel as if you are 'better' or 'worse' than they are? If God created all things as perfect, then what are you judging as imperfect?*

- *What are your hobbies? Do they make you happy? Is it the hobby that makes you happy? Or is it your experience of existence while doing the hobby that allows you to be happy? If God is the only source of Love and happiness, why do you think that your hobby makes you happy?*

- *Do you like sex? Do you have sex for procreation (which is a holy act), or do you have sex for recreation (which is for the ego's pleasure only)? Do you Love the being whom you are with? Or do you intensely like the physical attributes that they have? Do you worship and Love the purity of their Spirit, or God? Or do you worship material things such as the ego and material things? Ask yourself why you have sex?*

- *Is sex necessary to express love? If one loves their*

children and parents, do they need to have sex with them to express it? Or can it be done verbally? Can it be done nonverbally? How would it make you feel if the being whom you were with never wanted to express their love to you with sex? If you would feel sad, then why? Is not God the only source of happiness that one needs? Is not God the only supply or Source of Love and happiness in the universe?

- *Do you like to read this book? Why? Is it satisfying 'ego will' (the ability to have power, control, or be special above others), or is it following 'Divine Will' (to Love all others unconditionally and to help all mankind spiritually evolve)? Why do you feel this way? Is there a part of your being that wants to say, "I am God," so you can impress others or feel powerful? Or will you be humble? Why?*

- *Do you treasure every instant of existence? Or do you hate life and all that is within it? Do you accept the different conditions of the atmosphere around you and love them all the same? Or do you hate rainy days and like sunny days? Or do you complain if it is too hot, too cold, too humid, too wet, too dry, too damp, etc...?*

- *Do you like or dislike interaction with other beings? Why? Do you like to help others at any cost, or do you like to stay self-centered and help yourself? Do you serve 'Divine Will' or 'ego will'? Is it not your nature to help all others and serve God? Why or why not?*

- *Do you like to think (an ego function)? Or are you attached to the very method of thinkingness? Do you derive pleasure from contemplating physical concepts or spiritual Truths? Are you pleased or displeased with your knowledge that you have acquired? Do your beliefs and knowledge make you feel like you are your own person, an individual with special qualities and traits that no other has but you? Isn't this pride?*

- *Do you open-mindedly research and compare beliefs*

in various religions while searching for spiritual Truths? Or do you compare religions so you can prove that one is 'better' than another? Do you feel as if your ego made you an expert?

- *Do you like the clothes you wear or hate them? Or do you have no opinion at all? Do you feel that these clothes help to reinforce your identity? When people see you, do they expect to see you wearing the same old clothes? Does the image that you have created for yourself have a preppy, dorky, alternative, classy, business, sexy, unkempt, uncaring, dirty, baggy, or beach feel? If someone suddenly said that you could never dress your usual way for the rest of your life, would you be happy, sad, depressed? If you were told that you had to wear an ensemble that you didn't like, would you be upset or uncomfortable wearing it? Is there an article of clothing, glasses, purse, watch, ring, or even makeup or way that you do your hair that you are attached to? If you lost that article of clothing, would you be upset?*

- *Is there a hangout spot that your friends associate you with? If you have been going there for years, or doing something for fun for a while, would you be upset if you were never allowed to go again? If it burned down, would you feel depressed because you would never be able to go there again? Or would you be concerned for the being who lost their business? Or would you be concerned if anyone got hurt? (Be honest, your first thought is usually the most important to you.)*

- *Do you like to see, hear, smell, touch, or taste things? Would you be saddened by the loss of one or all of your senses? If so, why? Do you think that your senses make you who you are? Do you think that you wouldn't exist without your senses? Are there any emotional attachments to your senses? Are there any memories that you can recall that used a method of*

*perception? Do you think that the pleasure of exist-
ence comes from the ability to perceive things? Without God you could not exist, without perception there
is still God's Love, which is infinite existence. So of
what benefit is perception, when God already has
supplied all that is needed? Is it simply a vanity?*

All of the previous questions allow one to see their emotional attachments and the structure of their identity. Be completely
honest and you will most definitely raise in consciousness level,
but if you are not even honest with yourself, then of what value
are these introspective questions? If you lie to yourself, or are not
totally honest in answering these questions, you will just reinforce your ego identity, thus lowering your current level of consciousness and falling further from God. So be honest and compassionate to all of your own thoughts and 'ego will.' After all,
you never meant to harm anyone, think the 'wrong' thoughts, or
act on the 'ego will,' since it was an impersonal attack due to the
control that the ego imposed, because of the intrinsic nature of the
ego's ignorance and the interacting levels of consciousness. So
forgive yourself for any sins and surrender them to God. All will
be, and already is, forgiven; all that needs to happen is for you to
realize that.

If you seem or feel very uncaring or have a lack of
compasssion after answering the previous questions, do not hold
yourself in contempt, for you will only lower your level of consciousness. Just understand your error in choosing 'ego will' and
then adopt the higher values of the 'Spiritual Will.' You cannot try
to get rid of negative thoughts, feelings, and 'will,' because that
would require one to force the negative energy out of one's auric
field (ego). Force (control/energy manipulation) is a product of
the 'ego will,' so this methodology is an illusory form of healing.
One may force the energy to move throughout the energy bodies
through energy work, but the energetic patterns will just recirculate and redevelop, forming new or old problems that need to be
dealt with once again.

Overcoming Duality

An observation of the manifest that displays itself to the perceptive modality of the ego mind is known as duality. The ego's sequential method of placing the perceived forms of reality, which provides for the possibility of separating, classifying, and judging things within the realm of the linear, helps one to feel a part of or within existence. Duality is an observation made on the paradigm of the linear reality with perception. It is the paradox that many believe to exist. That is why many are not enlightened: because of the truth given to duality. The 'seeming opposites' are really just a mentation of the ego. In Reality, no opposites can exist, because everything is One and formless.

Duality requires form, and the Unmanifest is formless. Duality requires the perceptive faculties of the ego mind to receive the seemingly distant objects of form within the manifest levels of existence, but neither the ego nor consciousness is within the Unmanifest. Without perception, the ego would not be reinforced as much, due to an inability to feel separated, through external means, from God as its own unique separate identity. Without identity, there is no ego. So truly without duality, there is no ability to perceive form. Without the possibility of form, the linear realm would never exist. If there were no form, structure, or possibility of having an energetic pattern, the ego and the manifest/linear could not truly exist. This is due to the ego, which is an energetic pattern based on a structured reality of a sequential, logical, and rational order of the world of form; thus it has no True (Unmanifest) existence.

This leaves the question that so many beings contemplate: "So, without perception, what am I?" The answer: one is awareness, Love, existence, peace, and stillness, which are all one and the same—so one (referring to the Higher Self, not ego-self) is the formless consciousness aspect of God. And beyond Awareness, one is beyond consciousness as the Unmanifest. The universal "I-ness" that one "Is," is the Oneness that provides and is Allness, which is beyond Beingness, but is still the essence of All That Is.

Understanding the False Polarities

Everything within the realm of the linear, or manifest, is placed within the arbitrary paradoxes that seem to make sense to the ego and also help one verbalize their positionalities and understand their 'likes' and 'dislikes.' These polarities are written about by many so-called spiritual masters and scientific minds, who inherently mislead society into believing that duality is more than a possibility, "it is a reality" (i.e., Yin and Yang). Any enlightened sage knows that duality is only an illusory mentation within the ego mind that is created out of false and arbitrary points of observation and positionalities on an infinite gradation of energy or realm of possibilities.

All seeming points or polarities were just randomly chosen on a scale that has endless gradations or expressions. These endless gradations of the scale are viewed by the ego's perceptive methods, which, by way of positionality, places points that are thought to be *opposites* on the scale, thus blocking out the realization of the infinite scale while only seeing what it believes to be the *highest and lowest points of that scale* (*opposites*). So only the uppermost and lowermost frequencies that the ego can perceive are believed to exist and thought to be *opposites*. Without the realization that duality is false, one will never become enlightened, for it is a prerequisite and a necessity for ego transcension.

These *opposites* are thought by the ego to rule or control the linear realm that is thought to be reality. The paradoxes include hot and cold, life and death, high and low, left or right, right or wrong, bad or good, male and female, tall or short, interesting and boring, smart or dumb, attractive or ugly, known and unknown, light and dark, and many more. In Reality, none of these are opposites; they are all One, but simply reflect a different quality of energy. For example, male and female are not opposites; they are just different qualities of energy that reflect a different quality of beingness. They are not opposite, just different. For example, what about transsexuals, hermaphrodites, and eunuchs? Where are they placed on a dualistic scale that supposedly has only two opposites?

When it comes to the most common opposites known by man, such as 'hot and cold' and 'light and dark,' this is just arbitrary terminology that helps one identify and communicate the perceived differences within the linear dimension. For 'light and dark,' what is light and what is dark? How do we measure 'darkness' or 'lightness'? Since darkness is the absence of <u>visible</u> light, then the presence of light in varying powers obviously is perceived as bright, brighter, brightest, blindingly bright, and stunningly bright. So with darkness, when the presence of <u>visible</u> light is taken away in varying powers or intensities, the ego's perception labels this as dim, dimmer, dimmest, dark, darker, darkest, and no <u>visible</u> light, obviously showing a limitation of perception.

Furthermore, if one is confined in a room with no windows that allow natural light, and the lights are off, that room feels and seems dark. Then as one goes outside at nighttime, it is also called dark. This is because the moon adds natural light, which illuminates the outside a little. However, if the moon's light is taken away, the streetlights are turned off, and all of the electricity in homes and shops on the planet is turned off, the ego labels this as "pitch black." But even when all of these lights are turned off, light still exists, although at a frequency that the ego cannot perceive, interpret, or comprehend. Atoms produce light and energy called subatomic particles; the subatomic particles give off subtle energetic light qualities. But since the ego cannot see the subtle light, it does not recognize its existence, therefore labeling it 'pitch black' outside. Just because the ego or scientific equipment does not and cannot pick up certain frequencies does not mean that they do not exist. However, this is exactly how it is interpreted.

So then arises the big question, "What then is dark, if what I had thought was dark is really not as dark as what I just experienced?" The answer is that there is no dark. Darkness is the absence of light, and an absence of light would mean an absence of existence (God), which is an impossibility. This helps one realize that only light exists in varying levels. Similarly, one's existence is simply a light that is illuminated to a certain extent. It is either a light that is infinitely bright (God), or it is a light that has been dimmed by the presence of the ego (light still exists even if an ego won't see it).

Just the same, the presence of heat in varying levels creates the seeming duality of the paradox, 'hot and cold.' Even scientists know that only heat exists and that coldness is an impossibility. As a sun shines from billions of light years away, the heat on a planet (figuratively speaking) may be -700 degrees. However, if a sun shines from 2,000 light years away, the temperature or the presence of heat may be +1,000 degrees. So coldness doesn't exist; only heat does, although in varying intensities. For example, to go from -700 degrees to -701 degrees, a unit or measure of 'heat' would have to be taken away. One cannot add 'coldness,' for it does not exist. It can be viewed the same as the false paradox of 'light and dark'; 'darkness' does not exist, but light does in varying intensities.

Within the concept of life and death, one can see that it is only an illusion, because God is infinite existence; therefore to die or to go out of existence is an absurdity. Death in the physical realm implies that something has ceased to exist, for example, "a person who dies must go out of existence because the body lies here lifeless." The body can be compared with a car; it is only a vehicle for transportation. At first, the vehicle is new and fascinating, but as time passes (so to speak), the vehicle becomes more and more uninteresting (for most egos) and eventually breaks down. This prompts the soul to leave the body and to transfer to the next realm of the spiritual manifest, leaving an empty or vacated shell known to this linear dimension as the 'physical body.'

The Spirit/Self/God can never be destroyed; it is infinite. Therefore, the Spirit exists infinitely and is not subject to non-existence; neither is any other type of energy. Just as light exists and darkness is an illusion, life exists and death is an illusion. Death, a term of the physical dimension, is simply the soul's abandonment of the physical body to carry on with life in another energetic plane of existence, whether within the spiritual manifest (heavens or hells of form), or as One in and as the Unmanifest.

Similarly, tall and short, ugly and beautiful, interesting and boring, smart and dumb, left and right, and right or wrong are just relative points of perception created out of the false mentation of positionality that was based on a purely arbitrary scale developed by the ego to help one delineate and categorize the energies of the manifest. Just the same, the words chosen are arbitrary. In actuality, they have no significance or meaning except to the preprogrammed ego mind who tries to compute the information as fact, truth, or reality.

These are all just relative points of view that are compared with one's internal template, which has been previously learned or programmed as one's being by the current log of past knowledge and experiential events. In other words, what is tall to a 3-foot-tall person is short to a 7-foot-tall person, just as a person facing you will not understand directions if you use your current point of view of 'left and right.' You must put the content (the directions being given) into the proper context (understandable meaning) for a being to understand.

Just the same, a person may be beautiful to one being, but ugly to another. Beauty is a product of God, because God is the source of love, happiness, peace, perfection, and beauty. As one claims that something or someone is ugly, they are judging God's creation as a 'bad' creation. But as the Bible states, "God saw all that He had made, and it was good" (Genesis 1:31 [NIV]). This states (while not minding the duality of Creator and created and 'good,' which allows for the ego polarity 'bad,' plus the gender reference of He, and the terminology "saw," which denotes an ego function only) that all of creation is 'good.' This means that there is no 'bad,' because "all is good." Therefore all is perfection, without mistake. So all problems do not even exist, except within our own ego mind. (It is important to note that the Bible was written with much dualism, due to the lack of intelligence of the individuals at that time. There was really no other way to express it with understanding.)

Creation vs. Destruction

Probably the most confusing topic for spiritual aspirants to understand is the seeming polarity of creation vs. destruction. These two views are different due to dissimilar positionalities. To one ego's positionality, something destructive may seem creative, and to another, the opposite. This is simply due to both of their egos' view points and levels of consciousness, which make one see things differently. For example, the environmentalist sees things differently than the government bureaucrat. One sees ripping up grass lands to put in a paved road as destructive, while the other sees it as creative and efficient (respectively speaking).

Similarly, one individual at a low level of consciousness may see breaking mailboxes as constructive with one's time. However, another ego who resides at a higher level of consciousness (unenlightened) sees that this is a purely destructive energy. While these two beings may debate what is constructive and destructive, the enlightened being, who knows everything to be a creative act, sees why these two think this way and therefore steps in to bring peace to the issue at hand because neither is wrong. In reality, they are both confused because of their differences in opinion that create an internal positionality from an emotional response to a situation that was programmed by their level of consciousness.

Just the same, everything is in the process of, going through, and subject to creation during every instant of existence. There is no way to escape creation. So as one 'destroys' a mailbox, it is actually creation that allowed for it to be 'destroyed' (just think of it as the atoms being rearranged due to creation allowing it to happen). So destruction is actually creation, because all that is within existence is within creation at every instant of its existence. Since God is infinite existence and continuous creation, then no 'thing' can happen outside of God as Totality. Therefore, All is creation and constantly creating at every instant, since God is creation.

To clarify a bit more using another example, a bomb that is set off that destroys 200 square miles was only allowed to happen because God is creation. So when that bomb goes off, every molecule that is set into motion by the bomb is guided by the laws of creation. Remember that under scientific law (Newton's Law of Conservation of Energy), "energy cannot be destroyed." So this means that energy is within creation infinitely and cannot escape it. The creative power of God is also responsible (besides the ego willing it into expression) for all action that could ever be set into motion. This means that all 'things' possible are due to God's allowance. So the bomb is not destructive; it is creative. However, the beings who use this so-called 'destructive force' of the bomb have what they think are creative or constructive uses for it. These will be judged, by the ego, to be either constructive or destructive in nature. But to God, or higher beings, the bomb simply is what it is: a perfect expression of its level of consciousness and use of potentiality that actualized exactly as it was 'willed' (by ego) to be.

Relativity

The term *Relativity* means that the quality and extent of an experience are limited by the experiencer's level of content (thoughts, emotions, and beliefs) that is processed within the level of context (consciousness level) that is already known and that one is able to be aware of. Simply put, every experiencer will experience reality and the events within it differently due to one's differing ability to perceive, understand, and realize. Regardless, 'relativity' only denotes an experience within the dualistic/linear dimensions.

For example, as a person walks through a room and a smell is picked up, they think that the scent is how the whole room smells. However, that being may have only picked up a scent that covers 5 cubic feet of a 100 cubic-foot room, therefore tricking them into believing that the whole room smells. Just as the sky has 'air pockets' that planes frequently fly through, rooms have scent pockets. Not all scents diffuse throughout the entire environment; however, the ego will believe the event that it experienced exactly how the ego experienced it. So the ego's perception is that the whole room smells, but the truth of the matter is that just a portion of the room smells. This is due to the ego's perceptive limitations, which will not allow it to experience the reality that actually exists.

If two people walk through the room, one may smell the scent, while the other smells nothing. The same goes for sight, touch, taste, hearing, and the overall awareness of existence. No two souls experience exactly the same level of reality, nor are they experiencing the same level of awareness, nor can one process the same level of knowledge in exactly the same way as the other.

Many beings believe that they experience life the same

way as most others; however, this is not so. As one walks down the street with their thoughts and beliefs, as well as their overall level of consciousness and awareness, they affect life and existence around them completely differently than other beings. Just the same, each and every being interprets reality differently. As every (content) thought, action, word, idea, and context (level of awareness) of one's being influences how one experiences reality, it can be noticed that no two people experience existence in the same way, although there may be many similarities. Perception, as well as experience, is merely relative to the viewer and the level of consciousness within which they currently elect to reside.

Focus on the Context/Reality

As the ego experiences life, it tends to focus only on content, or what is seen, touched, tasted, smelled, heard, or thought of to be actual reality. As described above, the ego's thoughts, ideas, concepts, theories, words, actions, and feelings are the content of a being. Unfortunately, all content is illusion. Only the context, or the level of awareness that is experienced that allows the content even to be thought of, is the closest to reality. Until the context, or one's level of awareness, has been increased to the extent that the individual is considered an enlightened being, one does not experience and has not truly experienced Truth or Reality. So by one directing their awareness inward and introspecting, or questioning the ego's existence, the focus recedes from the previously concentrated-on content (illusion) to expand the level of awareness (Context). As light, or the answers to the questions of why one is or how one acts are (added) answered, one's awareness or context is increased, allowing one to witness and reflect on how one had previously thought, willed, and acted.

So as the content, or the illusory, has the pleasure and energy of focus diverted away from it and placed on the higher context (Truth), awareness becomes energized. This energizing of awareness is like blowing air into a balloon. At first, one looks at the balloon and admires the color, the texture, and the concept, but after a while, one blows air into the balloon, which energizes and expands one's experience of existence. This increase in awareness increases the joy experienced in life as existence, because of the added or realized and concentrated-on truth that ensues. So instead of wasting energy on meaningless illusory objects or thoughts of the manifest (content), one can simply place importance on the meaning (context), or level of consciousness that provides for the (objects).

Recontextualization

This is the process of rearranging words (archetypes/energetic patterns), so that the ego, from whom the words came, can reanalyze the sentence structure that has had the higher context (meaning/light) added by an enlightened being or the presence of Truth. This additional Power that has been added to an ego's energetic field can change the viewpoint of an ego significantly, possibly even enlightening the individual. This matter is discussed further in the chapter '*Analyzing Ego Linguistics*' (Chapter 14).

Causality

Causality is linear/dualistic terminology that is used to describe the seeming interaction of the manifest that was objectified, or crystallized energy that is perceived to propagate something else's motion and sequential actions, or a chain of events. It is an attempt to explain why, what, how, and to what extent something has happened or taken place by judging the interaction of the manifest energies. It is a means to try to measure and objectify, which is thought to bring forth the understanding of an energetic event or sequence of events that has taken place on a manifest plane of existence that has been thought to interact in the manifest dimension only. Thus it excludes Nonlinear energies, universal influences, and the ego's dictatorial energies that determine one's occurring and remanifesting events, which are unknowingly or knowingly chosen by one's own 'free will.'

By any means, causality does not exist, except within our minds. It is a false mentation of a 'specific' or 'certain' <u>cause</u> of something that is perceived as an event, or a chain of events. It only *seems* to exist due to the ego's lack of perceptive and subjective abilities. When one takes into account the context of the Nonlinear, metaphysical (the study of karmic potentialities and probabilities that influence one's direct energetic system known as the aura, the energies contained within, and the interaction of the spiritual energies of the spiritual manifest), and physical, it can be known that no one event or object causes, creates (besides God, but without intervening to cause, and ego will), or perpetuates any one outcome witnessed or perceived to be an event that was caused due to a manifest energetic interaction of the seemingly logical and rational.

In Reality, there is only One. Therefore, there is no thing that can cause another thing or an event to happen. All souls unknowingly or knowingly ask for their own lessons by willing to be an expression of a certain level of consciousness, so there is 'no thing' that has happened to them that created this misery by mistake; all happened on account of one's karmic potentiality and exercise of 'will.' As one examines the Truth of a matter or event, it is known that the so-called event was only allowed due to the county that it happened in, the city that provided for the county, the state that provided for the city, the country that provided for the state, the planet that provided for the country, the solar system that provided for the planet, the galaxy that provided for the solar system, the universe that provided for the galaxy, the universal karmic potentiality, the personal karmic potentiality, the negative energetic patterns or external influences, as well as positive, etc… So the universal influences, personal influences, circumstances, capabilities etc…, of a being were all factors that helped manifest the event that occurred. In totality, everything influences everything within the manifest level of creation. So the 'seemingly isolated act' or 'witnessed event' was really just one of many, as One synchronistic creative act in the Now.

It needs to be known that all happens at once within the current, present existence of Now. There are no separate events that are happening as such. All is not connected, but instead is One. So All events that are seemingly independent to the ego are really All of creation being witnessed as one simultaneous creative process. The manifest wasn't created; it still currently is creating in every approximate instant of Now.

In Reality, as Unmanifest, nothing occurs at all because All is still and unmoving. How can something happen when there is no other that something can happen to, no searcher who can search for anything, no reader who can read, no runner who can run, no talker who can talk, no abuser who can abuse, no backtalker who can backtalk, etc... There is no manifest energy in the Absolute and Unmanifest. Therefore, only an infinite energy that is an infinite potentiality can allow for the manifestation that provides the events that may be witnessed by the ego mind to be separate and independent events happening, due to something external causing them. So *causality was created by the ego* objectively witnessing the external interaction of all of the manifest properties simultaneously creating as such; it is an illusion and therefore not Reality.

The Experience of Now

To understand existence as a continuously creating event, one must experience the Now. This means <u>not</u> to use the mind to try and comprehend an experience, but just to live it within every moment. Just as no animal has to study what it is in order to enjoy its existence, neither does anyone else. In fact, thinking about experiencing life actually takes happiness and enjoyment away from the experience itself. Just think back to when you were a child: everything stimulates you, everything is fun and enjoyable. When the ego mind learns and judges what it thinks is fun and what it thinks is more fun, it tends to put a damper on life as an experience itself. So with every breath one takes or every move one makes, life should be enjoyed. If not, then the ego is trying to rationalize the event and compare it with other events that it knows will make it happy. This comparison makes one feel as if they would rather do what they just thought of, instead of what they are currently experiencing.

Keep in mind that a child enjoys walking, running, skipping, spinning, sometimes sitting, and just 'being.' Now ask yourself, "Do I? Or would I rather be doing something else?" If you would rather be doing something else, then you are not enjoying the experience of existence in the Now. Every thought that the ego has robs one of the enjoyment of existence. Happiness is lost when the ego tries to rationalize, comprehend, or think about an experience or any other concept at the time of the experience. When the ego wastes energy on thoughts, fears, or regrets about the past, present, or the future, enjoyment is lost, as well as peace and the ever-present ability to experience love and happiness to the utmost capacity.

Even Jesus states in the Bible that it is better to plan for *today* than to think about events that are not currently happening (such as past and future), and to pray to God for help and assistance *just for today* and not for one's whole life. Just the same, Jesus tells his disciples not to bring in the harvest for the whole year, just prepare for *one day* at a time. This basically emphasizes living in the Now and not preparing for or worrying about the future.

Every moment of one's life should be experienced as an instantaneous moment in creation that is taking place because of God's Grace, Love, and infiniteness. Don't think about an event as a creation, but instead think of every instant of every millisecond of that event as creation. Enjoy the ability to breathe, talk, hear, smell, touch, feel, move, think, experience, and just 'be.' Don't take these repeated tasks one does in life for granted. For without just one of them, what quality would your life have? The Truth is that one does not need any of these abilities to enjoy every instant of life. But since humans are blessed with these gifts, which allow for a more 'in touch' experience of reality, thanks to God should be given continuously throughout one's existence. After all, God is existence and all that one can experience.

If one feels as though the joy of existing is gone or dulled, then just slow life down that instant and say to yourself, "Live in the Now, experience the Now; the Now brings the happiness and Love of God without the restrictions of the ego." As you say this to yourself, try to enjoy the experience of movement, speech, touch, or any of the other perceptive faculties right then and there as Now. Become aware of your hand and your arm, while silently noting the fact that they remain completely intact and do what the ego thinks it wants them to do—how magnificent. Try to see your hand as it moves through the air, and hold in mind that without God's energy as existence, the hand would never move, or exist. So it can be seen that all things that you are allowed to do are due to God's allowance. Remember that, and try to see life as a perfect, delicate, and harmonious dance of energy within the infinite cosmos. The more that this is done, the more that one will feel at One with the Universal Whole in the Now of creation.

Ignoring Perception

Just as discussed in the earlier section, *'Levels of Identity Reinforcement,'* the many ways that the ego perceives simply enhance one's feeling of individualism in the universe. To bypass this drawback, a being needs simply not to focus on the events that occur in the physical manifest as much as before. The mind needs to be held clear, so that the many thoughts and perceptions may pass through, although still registering as existence within the manifest, but not as concentrated on as before. To focus on the manifest draws one to the lower manifest levels of consciousness; to focus on the Unmanifest brings forth enlightenment. So one should practice being 'aware' of reality, rather than critiquing its form.

Various methods that still the mind may be practiced, such as meditation, breathwork, and soft gazing. Instead of being in the habit of focusing on the little details of the manifest, one needs to simply shift focus onto the never-changing context of the Unmanifest Self. For instance, ego focus would be examining every change within the environment, but the awareness of 'pure consciousness' would remain unchanged and simply be aware of the never-changing surroundings. For example, at a racetrack, the ego would focus on the cars, the people, the birds, the grass, the asphalt, and so forth, in detail, but the 'pure consciousness' would just be aware of the racetrack and its intrinsic factors without being partial to one above another. By this method, a being may practice using awareness, which is an aspect of 'pure consciousness,' rather than using the judgmental and focusing aspect of the ego. This will help one not to judge people and things, which is a requirement before enlightenment. And with practice, and the inevitable release of consciousness itself, the Self as the Mind of God as the Unmanifest will be experienced as existence itself.

Meditation can be used to practice shutting off the ego mind. The very faculty of 'thinkingness' creates the false views or positionalities that despoil a being's mind. Therefore, shutting down the process of thinkingness, or what prompts the product of the manifest to enter a being's mind, can reveal an existence of formlessness. This is an experience of the Unmanifest qualities of the Self.

All energetic structures that do not present Truth do in fact empower the ego in its various endeavors, clouding one's mind with the illusory fantasies that are inherent in its lower levels of consciousness. So to still the mind is to experience the Mind. The benefits can obviously be seen, or rather known.

Chapter 14
<u>Analyzing Ego Linguistics</u>

Projectile Communications (Words)

The 'speaking of words' is the form of communication that the ego chooses, which seems (to the ego) to travel across time and space to describe an image or energetic stimulus that encourages languaging, or the expression of internal and external positionalities and emotional states. Languaging can only occur between two egos, not between an ego and God. Only exercising 'Spiritual Will' communicates with God (so to speak) via revelation, which uncovers Truth and knowingness that are and always have been present.

Due to the ego's inherent structure and qualities of form, it is only capable of understanding that which is of the same energetic value or quality of form. This style of communication was developed within the manifest dimensions and can only be used by way of the ego in the manifest/linear/dualistic realms of existence. Words were developed by the ego to travel across time, space, and distance, and are thus the portrayals of the linear and dualistic mechanism known as 'expression.'

Words not only are form and within the realm of form, but they are dualistic expressions of positionalities that the ego identity is and is an expression of. To be form is to be dualistic. This indicates the illusion of the paradoxical, such as the 'knower and the known,' the 'thinker and the thought,' and the 'speaker and the spoken (or spoken to).' With the understanding of the 'expresser, the expressed, and the person to whom it was expressed,' it shows that merely 'expressing' is dualistic. So the ego and all of its capabilities, expressions, thoughts, and communication styles are dualistic by their nature alone.

The previous explanation indicates that all words are illusion, due to their nature of form and dualism. This means simply to state the word 'I,' which is a noun that describes 'beingness' and existence, brings up the duality or opposition of nonexistence, which is an impossibility. Therefore even to state that one exists brings one to that delicate conundrum. One must simply be aware of existence, not vocalize it. The same can be said about referring to another person or object using words such as "you, this, that, he, she, or it." This shows that the 'experiencer' is a 'viewer' who obviously used the mechanism of perception, which is a dualistic quality of the ego that references where, who, or what something is. It directs the objectivity of the ego towards a focal point that establishes a sense of reference, direction, or position within the universe. This also brings up dualistic opposition: something must be able to exist *outside* what one currently knows to be existence, if something can exist *within* it. Likewise, adjectives that describe 'things,' nouns that are 'things,' verbs that describe action or 'doingness,' and adverbs, pronouns, and so on, are all dualistic by nature simply because of their nature, which is form, which is only noticed by objective perception that is *only* a quality of the ego.

Words were developed and used by the ego to convey ideas, concepts, emotions, feelings, perceptive stimuli, etc..., and to coordinate, organize, synchronize, and receive and give input that would benefit the evolution of the manifest ego soul. Due to one's lack of 'knowing of' the ego's reason for existence and its True Nature in the Nonlinear dimension, 'knowingness' was not known; in fact, the Unmanifest was believed not to exist at all. Therefore, in the beginning, the ego felt and was separated from God and thought that the linear/dualistic/manifest dimension was reality. This prompted the ego to develop a form of communication that would travel throughout this perceived 'reality,' which operates within the dualistic observation of time, space, and distance (linear qualities). So for words actually to travel across time, space, and distance is an impossibility within the Absolute Reality; it is only a false mentation of the ego mind. In other words, the thought that words (a type of form) exist and can be used is an illusion in the ego mind, or just a *thought*, nothing more.

Archetypal Energy Patterns

Archetypes are energetic patterns that carry a specific frequency into the province of a being's mind. The pattern carries within it a charge that is either (to the ego) considered positive or negative. But really it carries a charge that only denotes the level of love or Truth in varying amounts. This can be equated to the level of light that is brought into a dark room; it is either blindingly bright or very dark, or endless levels in between. When the level of love is rejected, the emotional state of hate, anger, and irritation ensue, which are currently known to the ego as negative energy.

The frequencies of these archetypal energy patterns energize the soul and can clear the subtle energetic bodies of this negative debris by adding light to the dark or stagnant areas. One may use crystals, stones, and gems, or simply use the mind to create an archetype through visualization. Everything in the universe has a frequency, but the physical items are not necessary. The Mind and the Will are all that are needed to add the Presence of light to any situation, emotional or mental state, or state of physical health.

If one chooses to use the mind, visualization is key. One may visualize the ocean to bring in the frequency of water, which is beneficial for harmonizing and clearing the chakras. One may visualize fire or the sun in order to clear the chakras, while energizing the 'ego will' as ambition and drive (which can be used to energize the study of Truthful text). One may visualize the earth in order to feel more secure and balanced. Or one may focus on the element of air, which brings in peace and love while increasing awareness. Or, if enlightenment is the goal, then Spirit alone is all that is needed to attune one's energetic frequency to Truth. One may visualize Jesus or Buddha (who are very high in energetic value), or simply say the names as a word ('Jesus'), which does the same for one's evolution. Always keep in mind that to become enlightened is to relinquish the use of the ego mind; no visualization is really necessary. However, positive visualizations by way of the ego mind can at least empower one's self while they are gathering courage to trust in God fully.

It is important to note that the image or word itself does not carry the frequency; instead, it is the 'will' or 'intent' that currently empowers it, or that has charged it in the past and stored it (with that charge) as a universal symbol or 'representation of will.'

An 'ego will'–charged archetype is low powered and negative, but a Spiritual Will–charged archetype is high powered and positive. That which exists in the manifest physical and spiritual dimensions of form is a low level of truth, but it is still truth (a lesser quality or a lower level than Absolute Truth, due to ego distortions). So only that which is denying God/Love is absent in that quality of Love, Truth, or truth (Truth with some fallacy).

To understand which archetypes are 'negative' or 'ego will'–powered, one must recognize and understand the qualities or levels of consciousness of the ego. When one visualizes a battle scene or a fight, a negatively charged archetype is formed that affects a being instantly. This reduces or lowers the karmic potential of that individual, thus taking their ego further from the ultimate realization of Truth. Likewise, when an ego visualizes getting a lot of money, or lusting over sex, or fulfilling cravings or wants, the same outcome is apparent. So if one always craves a cigarette or just thinks about having one, their karmic potentiality lowers them further into a state of denying God, light, love, or existence, because they would rather have that craving or fulfilled desire instead. So it can be seen that an ego who intends to revisualize continuously a past mistake or perceived problem will reinvoke the same emotional response, due to a lack of understanding of the event, the nature of the ego, and the refusal of God as sustenance and the reason for existence. By this, the ego chooses to stay in their own personally created 'hell' or suffering by that incessant lowering of consciousness, whether knowingly or unknowingly.

Just the same, 'positive thinking' can be used to stay positive and to raise one's karmic merit, which erases (by filling in with Light) karmic debt, helping one to stay in a positive frame of mind and not pick up the negative aspects of the egos around them, events that occur nearby, or events with the individual in them.

The more an individual attunes with an archetype that can provide them with a frequency that they need, the happier the life they will have. If the frequencies are always higher than the individual's current karmic resonance, enlightenment is more probable within this lifetime. If the archetypal energy pattern carries a lower quality of the 'ego will' frequency, such as wanting a nice car or house, wanting to be 'cool' or 'hip,' or wanting to be successful in worldly terms, then the being is charged with 'ego will,' which is not beneficial for the enlightened endeavor. If these thoughts are integrous (which shows a mixture of 'ego will' and Spiritual Will), then positive, but not high frequencies, are added to the ego's energetic field (known as distorted Truth, or truth). If these thoughts are nonintegrous/untrustworthy/dishonest, then the 'ego will' is negatively charged (showing almost a complete absence of the presence and mixture of Spiritual Will) and can bring forth the soul's demise.

So to be enlightened is to attune one's self continually and incessantly to the frequency of Truth. The majority of beings use the energy that has been left, or is still residing, in the universal energetic field, such as Jesus, Krishna, Buddha, etc... So for one to use any of these spiritual masters' energy will suffice, as long as one's karmic potentiality has been reached and is sufficient for enlightenment. Similarly, many have used mantras or repetitious patterns that have a high power or level of Truth in them. Likewise, prayer has the same effect (if integrous and selfless).

High-Powered Mantra Archetypes and Prayers

These are archetypes as word patterns that are at a very high frequency and capable of bringing about change. Enlightenment has come about for individuals who have said, sang, chanted, or even hummed the following statements repetitiously. I have also used these as well. The paramount high-frequency archetype is to pray for all of humanity selflessly and with humility. A true enlightened sage cares not for himself, but instead for the well-being of all others. So to unprogram one's own selfish thoughts reveals the enlightened sage or Higher Self within all of us, thus helping others. So pray and chant to amplify your frequency, but do it selflessly and to benefit all beings.

These prayers or chants can be likened to a 'lightbulb.' As one says them, the lightbulb goes on and brightens a part of their aura. The more that they speak the prayers or chants, the brighter they get. It is not uncommon to see a spiritual aspirant repeat a chant 400 to 500 times a sitting, then pray for about an hour, walk with Mindfulness and chant some more, and then pray and end the session, only to spend the rest of their day contemplating the significance of existence while devoting their life to God. This means that for the entire day, the spiritual devotee turns on a lightbulb that illuminates a section of their aura. The more they are attuned to holy things, people, or archetypal phrases, the more they Will for the Light and Power of God to enter their energetic field, thus illuminating their entire energetic field and expediting their spiritual journey, and maybe even concluding their ostensible search for enlightenment.

Archetypal Chants
"Ohm Mani Padme Hum"
"Jesus, Buddha, Krishna"
"Self is All, All is One, One Love, One Life, One existence"
"God is Light, Love, and Peace—Self is God, 'I' am God"
"Ohm" (drawn out like 'OOOOOOOHHHHMMMMMM')
"AUM" (pronounced as 'awe' and 'm'—and drawn out)

Archetypal Prayers
"God (sets higher intent), I pray to become a clear and direct channel for Divine Will. I pray that the Higher energy flows through me and affects the universe in a positive way. I pray that I bring peacefulness to an upset situation, love to resolve hatred, happiness to assuage sadness, and joyfulness to alleviate depression."

"I devote my life to God, because God is existence, and 'I' am God."

"God, I pray for all beings to become Self-Realized and for all to love one another unconditionally with understanding."

With hands in prayer position over the heart chakra, say, "God, I pray for all beings to willfully accept Reality, to realize that they are already blessed and loved unconditionally, and to help all beings at any cost." Then move hands in prayer position over the crown chakra and say, "God, I willfully accept to know Truth (move hands over brow chakra, or third eye); God, I willfully accept to see Truth (move hands over throat chakra); God, I willfully accept to hear and speak Truth (move hands over heart chakra); God, I willfully and graciously accept to feel Truth and be Truth, because 'I' am Truth."

"God, I will humble myself before man as I humble myself before the infinite Presence. I pray to serve the universe as a vehicle of Divine Love and peace, and to display the qualities of the Divine Presence at all times."

"I accept any and all spiritual gifts that are given, as I realize that life in and of itself is a gift at all times as well."

"I realize not to ask for anything, because all has already been supplied in the perfect amount and quality. So with this being realized, I ask to be a channel of God and to serve only Divine Will in any way I can. Whether it is to pick up trash off the floor to clean and protect the earth out of respect, to serve my enemy until they feel loved in life and realize God's Presence, to pray for humanity or for beings in hell, or to serve as a counselor to all beings, whether animals, plants, bugs, people, or souls without body. I dedicate my life to love all beings unconditionally."

"To serve God's Will, I choose to obey or to understand my parents with compassion as I choose to respect all of humanity with understanding. I choose to serve a request of an ego as if God had asked me to do so, but only if it is an integrous request. I choose to play the game of earth with humor and humility so as to make all other beings feel comfortable with life, myself, and others. I choose not to act on behalf of my 'ego will,' for this denies God, which is happiness, love, and peace—my very essence. I choose to love all beings unconditionally because God does and is this as well."

"I will not harm life; instead, I will love life. No matter

how big or small, no matter how significant or insignificant, I will respect all things because all things have a purpose."

Building Thought Forms (negative and positive)

As 'will' or 'Will' charges a thought form and is thus manifested, it adds to the totality of the universal karmic charge, which helps to govern and influence universal outcomes as well as the destiny of seemingly independent egos. All thoughts that have been created are charged with a varying level of distorted truth or the Higher Truth. The thought forms that have been manifested with a lesser quality of truth, or in complete denial of Truth, will stay at their inherent or intrinsic frequency, which affects and reacts with the universe as a whole, as well as the ego's seemingly independent reality. These charges created within the thought forms are permanent, unless the understandings that bring about realizations are recognized as such. This would deprogram the thought forms that contain 'lesser truths,' while bringing the Presence of Light to the lesser karmic charges that were so adversely affecting humanity and the universe. If this happens on a universal scale, it is what I term the "Universal Reveal," or "Mass Enlightenment."

So in actuality, all thought forms are permanent, and affecting that dimension, until the ego, which willed a 'lesser truth' thought form into expression, recognizes why it was created in the first place. The realization that ensues after the recognition of the 'lesser truth' thought form, with the understanding of the thought form development that the ego perpetuated, raises one in frequency or to a higher quality of truth—hopefully Truth. Therefore, all nontruth thought forms that are created can be changed in frequency by the (seeming) 'ego creator' who first put those specific thought forms into action. Just the same, an enlightened being with that realization, which is its being and which continually radiates from and as the Presence, has the capacity and ability to recontextualize the first programmed charge or contextual meaning that was instilled by the 'ego creator' into a higher frequency, thus adding the Higher Truth that sheds light on the naïvely created lower energetic ego pattern.

This means that one who has created many 'bad thoughts'

in the past can delete them by simply understanding *why* they created them previously. By adding spiritual Truth to a 'lesser truth' thought form, the 'negative' effects of the pattern will be stopped by the raise in frequency, negating the past thought form as if it had never happened. As that being becomes enlightened, which means that their personal karma has been transcended, the universal karma then becomes rectified by the addition of the Presence of God as Light. Therefore, one takes a low level of consciousness 'thought form,' or energetic pattern, and remanifests it (so to speak) into a positive and uplifting 'thought form' that can be used by other ego beings as lessons, instead of as hardships or conflicts.

An example of neutralizing a negative thought form or action is for one to hear what another person says or does, and then to correct them *humbly,* in order to show them that life is not as negative as they feel it to be. Do not correct them pridefully, for they will become more irritated, maybe even enraged. If they throw trash on the ground, pick it up and throw it in the trash can to show respect *silently* for all things. If they make fun of someone, explain that all are equal in Reality, that there is no possibility for differences. Simply lead by positive example, and reinforce other beings' thought forms with positive energy patterns, whether with voice or presence, thus surrounding them with Love. Further examples are discussed in this chapter, in the section on '**Recontextualization.**' (17 pages down)

When one speaks with 'good will or intention,' this balances out the negatively created or willed thought forms. It is almost as if one positively charged thought form can heal, which then negates or cancels out many other negative thought forms that were also created in parallel by the ego. For example, if 1 million egos stated, with no truth at all, "I hate stupid people," an enlightened being might spend about a day chanting, "All beings are perfect; hate is but an illusion that blocks one's ability to Love and to receive Love. May all beings Love one another unconditionally and be compassionate to all." If the enlightened being states this verse about 4,500 times, it would negate or cancel out the 1 million ego statements of "I hate stupid people." Because the Power of the Sage is so high in frequency and of a different quality of energy, it can cancel out a much greater number of negatively created thought forms.

Remember that the Power of God is far greater than the powerlessness of illusion, which is known as force. So it doesn't take as many positive thought forms to cancel out the negative (illusory) ones. One little spark of light is sufficient to light up a dark room—look at a candle, for instance. One may either choose to put a light in a dark room or keep it dark forever; it is only a matter of choice and will. Keep in mind that darkness cannot extinguish light, but illusion can block it from view or knowingness. This means that limited illusion cannot take over or destroy that which is indestructible and infinite.

Many beings tend to think that chanting or praying is worthless, but it is not. Prayer is always answered, just not in the way that most egos think. For every positive thought that is spoken, many, if not hundreds or thousands, of negatively willed thought forms are canceled out by the spontaneous resolve of adding light. Think of every positive word, idea, or thought as a spark that adds light (truth) to a dark room (thought form). Eventually, if enough light is added, the room will be completely lit and absent of any darkness (negativity). This applies to individual or personal karma in the same manner that it does to universal karma. So now it can be understood that for the universal karma just to be on a teeter-tottering level (which it is) of integrity and truth (positive, but close to negative) shows that there are far more negative thoughts, words, and ideas that are being chosen to be 'willed' than positive ones. Although just a few enlightened beings can offset all of the negativity in the universe, to shift more towards the positive, additional beings must become Self-Realized. So if one is not enlightened, every thought, action, intention, idea, or spoken word is still a part of the universal karma, affecting the balance of the universe in a negative direction. This is why prayer and 'positive intent' are so important to keep the universe positive.

Creating Heavens and Hells

It is important to note that all thoughts create, or are reflections of, astral dimensions that can be either perceived as 'heavens or hells,' depending on the level of consciousness that is being focused on. If one ego thinks about a 'negative thing or event,' a corresponding hell will be created. So as one 'self-proclaimed visionary' creates a movie about a fictitious demon, that 'thought-to-be' fictitious demon can now be perceived as real in the lower astral dimensions known as 'hell.' As one is 'astrally projecting' (leaving their physical body) throughout the lower or upper dimensions of hell, they can see a demon looking like something from a fake cartoon chasing poor souls; even though the soul believes that the event and being exist, it is really only within their own mind. In Reality, it doesn't exist at all. The soul is only afflicted by its negative thoughts and the belief that it is not a good soul who deserves heaven. Therefore, it has created this 'hellish condition' or perceived reality that it believes to be happening. So as the ego thinks it deserves this affliction, it is done. But it is only done in fairness. This gives a whole new meaning to the statement, "Be careful for what you wish for; you might just get it."

The above affliction describes someone who is an integrous or trustworthy soul, but who unfortunately believes that they deserve worse for eternity. These beings can be shown the way out of their own personally created hell, but a soul need not go through such an unpleasant situation. Unfortunately, a nonintegrous soul is not only subject to their own 'hell-created' thoughts, but to other nonintegrous souls who only derive pleasure from torturing souls. They may come in the form of the worst imaginable feelings or sights, feelings, and intentions. Their only purpose is to watch one suffer.

Fortunately, these 'hells' can be deleted by adding the Presence of Light to a situation or thought form, just as it may be added to negative thought forms. So resolving one's own karma not only raises the frequency of your own personally created hells and thought forms, but also adds the Presence of God (as Light) into other egos' personally created hells and thought forms. So an enlightened being actually raises the frequency of every ego, situation, thought, and hell. And by the addition of Truth to a lesser truth situation or thought form, the perpetuation of positive thought forms, as well as the resolution of the negative thought forms, lessens the karmic debt of the universe. This means that an enlightened being adds Light, by way of the Presence of God, to a negative situation, thought form, and within the dimensions of hell, at the same time adding Light to the earth and all its inhabitants.

Not only does the enlightened being transmute the negative energy into positive, but more heavens are created continually. This is because only positive thoughts, in essence, radiate from an enlightened being as the essence of God as Truth. These thoughts are prompted and perpetuated by Divine Will only. Similarly, other beings may do the same by following Divine Will and thinking only positive thoughts and doing only positive actions. All that comes from God is pure love, which instills peace in every being if used and recognized as such—this is Unconditional Love.

So in the end, it is all just a choice: a matter of will. Is it ego will or Divine Will? Does one create 'heavens' or 'hells' with their mind? This 'seeming' balance of the universe depends on everyone's interaction and choice. So make a point of thinking only positive thoughts, no matter what the situation. Create more heavens for one's self and for others. If one chooses *total enlightenment*, then they are beyond heavens and hells, because they are one with God and God is beyond heavens and hells. And at the same time that an enlightened being creates heavens for all other beings, they also neutralize the negative energies and hells created by others.

The Damaging Effects of Words

Not only does the use of words reinforce the belief of living in a linear/dualistic reality, but most words that are spoken today within communities or society are not manifested with a high level of consciousness. Therefore, those words that are spoken will affect the ego who is speaking and the ego who is listening in a negative way, through a lower level of consciousness that coincidentally contains a lesser quality of truth, which further distorts their view.

So with every word spoken to one's self, or an animal, or a plant, or a person about a situation, or about a topic in general will influence the way reality is felt and perceived. It will either feel more positive and peaceful, or more negative and worrisome. Not only do these negative thoughts affect other egos in a negative way, they shape the way reality is subjectively and objectively felt and known. So negative words block Truth from being known, and positive words help everyone to become enlightened.

Perpetuating Negatively Charged Thought Forms

Many egos get involved in the trap of perpetuating negativity. For example, when one ego says a negative thought or comment out loud to another, then other nearby or interacting egos join in with negative comments. The comments get increasingly negative and therefore generate more fallacy.

Example #1:
Ego #1 says, "Jack is sick."
Ego #2 says, "Jack has a fever."
Ego #3 says, "Jack has a 103-degree fever."
Ego #4 says, "Jack is so sick that he has to have surgery."
Ego #5 says, "Jack is so sick that he has to have surgery or he could die any day now."

Example #2:
Ego #1 says, "I did okay on my test." (really a D+)
Ego #1 says again (due to pride), "I got a 95% on my test."
Ego #2 says, "He got the highest grade on the test and in the class."

—As this is being said, both egos know that the child is failing school and has failed the test. The comments don't seem to be negative, but they are charged with the 'ego will' of pride, embarrassment, and denial.

There isn't an ego out there who hasn't lied just a little to make an event seem more fun, a word seem more hurtful, an action seem more heroic, and so forth. ***The ego loves drama***. Therefore, the ego must make life seem dramatic, fun, and interesting at all times. The ego can take a boring event and make itself believe that it is having fun. It constantly lies to itself to make reality seem interesting. The ego also lies to others in order to build itself up, so as to make it feel more important, admired, or respected, or maybe even to make others feel pity for it. When analyzed closely, the ego can be seen to lie continually throughout one's lifetime to achieve various recognitions, whether by one's self or others.

Unfortunately, these thought forms can take on a reality of their own. Since reality is shaped by our mind and our perceptions of it, then as thoughts are created and words are spoken, the destiny of one's self is ever-changing as one becomes attuned to the vibration or frequency of a thought. So when Jack is sick, it may be minor; however, when other egos make the scenario worse in their minds, they crystallize these negative energy patterns, which could actually make Jack more sick. So one shouldn't be surprised if Jack actually has to go to the hospital for treatment.

The same goes for one's life; if their life view is acceptable but only 'so-so,' they can make their perception of reality worse and more undesirable if they exaggeratedly tell everyone how bad their life is. It is actually common for one to lie to one's self and then persuade themselves to believe in the false reality that they wanted to believe in by exaggeration. This perpetuates their own negative condition, which has been shaped by the mind to be negative by constant pessimism. Around 90% of society is lying to themselves on a daily basis, and that is why around 90% of society does not even think that enlightenment is a possibility. If one thinks something is not possible, it is then not possible. The 'mind' controls reality by perception and programming, but the 'Mind' (Unmanifest) is Reality.

An Analogy for Thought Form Transference
The following analogy explains the ability of thought forms to penetrate into another being's energetic field due to weak-mindedness; this is also called 'auric permeability.'

Egos are a saturated mixture of various thought forms. To say the least, these thought forms are contagious, especially by the weak-minded ('easily believable,' or gullible).

Negative thoughts can be likened to a flu or a virus. If an infected person walks around and interacts with society, they spread the virus. Even though an ego has what it believes to be 'good intentions,' their negative affliction may and usually does spread to others, whether knowingly or unknowingly, especially to those with a weak immune system (which is parallel to being weak-minded). The individual who is infected with the flu (a negative thought form) doesn't know it at first. Perhaps the individual doesn't even feel the effect for a couple of days, or maybe their mind tells them right away. And as life continues, the effects of the flu are felt. Maybe the individual knows how they got it, but usually not. They usually come up with a theory that can sound like a logical and rational reason for how and why they got the flu.

This flu or 'negative thought form' can affect many individuals, not just the 'carrier monkey' that it originated and perpetuated from. Just as the flu afflicts one and worsens the quality of life, it can be remedied by medication. Similarly, the medication for the 'negative thought form' is Light. This Light is added to the seeming darkness (low level of light) of the thought form in the ego, and remedies the affliction. Once the ego has learned the reason for the illness and how to prevent or cure it, it transcends a little bit further from its misery. Much to its surprise, happiness is understood to have always been just a realization away.

This medication can be given by the previously ill, but now healed (enlightened), to other beings who get the flu, just the same as the Presence of God as Light can be given to an individual with a 'negative thought form.' But just as the ill must accept and want to take the medication to cure themselves of their affliction, a being must Will to cure themselves and accept the Presence of Light as the one and only cure. It is important to note that the ego cannot and will never heal itself. All that the ego can do is relinquish control and allow for the Divine Will to come through and manifest healing.

Analyzing the Error in Speech

Every ego who speaks is in error. The error is not mainly the content, but also the context (underlying meaning/level of consciousness). The context is the charge that is either a product of ego will or Divine Will by choice. Many enlightened beings do not speak much because of the realization that it is not necessary; all is already as it should be, and there is no need to put into language any more illusory ideas, thoughts, or words. It is also impossible to put into language or express the Nonlinear in its entirety. There are enlightened beings who choose to speak, and they are known as teachers of enlightenment; but many do not. The content, or actual verbiage, may appear similar to an ego, but the context or underlying meaning of what is being spoken is profoundly different. This context, which an enlightened being knows and is, is Truth from the Higher Source, which is of a higher expression (God), or the Light of heaven that illuminates all beings.

Analyzing Ego Linguistics
This section shows the errors in ego speech.

In Reality, the very first error in language is the denial of God, which leads to the soul's evolution within the dimension of the manifest, and its use of form to understand itself and the reality that it is interpreting. The second error in all sentences, besides the form of the words themselves, is the feeling that the illusory ego must speak to express itself or put itself into language. Speech seems necessary (to an ego) to travel across illusory time and space to penetrate another separate ego's mind. Without the ability to interact, the ego would feel lonely, due to the rejection of God's Love and the inability to know that everything is One and no language is needed. This 'lonely' feeling (created by unfulfillment) is the sensation of the loss of God's Love; the ego just doesn't know this.

The third error is the ego who 'thinks' (also an illusion) it creates something, which is an impossibility. The ego not only thinks that it controls its future or destiny, but it feels as though only its action controls what is ahead: not words, feelings, beliefs, or ideas. Therefore, the ego thinks any and all thoughts, no matter what the content or context, which inherently dooms it in this illusory dimension, because it does not know that all thoughts affect the universe. For an ego, this is not beneficial. Through this, only suffering is an ego's outcome or possibility.

The following errors occur after the errors above are made.

- **I am cold.**
   Error #1
      The ego's belief that it has its own independence from "I," which denotes indivi<u>dualism</u> and separation.
   Error #2
      The use of the word 'am,' which denotes the essence of 'beingness,' automatically brings up the opposition of 'nonbeingness' (duality).
   Error #3
      The use of the word 'cold' signifies the way that the 'individual being' perceptively feels as a separate self, and brings up the opposition of 'hotness.' Not only is 'cold' a dualistic term, it reinforces the ego's feeling that it really is separate from others, due to other egos' differing opinions. This makes the ego feel that what it is and feels belongs only to it, and its feelings, thoughts, and ideas cannot affect other beings.

- **I hate these types of people.**
   Error #1
      The ego's use of 'I.'
   Error #2
      The use of the emotion 'hate' shows the ego's low level of consciousness that is being used at that moment. As this word is used more frequently, a being may lower themselves to this level of consciousness permanently. The use of the term 'hate'

365

shows severe judgment that displaces attention from the ego's own faults and onto the other being; it is also dualistic.

Error #3

The use of 'these' shows separation and reinforces the dualistic nature of the ego and perceived reality. It also groups beings or things as identical or the same.

Error #4

The use of the word 'types' signifies that things or beings are put into a group as being the same, but different than the self who is making the statement (judgmental).

Error #5

The placing together of the words 'types of people' denotes that the individual is stereotyping all these types as the same. This blinds one from seeing that all illusory egos are different; there is no possibility for them to be ego identical. At the same time, one is blocked from realizing this 'ego illusion' and seeing that every soul has the same Spirit. The separation of one's self from the others' beingness stereotype shows that the ego is protecting its identity by judging others as undesirable.

- **I'm right and you're wrong.**

Error #1

Using the words "I'm" and "yours" shows separation and duality, which reinforces the ego identity that places one within a certain location in the universe.

Error #2

The use of the word 'right' is more than a word; the ego really feels that there is a right or a wrong. This is a classic dualistic opposition. There is no right or wrong. There are only various levels of spiritual truth, and all so-called truths within the physical are based on the manifest, which is an illusion.

Error #3

The ability to say who is right or wrong takes judgment from the ego. The ego only judges in order to place itself within the universe. To claim that it is 'right' is to give itself importance. To claim that the other ego is wrong is to feel in control of the situation by putting the other person in their place, so to speak. For example, "I'm right, you're wrong, so you need to listen to me."

- **I know this, I know everything.**

Error #1

The use of 'I' shows separation and duality, and reinforces ego identity, which places one within a certain location in the universe.

Error #2

The claim to 'know' is illusory. Only the ego 'thinks' (which is also an illusion) that it can know anything. Real Reality is not 'known' by an ego but experienced by the egoless and willing.

Error #3

To 'know everything' is a claim that either a knowledgeable ego makes to reinforce its feeling of control over egos who don't know as much, or that a less knowledgeable ego makes in order to mask its feeling of knowing nothing or feeling stupid.

- **This is a waste of my time.**

Error #1

'This' or 'that' signifies a dualistic realm, with the separation that would require these terms to denote locations or separate things with a 'this' or a 'that.' If everything were seen as One, then there would be no separate labels for anything.

Error #2

The term 'is' shows that the ego feels that the cir-

cumstance affects it, when in Reality, nothing can affect Universal Oneness.

Error #3

The use of the adjective 'waste,' which means to 'consume gradually or to wear away,' indicates that the individual feels as though they are losing something; in this case, it is time. In Reality, nothing can be lost or wasted, because everything already is in an equal and everlasting state of existence.

Error #4

The use of the concept of 'time' shows how the ego feels as if it were running out of time. This is because the ego feels as if existence is limited and time is the big factor. If it felt as though time were to 'run out,' it would then feel that it would cease to exist. This is because the ego can only have a 'limited run' in the realm of form; however, the Spirit is everlasting and permanent. It cannot waste away.

Error #5

The use of 'my' shows that the ego feels ownership towards the concept of time. To all egos, it can be rationalized that time is equal and ever-present to all without ownership. In Reality, time cannot and does not exist, because time is a form or concept of measurement that the ego developed to delineate its perception of events within the physical. In Reality, there is nothing to measure, no place to go, nothing to waste, and no form, because it is Nonlinear and formless.

- **You're too stupid to be spiritually advanced.**
  Error #1

  The judgment of 'stupidness' makes the ego who says this feel in control of the situation, and also makes them feel more important. This portrays them as covering up their own insecurities by pointing the finger at someone else's insecurities.

Error #2

This signifies ownership of 'stupidness' by stating "you're."

Error #3

The claim 'to be' states that one is in the process of becoming, and then becomes something. In Reality, everything already is; there is nothing to change, nothing that can become, because everything already is complete and total.

Error #4

The claim that one can be 'spiritually advanced' is impossible. This says that something has become something else. In Reality, nothing can become anything, because everything is already complete and total. If one is an advanced spiritual devotee, one is simply more aware of their True Nature; that is all.

Error #5

Whether one is smart, intellectual, scholastic, or even a genius does not mean that they have realized their True Nature. To be Self-Realized, one doesn't need any knowledge or intellect; they just need to be aware of Truth. A 4-year-old child has a better chance of Self-Realization than a 60-year-old rocket scientist. In fact, many beings who come to this earth who seem to have mental disorders, such as autism, retardation, and so forth, many times have higher levels of consciousness than the average person. Their purpose is to bring the Light that harmonizes, uplifts, and reinforces the universal energetic field and the individuals who are within it. Where modern science regards them as 'hopeless' or 'a lost cause,' enlightened beings revere and respect them as helpful and beneficial.

One must also remember that knowledge is a construct. It is form because it resides within the linear/manifest/dualistic. So the more knowledgeable one becomes, the more that a block to the realization of Self comes about.

- **You don't look enlightened.**
  Error #1

   The dualistic separation of the terminology 'you' reinforces the seeming individualism of all beings in the universe.

  Error #2

   To say "don't" brings up the opposition of "do." In Reality, there is nothing to do, and to 'not do' or "don't" is an impossibility. No negatives exist in Reality. So "not, can't, don't, or false" are impossible because only Truth (which is ever-positive [for ego understanding]) can exist. The absence of Truth is impossible, because that would require the absence of existence, and existence is infinite, because existence is God and God is infinite.

  Error #3

   Only the ego, which has perception, thinks in terms of looking or perceiving to identify something. If something is not perceived, it does not exist (says the ego). So as the ego uses the verb to 'look,' it signifies that it is trapped in its own illusion of thinking and feeling that what it perceives or is visible is real. Enlightenment is an invisible realization that one already is and has been Unmanifest, whether knowingly or unknowingly. It cannot be witnessed or experienced by the perceptive faculties of the ego.

- **I need to work out or I'll get fat.**
  Error #1

   The use of the word 'I' signifies separation, duality, and independence within the universe. This reinforces the belief in the illusory self, or the ego.

  Error #2

   The claim 'need to' is also an illusion. The Self has

no needs, claims nothing, and has nothing, but is the Source of All That Is.

Error #3

The experience that an ego feels it needs to do, such as 'work out,' is thought to be an external source of happiness, which by way of results (fat loss) satisfies the ego's ever-feeling and ever-present loss or emptiness due to the denial of God's fulfilling Love.

Error #4

The ego actually feels that the self who gets fat is the only self that exists, therefore denying its True existence: the Self, which is formless and 'unseen.'

A Heightened Context

When an enlightened being speaks, it is usually on a spiritual topic. However, at times they may need to speak in 'worldly terms,' such as about the weather; someone's job, lifestyle, and living conditions; or political issues. The enlightened being tends not to express viewpoints on political issues such as war, presidents, governors, materialistic issues, and so on, because everything is 'just is as it is': a perfect expression of its current level of consciousness. As an act of humor, the enlightened being may participate in some worldly events, but sees no need except to satisfy or bring happiness to the ego with whom they are interacting. In actuality, they would rather be praying, chanting, reading spiritual texts, going to a temple or place of worship, teaching people Truth, teaching yoga, teaching meditation, and so forth. The enlightened being tries to keep the Absolute Reality in context—this is happiness.

As the enlightened being interacts with society, they await a signal or indication from the other ego's willingness, so as to help them to stop suffering. The enlightened being compassionately responds to any moment of suffering that is being 'willed' to be given up, and they understand the individual's pain because they have experienced it before at lower levels of consciousness, when they were an ego. The enlightened being provides the energy that can lift and reinforce each and every individual's ener-getic field, as well as the universal field. With every word spoken, they energize themselves, others, and the universe. This is not due to the content of the word or the spoken form, but instead to the context, or deeper meaning (Higher Truth) of Reality that silently transmits with the word, or their Presence, which transilluminates all that is near.

These beings works off all the universal karma that was provided by others, thus liberating the world from its own sins. They are capable of transfiguring any being's lifestyle by only their presence, which brings the Presence of Transfinite nature. God's energy, of which they are a direct channel, brings only positive change. Every word that brings with it a greater meaning stimu-lates positive change in the individual who is listening to it or near it, or for the universal karma as a whole. Change may come rap-idly, or it may dwell within the ego's energetic field waiting for the appropriate time to be expressed. It all depends on the willing-ness of the individual to let go of the sinning nature (ego) that it has become so accustomed to. When that transient moment arises, healing begins.

Comparison of Context

- **An Integrous Ego (Preacher)**
  Words Spoken/Content: *"Pray to God every day."*
  Context/Meaning: *Every individual should pray to God in*
  (Illusory)   *Heaven that is far away from earth every*
           single day, so God doesn't judge you and
           send you to hell.

- **An Enlightened Sage**
  Words Spoken/Content: *"Pray to God every day."*
  Context/Meaning: *May all beings recognize their Unmanifest*
  (Truth)   *Self, which is the same as the 'One*
           Spirit,' as well as God Immanent (In-
           dwelling) and God Transcendent (Total

and Universal—All), which are one and the same. God does not judge you and send you to hell; you condemn yourself by your false thoughts and livelihood. Heaven and Earth are not in two separate places; they are superimposed as one.

*   *   *   *   *

- **An Integrous Ego (Preacher)**
  Words Spoken/Content: *"It looks so gloomy outside, so cloudy."*

  Context/Meaning: *I hate rainy days; they make me feel so*
  (Illusory)   *depressed. This shows not only a belief in duality, but that it controls one's life, feelings, and way of expression. It also shows that the individual allows their feeling about the weather (hating it) to block God's Love, thus making them feel depressed about the day. Isn't that ridiculous?—allowing the way a day looks to control the way one feels, happy or depressed and sad.*

- **An Enlightened Sage**
  Words Spoken/Content: *"It looks cloudy outside."*
  Context/Meaning: *Every day is how it is, a perfect expression* **Truth** *of itself and the local conditions. Rain is perfect, clouds are perfect, temperature is perfect, as the weather is perfect. The physical day doesn't really exist; it is an illusion. The Real Day is a moment. It is ever-present, all-fulfilling, and continuous creation. All is perfect, because All is God.*

Recontextualization

This is the method of an enlightened Sage, by which their 'beingness' or 'interactive processes' adds meaning/Truth or higher context/consciousness to an illusory statement spoken by an ego. The statements from the ego are judgmental, biased, false, and a sin in and of themselves. So the enlightened Sage may correct much of what is said by the ego; however, the Sage shouldn't add input verbally when it is apparent that it is not wanted by the ego. To result in the utmost in healing, the ego must accept it, or 'will' it so.

The enlightened Sage may rearrange words, so as to show the ego how to rearrange the content of the energetic package, which changes the context as well. The context/meaning will not only be in the newly rearranged content/words, but the nonverbal transmission or the Presence of God (Truth) channeled through the presence of the Sage, by action and words, stimulates transcendental change. This means that as the words are rearranged by the Sage, the energy of God as Truth in the form of consciousness is imprinted on the energetic properties known as 'spoken words,' which are form. Although the form may appear similar, the level of consciousness has been vastly increased by the addition of Truth.

It is important to keep in mind that consciousness is still form, although it is the highest level of form. It is necessary to witness linear events and recognize the existence of form. This 'rearranged' and 'reimprinted' energetic pattern that the Sage allows to flow forth is now capable of resolving the impeding qualities of the ego. Hopefully, the ego will not only understand the rearranged energetic package (words/content), which reveals a deeper meaning (context), but will also reuse it when they hear another ego misconstrue the True Reality as illusion by wrongful content and context.

The higher context (Truth), or deeper meaning of existence, is continuously channeled by way of the Sage as compassion and peace, which are capable of permanently transfiguring one's view of Reality as experience. These beings choose to help all others experience the Truth better, no matter what the cost.

They have given up the life of fulfilling their own selfish desires to help all others experience God. By the Presence that they radiate through existence, thought, and words, all illusory life views are then transpierced, resolving the illusory conflict within their mind.

Examples of Recontextualization

- **An Ego**
  Words Spoken: *"This person is so mean; he is very bad."*

- **An Enlightened Sage**
  Corrected Speech: *"There are no mean people; they are only misdirected, misguided, or confused."*

*   *   *   *   *

- **An Ego**
  Words Spoken: *"I am having a horrible day."*

- **An Enlightened Sage**
  Corrected Speech: *"There is no such thing as a bad day; it is all only an error within your perception."*

  OR

  "Two people go on a roller coaster; one loves it and the other is terrified. It is not the event that is terrifying, but instead, one's perception of it."

*   *   *   *   *

- **An Ego**
  Words Spoken: *"My child is so stubborn; he won't do anything that I tell him to do."*

375

- **An Enlightened Sage**
  Corrected Speech: *"It is not necessarily that your child is stubborn; is it possible that you may just be too controlling? And this lack of control scares you because you are unsure of his survival and security."*

  OR

  "All beings choose their own path; it is either an expression of the 'ego will' or 'Divine Will.' Allow him to practice choosing, rather than controlling his options. A parent's job is to be there for guidance, not to force him to do something."

  *   *   *   *   *

- **An Ego**
  Words Spoken: *"This person is so irritating."*

- **An Enlightened Sage**
  Corrected Speech: *"It is not that they are irritating; it is just that you've run out of understanding."*

  OR

  "Expectation is the leading cause of irritation. If you expect something to happen in a certain way, or expect someone to be a certain way, then you are actually attempting to make the external environment conform to your ideals of what you believe it should be like. And when this expectation of how you view the 'event to happen' or 'person to be' doesn't occur exactly how you want it to, then irritation ensues."

  *   *   *   *   *

- **An Ego**
Words Spoken: *"That person just cut into line. How rude."*

- **An Enlightened Sage**
Corrected Speech: *"To act in accordance with God, one must present their life, actions, and all thoughts as a gift to others. Therefore, consider that spot in the line in front of you a selfless act and considerate gift."*

* * * * *

- **An Ego**
Words Spoken: *"I hope that mean person gets a "D" on his next test. That way I'll get a higher score."*

- **An Enlightened Sage**
Corrected Speech: *"All karma is connected. So to wish 'bad' upon another is to wish bad upon yourself. As you sow, you shall reap."*
OR
"If you wouldn't want someone to judge you poorly and wish you 'bad,' why would you wish bad onto another? You should always wish the best for others, no matter what the conditions."

* * * * *

- **An Ego**
Words Spoken: *"War is very bad. No one should have to go through this."*

- **An Enlightened Sage**
Corrected Speech: *"War is an expression and reflection of the conditions of the two interacting forces at two individual levels of con*

377

sciousness that are perceived to be in conflict. Since earth is a place of learn ing, levels of consciousness will inter act and express themselves as needed for each ego to learn a lesson."

*   *   *   *   *

- **An Ego**
  Words Spoken: *"That person is cheap; they didn't leave me any tip."*

- **An Enlightened Sage**
  Corrected Speech: *"To have the opportunity to serve them was a gift in and of itself. Rewards for self less service are great in heaven. So you didn't make any money; instead, you worked off about a lifetime worth of karmic debt... but only if <u>not</u> done in contempt."*

  OR

  "Not everyone has the money to give. It doesn't mean that they are cheap or selfish. They may have children, their parents, or a house, car, or school to pay for. They may be in debt as well. Would you selfishly take a couple of dollars from a soul who is suf fering due to their lack of money? Would you take food from a starving child?"

*   *   *   *   *

- **An Ego**
  Words Spoken: *"I don't like ants; they are in my house."*

- **An Enlightened Sage**
  Corrected Speech: *"Why not? Every soul is equal in the fact that it radiates Divinity and was*

*created.Do you feel that ants are infe
rior to you? Do you feel that dogs are
inferior to you as well? If so, where do
you draw the line? What beings or life
forms have you deemed all right to
spare and love, and which ones have
you deemed as all right to be killed?
Tell me, without your body, personality,
perception, what would you be if there
was no possibility of nonexistence? You
would be existence. Since all beings are
only using a body, whether bug, animal,
or human, it is only fair to treat each
with respect and value its life. In Real
ity, there are no forms. So in essence,
your body or perceived status holds no
importance, because it is not real."*

* * * * *

- **An Ego**
  Words Spoken: *"That person is ugly."*

- **An Enlightened Sage**
  Corrected Speech: *"That person is beautiful; God only
  creates beauty and is the 'Source of
  beauty."*

  OR

  *"As you cast judgment on another, you
  shall receive it on yourself."*

  OR

  *"That person is not ugly; she is a perfect
  expression of who she is, a child of
  God."*

  OR

  *"Beauty is in the eye of the beholder.
  What you perceive to be beautiful,*

*another may not. It is just the same as
if you like to eat chocolate and another
does not. So it is not the object that is
undesirable; instead, it is just your
perception of it."*

As a Sage or a spiritual aspirant recontextualizes what an
ego has said, a simple rearrangement of the sentence may be used,
or a paragraph. It depends on the willingness of the ego to listen,
or whether there is time to speak. Perhaps there is no time to speak
at all; prayer for that person may be used. The Presence of the
Sage is sufficient, because God's energy is ever-present and continuously flowing throughout the Sage's body. An unenlightened
spiritual devotee should use a prayer, since the power that flows
through them is limited. If an ego is willing to change or to learn,
then no words are needed; just the Presence of the Sage is sufficient. If an ego can be spoken with, the Sage may be a source of
inspiration; the ego may spontaneously accept the Truth, either
completely or partially, depending on their 'willingness' to release
impediments with humility. Only then will happiness, unconditional love, and peace be experienced completely.

Chapter 15
<u>Thinking Mind</u>

The Ego Mind

The term 'ego mind' is actually redundant, for the ego is the mind; however, this provides a ground for clarification between the universal mind and the ego. Although they are both one and the same, an ego cannot truly comprehend this notion. Therefore, to ensure one's ability to understand and decipher the difference between the universal consciousness and the ego's (claimed) immediate consciousness, the word 'mind' is added after the term 'ego.'

The ego mind is basically a point of perception that moves about freely, but with some limitations and restrictions, and that interprets various external and internal stimuli in order to gain an understanding of that which it believes reality (the manifest) to be. The Unmanifest Self (Nondualistic) never moves, due to the manifest's dualistic requirement of the 'mover and that which it was moved to.' So the Self is immobile and an ever-present, infinite Source of potentiality that is always present throughout all of creation as the Unmanifest.

The ego, however, doesn't believe itself to be infinite. So it feels as if it must move around and understand the dimension that it currently dwells within and is limited to. So every ego that is imprinted on a physical body, and ingrained upon and activating their physical brain, is just the _point of perception of one's Self moving around_. When one realizes that they are the Self, which is the very essence of All That Is, then the desire to move around to see the sights of the world tends to be drastically reduced. Why travel to see the sights, when one is the sights? There is no need; it is all an illusion.

As the ego moves around as the point of perception, it develops a type of beingness that is called 'thinkingness.' This is most often misidentified as a trait of the ego, but it really is the beingness of the ego itself. This is why the ego is termed the 'thinking mind'; pure consciousness (Higher Self) as 'Aware Mind,' and the Unmanifest Self, which is beyond all consciousness, is termed the Pure Mind of God (or Mind), although even this is usually surrounded by much confusion, even by some enlightened Sages.

'Thinkingness'

The ego thinks; that is what it does. Thinkingness is really one believing that which is held within the illusory mind of the ego is who they actually are as self. So by this, it can be seen that thinking is just an illusion. It is not a product, or a quality of the Higher Self. The Higher Self is 'Aware Mind'; the ego is thinking.

Since the ego mind is connected to the universal mind, one's self is a direct expression of their level of consciousness, which exhibits a certain set of character traits and beingness. One's will selects the level of consciousness that they opt to be connected to, or be an expression of, but the 'thinking mind' is what gets to select the traits as the thoughts are running through their being. It can be said that the 'thinking mind' is a type of filter of some sort. It simply selects whatever is relevant to the situation that the ego is currently undergoing, thus seeming 'sane' in the 'right' situation. However, a 'wrong' selection of traits, words, thoughts, actions, or beingness in another situation will create the effect that one is 'crazy,' or momentarily 'not with it.' And in fear of being in error, the ego tends to point fingers at others so as to take the blame off one's self, an obvious exhibition of embarrassment and pride (lower qualities of the ego).

Thinking, as it is thought to be by the common ego, is one's <u>creation</u> of energetic patterns that are thought to have originated from the being who 'thought of it.' One must keep in mind that only that which is formless can produce form. Just the same, an atom cannot produce another atom, although atoms can be added together to produce larger elements such as molecules. But this is not creating; it is simply *willing* two separate elements of nature to be expressed in a certain way when combined. It is really just two qualities of energy expressing their current influence to be a different quality of energy by an external (in the manifest) force.

So the ego doesn't create anything, because it is form, and form cannot create. But the ego can use the faculty of its being known as 'will' to intend for an expression of energy to display its character traits, or specific inherent energetic qualities as such.

One of form's (with respect to the ego) greatest limitations is not being able to create anything. It can only 'will' things into an energetic expression, nothing more. There is only one creative source, and that is God as Unmanifest. The only reason that the ego thinks it can create things is because this is an illusion that it is misled and confused by. The ego can only select out of the already endlessly created forms that are contained within the universal consciousness.

Thinkingness, as used by the ego mind, is actually a delusional act that claims an already created energetic form as its creation. So the 'thinking mind' only claims or steals thoughts from the universal mind. Because the ego is in love with its creation, or so it thinks, it cannot fathom that it is not the originator of its expression or portrayal of beingness. So in less than a fraction of a second, one's own 'will' connects one to a specific level of consciousness that selects a wide array of opportunistic expressions; that which it selects, it claims as 'its own' if it is desirable, or denies as 'someone else's' or 'mental garbage' if it is not. These unconscious and subconscious functions all occur beyond one's knowingness.

The Thinking Processes

This section clarifies the many ways in which the ego likes to think. Since the ego is form and only knows of form, it keeps the mind preoccupied with all manner of form. It does this in many ways; some are known, while many others remain unknown.

For most people, when they get out of bed in the morning, they think about the events coming up in the near future, such as work, family, friends, eating breakfast, getting back to yesterday's clients, going over yesterday's problems, anticipating the day's events and forthcoming problems, and so on. They may even turn on the television or radio so as to flood the mind with all of the elements of form and all of its connected nature (lower levels of consciousness). Unfortunately, all these 'thought-of' forms keep one focused on the world of form/illusion, keeping one from experiencing their True Reality as the nonform/Unmanifest.

With this known, one can clearly realize that slowing down the process of the thinking mind is the way to go. If one can rely less on the ego mind, then one's True Nature is revealed as a by-product. When the analogy was made about the "ripples in the pond that distort the reflective nature of the water," it was to express the disruption of the Self (still water) by the 'thinking mind' (ripples). Practices such as Zen Buddhism were developed to help instruct others on various methods to still the mind, so as to reveal the more profound levels of awareness and, hopefully, the Mind/Self. The true practive of Zen is to be the Self, which is selfless.

The many ways in which the ego mind likes to keep busy:
1. *Current tasks (talking, job, interacting, analyzing, listening to a radio, dancing, learning, typing, etc...).*
2. *Lifestyle (what one likes and dislikes about life and one's self).*
3. *Habits (concentrating on habits: biting nails, tapping fingers).*
4. *Past mistakes (rethinking erroneous ways).*
5. *Remembrance (past situations, things, textures, feelings, events, people's faces, previously learned words, etc...).*
6. *Anticipating future events (worrying about what's next).*
7. *Rethinking problem-solving formulas.*
8. *Organizing, categorizing, and selecting thoughts.*
9. *Focusing on form and logic.*
10. *Storing information and accessing it for recall.*
11. *Activating, energizing, supporting, and moving the physical body.*
12. *Interpreting physical stimuli.*
13. *Interpreting spiritual stimuli (from unconscious and subconscious interactions with the universe and*

egos, as well as the conscious mind).
14. *Maintaining false belief in separate identity.*
15. *Dualistic speech patterns.*
16. *Controlling and regulating energy flow through chakras and auras.*

So one should analyze their ego's current state of thinkingness and try to pinpoint their ego's most valued mental assets. By recognizing which mental functions are used the most, one can realize that which is keeping them from Truth. By analyzing why one tends to rely on one function more than another, it progressively begins to become easier to slow the 'filling of the mind' with form. This allows one to transcend thinkingness and realize one's true awareness. So remember to stop whatever your ego enjoys doing; that is when true happiness reveals.

By merely answering the many questions of the ego, the need for thinking is reduced to a large extent. After all of the questions are answered, one's level of awareness can then be one's existential point that is beyond the normal limitations and burdens of thinkingness, filling one with serenity and peace for all of their existence.

The Nature of Thinkingness

While the creation of the ego is the beginning of dualism as the belief of the separateness of existence, thinkingness is pure dualism itself: for example, the 'thinker and that which is thought of.' The illusion is obvious.

The ego has an ingrained subconscious dualistic view that entrains one to operate only on that level of existence. So when the ego just exists, it is dualistic; and when it thinks, not only is it dualistic, it also continually reinforces the dualism of one's self. For example, for one to state, "I hate you," one must also realize the dualistic paradox, "You love me." Just the same, for one to make the statement, "I love you," one must realize all of the 'things' that they love and hate in order to place that very thought and/or verbal statement into context. This is because if no dualism existed, then why even make a statement in order to clarify how one felt in the first place? That's easy: to make sure that one does not mistakenly place a seemingly undeserving being, item, or event in the 'wrong' (dualism itself) category, such as placing one's beloved wife in the 'hate category.' To the ego, not to know its 'likes and dislikes' would cloud its perception of itself, resulting in the confusion of its identity.

To clarify further through another example, to state, "This is a table," one must first realize what a "nontable" is. One cannot know what a table is without knowing that there are other 'things' out there in the world that are not tables, thus creating the dualistically voiced opinion that states "table."

So speech is actually not even a necessity to exist; it is merely an option that one has to express their opinions, thus clarifying 'likes and dislikes,' which inherently helps them to define themselves as a separate character with their own traits. Making dualistic statements also energizes and reinforces the concept of dualism, which inherently sets the trap that keeps one from their very nature: the Source/Self/Unmanifest/God.

Why All Thinkingness Occurs in the Past

Many believe that the quality of thinking is actually a task that can only be practiced in the present. However, this is not so. Thinking is always a past-time event. It is never exercised in the present.

First, all information that is interpreted and analyzed is really done so at the unconscious and subconscious levels. As it surfaces in the conscious mind, it then is the aftereffect that describes the past event, while just thought to be current or in the present. So when the aftereffect crystallizes to an extent, it is seen in the conscious mind as a thought. The thought, however, occurred in the past and was just recognized later by the conscious mind, but still thought to be in the present.

Furthermore, existence itself is actually an experience that happens in the Now, but when the faculty of the 'thinking mind' is placed over it, it then becomes a past event. The only experience that occurs in the Now is that of residing in the Unmanifest/Self, which is pure existence without any distortion. So as soon as conscious mind has to interpret the energy, there is a delay.

The delay is known even in the scientific realm. For example, when one perceives a flower with their eye, the energy has to first reflect off the flower as energy and enter the eye. After that, it needs to be interpreted by the brain, which is imbued with and activated by the ego mind. After the ego interprets the energy of the external environment, it must judge, classify, and categorize, and then finally the ego may be able to experience the thought as such, which it feels is the present but is really just an experience or an after-effect of the past.

Second, all terms that may be used within the present were learned in the past—for example, when one was a child and had to learn what a 'table, bottle, diaper, tree, and mother' was. Not only did this act reinforce one's inherent nature of dualism, but it energized the ego mind to the extent of having to remember the past learned energetic patterns—words, thoughts, images, feelings, etc…—thus creating a seemingly never-ending, continuously creating cycle of learned programmings.

Existence simply is this: on a manifest level, ostensible 'things' are objectively perceived and subjectively felt to exist, prompting one to develop a way to remember these 'things.' This is done by creating a label that can be placed on the many 'things'; the label helps one to judge, classify, categorize, and delineate various energetic patterns. It is thought that knowing what all 'things' were and are would help one understand what reality was and is. Unfortunately, it makes the soul take its focus off the True Reality of the Unmanifest and place it onto the illusory realm of the manifest, perpetuating the already negative condition and increasing one's karmic debt.

So all the 'labels of things' that are used (by thought) within the present actually force one to live in the past by remembering the past in the form of memories, words, concepts, morals, dogma, and so forth. Thinkingness occurs about one second after the Now has passed. So to truly exist within the Now, one must abandon the 'thinking mind' that corrupts the experience of the Now as pure existence, allowing one to just be existence as Aware Self.

Chapter 16
Ego Stretch Mechanism

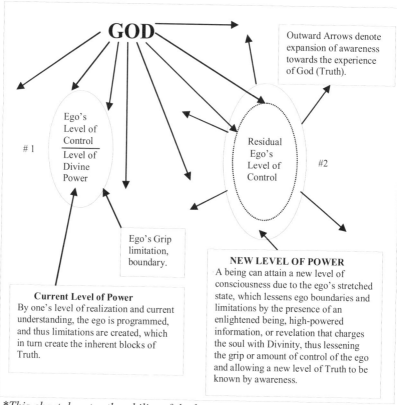

GOD

Outward Arrows denote expansion of awareness towards the experience of God (Truth).

Ego's Level of Control / Level of Divine Power

#1

Residual Ego's Level of Control

#2

Ego's Grip limitation, boundary.

Current Level of Power
By one's level of realization and current understanding, the ego is programmed, and thus limitations are created, which in turn create the inherent blocks of Truth.

NEW LEVEL OF POWER
A being can attain a new level of consciousness due to the ego's stretched state, which lessens ego boundaries and limitations by the presence of an enlightened being, high-powered information, or revelation that charges the soul with Divinity, thus lessening the grip or amount of control of the ego and allowing a new level of Truth to be known by awareness.

This chart denotes the ability of the being to transcend the ego by the process of adding the Presence of Light, which is Truth provided by God.

The ego's boundaries and limitations that it has set for itself usually do not change much throughout one's lifetime. However, if one seeks enlightenment and walks the path of Truth, by way of introspection, meditation, and 'rightful acts,' the ego's boundaries are then reset and the ego's grip lessened by the addition of the Presence of Light. That Presence is God as the aspect of Higher Self (the higher levels of consciousness—beyond ego control).

Whether it comes from the acceptance of God and the total relinquishment of the ego, or from a powerful Nonlinear catalyst that is made available within the realm of the linear, enlightenment becomes Reality. If the ego is not totally surrendered to God, then baby steps may be taken to loosen the grip of the ego (typically known as purification) until complete faith then resides unwaveringly. These steps are the most common ones taken towards enlightenment. They involve seeking out an enlightened being and taking refuge in the master (borrowing their energy frequency), following enlightened works or texts, being compassionate towards all beings, practicing yoga, using crystals or other higher (than one's current frequency) frequency objects, learning Nonduality (Advaita Yoga), practicing introspection and forgiveness, meditating, and acting as a selfless channel of Divine Will at all times.

All of these methods should consume the mind almost as an obsession: a full obsession to, for, and all things that represent and are God. This is called attunement, or keeping one's mind in constant alignment with a certain 'will,' whether 'ego will' or 'Divine Will.' If one is attuned to 'ego will,' the sins will be exhibited or portrayed by the mind, due to the lower frequencies that it is. If attuned towards God, selfless service will be shown, because the Divine Will's higher frequencies were chosen. As the mind attunes to something, that frequency flows towards one's self and energizes their whole being; so prayer is effective by way of attunement and also by creating positively created and reinforced thought forms.

The worldly or material realm that egos continually operate within is a lower frequency of the 'ego will.' Jesus said, "A worldly man cannot get into the kingdom of God" (NIV). This means that a being who is overinvolved with or overindulged in the material/linear/dualistic/manifest realm cannot be following Divine Will, since the worldly realm is at the frequency of the ego and not Absolute Reality (God). This is simply because the lower frequencies of the material/manifest realm dominate one's life as 'ego will,' leading to an 'ego will'–charged being who is not aligned or attuned with God Reality, but instead with ego reality. The desires, positionalities, emotional states, mental states, and attachments to the physical body, manifest realm, personality, emotions, and overall identity fuel the 'ego will,' thus slowing realization. Even so, there are frequencies that can be used by an ego being that are qualities of creation within the manifest (crystals/oils/herbs/incense/etc.) that have been preprogrammed with a higher frequency than any ego could ever be at. This makes purification of the ego or enlighten-ment a possibility within this lifetime.

The elements are higher frequencies, yet are a product of the material/ego/linear/dualistic/manifest realm. The elemental frequencies, respectively, in increasing order of power, are Earth, Water, Fire, Air, and then Spirit. Consciousness, an aspect of the Spirit, is the highest level of form; it is so abstract that it cannot properly be denoted as linear and manifest due to its irregularity of pattern or structure—although it is still form and within the linear. The element of Spirit, which usually refers to consciousness, is capable of recognizing form; therefore it is form and within the linear. However, this book usually uses Spirit in reference to and as the Unmanifest. That which is form (consciousness) and within the linear dimension is the only mechanism, or mode of awareness, capable of recognizing or being aware of form. This demonstrates the connection of consciousness to the manifest, because that which is formless or Nonlinear is not capable of recognizing or noticing any form/ manifest/dualism/ego/hell/sadness/positionalities/etc. So that which is Nonlinear/Nondualistic/Unmanifest/heaven/happiness/love is what Spirit is, the Unmanifest Self as God (limited qualities of this energy are in the Higher Self).

Balloon Analogy

The ego can be viewed as a balloon. The material of the balloon itself represents the limitation and boundaries that it sets and is. The air within the balloon denotes the level of awareness, which is the level of consciousness that inherently shapes the reality viewed by the ego. Thus a smaller balloon cannot experience the level of awareness (Truth) that is experienced by a larger balloon, because the larger balloon contains more awareness, which allows one's self to experience life or existence on a much more grand or Truthful scale.

This balloon (ego) is either content with its being, or it strives for something new. As its first realization is made, it searches for change, usually seeking the help of an experienced master (or maybe a book). As the master comes in contact with the student, the student's (smaller) balloon inflates, due to the level of awareness blown into the student's balloon by the master. As the student's balloon increases in size, it experiences a new level of awareness that feels pleasant and peaceful, and at times overwhelming and overflowing with joy. The longer the student stays near the master (an unlimited source of air with no balloon), the smaller balloon gets more and more inflated, thus increasing the capacity for the student's experience of reality as Reality. This is so because as one's awareness increases, one is more *aware* of Reality on a different scale or higher level of consciousness.

These new experiences that reveal the ultimate Reality intrigue the student, while making them dedicate their life to God. Unfortunately, as the master's unlimited supply of awareness (Air), by way of the Presence of God, is taken away from the student's smaller balloon, the balloon deflates, and awareness is lost to some extent. (The feeling of loss is where temptations to sin are the most prevalent.) This shows the student *close to* where they were existing, before the master and the realizations increased their level of awareness (by blowing up the balloon), and how the master helped them. They are encouraged to pursue the path of enlightenment or to (so they think) acquire new 'highs on life.'

Every time the student's balloon nears the master's unlimited air supply, the balloon first goes back to the prestretched state where it was the last time the master was near. Then the balloon is increased a little bit by the master's presence, or by the level of power within the teachings that are spoken. By this process, the student's balloon gets stretched just a little more, lessening the ego's previous limitation or boundary and increasing the amount of awareness that can be experienced.

The peace, tranquility, unconditional love, and stillness that the being feels by the increase in awareness drive them to seek the meaning of existence. But from the ego's standpoint (the balloon), one seeks to acquire happiness and peace as though it were external, thus bringing *periodic* attunement to God and increasing one's frequency and level of awareness by the alignment with the higher power. As the frequency and level of awareness are increased further, a more permanent fixation on God (an almost permanent attunement) takes place, thus energizing them with spiritual Truth every time. As the fixation on God, by way of attunement, becomes permanent, the balloon explodes (pops), and the limitations of the ego are broken and transcended.

Even though the ego is broken and transcended, its remnants can occasionally flow through one's consciousness, but these are observed with the full level of awareness that brings light to the previous ego mind energies. This helps one to be aware of the fact that they were a victim of their own choice, as they were also the being responsible for, and an antagonist of, all the subordinate levels of consciousness (egos) that exist in the manifest realms. Thus one helped mankind suffer when they were an ego, and consequently helps them transcend their karma when their own ego is dissolved, whether only by a minute amount or completely.

This massive realization brings about an awareness that is energized by the quality of unconditional love known as com-passion. Compassion allows a being to understand all points of view that any one ego has, without judgmentalism. Thus a selfless enlightened being now knows how to stop all egos' suffering, while simultaneously bringing the Presence of Light to all newly witnessed situations, whether silently, vocally, or by prayer. Without the restriction of their balloon (the ego), they find it easy to bring unconditional love to any situation through a high level of power that tends to bring peace to each individual, as well as the entire world. This allows them to be the unlimited source of air (Spirit) to another balloon in search of temporary or permanent inflation, which leads to the universal Truth of Oneness when the balloon explodes (pops) and the balloon's air fuses with the Source.

It should be noted that even though an enlightened being has transcended the ego, it can be 'willed' back as the focal point of existence at any time. The profound sense of loss and sadness will depress that being so much that it would be quickly rethought and rectified. However, there are some souls who become infatuated with the temptations and lures of the manifest, such as power, control, lust, and so on. If this being does decide to sin, then their ego will compare how it felt with happiness and how it feels with the sadness that it has so newly reacquired. Therefore, the soul will most likely become depressed, if they are not helped by another. To deny Truth again is a catastrophe that will be noticed as such.

Increased Awareness, But Capable of Sinning?

As one devotes their life to God, their awareness increases, allowing Truth to be known. However, occasionally that being may sin. Even though these sins are minor in nature, they still constitute a denial of God's Love for 'ego will' (external fulfillment). As the ego is stretched by the addition of light, awareness is stretched beyond the normal boundary. If 'ego will' is chosen, that being will then feel a slight regression, which may bring sadness, depression, or the feeling of abandonment by God. These symptoms may last for a couple of hours, a couple of days, or until the 'sin' is realized.

Flux in Consciousness due to Sinning

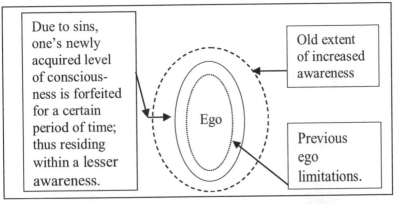

Due to sins, one's newly acquired level of consciousness is forfeited for a certain period of time; thus residing within a lesser awareness.

Old extent of increased awareness

Ego

Previous ego limitations.

This chart denotes a being's level of awareness as it decreases due to 'ego will' being chosen for expression.

The natural occurrence of the ego (sin) re-entering an enlightened being's existence is what I call "Ego Re-Entry." This usually occurs when one is being tested (by their own Will to transcend further in consciousness) in a 'trial period' that would propel them into a higher level of enlightened consciousness if they pass, or send them to a decreased state of awareness if they fail. Some of the 'sins' of temptations may be noticed, but others may not; thus, the latter are the obvious way that the enlightened being may allow the ego to 're-enter' its beingness. Usually, in a couple of days, a being is back to their previous enlightened state of consciousness, and they are presented with the 'trial period' only if they Will again to go higher in the consciousness of the Self. If not, the enlightened being will reside at their current level of enlightened consciousness for the remainder of their existence.

The nature of the devotee's sin is usually very minor. In fact, by an ego it is not even seen or known to be a sin. However, the exhibition of 'ego will' can be seen in seemingly harmless events, such as trying to heal another by directing energy to them. To direct energy is to use the 'ego will' to force it somewhere. This is obviously a product of the ego portrayed as *control*. No ego can truly heal someone; only God/Truth can. So to direct energy into someone's being, through the 'healing with the hands' technique, for instance, is actually 'ego will.' To use breath and visualization is to try to harness energy and make it do what one wants it to do (the act of manipulating energy or forcing change). Other small, and many times unnoticeable, sins are as follows: **wanting to** dream, astrally project, psychically communicate, experience spiritual phenomena, do Yoga, and so forth. There is a difference between doing things out of one's love for God and the willingness to serve, or because one's ego does it because it likes to do it. The same goes for wanting to eat, which is a sin if the mind pursues it for pleasure or satisfaction, rather than survival.

True healing comes when a prayer to God (higher attunement) is made, while asking (willing to be Truthful) God to heal the other being (humbly), while simultaneously giving up 'ego will' (both parties need to do this with absolute sincerity).

A New Type of Search

As the spiritual pathway towards enlightenment is chosen, a new type of search is under way—a search for the highest of high frequencies. In this search, the soul encounters things with intrinsic power due to its nature of creation. Although these manifested 'items,' which have varying frequencies that are many times higher than the ego self, can help to add light into the auric field of the spiritual seeker, the power is limited. Therefore, it is really a quality of linear force. Even though these frequencies are limited and are really a quality of linear force, they will seem to be unlimited power, because the frequencies are higher than the ego that is using it.

The power of God allowed force to manifest; therefore it is not 'bad' (although it is very limited), but it is just a choice that some took and others did not. For example, there is the angel who never made the choice to separate from God and the human who decided 'free will' was a good option at the time. We know that we deceived ourselves by taking this 'free will' (ego) option and are now trying to transcend the choice that we made, which created the 'fall from grace.' It is not 'bad' that we decided to 'test the water,' so to speak, because this now actually allows the ego to see that we have made an illusory mistake, so to speak, to live a life of suffering that inherently yields a greater appreciation for God's unconditional Love. If it were 'bad' to separate from God, God would have never allowed for 'free will' or the creation of the ego.

Many spiritual seekers may seek spiritual texts, crystals, psychic healings, psychology (as long as the psychologist is of a high spiritual frequency), crystals (which vary in frequency), preachers (as long as the preacher is of a high frequency), yoga, meditation, introspection (of high-powered texts, theories, concepts), nature, classical or new age music (of high frequency—not rap or hard rock or pop), psychic schools, or an enlightened master. One may not recognize which frequencies are high and which are low, and until known, attempting to decipher them should be avoided. This is when one should depend on the wisdom of a sage. The chapter on "**Raising Consciousness Levels**" explains this in detail. People may even intuitively feel that they should seek refuge in a certain part of the country that contains high frequencies, such as the mountains of North Carolina and South Carolina, the beaches in Hawaii, or the massive energy vortex at Sedona, Arizona. Whatever the method, the spiritual seeker's search for elevated frequencies is just like the ego's search for the lower frequencies of obsession, addiction, arrogance, abhorrence, pride, hate, and so forth.

To the same effect, while searching for higher frequencies, many spiritual seekers actually forget to attune themselves to God while trying to 'find' the highest amount of power. God is the highest (so to speak—Infiniteness) amount of power and obviously should not be neglected. God is first and foremost; the other manifest items with higher frequencies should supplicate (although not really needed) to the unlimited and infinite power of God. Keep in mind that the complete surrender of the ego to God, which allows for the power of God to be realized, is all that is needed, nothing more. However, these high-frequency 'items' can help increase the rate of spiritual evolution, while aiding a being in the ego's resolution; just don't forget to stay 100% attuned with God's Will.

Section Five
Initiating the Higher Power

"One can only realize the Self if complete and
unwavering trust and love is their beingness."
                                                    —BN

Chapter 17
<u>Self-Revealed</u>

The Journey

The process of enlightenment can be likened to a very long flight of stairs. One may choose to progress up the stairs, or stay at the bottom. One may choose to run up the stairs to see what is at the top, or one may choose to walk very slowly while pausing at intervals between levels. Nonetheless, the end result is the same whether one takes the scenic route or the expeditious.

The Stairs Analogy

The first step is physically easy to take, but the mental or ego resistance is exceedingly great. This is due to the number of stairs that are seen before one has decided to undergo the journey. One must force themselves up the first couple of steps in order to create momentum, which in turn doubles the amount of motivation. One must also feel able to succeed. If the feat seems too great, the ego will deny the challenge or give up in the middle.

If one can bypass or progress past the resistance of the ego, then the journey may begin. As the second step is taken, a sense of accomplishment is felt synchronistically with a feeling of apprehension, the fear of noncompletion, the fear of an unknown goal (outcome), and a sense of guilt and trepidation for what is being left behind. If the ego allows for it, the journey is continued due to the ego's increase in inspiration, motivation, and curiosity for "what else exists?" beyond what has been taught previously. As it progresses, if fear and apprehension have not made the ego falter or turn back to the familiar and known, it becomes intrigued with the newfound discoveries of what lies ahead.

If the ego's sense of exploration, achievement, and curiosity stay peaked, then a very satisfying journey lies within reach. At times, the ego will become apprehensive about the next step towards spiritual evolution and it may want to 'sit down' and rest, or think about what it wants to do: progress, stay, or recede back to familiarity. The ego may even convince one that there is no way to experience God (get to the top of the stairs), or that one is wasting time while simultaneously giving up the happiness of the material world.

At times an ego may pass by or meet other "Spiritual Journeyers" (SJs) who are on their way down, staying put and content, or coming back from the top without having reached it. This creates various positionalities and opinions that may be expressed about and during the journey, some negative and some positive, depending on their level of achievement and motives for mankind and themselves. These SJs may convince others and teach them how to progress upward towards the goal (Source) with their positive experiences and wisdom. SJs may have progressed to near the top of the stairs (the Higher Self) but have not experienced what is there. They will then either tell everyone that they are disappointed, there was nothing there, and it is all a hoax, or they may teach others the extent of their knowledge as Whole Truth.

These SJs teach their level of experience as the Whole Truth, simply because to them it is the whole truth that they know of and have experienced. They usually claim to know just as much as the SJ who has actually experienced the top of the stairs (the Higher Self), or that they themselves have experienced the top of the stairs. This in turn collects followers who believe in every word expressed by the SJ, who is falsely expressing their experiences of and as Truth, inherently leading their followers to the SJ's limited extent and no further. This obviously makes the followers ask questions such as, "Why am I not enlightened yet?", "Have I been following the master's way correctly?", "Am I not worthy enough to be enlightened?", "Does God not want me to be enlightened?", "Does this teacher know what they are doing?", "Am I traveling the right direction?", "Is God where I used to be, or is God really up there?" This can discourage many egos and cause them to retreat back to the familiar and known material world that provides comfort and tangibility.

As one nears the top, many emotional, mental, physical, and spiritual blocks appear and may make the final part of the journey very difficult. As the problems resolve themselves, one's identity tends to fade a little, as does as the ego's grip on the soul that casts the illusion of the dualistic and linear. Some beliefs, thoughts, emotions, and way of life just seem to be a memory and not who one is anymore. This creates the fear of, "If I am not who or what I had thought I was, then who or what am I?" This fear originates from the ego's fear of being nonexistent, while also bringing curiosity and motivation just to cross over the top to see what it is all about. The fear creates the biggest and most influential crisis in the spiritual journey: the 'fear of loss' of who one is. Many times, a soul decides not to complete this journey due to the feared loss of what they are most attached to—themselves (identity).

If a soul decides to abandon every thought, belief, idea, concept, way of life, and mental/emotional attachment that they are familiar with, the Truth at the top of the stairs is revealed in all its glory. As the last step is overcome, all fears, worries, stressors, inhibitions, and apprehensions disappear suddenly without warning as one transcends the stairs (ego) completely. One then finds Truth, but remembers that it feels all too familiar. For the 'place of Truth' is where one once lived, and with infinite and unlimited joy and happiness, one has found the way back home, wishing that they had never left in the first place.

With this newfound (but always have been) Truth having been discovered, peace, stillness, joy, happiness, and perfection of life are uncovered by the removal of the ego. One now sees the stairs (ego) as the source of illusion and distortion of Truth, the only block to the realization of what one is—God/Self/Unmanifest.

Understanding the Equality in the Levels

These levels of consciousness are like stairs; it is not better or worse to be on one level or another. They simply are what they are: a perfect expression of the frequency of that specific level. The stairsteps just denote different levels of learning, emotional states, mental states, beliefs, ideals, thoughts, intentions, will, and identity, i.e., who one is currently in this life. Whether one is on Step 1, 50, or 2,000 makes no difference. It shows a difference in levels, which is a difference in 'knowingness' that is beingness, not in importance. All beings have had to proceed through all of the steps of life and consciousness; therefore, no one is better than another, they are just on another level than some others. Farther along the road of life, these beings who were once below one's level may rise above them. Then, if one previously judged them for being worse than themselves, they would have to judge themselves equally harshly.

Just as the different levels of steps are no better than another, the same goes for the various levels (heights) of clouds, the different depths of fish, the different levels (densities) of gases, the different distances that planets are from one another. These observations are just what and where they are: observatory and judgmental. But eventually it will be known that the levels simply denote where beings are in the levels of consciousness, or analogously, where 'things' are in the universe. When used (intellectualized/rationalized/understood) improperly by a self-serving being, an ego judges themselves as better than another being who is at the lower levels of consciousness; that ego would feed off and fuel their pride and selfishness. When used (realized) properly by a selfless/serving being (a saint), it is a benefit that allows one to know where others are at, allowing them to understand what needs to be said to one in distress, or how they need to be helped to end the suffering that they currently endure.

Difference in Understanding

An ego and an enlightened being experience different realities. Respectively speaking, one perceives that which it thinks is real, but is illusion, while the other knows Truth by way of subjective reality because they are the very Truth and emanate it continuously. Basically, one knows or thinks they know truth but have deceived themselves, and the other knows Absolute Truth. The difference can best be summed up through an analogy.

Perceptive and Perspective Limitations

Imagine yourself as an ego in the center of a big city. You feel the solid concrete underneath your feet, while you see all of the tall commercial buildings along the road. As you walk through the streets, you smell the sewage system and see the lights of the cars. You can feel the wind against your body, but can't really tell which direction it comes from. You see the cars, but don't really know where they are going. From your understanding, you obviously figure that the people in the cars are going to work to make money (an internal positionality). You are also limited in knowing where they work and live. It is also noticed that the extent of your experience is equal to the extent or limitation of your perception and perspective on life and the events happening around you.

Now, as an enlightened being, you think back to the days of the ego and understand what it would be like to be on ground level. With these experiences in mind, you realize that one can simply think about it and remember the events or perceptive phenomena and experience them as if you were there. You realize that all was a product of the ego's perception, but its limitations stop one from noticing the actual reality: that of existence and the 'Big Picture.' You realize that for anyone who thinks it is reality, it is to them, but if thought is stopped and forfeited to God, the experience of Truth then becomes Reality. As an enlightened being, one's level of consciousness pulls one's self off the ground level, which has limited the ego's views, and onto the very top of the tallest building.

And as one transcends the ego, one may notice not only the remembered traits and experiences of the ego, but also have the knowingness of 'why things are how they are' because they see the 'Big Picture.' With this realization of and perspective on the True Reality, that which is going on down below, on the ground level of the city, is seen now to have meaning (but only to help one realize the universal Truths, nothing more). So every encounter with people or events brings about new understandings and lessons that are learned, breaking down the previous limitations that were imposed on a soul and revealing existence as a glorious sense of perfection, harmony, and Oneness. This previous limitation, called the ego, is now seen for what it is: a nuisance and a block to realizing the Truth, while simultaneously bringing about all of the seeming downfalls of life.

With the ego transcended, the enlightened being rejoices in this newfound Reality of being One with All, while hoping that they can help other beings realize that sadness, limitation, and loss do not have to be a part of existence. In fact, they are not even part of True existence. They are all just an illusion that needs not be experienced, just recognized as an illusion and transcended as such.

Do Not Become Discouraged

Many souls who have searched for Truth, whether for months, years, decades, or lifetimes, have become discouraged and disheartened by not finding it when they wanted to, and maybe are currently dispiriting others by talking down the path that they have chosen. There may be newspaper clippings, media reviews, broadcasts, reports, or interviews that bash the idea of becoming One with God. These writings can discourage a spiritual devotee and abolish any shred of hope they may have. But anyone who says that one cannot become One with God is obviously not en-lightened and speaking of their ego's traits (manifest/linear/dual-istic) with their ego's logical and rational understanding, which is inherently not capable of realizing God (Unmanifest/Nonlinear/Nondualistic). So they are limited in knowing God.

These disheartened souls (ego) will commonly use dualis-tic terminology: for example, God is over there, or back in time, in heaven, and not in the world. They may judge one and call them a heretic, 'sinner,' or a 'bad soul.' They will make one think that they are 'sinning,' but just examine who they are and how they speak; it can easily be seen that they are the ones who are 'far from God,' but only because of their dualistic mind. If they are willing to sacrifice their dualistic mind (the feeling of separate-ness), then Wholeness or Oneness will be realized and the 'far-from-God' complex will be dissolved, revealing itself as an illu-sion.

These disheartened souls try to discourage many who fol-low the path of becoming 'God-Realized' because of the simple fact that they themselves have not become 'Realized' either. These beings are so disappointed by not spiritually evolving themselves after all their years of dedication that they are convinced it is impossible to be One, and conveniently say that it's a "fool's goal." Many times they feel that with more knowledge of God, they are nearer to God. However, knowledge is a pattern, patterns are structures, structure is form, and form is linear/dualistic; God is Nonlinear/Nondualistic and formless. Therefore, their path is one of ignorance.

These beings may come out with new theories, while misinterpreting the teachings of spiritual masters, such as Krishna, Marharshi, and others, and they usually try to disprove Buddha's and even Jesus' teachings at times. They are ready to bash any idea of spiritualism or religiosity that is not what they believe. This prideful ego in turn develops a following of disheartened and nonenlightened beings, who are convinced that their leader is enlightened and the way to salvation. This creates a new "quasi-guru" who claims to know all about the universe. They are trying to popularize themselves and possibly their own religion, in which devotees follow the 'guru' in a new 'self (ego)-found' false religion, instead of Truth.

These gurus may walk the walk and talk the talk, but their intentions are less than integrous. Their nontruthful ways are presented in a logical and rational way that adheres to the mind of the devotee. These religions of nontruth were created by a nonenlightened, nontruthful, nontrustworthy, nonholy, nonspiritual, and purely egomaniacal expression of the lower self. The gurus may try to dress in 'garb' (whatever clothes are expected to be worn by their devotees), eat very little, act holy, and even write a book or produce a meditation CD. However, when the Presence is not emanating from their energetic field, they just *act* as though they are enlightened.

Truth comes from God because it is God; God can only be expressed by way of Power. Power is infinite and is God; force is limited and a product of the ego. Power 'just is,' and force tries to prove that it 'just is.' That which is All need not prove anything. That which acts (to act like something is a sign of force/ego) as though it is All desperately tries to prove (force others to believe) that it is All. That which has the Presence of God and is truly enlightened is humble, because that which 'just is' needs no explanation or proof to persuade others that it truly is (a magnificent book that describes Power and force in detail is **_Power vs. Force_** by David Hawkins, which can be purchased at veritaspub.com).

We don't need another 'guru'; we have plenty. All that is needed is for people to follow the path of Truth—that is all. Truth in literature is already provided in copious amounts. Authors who generate additional books of Truth significantly increase the frequency of a reader coming in contact with the Truth, thus helping all beings spiritually evolve to the highest degree of enlightenment. So, in essence, this book is not needed if one knows the path of Truth, walks the path of Truth, and is the conduit of Truth, or reads other books that contain an assured level of Truth that is equivalent to the frequency of enlightenment. But some resources that express Truth may be easier for one to comprehend than others, so selecting a book that expresses the utmost level of Truth that one can understand is important. After understandings are reached, then realizations will follow. So one should pick wisely and follow their heart to the path of realizing Self. Truth is Enlightenment, Self-Realization, or Oneness with God. There are no exceptions to the rule or alterations possible.

All Books Are Not Created Equal

Intrinsic Energetic Value of Books

One book on enlightenment is not necessarily equivalent to, or as high in frequency as, another book on the same topic. In fact, every book that has been written on the topic of enlightenment differs in its energetic frequency. Some contain half-Truths, while others are known as the "Word of God" (or God in writing), or just Higher Truths. Whole or Absolute Truth is the only acceptable Truth. There is no other or alternative truth. There is only one Truth; however, there are many alterations of Truth that should never have been published. These Higher Truths are called Absolute Truth by the ego, although they usually are not. Absolute Truth is only Absolute as the Unmanifest Self. So when an enlightened being expresses it, whether in writing, speech, action, intention, or in pure silence (called 'nonverbal transmission'), a slight alteration is made. Just as stated previously in this book, there is no way to express Absolute Truth in writing or in words, because form cannot properly express formlessness.

The expression of Truth should pertain to the Nonlinear and Nondualistic. However, it is all right if it speaks in some dualistic terminology only if the Nonlinear/Nondualistic is what is trying to be expressed for ego comprehension. The book must be dedicated towards helping one understand and eventually realize the Oneness as God-Consciousness, or being the Higher Self. It must also adequately express the different levels of consciousness that help one understand their nature and where one's ego is currently at. It must explain the genesis of the ego, the function, the identity, and security measures. It must also explain what one can do in order to transcend the ego. The book must be dedicated to teaching people how to serve God/Truth as unconditional love, compassion, and to be willing to help others make a positive change in their lives at any cost (within the boundaries of integrity). And if the book states that consciousness is what God is as Unmanifest, then put it back and disregard the reading. The Unmanifest is beyond consciousness. Consciousness is just an aspect of God as Totality.

Energetic Transmission of the Author

The author's energetic transmission is often overlooked, but it is the ***most important*** quality of the Presence that is imprinted in the pages of a book from the Higher Self of an enlightened being. The level of Power is silently imbued in and imprinted on the book as a silent blessing that actually acts as a catalyst for increasing the rate of enlightenment for the spiritual seeker who reads or picks up the book. It is almost like enlightenment medicine: read a page or two of the book and increase one's energetic field with the Power of God, thus dissolving one's karma and ego by a minute amount. The more that one reads the book, the more likely one will become enlightened within this lifetime.

The Presence of God within the consciousness (Higher Self) of an enlightened being will and can spontaneously resolve issues or dilemmas that had previously been roadblocks for the ego. The energy that this book contains is powerful because of the content of the book and the overall energetic imprint of the enlightened sage. Thus, a book on Absolute Truth is truly absolute (for our realm) when enlightened material is within its confines and it was written by an enlightened sage who channels Love as Truth to all.

The utmost level of Power, or Absolute Truth, is a very transforming energy that by mere contact is capable of enlightening someone. As one reads the book with this frequency of Truth imbued in it, enlightenment is almost surefire and imminent. Even though it is not necessary, it can be helpful to one's overall comprehension and realization if one studies many different texts comparatively. It must be kept in mind which books are Truth and half-truths, as well as complete fallacy. This will not be known to a beginning spiritual aspirant unless the books of Truth are studied, understood, comprehended, realized, or at least recommended by an enlightened sage.

If one is interested in analyzing various texts that differ in nature, then one must compare the books one is 'unsure' about with already known books of Truth, and not the other way around. Since Truth is the backbone of all religions and spiritual texts and masters, only books of Truth should be the backbone of one's spiritual practice. There is only one Truth that is provided accurately in some books; thus all other books that are half-truths or fallacy can be compared with those books of Truth. Those books will then bring light, understanding, and possibly realization to readers of the other books with very cryptic writings or occluded truths.

Chapter 18
<u>Spiritual Will</u>

Divine Alignment

As a being decides to forfeit an aspect of the ego identity that they previously assumed to be themselves, then the Spiritual Will is initiated. This means that the ego takes a back seat for a brief moment of its existence and allows Spiritual Will to come forth and present the radiance of God. This higher Will is like a positive magnet that attracts positive life situations, whether people, events, jobs, or karmic merit. Just as the ego brought negative stimuli or situations, the Spiritual Will brings the gentle loving essence of God, although in a smaller amount, due to the preset restrictions of the ego's limitations and boundaries.

As the Spiritual Will takes the majority of control (51%), an integrous or honest and trustworthy being emerges. With this newfound presence of light and love, more integrous and honest actions are prevalent. Just as the 'ego will' prompts one to be self-serving, the Spiritual Will prompts one to help others while thinking positive, loving, and compassionate thoughts.

The presence of Spiritual Will does not mean that the ego has been transcended. It simply denotes that the predominant energy is one of a higher power that helps one to see the whole picture (so to speak). Similarly, one may watch just one raindrop (the presence of some Truth), focus on the shower in its entirety (the Presence of All Truth), or ignore the rain (Truth) and focus on one's self, life, or feeling about the rain. With Truth in mind, the ego loosens its grip or control over the soul, allowing the radiance of the Spirit of God to shine forth in varying levels; from dim to brilliant to blinding. The popular Christian song, "This little light of mine, I'm going to let it shine, let it shine, let it shine, let it shine," illustrates that the presence of Spiritual Will is an option; whether one wants to let the light shine through them or not is their prerogative. Just as 'free will' was practiced to form the ego, 'free Will' must be practiced to allow the Divinity to shine through all aspects of one's life.

The option to allow for Spiritual Will to flow freely through one's being is the Presence of God working quietly within oneself. God is the ultimate in subtlety. God's presence can be felt and known, or it may be felt as if it is nonexistent; it all depends on one's level of awareness. At a higher level of consciousness, it is easier to feel the Presence of God. Many egos who are not religious or spiritual do not feel this Presence, nor do they believe in God or feel that God is everything and All. This is simply because their ego is blocking the ability to realize the Presence of Divinity in everything, whether in people, air, nature, and so on.

So, in essence, the presence of Spiritual Will in an unenlightened being is the choice to be honest with one's self and others, for the most part. This does not mean that an individual will be 100% honest or truthful. It only means that their ability to tell the truth or be honest is more common, at best about 51% at the lowest levels. Thus a trustworthy being at a lower level of consciousness will still lie to themselves and others about 49% of the time. This doesn't seem to indicate an honest individual, but it is better than lying that extra 1% or more. Due to the presence of faith and courage, that being believes there is a *reason* or a 'good purpose' for being nice, honest, or integrous, because of the unconscious or conscious knowingness that God exists and is love.

Though the ego may convince one to believe that they are a 'good person,' the lie (ego) that covers up their true being will slowly begin to resolve as the presence of Spiritual Will increases due to their faith in God; so does their level of integrity, love, and honesty. This creates a more honest, loving, and giving individual, which leads to a more honest, loving, and giving society.

The varying levels of Spiritual Will denote the varying levels of the Presence of God that are there by way of acceptance due to ego surrender (humility). This Will acts as a catalyst and perpetuates a positive magnetic effect on the higher frequencies of existence, stimulating a spiritually charged being to act on any situation within the proper context of the Presence of God; therefore, they are being driven by God's Will and very little of their ego will. As transcension (enlightenment) finally occurs, the 'ego will' is completely abandoned and replaced by the Grace of God, while continually radiating the Presence at all times. So an enlightened being is 100% Spiritual Will, with little possibility of return of the ego will. This obviously leads to a greater seemingly Divine Ordinance on the material realm of the physical dimension known as earth. Just keep in mind that everything always happens within Divine Ordinance, even though it may not seem so to the ego.

Levels of Divine Will

Just as the ego has varying levels of consciousness, ranking from the lowest to the highest, so do the levels of consciousness represent the Presence of God/Truth (Divine Will). As the ego allows the Presence to take control of its existence (which requires faith and courage), the level of consciousness increases due to the amplification in frequency that is supplied by the higher power. So the Presence of God, less restricted by the ego than before, is allowed to affect humanity in a heavenly way. With that said, one can clearly see that God can only be experienced when one has undying faith and courage to allow God to control their soul's path. As God is given the complete ability to flow freely and unrestrictedly throughout one's being, then enlightenment becomes a Reality, allowing one to experience and express God as Divinity and Truth.

Levels of Consciousness of Spiritual Will
Ranging from the lowest (after Pride)
to the highest (enlightened)

Faith
This is the level where one decides to allow the Higher Will of God lead them in their destiny. They still feel as if they are in control of their life and that other people cannot make them do something against their will, but they are trusting enough to allow other people's opinions to intervene. At times the ego will reject an opinion, but in other instances the ego will accept it as 'good

413

advice.' Faith is when one trusts in God that all is OK. One feels as if they are in control, but God helps out once in a while, such as directing them in a certain beneficial pathway, with money, relationships, etc.

Courage and Empowerment

As one decides to 'change for the better,' then Spiritual Will energizes and fuels them with the power to 'take a chance.' This is an attempt to see if what they believe to be the 'right' decision is correct. As faith leads to empowerment, it then fuels a being with the courage to allow faith to be trusted as the next step that the ego believes to be true.

Trust

When the Spiritual Will brings forth positive change, which the ego has come to agree is for the 'better,' a being begins to trust themselves. If one makes what they think is a 'good decision' (but unknowingly for self-gain) and 'bad things' happen, then one will never stay at or reach this level. If one has the best intentions at heart, then only 'good things' can happen, whether the transcension of past karma, a job promotion, or maybe getting fired from a nonintegrous job (which may seem 'bad' at the time) and finding a new, integrous job. Trusting in Spiritual Will only yields a positive outcome; however, although it may be a positive change, the ego may not see it that way at the time.

Willingness and Intention

As Spiritual Will flows, freely yielding its positive effects, one begins to understand that only the positive comes from believing in and serving God's Will. This creates the spark of Willingness to allow it to happen again and again. Furthermore, this Willingness creates the intention of 'doing good' to others because it is the 'right thing' to do. So Willingness is the acceptance and readiness to allow the Spiritual Will to flow through a being, while stretching the ego's limitations and expanding awareness. This infers that Intention is a knowingness that following the Spiritual Will provides only positive outcomes, making one want and intend to follow God's Will during their lifetime.

Optimism

As one trusts their life to God and intends to do acts of kindness throughout their life, then positive changes come about in an overflowing quantity. This leads one to understand that the future is looking 'pretty bright,' helping one to have a very optimistic view of life.

Acceptance

At this stage, an ego starts to analyze some or perhaps all of their sins in full context. They understand that they are 'sinners' (egos) and that they want to rectify what they have wrongfully done. They accept that they are not perfect. In fact, they understand that to sin is the nature of the ego and a common occurrence. They also accept life 'as is' and without as much analyzing as they did before. They realize that there is a plan for everything and that no one can control the external world around them.

Forgiveness

Acceptance lessens the fear of 'fessing up' or admitting sins, helping one to forgive themselves and others. When an ego has its full grip on the soul and duality is reality, God is thought to be far away, which leads the ego to believe that they can get away with some of their sins and not get caught (as if God might have missed something). As the ego begins to realize that God is everywhere, *all* sins are seen for what they are and known to be forgiven.

Release

As an ego begins to be fully honest with itself, old conditionings and past karma can finally be released as the process of forgiveness is under way. As sins are understood and forgiven without contempt, these negative energetic patterns can be released from the energetic system, which helps one transcend their ego, the very source of sin itself. This makes it easier for a being to love and understand others better, without judging as much as before. That being forgives all of the 'wrongdoings' done to them in the present, past, and future.

Understanding

As one really starts to be aware of who and what they are as ego and Spirit, an almost full realization occurs. This realization is not only a way of understanding others and one's own nature of sin, but also a way to understand the nature of consciousness itself. This understanding is a combination of the knowingness of the ego and the realized reason for its ignorance and bondage. Then one begins to understand that choosing Love is an option, just as choosing the ego is also an option. Everyone can judge someone or something, but few can understand everyone and everything enough not to judge.

At this level, a being doesn't really have to forgive because they don't see anything as 'wrongdoing.' They simply see creation unfolding exactly how it is supposed to at the various levels of consciousness. They have a divine understanding of why all things happen; there are no mistakes, and all is perfectly occurring. When all 'things,' people, or 'events' are understood, there is nothing to hold in contempt; therefore, there is nothing to forgive.

Love

When the previous observation is made by a series of realizations or revelations, Love is then chosen above all other options of the ego. One now begins to realize that the Love the ego experienced during its previous existence was not of its own origin; instead, Love was the Presence of God that the ego just claimed to own. This shows that the ego is not true divinity, but rather, it can be seen for what it really is: 'sin,' or the rejection of Love/God/Truth. This revelation usually prompts one to become fully enlightened, totally abandoning the ego and its deceptions. The realization also helps one understand that all people, or egos, think that to be sad and happy, truthful and deceived, upset and peaceful are the basic and normal emotions that humans have to be or experience to live, with no exceptions. Thus it perpetuated the belief that humans have to go through the 'roller coaster of life,' or the 'ups and downs.'

At this level of awareness, the previous ego positionalities are seen for what they are, an illusion, prompting one to choose a loving and compassionate viewpoint on life. However, one usually focuses this viewpoint on their own life and family the most, because judgment is still a possibility and a common occurrence.

Reverence

As the predominant energy of Love prevails, a new beauty is felt throughout existence; this is the Presence of Divinity. It is a **knowingness** that everything big or small is an integral part of existence. All 'things' are now felt to be connected in some way. Even if one has read some Truth about Oneness, the ego still restricts the whole Truth from being known, or else they would be enlightened. Therefore, only the almost completely transcended ego is allowed to experience a feeling of connectedness, as an infinite number of 'things' that are connected by the Presence of God (although still showing dualism and the possibility for judgment and the classification of importance). At this level of consciousness, one may walk slowly so as to not crush any ants, or they may internally Will Love upon others. They may carefully hold and admire a rock or dirt, while starting to realize that all life or existence is of equal importance, with no exceptions.

Unconditional Love

If the realization of equality becomes a Reality, then one arrives at the level of consciousness known as Unconditional Love. This is where 'snap judgments' begin to slow, and the prevailing qualities of Divinity within all beings shine brightly with all their beauty. This is the compassionate view that very few beings in this world have (about 4%). Also, it can be witnessed that other egos at lower levels of consciousness always seem to claim that they are loving and caring, or that they do not judge, but this is all a fallacious claim of the ego in an attempt to preserve its ego identity as a 'good person.'

This high level of love slowly fades away the dualistic reasonings that one so depended on as an ego. It resolves

417

judgmentalism, stereotyping, and other linear methods of measurement. This love begins to be known as the One Source that is intrinsic to All. Unconditional love will soon prevail, while providing a comforting sense of peacefulness.

Peacefulness

Love, or the Presence of God, is the Source of peacefulness, joy, happiness, and stillness. The peacefulness is within the Mind of a being and not a product of the ego mind. This ever-present stillness, which brings and is peace, is the quality of Unconditional Love that God is. At this stage, the ego mind begins to shut down and give up. As the surface mind quiets and clears, the brain waves of the individual may actually slow down to an extent, to the Alpha state (a light meditative state). These slowing thoughts help one feel as if they are a clear vessel getting ready for the Divine Will to flow freely throughout, which also helps them devote themselves further to the service of God. At this level, fear and anxiety are replaced by peacefulness.

Increasing Levels of Enlightenment

(1st Stage) Enlightenment (1st Stage Violet)
Experiencing Reality as Unconditional Love

As peacefulness is selected as an option, and the ego is discarded as the source of unhappiness and suffering, a being becomes illuminated with the 'Grace of God.' This realization of illumination is enlightenment. It is an all-encompassing sensation of a knowingness that God is everywhere at all times. The revelation that God is One and that they are also One with All of Totality is now understood always to have existed. It is just that the ego, or their belief of themselves to be separate, had blocked that realization of Truth.

This state is very peaceful, loving, relaxing, and comforting. It can be likened to the trancelike warmth and comfortableness that can be felt during meditation, but at all times without having to meditate. Now it is understood that the Source of Love is God, which is One and All. Within this state of awareness, personal karma (ego) is completely transcended. Therefore, universal karma or other egos' personal karmas (collectively) is what the Light of Self (not showing ownership or attribute of identity) relieves by adding the Presence of God as Love to any and all situations.

This enlightened being is a walking blessing for all other beings in this linear/dualistic realm. Fragments of the ego can be pulled back to affect the individual negatively, if any emotional attachments are wanted to be remembered and felt. This is the ever-present temptation that all enlightened beings must confront. It is not difficult for an enlightened being to deny this 'sin' and to stay in the Light of God, though; it is simply a matter of choice.

(2nd Stage) Blissfulness (2nd Stage Violet)
God's Love Intensified

As the enlightened state of awareness increases in frequency or Power, a blissful state ensues and becomes felt as all-pervading and at times incapacitating. It is also known as 'complete absorption into the Self.' Many times, in this state, it may be difficult for one to operate in the regular ego world, but with practice comes ease.

During an enlightened state, one notices that the world seems similar to a play that has preplanned consequences due to the chosen karmic vibratory packages that one has assumed, whether these were selected knowingly or unknowingly. One realizes that all choices are planned and outcomes are already taking place. It is seen that until egos realize why that path has been chosen, no change will take place.

At this level, suffering is now seen within the ordinary world as an option, not a guarantee. If this is said, other egos may think that a being is crazy, unless it is explained in detail. Sometimes one may explain in an effort to help egos transcend their own karma, while other times a being may say absolutely nothing with the pleasure of not caring what anyone thinks of them. This is only possible because one realizes that there is no longer an ego identity to prove, preserve, save, or build up. So with humor, one plays in this linear realm as in a game for fun, while understanding the actual context is God at all times. This blissful presence, or prevailing quality of Love, makes one peaceful, and others tend to feel peaceful when around them.

(3rd Stage) All-Beingness (3rd Stage Violet)
God's Love and Mind Manifest (Oneness)

This state of awareness truly allows one to feel as if they are the Oneness of the universe. It is similar to the earlier stages of enlightenment, which allow for the *feeling* of Oneness from a sensation of blending into the entire universe with love as One; this is considered 'I Am Presence,' or when one actually knows that they are the 'Light of Existence,' partly due to the intense blissful state, triggered by the Nonlinear Love that seems to blend one into the world of duality and Nonduality simultaneously. One truly feels themselves to be God-Consciousness. This is the first stage of the Sage.

One feels compassionate for all others and compelled and driven by the Divine to help all others become enlightened. These beings look forward to helping others with intense lessons of Truth and blessings. This advanced level of awareness has typically been called 'God Manifest,' which describes the manifestation of the Self that roams the linear with Nonlinear wisdom. The title refers to a 'purified (consciousness) being' with a transcended ego, who is truly Self-Realized to a very high degree. This being emits Unconditional Love and Peacefulness that can be felt by other beings (if the ego so allows). These beings also radiate a strong purity that strongly connects with others, while allowing them to notice that they really do understand the ego and its troubles (and can help resolve them as well). In this stage, peacefulness tends to overpower the blissful episodes of overwhelming love, providing a more stabilized state of awareness that yields more wisdom.

(4th Stage) God as Sound or Word (4th Stage Violet)
God as subtle energetic sound (beginning level) -Beatified

God as subtle energetic sound is a higher frequency than that of subtle energetic light, which allows the manifest linear dimensions to crystallize and form. It is simply a higher level of consciousness or awareness because of the intense amplification of frequency from subtle light to subtle sound. This being, who is an expression of God as subtle energetic sound, emits and radiates a brilliant-sounding hum, which can be heard by the 'tuned-in' clairaudient. The subtle sound mixed with violet and created gold.

The constant high-energy frequency heals egos' problems almost spontaneously. Some beings may also instantly enlighten when in the Presence of such beings. When an ego leaves that higher-energy field, the enlightened state often fades away, allowing them to realize that one can exist without the ego and help others by simply existing. This 4th stage enlightened being speaks and is the 'Word of God,' such as, "If God had a voice, God would say this..." Their words are a very accurate Nonlinear transmission of verbal material and languaging, as well as the nonverbal (silent) energetic transmission that elevates the consciousness of all other ego beings. This is why the Bible (Lamsa edition) is considered the 'Word of God,' as are other sacred texts of Truth with similar formatting, such as Buddhist and Vedic texts.

This being is also considered beatified, or able to give blessings. Due to their presence being so high in consciousness, they continually heal others by simply existing. This being can pray for others that they have never met and heal them (to their ego resistant extent) because they realize that the other being is just another manifestation of oneself. This enlightened being does not pray across a distance (like the ego attempts) to heal another being, instead they simply 'think' using their universal mind and heal that aspect of their mind. At this level of consciousness, one can raise the frequency of an object, person, or animal... but only as high as that being is willing to go for the ride, so to speak.

(5th Stage -beginning) (1st Stage Gold)
God as Universal Identity
Higher Enlightenment (subtle sound dominates)

This is the 'Universal Identity' known as 'Buddha Nature,' 'Christ Consciousness,' or 'Transcendental Krishna.' The condition ensues when the aspect of a being, known as the Higher Self, is realized to be One with all levels of consciousness, and they now see themselves as the Universal Mind itself. This means that a being sees everything as a product of the Self as the Universal Mind, and knows the utmost Truth in this dimension of the manifest. But bear in mind that they are still beginners in the next realm of even higher consciousness.

This being is 'pure consciousness' and is capable of many seemingly miraculous things. But these miracles are seen and known to the high-level Sage as normal and in need of no comment. This state of existence is known as the Avatar, or God as Universal Mind on earth. This being is typically called the 'Savior' because their purpose is to save all beings from their own sins, whether through action, prayer, or their Presence. To be around this being is one of the highest blessings that one can attain in the limited linear dimension.

(6ᵗʰ Stage –'mid-power') (2ⁿᵈ Stage Gold)
God as Universal Identity (subtle sound - mid level)

While the previous stage is when one becomes aware of being the Universal Mind, at this stage one becomes even more aware of that fact. They almost go from being aware of that fact to being that fact. The revelations that come with this level of enlightenment are utterly amazing and cannot really be summed up or explained. All that can be said is that this being now knows that they **are the Universal Mind**, while the previous stage of the Sage just **knew of the connection** of the universe as Oneness.

(7ᵗʰ Stage –'high-powered') (3ʳᵈ & Final Stage Gold)
God as Universal Identity (subtle sound highest level)

This is a rare stage of enlightenment that few have ever experienced. Termed the 'final nirvana,' it is the last stage of enlightenment that can be experienced by a being in this realm of existence. Not much can be said about this stage, because few have ever attained it, such as Jesus, Buddha, and Krishna, and this level of enlightenment is nearly impossible to language. It is said that it can only be experienced when one is already close to this level of enlightenment and is leaving their physical body in the dying process. This is how the Buddha stated it.

Chapter 19
Raising Consciousness Level

Align the Mind

Aligning the mind is the first and foremost step that should be taken every day in the morning and at night with prayer and meditation. Just as well, Mindfulness can be practiced all throughout the day in order to stay aligned, or to realign. To align the mind is to attune one's energetic frequency to that of the Divine Will, or God. It can be done through praying, meditating, having an unspoken knowingness, reading a book of Truth, talking to others about Truth, Mindfulness, doing 'good deeds,' and so forth. This in effect brings the higher frequencies of Truth into one's energetic field. Whether one wants to use the frequency of God, Allah, Jesus, Buddha, or Krishna makes no difference; it is all one and the same. One may also pray and ask for energetic help from an angel (never incarnated), or an enlightened being who is currently incarnated or has left the physical plane. Just be sure not to attune one's mind to that of the 'lower ego will'; that would be detrimental to one's spiritual evolution, possibly damning.

To attune one's energy in order to raise in frequency, visualize a high-powered guru, sage, saint, avatar, and so forth. For instance, one may visualize intensely an external (a picture on a wall) or internal (from memory) picture of the enlightened sage Buddha. As one holds this image in mind for about 15-30 minutes, a transfer of energy commences. It can be likened to telephone lines; it is a direct connection to the Higher Self through one who has already connected before and currently is. It doesn't matter if one is not sure whether the image being focused on is correct or incorrect; the Will is what sets intention, charges the action, and connects one with the Self through that entity, not the image. The name of the sage or spiritual master can be used as well.

Many devotees focus on the image while chanting the many names of God. One may also simply say, chant, or hum the word,

"Ohm" out loud or internally with the image. It is important to note that an external image is not necessary. One may simply visualize the figure in their mind. Many devotees visualize an archetypal figure (Jesus, Buddha, etc...) and chant, "Ohm," while others simply pray for the 'good' of humanity. Whatever your method, it is just a means to choose Divine Will over ego will. The more a being chooses God's Love and Will over their own ego will, the further one will advance spiritually. Enlightenment is certain if a being devotes 100% of their life to God and surrenders all of the impediments and vicissitudes of the ego to the Source.

Daily Prayer Format

This is to be done in the morning after one is sufficiently awake, and then done at night 1 to 2 hours before sleep.

1. *Go to a quiet room and adjust the air temperature to a comfortable level.*
2. *Sit in Indian style, lotus, half-lotus, or gasho position.*
3. *Take at least 5 deep and slow breaths, while adhering to the pranayama format, to relax and calm the mind and balance one's frequency.*
4. *Place hands in prayer position in front of the heart chakra.*
5. *Pray to God to release and surrender the old conditionings and programmings of one's being (be humble).*
6. *Pray the following: "I pray to be a clear and direct channel of Divine Will, so that I may bring Divine Will to an 'ego will'–dominated situation, that I may bring peace to an unpeaceful or upset situation, bring love to an area of hatred, bring happiness to an area of sadness, and bring joyful bliss to a person who needs to feel it in order to find the value of living."*
7. *Pray for clarity and understanding, or strength when you feel weak and upset.*

8.   *Pray for all beings to become enlightened and to choose Divine will over ego will (chant about 25-50 times to reinforce thought forms and intent).*

9.   *Pray for one's family and friends, or people in need, to feel at peace with themselves and all others, to feel loved throughout the day, and to respect all beings.*

10.   *Ask for guidance, then place hands together in lap or hold mudra while meditating.*

Meditations after Prayer

Extreme Novice Stage
(no prior understanding of metaphysics)

- *Whole-body tensing*
- *Chant a Mantra (200 times with open eyes)*
- *Pranayama, 20 breaths (closed eyes)*
- *Breath Awareness (5 to 10 minutes) (closed eyes)*
- *Open-Eye Peripheral Gaze (5 to 10 minutes)*

Novice Stage
(with little understanding of metaphysics)

- *Progressive Muscle Relaxation*
- *Chant a Mantra (200 times with open eyes)*
- *Pranayama, 30 breaths (closed eyes)*
- *Concentrate on heart center and breathe in and out for 10 breaths (closed eyes)*
- *Then on the throat center, 3rd eye, and then the crown*
- *Breath Awareness (closed eyes)*
- *Open-Eye Peripheral Gaze, with pranayama, then with*
- *Breath Awareness (Open-Eye Peripheral Gaze)*

Beginner Stage
(just starting on the path to Enlightenment)

- *Progressive Muscle Relaxation (closed eyes)*
- *Chant a Mantra (200 times), then another one (200 times)*

- *Pranayama, 15 breaths, then (closed eyes)*
- *Use chakra charge and clear meditation (BROYGBIVWG)*
- *Concentrate on crown chakra while breathing in and out, then third eye, then throat, then heart.*
- *Breath Awareness (still closed eyes)*
- *Breath expansion—through body, aura, room, house, world, Universe, and so on*
- *Open-Eye Peripheral Gaze or Inner Sound Technique*

Intermediate and Advanced Stage
(close to Enlightenment)

- *3 deep breaths to relax with whole-body tensing*
- *Bandha Technique (open eyes)*
- *Chant a Mantra (100 times), then another one (100 times)*
- *Pranayama 15-25 breaths (closed eyes)*
- *Kundalini Technique (closed eyes)*
- *Energy body expansion (closed eyes)*
- *Breath Awareness (closed eyes)*
- *Open-Eye Peripheral Gaze*
- *Chant "I am God" (with proper context, of course) 100 times*

After Enlightenment

No meditation practice is really necessary, because all of one's focus is always within the proper context and life seems to be a constant meditation. Meditation enhances the blissful feeling extensively, sometimes bringing one into a catatonic state. Meditation can be used to shift one's focus from a lesser level of the energetic body to awareness that resides in the outmost layer and crown chakra, softening views in the physical and strengthening one's awareness and joy.

After enlightenment, one usually seems to be compelled and inspired to chant and pray. Meditation is not really necessary, but thoroughly enjoyed when practiced with humility. The Sage finds more value in reinforcing the positive thought forms of the universe by chanting and praying, rather than enjoying the benefits of meditation. This usually prompts one to start teaching individuals, groups, or the world, depending on one's mission in life. One may even not teach, but walk around or travel to different parts of the world, chanting and praying for all beings to become Self-Realized, thus providing energy to the world via the Presence of God as Truth, Love, and Light.

Practice Mindfulness

As one devotes their life to the service of God, it is natural to become more Mindful of life and all of its wondrous forms. Throughout one's day, it is important to practice mindfulness. This includes walking very slowly while watching the ground to make sure of no untimely deaths of any bugs or insects. It includes respecting what the bugs do for us, how they balance the earth, how their energetic levels of consciousness affect the universe, and how we are all supposed to share this physical dimension together. Humans don't own it; they just like to act as though they do through power trips or exhibitions of control over the 'thought-to-be' lesser forms of life. Mindfulness is the understanding of how all 'things' just are, and that there is no need for change: just the realization of the Truth, or the greater meaning of existence.

Mindfulness is an attempt to respect not only other animals and insects, but to respect other people as well. Then as we walk on the earth, respect should be given to the dirt, the rocks, the core of the earth, the planetary forces, the sun, the trees, the plants, the water, the moon, the stars, the grass, your body, the ability to express one's self through voice, action, thought, and so forth. Mindfulness comes when one minds what everything in the universe is doing as a whole, or 'seeing the big picture.' It is knowing that all seemingly independent 'things' are really functioning as a whole, that all things either increase or decrease the level of consciousness. To kill a bug willingly is to add the frequency of hate or disrespect to the universe, which in turn lessens the overall frequency of mankind, or lowers the level of consciousness of one's self and all others. So to be Mindful to seemingly individual beings is to respect and to be Mindful of the Universe as a whole.

Mindfulness requires knowing that all beings who proclaim their separateness really have the same Spirit, which is God: that all are one and the same. That every breath is every other being's breath, that every thought affects every other being's thoughts, actions, words, and so forth. It is to know the Truth about existence, and to keep it in Mind at all times. To respect All That Is because All is God. Not to respect one 'thing' is not to respect God.

Practice Good Will

This entails not *trying*, but *doing* 'good things' for others, such as helping someone across the street, picking up what they've dropped, giving them 50 cents for a phone call, complimenting a stressed store clerk for doing a wonderful job, telling someone who doesn't like their hair that they are beautiful, giving a plant a compassionate touch, pushing a shopping cart that is not yours back into the store, picking up trash that is not yours, spending extra compassionate time with an ego-centered being because it makes them feel better, and so forth. If one doesn't have the opportunity to help someone physically, then 'good deeds' can be done through mind or thought, as well as prayer. Remember that the intentions make the biggest shift in consciousness, not the actions. So if one is feeling contempt for mankind, then possibly this is not the best time to try to be nice to others. This is because one's intentions may harm others on a subconscious or unconscious level, the very thing that we are all trying to help raise—consciousness itself.

Kindness should not be forced, for force is the product of an ego being exhibited as control and manipulation. It should flow freely and infinitely as what it is: a product of Divine Will. At first it may feel as though one is trying to be nice (this shows the ego's resistance), but after a while, kindness just seems to flow continuously (this shows that the Divine Will is beginning to dominate). When one is enlightened, kindness flows out of every part of their beingness as Divinity, affecting all beings positively and

Divinely just from one's very essence, which radiates forth as compassion, love, and peace.

Keep Thoughts Pure

Every thought charges one's being and affects the whole universe and its karma. The more negative the thoughts, the more negative the mind, the being, the world, the universe, and so forth. Because 'like attracts like,' it can be understood that one negative thought attracts another, thus lowering one's level of consciousness and the beings around them. So don't focus on the negativity of the universe and the beings in it, but rather, focus on understanding why the mind views it as a problem in the first place. Keep in mind that only the ego 'sees' and 'knows' problems. So if one is trying to transcend the ego, then the individual must look past what the ego can only see—problems.

As a thought enters one's mind that is impure or distorted in nature due to its charge and will, surrender it to God and ask for help. Ask God/Universe to give insight into why one feels compelled to think it. Ask God to take it from you and to give you light instead. If you pass by a billboard or advertisement that promotes sex, drugs, drinking, and so forth, then look away and say, "I choose God/Truth, not my desires/illusion." Every time one denies the ego, the connection to Spirit grows stronger.

The process of introspection deals mainly with dissecting negative thought forms and belief patterns, which brings light to the situation. It is a method of becoming and staying pure in Spirit. After much questioning of 'thyself,' or the ego's discord, the mind begins to become unraveled and healed, quieting the thinking mind and revealing Truth in and as the Aware Mind.

If the mind becomes too impure or bothersome, then chant a spiritual saying over and over until the thought form clears. One may pray as well. In doing so, the negative thought forms tend to dissipate by the addition of the Light of God by way of attunement. As one attunes one's self, they elect to be on a higher frequency than the current (low) one being expressed, either outwardly as actions and words, or within the mind as thoughts, intentions, or temptations. Positive chanting will also uplift the universe.

Study Books of Truth Daily

There is almost no better way to attune one's energetic field to God than constantly flooding the mind with Truth. The words themselves are not Truth, but due to the higher energy they bring, they are able to disassemble the ego mind, revealing Truth. Just make sure that the book has been written by an enlightened sage, for the accompanying energy field imprinted on the book's content is more beneficial than the words themselves. Make it routine to read, study, and understand the concepts presented, for liberation from suffering is the gift that one receives when they are realized to be Truth itself.

Every instant that one reads a book of Truth, they are raised to their current maximum potential of consciousness (the ego-stretch mechanism discussed in an earlier chapter). After one is raised to their maximum, the progression through the book's lessons stretches the previous limits or boundaries set by the ego. Thus, an obvious expansion of awareness, which is a raise in consciousness, ensues. If one cannot read well, then just absorb the book's energy.

In fact, while one feels a bit depressed or in turmoil, a book of Truth can be read and the feeling tends to dissipate with the addition of light. Reading the book will raise one's vibratory rate and shift them into another, higher level of consciousness. The depression or problem seems to fade as God's Grace surrounds one's self as Self with Love and understanding.

As one holds a book written by an enlightened being, the enlightened energy works on the ego silently; but as one reads the book, the energy transpierces one's energetic field, bringing realizations more swiftly. As one studies a book of Truth, the energy from the sage and the Truths presented within merge with the soul. And as one **realizes all** of the Truths in the enlightened teachings (or this book), enlightenment is then known as one's self as Self.

This profound Truth that becomes one's being, but has always been one's Self, is one's expression as Divinity and Truth. It is important to realize that to understand a concept is not the same as realizing it. A realization is a revelation, or Truth revealed by God as a gift that has always been, but just not recognized as Self.

In contrast, an 'understanding' is a familiarity with the concepts, yet yielding little or no Truth. Many understand, or at least think they do, but few are realized or capable of realizing Truth.

The Enlightened Being's Presence

If one knows an enlightened being, then seek their guidance, affirmations, and frequency. Their Presence alone is sufficient to enlighten anyone who is willing to completely surrender their ego to God. Many skeptics argue that if an enlightened being can enlighten anyone, then why don't they? Or "they must not want anyone to become enlightened?" The fact remains that all sages intend the best for all beings and will help anyone trying to transcend the ego. The block is not God or the enlightened being not supplying enough energy; instead, it is that the ego who seeks the help (Truth) does not completely want to give up their illusory identity. There may be a past or current remembrance or problem that they are just not willing to give up. Many beings don't cross the 'border' that separates the enlightened and the unenlightened because they are holding onto a negative thought form, old conditioning, or a previous belief system. It only takes **one** ego thought form or ego structure to keep one from complete liberation and freedom.

There are many 'spiritually advanced,' but not enlightened, beings who seek a sage's help, but their pride usually keeps them from using the energy. To be *spiritually advanced*, the feeling of 'knowingness' becomes predominant. This creates pride and makes that new aspect of one's self, intellect, or knowingness, a force that doesn't allow for surrender to God. Practice being humble before man, as one would before God. After all, Divinity is within us All.

One of the most common blocks to becoming enlightened, besides duality and causality, is the fact that a being feels as if it were impossible for them to become enlightened. This is an instance where the ego mind creates the boundary that stops the transcension process. If one doesn't think or believe that they can become enlightened, then they can't. They have thus condemned themselves by that very thought. Remember that the ego creates the limitations. So, "Think not and be affected not." Always believe in what seems impossible to the ego, i.e., "Where there is Will, there is a Way."

Practice Nonattachment

Physical Attachments

All physical things are impermanent, meaning that within a certain period, whether 2 weeks, 20 years, or 200 million years, it will cease to exist. For instance, in 2,000 years, the buildings of today will not be there because of structural instability, damage, or an improved design that calls for a new building. A building may just wither away like an old flower due to erosion by the elements, such as water that wears down stone or concrete. So because of the impermanence of physical manifestations, one should not become too attached to the withering dimension of form. And due to the manifest dimensions being those of lesser truth, one needs to realize that Absolute Truth is formless. So, just as the ego is transcended, the physical dimension should be, too. This does not mean that it is okay to kill one's self to become nonattached to the body, ego, and the physical world, as many cults seem to misunderstand through their practices. It does not even refer to one detaching themselves from the physical world, for example, withdrawing from society. It simply refers to a state of mind or an attitude that one has while functioning in this world. To see things as they are, absent of Truth to the ego, is therefore meaningless; but in Reality, the unchanging, stable, and permanent substrate that is within all form is that of the Unmanifest.

If one is overly attached to something, such as a new race car, a television, or the way they dress, then it should be forfeited during the time that it takes one to become enlightened. This does not mean that the item should be thrown away, set on fire, or sold. It just suggests that it should not be used, focused on, or thought of, for this re-energizes the ego will. Only the ego thinks it needs a car; God doesn't. So if God doesn't need a car, then one's being should not fixate or attune one's 'will' to that lower level of consciousness; rather, one should forfeit the desire to have a car, relinquishing the attachment that was holding them back. To fulfill one's desires or to seek happiness anywhere but within one's Self connotes that a being is searching for an external means of satisfaction, rather than accepting God's Love as complete, total, and within.

If one feels like giving something (their *pride and joy*) away or selling it, it can be done. That signifies a permanent detachment from the item; however, the mental attachment may remain. This can be known by an ego thinking about it, having the desire to show it off, wanting to have it, wanting to experience using it, and so forth. The more frequent the memory or thought, the more attached one is. If there seems to be a *craving* to do it, have it, or be with it again, then it should be surrendered to God as an illusion and a problematic attachment. As the realization ensues, by way of a revelation, the illusory bond will disengage. After that, it is a matter of 'will' not to think of it anymore, or the effect that the attachment had on one's life.

One can diagnose attachments by introspection. Just ask your self what physical things make you happy; those are the attachments. If one were to forfeit the attachment, how would one feel? If sad, then the attachment tends to control an aspect of one's life. For without it, one believes that they would feel not as happy as they could have been. This is an illusion. The fewer physical attachments one has, the more God's Love is realized and the happier one really is. The objectified physical dimension brings about many attachments, but the attachment is actually not physical; instead, it is emotional and mental. For without the ego mind and physical body, there would be no possibility to see, hear, feel, smell, or touch anything. Therefore, no attachments could even be made.

Emotional Attachments

As the ego objectively (externally perceives) and subjectively experiences its perceived reality (experiences the energetic response patterns in the mind), energetic responses known as emotions arise. These emotions create attachments, whether they invoke a 'desirable' or 'undesirable' response. One may become emotionally attached to a happy event just the same as a sad one. If one sees a beautiful mountainside and feels as if they want to live there, a strong attachment is made. If one sees the mountainside and leaves its magnificence, but constantly thinks about it to relive the pleasant emotional state and wants to go back, then a very strong emotional attachment is made. At this point, a conundrum arises; it is the possibility of the ego not seeing the mountainside again, which brings fear and a feeling of loss or disappointment.

The ego ignores these unpleasurable moments, thoughts, or feelings so as to not relive the seeming tragedy that inherently lies in its objective and subjective positionalities. The same goes for other instances within the mind that create the feeling of 'wanting,' which also brings up the 'possibility' or seeming duality of 'loss.' Such instances are as follows: an ___intense wanting___ to feel 'cool,' be pretty, lose weight (for self-satisfaction instead of health), get beautified (manicure/pedicure/waxing/hair/etc.), have a car, house, motorcycle, person, friendship, shoes, clothes, food, cigarettes, alcohol, drugs (illegal or legal), herbs (such as stimulants or depressants), be famous, be sexy, work out to have the ___best___ body, toys, presents, compliments, etc… An attachment can be noticed if there is a ___want___ that is in ___overdrive___ that consumes the thought faculties of the mind, or that depresses a being if it is not acquired when desired. Simply surrender that constant plaguing thought to God and say, "I choose God/Truth over this form of temporary happiness that attempts to replace God's Love for me." If one likes motorcycles and has always looked at them in the past, now is the time to ignore them as they drive by. If one continuously shops for a bigger house than they currently have, then now is the time to stop searching and be happy with what one has, while simultaneously existing within God.

From a psychological and holistic standpoint, it can be seen that the ego has difficulty in releasing any negatively charged energetic patterns. These negatively charged emotions or positionalities are felt to be a part of the ego's past. Therefore they are felt to be needed in order to be part of the present. After all, without any memories of one's past, the ego won't understand who or what it is. So due to this fear of a 'lack of identity,' these positively and negatively charged emotional states are held tightly, to allow the ego to 'know itself,' or so it thinks.

In Reality, these thought formations that evoke the emotional states actually block one's True Essence from shining through. This is a block that many cannot overcome. For example, an ego has a hard time forgiving another for raping them at a certain period in their life; just the same, another can't seem to forgive someone else for robbing them and murdering their sister. Even though these are hard lessons to go through, one must understand that due to both of their levels of consciousness at that specific time, it was necessary for both souls to go through the undesirable event. It should be understood that if that ego does not release that unpleasant emotional energy, it will keep their level of consciousness down, near what they were when they experienced the past traumatic event. This keeps one's wounds open, whether knowingly or unknowingly, and invites another attack. In this case, ignorance is not bliss.

To truly overcome any of these energetic blocks that were created by the ego's emotional states and positionalities, and that inherently create attachments, one must surrender *all* to God. This means that one should not hold a grudge, which many egos feel is needed in order to justify anger and resentment towards another. As anger and hatred are held in mind about another who has wronged one's self, one is telepathically (so to speak) linking one's self to the other ego's karma. This signifies the importance of *not* holding a grudge, but simply releasing another from their emotionally traumatic ties to one's self. As this release is made, tears may flow to signify the emotional discharge that had held one back in life. After one disconnects from another ego's lower level of consciousness, a revelation is experienced with joy. This frees one from their own bondage that was created by linking their karma to another being's karma. So, "To release is to *Live*."

Many times, spiritual devotees write down all of the names of those whom they have 'done wrong to' from their first memory to the present, but only to ask for forgiveness and release the karmic connection. Just the same, they write down all of the egos' names who have 'done wrong' to them, but only to give forgiveness and release that 'untruthful' energy. So release all karmic bonds bound by trauma; this brings happiness and revitalization. To hold onto a past traumatic event is to hold onto the traumatic emotional states evoked by the event, the offender, and the specific karma of the overall package. To do this is to ask for suffering, pain, and misery day by day.

Mental Attachments

The ego is mind; therefore, it is thinkingness. All the ego does is evaluate circumstances, events, things, people, days, etc… Its job is to make one feel important, whether by receiving endless praise or pity. It not only needs to be the center of attention, but it needs to feel as if it controls its destiny, as well as current events. The control that the ego implies is that of the thought processes, also known as mentation. In order for the ego to feel in control, it takes credit for one's thought processes and brain activity, even though one can walk without 'thinking' about it; the heart beats and the body breathes without conscious thought as well. When the soul leaves the body, suddenly the brain deactivates and a being is declared dead. The infinite thought forms and emotional states are prevalent within the ego's level of consciousness, indicating that thoughts come from 'without,' not from 'within' or the ego's initiatory process. Not only does the ego initiate low-powered thoughts, but it also elicits an emotional response that makes one feel subjectively as well as objectively involved in life. And by this, it can be said that the ego uses the emotional responses to make one feel attached to thought. This convinces the ego that it thinks because it feels involved in the thought process by initiation, acceptance, and rejection. For it feels that what it thinks, it is.

It is important to remember that the ego does not think; it just 'thinks' it does (sorry about the contradictive humor). Thinking is automatic. Depending on the concurrent level of consciousness of an ego, thoughts are selected and continuously filtered through the mind. In extreme states of intensified and amplified energy, thoughts are expressed as a visual display called personality, for as one thinks, they feel they must be that way. This prompts one to be who they think and feel they are. Each individual expression of one's self is known as a character trait. These are small things that one does or exhibits that collectively make up their character or personality. One's personality and character traits are a direct reflection of their inherent level of consciousness, whether solely expressed by the ego or by the overall karmic pattern via karmic interaction, which influences action, thought, and personality.

It can be seen that when the ego is drifting off in thought, it loses concentration on its current activity, whether this is driving, sports, and so forth. Just think back to an event when the mind seemed not to concentrate, but everything came out exactly how it would have, had there been full concentration. For example, remember driving; there has surely been a time in one's life when they felt as though the body, without the mind, drove itself while the mind just sat back and watched the event, or maybe it was off doing its own thing, 'daydreaming.' The same goes for speaking. Many people describe situations where the words just seemed to flow out of their mouths without any prior planning, as if they were spoken through them, like a channel. This happens more often than most people think; just analyze one's self while speaking and it will become apparent.

To stop the thinkingness of the ego, one may practice pranayama, or deep rhythmic breathing that emphasizes the concentration efforts on the flow of energy as seamless and fluid. It is similar to **breath awareness**, but is not the same. "One-pointed" mindfulness may also be practiced. The ego concentrates for about 15-30 minutes on an archetype, the repetitious chanting of one word or sentence, or an external image. One may focus on a flower, picture, mandala, or religious figure. By concentrating on something for an extended period, the mind grows silent as the various thoughts that do not pertain to the task are ignored. Thoughts only grow and intensify as one's mind concentrates on them. So by diverting one's attention to something besides the ego mind and its sea of thoughts, thoughts will reduce in quantity, freeing one's self from the constant thinkingness that had enslaved them.

As thoughts reduce, the shift from detailed focus to awareness occurs. This is the shift from (ego) mind to Mind. As mentioned before, the process of introspection deletes the reasons for thinking (only if one is true and honest with the self and Self) by solving the seemingly problematic. It adds light to darkness, so to speak, which resolves the empty feeling that accompanies the ego's use of its intrinsic 'lower will.' The more that thoughts are looked into and solved, the fewer thoughts one will have, due to the lack of needing to think those very thoughts or questions. So in a way, this is a way to use thinkingness to delete the need for thinkingness.

Stop the Ego Before It Starts

Stop the ego before it takes control—not by control, but by diversion and a shift of emphasis. If an ego has to perceive the world around it to understand its place in the universe objectively and subjectively, then shut your eyes and meditate to still the mind for about 2 hours a day. If the ego has to judge whether it likes or dislikes something, then understand why it is important not to judge. Try to see things as equals, for example, all beings are egos who are trying to find their way back home to the Source. And if the ego wants to express its own 'will' and self-centeredness, then do something for others out of kindness and compassion. If an ego does not want to pray, then pray every day and night to God. If an ego thinks it rules the physical dimension, then every day practice mindfulness and respect for all of the bugs on the plants and the wasps in their nests. See all as a perfect expression of its essence.

If one knows they will become emotionally involved in an ego-centered and controlled event or conversation, then do not participate or become involved. Perhaps one could even go to a church or temple that will not bear witness to or house such emotionality or a display of character. And maybe a being there will actually illuminate your current ideologies or belief systems. If one feels as though they need to have revenge on another ego who has 'wronged them,' then spend *all day* in prayer. Try to see that your own level of consciousness has brought this event to you and attracted the giver of the trauma. Stopping the ego is simply an attitude to live for and to serve the Divine Will and not the ego. It is a way to become nonattached to the ego's trappings: lower energies (consciousness).

Be Surrounded by Positivity

Throughout one's life, one can choose either to be surrounded by negativity or positivity. This is what the Bible meant when it stated that one should not "yoke themselves unevenly." Someone of positive energy who is trying to choose Divine Will should not be around those who are operating under ego will. This is only because a positive being not only would be tempted to 'sin' by a nontrustworthy ego, but would unfortunately pick up some of their negative karma just by being in the same place. Keep in mind that karmic debt can be linked unconsciously; it is the same as if an enlightened being unconsciously sends positive energy, or karmic merit, to an unsuspecting ego. Energetic exchanges occur on all levels, not just conscious ones.

One may go to a place that supports a higher level of consciousness, such as a church, temple, New Age bookstore, and so forth. If beings go to a place to pray or practice being integrous and kind, then it may be safe to assume that it is emanating a higher level of consciousness than most other places, such as a mall, night clubs, rock concerts, etc... And if one has many confrontations or conflicts in the home, then it is surrounded and saturated with negative energy. It would then be wise to leave the house when one feels depressed or irritated.

Similarly, try to be around 'like-minded' people. If one is not enlightened, then they are subject to *all* the other ego's negative influences. As one becomes enlightened, then the negativity does not affect their state of mind or energetic levels. They will then permanently radiate positive energy, which uplifts all of humanity. Therefore, at that time, they may go into negatively charged places and be around egos while not picking up their karma, and the Self that emanates from them will resolve the other negative thought forms and increase all beings' level of consciousness.

House Clearing

One's home picks up much residual karma that is and was imprinted on the walls, floor, furniture, and so forth, by the egos who dwell in it. It is necessary to cleanse this energy to instill a feeling of peace throughout the house. It is important to note that one cannot remove negative energy, only alter its resonance. Analogously speaking, one cannot remove darkness by scooping it out with their hands; they can only add the presence of light, which raises the wavelength or frequency of darkness to that of light. Just the same, one can only raise the frequency of energy by adding light, not by removing negative energetic patterns. To raise the energetic frequency of something is to bless it. To lower a level of consciousness by an excessive amount is to damn it.

There are many ways to bless a house. Prayer is beneficial and the most commonly used method, but there are other not so common but effective ways. High frequencies are not only within words and thoughts as intentions, but within some crystals, herbs, prayer flags, symbols, and so forth. They are all used as a means to raise the level of consciousness in a house or even that of a person, hence the wearing of jewelry such as crystals, gems, and diamonds.

Herbs such as sage, white sage, lavender, and frankincense are probably the most commonly used throughout the world. There are also high-frequency stones such as moldavite, amethyst, tektites, and many more, which have been used in raw form or set in oil so as to imprint their frequencies within it. The oil is then taken up and put into a vial or into wood chips that may be sold as an essential oil or incense, respectively. This oil may be diffused throughout the house, or the incense may be burned.

Another common method of negativity neutralization is the use of Prayer flags. Prayer flags may be posted on the front and back doorways to neutralize any and all negative thought forms that may penetrate the positive barrier thus far established. Hopefully, any egos entering one's house may read the flags and raise their vibratory rate as well.

Crystals and Oils Aid in Spiritual Evolution

Not only do high-frequency crystals and oils help to raise the overall energetic pattern of a room or area, but they can also be worn. This can help to lift and reinforce a spiritual devotee's energetic field, helping them to stay in a higher frequency and expedite their spiritual journey. Since early mankind evolved, it has been intuitively felt and known that the various natural products of the world have healing powers. One can easily witness the elaborate headdresses, the beaded clothes, and the use of crystals, all of which show the importance of precious and rare gems and stones. Not only did the first humans feel this way, but to this day many beings carry on this sacred tradition, for instance, the diamond wedding ring, gold necklace, rare gems placed in jewelry, and so on. Although initially importance was placed on the healing powers of these items, the focus seems to have shifted to their monetary value. This still shows their importance; however, it is misplaced and misunderstood.

Many skeptics argue this point and say that these gems are important only because they are rare, and therefore the supply is limited. And as the ability to obtain them decreases, their value tends to increase, and thus their importance increases as well. However, before these gems were known to be limited and rare, Indians, tribesmen, and various cultures wore them religiously or every day, and especially for ceremonies. Shamans used to cut up crystals and grind them into a powder, then cut themselves and rub the powder into their wounds. They did this because they knew that crystals amplify energy, which fortunately for them, would amplify their spiritual powers. The shamans certainly did not do this just because it was the 'thing to do at the time,' because then other people in their culture would have done the same. It was strictly spiritual, not for the undedicated to do, or to understand. This was considered sacred knowledge.

Just the same, as previously discussed, priests, pastors, and other religious leaders use the power of water and oils such as frankincense to anoint or energetically cleanse and bless something or someone. They typically use the oils on the pews in the church before a service, or on the foreheads of religious followers; many times 'holy water' is used instead. 'Holy water' is no more than normal water that has been prayed over by the priest. So in essence, the water is reprogrammed with a higher frequency by way of the 'good will' that is imbued on it by the blessings of a religious figure. The water that is blessed is usually only a little bit higher in frequency than water itself, because the priests or pastors are usually not themselves at a very high frequency; they may be higher than the majority of the congregation, but not as high as an enlightened being. The water would be at the frequency close to Jesus or Buddha if an enlightened being were to bless it.

The intrinsic, but limited power in rare gems and oils is known as 'force.' This force is at a very high level of consciousness, but because it is limited it cannot be properly called the power of God (which is unlimited). Most frequencies are thought to be capable of healing on emotional or mental levels, while others mainly heal the spiritual levels. It is important to note, however, that while healing on emotional or mental levels, the spiritual levels are being simultaneously healed first and foremost. One cannot truly heal an emotional or mental aspect of the ego without healing some aspect of the spiritual. This does not imply that the Higher Self is being healed, but rather that the faulty spiritual belief patterns are being relinquished. So by the release of the fallacy, the Truth (Self) then prevails. The Self as Unmanifest is perfect; there is no need for healing. There is only a need to heal the way one thinks they are. Perception, perspective, and beliefs are the illnesses.

Similar to crystals and oils, many people have tattoos of spiritual sayings, prayers, and so forth, put on their body. This is not necessary, and neither are crystals or oils, but it can be very helpful in attuning one's vibratory pattern and raising their current level of consciousness. The everyday recognition of a tattoo will align one's intention with the 'greater good' of humanity. It will help one remember to serve Divine Will and not to be tempted by the ego.

Tattoos are effective ways for increasing one's energetic frequency, although only if the proper content is within the proper context. So if one is getting a tattoo to be 'cool,' respected, admired, or the center of attention, the exploitation of improper context is used. Even if a spiritual symbol tattooed on one's skin is of a high frequency, the improper use of context will be overridden by a lower positionality of the ego, canceling out the healing properties of the tattoo until the mistake is realized. Remember that the healing energy of a high frequency cannot enter one's energetic field unless a negative quality of the ego is given up in exchange. Whether one wants to give up or surrender to God the pride in one's self, or shame, false beliefs, old conditionings, and so on, doesn't matter. It is up to the ego to make the trade. **The larger the trade, so to speak, the larger the reward will be**.

*Caution: Learn how to use the healing powers of crystals before trusting their effects. Never use them directly after buying them from a store. Always clean them first with sea salt, earth, water, oils, reiki, Good Will, herbs, white or gold light, etc., before use. If not, negatively imprinted energy will be picked up by one's self.

Teach Others Truth

Perhaps the best method for increasing one's level of consciousness is to teach Truth to others. Even though one will be limited in their understanding and realization, one's level of consciousness will recirculate and redirect the spiritual Truths that were learned back to the teacher, thus sharing that level of energy or Truth with another and enlightening one's self more by the amplification of energy. As this energy is recirculated, the level of consciousness that one (the teacher) is trying to express will flow through a being as words are spoken and Will is conveyed. This brings forth new Truths that the teacher was not even aware of themselves. So these new Truths that become 'spoken words,' or instruments of healing, will then raise in consciousness both the one teaching and the one being taught. Thus, both become more illuminated, maybe even enlightened. So in effect, the teacher is not only teaching others, but teaching themselves as well.

Stop Learning Linear Concepts

As one continues to learn in the linear realm, the lower frequencies of that information will lower one's level of consciousness. If one must learn linear material, or focus on a linear task, it is important to keep in context the True Reality instead of the linear. This does not mean that one should never learn another linear concept; it just means that one should see the 'whole picture' and not just the linear facts or evidential proof that is available for experience. True Reality is beyond proof, rationalization, or justification. The main focus of the spiritual devotee should be on the Nonlinear Truths that bring forth the realizations that reveal the Self. Thus all actions and thoughts of the linear are kept in the proper context of the Nonlinear. This is how all actions of the ego can be sanctified by God as holy.

Practice Being Nonlinear

Throughout the day, every linear event or action should be experienced in the proper context of the True Reality. This means that, at all times, the greater meaning of life should be kept in mind, coloring all activity that is undertaken. If done properly, all of life is a holy event. Some easy examples are as follows:

- *While walking or driving, feel as if you are moving throughout your Self, because all is God.*
- *When breathing, eating, or drinking, notice that you are consuming your own manifestations of your own Self.*
- *When talking to others, understand that all beings are not awakened yet, so be compassionate with them in hopes that they may realize the Truth some day.*
- *When talking to others, realize that they are not talking to you. Instead, their level of consciousness is simply using the human body as a sock puppet, reflecting their level of consciousness as action and voice.*
- *When someone becomes angry and physically violent, understand that it is not a personal attack. In fact, they have no control over it. All that is and can be seen is the outcome of two levels of consciousness interacting. So no one person has been done wrong. Both have given punishment and received punishment equally.*
- *Understand, when a mishap seemingly occurs, that there are no mistakes, chances, or coincidences. That would*

require them to happen outside an infinite God—an impossibility. All is manifesting itself perfectly; there are no accidents.

- *Try to see the world as a 'spiritual training ground,' a world that allows all beings to learn how <u>not to judge</u> and to <u>love all others equally</u>. The real lesson is to remember who and what one is, to realize that everyone has the same Spirit. Look at a bug or a criminal and understand that your Spirit is exactly the same, whether you like it or not. So you can either deny that fact, or accept it with love and compassion.*

- *As one does the necessary actions that are required throughout the day, act as though you are operating on an astral level (less dense), not a physical level. Try to serve the other being's soul and higher purpose, not their physical body or reflective consciousness level. In short, ignore their actions and words and serve their soul.*

Be in Nature as Much as Possible

Nature is very healing. Not only does it represent the many frequencies that make up the energy bodies, but it is what these bodies run on. The root chakra runs on earth frequency, the navel on water, the solar plexus on fire, the heart on air, and the throat, brow, and crown on Spirit, known as aether (pronounced 'ether,' latin for spirit). In one's home or office, the energies tend to become stagnant and unmoving. This creates old energetic patterns that radiate a low level of consciousness and can block one from a comfortable spiritual journey. These low-level energetic patterns bring forth discomfort, while making the devotee feel as if they are going in the wrong direction. This is just an illusion, though.

In nature, the energies may be free flowing, liberating, and energizing. The various energies that nature is composed of have been known to bring and be healing energies. For example, ask yourself, "Why do so many people take vacations?" Not only to get out of work and relax, but to be in the wilderness, in the trees, near the lakes, while taking in the view of the mountains. Perhaps one may go to the beach, or to the desert. Whatever your pleasure, it is simply a reflection of the energies that are needed in order to heal yourself at that specific time. One can notice that after a vacation, a relaxing and peaceful sensation is felt throughout the body. It is recognized as such—healing to the body, mind, and soul. But above and beyond all, God is really the only Source that is needed for existence, and God is beyond all frequencies. The frequencies of earth, water, fire, and air are just the energies that universally manifested for us to be and remain balanced if and when needed.

Devote One's Self to the Service of God

By keeping the higher context in mind at all times, the service of Divine Will becomes a natural by-product. It is not something that needs to be focused on. It just is what one is: a vehicle of Divine love and peace. Just as if one is at a low level of consciousness, the by-product may be shame, pride, hatred, and guilt. The higher levels of consciousness reflect only higher actions, words, and Will. By dedicating one's life to the service of God, enlightenment is the automatic by-product, because that which is the Will of God makes one God-Realized. By comparison, if one expresses a viewpoint of pride repetitiously, they become a vehicle of pride and are later consumed by and are pride in and of itself. Similarly, expressing too much hate makes one become hatred. So the emotion or positionality becomes the being. This is why expressing unconditional love and Truth makes one become enlightened, because the enlightened simply are that.

Be True to Your 'Self' and Others

This requires one to be compassionate towards the views that their ego has, and to understand why they are what they are. By understanding and being compassionate towards the nature of the ego, one may be true to the Self at all times. It is important that all actions, thoughts, and words be in the greater context of the Higher Self. If actions and thoughts are not in the proper context, the possible outcome may be damning. Not to keep actions in their proper context is to deny God for one's own pleasure or ego will. When all actions are a direct expression of the Divine Will, life is sanctified and pure. This constantly raises one's level of consciousness at any given moment.

Likewise, since one's own Higher Self is everyone's Higher Self, it is important to understand that when interacting with society. Not to be True to someone's Self is not to be True to your own Self. Each individual is only showing various expressions of their ego; they are not showing different expressions of the Self. The Self is beyond expressions, but the *manifestations* of the Self do have expressions. All beings have the same Self and are plagued by their own damning choice: to be an ego. So since one can see that we all have the same problem (the ego), the same solution (to transcend it), and the same Source (God), it is easy to ask, "Why are there so many conflicts, when we all have the same problems that can be worked on together as a whole?" The answer is easy: no one knows that they are plagued by the ego and have the same problems, the same solutions, and the same God. Everyone thinks that their God is so much better than another's God, when in actuality, we all have the same God, which is existence/Truth/love, which creates and supports All That Is with love and peace. Because God exists, we exist.

Chapter 20
Living a Spiritual Lifestyle

Don't Deny Your True Nature

The ego's rampant lifestyle is all seen in hindsight as a meaningless illusion that never needed to happen. In essence, it was selected by choice, which by the same measure can be transcended as well. Do not put faith into the ever-changing variables of the manifest; instead, focus on the never-changing, always has been and is, ever-present constant of God. This keeps the mind constantly aligned with the higher context. Variables come and go, providing temporary happiness, but God's permanent Presence is happiness, love, and peace, which never leave, and are always accessible to any being no matter what type of 'sinner'; one just needs to recognize it.

To choose the ego is to deny God. To deny God is to deny your Self. To deny your True existence is analogous to a blade of grass denying that it is part of the lawn, dirt and trees from a safari, leaves from a tree, an atom from the atmosphere, a piece of concrete from the pavement, sand from the beach, and so forth. It is simply to deny yourself from knowing your existence as the Whole. The ego, which is the proprietor of limitation, denies because it is afraid to know. This would obviously contradict everything that it currently believes—that each individual is exactly that, an individual with limitations—which would signify the end of the ego's existence.

So to retreat from the ostensible protection of the ego is to simply merge back with the Source, to become One with the Whole, or to be One's True Self (Self-Realized). It is to know that one's True origination is that of God, not only as a part, but as God as the essence of All, as well as All That Is.

Keeping Life in Proper Context

As one carries on with their day, it is important to keep the mind aligned with God. This means that all actions and thoughts must be kept within Divine Will (and as a product of), and one should not give in to the temptations of the ego.

To understand the nature of sin, one must understand the nature of the ego. However, since this aspect was analyzed in previous chapters, it will be simplified to a daily and instantaneous task.

While the day proceeds, witness the actions, thoughts, and will of the ego. Then with ease, just say, "Does God want me to do this, or does my ego?" Then specific actions such as watching television, reading a magazine, playing video games, excessively combing your hair, driving a sports car, racing a motorcycle, making money, and so forth, can be questioned. And in doing so, one can keep life in the proper context. For instance, only the ego wants and desires things; God doesn't want or desire anything, including the world to be a better place, because it is already perfect. The earth is not a heaven; it is a purgatory, or a place to live life and learn lessons. It is supposed to be full of people 'sinning' and people choosing the Divine aspect of existence. This is why one ego killing another is not really to be considered bad; it is simply a reflection of an ego's current level of consciousness. The expression of that level of consciousness was portrayed by one and asked for by another ego level of consciousness. So in essence, one ego chose to kill, and the other chose to be killed, whether knowingly or unknowingly. If this is not known, then witnessing egos can be seen to blame God and wonder why it happened to such a nice woman and say, "It's just not fair." All is fair; one gives and one receives, but only because in a previous life or another they were the giver or taker.

The higher levels of consciousness are always available; they are not for special people. Heaven is not withheld for a special breed or type of person. Like the universe within which all exists, its energy is available to all, and no one is shunned, no matter what sins plague their life. So one who chooses to exist in the higher frequencies is one who chooses to live a 'sinless' life with God. If things or events in the world look grim, it is because one's ego wants to see it that way. If one transcends the ego, then only heaven will be experienced for every instant of existence. So to exist and experience heaven or hell, or the physical or astral dimension, is simply a choice, nothing more and nothing less. However, one thing is certain: to know and understand the traits of the ego and True Reality are much more beneficial than to go about life naïvely, not knowing what sin (ego) is, or at what level of consciousness they are currently existing.

Likewise, to understand content (form) reveals the greater context (meaning). Thus one can analyze their own thoughts and actions, and by way of understanding their own ego-motives, the many layers of the ego-self peel back like an onion, revealing the Self. It will then be known that if one does a selfish act, then the ego is in control. If a selfless act of love and peace is dominant, then God is expressing Divinity through one's being without the restrictions of the ego, yielding the aspects of the Higher Self.

Have Faith

Throughout all of the perceived "ups and downs" in life, it is important always to have faith in God. Not to have faith in the higher Truths and the Unmanifest is not to have faith in one's Self, which is part of the 'whole.' Realize that all 'trials' or depressed periods of time in one's life may be a prerequisite, or a condition that needs to be experienced in order to transcend the ego a little bit more. Often, one will experience depression, despair, or loneliness for an instant, a couple of hours, or a couple of days before happiness, by way of a revelation of the Self, is experienced. That depression is a moment of the clinging of the ego before it lets go of that aspect of its self. The sadness that accompanies it is the fear of death of that aspect of its self. It knows that it is being disassembled and thus transcended.

Remember that God is always available and always present. One is never alone or going through this alone; all beings are going through this. The only difference is that some beings have chosen to transcend their karma quickly, while others have chosen to reside in a certain aspect of the self. They would rather suffer than be happy and at peace. This can be seen in the 'emotional dumper,' who feels that if they are troubled, all of society must know. If they don't tell enough people, the anxiety builds up and their ostensible caring and sincerity are not reciprocated, leading to a more troubled and unhappy soul. These 'emotional souls' usually do not want to give up their emotional attachments in the world. They unknowingly choose to worship the vicissitudes of the ego, thus suffering when not needed. There is typically no hope for them in this lifetime.

Speak Only Truth

In business situations, in family life, or with friends, the ego is forced to resurface in order to communicate with the egos in the manifest. In so doing, however, it will cause one to shift emphasis from the Nonlinear and onto the linear. If possible, try to keep in the proper context of the Higher Self.

This can be done by listening to what an ego says and then making a statement that will reveal the error in thinking, not to show them that they are wrong (because no ego likes that), but rather, to show them another way to look at something. Study the chapter on "**Ego Linguistics**"; this will help to keep one's mind attuned with Truth while communicating with the world.

Also, if another asks about the physical dimension, it can be spoken about in the proper context, even if the conversation has an egoistic quality. For instance, if someone says, "The flowers are beautiful," one can say, "Then thank God for them, for God is the source of beauty and perfection." One may simply agree with a nod, but internally thank God for All That Is.

If an ego tries to bring one down to the lower emotional states by wanting pain or sadness to be felt, then stabilize it by bringing into consciousness a positive statement. For instance, if an ego says, while crying, "A robber stole my watch. I hate him; I wish he was dead," the following statement can be said to counter it: "A robber robs in order to fulfill a void of sadness. Do not look at it as a person taking from you, but rather you giving a gift of happiness to a sad being that made his day feel a whole lot better. Is not the gift of happiness due to all beings?" If one is a spiritually advanced being, then the following can be said as well: "Besides, time doesn't exist anyway, so why do you need a watch in the first place?"

The former is the better alternative, instead of sympathizing with the ego and doubling the effect of negativity by saying, "I know, I know, that robber should be shot. How could someone do something like that? What a jerk! I think that all robbers should go to hell. Oh, I am so sorry for you. I liked that watch too; it was a very nice watch. I can't believe it was stolen. You must be so sad." If these statements are said, then the ego will feel even more negative and create a negative bubble around themselves that won't allow them to feel happy for a while. This negative bubble will also affect all mankind and the universe in a negative way, by adding sadness and pain to the world.

Adopting Higher Values

Remember that the ego cannot get rid of its lower values or attributes, because that would be the ego trying to extinguish its own existence, something it just won't do. This is comparable to a 'trash can' trying to take itself out to the front of the house for 'garbage day.' It won't happen. Remember the analogy, 'Water cannot get rid of itself by adding water.' Instead, one must simply adopt the higher values or qualities of existence, those being love, forgiveness, and peace. The following describes the qualities of energy to practice being an expression of, and how to apply them.

- **Compassion**
  Seek to be the healer of any situation. May your words provide comfort and your energy manifest a healing in others. Try to understand all beings' 'frame of reference,' meaning that one should try to see the motives that the ego has so blindly chosen, not because they are mean, but because they were not aware of any other options. This is also the practice, until it becomes one's Self, that allows one to accept anyone without passing judgment on them. Also, all beings want to be accepted by someone… so be that someone.

- **Unconditional Love**
  Realize that all beings are an expression of their level of consciousness that is an expression of God on some scale. To deny loving any being, no matter what level of consciousness they operate within, is to deny loving a part of God or the universal Self. Keep in mind that most beings, if not almost all, do not know what Reality is, nor are they aware that they have either knowingly or unknowingly opted to be an expression of a lower level of consciousness. So love them for who they are; they are more than likely not even aware of how they are acting, or that it may be disapproved of by most. So be their source of understanding and love; you may be, to their knowledge, their only 'known source.'

- **Understanding**
  This can be accomplished by realizing that we are all in the same boat, so to speak. We are all egos who have lost our way back home. Some have decided that their route is the best, while others seem to disagree, developing their own methods for increasing their stored surplus of happiness. Do not judge, but rather, see where they are coming from. Remember that all want love and happiness (because that is their True being), but many don't know how to experience it. So by understanding others' beingness, one can better serve them, thus helping them connect with the Source and become a servant of God, which prompts them to dedicate their life to helping others.

- **Selflessness**
  Practice being a 'giver.' This means that before one thinks about what they can do for themselves, they should ask themselves, "What can I do for the universe?" There are many ways to practice being selfless, giving, and caring. Just say to yourself over and over, "Serve others, then myself."

- **Prayer**
  This is one's sacred time with God. There needs to be no other to pray with. Just shut one's eyes and sincerely and honestly pray for all beings to become Self-Realized. There really is no other goal or 'thing' to ask for. If all beings were Self-Realized, then no misery or 'evil doings' would be done; there would be no illness and all would be peaceful and happy. One may also ask for strength to deny temptation and to be a clear channel of Love and Peace.

- **Being a Vehicle of Peace**
  Examine life instances that seem to be abrupt or unpeaceful. And as it is seen that peace is needed, identify what role one can play. Sometimes, a person only needs to interrupt and ask for the time, and other times a compliment may be in order. Sometimes an observation may be used, such as saying "The sky is absolutely beautiful, don't you think?" By directing the statement towards the two 'opposers,' one is prompted (not forced) to answer. If it is obvious that nothing can be said or done to calm the situation, then prayer can be silently said within; it is more powerful than most realize. If a child wants money to have candy, but no one will give it to him, give him the money; however, don't overstep the boundaries of the parents. Throughout life, many instances to be a vehicle of peace can be seen, but very few will act on them.

- **Always Be Grateful**
  Life itself is a continuous gift that is always giving. Just to be a part of existence is spectacular in itself. If one finds themselves wishing certain aspects of their life experiences did not exist or never happened, then they are just blocking gratitude and acceptance in order to be self-centered, judgmental, and irritated. This obviously further reinforces the ego's structure and makes one feel more separated from the Source.

  So on awakening, one should give thanks and gratitude

for the Source, the sun, one's body, the ground that is walked on, the air that is breathed in, and so forth. As soon as any of existence is taken for granted, life becomes irritating and unpleasurable. Take time out of the day to imagine how life would be without legs, arms, or any other organ. Try to see how life would be perceived then. Then be grateful for everything in your life, and learn compassion for those who would be perceived as 'less fortunate.' Be grateful for your 'up times' and your 'down times.'

Methods To Increase Connection with Self

Only Truth is needed to transcend the ego; however, there are various techniques that can increase one's circulation of energy. The following are some of the methods that aid in releasing negativity and becoming positive:

- **Meditation**
  This is the time that one takes to practice pure devotion to God. Prayer may take a couple of minutes to a couple of hours (whatever the preference), but meditation is complete devotion to God that is shown by complete silence and mental fixation on the higher Truths. It is a time for reflection and learning, as well as for prayer and healing. This is the way for one to bask in the glory of God and absorb the higher Power, which is Self.

- **Breathwork**
  *By learning the proper mechanics of breathing, one may begin to understand how to relax the body entirely. Deeper relaxation leads to longer and more powerful meditation, which yields an increase in the flow of revelations. The various types of breathwork can be practiced throughout the day, and there is no need for complete silence when practicing them. The most beneficial technique for receiving revelations is the practice of **breath awareness**, which is described in the chapter on **"Understanding Meditation."***

- **Chakras**

  These energy centers are one's direct pathways to releasing negative energy and pulling in positive energy. In other words, they are capable of pulling in the frequency needed for Self-Realization, which resists the influences that are inherent in the lower levels of consciousness, signified by the lesser colors on the <u>BlackROYGBIVGold</u> scale. These energy centers have been talked about and explored for thousands of centuries. They are the spiritual keys that can help to balance one's life.

- **Kundalini**

  *This powerful energy lies latent between one's lower chakras, namely the sacral (below the navel) and root. When it is released, spontaneous Self-Awareness may occur. However, the **Bandha Technique** is the only method of Kundalini release mentioned in this book. It is, however, sufficient in and of itself, with the presence of Truth, to produce enlightenment.*

  *If an advanced practice or methodology of Kundalini release is desired, then an advanced Yoga Institution should be sought. This is because any other practice besides the **Bandha Technique** could prove harmful to an individual on many different levels: emotional, mental, spiritual, and physical. The Bandha Technique is, for the most part, safe and sufficient.*

- **Yoga**

  Yoga means 'Union.' While many practitioners believe that it helps their physical mind (brain), body, and soul become connected, it actually refers to enlightenment, or the realization of the union between all things, especially that of the Self and God as One.

  Not only does this practice help the devotee relax through the various postures and breathing, stretching, and meditation techniques, but it also provides a philosophy that helps one to become Self-Revealed. In addition, the prac-

457

tice of Yoga allows one to work with the chakras and ener-getic field, if taught by an educated teacher.

Dedicate Life To Serving Others

A True channel of God will strive to help others at any cost. No matter who a being is, they will pray for them, and if possible help them realize Truth while in the manifest realms. Also, being a channel of Divinity requires always accepting the love that flows through one's Self while directing it towards an individual in need, whether by prayer, word, or action. It requires one to inspire those who are around them to wake up and take action in their own destiny. With all of this said, it actually only requires one thing: to be a channel of God's Presence who willingly serves others through whatever means are necessary at the time.

Follow Intuition

At first, intuition may be hard to discern from ordinary thoughts, but in time, it will become progressively easier to pinpoint and tune into, for it always yields important information. Intuition is a brief flash of knowingness, the same as a revelation. It seems to come sparingly, but in actuality, this is only because our minds have been trained to block most revelations out, or maybe one attributes it to something else, such as 'nonsense' or 'everyday thoughts' and imagination. So with hindsight, it can be seen that an ordinary individual actually blocks out the many revelations, or intuitive flashes of Truth, to operate the ego instead. So progressively, as the ego is transcended further, intuitions not only are easier to identify, but also seem to come more frequently.

Most intuitive flashes come during the **breath awareness** meditation, which follows the introspective meditation. The introspective meditation charges the Will to a specific question, then the breath awareness meditation allows one to focus on remaining a clear channel through which the revelations may flow. As a revelation comes into awareness, the individual usually identifies it as an 'intuitive flash' if it pertains to a relevant situation that one is currently going through, but it is marked as a 'revelation' if it pertains to the highest of Truth, or an answer that reveals existence more clearly. They are, however, both the same.

As one's intuition becomes more trusted, it can be known that much needed information has been delivered and can be received with ease. The high context of Truth is that which can profoundly change one's experience of reality. It guides one to their ultimate path, Self-Realization.

Don't Deny an Opportuny To Be a Channel

The Source of all beings is love. Not only is this everyone's source that provides for existence and brings happiness and peace, but it can be expressed through anyone who chooses to be a vehicle of love. Since existence is love, then all beings who exist are love as well. Some deny their existence, which inherently lowers their ability and capacity to express and feel love, while others choose to accept love as their existence. The more that one accepts love as their Source, the more they are used as a channel of God as love.

Unfortunately, the ego will always find ways to justify why it shouldn't give love to others or accept love itself. For example, when someone has 'wronged' them, the ego says, "They don't deserve my love; I would rather hate them." By not allowing (restricting flow) God's energy (love) to flow through one's Self to the other is denying God's love for one's self and the other, therefore casting one's self into the ultimate depths of consciousness and asking to feel pain and suffering, just as one's self has also wished on the other. To forgive another's 'wrongdoing' allows God's love to flow through one's being, bringing peace and love to another as well as one's self.

The *first step* in allowing love to flow through one's self is to forgive all beings for any 'wrongdoings' that they have done against one's self. The *second step* is to wish well for all others whom one has just forgiven, as well as anyone else, whether known or unknown. One does not have to know anyone to willfully be their channel of love and sustenance. The *third step* is always to help others at any cost, no matter what; humor them, play in their game, even if you know that it is an illusion. The *fourth step* is not to allow the ego to justify why someone doesn't need love.

Not to have love is not to be in existence; therefore this states that no one can exist without love (keep in mind that 'nonexistence' is not a possibility because God is *infinite* existence). Not to allow love to flow through one's being not only denies or rejects God, but also wishes one's self and all others who are denied love to exist no longer. So in essence, one is actually wishing one to 'not exist' if they deny being a channel of love for another. And since nonexistence is an impossibility, then clearly the absurdity of this illusory intent that is willed forth by the ego can be seen. So give and receive freely; it is the very essence of everyone's being as existence.

Chapter 21
<u>Healing Meditations</u>

This chapter offers a brief summary of some useful meditations that can help one transcend the ego by increasing their frequency and/or intrinsic quality of light. The 'meditation format' is found in the chapter **"Raising Consciousness Level."**

Whole-Body Tensing

This technique helps one to relax the physical body deeply, which in turn redirects one's external focus inwardly. It is very basic and a technique that anyone can do.

Simply sit or lie down in a meditative posture and take a few deep breaths. After 5 long, deep, relaxing breaths, tense the entire body at once, from the toes to the top of the head. Do this for about a **5-second** hold while breathing in, and then exhale (**6 to 8 seconds**) very slowly while relaxing the body in a dreamlike manner (slow and soft movements). As this is done, allow all of the muscles to relax and drop freely (concentrate on the relaxed feeling). Repeat **every 20 seconds** or so. This should be done about **3 to 5 times** at the beginning of a meditation, before any other type of meditative practice has begun. When completed, just focus on the heavy, deep, relaxed feeling and allow it to increase with deep breathing, known as *pranayama*.

Very Important Muscles To Relax
- *Face, head, neck, tongue (but do not neglect all of the other muscles either)*

Pranayama

This is simply deep, rhythmic, controlled breathing: nothing more. While breathing, one should remember to take a deep or full breath, not just a half-breath. Most people forget to fill the entire lungs and just breathe with the upper half. With Pranayama, one should focus on the counting (visualize) and the breathing, as well as the control. By doing this, one will make both hemispheres of the brain sync-up, which in turn creates a more peaceful meditation. Refer to 'hemi-sync' in the chapter **"Understanding Meditation."**

After the ***whole-body tensing***, one should then begin with ***pranayama***. While the beginning meditator may have trouble with this, it will become easier with practice and familiarity. So one should just sit and ***breathe deeply*** while ***counting*** and ***visualizing*** the numbers in their mind as they are counted.

For example (use whichever of the following is the most comfortable):

- *Inhale 4 seconds, Hold 3 seconds, Exhale 4 seconds, Hold 3 seconds*
- *Inhale 6 seconds, Hold 4 seconds, Exhale 6 seconds, Hold 4 seconds*
- *Inhale 8 seconds, Hold 5 seconds, Exhale 8 seconds, Hold 5 seconds*

Obviously this practice can be drawn out for as long as one remains in control of the meditative practice. If one begins to feel out of breath, then they may slow their count and breath. For most meditators, a trancelike state is felt in a matter of minutes, usually about 10 to 20 minutes if concentration is held firmly. Pranayama should only really be exercised up until the point where one is in the trance state and increased awareness.

Color Breath

After one has been through the previous stages of meditation, ***whole-body tensing*** (or progressive relaxation) and ***pranayama***, then the color breath may be used. If one is very new at meditating, chakra work, spirituality, or the pathway of enlightenment, then one could meditate using the ***ROYGBIVWG*** scale by breathing in the colors while allowing them to saturate their entire energy body. But if one is very wise in most of the techniques that the spiritualist uses and/or has been on the path of enlightenment for a long period, then they should more than likely use only the colors white and gold. These colors cleanse and balance the energy bodies and chakras, as well as spiritually renew and direct one in their path towards enlightenment.

The practice is relatively simple: just meditate and breathe in the colors through the mouth and mentally direct the frequencies throughout the physical and energy body until complete saturation occurs. Start at the lowest frequency that should be used by one's current overall level of consciousness, and then proceed to the higher frequencies that will aid in helping one to expand their awareness and increase their frequency.

While chakra work, described below, is relatively more advanced, this practice is easy for anyone to do. Just breathe in each frequency (color) until it is easy to visualize, or until the color is felt throughout every part of one's beingness. If the colors are hard to feel, then just do about 5 to 10 breaths of each color. In the beginning, this may be the more beneficial way to meditate, and as one becomes more advanced, the intuitive sense of knowing when it is 'time to move on' can be used. As one practices every day, what is needed will become apparent.

Breath Awareness

After most of the meditative techniques have been applied, then one can just relax and focus on *breath awareness*. With this practice, one simply relaxes and allows the body to breathe by itself without any help from the mind. Just go with the natural flow of the breath *without* trying to control it whatsoever. Get into the rhythm and let it take over. Try to have *no* 'stop' or 'start' break in the breath; feel it as if it were 'whole' and 'circular.' This practice helps one to be receptive towards revelations: the realization of Truth.

Breath Expansion

To increase one's energy body, which aids in energy expansion, one should just take a deep breath **in,** while bringing all energies that are around them into themselves, and then exhale while allowing all of the energies to expand to the edges of the room that they are in. After this, inhale the energies back to the body and then exhale the energies back into the world, while surrounding the house that provides for the room. Then repeat and expand in the following order:

- *Neighborhood that provides for the building*
- *City that provides for the neighborhood*
- *State that allows for the city*
- *Country that allows for the state*
- *World that allows for the country*
- *Ozone that encompasses the world*
- *Solar system that encompasses the ozone and world*
- *Galaxy that encompasses the world and solar system*
- *Universe that provides for and encompasses the galaxies*
- *Consciousness that provides and allows for the universe*
- *Unmanifest that provides and allows for consciousness and the universe*

With this, one should always bring the energy of the breath back to the body and then expand it each time to the 'new level' of awareness that one is attempting to experience and understand. Try to feel the infiniteness of the universe while keeping the Unmanifest in the proper context at all times.

After the energy has been expanded to the utmost extent with each breath, then bring the awareness back down to the first level of the body. After this, take the awareness to the smallest energies in the universe, for example:

- *Body to the organs (pick one organ)*
- *Take the many cells out of the organ (then pick one cell)*
- *Then take out all of the DNA of the cell (pick one DNA)*
- *Then take out all of the atoms in the DNA (pick one atom)*
- *Then take the atom apart into subatomic particles*
- *Then take apart the subatomic particles into subtle light*
- *Then take apart the subtle light into subtle sound, then consciousness*
- *And then into the Unmanifest, which provides for ALL*

Open-Eye Peripheral Gaze

With this type of meditation, one just gazes off into the distance, while not focusing on that which is directly in front of them. One actually uses their peripheral vision to look to the left and the right at the **same time**. While the eyes are not meant to focus well on anything to the extreme sides, this practice forces the mind to _**not focus**_ on anything, allowing it to remain relaxed and unfocused.

While the mind tries to focus on that which cannot really be focused on, the mind exerts all concentration towards one point, and by this, all thoughts wither away due to the lack of focus on them. This clears the mind of its many distractions, while aiding the spiritual aspirant in clarity by shutting down the thinkingness of the ego mind. It is also best done in a nonmoving atmosphere.

Subtle Sound Focus

Just the same as *peripheral focus*, this technique quiets the ego's thinkingness. One needs simply to shut their eyes and listen with the **utmost concentration** on all of the sounds around them **at once**. Obviously when all sounds are focused on, the mind goes into overload; paradoxically, this quiets the mind.

While doing this technique, though, one should actually not try to focus on all 'little things' as their focus; rather, they should hear **all sounds as 'one'** while focusing on that which cannot be focused on. This is known as fixing concentration on the 'subtle sound,' or the 'sound underneath the sounds.' Most try to concentrate on the high-pitched, ringing noise in their ears while also listening to **all** sounds **at once**. If this is done for about **5 to 10 minutes** with **absolute** concentration or 'fixity of focus,' then the mind becomes silent and one's energy expansion increases dramatically. While this is felt to a degree by someone who is not yet fully enlightened, the enlightened being overwhelmingly knows and feels it.

This technique, as well as the *peripheral focus*, should be practiced after about **10 to 20 minutes** of meditation, longer if desired. Breathing should also be very slow and controlled. If one becomes distracted with thoughts, then start over.

Chakra Work

This book does not focus on the chakras. While they do regulate energy flow and allow for a much more peaceful existence when balanced and cleansed, just undergoing the path of enlightenment will cleanse them as well. So there is no real need to cleanse them through elaborate chakra work; introspection will heal all energetic imbalances. For instance, each chakra runs at a specific frequency, so these inherently regulate various levels of consciousness. If there are any problems in any of the chakras, one could just simply add the frequency needed by the 'color breath' technique, or resolve the lower energy thought forms that are depleting and lowering the frequency of the chakra and being as a whole. By resolving the lower energy thought forms through introspection, one clears the chakra and raises its frequency and their beingness. Thus, no in-depth 'chakra work' is really needed.

- **Chakra Breathing**
  *After understanding the basic location of each chakra, one can just breathe in the appropriate color that is needed, or that the chakra operates on. By breathing **into** the chakras, which means pulling in energy through the chakra with each breath as if the chakra were breathing itself, energy begins to move, freeing up a stagnant or unmoving chakra condition by raising its frequency and directing flow.*

- **Chakra Clearing**
  With this technique, one needs only to use the upper frequencies of Violet or Gold to cleanse and bliss them out. Do this by directly adding the colors through breath and mentally feeling the increase of energy in the chakra.

- **Chakra Charging**
  By continuing to add the color that the chakra operates on, it then is charged and cleansed to a degree.

- **Basic Tune-Up (Circular)**
  Once one learns how the chakra works and moves, then they may opt to give it a 'tune-up' by mentally feeling it rotate in the desired fashion. As one will learn, a chakra that rotates 'clockwise' or 'counterclockwise' denotes a difference in a being's overall energetic expression.

Kundalini

This is perhaps one of the most talked-about energies that cleanses the soul. It is capable of doing so by rising from the lower chakras and 'blissing out' the upper chakras. In essence, what one is doing is intending or willing the lower energies, which operate the lower chakras, to raise and supply energy to the upper chakras. By this act, in and of itself, one intends not to operate on the lower energies as they simultaneously ask or 'intend' to be a channel of the Divine Will.

The Kundalini energy is located at the bottom of the spine, between the lower root chakra and the sacral and navel chakras. The sacral chakra, a slightly smaller chakra, is right below the navel. It is not spoken of often, but it does indeed exist in that area.

The ***Bandha Technique***, a practice that is applied to the lower chakras and the Kundalini zone, helps to bring out this powerful, evolutionary energy. By each session, or use of the Bandha, one will raise in level of consciousness. While the raise in one's level of consciousness may go by unnoticed, the blissful feeling may be very strong. The 'blissed out' feeling can be strong, but it comes infrequently. It also is important to note that **no more than 1 session per day** should be practiced. This technique is far more powerful than most give it credit for, and if one evolves too quickly, they may have many emotional, mental, and spiritual imbalances. These will not be pleasurable. In fact, they may be depressing. But do not worry; the depression, if felt, will only be temporary.

The **Bandha Technique** practice is as follows:

1. *After **whole-body tensing**, breathe into the lower*

467

chakras to charge them up (inhale energy with those chakras and direct any other energies in the body to those chakras as well).

2. In the 'core' of the lower body, as well as between the root, sacral, and navel chakras, focus with one's mind to feel the area increase in energy (one may feel warmth, heat, tingling, pressure, etc...). The energy may feel localized or come in waves.

3. After about **5 minutes** of charging the lower chakras and the Kundalini zone (<u>within</u> [inside] the core of the body), one should **exhale all air** and drop their head to their chest (chin to top of sternum) while 'pulling in' (contract muscles) the entire abdominal section with a 'locked suction' (one tries to inhale but cannot because of not allowing one's self to inhale).

4. At the same time, one should contract their 'PC' muscle. This can be located when one urinates or defecates; it is what allows one to stop in the 'middle of flow' or action. Just 'squeeze' the entire area for **5 to 10 seconds**. With this technique, one should not just act as though they are 'stopping the flow' while in meditation, but should couple it with the 'locked suction' technique, creating more of an internal pull. Mind you, this occurs while the breath is 'held in'; it creates a strong inner pull that helps to energize the area and escalate energy up throughout the main nadis or Sushumna. Think of it as the main meridian or energetic pathway that all subtle energy uses to go up throughout the energy body.

5. Then while releasing all contractions, or 'inner pulls,' breathe **in** (while pulling the chin off the chest), and guide the energy in the Kundalini zone up throughout the Sushumna, up to the higher chakras. Allow it to exit through the chakras to the outside of the energy body. Feel and intend it to cleanse the chakras. **Always** pull the energy up to the crown chakra and allow it to exit there, while mixing in violet and gold light as it exits the crown. Then take this energy around the outside of the

body to cleanse it.

6. *Do this technique about **3 to 5 times per session** and **once per day**, then stop and meditate with **breath awareness** to allow the energy to dissipate freely and evenly.*

Crystal Therapy

With this type of therapy, one should just place a high-frequency stone on a chakra that needs healing. It is wise to use the highest-frequency stones, crystals, or essential oils on the higher chakras. When trying to attain enlightenment, one should just focus on the higher chakras to attune them to the higher Source. The lower chakras will cleanse eventually.

As the higher vibrational stones, crystals, or oils are used on a specific chakra, just relax and breathe in through them and circulate the energy to all parts of one's beingness. **By placing a moldavite stone on one's head (the crown chakra) and <u>breathing in through it</u>**, one can usually detect a huge shift in awareness in just 5 to 10 minutes. Likewise, placing a high vibrational stone on the brow chakra usually has the same effect.

Using the Mantra

Simply state the following Mantra: "I **will not harm** life. Instead, I **will love** life. No matter how big or small, no matter how significant or insignificant, I will respect **All 'things,'** because **All 'things' have a purpose.**" Many variations can also be used, such as the following:

- *"I **will not judge and hate** life. Instead, I **will accept and love life**. No matter how big or small, no matter how significant or insignificant, I will respect **All life**, because **All life has a purpose.**"*
- *"I **will not create upset**. Instead, I **will resolve upset**. No matter how big or small, no matter how significant or insignificant, I **will respect all situations**, because **all situations have a purpose**."*

Refer to the 'hemi-sync' section of the chapter, **"Under-**

standing Meditation," and apply it to the mantras.

Color Meditation To Cleanse and Protect

When one is trying to evolve spiritually, feeling energetically imbalanced becomes a common occurrence. This is because before one transcends up throughout the higher frequencies, a 'dip' or a lowering in consciousness is usually felt beforehand. Thus, to stabilize the effect of the seeming downfall or backwards evolution, one must pass their 'trial' or 'temptation period' in order to completely resolve the issue at hand, which helps one transcend to a higher level of awareness. However, some trials can be very difficult to transcend, so a means to balance these undesirable energies can be sought through meditation as a temporary healing. Remember that True healing is from God, or realization of Truth, only.

A basic meditation that allows one to balance and purify one's chakras and energetic bodies is first to do the ***whole-body tensing***, then the ***forced exhale breath*** (3 times), then ***pranayama***, and then meditate by surrounding and saturating one's self with white. White is the complete spectrum of all 'pure colors.' So by using this ***white light meditation***, one brings forth the energetic values of the many colors in one's energy body and chakra system as the purest in quality and expression. To amplify the effect and healing process, just breathe in the white light and send it throughout the physical and subtle bodies with the intent to heal. To amplify even more, one should try to visualize themselves in their astral body in an astral dimension that completely saturates the body with the white light. If one so desires, mentally fly through the astral dimensions (in mind) with the mouth open, allowing the white light to enter and then exit through the soles of the feet, which removes all negativity from one's beingness. Feel it radiating with warmth, purity, and love. Sit in white light for about **10 to 15 minutes**. Then one may conclude the meditation by adding 'gold sparkles' or end it with a high-powered mantra or prayer.

Also, before an ego enters a 'negatively charged' place or becomes involved in a negative situation, one may meditate and saturate and surround one's self with white light for protection from the lower energies. Picture a 'bubble' of white light that stays with one's self.

Section Six
<u>Revealing Truth Now</u>

"To recognize Truth in All is to realize one's own Self in All."

—BN

Chapter 22
Questions of Interest

Frequently Asked Questions

1. How can one be patient?

By realizing that all actions that one does can either be initiated by the ego or the Divine, which is basically being selfish or giving, respectively. One needs always to keep the mind aligned with Divine Will; then anyone who was previously seen as an irritating delay can now be seen as an opportunity to be an expression of peace and love. For if one has peace, one has patience; and if one has love, then one has compassion. So if one is truly serving Divine Will, then they will not be impatient.

To be patient, one needs to understand why it is of some importance. When the realization of an infinite existence of the soul is made, the reason for 'hurry' is somewhat dulled. When the realization is made that the soul has usually already lived millions of lifetimes, the need to quicken one's pace and 'finish something' loses importance as well. Focus needs to be directed on the path or the journey itself, and not on whether one gets to the *desired location*.

If one is late to work, it is no one's fault but the choices that they have made themselves. There is no reason to get mad at traffic that doesn't move at a fast enough *desired* pace. If one stays focused on the journey and not the destination, anger will remain nonexistent, because one won't notice the previously irritating action that blocks one from reaching their illusory destination. For instance, if one is visiting North Carolina, they will take their time to see and enjoy the sights at their own slow pace. If someone speeds by them, it is not noticed as much because they hold a different intention: to take their time, enjoy the journey, and relax while seeing the sights.

The next time someone pushes you out of the way when you are standing in line, just pause and say to yourself, "They must have a very important place to be right now and need to get there in a hurry. I hope they get there safely and accomplish what they need to." By doing this, one switches their intention from irritation to understanding. It is not what happens to you that makes or breaks the day, but the way in which you perceive it. When one has understanding and is at the consciousness level of unconditional love, it is termed 'compassion.' This is a combination of understanding the motives, intentions, and positionalities of an ego, while not judging them, and *deeply* caring in the same way for all beings in existence. This allows one to know why the ego does something, even when the ego doesn't know. Thus one sees a being in need and not one who should be condemned or cursed at.

2. Is it necessary to believe in God?

Whether one believes in God or not makes no difference to God. It is like one of a person's skin cells trying to deny it is part of the body. The body does not care about such ridiculous claims or theories, when the Truth of the cell's existence has always been known and 'just is.' It is simply a foolish belief that the cell has created about its existence. It is the same if an atom in the sky tries to convince itself that it is not a part of the universe. This is clearly a false theory of existence that the atom makes itself believe. Even so, the universe loves and accepts it as itself. The universe does not deny it love, because then atoms would continuously be disappearing due to the loss of existence (which is love). In the same manner, think of all of the souls in the physical who would be continuously disappearing due to the denial or lack of God (love). Souls cannot 'not exist,' due to God being 'infinite existence.'

Keep in mind that love is God. So to deny God or love is to deny existence. One can create the concept that they are not a part of God or One with God, or even that God does not exist, but this would be denying their True Nature: existence as Oneness, or the simple fact that they even exist.

No 'thing' can exist outside of or without God. Not only is this a concept of the linear/dualistic reality (inside and outside), it is an impossibility because it would require one not to believe that existence exists, or that God is the Unmanifest potential of creation, All of Creation, or infinite. If God is infinite, then God is All. So there cannot be anything that exists outside of God. Any theories that one has of being 'away' or 'separate' from God are fallacious and will lead to the demise of the soul.

3. Is there a hell?

The lower astral dimensions are termed 'hells' by most religions. According to one's total 'lifetime karma' (really a product of Now), acquired by the totality of expression of choice that is prompted by will, one's predestined dimension is selected as a result of one's own corresponding frequency, which creates their reality. This basically means that if one adopts the less-than-honorable ways of the ego, then the 'hells' are more than likely to be selected for the afterlife.

Nondualistically speaking, hell isn't 'bad.' Although it may be undesirable, it is a product of the ego's choices that it has made throughout its past lifetimes. So the ego has actually selected hell for the afterlife as a result of its own choices; being ignorant of that is purely their option.

If one has lived a life where they always wanted or craved something, then the afterlife would be in the lower astral dimensions (hell). This dimension would be one where endless needing and wanting would be one's reality. And unfortunately, in the astral dimensions or 'hell,' these needs or cravings would never be fulfilled and all that would be experienced is an endless feeling of loss. Since time stops in the astral dimensions, they will feel infinite and be eternal. This hell that is experienced as reality would be different than the hell that is experienced by a murderer or rapist, who will more than likely experience the same torment and pain that they caused others for all of eternity.

What is called eternal is infinite. It is infinite as long as the ego is willing to go for a ride (so to speak). This means that the ego has the option to go to another dimension with lesser 'penalties,' if karmic propensities allow. But this can only happen when the karmic lesson is learned, understood, and then realized. Conversely, though, the perceived and experiential reality that the ego goes through will feel so real that it will not have much of a chance to transcend, because the ego may not recollect that there is a God to surrender to. They also usually feel as if they hate God in the lower astral dimensions. So potentially, hell can be infinite and eternal if the soul doesn't surrender all to God. But if the soul who is in hell surrenders all to God, they will transcend to another level of reality, an energy realm of purgatory like a lesser hell, possibly even a lesser heaven. If the entire ego is completely surrendered to God, then transcendence to the level of enlightenment is possible.

'Hell' is basically a reality that has been created, pre-selected, and predetermined by the choices of one's lower self or ego. This means that by one's own choice, one chose to go to hell, whether this is realized or not. As a collection of energetic influences that were in one's own karmic resonance, a 'special hell' has been created just for them. If one set someone on fire in their previous life and killed them, then they may feel the pain of that death for all of eternity; one may even burn in an 'eternal fire.' If one always liked to put people down and humiliate them, then they will feel the same pain and torment for all of eternity. If one just likes to get compliments that reaffirm how one feels about themselves, a lesser hell will be selected where one will feel the same, but will have no one to talk to and get their affirmations from. This will create a feeling of loss and emptiness, because without affirmations the ego will never be satisfied. This hell is created to help one wake up and take the next step, which is faith, trust, and courage. As this is done, they will transcend to the next level, a lesser hell, or a lesser heaven in which the next lessons can be learned.

4. So are 'Heaven' and 'Hell' in different places?

Two of the ego mind functions are to separate and to categorize. This means that the ego judges things in order to decipher what it likes and what it does not like. As it does this, it places these 'things' into categories, which feel separate, different, and distinct, at least in the ego's perception.

Since the ego can only operate in the perceived linear/ dualistic/manifest reality, it can never realize the Truth, which is the Nonlinear/Nondualistic/Unmanifest Reality. Since the linear perceived reality of the manifest can be measured and perceived, the ego always sees separation between things within it, thus showing duality. Because the ego cannot even conceive of the True Reality where All is One, it just expects heaven and hell to be in two different locations (showing space, distance, time, and perceivability). As the ego is transcended, this illusion will fade into the True Reality of Oneness and heaven will be experienced everywhere at all times, which is beyond time.

5. Hell is darkness; wouldn't it be in a different location than light?

The 'Light' is an aspect of God as Totality, known as consciousness. Within consciousness, the many forms are given the ability to exist as the manifest. And since God is infinite, this means that All is God and nothing can be outside of God because God is infinite existence. God is *existence*, so nothing can *exist* outside of God (there is no 'outside'—duality with 'inside'). Due to the fact that God is infinite and ALL, ALL is existence as varying levels of truth, such as the upper and lower heavens, upper and lower hells, and upper enlightened consciousness. Without God as existence, hell could not exist, which means that hell actually needs the light of God in order to exist.

Remember that the ego's purpose is to make sure that its identity is strengthened, secure, and independent. So essentially, the ego is making itself believe that it is separate from God, and that there is a possibility that it can escape God, such as going to hell to escape God's light, love, and/or existence. This is nothing more than a myth or an illusion that was created by the ego in order to give itself a seeming amount of control, which ultimately disguises the soul's existence as a separate entity.

As the ego creates the perceived reality, it thinks that what it has been shown or 'knows about' is the limit to what can exist or be experienced. So the ego cannot think past its own boundaries that it has set for itself. What one's ego is, is the extent of what one can be (or until altered), because that is all that it has been programmed with or to know.

Knowledge creates the ego's construct that is the boundary of what can be experienced or perceived as real. This would obviously affect the amount of control that the ego could have over the soul and its perceived reality. Every thought, belief, ideology, and point of view, as well as personality, social and economic status, and connection with the physical body strengthens the ego's sense of independence and tricks it into believing that it is separate from God; therefore it feels able to control its life and destiny without further confusion and complications, while feeling in total control. This is all still an illusion that needs to be realized.

These same thoughts carry over to the afterlife, which still makes one feel as if their identity is separate and independent. This feeling is what the ego craves and lives for. This is why, when one goes to 'hell,' it is still seen as a reality. It will also make the ego feel contempt and hatred for God, which does not improve their chance for spiritual evolution or 'change for the better' (dualistically speaking).

This dualistic mind of the ego is what thinks that heaven and hell are separate. So as the ego thinks that this is so, it believes that hell is 'down there' and heaven is 'up there.' These terms are expressed in linear concepts, which is the only way that the ego can understand. By knowing where 'things' are, it tries to understand its place in the universe, thus making it feel more independent or its own entity, although maybe within something 'universal.'

So the concept of heaven being 'there' and hell being 'elsewhere' is expressed in linear terminology, so the ego can conceptualize its place in what it perceives as 'existence,' blocking 'true awareness' of everything being within God, or all being one and the same. It can now be understood why the ego would see heaven and hell as two separate places, a linear conceptualization.

Within the energetic field is the created reality that can be perceived in the astral dimensions. This means that within God's infinite energy, one's ego blocks the True Reality and selects a corresponding reality from the 'superimposed whole' that it can identify with. We label these different realities that have been created as astral dimensions, or perceived realities within Truth, although lesser levels of truth.

This means that one's energetic field is almost like a multidimensional screen in a movie theater that extends infinitely and shows a movie for all of eternity. The movie being shown is the consciousness level that the ego currently corresponds to. Luckily, in the physical dimension the movie is in our head, but in the astral dimensions the movie is perceived and experienced everywhere as waking reality. So depending on the karma that was created during one's lifetime, the determinant movie will be selected and experienced as the only reality. This movie comes complete with emotions that one will feel, scenery that will be seen and felt, and, if one is in hell, an infinite feeling of loss, rejection, fear, pain, and emptiness.

Unfortunately, everything will not be experienced as a movie, but as reality, with no other options or known possibilities of escape or redemption. This is referring mainly to the 'hells' or lower astral dimensions, which are the most difficult for one to realize their way out of due to the ego's strong grip (control) on one's being. Heaven will only be experienced as the ego allows it to be; since the ego still has not been transcended, the soul is at its every whim. As the ego is transcended, all will be experienced as pure, perfect, and complete, with no distortions of Truth, happiness, love, or peace. God is purity, but the ego distorts existence to a point where it can no longer be felt; thus 'hell' is experienced.

Even though the ego sees itself as separated from God, Truth is just a realization away. So as the ego creates its version of one's own personal hell, merely to experience it shows existence. The 'hells' are still within all existence, even though the illusion stems from the ego or within the energetic field. This clearly means that one could not even _exist_ in hell if God's energy were not present at all times, simply because **God is infinite existence** and there is no place one can go to escape God. God's energy keeps one in existence so that the ego may learn lessons and hopefully realize Truth.

God does not punish people by placing them in a hell if they were 'bad.' One creates their own version of what is allowed to be experienced and perceived because of their corresponding consciousness level. This means that in concordance with one's actions, intentions, beliefs, conditionings, ideas, thinking processes, desires, wants, cravings, and feelings of being separate and independent, an energy plane of existence and perceived reality are simultaneously created at 'will' to experience what they feel they need to experience.

6. So then, we are not judged by God?

That is correct. There are no 'things' to judge, because all things are expressing themselves perfectly at their own level of consciousness. This shows the ego's limited linear mind of separation and a world of duality such as 'good or bad' and 'deserving or undeserving.' It would therefore still be an illusion to believe that God judges something, because that would require separation between God and the individual being judged (duality). God is all, which is One and refers to everything being included. Only the dualistic/linear ego mind could think of judging, because it sees separate things that it can judge and classify.

As a result of our choices and decisions in life, karma, or the levels of consciousness, is created and expressed simultaneously as the 'will' is exercised. This means that what the ego perceives as God judging us to go to hell or heaven is really an illusory product that we created by our own 'free will,' which is our karma or level of consciousness expressing itself. So all beings pick their fate and destiny by their own choice.

7. Is there a heaven?

The Self is heaven; it just needs to be realized as such. As the ego transcends, the Self shines forth and heaven is revealed everywhere in All. Hell can be compared with the lower reality of the ego, while heaven is the Higher Truth of the Self. Heaven is not 'somewhere'; it is 'everywhere' because God is everywhere. The ego is the only block to that realization, and as it dissolves, Truth is known and felt to be everywhere. Jesus said, "Heaven is within." This means that the Divinity of God is within and is All beings, and it depends on one's realization of Truth, which allows one to understand and feel the Presence in All. The only reason Jesus had to say that to anyone is because he understood that no one realized it. Beings knew that God was outside or beyond, but no one realized God was inside as well.

This clearly indicates that God is not only within All, but is All as well. The ego just changed or distorted the Truth into an illusion that manifested from its own perception and ideals of what it thought was truth. So the ego distorted Truth and converted the Real Reality into its own version of a linear/dualistic reality, trapping one in the illusory realm of the manifest/linear by the dualistic observation of separation.

The ego separated and categorized all 'things' as being in different locations and having their own existence 'outside' of God, while worshipping a God that is 'elsewhere,' creating the distorted perception of reality, with 'hell' being somewhere and 'heaven' being somewhere else. Because the ego brings bondage, suffering, needs, and wants, and it thinks that happiness is something to be acquired, it can be seen that the ego is the source of what would be perceived as a 'hell.' The level of consciousness of the ego creates the 'hell' that will be experienced. As the majority of the ego is transcended, so are most hells, thus revealing heaven.

8. How can I be a good person?

In Absolute Reality (Nonlinear), there is no good or bad. This would show a polarity or opposites, a linear concept. For opposites to exist, there must be judgment and a linear reality. If judgment is a part of one's life, then the ego is currently controlling one's life and view of reality. Since the ego does not exist in the Absolute Reality, judgment can and will be made in order to better understand its surroundings.

In the Unmanifest, there is only one and not two. Judgment can only occur in a dualistic and linear reality. That reality is a false reality, or a lesser reality that is perceived by the ego. Each level of consciousness is the karmic condition of the ego, which allows the reality to be perceived at that time or current stage in one's spiritual evolution (showing a dualistic/linear reality). These different levels of consciousness display the inherently different positionalities, emotional and mental states, and spiritual awareness. In the Unmanifest, all is perfect, unconditionally loving, and peaceful. There are no other emotional or mental states. Therefore, there is no 'good' or 'bad' thing to do, act, feel, and so forth, even though the ego perceives it this way in the linear.

So to be a 'good' person, one must intend to do so. This means to allow the Divine Will to operate through one's self as Self at all times. Will provides the level of consciousness that is displayed as love and acceptance. As this state of awareness is portrayed, all beings who come in contact with it will heal to a certain degree. All of the old conditionings must be dropped in order to allow the Will to flow freely and unobstructedly. This means that judgment, hate, regret, revenge, pride, discouragement, blame, distrust, cravings, desires, aggression, despondence, and discrimination must be surrendered to God for Truth. These prior positionalities cannot easily be dropped, and one cannot simply will them away. One must look into the ego's intentions, motives, positionalities, wants, desires, and cravings in order to understand why 'things' are perceived to happen the way they do. As these inquiries are answered, understood, and realized, Truth will prevail and become the predominant energy in one's energetic field.

All wants need to be surrendered to God as a sacrifice for Truth. As Truth is adopted, then so are love and acceptance. This allows one to be more giving, understanding, compassionate, loving, and healing (helping other beings transcend negative karma). Not only will it correct one's negative karma, but it will also predestine one's afterlife in the upper astral dimensions (heavens).

First and foremost, however, one must just decide to be honest with one's self and others, and to practice *truthfully* analyzing one's motives and perceptions of reality. As situations come to light, one's awareness expands, which increases one's capacity and capability to love others.

9. Is God forgiving? Loving? Angry? Happy?

God is All-merciful. God has already forgiven all that has been and is currently done, said, thought, and willed; sins are due to the ignorance of the ego. All less-than-integrous 'things' are done because one does not know 'better.' So the ego actually is innocent in all actions done. This pure innocence still acquires karma, though. This is simply due to the ego, which has created the illusion that it knows what it is doing, but it is nothing more than a confused soul. With this said, one can understand that God is unconditionally loving and always peaceful; the source of peace, understanding, love, and compassion is God as Unmanifest. The source of confusion and suffering is the ego.

Nothing that the ego does affects God in a 'bad' or 'negative' way. 'Negative things' only affect other souls and the ego who created the negativity. There is Universal Karma, which is the totality of the 'positives and the negatives,' and it affects all souls in totality. God is never negatively affected, however, because God is the unlimited and infinite Source of positive energy (love, peace, happiness). Just as God is infiniteness, the ego is the limitation that will not allow a being to experience the Nondualistic, infinite, and Nonlinear, as well as unconditional love. That which is limited can never overcome or torture the unlimited.

So since one never hurt or offended God, there need be no apology. The only one the ego hurts or negatively affects is itself and other souls. Therefore, God will never become mad or angry at anyone, no matter what they say or do. **Form never affects or interacts with nonform.**

10. What is God?

God is nothing more than pure, unconditional love, stillness, and peace that radiate infinite potentiality as the Divinity of the Unmanifest, which expresses itself as the manifest (within the aspect of consciousness only) when the conditions of the universal karma and levels of consciousness of (the seemingly) individual souls become a necessity. God is the intrinsic power or value of existence as Unmanifest, as well as its other aspects simultaneously, being those of the manifest and universal consciousness.

11.Could you elaborate more on God?

God is beyond the manifest, the linear dimension, the spiritual manifest (astral), frequencies, colors, thoughts, hells or heavens, spiritual phenomena, chakras, auras, and psychic phenomena, yet God as Totality includes All of these.

God is beyond the Immediate-Self and the Transcendent-Self, but is also both as One as consciousness. God is beyond duality and nonduality, yet is both the nonform substrate and the structured reality of the manifest that allows for the objective perception of the ego. God is beyond physical form or formlessness, but is both as well.

God as Unmanifest has no attributes of the ego at all. God does not wish 'bad' on anyone, nor does God try to hurt anyone. God does not favor anyone or any outcomes. God does not need one to appreciate or worship God. God is beyond all gender and positionalities of the ego. God cannot be affected negatively or positively by any acts of the ego. Because God is infinite, God's energy can never be decreased or overcome by any ego, demonic soul, satan, or any other type of limitation. God does not control one's destiny and send them to 'doom,' but rather, the direction of life simply flows as never-ending creation due to the level of consciousness that a being chooses with wisdom or blindness. All egos create their own fate by choice; God neither judges nor condemns. God doesn't want anyone to go to 'hell,' be shot, injured, be avenged, win a war, or kill for any purpose whatsoever, *including killing or punish-*

ing oneself or others *for God or because one feels it is justified*.

God does not intervene in the physical world by striking one dead to save another. God does not burn down houses, towns, or forests, because one prayed for it. In the same manner, God does not create floods that will destroy people, villages, or continents. God is the *same* unconditional love that is equally available for the saint and for the sinner.

Just the same, God does not turn staffs into serpents, or vice versa. God does not burn or etch phrases or commandments into the sides of the mountains. God does not strike people dead with lightning. God does not help a sports team win over another team; after all, both sides usually pray to win. God does not wish for us to have a 'better' life, because God already knows that all is perfect as is, and it was all chosen by our own free will.

12. How does one control the ego mind to stop thinking?

Control is a product of the ego and should not be administered. The process of control brings limitation and hinders the evolution of the soul by strengthening the ego. It is not that one must control or actively try and stop the ego mind from thinking in order to acquire 'no-mind,' but rather, one should simply delete the arbitrary and pointless reasons for thinking. Thoughts are systematically deleted when the understandings and realizations become one's Reality.

Self-Inquiry, the process of looking within to find out and understand the reasons for all of the motives of the ego, should be practiced with commitment and devotion every minute of the day. This will provide an endless day of karmic release. As negative karma, which is the ego and the reason for thoughts, is released or transcended, the state of existence known as 'no-mind/ego' or enlightenment ensues. Instead of thinking, one simply is what 'just is.' This is also called the 'I AM' presence, or state of existence.

13. What is one step that I can take to reduce the amount of thinking that the ego does?

Focus on existing in the Now. The ego likes to regret and rethink the past, while simultaneously fearing and planning for the future. The ego mind is constantly cluttered with all of its random thoughts and pointless ideas and fantasies. It does not need to think of the past and future while currently thinking and operating in the present as well. As one realizes that the future is already planned and so is death, the need to think about the past and future lessens to a degree.

The process of living in the Now has been documented in the Bible and spoken about by many enlightened beings. It makes no sense to worry about something that cannot be changed. One should just trust that they will make the proper choice when given the option. If one devotes their life to serving and following Divine Will, only positive (raised consciousness levels) outcomes are available. One must simply observe every instant that one is in and experience it as perfection. True happiness comes from existence itself. And as one spiritually evolves, it is discovered that thinking takes away from the very experience of existence itself, thus lessening the degree of happiness and joy that is experienced at every passing moment of Now.

Try not to see life as just pointlessly occurring, and to think that events need to be experienced in order for one to be happy. Events don't bring happiness; one's subjective experience does. So as one is driving down the street, try to experience every passing moment as creation. As the road is zipping by, say to your self, "This is creation (second #1), I am experiencing creation (second #2), creation (second #3), creation (second #4), etc...," and try to see and feel it as a continually unfolding creative process.

It is a way to remind one's self that creation is constant and continuous. After a while, the true pleasure from existing comes in every instant. So one will not feel compelled to search and plan for new things or events to be experienced every second of the day. These events, as well as the ego's thinkingness, will be seen as the illusion that blocks true happiness from being experienced; although it does give some remedial form of temporary happiness, it is not permanent.

14. Why should I be a good person when I don't believe in God?

Do you believe that you exist? (Answer: Yes.) Then you believe in God; you just don't know it yet. God is infinite and God is existence. Therefore, all is existence and you are in existence, which means that you are within God; and since nonexistence is an impossibility, you have always been, will always be, and are currently within God as existence. So why be a 'good person'? It is an expression of being true to your Self, or nature of existence, which is love. Why deny it?

15. Why did God cast the plague upon earth?

God did not cast any plagues on the earth, just as a loving father would not blow up one of their children, or one of their children's prized art projects. God does not favor one child over another, so God would not choose to kill, injure, or maim any of them. If God did, this would show *conditional* love, which is only a *restricted* and limiting nature of an ego, contradicting infiniteness (unlimited).

The world is unraveling just as it should, perfectly. Due to the many levels of consciousness that are interacting, the expression, result, or outcome is inevitable. And all happens exactly how it should: no differences, no mistakes, no chances.

Due to mistranslations of the Bible, egos misconstrue it

further by their belief in the misinterpretations. For example, when Moses supposedly 'parted the Red Sea,' it is now known that this was a mistranslation in the Bible; instead, it was the "Sea of Reeds," a much smaller sea. At the same time in history as this seeming miracle, it was found that a volcano erupted, creating a tidal wave like the earth has never seen. As the tidal wave progressed, it sucked up millions of gallons of water for many minutes (sufficient for thousands of people to walk on the ocean floor as if it were dry land) until it came to shore and crashed on the land. Researchers know this because volcanic ash from the volcano, found embedded in the shoreline, was carbon-dated to that exact period.

Plagues of flies, locusts, frogs, and so forth are common occurrences in that region. Even today, plagues such as leprosy are common in places such as India. So if plagues happen today, it is safe to assume that they have happened before. Science now knows that plagues happen in a certain order in the physical dimension. For example, on earth, the plague would have unraveled exactly the same way as in the Bible. There is a difference between God casting a plague on earth and Moses foretelling the future and knowing what was about to happen, thus using it as leverage to 'free his people.'

Many times, precognition, or knowing future events before they happen, was taken as a literal word from God, a sign from God, or a punishment from God. In actuality, it was really just a glimpse of a message from the universal consciousness that stores all facts, whether large and noticeable, or unnoticeable. Just the same, 'déjà vu' and a message from an astral being are commonly mistaken as a message from God. Sometimes an astral being will say that they are God in order to fulfill their own prideful feeling. Remember that God is everything. So *God does not claim identity*, because identity (ego) is false and an illusion in and of itself. When one is everything and infinite, then there is no other to identify one's self to; identities are linear/dualistic concepts of separation that are not a possibility in the Nonlinear and Nondualistic.

16. Why then does the Bible say that God is vengeful, judging, punishing, fearful, and angry at sinners?

Most religions have put the traits of the ego upon God because they just assume God is like them, but in a greater sense and with more power. For example, the ego believes God to be a person or a spirit being, to have traits of the ego (anger, hatred, remorse, judgment, vengeance, etc…), to be both limited (physical form) and unlimited (but still in form), to be somewhere besides earth or the universe (such as heaven), in a totally different dimension and time zone, to have a physical voice, to be someone you can make a deal with, to be someone who judges us when life is over, etc… Because this is the way that the ego operates and feels, it assumes that God must be somewhat similar. This leads to Truth being distorted by the ego and written in a sacred text as holy and true. Because the text says it is the only way to God (getting to God, which is dualistic and an impossibility), people who read it believe it to be the only source of Truth provided, while all others are false, leading to religious differences, wars, terrorism, and social problems.

God is nothing but the pure, Unmanifest creative potential that is unconditional love, while simultaneously being the manifest, or All That Is. The ego is limited, but God is infinite and unlimited. God has no feelings to be hurt and cannot be injured, and therefore needs not seek vengeance, punishment, retaliation, or have remorse for what 'He' has done. God is not limited to a physical body or gender. God does not look at or favor things, events, or people. God has no pride, because there is nothing to prove and no one to prove it to. This is due to the fact that God is All and One. Only the ego thinks that separations and judgments are possible.

17. Is Jesus better than Buddha?

One is not 'better' than the other; both are on the same level of consciousness, God-Realized. The word or description 'better' is a means for the ego to judge, classify, and categorize, therefore placing itself among the seemingly respected scale of earthly importance, while knowing its own and other people's standings. This provides the 'ego-concocted theory' of "who's the most important." The linear ego mind thinks that 'things' or 'people' are either better or worse (dualism). In actuality, however, beings only appear different to the ego because they are on different levels of consciousness, just being and displaying themselves perfectly for who they are. Unfortunately, the ego judges and separates by importance, thus placing one above the other.

Jesus and Buddha were different people in different parts of the world, but were doing the same thing: helping people realize the Truth of their existence. They were both enlightened beings who were completely egoless. They both knew the same level of Truth, but taught it a little differently because of the region of the world, the time, the acceptance of the people, the resistance of egos, the education of the people, the kings' restrictions, and the restrictions of the predominant religion. Due to these factors, the lessons had to be shaped so that people could understand what was being said. This led to two separate teachings that were fundamentally similar, but sounded different.

Jesus taught how to purify the ego, meaning to release the lower will of the ego and devote one's life to God. Jesus knew that the people of that time were in need of salvation, meaning 'securing a place in heaven' (so to speak). Buddha taught total relinquishment of the ego, or how to transcend the world of illusion and become enlightened. He felt that there was no reason to live in this world of suffering, prompting him to show people the way of enlightenment. Jesus taught the lessons that were accepted the best at the time when he was incarnated, and Buddha did the same.

18. If it's not God who tells people to kill others, then who is it?

Too often, people misunderstand what God is. They expect God to have a voice that speaks to them. This would imply, however, that God is a being who is separate from them, which refers to a dualistic reality. One must keep in mind that God is Unmanifest, and that there are no separations that would infer that God is somewhere else and talking (with a voice that has sound waves—form) to someone (through space) in a different location. This would also create a reality of perceivability; ego perception is only based on dualism/separateness. The ego cannot comprehend that God is Nondualistic and Nonlinear, or infinite.

Many people misunderstand which spiritual phenomena are positive and which are considered negative. Most people don't ever hear or see spiritual phenomena in their lifetimes. So when and if any spiritual phenomena are experienced, a being usually wants it to be from God or a positive message. Many times the message is just from a soul who has passed over and is trying to connect with anyone.

The astral soul may spread 'good or bad' messages to the being who is listening. However, many messages that sound positive could be very negative in nature. If a person prays (which is just setting positive intent) and asks for help, they are summoning any and all souls to answer. If one protects themselves with God's energy before asking for answers to a problem, then they will be considerably protected from negativity. Unfortunately, many individuals think that they are attuned to the vibration or energy of God when asking for help, but are not. This allows all types of souls to give messages that range in spiritual Truth, some of which are complete fallacy.

Due to a lack of understanding and realization of Truth, these messages are accepted as a higher level of consciousness or of a higher power. People will often believe any spiritual phenomena as Truth just because they were never before experienced; therefore, they feel that it must be of some importance for them to be given this gift of knowledge.

A large percentage of the souls who do come through provide knowledge that is no greater then the average of society. Because it is perceived to come from 'up there,' the knowledge is expected to be of spiritual importance and to be positive. If a soul is of a lower level of consciousness, messages will be conveyed to all those who can perceive the advice, along with the correlating level of fallacy. Therefore, when one is praying and asking for advice from the spiritual manifest (including heavens and hells), all spirits are invited to communicate if one is not properly protected by God's energy. Just because one prays to God doesn't mean that the information comes from God. In fact, Christian followers feel that any messages that are perceived from the spiritual are positive, just because they are Christian. They usually proclaim that it is Jesus' voice, just as Muslims say that it is Muhammed or Allah. Due to the ego's misunderstandings of Truth, mixed messages will be perceived and usually acted on because they are felt to come from a 'good' origin. So if this voice says to kill someone for God, then it may be done and believed to be 'in the right.'

One should remember that if a spiritual voice is talking to them, it is not God. It is usually believed to be God, but it is not, because of the linear relationship that is felt to exist by the ego/mind. By comparing the Nonlinear and the linear, it can clearly be known that God can only be experienced by the realization of the Self (Enlightenment) as One with the Nonlinear/Nondualistic Reality, which God 'just is.' When an understanding of the difference between the linear and Nonlinear is reached, then no misunderstandings of the Reality of God can exist. Thus no misinterpretations or misunderstandings of the Truth will occur, providing society with positive messages coming from positive beings, or just a worldwide realization and no need for messages.

19.Is there a spiritual answer to everything?

There is only one answer that applies to everything, and that is the realization of Truth. When the realization of Truth is experienced, then all of the illusions of the ego's problems disappear, and the world is seen as it is: perfect and problem-free.

Problems are seen and thought to exist because of the constructs of the ego mind that think 'things' are separate. Therefore, when something that is undesirable is seen, it is perceived as problematic. When All is experienced as One, then there is 'no-thing' to fix or solve, only the perception of the ego, which is the dualistic source of the 'so-called problem': separateness. God is spiritual, God is All; therefore All is spiritual, including answers. The only answer to all illusory problems is the transcension of the ego.

20.How do I cope with death and old age?

To understand the True Reality brings comfort in itself. Studying theology can bring about uncertainty due to the lack of Absolute Truth. To study the path of enlightenment and metaphysics can bring one a sense of peace because the levels of Truth are higher than those of religion. Understanding the levels of consciousness, as well as how the astral dimensions are developed, will allow people to know what is on the 'other side,' or better yet, allow them to know the 'spiritual laws' (karma) that govern where one goes after life in the physical incarnation is over.

Death is only feared because one does not realize the Truth, due to the obstruction and distortion that the ego provides and is. When the ego is abandoned, Truth will be known and death will not be feared. For those who seek comfort and understanding about the 'afterlife,' or 'life on a different level of reality,' one may try astral projection, although this is not recommended because it lowers one's level of consciousness. It will allow the ego to have proof that the astral dimensions (heavens and hells) do exist, and will make a believer out of anyone. It can instill a profound sense of faith, which will diminish any signs of fear that one might have of death. But enlightenment takes *all* fear away.

The aging process should not be looked at as 'good' or 'bad.' It is just another level of the ego's perceived reality that doesn't really exist in the first place. Since the constructs of the ego created the perceived reality that is called the physical dimension, aging should be looked at as an illusion and not Absolute Truth. Therefore, it is a false reality; the True Self is infinite and can not die.

The Higher Self is the Truth; the ego is the distortion. When one ages, their physical appearance changes and so does knowledge, but the Spirit remains unchanged, pure, and perfect. So aging is not a negative or a positive condition, but instead is just a reflection of more time to learn lessons on earth. Whether one is Self-Realized at 20 years old or 75 years old makes no difference. In the same manner, it doesn't matter whether it takes 10 lifetimes or 1.8 billion lifetimes to enlighten; the end result is the same.

When one is enlightened, all beings will be seen as the Self, and age, gender, race, or separation will not be noticed.

21. How is the world to be seen as perfect, when problems abound?

Earth is a place of learning, where many beings are all learning different things due to their different levels of consciousness. Different levels of consciousness denote different karmic levels, which inherently bring forth a variety of lessons to be learned. This is why many beings at higher levels of consciousness, within the confines of the ego, see other beings at the lower levels as problematic, when in essence, they are all just being who they are on their concurrent level of existence. The different levels of consciousness in this world create the ego's seemingly justified grounds for judgment. This allows the ego to make statements such as, "There are problems," or "How can someone act like that?" In Reality, all beings are 'being' themselves perfectly and the world is evolving just as it should.

22. With age comes knowledge. So isn't knowledge important?

Knowledge is stored energetic patterns (form), termed 'information,' which the ego mind holds onto because it makes rational and logical sense. Knowledge makes the ego feel educated and therefore more secure in its survival. Security comes from the ego knowing that it could handle many different situations because of its knowledge and intellect. An excess of knowledge makes one worry less, because the ego knows it could take on tough challenges if they were to arise.

Knowledge is helpful in the physical and spiritual manifest, but not in the Unmanifest. Knowledge is basically 'stored form.' The Unmanifest is not form; it is formless. Knowledge, or the storage of lesser truths, will slow one's enlightenment. However, knowledge of the ego transcension process is very beneficial because it deprograms the knowledge that the ego has led itself to believe as real, in turn revealing the higher awareness.

23. What if death is the end?

Death is only a term created by the linear mind to describe when a spirit leaves the confines of the physical body. Most people, however, see it as the end of life. In actuality, the end of life is an impossibility because God is infinite existence; which we are. The Higher Self is the only part of one's immediate (excluding the Unmanifest) existence that is not a heavily distorted illusion, and is aware that it cannot die.

The Spirit has always existed, although the ego has had a (felt to be) limited run. The only death is that of the ego and physical body when they are transcended and abandoned, respectively. And this is still an illusion because the ego and the physical body are an illusion as well. So illusions cannot die, but can be passed by as a whimsical memory of fallacy.

One must have faith in the Absolute Truth and realize that a greater power has already planned the physical life's outcome via the interaction of universal energies and a being's free will. Faith is the prerequisite that helps one understand that the soul is not subject to death; only illusions are.

The ego, an illusion, sees death as the end because it only sees in the linear, or within the extent of the measured and perceived reality. When the ego cannot see or perceive something, it is then feared. When 'concepts' are feared, the ego places its own beliefs and positionalities on the subject. This further distorts the subject at hand, usually making the ego more fearful. The ego basically takes a simple, unknown fact and distorts it into a fearful perceived reality. That theory or belief spreads to other like-minded beings, making them fear the same problem while placing their own imaginative twists on the concept. This feared concept of death is prevalent throughout the world, except for those who are spiritually advanced or enlightened... they actually welcome death and will enjoy the experience.

24. What can I do to understand people a little better?

Understanding the nature of consciousness allows one to have an understanding and compassionate view, rather than a judgmental view. When one realizes that all beings' personhoods, personalities, and traits have been created and shaped by the ego and therefore are an illusion that was a product of karma (which inherently was created by the ego as well), one can understand that the ego is like a virus or distorted program in a computer that makes one seem different from who they really are in Spirit: pure, accepting, and always unconditionally loving.

Everyone's ego acts, thinks, intends, wants, needs, speaks, looks, and is different because of the totality of karma, personal and universal. So because the potential energy of creation of the Unmanifest allows for the ego, which allows for consciousness and the manifest, which allows for interaction between things (duality and linear reality), which allows for karma to be acquired, which allows for the shaping of destiny, it then changes all that is experienced between a specific ego and the universe to its own perceptive rationalizations and idealizations. So each ego is at the whim of all collective karma. Therefore, it can be seen that all pure souls have been distorted or corrupted by the ego (a virus) to a certain extent.

All egos have been influenced in their growth and programmed by the totality of karma and creation, from the Unmanifest, manifest, karmic debt and merit, galaxy, universe, solar system, constellations, planet, continent, state, region, city, county, neighborhood, amount of oxygen in the area, atmospheric pressure, humidity level, birthday, time of birth, health at birth, type of physical body, health and wealth of family, family itself, relatives, friends, schools, social and economic conditions, population, hearing other people's problems, speech patterns, language, books that are read, TV that is watched, jobs that one holds, and interests that one has. All of these shape the individual or ego to what and who they are. So one cannot blame them for who they are but rather, one should understand them and offer help whenever it is needed.

All of the previous factors have shaped the ego and set

it at a specific consciousness level that displays the present personality of the ego. So one cannot expect anyone to act how someone else acts, or to think how someone else thinks. That is like expecting a turtle to run as fast as a cheetah. It is not going to happen, at least in this stage of their evolution. So one needs to stop wishing for all others to act or think in certain ways and simply accept them for who they are. Just keep in mind that they are exhibiting perfectly who they are at their programmed level of consciousness. One cannot be upset with perfection. To attempt to make someone conform to a certain criterion or identity is to control them. Only the ego tries to control reality or what is within it.

25.How can I stop getting irritated?

By remembering this phrase, "Expectation is the only cause of irritation." What is meant by this is that when one **expects** the outside world to go their way, or a person to conform to who they want them to be, their ego's control factor is surfacing and playing out. So when the event goes their way, or the person fits their ideal mold, they are happy. But when the world or person does not conform to their ideal or belief of what they should be, they then become irritated and upset, disrupting their peaceful state and bringing forth a negative demeanor that affects themselves, others, and the entire universal consciousness.

So for one always to be at peace and not irritated, one must not **expect** the world to go a certain way or a person to be a certain way, for when the ego cannot control the outside environment, irritation usually ensues.

Irritation also stems from a lack of understanding. When the ego does not want to understand a certain situation (i.e., why it had to happen this way), world event, or type of personality, they choose to block out love, peace, and acceptance (God), and choose to be an expression of the ego as dualism, judgmentalism, criticism, categorization, anger, and control. This also reinforces their feeling of being separate from the Source and being independent.

The ego believes that the source of happiness is elsewhere, or outside of its self. So it searches dualistically for that perceived source of happiness. Unfortunately, this leads to the ego empowering itself with more dualistic energy (belief in separateness) that creates an ever-present feeling of emptiness and being unfulfilled. And with this feeling, the ego observes external events and beings and places itself within the ideal type of existence that it wishes that it has or was. And when this mental projection doesn't manifest in the exact same way that is desired, the ego gets irritated. For instance, a checkout line that doesn't move fast enough would require one already to have an **expectation** of how fast the line should move. In another instance, a being who is always being negative would require one already to have an **expectation** of how positive they would like them to be. Remember that a turtle cannot be forced to run as fast as a cheetah, or one cannot be stretched beyond their means, limitations, or ability… so don't **expect** it to happen. An ego is who it is based on its level of consciousness. It cannot be at a higher level than where it currently is. A solid cannot become a gas.

26. Why does my family have cancer?

As even the medical field agrees, around 80% of illnesses are created from the mind. The word 'disease' actually came from the explanative, 'dis-ease,' or not at ease. This actually explains a lot, since about 80% of the population is in karmic debt, thus exhibiting a primarily negative personality and attributes. These lower states or conditions of the ego are pride, lust, desire, constant wanting, hatred, unforgiveness, retaliation, revenge, guilt, blaming others, grief, despair, hopelessness, shame, lack of remorse, being untrue to one's self, worry, irritation, agony, anger, resentment, fear, and many others. Along with all of these, the ego constantly regrets and rethinks the past, while trying to control and harness the future with constant worry and fear. All of these lower emotions and viewpoints on life make one's energetic system go weak and become drained, bringing on complications of health and displaying themselves as 'dis-ease.'

This constant waste of energy—which is provided by feeling, displaying, and being the conditions that were set by the lower states of the ego—creates 'ill health.' Since the (positive) energetic system is low on energy due to the (negative) ego's constant use, the rest of the body and energetic system feels a lack of energy. Thus, if energy is wasted, a liver in need is going to have to wait for energy to be made available again to repair itself. However, if energy never becomes available because it is constantly wasted by the ego, 'illness' and 'dis-ease' are the result, and the liver will degrade slowly with time. This brings about possible disease or the loss of the liver, and the question, "Why did God do this to me?" The answer is that all illnesses are created by the ego, and that God never wishes one ill.

People only get the diseases that they are programmed to receive. Since the ego does not want to blame itself, it finds another being to blame, such as God.

27. Are priests and preachers righteous?

(Try to stay away from stereotypes, grouping is an illusion). Not necessarily, but they can be, depending on their level of consciousness and the 'ego will' that is being used at a specific time. Some preachers understand that when the term 'righteousness' is mentioned in the Bible that it denotes following the 'right way' or God's Way. Unfortunately, many others feel that the term 'righteousness' is the Bible expressing a follower's right to be prideful while condemning other religionistic viewpoints, as well as 'loving the heavenbound' and 'hating the sinners.'

28. Is homosexuality wrong?

As the creation of the world continually unfolds, new lessons are readily learned by some, while others do not feel the need, or do not even want to learn. The main problem is that of judgment. As we judge others, we place a sense of importance on ourselves, while simultaneously devaluing the integrity or intrinsic value of the 'thing' or 'person' being judged. The main goal that society needs to realize is that we are all one, that there is not two, so there is nothing to judge or discriminate against. The separations are a product of the ego, which clouds Truth and makes us all feel independent and special.

The purpose of the visible differences in the physical manifest is to help all beings who inhabit earth to learn to live together without judging. (All differences are a perfect exhibition and expression of the potentiality of the Unmanifest manifesting its level of Divinity and intrinsic value, as well as its 'willed' current level of consciousness [karma] and environmental factors.) This is to help us overcome the barriers of the ego so we may learn to feel whole or One. As the barriers of the ego are overcome, the seeming separations that it sees will dissolve and all will feel connected as one. The problem is that as some souls are learning not to judge and usually treat people as equals, there are many souls who like to judge and discriminate against others.

As current conditions, races, and social classes become tolerated and hopefully understood to be equal, this brings forth new change that will help teach souls (even those who understood the last lesson) to understand with compassion and without judgment. This world is full of different people (because of the egos). All people are born into different cultures and have different backgrounds, not to mention different levels of consciousness. The traits of the ego are to be understood and seen for what they really are: illusion. When the ego is removed, all will be known to be One. So until the lessons of equality are learned, new lessons will be unfolding continuously. This means that all ego beings will continually differ because beings on earth aren't trying hard enough to understand that all are equal.

Just as 'blacks' and 'whites' continue to work out their differences, now 'heterosexuals' and 'homosexuals' have to work out their problems of judging each other as well. Homosexuals have been around since the dawn of time; it is just that they feel more comfortable in letting others know that they are 'gay' because they have seen how people are now adapting to other discriminatory factors, such as color. As long as beings still have an ego, there will be many lessons to be learned. As the ego is dissolved, all is realized as perfect and One, with no judgments to be made.

29. How can we overcome jealousy, anger, and hatred towards people?

By simply choosing the Divine Will over the ego will, which eventually eradicates the false notion that duality exists. With duality, the ego compares with judgment, allowing it to tell the difference between what it views as 'rich and poor,' 'lucky and unlucky,' or 'ugly and pretty,' which propagates jealousy if one is on the 'lesser end,' or if one feels that they have a void to fill. Without duality, this is seen as an illusion; therefore no judgment is made and no lower emotion felt.

To overcome anger, one needs not to hold an expectation of what they think society should conform to. As society breaks the mold, the ego gets irritated, sometimes enraged. This is due to the ego's feeling of 'loss of control.'

30. Is technology killing our spirituality?

Technology is not 'killing' our spirituality. Spirituality can never be destroyed; technology, however, could be considered a boundary or a limitation because it attracts the ego and could be an attachment for some. But on the other hand, it allows spiritual information to be sent out via email, the Internet, television, radio, and so forth.

Technology intrigues the human mind, which may make people physically and spiritually lazy. Or, plainly put, it can make human beings not take care of the physical body (a temple) or spirit. Most people would rather watch TV than read the Bible, go to a temple, or study spiritual texts. Fast cars, big houses, new clothes, beauty treatments, boats, planes, motorcycles, computers, radios, etc..., are creating new lessons in loss, fear, pride, and mental and emotional attachment.

Whenever the ego acquires something, it becomes so attached that it creates pride in having and owning it. This overattachment results in the ego simultaneously fearing it would get lost, stolen, damaged, or someone would not admire the object as much as it does. If the ego loses the 'attached object,' it feels as though it has lost its source of happiness, thus leading to depression. The feeling of loss that brings depression and sadness is the reason why the ego doesn't want to give up material possessions in the first place. The ego doesn't realize that the object didn't bring the happiness; instead, it was the ego's enjoyment of existence while using it. This is why not everyone likes the same things or has the same tastes. For instance, two people go on a roller coaster; one loves it, and the other is terrified. This is due to two different perceptions and perspectives that the ego has on the event or circumstance. One's feeling about that which is perceived or experienced as existence is what brings happiness, not the object itself.

In short, most technology is creating new obstacles that have to be overcome in order for one to become enlightened or Self-realized. The main lesson that will become increasingly difficult to learn is that of nonattachment: the process of looking within for happiness and releasing the external objects that make the ego feel more concrete or real. Every object that the ego acquires further reinforces the feeling of separation or duality, and the illusory feeling of ownership. It is impossible to own something when all is God.

It is important to keep in mind that technology can be used for many beneficial advancements in society. For instance, one can have an Internet site or television program that promotes Truth.

31. Does this mean that technology should be avoided at all costs?

Technology isn't the enemy; the ego's feeling of attachment is. One can use technology for what it is, while remaining emotionally uninvolved. When emotions arise, such as desire, want, or a feeling of need, then the ego is forming a bond with the object. This emotional bond is an emotional tie that creates and is attachment. This does not mean that one should try to be miserable while using technology, but rather, watch one's involvement with it.

One should enjoy technology and be happy with it for the current use at hand and then walk away. If any feeling of wanting or desiring to go back to it arises, then attachment is taking place in the form of a 'craving' or 'desire.' If one is overly attached to a computer and the thought of computers is constantly in mind, then it would be wise to step away for a couple of days, weeks, or maybe months, until the emotional attachment has subsided. When one does not care whether the computer is used or not, the emotional attachment has been relinquished and the use of the computer may be resumed.

32. Are we more important than other animals?

By analyzing the error of life, one can see that the ego's ignorance is at fault. The thinkingness, emotional states, ideologies, and judgments create and reinforce a seemingly dualistic reality, helping us 'dig our own hole' that we can't see our way out of. This illusory view on life is what makes human egos feel superior to all other beings.

As previously stated, one can see that animals are no less important than humans due to their lack of intelligence. In fact, the ego's intelligence actually reinforces the feeling that it knows everything, thus reinforcing the predominant energy of 'pride' in the energetic field. This creates the inability to surrender one's ego, knowledge, viewpoints, idealistic values, and so forth, which keeps one from God's Love and Truth, which are all one and the same.

Many humans feel as if animals do not have the same capacity to love as they do. This is incorrect. Many animals are at a higher level of consciousness than most humans, thus increasing one's ability to give and receive love. One knows this when a human becomes 'horribly disfigured' in a car accident, but their dog still treats them exactly the same. Just the same, one may have abused their dog a couple of times, but it keeps on coming back for affection, which is an expression of their unconditional love.

Animals also seem to know when a human is feeling depressed, which prompts them to give love in order to cheer up their 'master.' Just as humans feel that they have lessons to learn and missions to complete, so do animals. In many instances, the animal's mission is to provide their 'master' (and the universe) with unconditional love.

Humans often think that they must be more important than animals because they are bigger. If this is true, then a 7-foot-tall, self-centered basketball player must be more important than a 5-foot-tall doctor and philanthropist. Just as this concept makes no sense between people, the same goes for the comparison between animals and humans. A small animal, a smaller animal, or even a bug is no less important than any human. All are souls in a body of some shape, size, color, and so forth, who are trying to learn a lesson in this lifetime. With this said, it can be clearly seen that all life forms should be respected, helped, and loved unconditionally. After all, we all have the same Source and the same ultimate goal; enlightenment. Humans are just animals who use tools.

33. Are there other life forms in the universe than on earth?

Out of the endless physical galaxies that do exist, it is foolish to assume that ours is the only one with life forms. Even scientists will tell you that they are positive that other planets just like ours have life forms or beings who operate on their own universal laws, not too different from those of earth. The problem is that no one knows how to travel in light years yet, so the chance for us to prove this theory is still far from our understanding. However, one may visit other dimensions of reality through astral projection or an OBE. It is possible to astrally project to a far-off, distant planet in another galaxy, while visiting other beings who inhabit the planet. Unfortunately, it is not as easy as it sounds to direct out-of-body travel when one has never been to that specific location before.

Whether one wants to believe in otherworldly life forms or not is entirely up to them. This will not inhibit one's understanding and realization of Truth. It is only a side avenue of specific interest to some people. When focusing on our physical dimension, other beings' dimensions, or the spiritual manifest, it will just slow one's progress in their spiritual evolution because the linear mind of the ego would have to understand and focus on form. This would strengthen the ego by directing the focus onto its nature, which is form. Basically, when the ego is concerned with dimensions of form, it strengthens the ego, because that which is focused on (the material world, or form) strengthens that which it is (ego structure, or form).

34. What are facts? And what are beliefs?

Truth is fact. The ego's perception or positionalities of the Truth are beliefs. A belief is the ego's take on Truth, which then turns it into a lesser form of Truth known as truth, or even complete fallacy (denial of Truth).

35. Is God a fact or a belief?

God is fact/Truth, as the formless Unmanifest potentiality of creation. However, once the ego's traits are put on God to make 'him' (showing gender) seem fearful, angry, righteous, prideful, vengeful, intervening, showing favor, separated from us (showing duality), punishing, or judgmental, God then becomes a belief. A belief is an ego's distortion of reality that it thinks is the real reality.

Truth is not a belief; it is a fact. There is only Truth, or the distortion of it. A distortion is the ego's perception of what it thinks Truth is. Because the distortion makes rational and logical (linear/dualistic) sense to the ego, the ego accepts it as Truth. However, God is Nonlinear/Nondualistic, irrational, illogical (to the ego), unprovable, and immeasurable, so the ego just falsely creates some 'thing' that it believes to be God, with all of its own dualistic/linear traits that it projects on the traitless Unmanifest Source. Therefore it constructs its dualistically perceived reality of a 'superbeing' with ego traits (but more powerful) that created (showing past tense, or time) this planet a long time ago, while always watching and judging us, as well as simultaneously loving the saints and hating, condemning, and punishing the sinners. This shows conditional love, which is a limited trait that contradicts the infiniteness of God, which is unlimited and unconditional love.

God is infinite and unlimited, so placing ego traits on God would attempt to limit that which is limitless. The absurdity lies in the contradiction. For example, if God hates sinners, then the supposedly unconditional or unlimited love would be limited and therefore not available for sinners. This indicates that God would not be infinite, due to the inherent limitations of loving capacity.

36. How can you accept the death of your family and friends?

By realizing that everyone's death is planned by karma, meaning that all beings unknowingly choose their own death by every choice that is exercised by their own 'free will.' As karma changes, the seemingly preplanned death that would have been experienced changes as well. So as tragic as the death may seem, that soul needed to experience it because it was in concordance with their karmic levels.

37. How can you accept the sudden death of an infant?

An infant already has karma acquired from past life choices. This karma determines what the soul needs to experience in the new lifetime; perhaps the soul of the child had an abortion in a past life, or maybe it neglected its child when a parent and the child died.

Some babies are born into this world with a very high level of consciousness and are supposed to die suddenly after birth or within the first year or two of life. This is because their role in the evolution of mankind was to bring that high-frequency energy into the universe to uplift the overall karmic vibration of the world, thus bringing light to the world and helping all mankind save themselves from their own sins, and not to stay in the physical.

38. How is that fair to the parent of the child?

Everything is fair. God is the ultimate in fairness. To say that God is not fair is to assume that God is judgmental and imbalanced, or has 'ill will' for others. The only reason these parents had the privilege of having a child, whether it passes away suddenly or lives a long life, is determined by the parents' overall karmic package (as well as the child's).

Each parent's karmic vibration is set at a certain level of

consciousness, which selects the child's soul by its karma, thus creating the appropriate life that it needs to live. Not only does the child receive the 'perfect' experience that it needs to have, but the parents do as well. All happens in perfect accordance with Divine Will. No accidents are possible. Life unravels as perfection via universal and personal karmic levels of consciousness.

39. How can it be explained if 'good' parents experience a 'sudden death' of their child?

The term 'good' is a purely subjective word. What is good to one person is not good to another. Just because a being is perceived by the ego to be 'good' does not mean that they are at a high level of consciousness. 'Good' people can have low levels of consciousness: thus the symptoms of the perceived 'karmic disorder' of "bad things happening to good people." Keep in mind that all happens within the Divine Order of God as manifest expression.

40. If someone gives money away all of the time, doesn't it make them a 'good' or giving soul?

Not necessarily. It really depends on the intention or motive that they hold at the time of giving. Was the act inspired by the Divine Will? Or was the act forced by the ego? Many people give money away because they want to be seen as giving. However, this does not really make them a giving person; in fact, it makes them fall victim to greed. They are actually exhibiting self-serving traits because the ego thinks it can give something (money) away, but then get something such as admiration, respect, loyalty, compliments, etc…, in return.

So the motives of the ego are not really to give, but to trade. It is almost like buying respect and admiration from the beings who saw the so-called 'giving act.' A very large percentage of the world's population of 'givers' really just wants attention paid to the fact that they are 'givers.'

If one truly is a 'giver,' an anonymous gift (money, love, kindness, prayer, intention, respect, or advice) will be given and nothing will be asked for in return, not even a 'thank you' or recognition for the act. This is because the giver feels Divinely inspired to do so. When one just realizes that it just should be done, there is no feeling that anything needs to be acquired: no emotions (respect, admiration, compliments), or material objects. The essence of the saint is to give purely all of their life as a contribution to helping humanity evolve spiritually. This being has no wants.

41. Which religion is more correct?

By stating which religion is correct, it is indicating which religion is better than another, showing the ego's judgment. No religion is better than another; different religions simply teach different levels of Truth. Some have more profound levels of Truth, while others have been greatly distorted by the ego's perception. Just as the first and original Buddhism teaches the path of enlightenment, many other branches of Buddhism have been created because of various egos' distorted perception of what they thought truth was instead. Or maybe they thought that they had a 'better way.'

There is only one Truth, so why are there so many religions? This is because many different egos had their own distorted theory of what they thought Truth was, thus changing the one and only Truth into many sub-branches or lower levels of Truth, known as 'truth.' These are really just an illusion. There is no point in studying or following illusion.

42. Is eating animals wrong?

It is not wrong; it is simply a way of life that has been adopted throughout human evolution. The fact that humans evolved with bigger brains and dominated the planet was because they started to eat animal protein. First it was bugs, and then came animals. Much nutrition comes from animals that are eaten. For instance, animal meat provides different micronutrients such as vitamins and minerals, as well as macronutrients, carbohydrates from blood glucose and stored glycogen, fats that give large amounts of energy and can help keep one warm when stored in adipose tissue, and proteins that help to repair all of the tissues in the body. So, certainly eating animals is all right for the evolution of the human body. But what of spiritual evolution?

One can still spiritually evolve while eating animal meat, but it can take longer. For one, the pain of the animal as it is slaughtered is imprinted on their beingness and physical body. So when one eats their meat, they pull in all of the negative karma that was produced by the animal's past life, its terror prior to slaughter, and the actual murder itself. This slows one's spiritual evolution by adding the negative karma to one's energy field, which they are trying to get rid of. It makes no sense to be on a path to purify the ego, but then add negative karma to oneself on a daily basis by eating meat.

In addition, it is very hard to have compassion for all life when one is mercilessly slaughtering and eating it. Imagine petting a cow on the head while eating a hamburger. That just seems inhumane, doesn't it? It is like being the ultimate hypocrite. This is really no different than one saying that they love animals, but they are also carnivores. Sometimes the ego even likes to feel as if it is not participating in the slaughter, by blaming the slaughtering company for doing it, or by acting as if it didn't know that millions of animals gave their lives on a daily basis. If you eat animals, you are contributing to the mass slaughter of millions of beings. This is why it seems that one should cut down on the consumption of meat: to save souls from torture.

On the other hand, most animal souls need that experience in order to evolve to the next consciousness level, or they would have not been born into that specific 'animal body' within the prior conditions of the slaughterhouse. So technically, to stop eating animals will slow the progression of spiritual development for those souls. However, showing love to the animals being slaughtered and the slaughterers who have no compassion for any animal life would help them to evolve spiritually as well. So life seems to be a delicate conundrum. Although, it is comforting and beneficial to know that there are infinite dimensions and energy planes that infinite souls may incarnate into, some souls need to experience that lesson, so is it wise to rob them of that lesson?

To benefit all souls, it would be more beneficial to stop eating meat and slaughtering animals, while showing these souls who have a lower level of consciousness love and compassion. This helps the animals learn compassion and kindness, which raises their level of consciousness to a new high. The same can be done with the slaughterers. By doing this, no being would have to go through the lesson of terror.

43.How do I know when I am being a bad person?

What you mean to say is, "How does one know if they are allowing the ego to control their life's path?" It is simple: if one is being self-serving, then the ego is currently dominating. If one cares for the well-being of others before their own self-gain, then Divine Will is the influencing factor. All one must do to be in Divine accordance is to act, speak, and intend with honesty, truth, and integrity. If one is exhibiting the traits of the ego, dishonesty, pridefulness, selfishness, and a lack of respect, love, and compassion for all beings are displayed. This is what the society of egos has inherently labeled as 'bad.'

44. Is atheism incorrect?

Not to believe in God is not to believe in your Self, existence, love, happiness, or peace. Most atheists believe in God at different levels. For instance, they believe in existence and love; it is just that they don't usually believe in the modern religious representation of God. But for others, they may just simply not believe in a higher power.

45. Why do preachers always ask for money?

Many churches get some financial support from government grants and other contributors who want the affiliation and recognition of being a provider for a 'place of God.' To become a member of a church, one must give 10% (which is tax-deductible) or more of their income to the church. Just the same, the churches always ask for money at the services as well. This allows not only the church to be supported, but also the pastor, bishop, or priest.

Other services need to be funded, too, such as daycare, nursery, lawn care, maintenance, mission trips, and so on. The fact remains that most churches will still ask people for more money, even when those expenses have been paid. Some of them say that they are just saving up for future expenses, but sometimes the money can be in excess of $100,000 to more than $1 million.

Some churches even cost more than $20 million to build. This is due to the greed of the church leader. Their ego is displaying their greed and pride, which shows that they feel image is important. Just as they feel that 'churchgoers' should dress and look a certain part, they feel that their church should look bigger than others. They still think that 'bigger is better,' or that it shows they care more about God than other religions do. They also feel as if it is a tribute to God, and that God will appreciate them more for what they have done, thus reserving a place for them in heaven.

The followers are often coerced by the preachers to give as much money to the church as they can. They will say that the more money one gives shows how much one loves God. The preachers have said that if one doesn't give all they can give of their money away to the church, then one is being greedy and sinning, and will therefore go to hell. This in turn makes the followers feel guilty for not giving money and forces them to give what they have. This misconception stems from the ego, which makes one always feel that they need to try harder to 'prove' to God that they worship and idealize him. If anyone tries to coerce or convince one to give money to the church, then leave that place and ignore their teachings. Money should be given as an act of free will, givingness, and selflessness. Money can always go to other organizations that help people, such as other nonprofits.

A Spanish man in Florida just received over $7 million from the government to start his own 'Spanish Appreciation Center'; doesn't it make sense that a church would get more because people fear God? Not only does a church get money to start up a church, the church can apply for government funding. Unfortunately, many church leaders have been caught embezzling money from churches. This means that the preacher or pastor has been taking money from the offerings that are passed around every Sunday morning and increasing his annual paycheck by $10,000-50,000 or more.

The religions that teach the highest level of Truth ask for the least amount of money; for example, in most Buddhist temples, the Buddhist monks don't get a salary, but the priests, pastors, and bishops do. The Buddhists monks' food comes from the people who donate it, or who provide the money to buy it. They accept donations, but they ask for no money, because it is not needed for extravagant extras. This is why many Buddhist temples grow their own food (vegetables and fruit). For one, they don't spend money on $5 million to $20 million churches. They conserve money and may spend $1 million or even less on a temple. Most monks realize that the only necessities are food, shelter, and water. They live on the bare minimum, because that is all that is needed and nothing more is wanted; it is because the teachings of the Buddhist monks contain higher Truths, unlike many other religious leaders, who are usually only versed in lower levels of truth. In fact, many church leaders cannot even be considered 'ego-purified' beings, where their level of consciousness is at the level of unconditional love and nonjudgmentalism. The pastors of today are controlled by their egos, which control their lives and hold onto the capacity to sin and the presence of sin.

46. Why do people feel more comfortable in a big, overdone church rather than a small church?

Churches are always competing for followers. The bigger and better a church is perceived to be, the more people will be impressed and continue their relationship with God through that specific church, thus increasing the number of followers, the feeling of leadership, and the church's income. The ego is always impressed with 'bigger' and 'better' things. When one outdoes another, then the small and seemingly insignificant things are ignored.

The ego also thinks that God cares how big a church is, as if God were impressed (an ego emotion) with physical things. When God creates All that Is, a big church still remains almost invisible to the infinite creation of All. However, All is important to God and is cared for equally, no matter how big or small. Whether significant or insignificant, all things are respected, loved unconditionally, and accepted because everything has a purpose in the universe.

When people stop putting so much emphasis on the physical world of impermanence and illusion, the linear and dualistic, or the world of the ego, Truth will be revealed and realized. At that moment, people will stop trying to 'outdo' each other by having the 'biggest' and 'best.' Instead, they will realize that importance should be placed on existence itself, the source of infinite and eternal love and light.

47. Why do I have to dress up for church, just to learn the word of God?

Most churches and religious leaders equate a clean-cut, well-dressed person with being respectable and showing respect for the church, the pastors, and God. Clothes help to shape the ego's identity, giving strength to the illusion that they are separate from others in some special or unique way, such as the way they dress. Integrity and holiness are not expressed through clothes. In fact, most people who dress up are not integrous, honest, or trustworthy people.

Just look at businessmen or salesmen; they wear a suit, and they usually tell 70-80% truth about what they are selling, then twist it a little to make someone buy. They do not usually respect the customer; they are just using them to make a sale (money). The anger of the salesman can be witnessed when the customer does not buy.

So during a sales pitch, they act as though they are the customer's friend or buddy so they can win their trust and confidence. Then they usually manipulate the truth to make the sale. They are pressured to do this because if they miss the sale, they have to explain to their 'higher-ups' (bosses) why they have failed. A true friend will be happy when the other friend stops in to say hello, with no pressure or expectations to do or buy anything, and then can leave while both parties are still happy.

Dressing up in really nice clothes with extravagant jewelry is just another illusion that the ego wants other egos to see and believe in. An enlightened being can walk into a church wearing shorts, sandals, and a T-shirt, but have more good will, good intention, unconditional love, compassion, and respect for all beings and God than all of the congregation as a whole.

48. Why are we here on earth?

The only purpose that one has on earth, or any energy plane for that matter, is to evolve spiritually or enlighten. This means that one has to learn their lessons while raising their consciousness level until the ego is totally transcended, thus revealing Truth. As the consciousness level is raised, karma is transcended. When all personal karma is transcended, all personal lessons have been learned. When one learns all lessons, then there is no reason to incarnate again. This marks the last physical incarnation, unless one later chooses differently.

Many beings feel that the purpose of being on earth is to be born, go to school and become educated, make friends, get a career, get married, have kids, buy a nice house and car, and live in a nice neighborhood. These ideals are the main purposes of the 'earthly incarnation' that the ego perceives, because they are fulfilling and satisfying to the ego. Because the ego always feels a sense of loss, due to lack of God's internal fulfillment, it always tries to find 'external things' to acquire. The ego thinks that it will fulfill itself and have a sense of satisfaction when it gains material objects. Unfortunately, the sense of satisfaction is always impermanent and temporary, making the ego search for new and better things to acquire. This continual cycle brings the ego a constant sense of 'gain and loss,' which always makes the ego feel unfulfilled as the 'loss' is experienced.

When material objects do not bring the same fulfillment to the ego, it searches for other 'things' that could equal or surpass the level of happiness that the last possession gave it. Sometimes the ego looks to religions, philosophy, culture, or belief systems to find something different that it can explore, in hopes that these will bring happiness as well. This is the ego's first attempt to find real Truth, although it looks at it as another source of external happiness. All of the preceding does bring a sense of happiness and fulfillment to the ego, but it is limited. The limitations prevail until the confines and restrictions of the ego have been completely dissolved.

49. Aren't enlightened beings considered extremists?

To be an extremist, there must be a duality. For instance, a duality is showing two polarities, such as conservative and radical or liberal. A conservative and liberal are not two opposite people (even though it seems that way), they are just two different people at two different levels of consciousness expressing themselves differently. And because they are both within our view of what we have seen people to be, then they are marked and labeled as opposites.

Duality or polarity shows that there are two points that one can go to, which is an illusion of the ego. From what point is one an extremist, if there is no other polarity?

To an ordinary unenlightened ego, an enlightened being is usually viewed as an extremist, is "off his/her rocker," has "gone overboard," has "lost touch with reality," or has "abandoned the world and responsibilities." On the contrary, they realize the actual Reality while simultaneously observing egos in the world as lost and in need of help. To an enlightened being, they are simply being what they are and are not denying their True Reality (God). If an ego wants to label them as an extremist, they should see them as an extremist for God, love, serving others, and bringing happiness to all, or devoting their entire existence to that which is True and not believing the illusory dimensions of lesser truth or complete fallacy.

50. If God is so good, why doesn't he take away all of the pain and suffering; why doesn't he make all of the unenlightened...enlightened?

It is simply this: because egos don't want God to. They

would rather suffer. If they didn't will that to be so, they would already be enlightened and would never have suffered in the first place. God didn't 'will' for 'hell' to be created (analogously speaking), the ego willed for God to create hell, so God allowed it. God never condemned us; we have condemned ourselves. "Our ignorance is our condemnation," as the Buddha said. The energy of God has always been available; it is just that we have denied it and chosen suffering instead.

To begin on the path towards enlightenment is to understand this very concept. God is innocent; our ignorance is to blame. This is stated because many egos are still continuously blaming God for what their ego has done to them.

51. If one 'tries' to become enlightened, which is obviously a type of ego control, how does one not use this energy in their quest?

The ego should be looked at as a tool that helps one energize the direction of their journey. One should allow it to motivate them to study books of Truth, meditate, listen to teachers of Truth, and so on. Then, after the ego has been used to an extent where most of the 'internal burning' questions of existence have been answered, it shows that the ego is almost completely shut down. After the ego mind quiets in its nature and the quality of thinkingness lowers in frequency, it is then advisable to stop using the ego to try to attain (which is an obvious dualism—'the attainer and that which is attained') the goal of enlightenment, but rather surrender all to the Source and allow for the Higher Power to dissolve the ego.

The ego can only start the search and study the path, but it cannot cross over into the aspect of Self, for it is the 'no-ego zone.' So one can only use the ego to get to the 'final doorway' of enlightenment, then the Higher Power takes over.

The natural fear that one has is that they worry about doing all of this 'spiritual work' and then ending up right where they started, by giving up and then sinking back down in level of consciousness. But one should just remember the spiritual law of 'like attracts like.' So if one has transcended most of the ego, then positivity prevails. And this positive nature of one's self will connect with the highest nature of the universe and will automatically pull one over (so to speak) by the 'like attracts like' rule to the nature of the Self. Just have faith and trust in God.

It should be kept in mind that one cannot transcend the ego if they currently have attachments, whether to family, friends, animals, itself, etc…, or to the emotional or mental aspects of life. One must analyze all attachments that they have and realize why they are not as important as they had led themselves to believe. If one is not enlightened, they are attached to the ego itself and its other subconscious and conscious attachments of being a separate individual.

52. Can you elaborate more on that?

The ego, when fully charged, is pure negativity. So as one transcends throughout the many levels of consciousness, the ego loses negativity by the addition of positivity (divine will). So since the ego is the source of negativity and limitation, it cannot go into the Source of positivity and unlimitedness.

The ego can be looked at as a car. When completely fueled, it runs very well. But when it runs out of fuel (negativity), it loses momentum and eventually stops. And if the car keeps on running, then one cannot stop it. So one must allow themselves to be filled with positivity by serving only Divine Will and not giving into the various distracting temptations of the ego, for this will refuel the ego and keep it going. So naturally, when one's vehicle stops, it prompts one to get out of the source of limitation (car) and experience the real Reality that had been shielded from them. Just remember this phrase, "A car (ego) can't run without fuel (negativity/dualism)."

53. What are the fundamental blocks toward attaining enlightenment?

On one's path towards transcending the lower self, the major blocks are those of, from lower to higher, (1) releasing the lower qualities of the ego, (2) having faith in the unseen (higher power), (3) having a basic familiarity with the teachings of Truth, (4) understanding that all things are equal, (5) stopping the judgment process of the ego, (6) realizing that duality is an illusion, (7) releasing all attachments of the ego, including itself, and (8) having faith that the ego will be transcended without trying.

54. When one is enlightened, can the ego take control?

This is what I term "Ego Re-Entry." This means that the enlightened being has chosen, usually briefly, the sinning nature of the ego. A common misconception that most people seem to have is that enlightened beings can't or don't sin. This is incorrect. The option of 'free will' is always there, just as it is for all egos. It is just that they do not feel motivated to act on it. But an enlightened being is often tempted to 'fall from grace.' This is usually denied and seen for what it is: an illusion and diversion from the Truth. Just read the Bible or any other sacred text and one will find enlightened beings facing many temptations from the 'other side,' for example, Jesus and Satan, Buddha and Mara.

While enlightened beings do not usually sin, it is still a possibility if they so desire. But this could cause a re-entrapment from the ego, which may never let go. Due to this knowledge, as well as knowing Truth, being One with God, and already feeling eternally fulfilled, they can deny temptation very easily. If an enlightened being is going through a 'trial' (a test before they increase in power), then they may feel a moment, an hour, a day, or a week of being away from God. At this time, it is easy to sin. But the karmic repercussions are known and not desired.

Ultimately, they realize that if they were to sin, they would just worsen the universal karmic debt, the very thing that they are trying to erase. And in knowing this, they avoid using the ego, to keep the universal karma where it is, and also stay as a 'higher power' that will help to resolve other beings' negativity within and as the universal whole.

55. What if one's career causes harm to people?

There are some jobs that require a nonintegrous viewpoint in order for one to succeed while remaining employed. Only a less integrous and selfish ego would try to stay employed at such a workplace, if the job were to require what no job should: relinquishing the positive virtues of the soul, such as truth, honesty, respect, selflessness, and integrity. These virtues are given up for a selfish exchange of money. If one pays another enough money, they will do just about anything. If the job compromises the health, well-being, or integrity of people in the world, it then needs to be looked at for what it is, whether self-destructive or world-destructive. Creation is of God, but the intent to be destructive, selfish, and not care about others is a lesser virtue of the ego.

All of the lesser emotional states, intentions, and viewpoints of the ego will create more of a karmic debt that the soul will just have to transcend later. If one knows that they are making blueprints for a new type of bomb, then the karma will be attached to the action and intention of the ego. If the ego tries to justify the act by saying, "Well, we need protection from foreign invaders," then they are just ignoring the truth that they are not helping mankind but destroying it.

One cannot ignore truth or deny that it has any part of something destructive when it is; this is just an attempt that the ego makes to convince itself that it is right when it may be 'wrong.' No one can trick the Self, but one usually tries anyway. This will actually result in more negative karma by compounding illusion. When one knows that they are doing 'wrong' and they try to justify it or ignore it, the fact still is that they are still doing something that is less than integrous and is a part of mankind's destruction. Unless one does not care about the evolution of their soul, and others, then a new job is definitely suggested.

Chapter 23
Student Discussions

1. **Is God really 100% in control?**

   God is actually not in control in the way that the ego thinks. The ego expects God to make happen what God wants to occur in one's life, regardless of the ego's choice. The fact of the matter is that God provides the energy, which provides for the circumstances that allow the lessons to be learned, the physical and spiritual manifest dimensions to exist, and the 'will' to be used. God wants and needs nothing; God is All.

   The very fact that the ego has 'will' shows that God is not controlling it. The ego actually decides what is going to happen next in one's lifetime through one's consciousness level. Every unfolding of creation that is experienced as existence in physical life is due to the ego willing it so.

   If God were controlling, egos would be forced to be and live a certain way. Because they are not, it can thus clearly be seen that God provides the energy that creates every instant in one's life as it is willed by one's self to be. If God were controlling all beings, then they would never have been given this 'free-will' opportunity. It is important to remember that *control* is an aspect of only the ego, not God. The term *control* means being forced to do something or act in a way that is against one's will. Since every instant of creation in one's life is an act of 'will,' then it very easily can be known that the ego guides its own destiny. Without God, however, destiny as well as existence would never have been a possibility.

2. **So then, if the ego is just reflecting what level of consciousness it is at, is one not responsible for their actions, thoughts, and intentions?**

One may not be able to control the continual channeling of one's level of consciousness, but one is responsible for the 'will' that is exercised. The ability to 'will' something to occur or be expressed is a very important responsibility that could alter the manifest existence of one's self and others, and the universal karmic energy patterns. So to say that one is not responsible for something is false. One is responsible for 'willing' it to happen; God just allows it to be done.

3. If God loves us so much, then why were such perceived realities as hell, pain, torture, and suffering allowed to be created and then experienced?

The ultimate level of unconditional love allows for free will. It allows each and every soul to create and then experience its own level of reality that it feels should be experienced at that time. Just as God never asked us to choose to separate and leave divine grace, God never asked us to create the hells and tortuous dimensions. The ego 'willed' each and every negative event to become a possible reality, and because God loves us so much, this was allowed. It is not God's fault that egos are ignorant and do not know what they are getting themselves into. To think that is ignorant as well.

As the ego first 'willed' to be separated from God, or so it thought, this created a feeling of loss. As this feeling of loss was experienced, a 'hell' of that empty feeling became a reality that could be experienced. As the first animal or human felt that it was necessary to kill or maim another, that corresponding 'hell' was created as well. Unfortunately, the ego has another aspect of itself that continuously blames others for seemingly negative experiences, prompting the ego to blame other egos and even God for one's own willed misfortunes. So egos are to thank for the suffering and misery, not God. God is the light (positivity), and the ego is the darkness (negativity).

4. So then, how does all negativity become light?

If all egos choose to transcend themselves, they must choose to be a pure channel of Divine Will, rather than ego will. This adds Light to their ego, which raises in level of consciousness and then dissolves into the infinite Presence of Light. As egos are healed by the addition of Light, the negative thought forms that were created by those very egos are healed as well—therefore, in a manner of speaking, deleting the egos and the hells that they willed to be created.

Unfortunately, some egos love the feeling of misery, control, pride, or torturing others. These beings will more than likely not choose Divine Will. They actually derive pleasure and strength from seeing people suffer. In the astral dimensions, tormented souls will follow other souls around while trying to torture them with 'spooky' sounds, sights, or feelings. Beings in 'haunted houses,' or souls who are trapped in this dimension, try to 'spook' others currently dwelling there. It is also important to note that not all souls trapped in this dimension are nonintegrous and tormenting. Some are just lost and confused. Really, all egos are just lost and confused.

5. Should dreams be taken as prophecy or Truth?

No. In fact, many dreams are just the ego's reflection of the events, thoughts, actions, and feelings from the previous day. The information from dreams comes from the astral dimensions, which contain a large variety of souls from high to low levels of consciousness. The information received in dreams is almost 99% inaccurate and cannot be trusted. Very rarely is a dream accurate. If an accurate dream occurs, it is usually clouded by metaphors and analogies that cover the Truth. To be skilled enough to decipher dream symbols and meanings is a rare talent; many claim to have this talent, but are deluded as well.

If one analyzes their dreams, they are usually a compilation of the ego's fears, anxieties, emotional and mental states, as well as different internal and external positionalities. To trust in a dream is to trust an illusion. Remember that pure Truth is formless; dreams are obviously a product of form. This can be seen in the various energetic structures that create a variety of different dreamscapes and scenarios.

The 'dream book deciphering kits' are usually meaningless and useless. This is simply because dream symbols are not the same for everybody, but instead have a different value and meaning for each person. Symbols are a reflection of a being's outlook on life; their meanings are really only known by the dreamer. Only a hypothesis can be given to a dreamer by another ego, not Truth. And anyone who has written a book deciphering dreams is an ego, not enlightened. Does one really want to trust the interpretation of their illusory dream to another illusory being with an illusory outlook on life?

This is why the Book of Revelations in the Bible cannot be trusted, because of the way in which information was gathered to create the scripture. Revelations was written by a man who simply copied down the dreams that his ego felt were truth. Unfortunately, these prophesies are more than likely false and not to be trusted. The book was in fact written dualistically within the linear, with judgmental and biased comments about God hating sinners and favorably picking out saints. Any spiritual devotee who has understood the basic spiritual laws that govern us all will know that this is false: the 'opposite' of Truth (contradictive humor).

Just the same, all throughout the Bible, statements that reinforce fallacy were written as fact because of a massive misinterpretation that many Christian followers had and currently still have. If all beings properly understood the manifest and Unmanifest, then all confusion about psychic phenomena, dream scenarios, out-of-body experiences, and so forth would never be misunderstood. Due to the ego's inability to understand Truth, mistranslations and misunderstandings have become a way of life. Plainly put, the ego is in an illusion and this is all that it knows, or has a possibility of knowing.

6. Is it actually possible to be a trapped soul within the physical dimension?

Yes, it is very possible. However, the dimension that souls are usually trapped in is not really the physical; instead, it is an energetic reflection and refracted copy of the physical manifest. This dimension is almost identical in that it looks the same, but it is slightly altered—hence the use of the word 'refracted.'

The difference between the physical and energetic copy is one of alterations. The physical dimension is solid and, for the most part, cannot be altered. But the energetic copy, often referred to by others as the 'real time zone,' is also a mental zone. Here a small thought that enters the mind can significantly alter the world as it is experienced by the soul. If one is caught up in a repetitious memory, that scenery and memory will be relived again and again until they are willed to cease. Just the same, an integrous soul who, for a split second, thinks about a nondesirable place transports there. This is the realm where thoughts are not sacred, but instead shared by all.

Unless one is enlightened, these multidimensional realities can be experienced for eternity with no escape. An enlightened being is able to go to any dimension (if they want to) that is at a lower level of consciousness than they are; this is very useful for helping trapped souls. As a sage rescues a soul from mental attachments, which creates the perceived reality, they may stay to instruct the soul further or transcend back to their level of consciousness as Higher Self. An ego does not have the option to be One with God; instead, it can only be that very expression of what it is. To surrender the ego to God out of love is to realize one's Self once again as God as One.

7. Why would someone deserve love or forgiveness if they have wronged another?

The ability and capability to sin is an option; however, it is an unknown option. It is unknown because the ego does not truly understand the karmic recourse, if any. The ego may be familiar with physical recourses such as jail or repayment, but spiritual karma is a very uncommon concept.

It is as simple as this: the ego doesn't know that it has an option to escape suffering by choosing Divine Will. It is still functioning in the survival and security mode, which entails living for one's self (selfishness), protecting its identity, protecting territory and reproduction, and staying alive. So these beings have not really intentionally wronged anyone; they have simply been misguided or misled into believing that what they did was the only option they had that would bring in happiness and block out the continual feeling of loss and emptiness. So these beings should not be hated and ignored, but instead, loved and helped.

So why would a being who has perceived another being as 'wronging' them feel as if they do not deserve love or forgiveness? After all, it is not as though that being owns love and will run out of it. Love is an infinite quality and property of God; no ego or enlightened being can own it. To claim to own a feeling of love for something is to claim to own God, because God is Love.

An ego who does not forgive another and send them love is usually protecting its pride, such as, "I'm right and he's wrong, so he doesn't deserve it." And in an attempt to express one's security, the claim might be, "If I send him love and forgive him, he may get close to me and do it all over again." In short, the ego can always find a way to justify any action, emotion, or way of thinking. Just because an ego can justify its actions doesn't mean that these were proven correct. In fact, it usually means that the ego has just come up with an illusory statement or belief system that backs up or reinforces how it feels. This reinforces the pride that the ego was feeling and brings in temporary happiness, thus denying God's love, which is Truth and permanent happiness.

Every single being is a channel, whether of ego will or Divine Will. So what a being wants to be an expression of is totally up to them. They can be a servant of God and be happy, or a slave to sin and constantly suffer. To deny being a Divine channel to and for another being who has 'wronged' one's self is to deny God's love that flows through one's being. This stops one's own flow, as well as that of others.

Not only would allowing and Willing one's being to be a channel of God raise one's level of consciousness, but the other being's level as well. This means that both beings would go up in frequency while feeling happier and more at peace. After all, a 'sinner' sins because they are trying to fill that empty feeling that is felt. So to send them love and forgiveness is to fulfill them, which would inherently allow God's love to flow to them and help them to stop sinning, therefore providing a more peaceful being, relationship, and world. To deny God's love that is channeled through one's being is to ask for one's self, the other, and the world to suffer.

8. How is it not possible to own anything such as love for one's child or family; to say that sounds insensitive?

It is important to keep in mind that God is love, and God is infinite. This means that everything within existence is a quality and intensity of love. That which is perceived as normal in society is seen as love, and a below-normal intensity of love is perceived as negative emotions. For instance, a being may love himself and nothing else, but he at least loves himself. However, the world would see him as a channel of hatred, when in reality, he has just chosen to function at a very low level of love and to deny most of it.

At the lowest level of consciousness, a being may love about 1% of existence but absolutely hate the other 99%. That 99% hatred is really just a 99% denial of God's love. So any love that a being experiences is allowed by their Will, but it is not a direct emotion or feeling that they themselves have. It is in fact a quality of God that they simply allow to flow through them by the faculty of will.

It is understandable that a mother would like to assume an identity as owner of a child; however, this is not so. God is both the creator and the created, the potential and the product, so it is false to claim to own both what God has allowed to manifest and the experiences that come from it.

The experience of birth is really what makes the father and mother feel like parents. They feel as if both of their DNA combined and created a child—their child. But without the energy of God that allowed for the DNA, the parents, the experience of life and its conditions, and the world to exist, neither the child nor the parents would ever have existed. To own something means having control over that property. When a child dies at birth or a young age, what control did the parents have over that circumstance? Just as everything is up to Divine Will, nothing can exist outside of God or Divinity. If nothing can exist outside of existence (a paradox), then God is the sole owner of everything (so to speak). God isn't really even an owner, because that would impose a dualistic relationship, the owner and the owned. Instead, God is the constant expression of love as existence. God is everything as One, total and complete.

So all beings are not even owned by God; they are simply various expressions that are portrayed as differing levels of consciousness. Each level of consciousness is essentially charged by one thing only: the amount of will (truth). The highest level of Will is One with God, the middle levels are viewed as the 'kind and loving' being, the lower levels are seen as 'normal society,' and the lowest levels are those of the 'sinners' who deny God's love and the Truth of existence. So it can be seen that All is God; any beings who think differently are simply expressing their level of consciousness.

9. How can one not own property such as a house, or a pet that was purchased for $700?

The act of purchasing is actually illusory. Nothing can really be purchased. That would require one to buy a part of God, an impossibility. The social agreements that civilized man has are actually illusory. However, because these are logical and rational-sounding to the ego, they are accepted and thought to be necessary. They also reinforce the ego rules, called 'laws,' that help to provide safety and security. Monetary values only exist in the physical dimension, not in Reality. If one wishes to live here, however, then the rules need to be abided by.

To pay $700 for a pet is more or less an illusory contract between two illusory egos. However, it can be looked at as a payment to free the animal, along with the ability to care for it with continual love. One could let it go as well. It may be wise to decide what would be of some benefit for the animal being.

Just the same, a house, or any property, is a product of God's continuous unfolding as creation. It cannot be owned; however, many egos would argue this point, because of the ego's dualistic nature, which feels that it is necessary to own or acquire material things to be happy. The ego feels that the more that it acquires (owns), the more that its level of importance goes up. When one becomes Self-Realized, at the very high levels of Truth, it can be known that the owner and the owned are self-identical, meaning that whatever one claims to own is really a product of them as well, for each individual's True nature is that of the Unmanifest, which provides for the manifestation. Thus, without one's Unmanifest nature, nothing would exist. When one is enlightened, it becomes comical at times to walk through nature while realizing that which is being walked through is really just a different aspect or expression of the Self, which is no different than themselves.

All is God; nothing can be owned. To claim to own something is to fall prey to one's own illusion of dualism. So while one is existing in the physical dimension, money can be used to purchase things, but keep in mind that ownership is a common fallacy that blocks one from True realization.

10. So since the ego cannot actually own anything, then the ego cannot really lose any-

thing either, right?

That is correct. The ego can only experience loss when it is under the delusion that it can own something, whether a child, house, car, money, and so forth. Fear also arises when the feeling of ownership is threatened or jeopardized. In fact, many egos become defensive at the concept of losing ownership. Defensiveness is an egoistically selfish trait that tries to deny the possibility of this loss.

The ego also builds up anxiety before this dreadful day when importance, pride, and happiness are seemingly lost. As the day approaches and loss is experienced through the revocation of ownership, depression may set in. So really, a whole array of emotions and positionalities branch out from this very illusory concept. To understand the Truth of 'ownership' resolves many ostensibly troubling concepts.

11. When it is said that everything is God, how can a table be God? Wasn't it made by man?

The table itself is not the totality of God, but just another expression of existence. The table was indeed formed by the ego; however, the energy provided was due to God allowing it so. The energy that manifested became noticed by an ego and then was manipulated or shaped to the appropriate form. Even if the ego made the table, how did the thought originate in the first place? Without God, no thoughts would even be possible. God provides for the levels of consciousness to manifest, which allows various thoughts to flood the ego's mind. As the ego claims ownership over the thoughts that allowed the table to be mentated, the product (table) of the laborer is also believed to be 'man-made,' thus ruling out God as the provider and the reason for its existence.

Furthermore, to say that God's energy is not in the table, or even in the molecules that allowed the table to be manufactured, would contradict the infiniteness of God. This would mean that God is not infinite, which implies limitations and boundaries. These are obviously not qualities of the

Unmanifest. Since God is infinite, it can now be known that God is All, the manifest and the Unmanifest.

12. Can it be said that the table has less of God's Presence within it than does a human being?

God is equally within all things, but an onlooker may find it hard to detect the appearance of divinity. This actually depends on the 'will' or 'Will' that has charged the ego of the person or the item, and on the level of consciousness imbued in it that allows the Presence of God to shine forth. A table that was 'hand-crafted' by an enlightened being who was charged with a high level of Truth would indeed carry a higher frequency than a human being who was selfish. It is important to note, however, that the availability of God is equally present to and in all things. It simply takes the individual to recognize that fact and to allow God to operate through them as a channel. With a material item, a being may pick up an object and charge it with their overall karmic vibratory rate, Divine Will, or ego will. And it then depends on what is done with it, whether blessed (holy water), cursed at (a VCR that won't stop blinking), or used for a nonintegrous activity (gun that is used to hunt, murder, or rob).

13. So is everything at a certain level of consciousness?

Everything in this universe of the manifest is a reflection of karma, meaning that all 'things' are actually programmed or imprinted with 'will' and 'Will' that have set their level of consciousness. All beings who inhabit the manifest program the 'things' that they walk by, touch, or think about. The same goes for egos. As they think positive thoughts about others, it positively affects them, but only if willfully allowed; however, the opposite is true as well.

So the car that one drives was charged by the materials that were used, the area that it was built in, the egos who assembled it, the dealership that it resides at, and the various salesmen and customers who sat inside it. Furthermore, the being who decides to purchase the car charges it with every thought and emotion that they have while driving around town to various locations. The same goes for all 'things.' This world is like a computer that is programmed, but it can be reprogrammed within every instant of existence just by will.

So it is easy to see that if all beings became enlightened, or close to it, that all 'things' that once carried a negative charge could be reprogrammed to a positive charge. This would resolve the many arbitrary conflicts that seem to plague the ego's version of reality. Reality would then be a perfect expression of Divinity that radiates unconditional love for all of eternity.

14. Why do many egos claim to understand the Bible, but then when asked specifically about a matter, they divert to another issue?

The Bible, or the various transcriptions and points of view about what Jesus said or taught, comprises many fallacies. The error comes not from Jesus, but from the varying positionalities of the beings who attempted to transcribe Truth onto paper. If one chapter, or book of the Bible, was 100% correct, another written version by anyone else would not be needed. But many beings tried to keep a record of what happened at the turn of that millennium, and unfortunately these stories differ, sometimes greatly.

Beyond the ordinary, Jesus spoke within the Unmanifest context, which was very confusing to the common ego that attempted to understand. The fact was that Jesus spoke a very high level of Truth; however, the egos who tried to rationalize and make logical an irrational and illogical matter just distorted pure Truth into a lesser truth. Jesus spoke in parables, because Truth can usually be conveyed the easiest in that fashion. A high-level sage often cannot speak in an understandable way to an ego. The degree of understanding depends on the level of consciousness of the being who is trying to comprehend that Truth.

To the ego, an enlightened being speaks in riddles; however, to an enlightened being, the ego speaks and is an illusion that cannot comprehend Truth, no matter how hard it tries. On the other hand, an enlightened being can speak in parables to another enlightened being, and a full, comprehensive conversation would take place without an ego understanding one word. This is due to the ego's limited comprehension and the fact that the ego is illusion and can only understand that which is illusion. Truth to an ego is nonsense (non-sense). So Truth may sound foreign or incomprehensible to the ego, but is still every being's essence and reason for existence.

15. Why do egos refer to God as a He?

Egos only understand beingness in terms of gender. They do not understand nongender. The merely apparent existence of gender actually reinforces the dualistic relationship between an ego and other egos.

Jesus understood this; therefore he shaped the Truth to an ego's intellect for easier comprehension. If Jesus had said that God was just infinite Unmanifest potentiality, egos would not have understood. Back then, egos implicitly knew that the father figure was the provider. Therefore, since God is the ultimate provider (the creator), God was labeled as 'He.'

Due to the use of the ego's gender controlling 'He,' many religious leaders have now confused Jesus' form as that of God, and both are now thought to be "He's." And with that, many believe Jesus to be God because he is a 'He' as well. This is because religious followers have seen a man do miracles, not the Unmanifest power of God flowing through him; thus belief has been misplaced onto Jesus when it should have remained on God. Just the same, no enlightened beings have any power. They simply are a pure channel for Divine Will, which may manifest as the seemingly miraculous.

The Truth, however, was misinterpreted. The beauty and Truth of Jesus was not in his gender, the path he led, the miracles he performed, or the way he died; instead, the beauty was within him as Divinity, or the radiance of God. This beauty was genderless, formless, and undetectable. Just the same, all beings have the same undetectable nature of Truth.

16. What did Jesus mean when he spoke of the "broad and narrow paths?"

The broad path is the refusal of God, and the narrow path is the acceptance of God. The broad path has many roads that are the different ways to deny God's love, such as pride, shame, guilt, hatred, giving into the various pleasures that tempt the ego, and the very basic structure and nature of the ego. So whether to choose the pleasures of having sex, doing drugs, thinking, being prideful, hating someone, stealing, or just having a negative attitude is denying God's love and replacing it with the temporary happiness that is thought to be acquired externally by the ego. So basically, choosing ego will over Divine Will is the broad path, for there are many ways to sin.

The narrow path has only one option, and that is to be a vehicle of Divine Will by transcending the ego, thus serving God as an expression of love, compassion, and peace. To sin is to elect to go back to the broad path and to deny God once more. Constantly to choose Divine Will is to remain ego-free.

17. In Matthew 13:13, Jesus states, "Through seeing, they do not see; through hearing they do not hear or understand" (NIV). What is meant by that?

This means that the physical eyes cannot see, the physical ears cannot hear, and the ego mind cannot understand. The Unmanifest Truths cannot be perceived by the rational, logistical, dualistic, and linear ego mind, and the ego's way of perception cannot perceive that which is formless and unperceivable.

This was Jesus' way of stating that the ego mind is not

capable of understanding the Ultimate Truth. Furthermore, the following verse states, "People's hearts have become calloused, they hardly hear with their ears, and they have closed their eyes. Otherwise they might see with their eyes, hear with their ears, understand with their hearts" (NIV). Here Jesus states that man's heart is closed and unloving due to its self-serving purpose. To choose to be self-serving is to deny God's Love. So people's hearts were calloused by the denial of God's Love that was initiated by choosing ego will. The ego is what blocks Truth, which is Love, and reinforces the illusion.

Similarly, in 1 Corinthians 8:2-3 it is written, "The man who thinks he knows something does not yet know as he ought to know. But the man who loves God is known by God" (NIV). This means that the ego mind cannot know God because the ego's linear structure and interpretive abilities can only know form, not formlessness. It is important to note that only the ego claims to know God, but the enlightened being is an expression of God as love and Truth.

And when the Bible states, a "Man that loves God is known by God," it means that to know love is to know God, because God is love; and vice versa. So transcending the ego, the illusion that keeps one from knowing unconditional love, allows for the Self to shine through, thus revealing one's source (God) as Truth, which is peace and love.

18. Does the Bible reference anything on impermanence, of which the Buddha spoke?

The verse 2 Corinthians 4:16-18 states, "Therefore we do not lose heart. Though outwardly we are wasting away, yet inwardly we are being renewed day by day. For our light and momentary troubles are achieving for us an eternal glory that far outweighs them all. So we fix our eyes not on what is seen, but on what is not seen. For what is seen is temporary, but what is unseen is eternal" (NIV). This clearly states that the world of form is withering away, so one should focus on the formless, or the Unmanifest (permanent). This act of faith brings one karmic merit, love, and peace, which are all properties of God.

19. In the Bible, where does it state that God loves all beings the same, no matter what the sin?

Many scriptures in the Bible state that God is unconditionally loving. The statement that proclaims God is 'unconditionally loving' shows that God cannot and will not judge anyone for their sins, therefore implying that God loves all equally, with no exceptions.

The ego is incapable of understanding what unconditional love is due to its very nature, which is to judge and compare all things. The ego does not know how not to judge; therefore it feels as if God must be a being who has a higher capacity to love, but still judges. This makes the ego believe that God must hate sinners and love the righteous. But in Matthew 5:45, Jesus states of God, "He causes the sun to rise on the evil and the good, and sends the rain on the righteous and the unrighteous" (NIV).

Even though the Bible states many times directly and in parables that God loves all unconditionally, the ego still seems to think differently. Many religions create a competition of who is the most spiritually advanced, which by an ego's standards is believed to show who God loves more, when in essence God loves all equally and provides love to all equally. Only those who transcend the ego can completely feel this love. All others will continue to judge everyone else consciously and subconsciously, making them feel as if God only loves and selects some beings for heaven, while damning the rest.

20. Can you explain what the ego mind is?

The ego and the mind are self-identical. The term 'ego mind' is used to clarify the difference between that and the Unmanifest and Aware Mind. The ego is an illusory program that believes that it is a separate being with its own identity. It is basically an illusory thought, nothing more. To understand 'ego mind,' it is important to understand what Universal Consciousness is.

The *Universal Consciousness* (transcendent God) consists of the many levels of consciousness from the lowest to the highest (please forgive the use of duality). Analogously speaking, the transcendent God can be climbed like a ladder of frequencies, from the lowest (form and ego) density to the highest (formless and Self). Any being's mind is simply a program that can be reprogrammed at any time to be a product of any level of consciousness. So a being can choose by 'will' whatever level of consciousness they currently desire to be a part or an expression of. In essence, then, the ego is a faulty belief pattern that creates a false focal point of existence, which reinforces its perception of its self as a separate and unique identity. In other words, it believes that it is somewhere that it is not.

To sum up, every being chooses what level of consciousness to operate at and where to believe they currently exist. This level of consciousness that they choose to exist in is expressed as various character traits, which shape the identity that they feel to be their own selves. As an ego chooses the reality that it currently perceives, the energy becomes condensed and therefore denser. As the energy becomes denser, the ego lowers its level of consciousness into the denser realities. If a being chooses Divine Will and bypasses the temptations of the ego will, however, the higher frequencies or less dense energies are selected to express as their reality. So as higher frequencies (love, peace) are chosen, that being raises in their level of consciousness, thus bypassing the perceived realities of form (lower levels of consciousness) and becoming Light rather than solid form.

21. So then, what exactly is consciousness?

The 'Transcendent God' is the universal consciousness. It is the totality of all universal karma, which comes in a variety of frequencies that makes up the various levels of reality that one can climb up or down (so to speak). It can more properly be connoted as a selectable reality that any being can choose to exist within and as, thus providing their concurrent experiences thereafter.

'Pure Consciousness' (Higher Self) is the highest level of form that is capable of recognizing form. It can be said that consciousness is an energetic structure that is capable of interpreting the various frequencies. Remember, that which is form is capable of recognizing only form. Consciousness allows for realities to be experienced as such. Only the Unmanifest, which is beyond consciousness, has absolutely no distortions.

22. If there wasn't a physical dimension, where would we be right now?

All egos would be existing in the astral dimension at the corresponding level of reality that was shaped by their karmic propensities or current level of consciousness. A being will feel the astral reality to be as real as the physical; there will be friends and real-feeling situations. Family, birth, and death, however, are purely physical world situations.

An enlightened being, though, would exist within the Higher Self and be aware of the Unmanifest; since they have bypassed all of the games and entrapments of the ego mind, they are not subject to any of the astral influences.

23. If families are only a physical world situation, then why do egos refer to Jesus as Son of God?

All beings who choose Divine Will over ego will can be properly known as a 'child of God.' These beings choose to reside within the light of God rather than the darkness of the ego. That phrase was created to help all egos realize that they are all allowed to be 'children of God' if they just choose to.

The term 'children' is used because it is easier for egos to understand than an impersonal Unmanifest energy. Remember that God is impersonal because relationships can only occur between egos (dualism). After all, there is nothing to have a relationship with when there is only One. Since egos know God as the 'Father,' the concept of 'the children of God' is comprehensible and makes one feel closer to Truth and further from 'sin.' This sense of accomplishment in becoming a 'child of God' also helps to keep one on the 'right path.'

Religious leaders call Jesus the 'Son of God' because of the virgin birth. For if there were no human father, then God is it, the ego assumes. However, God did not elect to send someone to help out humanity. The earth was not being 'done wrong' by people. The overall level of consciousness of earth was in fact very low, but God has already supplied the loving energy of Truth for transcension <u>at all times</u>. So the world and its people did not need to be saved; it was just that egos needed to pick God over selfishness and sin. If beings were just to choose God over the ego, then all sin and suffering would be transcended. This allows one to feel loved unconditionally and infinitely when it is realized that God has always been there for them.

So God did not impregnate the 'Virgin Mary,' but rather Jesus, an enlightened being from another dimension who never had a name, nor incarnated before, chose to come to earth out of sheer compassion for souls who naïvely chose to suffer rather than to be in peace. Jesus chose to help earthly souls transcend their egos (sin); God is and always has been present, and has never neglected anyone, no matter what the circumstance. Since egos had chosen out of ignorance to live a 'sinful life,' it was not known that a peaceful life could be a reality, nor that God and happiness were just a realization away.

So it was seen, or falsely perceived, to be God coming to earth, but in reality, Jesus, who was One with God, decided out of pure compassion to help direct mankind to Truth, *that is love*—to elect to suffer in order to help other egos find love. Not one ego would truly do this out of their love for all beings and love for God.

24. When one is enlightened, is it possible to feel bad, irritated, or abandoned by God?

If one chooses an ego temptation, such as wanting to dream, leave the body by projection, psychically communicate, control energy with the mind, and other various nonharmful 'sins,' then that being, depending on the nature or intensity of the sin, may feel energetically imbalanced; at times this may feel as though they have been abandoned by God. As an enlightened being knows that they themselves chose 'ego will' over Divine Will, they clearly know that God did not punish them, but rather, they punished themselves by denying Truth once more.

It is important to remember that an enlightened being has transcended the ego, not destroyed it. So at any time, which is very unlikely by the enlightened, one may simply 'will' it so. The enlightened being knows that to choose the ego is to deny God's love that they experience every instant of their life. This is why it is so simple to deny temptations; it doesn't feel as if they are needed, or wanted. However, in some instances an enlightened being is tempted by a 'low-level' force, which may be called a 'demon' or 'satan/mara,' that tries to convert them into an ego. If an enlightened being fails to deny the temptations, the after-effects will be very undesirable. But if they deny the temptations, a new level of awareness is experienced, and thus they transcend to an even higher state of enlightenment.

If an enlightened being denies *all* temptations of the ego calling them back through never-ending desires, wants, and pleasures, they will become Self-Realized to the degree of an 'Avatar.' In essence, they will be the frequency of Jesus, Buddha, and Krishna while incarnated. This being is the 'Pure Mind' of the Universal Identity, the highest level of enlightenment that can be achieved in this earthly dimension.

25. I thought that enlightened beings don't sin?

There are many different intensities of sin. There are the

very energetically dense, lower-level-of-consciousness sins, such as hatred, lust, torture, shame, and so forth, and there are less energetically dense sins, such as 'willing' to dream or to think about the "what if I were an ego?" questions. Sin shows attachment to the ego that needs to be shed, for it only holds one back from further spiritual advancement.

So the sins that most egos feel are 'real sins' are those of murder, rape, molestation, abuse, abandonment, stealing, and terrorism. But the sins that egos do continually, which they themselves do not properly recognize as sin, are feeling pride, feeling ashamed of themselves or others, holding anger and resentment towards others, giving truth to their illusory self and physical body, believing in duality and the linear as real, not serving God and all beings, trying to control their family and friends, manipulating the business in which they work, not respecting other people's feelings, searching for happiness outside of themselves, not believing in God, not believing that we are all One, judging others for their appearance and personality, not respecting animals' or insects' lives, trying to fulfill the constant cravings and desires of the ego, becoming attached to the physical environment, becoming attached to the emotional and mental states, and believing in and reinforcing their ego identity. These are all sins. Now it can be clearly seen that all of society unknowingly believes that sin is a way of life that reinforces who they feel that they are. For without sin, the ego thinks that life would remain uneventless and boring, therefore convincing itself to deny God for all of eternity.

So in comparison, an enlightened being's sin is basically nonharmful to society, one's self, other beings, and the universal karmic resonance. If an enlightened being elects to leave their body by astral projection, it is to help other souls see Truth and to be freed from their own created hells. However, if the enlightened being caused the event by 'ego will' and not by God's Will, then it can clearly be seen that 'ego will,' which prompted the decisive action, was used. This may have been done to serve others, but the problem was that the ego decided to choose what to do and when to do it, not God. Since an enlightened being is still benefiting society and living life for others, the nature of their sin is more or less benign.

26. After one is enlightened, is that it?

Enlightenment denotes the transcension of the ego as the focal point of existence. As transcension occurs, one will not feel driven to increase in awareness unless Divinely inspired to do so. In this case, one may be inspired to write or teach. Many enlightened beings, though, right after transcending the ego, remain at the first level of enlightenment, which is within God's love and beyond duality. As one transcends the ego further, however, many different levels of awareness have the potential to be known. The *first level* of awareness, and the most common, is the transcension of duality that is reaffirmed by God's infinite love.

The *second level* is bliss, which is when God's love intensifies to an overwhelming extent. At this level of awareness, many enlightened beings are heard to proclaim that they are 'One with God' as the light of existence. They are heard to say, "I am," which denotes their intense feeling of blending into the finer energies of the Self, which provides for the manifest. They truly feel as if they are existence.

The *third level* is known by the enlightened being as the intense love shifts into a very profound peace that remains undisturbed in any situation. They often tend to be emotionless at first, but in time, they may seem erratic and uncontrollably joyful. They may shift from being still and quiet at a high level of awareness, but then suddenly get up and run around while laughing and playing with an animal, bug, or person. These beings usually teach others very high levels of Truth that are usually impossible for the average ego to comprehend. Because they simply are a very high level of Truth, it is in fact difficult for them to try to make information easy for the ego to understand. The latter stages of these beings' development bring forth the ability to bless 'things' and beings to a high degree. To be around them is to be blessed, but to receive a blessing from them is extremely uplifting and beneficial. Their energetic field continuously recontextualizes as it radiates Truth to all beings' ostensible problems. Many times, others feel at peace with life and self while with them. The *fourth level* of awareness that the enlightened being may go through is that of the 'Mystic.' Typically, many spiritual phenomena happen to them; these are seen as quite normal. For the average individual, sleep is quiet, but for the mystic, sleeping can be just like being awake, because their high level of consciousness stimulates dreamscapes, as well as prophecies, revelations, psychic experiences, and out-of-body projections. Sometimes dreaming may seem more energetically involved than the awake state, creating an energetic imbalance in the moments after awakening. Even though the dream scenario is usually ignored, it is as if the revelations or insights within can be picked out with ease; thus they can decipher which is false, and which is Truth.

The *5th to 7th enlightened stages* are simply when one reaches 'Buddhahood,' or the Universal Identity. These beings are the highest essence of the Self in this worldly dimension.

27. How do consciousness and awareness differ?

Consciousness is the essence of the ego and the Higher Self that provides for the awareness of form. But without the Unmanifest Self (existence itself), which provides for consciousness, awareness would not be possible. Consciousness is an energetic structure that is capable of recognizing form, and the Higher Self is one's awareness of existence. So to be aware of the existence of form is to use the energetic structure of consciousness. As one raises in consciousness level, the Self becomes more revealed, thus increasing awareness. As one's awareness increases, the fallacies and lesser truths of the ego's limited awareness can be seen and known with ease, allowing one to be aware of the lesser truths and eventually be the Self as the Unmanifest, which is existence itself.

It is important to realize that as long as one is within consciousness, one is aware of their corresponding level of reality that they are attuned to, or 'are.' As one raises in consciousness, whether within the ego levels or Higher Self, one increases their capacity and capability of knowingness, which is the increase in awareness. When consciousness expands, awareness expands as well. They are basically synonymous with each other except for the fact that consciousness is what allows for awareness in the first place.

28. Jesus always stated, "I tell you the truth"; aren't there many different types of Truth?

The Truth that Jesus spoke of is the Absolute Truth; no other ego statements or realities are properly considered to be Truth. The egos of today judge physical events and perceptions in the manifest world and then label what is witnessed as truth, thus claiming that which did not happen as a fallacy. This basically means that egos feel manifest perceptions can be truth, which is false.

The only Real existence of Truth is God, or the Unmanifest. Because this Truth cannot be witnessed or perceived, it provides a difficult ground for ego comprehension and believability, and has created many adversaries of Truth who deny God and reject what Jesus said.

Only Truth can exist, because Truth is existence. And since God is infinite existence as light and love, Truth can now be seen as God, which "cannot not" exist. God is purely infinite existence, which is Truth as love. All information pertaining to the manifest dimension is not Truth, but instead a distortion that can be called 'lesser truth.' In actuality, there can only be Truth; anything that proclaims 'fallacy' to exist is denying Truth. For not only does this create a duality, but it would require one to prove that 'fallacy' or non-Truth (non-God/existence) exists. If one were to prove that nonexistence existed, it would be a complete contradiction. This proves that only one thing exists, which is existence, or God (Truth).

29. What is an easy way for one to overcome the 'selfishness' that is inherent in the ego?

It is actually a very simple process. One must just do integrous 'things' for others out of one's love for God. At times it may be hard for one to remember that others should be served first, but a simple tool that will help to keep one aligned is the saying, "Serve others first, then myself." This will help one overcome selfishness and enjoy the process of helping others first.

The only reason for the difficulty in helping others first 100% of the time is that the ego is not used to this type of thinking or action. The ego has always been self-serving, so this new concept tends to instill fear within it. One of the ego's purposes is to make sure that one survives; therefore, it is only familiar with taking from others and thinking about itself. The ego feels that if it doesn't take care of itself first, it dies. Also, the ego thinks, "That sense of security isn't felt by helping others succeed."

One needs to keep in mind that fear may be felt initially. However, it will pass, to be replaced by a feeling of fulfillment and satisfaction. For every 'good deed,' one's level of consciousness will increase. A 'good deed' is never wasted, even if it looks as though the being whom one has helped doesn't care much. The 'good deed' that one performs has the power to shift their level of consciousness to a more positive one. Remember that only 'good' comes from helping others, even if one doesn't get the result that they were hoping for.

30. Can you explain in greater detail the reasons why the ego cannot see into all dimensions at once?

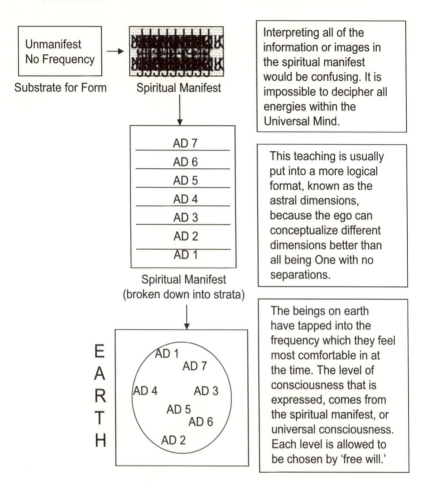

Unmanifest
No Frequency

Substrate for Form

Spiritual Manifest

Interpreting all of the information or images in the spiritual manifest would be confusing. It is impossible to decipher all energies within the Universal Mind.

AD 7
AD 6
AD 5
AD 4
AD 3
AD 2
AD 1

Spiritual Manifest
(broken down into strata)

This teaching is usually put into a more logical format, known as the astral dimensions, because the ego can conceptualize different dimensions better than all being One with no separations.

E
A
R
T
H

AD 1
AD 7
AD 4   AD 3
AD 5
AD 6
AD 2

The beings on earth have tapped into the frequency which they feel most comfortable in at the time. The level of consciousness that is expressed, comes from the spiritual manifest, or universal consciousness. Each level is allowed to be chosen by 'free will.'

A being 'wills' the level of consciousness that is allowed to be used for their current existence; this accounts for their level of consciousness. To perceive all stimuli in all dimensions at once, however, would not be pleasurable. Imagine experiencing all of the 'hells' and the 'heavens' simultaneously for all of eternity. This experience would be undesirable for anybody. It would simply be too much information to perceive and interpret at any given time. If one believes differently, they are under yet another delusion.

The diagram above illustrates that the mixture of all energy inherent in the Spiritual Manifest is actually how the universe is. All frequencies are actually superimposed over one another. The overall comprehensive compilation shows the various levels of consciousness that are a direct reflection of universal karma. To be an expression of the entire universe as a locus within existence would resemble the most insane being imaginable, but the word 'insane' cannot really describe it accurately. It would be something that no being has ever seen before; that being's level of confusion would more than likely confuse others just by karmic contact. It would be a nightmare to witness and the 'worst of hells' that one could possibly experience.

So the real Spiritual Manifest has been segregated into levels, from higher to lower, delineated by the inherent level of consciousness that is grouped by the frequency that it emits and is. In so doing, the manifest levels of the spiritual were made comprehensible by the ego due to its linear structure. And due to the faculty of 'will,' a being can simply elect the level of reality they would like to experience. What a perfect gift from God/Universe. So the ability to experience one frequency or level of reality at a time is a gift, not a disadvantage. Psychics cannot see into all dimensions at once, but rather, they have become more familiar with a method that allows them to experience the various levels of reality and the beings within them one at a time (known as 'tuning in').

31. What is meant by looking for wisdom within?

Typically, it has been taught that the Higher Self is the outermost layer of the energetic field, meaning that it is the border (so to speak) of the manifest and Unmanifest. Just the same, the crown chakra, which connects with the outermost layer of the energetic body, is said to be one's connection to higher consciousness. This is true because the crown chakra runs at the highest frequency, making it easier for one to connect with the Higher Self. Unfortunately, this has led many to believe that it is the only way to connect to the Source, thus leading the masses to confusion.

The previous belief contradicts the fact that God's Presence is infinite and ever-present. It would lead one to believe that the crown chakra and the outermost level of the energetic body are the only way that a being can connect with the Unmanifest. By noting that all of the manifest stems directly from the Unmanifest, it can be seen that one must just trace back one energetic manifestation to connect with God, no matter what it is. The following illustration will clarify.

If there were dualistic stopping points, All would start and end with God as the Unmanifest.

God as Unmanifest→which allows for Consciousness→ Physical Universe→Galaxy→Solar System→Earth→ Population→Individual Person→Organs of Person→All Cells of One Organ→One Cell from All Cells of Organ→Cellular Structure of Cell→Molecules from Cell→Atoms from Molecules→Sub-atomic Particles that come off Atoms→ Subtle Energetic Light from Subatomic Particles→Subtle Energetic Sound that allows for Subtle Energetic Light→Consciousness that provides for it→All that is superimposed upon **God as Unmanifest**

So if one connects to the Source, one connects to All that is within consciousness and the manifest. All seems to be in a complete, full circle of existence. The Source provides for All. (not 'cause and effect')

Just as many beings imagine the biggest 'thing,' such as the 'physical universe,' and then say "God encompasses that and beyond," many forget to do the opposite. They always seem to trace the smallest to the largest 'elements of life' to connect with God because they feel that infiniteness implies infinite 'bigness.' However, one should also attempt to find the Source of the smallest energetic element within existence. One needs to realize that God not only is infinitely 'Big,' but also infinitely 'small,' which is one and the same. Whether one traces the Source by following the increase in size, or the exact opposite, God is there as the exact same Source. As soon as one traces one element to the Source, which is Unmanifest, one connects with the infinite Presence of God.

So if one were to meditate on the smallest energetic spark of existence and then trace it back to the Source, God would be the connective, life-giving substrate. To do this, and then sit in meditation with **breath awareness**, would directly connect one to God, allowing revelations to flow forth at an increasing rate. Exactly the same, one may trace the largest elements of existence and understand that no matter how big something is, God encompasses All.

So to look within is really an attitude that denotes one should trace all existence, as it is known to the ego, back to the Source. This is the direct connection to the Unmanifest source of knowingness; wisdom is within God only, and God is the Unmanifest that provides for All That Is.

32. How else does the ego enter our lives?

It may come through television and radio in the same way that it comes from one's mouth and intentions. So one must choose what type of 'will' is allowed into a household, at get-togethers, in one's car, at schools, and so forth. This cleverly camouflaged 'ego will' is wrapped up in a seductive and desirable package that many cannot resist. All sin seems pleasurable at the time, or in the 'heat of the moment,' but is looked back on with regret.

So with the obvious statements brought into awareness by the previous, one can see that the 'ego will,' which comes by way of television or radio, can negatively influence a family or relationship as well. Energy can be transported in a variety of ways, such as from the lower ego minds of the creators of a film, the actors within it, the content and context of the film, the station that is relaying or transmitting it into households, the commercials between the sitcom or movie, and the limited level of awareness of the viewer (a child or adult).

This 'ego will' then subconsciously affects any being who is near it, as well as the universal karmic charge. As this 'ego will' lowers the universal karmic charge, it lowers the karmic potential of all beings in existence who are still subject to the ego's manipulative coercion, leading to more 'sinful' beings who will have a more undesirable journey and greater difficulty in transcending the ego (sin).

So this would obviously affect the relationship of a 'couple' or a family adversely. Depending on the susceptibility of the ego viewers, there would more than likely be an increase in tension, fighting, irritation, rebellion, and anger. This would create the feeling that one wants to run away from the situation at hand instead of solving it, thus running away from trouble and not 'facing their demons.'

33. If Jack stole Jill's car, then how could stating that fact not be true?

Anything that happens within the illusory is still illusory. Since the concern is enlightenment, only the Absolute Truth is focused on as Truth. Therefore, only the Unmanifest is Truth, and all manifest events, situations, or things, as well as relationships are false.

So if the illusory identity of "Jack" stole the illusory identity of "Jill's" illusory car within the illusory dimension of the physical manifest, then where is the Truth? Since all concepts of ownership are false, then one can see that being 'sad' just because the car was stolen is a waste of illusory time as well. One must focus on the never-changing, formlessness of Reality that provides for the illusory reality of form and variability; this is Truth (the substrate that allows the illusion to be 'willed' by the various illusory beings within consciousness).

It still needs to be understood that Jack stealing Jill's car is within the distorted levels of truth; however, it is just not

Absolute Truth. There are the many fallacies of the ego's perception and positionalities that distort Truth into truth. The manifest can never be Absolute Truth.

34. Since the ego is the source of perception and positionalities, would one who transcends it then lose their ability to perceive?

On the contrary, perception becomes more intense and clear because awareness is now mixed in with the senses. Awareness brings forth the Presence of Divinity within All that can be perceived. Thus the experience of perception can be quite stunning and overwhelming. At times, one may overload with the profound love that shines forth from all that is created.

When the ego is transcended, perception is not relied on as much; however, it remains a part of one's being, but is operated by Divine Will instead of the lower energies. Because a being now lives in the Now, they no longer desire to see, hear, smell, or touch things. Instead, they enjoy an experience as it happens instantaneously, without anticipation or regret. The ego, which relied on the perception of its senses, could not enjoy existence unless it could perceive the world of form—for example, when a being feels sad because they just lost their sight or ability to be mobile. An enlightened being, however, relies on awareness, which is the very foundation of existence as beingness. To simply state 'I' denotes that a being had to be aware of its existence before the statement was made. So first awareness must be recognized as existence, and then the perception of the ego can be used to reinforce its positionalities and separateness, whether by thoughts, verbalizations, sight, touch, or the ability to exercise will.

While the perceptive senses of the former ego used to control reality, the Divinity of God that flows forth from the 'egoless' being now controls the ego, using it as a machine that relays the message of Truth, whether through speech, action, thought, Will, or expression. It could be said that the ego is now God's interactive tool that brings the light of the Higher Self to the lower dimensions of darkness.

35. Why do people have a hard time seeing all beings as equals?

The problem lies in the ego, whose main function is to judge and understand that which is different. This reinforces the ego's understanding of what is a property of itself and what is not, which reinforces separateness. This means that the ego judges all without exception in order to know its value or importance in this dimension of form.

Typically, the ego judges that which is 'small' or 'less intelligent' as unimportant and expendable. Just the same, the ego judges that which is 'large' or 'intelligent' as the most important. So after judging all 'things,' it feels that it knows what it should respect or revere as important and what can be killed or disrespected as unimportant.

To an ego, the being with the 'biggest brain' is the most important, and vice versa. This is why a person can say without remorse, 'You are the scum of the earth,' in effect to show inequality, where in fact they are still showing perfect equality. Just the same, humans will kill animals and eat them without remorse. They do not usually feel for, nor do they care for, any other beings besides humans, only themselves and maybe family, close friends, and family pets (in that order).

Since the ego is the program that is formatted with the linear rules of the illusory, it can be said that the most programmed ego is the most deceived, or believes the most in the lie. This is because the human ego has been the most programmed to believe that this manifest dimension is real, while animal egos are not certain what reality is or is not. For example, when an animal dreams, they do not know what was real and what was the dream. The same can be said when they leave the body or die. Judgment is a trained response to reinforce one's self-concept.

36. On the subject of consciousness, do all diamonds have the same consciousness level?

From the pure beginning of the manifestation process, yes. But where a diamond comes from and the people who have handled it make a big difference. For instance, if diamonds came from Iraq, they would obviously be charged with the 'ill-will' that currently flourishes in that country. However, if the diamonds came from a deeply spiritual and somewhat untainted place, such as the 'heart' of Sedona, Arizona, they would be charged with the higher energies that they were capable of handling. This is why spiritualists usually purchase crystals that have come from there, instead of most other locations.

37. What accounts for the limitation?

The ego is the source of limitation. It is a program that has been formatted to run at a certain level of efficiency. It is only able to do that which it has been programmed to do. All other options that are not programmed within itself are the limiting factors that hinder 'free existence.'

The ego should be looked at as a computer game that can only do what it was programmed to do. Just because it is an impossibility for one program does not mean that it is an impossibility for another. Some programs are set to have learning impediments, others to have crippling diseases, while some are Olympic athletes who are breaking new physical records. So it can be seen that the only limitations are what one puts upon themselves (usually before incarnation).

As the ego is transcended, the source of limitation is disbanded and seen for what it is—an illusion. For example, Jesus broke the linear rules that limited other egos, such as raising a person from the dead, or feeding a crowd of 5,000 with two loaves of bread and two fish.

Those with the wisdom to transcend the ego become that very essence of God as Unmanifest—limitless and infinite.

38. Is any program possible?

Yes. One can assume any type of programming, but only if they are 'willing.' Such is the case with 'feral children,' who are children raised by animals.

There is a famous case of a Ukrainian girl, known as Oxana. She was neglected by her alcoholic parents; thus, for many years, she lived outside with the not-so-well trained family dog. Here she learned how to speak, eat, and fend for herself just like a dog in the wild. She also crawls on all fours while running, jumping, and urinating. After a long run, she pants to cool herself off while lying in the dirt or under a tree. If thirsty, she chooses a puddle on the ground over a water faucet. When she gets angry, she barks, growls, and then bites. To her ego, she is a dog and nothing more. She does not know the concept of being a human.

39. Why is it said that no one can 'become' enlightened?

It is simply because everyone already is, although in the higher aspect of Self. Each individual is All as beingness. This means that they would be the utmost bottom level of consciousness, as well as the top and the levels in between. However, one is simply a reflection of the level of consciousness that they have chosen. This can be likened to a bug in water. It may swim to the top or to the bottom, but wherever it goes, it is still a part of the whole. This is similar to the astral dimensions, which are separated into various levels by the ego to ease comprehension. Imagine one's self as a point on a chart that can go up and down at will. The 'point' is one's immediate reflection of consciousness, but the astral dimensions are what one is within the illusion as a whole. So choose wisely. To transcend the ego and consciousness itself is to transcend the astral dimensions as well, and to realize the Unmanifest Self.

So how does one become something when they already are it? A being does not think that they are enlightened, because they are operating at a lower level of consciousness with the restrictions and limitations of the ego that will not allow them to see the Truth in this fashion. So the Higher Self, which is a part of one's beingness, was simply not selected for the focal point of that being in their current existence, but rather, the ego was. This makes a being believe that they are not enlightened and must become enlightened in order to say so.

The Self is enlightened, but the ego won't let one know. This is why one is said to transcend the ego in order to *realize* that one already is enlightened, hence the use of the terminology, Self-Realization. It is all just a matter of 'will' or 'Will.' To adopt to the higher Truths is to 'Will' to realize one's True nature. To stick with the egocentric and selfish ways of the ego, however, brings forth suffering in the world of form and sin.

40. Why does enlightenment take so long?

What measure or extent feels long to the ego? Whether enlightenment takes 1 day, 1 year, or 100 years, it is still not a lengthy journey compared with a soul's average manifest existence (this is said in respect to the seemingly individual perspectives, not as the universal whole). A soul has existed within the manifest state of the ego for many thousands to millions, maybe even billions, of years.

The ego views this period as long because its current lifetime memory is only familiar with the average human lifespan of 60 to 100 years. So anything that may take 60 to 100 years seems to be a waste of time and a ridiculous journey. The ego justifies this feeling by stating, "Why choose the path of enlightenment? I don't know if it even is possible; and if it is, I will more than likely not accomplish it in this lifetime." This defense mechanism is obviously the fear of the ego becoming resolved, so it justifies the only answer into a seeming illusion.

Even though, historically, it has taken one many lifetimes to accomplish the goal of enlightenment, with the Truth that is present today, it would not be uncommon for one to become enlightened within less than a year, or possibly a few months. Time really cannot tell, for all that is truly needed is one's complete surrender of the self to the Source due to one's love for existence, which is Truth/Love/Peace. If this is present in one's being, then no study is even required. However, the ego will trick itself into believing that it has surrendered it-self to God, when it really hasn't. Just the same, it will trick itself into believing that it loves God unconditionally, yet there may be one thing in its past that the ego blames God for.

Due to the uncertainties, many beings actually start on the path to test it as a trial. Then, with time, when the methodologies have been proven as Truth, enlightenment becomes one's chosen path till the end of their days. It only takes one profound revelation to transfigure one's 'beingness' within this ego existence into pure Divinity, changing one forever into a pure channel of Divine Will as an expression of the Higher Self.

41. How does one motivate themselves to pursue the path of enlightenment?

Motivation is a product of the ego. To motivate is to bring forth the intense drives and desires in the ego to acquire external material gains that are thought to bring satisfaction. It can be seen in a court of law which motives the ego has acted on to obtain a material object, mostly money. So egos who claim to be inspirational speakers, who get people to take charge of their life and make money by selling real estate, creating pyramid businesses, having a better sex life, and so forth, are really just ego motivators.

Inspiration, on the other hand, is a powerful catalytic source of energy that brings forth positive change and creates a yearning for more, but only out of the pure love that one has for God. So merely to love God/Truth/existence brings forth inspiration and positive change. To search for Truth, to be an expression of Truth, and to devote one's life to Truth are the ultimate in inspiration. Not only will one be inspired to act constantly within the spiritual laws of Truth, they will help others to become inspired as well. The ultimate in inspiration is enlightenment.

Chapter 24
<u>In-Depth Explanations</u>

(Q) Could you explain duality a little more?

Within the word 'duality' lies the explanation. **Dual**ity is '**dual**,' meaning that there are two and not one. '**Dual**' can only refer to a **dual**istic or separated reality of the many. Within it, nothing can be unified or seen and known as One. By the very term 'indivi**duality**,' '**duality**' can be seen.

When one reaches the age when they are trying to 'find themselves,' they are really just using the ego to reinforce their 'indivi**dualism**.' This is not really 'finding one's self,' but rather, creating another identity that feels separate from others and the Source, that they think is real.

During the use of the ego's objective or external perception, it searches for material things that are not attached to itself or identified as one with itself. By the seeming separation, which is only witnessed as such by the ego's external perception, it then labels everything with a 'title' that it feels best expresses its reflection of energy. And the next time the item is witnessed by the ego, the mental label is then 'thought of,' which reinforces the seemingly separate reality.

Throughout time, many separate 'things' have thus been experienced and labeled based on the ego's limited perception. Within that limited range of frequencies that it can perceive, the ego then labels the highest and the lowest of the frequencies as real, and that which is not experienced or perceived as 'false' or 'imaginary.' So the ego, which relies on its dualistic mode of perception, has actually persuaded itself to believe that nothing other than what it can experience or perceive is real. This programs the mind to believe only in that which can be perceived (form) and to ignore that which cannot (Unmanifest).

And as the physical dimension is witnessed as heavily entrenched in dualism, it reinforces the ego's feeling of separateness with every thought (the thinker and the thought about), action (the actor and that which was acted and that which it was acted to), and beingness itself (believing that the ego is a being also brings up the dualistic opposition that nonbeingness is a reality). So all of the perceptions (ego) that can only interpret that which is separate from the individual are witnessed as opposites and dissimilar.

The sun and the moon are two different expressions of energy, yet they are said to be opposites by ego-based society. Just the same, light and dark are said to be opposites, but the light of consciousness comes in ranges that the ego can neither comprehend nor perceive and interpret. The ego, which is restricted by its very nature, cannot perceive all frequencies. So it can only label that which is within its perceptive range and nothing else. It is no wonder that the ego cannot know of anything that it cannot perceive, although it may 'think' it does. This is why the ego cannot know God; God cannot be perceived because God is not external, linear, manifest, or dualistic.

The various concepts that were created by the ego have entrapped and enslaved it into a delusional state of existence in which it believes that everything is separate and not One with itself. And unfortunately, these dualistic concepts are observed throughout its perceived reality of the manifest. So when the ego goes outside and sees the 'light' of 'day' provided by the 'sun,' it automatically knows of the 'dark' of 'night' in which the 'moon' can be seen. So the dualistic concepts that are an ego's beingness actually keep it from knowing the Source and prolong its existence in the manifest environment, which was 'perceived' and 'labeled' by the ego as separate and different, reinforcing its notion that everything is not connected in any way. This is why it is so hard for one to abandon the dualistic beliefs that seem 'real': because they are witnessed as real by the perceptive faculties of the ego, and are everywhere around it in the manifest dimension that it is currently operating within.

Some basic dualisms are as follows:

Knower and the known
Thinker and the thought of
Reader and the read, or that which it was read to
Writer and the written to, or written on
Seer and the seen
Doer and that which was done
Feeler and the felt
Speaker and that which was spoken of
Eater and the eaten
Drinker and that which was drunk
Listener and that which was listened to
Walker and that which was walked to, or walked on
Smoker and that which was being smoked
Existing and that which one is existing within
Existing and nonexisting
Love and hate
Peace and war
Acceptance and nonacceptance
Emoting and that which was emoted (emotions)
Sky and ground, or sky and nonsky
Friend and nonfriend
Girl and boy, or man (male) and woman (female)
Projective and receptive
Hot and cold
Light and dark
Moon and sun
Day and night
Birth and death
Manifest and Unmanifest
Skinny and fat
Glossy and flat or matte
Light and heavy
Shiny and dull
Rough and smooth
Clear and occluded
Fuzzy and nonfuzzy

Pointy and round
Force and that which was forced, or where it was forced to
Acid and base
Clothed and naked
Fish and bird
Hairy and bald
Tall and short
Large and miniscule
Strong and weak
Linear and nonlinear
Judger and that being judged
Separateness and oneness
Few and the many
Chaotic and controlled, orderly and disorderly
Visible and invisible
A specific color and that which is a different color

Even the nature of speech portrays 'dualism.' For example, when one speaks of the past, they must know of the future. Just the same, this would help one place in that 'timeline' when the present or the next few moments would be. As one describes their life, they often reference past, future, and current experiences that they have been through, for example, by saying, "I ran to the grocery store to get some apples." By stating "I" in their speech, they are trying to divide the experiences that they have had from all others. So to state "I" also means being dualistically split from everyone else, as well as the Source. To say that they "ran" would clearly show that it was a past event that is not current or future. So the ego, which presents its experiences to separate entities, would have to know what the past, future, and present (linear measurements) were in order to decipher the differences to explain it accurately to others.

The following examples will help to clarify this further: "Will you eat the apple," "I ate the apple," and "I am eating the apple." These statements clearly show the ego's use of words to explain future, past, and present actions, respectively. So does the delineation of time and chronological order, since the ego also feels that it must proclaim its independence and separateness by stating that which it has just done or is about to do. The very delusional thought of being separated from the Source and all others is what spawned this type of dualistic speech in the first place. As one transcends the ego, their speech may remain the same, but the meaning is profoundly different. In the enlightened state, one may not ever speak again because there is seen to be no need to language such fallacy.

(Q) Why are the many forms perceived?

All forms are simply a frequency that feels to be a reality that can be witnessed by a type of perception (the ego), which is able to interpret and understand a specific range of frequencies. So without the ego, which perceive these frequencies in the manifest as real, one would not perceive the frequencies I this way and would therefore experience a completely different type of reality that the ego in the physical has not yet even thought existed.

The ego can be compared with a piece of scientific equipment that is able to detect radio waves. It can only detect that which it is able to detect, and all else is not received by the device. So one who is tuned into the radio would believe that only what is heard or detected exists and that which is not detected is nonexistent. The truth of the matter is that there are many frequencies that the device will pick up and many that it will never pick up; the latter frequencies are simply out of its range. If the hardware components of the device were upgraded, a whole new range of frequencies would be picked up and realized to exist, in addition to the other frequencies that were already perceived. Thus one's awareness would be expanded into a new range of frequencies and one would experience a different aspect of reality that they had previously blocked out.

At a deeper level, one can realize that all form is simply a manifestation of the universal consciousness, which is itself a manifestation of the Unmanifest Self. So everything that can be perceived is really just an aspect of the Universal Mind that was willed into expression as a thought. Thus all form is a thought, nothing else. Clearly, then, for an ego to make the illusory claim that it has its *own* existence apart from the universe would be like one of an ego's 'thought forms' claiming to be apart or separate from that ego. This is obviously an illusion in which one gets to choose the part they would like to play, the 'thinker' (the Universal Mind) or the 'thought of' (the illusory ego mind). And as one transcends throughout the 'lower levels of consciousness' (the ego mind) to that of the Universal Mind, one then still needs to realize that they are beyond all thinkingness itself as the Unmanifest Self (no form and no thought).

(Q) Can you elaborate more on causality?

The theory of 'cause and effect' was created by not seeing the many influential factors that are 'behind the scenes.' As egos see an event, they naturally think about any physical influences or causes that have created that specific outcome. And because these egos are limited from knowing about any energies that are beyond their perceptive range, they believe that only physical influences determine the outcomes that are witnessed.

Similarly, 'white light' is the total and complete light that contains all frequencies that exist; it simply 'is' All light.' So when a frequency or color has manifested itself into a perceivable pattern of form, it is not caused by anything; it simply is another aspect of the 'white light' that has manifested into the realm of the perceivable. When egos witness actions, thoughts, beingness, or events, these are only attributed to that which is within the realm of the perceivable. However, all aspects of the 'white light' are just being expressed as the many frequencies that are manifesting as various aspects of existence, which are witnessed as coming from within the physical dimension.

Just as all of the 'perceivable' is an aspect of consciousness, all is an aspect of light because all light is consciousness. So all form is then just a reflection of its expression of energy as light, which is just another quality of consciousness; that is all.

And as the dualistic conceptualizations are now known to be an illusion, causality can be seen that way as well. This is because the caused and that which was causing the action are dualistic. There is no other to cause anything in Reality.

(Q) So what then of karma? Is it not causality?

It is actually not. Karma is simply the level of consciousness that one chooses to be an expression of that has its own qualities, which it simply 'just is.' If one is at a lower level of consciousness, the more they will display negative attributes and experience more negative events in their life. So when one is at a higher level of consciousness, they portray more positive qualities and experience more positive events. So the negative or positive experiences that occur in the physical are not 'caused' by anything. Instead, these qualities are just what one elects as their beingness. When one 'just is' positive, they can be nothing else but positive. They don't create or 'cause' positiveness; rather, they 'just are' it. Likewise, when one 'just is' negative, they didn't cause that expression of energy, they simply 'just are' it.

Fortunately, all beings have the option of 'free will,' which allows them to elect to be a certain expression of energy. Thus they are not 'causing' themselves to be another expression of energy; rather, they are just realizing that they already are the aspect of energy that was just beyond their previous perceptive range. And as the realization 'sets in' that they already 'are that,' then that aspect of their beingness is revealed. When the unrestricted, unlimited, and infinite Self is revealed, it is known as Self-Realization.

Because the ego can only perceive that which is form, rational, logical, or linear and dualistic, it does not know of the unseen karmic laws of the universe. Where the ego may think it has a 'clue' about karma, this is really just an idea that it has formulated and led itself to believe is truth. This is why all egos seem to believe that karma is 'cause and effect.' When one realizes the Self, all notions of karma are swept away as an illusion that had misguided them. Karma is then seen to be just what one is, a certain reflection of consciousness with specific restrictions that limit one's true 'beingness' from being known.

So if one were a rapist in a previous life, when incarnating into this lifetime, they would carry the same overall level of consciousness as in their prior life. The negative 'past deeds' did not cause them to acquire the negative karma, but rather, that same level of consciousness that they acquired in the past is still who they are in this current lifetime. So if they were to karmically have a negative life or perhaps be raped in return, they unknowingly asked for it by electing to remain at that level of consciousness, which is an expression of the lower levels of consciousness that bring forth suffering and pain. So their current level of consciousness is what unfolds in and as the manifest as their life progresses, not past 'karmic debt' catching up with them and 'causing' a seemingly negative phenomenon.

All reality is in the Now. There is no past. The 'past' is simply a mental concept that keeps track of the many experiences of the Now. As soon as the Now happens, it fades away as the newly experienced Now takes over. This is the simultaneous process of creation being always of the Now.

(Q) How can the created 'levels of consciousness' not be linear or judgmental?

The 'levels of consciousness' are referred to as 'levels' because this helps the ego understand something that is not logical, rational, sequential, or delineated by any means. The many 'levels of consciousness' are really just One superimposed and integrated whole that was dissected or taken apart by the seemingly different qualities of light. The levels are not above or lower than the others, although it is stated in this way to aid in comprehension. Because the ego cannot understand anything that is not presented in a linear fashion, the superimposed whole was split into many levels and termed 'higher and lower frequencies.'

Just the same, the levels of consciousness are usually separated and delineated into a descending and ascending scale, in which the higher frequencies are said to be more Truthful, and the lower levels of consciousness are then said to be various levels of distorted truth, known as illusion. And that which is completely distorted and in 'denial' of the Source is said to be fallacy. Obviously, one can conclude that the 'lower' levels of consciousness are heavily distorted truth and the seemingly 'highest' levels are the most Truthful. If it helps one understand the aspect of existence known as consciousness, then one may study the scale of consciousness that is presented in a vertical fashion. If this view of the scale brings forth judgments, such as which is 'better or worse,' then the scale can be inverted, or turned to the side. This way, there is no higher (better) and lower (worse), only left and right.

The separations were only shown to help the ego learn the differing qualities of consciousness that are within existence as One. This is no different than taking a whole human body and separating it by all of the differing qualities that it has, such as organs, bones, cells, and so forth. In Reality there are no separations, divisions, and/or differences, so there is no 'better or worse than' as applied to levels of consciousness. Rather, there are simply differing qualities of energy that can only be perceived by linear, dualistic, and illusory external perceptive means. Without the sense of perception, a quality of the ego, these levels of consciousness cannot be witnessed or even known to exist, unless willed to be seen.

(Q) The book is entitled 'The Ego Identity Crisis,' yet you speak seldom of any other type of identities that the ego may assume itself

to be?

This is simply because the ego is the only identity that creates and reinforces the separation between the 'seeming many.' All assumed identities such as 'doctor,' 'CEO,' 'muscle man,' and so on, are merely additional features of the ego that are used in order to reinforce the delusion of separateness. In a sense, these can be seen as the ego's defense mechanism, which is an identity attachment (assumed identity) over an already existing identity (ego—or the belief in 'being separate') attachment.

While the many identities that the ego assumes are indeed attachments, the only attachment is really that of the ego itself. When one reaches the 'final transitional point' where the ego is almost transcended, the ego is the only necessary relinquishment, nothing else. So the only actual attachment is one of the ego and all else is just additional, furthering the illusion and perpetuating the already negative condition of the 'lower self.'

(Q) What accounts for 'seeing' different energies?

While the ego is set up for an independently existing condition, in which it is able to 'see the sights,' this is merely because of the perceptive faculties that are a part of its beingness and interpret energy in that way, nothing more.

The ego's energetic structure is programmed to interpret certain energies. It cannot and will not interpret anything beyond its programming. But if the programming is changed, then a being's experience of reality will indeed be expanded.

(Q) So what accounts for the separated energies that are able to be seen and interpreted?

All energies in the universe, if seen as separate, are observed by an ego. The many energies that are being seen as separate are simply due to the manifestation of the universal whole (the totality of all beingness, emotional and mental states, and thought forms).

As the universal consciousness, the totality of all beings' conscious reflection (the one beingness), continuously 'thinks,' the many manifestations abound as seeming reality. They range from the realm of the visible to realms that are higher in frequency, which are visible to certain spiritual beings (at that frequency) but not to unattuned earthly inhabitants. So as the Universal Mind thinks (which is really just a collection of all beings' thoughts [which are from and of the One Mind] that 'gel together' as 'One thought'), creation ostensibly occurs. And that which is seen is noted as 'real' and vice versa.

All form is no more 'real' than if one were to look at a blank, white wall and mentally create an image. One may draw it if they wish, or just hold the image within the mind. Whichever means are acted on, the actual event of creation remains the same, where some energies are visible and others remain invisible.

All energies that appear as form are actually just random selections out of the infinite, unlimited whole. The ego mind just projects its own limitations on the infiniteness of the universe and brings this infiniteness to its own frequency by distorting the Truth (formlessness) into lesser truths (form) that are more comprehensible and operational. And without the quality of consciousness (which is the highest level of form), no form could even be registered, witnessed, or recorded and operated within. So no form would be detected at all; only infiniteness would be known and felt to exist as beingness itself, nothing more.

(Q) How does one practice being in the Now?

While operating in the 'world of form,' one cannot actually do that. This is because all form, whether visible and interpreted or just thought of, needs to be recognized by consciousness as being in the present. And as soon as it does that, it is the past. As soon as one thinks about being in the Now, the Now that it was thinking about is gone. It is impossible for an ego to be in the Now, because the ego isn't even in the Now itself.

To be in the Now, one must simply realize it as Self. This is done by transcending the ego, which distorts the Now into the past. In doing so, one transcends the 'thinkingness' that the ego just is, and one's true beingness is then revealed already to be in the Now as the Self.

(Q) If God is infinite, then why can't God be form?

Because all form is limited in some way; it may be restricted by size, shape, height, thought, etc... Only that which is not form is unlimited and infinite.

God as Totality is the manifest, the Unmanifest, and the aspect of existence known as consciousness. So God is truly All That Is. But the highest essence of God, whose quality is unlimited, unbounded, unrestricted, immeasurable, and unperceivable, is that of the Unmanifest. Because it is beyond form, it cannot be measured, perceived, limited, or restricted in any way. So this essence of God that is throughout all form, but remains formless, is that of Unmanifest Self, also known as **God as Unmanifest.**

Many egos want to believe that the Source (God) comes in form, so that they are comforted in knowing that a 'father figure' in some shape comes to greet them when they die and watches over them as they live. This 'family feeling' comforts them and also allows them to believe that God will interact and help them when needed (just like a parent figure). One must keep in mind that God is everywhere, in and as everything, and is existence itself, so there is no need for God to judge 'himself' in certain areas of 'his' beingness as imperfect or in need of a 'tune-up.' All is being expressed in a certain way because certain aspects of itself (egos) have 'willed it' so. So if egos ask for a certain type of reality to occur, then why would God intervene to stop it? This would also take a being who could recognize form (consciousness) and who judges everything it sees (an ego quality). ***God as Unmanifest*** is beyond consciousness itself, so it cannot even perceive any form, hear any requests (voice = sound waves/ form), judge anything that is form, have a viewpoint, have emotions, or have the ability to direct energy anywhere. How does one direct energy to somewhere when they are everywhere as everything?

One should keep in mind that all form is a manifestation of the Unmanifest and universal consciousness. But as soon as form manifests, Truth becomes distorted and no longer can be considered Unmanifest. When form develops, the linear, logical, rational, and dualistic realm appears and is clearly not 'nonform.' **God as Unmanifest** is pure and remains that way infinitely. But the many manifestations of the Self are indeed distorted and illusory, each to their own extent. So the God to whom most religions point in their sacred texts is the **Unmanifest Self,** or **God as Unmanifest**, and not the 'whole beingness' of **God as Totality**. Whoever believes that God created the universe must believe in **God as Unmanifest** being that Source of nonform potentiality and infiniteness (the Creator).

(Q) So how did the linear reality come about?

As the ego looked on the many manifestations in the realm of form, it judged the **space** between the many forms, the **distance** (length) between one form and another, and the **time** that it took to travel across space or from one energetic event to another (seconds, minutes, days, years, etc…). So linear measurements were simply an observation that were imbued in and integrated with a mental construct that helped the ego keep 'better track' of its environment and experiences. In essence, the linear system was really just an internal observation (judgment and viewpoints) that was made on an external observation (the world of form). And since form is an illusion, so are all of the observations made upon it as well.

(Q) Can you explain more about how the levels of consciousness are not linear and sequentially placed as better or worse?

In this physical universe, think of an endless number of radio waves that can be picked up and interpreted if tuned into properly. These radio frequencies are not above or below one another, even though their bandwidths differ; instead, they are simply superimposed over one another, as one 'set' that contains and is these many frequencies.

The levels of consciousness are much the same. One level is not better than another, just as one radio station's bandwidth frequency does not indicate that it is better than another. If one level is selected as more desirable than another, it is merely one opinion of one individual that was based on the use of a judgmental partiality. In Reality, there is no better or worse frequency; it is only seen this way by a judgmental being (an ego)—for example, if one likes radio station 93.5 and another likes station 105.1. This is obviously an instance where one finds one radio station (level of consciousness) more desirable than another. But clearly one is not better or worse than another; it is just an opinion.

Opting to stay in the realm of the ego while complaining about the negatively perceived conditions of manifest reality is like tuning into a radio station that one doesn't like and deciding never to change it. Therefore, from this analogy, one can conclude that a being only elects to stay an ego in order to complain about their various circumstances; while some egos complain daily, others do so seldom.

By this, one could analogously see that God is the backdrop in which the many radio waves are allowed to exist and express themselves without bias. Favoritism only exists in an ego's mind. This is similar to the Unmanifest as the backdrop for the universal consciousness. So one can see that without 'nothingness' (formlessness or God), the many 'things' (forms or illusion) could not be seen or experienced in any way. This is why form is visible. So thanks be to God for all experiences, as well as existence itself. Without God, no form would be perceived, no experiences had, no thoughts allowed, and no such thing as existence would even exist.

(Q) You stated earlier that 'feeling' is dualistic; so what is the difference between 'feeling' the enlightened state as love, peace, and happiness, and 'feeling' the ego's states of existence?

In reality, no one ever feels anything; instead, they simply are that level of consciousness that manifests as a quality that the ego labels as a 'feeling.' Egos then label these separate 'feelings'; because they experience so many emotional states, the 'labels' help them to express what they are 'feeling' in that instant of their existence, and also aid in recall.

The ego is under the illusion that it is a 'doer,' a 'thinker,' and a 'feeler'; so by this, one can conclude that it is merely an illusion to 'feel' anything. In actuality, they 'just are it.' One must keep in mind that they are just a channel of their level of consciousness, which expresses itself as a being selects what traits they want to portray. But as the ego thinks that it creates the emotions and thinks the thoughts, it is really only tricking itself into believing that it has control. In Reality, the ego has no control; it only thinks it does.

While an ego has the capability to 'feel' the many states that are within its realm of existence, an enlightened being is beyond all ego states of awareness and only 'is' what they are: peace, love, and happiness, which are one and the same. So the enlightened being doesn't feel a certain way; they are that way. This is their existence; their only expression is beingness itself. And it is not what they express; it is what they are. It will only seem like an expression to an ego because it doesn't know of any other way to understand it. The ego thinks dualistically: the 'thinker and the thought of,' the 'feeler and the felt,' the 'expresser and that which was expressed,' and the 'emoter and that which was emoted.' This obviously strengthens illusion.

All dualisms contradict infiniteness by creating the illusion of separation or 'the many,' and also deny one's True Nature as the Unmanifest. By this, the finite, fallacious, limited, restricted, sad, depressing, hateful, and unjoyful false existence resumes as 'real,' reinforcing the ego's existence and 'giving truth to the illusion.'

(Q) Why are labels developed?

To an ego, it must language its existence to better understand itself and other beings with whom it converses. 'Labels' are merely randomly selected energetic patterns that are applied to 'specific feelings' that the ego has in order to better understand and express itself in the linear dimension of time, space, and distance.

All 'labels' are actually distortions of the real Reality. But to an ego, they are the only way that it feels it can express itself. When a close approximation of expression occurs between the 'labels' and the 'meanings' that an ego is trying to convey to another, then language is developed and used as the proper means of conveyance. It is important to remember that 'labels' can only be applied to some other 'separate thing' that is dualistic and only of the ego's realm of existence.

Since the True Reality can have no labels (an energy structure or form), then the label 'God' is an illusion as well. How can one take that which is form and place it on the dimension of nonform without distorting nonform? That's simple; it can't be done. The Reality of the Unmanifest cannot be described, understood, comprehended, rationalized, felt, or 'labeled.' As soon as any of these ego traits are applied, the Truth (nonform) becomes distorted and manifest. Even to say the 'Unmanifest' or 'Truth' (labels) distorts Truth.

(Q) So if all 'labels' distort Truth, then why speak and teach others?

I don't have to speak; for me there is no need. But in order to bring the essence of the Truth to others, I speak. If one realizes the Self and never proclaims it, then no ego would ever search for such a Reality or, more accurately, try to realize it.

Words are expressed by an enlightened being in order to help others. This is not done because we want to 'hear ourselves talk.' Instead, out of our sheer compassion for all who suffer, we speak and try to express that which is inexpressible in an attempt to end all suffering and pain in the manifest. All enlightened beings truly feel for others; this is why they continue to teach and radiate the essence of the divinity. If one cannot speak, then they will bring forth the higher power by their very essence and prayer or intent.

If there were no egos to be saved, then no words would be spoken; all beings would be fulfilled as One, and no such thing as illusion would exist. Because egos naïvely hold onto the false dimension of the manifest, they elect to suffer. And due to the fact that enlightened beings know this, they offer help to all those who accept.

(Q) Who exactly created the dimensions of form?

God as Unmanifest provided and is the energy for creation, and the *universal consciousness* is what is expressed through frequencies, colors, and various forms. Creation is a universal process, not a 'cause-and-effect' scenario. So God did not 'cause' the world to be created and neither did egos. Creation 'just is;' it is and always has been a universal event. There is no start or end date for creation; it just infinitely has been and always will be.

But it should be understood that egos really just 'think' that the world of form exists. In Reality it does not. Because the ego is illusion, it sees, understands, and interprets only that which is illusion. And since all form is an illusion, it does not really exist. So there is no dimension of form. To say that there is would be an expression of the ego, which believes the world of form exists as real. Remember that an illusion is 'not real,' so there is no such thing as form in Reality.

(Q) So what then started the creative process?

To state what 'started' creation would then mean that there was a specific 'cause' that began the manifestation process. Since there is no 'cause and effect,' nothing 'caused' or 'started' the creation process. This would also create dualism, such as the 'beginning and end' or 'start and finish.' So obviously, it could not even be a product of the Unmanifest. Creation just always is, has been, and will be what the universe is. It 'just is.' It is an endless, as well as a beginningless, process.

The ego has a hard time comprehending this concept, because it can't. For this to be possible, the ego would have to know what 'infiniteness' truly is. And since this is only a quality of the Unmanifest, obviously the ego cannot know. This is why the realization of the creative process only becomes apparent to and as the beingness when the ego is transcended and the Self replaces theory with knowingness. Only an enlightened being at the higher states of awareness would be able to truly realize the infiniteness of creation.

(Q) From all of the suffering in the world, what is the main cause of irritation?

Expectation is the main cause of irritation (please excuse the dualism). This is because the ego expects the external world or egos to be, act, or speak a certain way. And when this doesn't happen in the way that the ego had mentally constructed, it becomes irritated at the other being, event, or situation.

Expectation is really the ego trying to control another being or event by placing intent, which is that of 'control,' on it. This is how the ego tries to conform the world to the mold that it has deemed acceptable. If anything does not conform to the mold, however, the ego becomes irritated and upset with that being and/or event.

Some examples are as follows: 'wanting a person to speak slowly and clearly,' and when this does not happen, the ego gets mad. Or 'expecting traffic to move fast and it moves slowly'; thus the ego gets upset with the traffic. Or 'wanting a person to be more compassionate.' Obviously, with all of these 'thoughts' that the ego had, it was really just trying to convince itself that the external environment was occurring just how it was controlling it to be. And when external events or persons do not conform to its mentally fabricated conceptualization, it then becomes irritated because it feels as if it is losing control. And as an ego feels as though it is losing control, fear arises, along with an identity crisis that brings up the question, "Do I really have control?"

(Q) You spoke once of a 'reality flux' or a refraction of the levels of consciousness. Explain?

While the frequency of physical light is lower than that of sound in the physical dimension, the frequency of subtle light is lower than that of subtle sound in the universal consciousness. Since it is beyond the measurability of scientists, they may never discover this. Instead, various theories may be cast as its replacement.

It is also important to keep in mind that subtle energy is a completely different type of energy than physical energy. The seemingly same 'light and sound' that are refracted are really just an illusory observation of two different types of energy with similar qualities. Keeping this in mind, the explanation will continue.

The effect of this difference seems similar to putting a pencil in water. While the top of the pencil that is out of the water is straight and its entrance point is known and obvious, the part of the pencil that is under the water shifts slightly and appears to bend as a result of a refraction (distortion) of light by the water. By this analogy, it would seem that at the level where the 'reality of the ego' and the 'Reality of the enlightened being' <u>meet</u> (the transcendental point), they actually change in appearance, frequency, and relationship to each other. It appears that the 'transcendental point' is the level that gives the illusion that the refracted energy shifts the appearance and locus of reality, just as the water refracts the light reaching the pencil.

By analogy, one could say that egos are living under the water, thinking that the 'bent and distorted' pencil is real, thus denying a higher reality that is just beyond their perception. It is important to keep in mind that we are discussing the dimension of form, so all refractions are merely observatory and illusory. This artifact of perception increases the ego's trust in the illusion and therefore can create believability in the distortion of the seeming reality.

Remember that the Reality of the Unmanifest is beyond all light, sound, frequency, and perceivability. So this observation and knowingness is still within the dimension of form and not to be trusted as Absolute Truth or as having the qualities of the Unmanifest.

(Q) If there is no such thing as 'chance,' then how do people win the lotto? Is that not chance?

There is no such thing as 'chance.' All happens of its own as a continuous creative process. Actually, the picking of the lotto numbers doesn't really matter. The ego doesn't pick the winning numbers, but rather, the universe picks the numbers in concordance with a being who is karmically deserving. So if one is supposed to win, they will win. But it is not up to the ego to deem who is 'ready to win'; it is a universal response. Just remember that the "ego doesn't pick the numbers, the universe picks the ego;" not as a personal selection, but karmic interaction.

(Q) I heard an enlightened being once say that there are no different levels of love; that

there is only one love because it is infinite; therefore implying that everyone that says differently is disillusioned. You express that love comes in many different levels, by your example and chart. What are your comments on this?

Each and every being has experienced a degree or quality of love. One cannot experience the infiniteness of love unless operating as the Higher Self, or enlightened. There is only One love, however, it is distorted by the ego of man and therefore experienced to that being's concordant level of consciousness. Thus, the veil of the ego covers up and hinders the experience of love as its Higher Self essence. So the ego can only experience its distorted version of love that it allows itself to feel.

One must keep in mind that the ego's job is to distort Truth, which is love. So unless one is enlightened, one can only experience the level of love/Truth that their ego allows them to. There is only one love, but the ego will only allow one to experience a certain degree of it. As one transcends their ego a little more, the experience of love increases for that being; thus, a more positive, happy, and peaceful feeling ensues.

If all beings experienced love at its unrestricted extent, we would not be discussing this because that question would never arise due to the Truth being known. The only reason why a being has to ask or state this is due to the fact that they are under a certain degree of illusion.

Love, like the Universe itself, has always been and is infinite. There are no boundaries for it and it is always accessible to everyone. One must simply choose to experience it by dropping the illusion that is consuming one's beingness. Just as the universe is infinite, but cannot be realized to be so until one realizes the Self, love is infinite, but also must be chosen to be experienced. Due to the fact that love and Truth is the same thing, one must transcend the ego in order to realize Truth, which is love. It is always infinite, but must be recognized as such before it is experienced as such.

(Q) Is it more beneficial to absorb Truth in silence, rather than in a meeting or a lecture?

If the ego were ready to surrender 'all that it is,' then yes. However, the ego is usually not that ready. In fact, the only reason an enlightened being speaks to an ego is because the ego needs to hear some 'proof' of why it should accept Truth in the first place. So the teachings of the Sage are brought down in frequency, or distorted to a degree, so that the ego can identify with the Truths that are being presented in a more logical, rational, and linear fashion. One cannot expect an ego just to absorb Truth in its Absolute essence; if that were the case, then all egos could be enlightened Now. So tell yourself, as you read this, "I want to be my highest essence. I surrender all that I think I am to the Source and allow Thy Will to flow through my being as an ever-present channel of God." Now, are you enlightened yet? Probably not. This is because the ego is just saying this with what it feels is sincerity and is making itself believe that it wants to transcend itself. Since the ego doesn't want to die, one can then realize that "feeling like you mean it," or 'being sincere,' doesn't mean much coming from the ego itself. An ego opting to transcend itself is an ego opting to die, permanently. So clearly an ego wouldn't really want this.

Enlightenment is a nonego reality. So the ego cannot be used to 'ask its way over.' The only way to really surrender the ego is to adopt the Higher Will and never give into the ego again. If the ego is not used, then the ego has no use and is not needed as the focal point of one's existence. So as a Sage speaks, the proper words are selected in order to convey the highest essence of Truth that the ego will accept at that time. And as the ego accepts various aspects of the Truth, a being then raises in frequency. As the frequency of that individual raises higher and higher, they not only express a higher frequency as their beingness, but they are also capable of realizing the higher Truths without having to be brought down in frequency as much by the Sage. So the lessons will progressively become more and more 'parable sounding' to other egos listening in, but clear to the ego being who has raised in frequency. So this book is very basic to a Sage, but not to an ego.

As the ego has raised a significant amount in consciousness, it then could just sit in silence with a Sage and absorb the higher frequencies. But that 'bond of trust' must be established first, before an ego could truly absorb the higher essence. If the ego did not fully trust the Sage, then the defense mechanism of the ego would 'fend off' the higher frequencies in an effort to maintain its survival as an ego. Only when one attains enlightenment will they fully realize that there is more Truth in Silence than in words. But this is foreign to egos, even if they say they understand. This is because the ego is form itself. So for an ego to say that it loves silence (nonform) more than noise (form) is absurd. This would be the ego wishing itself (form) to 'not exist.'

Just because the ego doesn't enjoy various noises in the external environment doesn't mean that it dislikes all form. In fact, many egos who claim not to enjoy external noises actually love to think. So really they are just creating their own noise inside their head (internal environment). They just prefer one type of noise to another.

About the Author

About the Author

Growing up in this physical dimension, Brian Nager has always been fascinated with the Truth. At a young age, he enjoyed conceptualizing about the meaning of existence and understanding the physical realm in which he existed. After he asked many questions, his parents bought him an "Ask Me Why" book in an effort to resolve some of his unending questions about existence.

As a child, Brian grew up with a Christian heritage, from the schools that were attended to the holidays that were celebrated. Even with this religious background, ever-burning questions remained for him that no one had yet answered.

In an attempt to have some of these questions answered, he asked the teachers of religion in his elementary school their opinions of his philosophical thoughts. Much to his dismay, the teachers could not give an acceptable answer. If the questions were too difficult, the teachers would just say, "Because that's just the way it is." In other words, they didn't know. They didn't even seem to have given it much thought. It was as though they had just accepted what others had taught them without scrutiny. Brian felt that he could just read the stereotypical religious books, rather than having a puppet parrot back to him what was already in them. So then it became clear to him that society was basically programmed with nearly the same thoughts and beliefs, at least in the regions that he knew.

As a result, Brian didn't feel that he could trust religion, preachers, or religious teachers. He also didn't see religion as 100% correct; instead, he saw many contradicting statements that were presented from various points of view that were somehow taken as pure truth by society. As a child, Brian viewed these preachers of religions as holy, because that is what he was led to believe by society. It wasn't until he started to compare the different truths that were expressed that the preachers were, in fact, found to be just as confused as he was. With this confusion in mind, he left the religious teachings that so many beings had become entrapped in, hoping to find Truth.

At this time in his life (8th grade), Brian had denounced all religions, but still believed in God. Luckily, he was about to be switched to a public school, instead of the private school that he had become used to. The new school brought many surprises, the first of which was that it had about a 65% minority attendance, differing greatly from about the 1% minority in his previous school.

This was actually the first time that he had truly realized that many different types of people existed in the world. The mannerisms, cultures, beliefs, and overall looks of the beings at his new school were completely different. This experience taught him that what one thinks about reality can completely change when one is placed in another circumstance with different surroundings. Unknowingly at the time, this helped him search for a way to express that all beings were somehow connected, despite their ostensible differences.

As the search for an alternate reality resumed, Brian unfortunately experimented with drugs temporarily in an attempt to experience something different. This was an internal prompting to see if it was as 'bad' or 'dangerous' as society had claimed. After experimentation with the first drug, he realized that what he had been led to believe was in fact not as bad as it had been portrayed; it just depended on one's view. This continual experimentation beyond the boundaries that were set by society led him to believe that there was indeed something more to reality, which the majority of society had not yet experienced or fully understood. It allowed Brian to make his own decisions and not to rely on other people's claims, no matter how insistent they were.

This experimental attitude led him to be more rebellious over time. When other beings told him not to do something, he ignored their advice and decided for himself whether the path was correct for him. Many times this led to the being who warned him responding, "I told you so," but the experience of the event was seen to him as the most important aspect of life. He did not care if he failed; to him, the most important part of existence was the experience of life, no matter what the outcome.

The use of drugs was obviously discarded due to its temporary high, which inadvertently increased one's feeling of depression when they were not being used. It was realized that drugs were not the way, which then prompted the next direction in the search for Truth. It was found in ancient Yogic studies and current metaphysical practices, which from his family's standpoint seemed odd and questionable, but to him seemed to be a breath of fresh air.

The journey actually began before he had even realized it, when his mother taught him how to breathe, visualize, and count to relax. She had learned this technique from her chiropractor. At the time, he saw no use for such trivial novelties, but as the years passed, he noticed that control and awareness of the breath was perhaps the most talked-about ritual that was said to lead one towards psychic development and possibly enlightenment.

Throughout the progressive and transitional years of his life, Brian noticed that metaphysics could train one to have seemingly great powers or abilities. This intrigued his ego, which then directed him in his path, the first being astral projection, the second being psychic development, and the final stage being inquiry and transcendence.

He enjoyed the metaphysical aspects of the spiritual life, which provided proof of an alternate existence, one of fewer restrictions, limitations, and boundaries—a world of infinite possibilities. He learned how to induce many spiritual phenomena through breath and other techniques, but as he progressed it became apparent that there was still a barrier of some sort. This barrier seemed to impinge on the level of happiness and peace that could be felt at all times. He had many astral projections and psychic experiences, but still he was not happy 100% of the time. This led Brian towards an avenue of spiritual research that he had earlier dismissed as false, or only for 'unskilled' and 'weak-minded' individuals.

As he shifted focus, he began to study many spiritual texts that seemed to have focused on simple details; the focal points in these texts were love and peace. He had wondered endlessly, "What could be the benefit of helping others whom I have never met before, or who have never helped me? What could I possibly owe them? Why?" Regardless of these thoughts, he pressed on and believed in God so much that he decided to love and help others, but out of his pure love for God and existence. After all, he thought, "I could still astrally project or induce psychic communication when I get bored with this." However, the life experiences that unraveled before him could never have been expected or prepared for. And through his search for enlightenment, the question remained in his mind, "What power does love have?"

After endless hours of study and meditation, he became so loving that he could understand an ant, or any other bug or animal. He began to also understand the reasons for suffering and how the mind worked. He felt as though he was beyond the world looking in and seeing how the world operated. The greater Truths of the universe didn't have to be researched; he just knew them as if he were them. It was as though an illusion had been lifted and the projector that had shown the movie of life was realized to be the source of existence itself. This wisdom came not from the knowledge that was studied, but from the revelations (egoless experiences) that revealed existence as Truth, which is God.

He no longer felt himself to be the previous identity that he had spent many years creating; instead, he was 'identityless' for the first time in his life, an experience that not many ever know. Through his devotion to help all others under any circumstances and to adhere to the Truth of existence, he did not *become* enlightened; instead, he *realized* that his True Self already was, has been, and was just ready to be recognized as one's Source, which is Self-Realization, known by egos as 'enlightenment.'

As the Self emerged, the once selfish, science-minded, materialistic, prideful, and knowledgeable, but suffering ego dissolved into oblivion and was realized for what it was: an illusion and the source of suffering itself. So the ego's traits, inherent in his being, withered away as the Truth shone through as love, which was no different from the Self. This revealed the True purpose for which all beings live: to become Self-Realized and merge back with one's 'Source' (God).

Brian's ego was previously programmed to dislike English class, but now he writes his own books. The ego was attuned for sports and bodybuilding, but now he works out just to be healthy and to live longer, only to carry the expression of Truth further. His ego used to drink with friends occasionally; now he is a vegetarian, and never drinks alcohol, smokes, or does drugs (legal or illegal). His ego used to care about what people thought of him, but now he expresses him 'Self' without care or worry about what others think of him. His ego used to worry about life and death; now he fears nothing and would be happy to die (return home).

The beliefs in duality and linear reality that were once thought to be true were also past ego traits that have been revealed as false. The past ego identity believed in helping out others sparingly, but now he travels many miles out of his way to help others without charge. His previous life centered around material and monetary possessions, but these are now seen as unnecessary.

These actions and thoughts are not forced, but simply expressed as what he now is. The changes in being did not take place within years, but instead within a couple of months.

By seeing the instantaneous changes that took place in his life, he now is a believer that anyone can change, but only if 'willing' to. Brian has now devoted his entire life to helping all others become Self-Realized. He speaks to individuals, as well as groups, about the process of enlightenment. He not only creates books that carry the frequency of Truth, but the Presence flows through him as a direct channel of Divinity. His only purpose is to help others understand Truth and merge back with the Source.

He understands that if he helps create 'inner peace' within all beings, world peace will become more than just a thought, but a reality. As all beings become enlightened, the Universal Reveal, or mass revelation on a universal scale, can now be under way. He states that all beings will have no personal karma, meaning that the universal karma can be dissolved like a tablet of illusion in 'pure' water. So it can then be seen that Universal Peace can become a reality, where the heavens uplift and the hells dissolve into infinite peace and love. Love is infinite; it just needs to be recognized as such. By this, love is allowed to heal and Truth allowed to reign.

—Jaron Krane (student)

Appendices

Buddha , Jesus, Krishna, 'this book' calibrates around here--------->

When enlightened beings become the Universal Identity (gold)---->

Less than 1 in 60 million beings are at this level of consciousness->

About 1% of egos are at this level of consciousness------------------>
Beings at the 'final doorway' (the last of duality)--------------------->
Limited level of peacefulness that the ego can experience----------->

A being that realizes God is Love and nothing else------------------->

Most Bibles resonate at this frequency--------------------------------->

Most psychic/spiritualists resonate around this level----------------->

Religious Minds are usually at this level of consciousness---------->
(About 8 to 10% of society are here)

A being that realizes God is mostly positive things------------------->

'Oprah Show' usually tends to calibrate around here----------------->

Trusts that reality will be alright when one releases control of it---->

A being that allows God to 'control' reality instead of itself--------->

Most egos are at this level of consciousness -------------------------->
(80% of society is at this level or below)

Egos that have a 'criminal mind' usually calibrate around here----->

Beings that are addicted to drugs, money, etc., are around here----->

Terrorist usually resonate at this level of consciousness-------------->

Most suicides occur when one is at this level of consciousness----->

Attributes of Levels	Identity Assumed	Color Stage
7th stage enlightenment	Universal Identity	Gold 3rd
6th stage enlightenment	Self as Purified	Gold 2nd
5th stage enlightenment	Self as Subtle Sound	Gold 1st
4th stage enlightenment	Self as Beatific	Violet 4th
3rd stage enlightenment	Self as Sage (peace)	Violet 3rd
2nd stage enlightenment	God's love intensified	Violet 2nd
1st stage enlightenment	Self as God's Love (One)	Violet 1st
Completeness	95% Giving & 5% selfish	Indigo 2nd
Serenity & Revelation	92% Giving & 8% selfish	Indigo 1st
Ego Peacefulness (limit)	90% Giving & 10% selfish	D. Blue 1st
Reverence & Respect	88% Giving & 12% selfish	L. Blue 1st
Unconditional Love	85% Giving & 15% selfish	Green 2nd
Love for Nature/Others	80% Giving & 20% selfish	Green 1st
Understanding Others	78% Giving & 22% selfish	Green 2nd
Love for self/Self	75% Giving & 25% selfish	Green 1st
Understanding self	70% Giving & 30% selfish	Yellow 3rd
Forgiveness & Release	65% Giving & 35% selfish	Yellow 2nd
Acceptance	60% Giving & 40% selfish	Yellow 1st
Optimism	59% Giving & 41% selfish	Orange 3rd
Inspiration	57% Giving & 43% selfish	Orange 2nd
Willingness	56% Giving & 44% selfish	Orange 1st
Trust	55% Giving & 45% selfish	Red 3rd
Courage/Empowerment	52% Giving & 48% selfish	Red 2nd
Faith in a higher power	51% Giving & 49% selfish	Red 1st
Neutrality	50% Giving & 50% selfish	1% black
Pridefulness	45% Giving & 55% selfish	**20% blk**
Insecurity & Control	43% Giving & 57% selfish	**30% blk**
Irritation	40% Giving & 60% selfish	**40% blk**
Anger & Hatred	35% Giving & 65% selfish	**50% blk**
Addiction & Craving	30% Giving & 70% selfish	**60% blk**
Fear & Anxiety	25% Giving & 75% selfish	**70% blk**
Grief, Regret, Despair	20% Giving & 80% selfish	**80% blk**
Blame, Guilt, Shame	10% Giving & 90% selfish	**90% blk**

*Blacks are various shades of gray (lighter at top, darker at bottom)

In the chart on the previous page, the subtle colors (not physical) that are the levels of consciousness cannot be seen by 'psychic sight.' This is because when one uses the faculty of 'psychic sight,' they usually can only 'tune in' to a few of the many levels of one's beingness. For example, if they can only tune into the lower three levels of the energetic field, then they will only be able to decipher what a being is on those levels alone. If they state that one is red, blue, and yellow, then that was just for the levels that they tuned into. This is obviously not an accurate reading; nonetheless, it is what nearly all psychics do.

An important side note is that almost all psychics can only tune in to about the first three levels of one's beingness, and usually cannot interpret high vibrational colors. So if an individual has the higher-frequency colors in their beingness, then the psychic cannot see them or comment on their presence in that person's beingness. The psychic simply will not see them. In addition, these subtle colors are very hard to detect and some look very similar to each other. So trying to decipher between 'dark blue,' 'indigo,' 'violet,' 'bluish-green,' 'light blue,' 'dark violet' (sometimes referred to as 'purple'), and other colors that are close in range, is typically very hard or nearly impossible.

So since 'psychic sight' cannot be used to determine one's level of consciousness, another technique must be used. This technique, known as 'kinesiology,' which is also called 'muscle testing,' has been around for thousands of years. It is a 'time-tested' technique that provides very accurate and reliable answers when done by an experienced practitioner.

The process of 'muscle testing' is simply this: when a muscle is tested while one holds an image in mind, recites a mantra, perceives an external image, or holds an object close to the body, then the muscle goes either weak or strong as another being forces one to resist an external pressure—such as if one holds their arm in front of them and another being presses (at the wrist) their arm down as they are holding an object or thinking a thought. Thus, as the arm is pressed down and the being who is resisting the pressure feels weak, there is said to be a 'lack of truth' in the object held or statement said. But if the arm remains strong, then there is said to be the presence of truth. This will not be gone into in detail here, however, because a book has already been written that explains this technique and has a 'perfect scale' already made: *Power vs. Force,* by David Hawkins. There is no need to create a duplicate scale when one without error already exists.

The only reason that this book discusses the 'scale of consciousness' described above is to help egos understand that these levels of consciousness are colors, and that they are not just indescribable energies—although some are very hard to describe. And since I recommend Hawkins' book to all of my students, I have heard a great deal about it. However, I have students who do not want to get involved with 'numbers on the scale,' so I have told them of a way that I use to calibrate various levels of consciousness. This method is finding out what color one resonates at. While I do not use the 'muscle testing' technique that Hawkins relies on, I use another type of technique, known as 'divination' (basically the same).

Divination is initiated by praying and aligning the mind with the higher Truth—for example, by stating the following prayer: -this prayer is not to ask anyone for help, but to set intent

"I align my mind with the highest of Truth and Will to be surrounded by positivity. I ask to connect to my Higher Self so as to get a universal response that yields only the correct answer, one with no distortion. I also ask to receive only Truth from my higher Self, without using the ego."

Then I hold a pendulum in my right hand (between the thumb and forefinger only) in the left side of my beingness (energetic field), while stating my question (in statement form) and waiting for the response. After saying my statement, I say "Yes," to confirm what I just said as true. Then I await (1 second) a response from the universal mind that confirms what I just stated as either "true" or "false." If my answer is false, then my pendulum swings in a clockwise (as if looking at the ground), circular motion to verify the statement as 'false.' And if the pendulum swings in a counterclockwise, circular motion, then it is a 'true,' 'yes,' or 'positive' response. This is the universal mind showing the presence of truth in the question that I phrased in a statement format. This yields the answer that tells me what I need to know: for instance, what level of consciousness someone is at, or where I am currently at.

The process is actually a little more complex than this, but this explanation will do for now. So when using a 'scale,' one must state the scale or have it in front (while placing the 'intent of use' upon it) of them, while putting the question in a statement form. And as this is done, anyone can find out what level of consciousness they are at, by noting the stage (1st, 2nd, etc...) of the color in one's beingness. This also will allow one to see what percentage of 'givingness' and 'selfishness' one is currently being an expression of.

It is important to note that the response is a universal one, so it is not actually probing the ego for answers. Although the ego can interrupt and distort the answer if the process is done for self-gain, if an action or question or intent is nontrustworthy, or if one is energetically imbalanced (whether from a fast rise or fall in consciousness) at the time. It is known to be a universal response because any experienced practitioner in any location in the world can get the same responses that another has received from the universe without conversing or discussing the test or results.

Furthermore, any being who is not at least above the 'level of neutrality' cannot calibrate anything, whether themselves, anyone else, an object, a thought, action, etc... So one must align their beingness with Truth before they can even get an accurate test response.

Books on working with a pendulum can be researched and then easily used. It may take several months to years of honest practice, however, until one can get accurate and reliable calibrations. In contrast, kinesiology can be learned a little more easily than the pendulum. This is why many beings seek out the use of 'muscle testing,' and this is why I always recommend David Hawkins' book, *Power vs. Force,* which explains it.

Opposing Forces (analogously speaking)

When a being resides at a certain level of consciousness without much change, it is because they use equal forces that stabilize them at that level of consciousness. Since each level of consciousness (below violet and gold) represents the amount of 'ego will' and 'Divine Will' that a being chooses to be an expression of, then it clearly shows the amount of selfishness and givingness that they choose as well. When a being is an expression of the higher levels of consciousness, known as 'enlightened states of awareness,' then they are only restricted by how many times they allow the ego to re-enter into their beingness, such as failing a 'trial period' that is a universal test brought forth by one's willingness to serve Divine Will.

It is important to note that the levels of consciousness really just denote the various expressions of energy. They are not opposing forces. It is just stated this way here to help one understand the resistance of the ego.

So by this, one can conclude that a being who is on the level of consciousness known as 'neutrality' is about 50% giving and 50% selfish. Likewise, a being who is at the level of 'love for nature and others' is about 80% giving and 20% selfish. So the only reason that a being is 'stuck' at the level of 'love for nature and others' is because they have some 20% 'ego will' that they are not ready to abandon in order to transcend further up the scale. In most cases, the individual is not even aware of being 'stuck' on a certain level of consciousness. They simply are naïve to that fact. So they then just carry on life as if that could not be so (that is their ego denying truth, though).

If one is at the level of consciousness of 'love for self,' then they need to realize why they are at that level of consciousness and then transcend it by releasing their previous beliefs. So this being would have to learn why not to judge every type of being as differing in importance and try to see them all as equals. If this is done, then they will feel a drop in consciousness first, signified by temporarily feeling an energetic imbalance; then, as the 'unpleasurable feeling' is offered up to the Source as 'false' and 'unneeded,' it releases from their beingness and allows them to transcend throughout the higher levels of consciousness with bliss, that being 'love for nature and others.' This level of consciousness is also termed 'unconditional love.' At this level of beingness, the individual sees everything as equal, with no separation by and of importance. So without the previous ego quality that used to judge everything in terms of importance and lovability, everything then is seen as a perfect expression of existence, which many times leads one to feel an overwhelming feeling of love for all (fewer than 5% of the world's beings calibrate at or above this level of consciousness).

If one refers to the chapters that describe ego levels of consciousness, both the seemingly positive (above neutrality) and negative (below) (which are just labels), one can realize what the next step in their evolution is. So it is imperative to study that which one is and what one needs to do to transcend higher in consciousness.

One should look through all of the traits and pick out the predominant qualities that they choose to be an expression of— that is, if they are not able to get an accurate response from kinesiology or divination. Remember that one could be at the level of consciousness of 'pride' even if one believes that they are not. Keep in mind that a being could have 30% of 'pride' in and as their beingness, but because this does not seem predominant, then they will assume that they are not that. This is the ego in defense mode. Nearly everyone whom I teach or talk to 'thinks' (ego quality) that they are a certain level of consciousness, and then when I calibrate them with my 'color scale' or Hawkins' scale of consciousness, they find out that they are not what they believe themselves to be.

Using a type of calibration technique is really the only way to get an accurate response. The ego **cannot** tell itself where it is currently residing, because of the fact that all egos would like to see themselves in a 'good light.' More than likely, fewer than 1% of the beings in the world could read the descriptions of levels of consciousness and find out their level. This is because egos are not honest with themselves; if this were true, then there would be no egos due to the complete resolution of all of their seeming problems. So learning a calibration technique is highly recommended. Don't trust your ego, or you may find yourself at the same level of consciousness 20 to 80 years from now.

If one cannot use the calibration techniques with any accuracy, then they should just follow the book's Truthful teachings without straying back into their 'old habits.' If one just stays aligned with Truth, love, peace, compassion, and serving divinity, then they will progress upwards in spiritual evolution. Calibration is not needed, but it can be very helpful to a struggling spiritual devotee. Enlightenment is really just keeping the ego out of one's life. The ego is suffering, so why not?

*   *   *   *   *

Calibration Services

Contact calibration@revealingtruthnow.com in order to be calibrated 'free of charge' (by a Sage) by your choice of either the **Hawkins Scale** or the **Color Stage Scale. (Once per two-month period**, please.)

If one would like to be calibrated once a month, once a week, once a day, or every 2 to 4 hours during the day, so as to track one's progress of raising in consciousness, one should check the calibration pricing guide at www.revealingtruthnow.com.

The funds received from this service will be put towards financing the building of a temple that will provide a meeting place for teachers and seekers of Truth. Furthermore, the proceeds that come from this book, or any of the products that are sold on the Web site, will be used to finance this project, and to support the spreading of Truth across the world. So these are not really payments, but donations to aid in the liberation of the universe.

Products and Services

RevealingTruthNow, at www.revealingtruthnow.com, is a dedicated provider of Truth, whose focus is to supply only high-frequency items to the public. Incense, books, lectures on CD, or any other products that are sold will assuredly calibrate in the upper levels of enlightened consciousness (Gold).

Each product that is sold will be blessed at least to the 2nd Stage Gold level, and also will be programmed or imprinted with the intent that the being who acquires the object will transcend the ego at a faster and more stable rate. This will help one remain at a more steady level of consciousness as they transcend, which will cancel out most feelings of 'downness.'

When one does not work directly with an enlightened being, there are many times when one can feel lost or depressed. So acquiring these blessed objects, which carry the Sage's imprint of the Self, are a way to have their energy aid one in transcension without the Sage being physically present. This is especially effective when one is at the 'final doorway,' where there are many 'ups and downs.'

Incense

All incense is carefully selected for its current level of consciousness and the level that it can be raised to. No incense will be sold unless it is for a specific energetic purpose that aids one in transcending the ego. All incense is blessed as soon as it comes from the manufacturer; thus it differs greatly from the incense sold in stores.

The incense will carry with it the energy of the Sage (Higher Self), to the degree of 2nd or 3rd Stage Gold. Most incense at stores calibrates in the lower, unenlightened levels of consciousness due to its being handled by many people (shippers, manufacturers, store owners, customers with various thoughts, intent, etc.). Just the same, by nature, most incense does not emanate the higher enlightened frequencies. So this way, one will receive incense that is at an already high level of consciousness, and that will be blessed further by a Sage (who calibrates in the upper Gold Stage) to emanate an even higher level of consciousness.

Enlightened Lectures on CD

Throughout Brian's travels, as he taught others, recordings were made to further convey the message of Truth to those who could not attend the meetings. These lectures speak of the creation process, the appearance of the Universal Mind's thoughts, universal consciousness, the ego, Higher Self, the universal consciousness, the ego, Higher Self, the attributes of the various levels of consciousness, prayer, blessing objects, people, and the world, recontextualizing the universe, living with egos as Self, meditation techniques, helping others, and so forth. These meetings ended when the last question was asked. They usually lasted for several hours and there was never a charge for attending.

These CDs contain the 2nd to 3rd Stage Gold levels of consciousness. The essence of these meetings was recorded on CD, and that in and of itself aids one in transcending the ego when one is near. As the CDs are played, the energy surrounds one's self, and when a being decides to accept it, transcension becomes more probable. To just continually play these CDs makes any place a more positive environment, whether one is in a car, house, workplace, computer, or headphones. Because most beings have their television or radio on throughout the day, lower frequencies go into their dwelling space and decrease their level of consciousness by karmic contact. So these CDs can be seen as a neutralizer of any negative energy in the universe, and an uplifter to all who listen to, or are just near, the power presented within.

Blessed Malas (Prayer Beads)

While one is on the spiritual path and transcending the ego, it can be very difficult to always surround oneself with positivity. When meditating and praying, holding a high-frequency item can be very uplifting and healing. Thus Malas (prayer beads) were purchased from the Tibetan people, to help them financially and to provide some support for their lifestyle, as well as to obtain high-quality, handcrafted works of art that have higher energies.

As each Mala is handcrafted by the Tibetans, a prayer and blessing are said to ensure that it resonates at a higher level of consciousness that will aid one in transcension. As the malas are received, they are furthermore blessed by a Sage to raise their level of consciousness to the Gold Stage. Praying with these Malas can be very healing and peaceful, and they are great meditation tools.

Appendix 1B. Karmic Packages

*This chart compares the nature of beingness of certain types
of people at differing levels of consciousness.

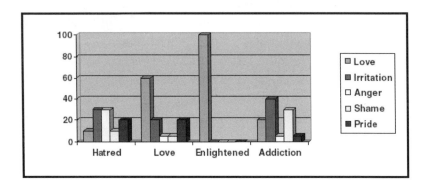

In the chart above, the being on the far left is the representative energy known as the consciousness level of 'Hatred.' While this being is predominantly the quality of 'Hatred,' this does not exclude them from having any other traits, such as love (10%), irritation (30%), anger (30%), shame (30%), and pride (20%) (these percentages were created at random to portray a somewhat similar and accurate description; they obviously vary for each being). Just the same, a being who is predominantly the level of consciousness known as 'Love' is not just love. On the contrary, that being is a mixture of energies (karmic package) as well, such as love (60%), irritation (20%), anger (5%), shame (5%), and pride (20%). But they are said to be at the level of consciousness of 'love' because they are predominantly that quality of energy.

Clearly, then, just because one is at a certain level of consciousness, it doesn't mean they are not capable of opting to be an expression of another quality of energy. Also, because so many egos are confused as to the nature of the enlightened being, the various qualities of that being's existence are placed on the chart to show that they are also a mixture of energies. So they are not exempt from being a mixture of various qualities, either, just because they have transcended their ego; it can be seen, however, that the mixture is basically within the Higher Truth or the upper levels of consciousness. This is because they may frequently be 'tempted' by the lower energies of the ego while going through a 'trial period.' Thus, when the ego re-enters, the lower qualities of energy are expressed through and as their beingness.

It is important to understand that only a few energies, representative of the qualities of the levels of consciousness, were used just to 'show a difference' in the expression and/or quality of beingness that comprise various types of beings. Many types of energies that are within and as one's beingness are not listed in the chart above. And just because these are not seen as a trait of an individual doesn't mean that they are not an expression of that individual's beingness itself.

Also, as an enlightened being who is currently an expression of the lower levels of enlightenment (1st stage) transcends further throughout the upper levels of enlightenment, then that being's 'beingness' will be purified even more. So the many 'ego re-entries' experienced in the lower levels of enlightenment (1st, 2nd, and sometimes 3rd stage) will not be experienced as much while one is in the upper levels of enlightenment (3th stage and up to 7th). Obviously, the higher that one transcends throughout the upper levels of enlightenment, the more pure they become.

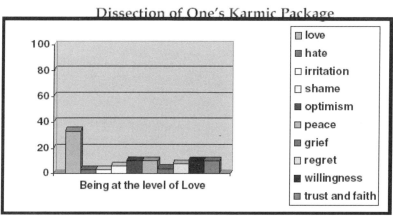

The chart above shows more accurately the 'karmic package' of one's beingness at the level of consciousness of 'love.' So they could barely have any love in them, or better yet, as an expression of them. So a being who is at any predominant level of consciousness could just have 10% of that energy in and as their beingness, and then have many other low-percentage energies as their beingness as well. **Note:** The numbers on the axis represent the percentages of used energy. A being at the level of 'love' is in the chart below.

Dissection of 'being at love' Karmic Package

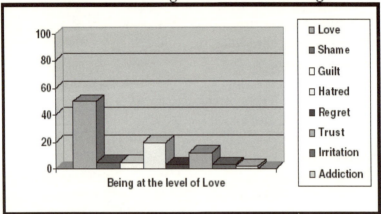

Enlightened Being who allows for *little* 'Ego Re-Entry'

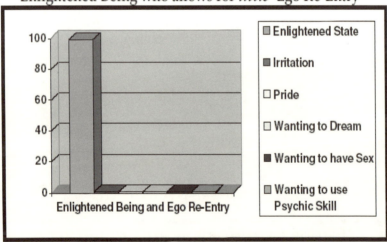

*If the ego re-enters, then it could grow and gain momentum. See the example below for this illustration.

Enlightened Being who allows for <u>a lot</u> of 'Ego Re-Entry'

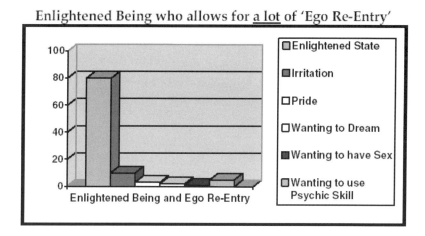

An enlightened being could eventually drop below the level of enlightenment, if they will it. So just as a being who is operating within and as the ego states could opt to be an expression of the higher states and eventually become (realize) that state of existence as 'enlightened,' an enlightened being could opt to be an expression of the lower ego traits, bringing them down as a result of their own 'free will.' Although it is rare that one would want to descend back into the realm of limitation and suffering, it is possible. All it would take is for the 'enlightened being' to give in to one temptation. And as that temptation lowers their level of consciousness, many more temptations start to follow. And as these amplify in number, it becomes increasingly more difficult to deny them, creating an environment or type of existence that is a lower expression of energy.

Often, while progressing throughout the path of enlightenment, an ego may bring forth many 'heavy-feeling' energies that tend to depress one's self if they are not properly dealt with. While earlier parts of the book speak about meditation, introspection, and other healing methods, this appendix describes some fast 'spiritual medicines' that help one to alleviate the energetically imbalanced sensations.

Examples of 'spiritual medicine' are as follows:

1. *Wake up and slowly (30 seconds) stretch while breathing deeply and slowly. Do Yoga if possible.*

2. *Slap yourself with both hands at a <u>fast rate</u> and medium pressure over every square inch of your body. Start with the head and the back of the neck, then the face, cheeks, forehead, neck, chest, shoulders, back, abdomen, lower back, sides, arms, legs, calves, and feet. This wakes up every neuron in the body and stimulates the subtle energy to move as well. (recommended daily)*

3. *Shake your head from side to side while saying "boogety, boogety, boo" (3 times). This will make anyone laugh, especially if they are looking at themselves in the mirror while doing it. (recommended frequently for a fast, uplifting effect)*

4. *Use the peripheral gaze technique while operating in worldly situations. This takes the extra focus off the illusion and places it on the underlying context that is a higher Truth.*

5. *Eat balanced meals. Do not eat excessive simple sugars (such as candy, ice cream, soda, juice, etc...). A sugar crash always imbalances the physical body. And the mental effect of noting how the physical body feels will then affect the overall state of beingness.*

6. *Use the 'Bandha Technique' and breathe the energy that is fueling the lower chakras and emotional/mental states up to the crown, third*

eye, throat, or heart chakra.

7. *Meditate or pray for about 20 minutes to align the mind with the Mind of Self. This shifts the emphasis from self to Self.*
8. *Think of a loving memory (i.e., cat, dog, pet, family, children).*
9. *Try a mixture of some of the previous.*
10. *Force a smile and laugh. This has been proven by scientists to uplift one's mood and create a more positive thought process and beingness. Staying in a positive mood has also been shown to help one increase their immune function.*

3 Basic Layers of Energy Body and Chakra System

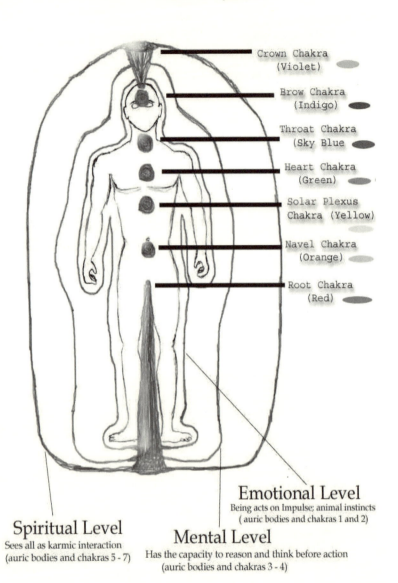

Crown Chakra (Violet)

Brow Chakra (Indigo)

Throat Chakra (Sky Blue

Heart Chakra (Green)

Solar Plexus Chakra (Yellow)

Navel Chakra (Orange)

Root Chakra (Red)

Emotional Level
Being acts on Impulse; animal instincts
(auric bodies and chakras 1 and 2)

Spiritual Level
Sees all as karmic interaction
(auric bodies and chakras 5 - 7)

Mental Level
Has the capacity to reason and think before action
(auric bodies and chakras 3 - 4)

The diagram to the left is of the auric levels which contain the 7 auric bodies. When tuned into with clairvoyance, 3 levels of energy are usually seen. Only an experienced spiritual being can tune into specific energy levels, chakras, pathways, and blockages. A spiritual novice may only be able to tune into 1 level, or perhaps none.

The closest level to the body is known as the Emotional Level. It is the lowest in frequency, which is the easiest to detect, and the most primal energy of our innate ego beingness. It prompts the ego to respond without thinking through the scenario before it is acted upon. Emotions over-ride logic. So as the emotions act through and as one's beingness, they tend to look juvenile or immature. Very low energetic impulses look animalistic and uncultured. This is what the current ego society rates or judges as 'evil' and disrespectful to all life.

As the ego evolves, it energetically advances into the outer levels of the energy field, from the Emotional Level to the Mental. Thus, the being now rationalizes its actions to figure out the consequences of the event before an action is done. This being typically allows for certain emotions to be felt, such as love, respect, trust, and so forth. For they see the benefit in feeling 'good' and not getting in trouble with others. As the egos move into this level of consciousness, they become more civilized and less animalistic. This is when their views and actions tend to incorporate others that are nearby, especially friends and family. These beings will serve themselves first, and after they have taken care of their needs, they tend to reach out to others that are around as to help them fulfill their needs. At times the lower levels of consciousness may resurface and summon the 'darker energies,' but they typically lead positive lives and help others when possible. About 10% of the world can be said to be in this range. (90% in Emotional)

As the being moves out of the Mental Level and into the Spiritual, they don't criticize as much because they are satisfied and at peace with nearly every outcome or appearance in their perceived reality. These beings see all that 'happens' as a karmic interaction of divine accordance. They see no mistakes; only creation. They live for the higher purpose and seek out to serve others rather than themselves. They may neglect the physical body, or forget that they have one to take care of, because they are so focused in helping others realize the True Purpose we are all here for.

For spiritual services, such as guest speaking or publishing inquiry, contact:

By Email: admin@revealingtruthnow.com

For revealingtruthnow's calibration services, contact:

By Email: calibration@revealingtruthnow.com

To ask spiritual questions and have them posted on the revealingtruthnow web site, contact:

By Email: askaspiritualquestion@revealingtruthnow.com

To share spiritual occurrences within your life and have them posted on revealingtruthnow's web site, contact:

By Email: spiritualphenomena@revealingtruthnow.com

To give a testimonial of how this book has changed your life, contact,

By Email: testimonial@revealingtruthnow.com

Or Visit the Web Site at:
www.revealingtruthnow.com

RevealingTruthNow.com guarantees that everything sold within the site will calibrate at or above the 1st Stage Violet level of enlightened consciousness. If blessed, it will calibrate at the 2nd to 3rd Stage Gold level of consciousness. Our purpose is to supply only the highest frequency objects or teachings that are imbued with the Presence of the Self as to help all beings transcend the ego and attain the state of universal awareness. So you can feel safe shopping here. Also, take time to tune into our Radio Archives of enlightened lectures.

Products Sold:
Blessed Incense, Blessed Malas (prayer beads), Books, Newsletters, and more. We only provide high frequency items!

On the web site, there is also a 'chat room' that can be accessed by anyone who wishes to speak with others whom are currently on the spiritual path. You may post messages there and meet others who have had or are currently having spiritual experiences that may help you understand your journey a little better. **Online Enlightenment Programs are also available.**

Book Notice:

The next book, **Being That Which Is**, is due to come out by the middle of 2005. Whereas **The Ego Identity Crisis** explains the process of enlightenment and exactly how to transcend the ego, Being That Which Is, explains how to get past the 'final doorway' of the ego's clingingness (for those who are stuck), as well as discusses the higher Truths that are known by only the enlightened beings at the 1st to 3rd Stage Gold level of consciousness. This book will help not only those on the path of enlightenment, but the spiritually advanced and the novices.

Whereas this book explains enlightenment more as a personal journey, with some references to its True Universal Identity, Being That Which Is only explains the energy of the Higher Self as the Universal Identity. While this book stimulates the revelation that God and Truth are the same thing as the Universal Mind, Being That Which Is only expresses what the Self is from the standpoint that all is Universal. It rarely, if ever, speaks of God. The second book is to help the being bridge the final gap that distorts spiritual vision which then yields the condition known as the Universal Identity (1st to 3rd Stage Gold). These are the final stages of enlightenment that all beings could realize they already are after reading the next book, Being That Which Is.

While this book, The Ego Identity Crisis, calibrates in the lower 3rd Stage Gold, Being That Which Is, calibrates in the higher 3rd Stage Gold. It is virtually pure and undistorted; at least for the level of consciousness that is able to be conveyed in this earthly dimension.

Being That Which Is, teaches the 'how to' of blessing, praying, recontextualizing, and serving the Universal Purpose. It will truly help all beings see All That Is as One.

Recommended Reading

Hawkins, David. 2002. *Power vs. Force: An Anatomy of Consciousness*. (Rev.). Carlsbad, Calif., Brighton-le-Sands, Australia: Hay House.

———. 2001. *The Eye of the I: From Which Nothing is Hidden*. Sedona, Arizona: Veritas Publishing.

———. 2003. *I: Reality and Subjectivity*. Sedona, Arizona: Veritas Publishing.

Maharaj, Nisargadatta. 1973. *I Am That*. Bombay: Chetara.

Nager, Brian. 2005. *Being That Which Is: A Lightworker's Guide to Recontextualizing the Universe*. Orlando, Florida: RTN Publishing.

All books by David Hawkins can be purchased at the Veritas Web Site, veritaspub.com, and spiritual bookstores. *I Am That*, by Nisargadatta Maharaj, can be found at most bookstores. Books by Brian Nager can be found at www.RevealingTruthNow.com.

Additional recommended books are:

- *The Truth Is*, by Papaji (Poonja).
- *The Yoga Sutras of Patanjali*, by Patanjali.
- *Holy Bible from Ancient Eastern Manuscripts*, by Lamsa.
  also known as the *Lamsa Edition Bible*. (the most accurate and high powered Bible to date.)
- *Collected Works* of Ramana Marharshi, by Jupiter Press.
- *Spiritual Teachings* of Ramana Marharshi, by Shambala (Pub).
- *Bhagavad-Gita*
- Any writings of Mahatma Gandhi